Thirty Years' War

Treaty of Augsburg	Spanish Armada defeated		Grotius publishes first book on international law	Treaty of Westphalia	Hobbes publishes *Leviathan*	Louis XIV begins to govern	Industrial Revolution under way
1555	**1588**	**1618**	**1625**	**1648**	**1651**	**1661**	**1750**
		Tokugawa Era of premodern Japan begins		Manchu dynasty founded in China			

Multipolar Balance of Power

U.S. naval squadron in Tokyo Bay demands U.S.–Japan trade	Charles Darwin's *The Origin of Species*	Dominion of Canada established		Spanish-American War	First manned flight		World War I begins	Russian Revolution
1853	**1859**	**1867**	**1868**	**1898**	**1903**	**1911**	**1914**	**1917**
			Meiji restoration begins modern era in Japan	U.S. imperialist period		Chinese Manchu emperor deposed		

Bipolar Era

U.S.–USSR Peaceful Coexistence

India and Pakistan independent — Cold war — Containment	Israel independent	NATO established — Chinese Communists take power	Stalin dies	Vietnam independent and divided	Ghana independent	European Common Market formed	World population 3 billion	Cuban missile crisis
1947	**1948**	**1949**	**1953**	**1954**	**1957**	**1958**	**1960**	**1962**
				Beginning of African independence				

Bipolar Era Ends   U.S. Dominance in an Era of Change

World population 5 billion	Berlin Wall opened	Germany reunites	War in Persian Gulf	Clinton in power — Yeltsin in power	NAFTA ratified — European Union begins	Cairo Population Conference — Genocide in Rwanda	4th World Conference on Women — UN's 50th anniversary	Kyoto Global Warming Conference
1987	**1989**	**1990**	**1991**	**1992**	**1993**	**1994**	**1995**	**1997**
	Tiananmen Square massacre		Soviet Union collapses	Earth Summit — Chaos in Bosnia	START II	Summit of the Americas	World Trade Organization begins	Kofi Annan becomes UN secretary-general

Ban Ki-moon becomes UN secretary-general

2007

Online Learning Center

Visit the Online Learning Center for
International Politics on the World Stage, Twelfth Edition
at
www.mhhe.com/rourke12
to access

INTERACTIVE EXERCISES
- Simulations
- Analyze the Issue
- Join the Debate
- Web Poll

NEWS ARTICLES AND LINKS
- Web Links
- Course-Related Headlines from the *New York Times*

QUIZZES
- Chapter Quiz
- True or False
- Essay Quiz

MORE RESOURCES
- Chapter Outline
- Maps
- Glossary

International Politics on the World Stage

Clockwise from top left:

1. The image of a Chinese soldier in front of the Olympic rings that herald the 2008 summer games in Beijing captures the tension between China as an authoritarian state and as an increasingly modern, economically liberalizing country.

2. The isolated polar bear on an ice flow is a reminder of global warming's many dangers, such as the melting of the polar ice caps.

3. The tragedy of Darfur in Sudan is etched on the face of this refugee.

4. The image of U.S. Speaker of the House, Nancy Pelosi, and Senate Majority Leader, Harry Reid, highlights both the problems of and protests against the U.S. presence of Iraq and the growing number of women in positions of power around the world.

5. Some see Venezuela's President Hugo Chávez as a dictatorial demagogue; others praise him for challenging U.S. dominance of the Western Hemisphere.

6. New UN Secretary-General Ban Ki-moon listens to a UN peacekeeper discuss the situation in the Democratic Republic of the Congo, the site of one of many UN peacekeeping missions.

About the Author

JOHN T. ROURKE, Ph.D., professor emeritus, is former head of the Department of Political Science at The University of Connecticut. He is coauthor with Mark A. Boyer of *International Politics on the World Stage, Brief,* Seventh Edition (McGraw-Hill, 2008); author of *Presidential Wars and American Democracy: Rally 'Round the Chief* (Paragon House, 1993); coauthor of *Direct Democracy and International Politics: Deciding International Issues Through Referendums* (Lynne Rienner, 1992); editor of *Taking Sides: Clashing Views on Controversial Issues in World Politics,* Thirteenth Edition (McGraw-Hill, 2008) and *You Decide 2008: Current Debates in American Politics,* Fourth Edition (Longman, 2008); author of *Making Foreign Policy: United States, Soviet Union, China* (Brooks/Cole, 1990), *Congress and the Presidency in U.S. Foreign Policymaking* (Westview, 1985), and numerous articles and papers. He continues to teach and especially enjoys introductory classes. His regard for students has molded his approach to writing—he conveys scholarship in a language and within a frame of reference that undergraduates can appreciate. Rourke believes, as the theme of this book reflects, that politics affects us all and we can affect politics. Rourke practices what he propounds. His career long involved the university's internship program and advising one of its political clubs. Additionally, he has served as a staff member of Connecticut's legislature and been involved in political campaigns on the local, state, and national levels.

International Politics on the World Stage

TWELFTH EDITION

John T. Rourke
University of Connecticut

Boston   Burr Ridge, IL   Dubuque, IA   New York   San Francisco   St. Louis
Bangkok   Bogotá   Caracas   Kuala Lumpur   Lisbon   London   Madrid   Mexico City
Milan   Montreal   New Delhi   Santiago   Seoul   Singapore   Sydney   Taipei   Toronto

The **McGraw-Hill** Companies

McGraw-Hill
Higher Education

Published by McGraw-Hill, an imprint of The McGraw-Hill Companies, Inc., 1221 Avenue of the Americas, New York, NY 10020. Copyright © 2008, 2007, 2005, 2002, 2001, 1999, 1997, 1995, 1993, 1991, 1989, and 1986. All rights reserved. No part of this publication may be reproduced or distributed in any form or by any means, or stored in a database or retrieval system, without the prior written consent of The McGraw-Hill Companies, Inc., including, but not limited to, in any network or other electronic storage or transmission, or broadcast for distance learning.

This book is printed on acid-free paper.

1 2 3 4 5 6 7 8 9 0 VNH/VNH 0 9 8 7

ISBN: 978-0-07-340388-5
MHID: 0-07-340388-1

Editor in Chief: *Michael Ryan*
Publisher: *Lisa Moore*
Sponsoring Editor: *Mark Georgiev*
Developmental Editor: *Ava Suntoke*
Editorial Assistant: *Briana Porco*
Marketing Manager: *Simon Heathcote*
Production Editor: *Alison Meier*
Manuscript Editor: *Sheryl Rose*
Design Manager: *Andrei Pasternak*
Art Editor: *Emma Ghiselli*
Illustrators: *Emma Ghiselli, John Waller, Judy Waller*
Photo Researcher: *Pamela Carley*
Production Supervisor: *Randy Hurst*
Composition: *10/12 Berkeley Book by ICC Macmillan Inc.*
Printing: *45# Pub MattePlus, Von Hoffmann Corporation*

Cover: **China Olympics:** © Associated Press; **Polar Bear:** © Paul Miles, Getty Images; **UN Secretary-General, Ban Ki-moon:** AFP/Getty; **Time to Change Course in Iraq:** © Associated Press; **Refugee in Sudan:** © epa/Corbis; **Hugo Chávez:** © Associated Press

Library of Congress Cataloging-in-Publication Data
Rourke, John T., 1945–
  International politics on the world stage / John T. Rourke. — 12th ed.
      p. cm.
  Includes bibliographical references and index.
  ISBN-13: 978-0-07-340388-5
  ISBN-10: 0-07-340388-1
  1. International relations. 2. World politics—1989– I. Title.
JZ1305.R68 2008
327—dc22

2007016456

The Internet addresses listed in the text were accurate at the time of publication. The inclusion of a Web site does not indicate an endorsement by the authors or McGraw-Hill, and McGraw-Hill does not guarantee the accuracy of the information presented at these sites.

www.mhhe.com

Preface

This Edition: Changes and Organization

Taking the view that our lives are inescapably affected by world politics, *International Politics on the World Stage, Twelfth Edition,* stresses the impact that world events and global interdependence have on your students' lives. In addition to highlighting this interconnection, the text points out how the events of current history relate to the theories of international politics that have been formulated by political scientists.

Each time I revise this text I think to myself, "The world will settle down and the next edition will be easier." Wrong! This edition proved to be a major challenge and effort. You will see that there is a continued emphasis on being current without being journalistic in order to engage the students. The struggle of the United States in Iraq and the conflict within the United States over whether or not to soon withdraw; the ongoing threat of terrorism; the looming threat of avian influenza; the genocidal horror in the Darfur region of Sudan; a new UN secretary-general; tensions with both Iran and North Korea over their alleged nuclear weapons programs; the increasing presence of China as a political, economic, and even military power; the impact on U.S. foreign policy of Condoleezza Rice, the first African American woman to serve as U.S. secretary of state; new leaders in France, Germany, Great Britain, and Japan and the impending ends of the presidencies of Vladimir Putin in Russia and George Bush in the United States; and other recent events are all extensively detailed. It is also important to be as current as possible with the massive amount of changing data on economic performance and capacity, weapons levels and transfers, and other statistical aspects of world politics. I have used original sources for my data when possible so that students will have the most recent information available.

The more I study global politics, the more I am impressed with the idea that the world is a primitive political society. It is a political system that is marked by little organization, frequent violence, and a limited sense of global responsibility. It is a world of conflict. But there is also a world of cooperation, a countertheme, based on a desire among states and their people to work together globally. Although it is still only a nascent desire, people have begun to realize that their fates are inextricably entwined with one another and with the political, economic, social, and environmental future of our planet. The organization of the text flows from this conception of the world as a primitive, but developing, political system. Therefore, the chapters not only analyze world division and conflict but also focus on cooperation both as a goal and in practice.

Indeed, the text's organizational scheme reflects this menu of choices. One group of choices is associated with the traditional way of doing things. This involves sovereign states pursuing their self-interests in an often inequitable and conflict-filled world. The alternative group of choices include cooperation in a system in which states are less sovereign and international organizations play a wider and more authoritative role. The options are not necessarily either-or picks. Your thinking needs to be more subtle than that. So think about whether the world should modify its traditional approach to world politics and, if so, how and to what degree to adopt alternative values and conduct.

To explore our menu of choices, the introduction to the text discusses the importance of world politics and the methods, theories, and purposes of political science (chapter 1), the evolution of the world political system and its current instability (chapter 2), and the three levels of analysis that need to be studied simultaneously—the system, state, and individual levels (chapter 3).

Beginning with chapter 4, the menu of choices organizes the remaining chapters of this edition, with usually alternating discussions of national conflict and international cooperation in successive chapters. In this way, equal attention can be given to the two roads without losing sight of the fact that they lead in divergent directions.

Chapters 4 and 5 deal with two divergent political orientations. The traditional orientation is nationalism (chapter 4); the alternative orientation comprises transnational ideas, identifications, and processes (chapter 5). Alternative ways of organizing the world politically are the subject of the next two chapters, with chapter 6 focusing on the traditional political unit, the state, and chapter 7 taking up international organizations, with particular emphases on the European Union and the United Nations.

Then chapters 8 and 9 explore divergent approaches to the conduct of world politics. Chapter 8 covers the traditional approach, national power and diplomacy; chapter 9 examines the alternative road of international law and morality. This pair of chapters is followed by another pair that introduce two approaches to physical security in the world political system: national security (chapter 10) and international security and other alternative approaches (chapter 11).

The text then turns to international political economy. The commentary begins in chapter 12 with an overview of IPE theory and of global economic conditions and trends. The main thrust of chapter 12, however, is economic nationalism, the traditional approach to the international political economy. By contrast, chapter 13 focuses on an alternative approach, economic liberalism, as part of the greater phenomenon of globalization. Chapter 13 concludes by reviewing the arguments for and against economic nationalism and economic liberalism and asking its readers to evaluate the two approaches. The final two chapters look into the traditional and alternative approaches to global human rights and dignity (chapter 14) and the environment (chapter 15).

Instructors who have used this text before will undoubtedly notice that there have been some changes in where material appears. Commentary that had been in chapter 5 on constructivist, postmodernist, and feminist theory has been moved to chapter 1. This brings those ways of thinking together with realism and liberalism (idealism) to create an earlier and more concentrated look at international relations theory. Another important bit of rearranging was to take the section on military power in chapter 10 and economic power in chapter 12 and move them to chapter 8 to create a more unified examination of all aspects of power in that chapter.

Writing Style and General Approach

The single greatest factor that prompted me over two decades ago to begin to write my own introductory text was the desire to use one that, in today's jargon, was "user friendly." Over the years, I have tried to accomplish that in a number of ways. One is to make my theoretical points in straightforward, "plain language," and then to illustrate them with an interesting and usually current example. Being up-to-date is a major goal of this book. Sometimes, heeding the advice of Mary Poppins that "a spoonful of sugar makes the medicine go down," I even occasionally take time to include a joke or tell a "story" that makes a point in a light way. This is meant to show the student readers that international relations can be fascinating, even fun. A third thing that makes this book user-friendly for students is the "road signs" to provide reference points and guidance during the journey through the text and semester. These road signs include an outline (a map, so to speak) to begin each chapter, lots of headings, an array of boldface glossary words, and judicious use of italicized phrases to highlight concepts and points. I am pleased to report that the feedback from instructors and from the occasional student who writes or e-mails me is that most students are delighted with the book's accessibility and readability.

Data and Graphics

This text presents students with an extensive array of tables, figures, photographs, maps, and other graphics to emphasize, expand, and give visual life to ideas. Each photograph is picked personally by me, and I have designed almost all the figures and tables, often making my own calculations to create them from the data. Another part of my approach is to present a significant amount of data to students so that they can see for themselves what the statistics indicate rather than accept my interpretations or those of any other scholar.

Research, Citations, Bibliography, and Suggested Readings

One of the aims of this text is to bring together a representative sampling of the latest research in international relations. Scholarly articles, so often ignored in survey texts, are particularly emphasized. This research is documented by extensive references using the "in-text" style and by a significant reference list/bibliography. In addition to recognizing my intellectual debt to a host of scholars, the references and bibliography also serve as a reading list for students, as explained to them in the "To the Student" section following this preface. As such, references are often meant to serve as suggestions for further reading and do not necessarily mean that the cited author(s) propounded what is being said at the point of reference. Using this approach instead of the end-of-chapter placement gives intellectually stimulated students immediate thoughts for additional reading. For those instructors whose organization differs from mine, I have taken care to provide a detailed table of contents and index in order to facilitate the integration of this text with your syllabus. You will find, for example, that:

> **Economics** is discussed, among other places, in chapters 1 (how it affects students), 2 (global economic divisions and trends), 5 (globalization), 8 (economic power), 12 (theory, general global conditions, and economic nationalism), 13 (economic liberalism), and 15 (sustainable development).
>
> **Terrorism** is addressed in chapters 1, 5, 9, and 10.
>
> **Moral and humanitarian issues** are taken up extensively in chapters 9 and 15 and also form an important part of the discussions of national interest, coercion, and economic challenges in, respectively, chapters 4, 10, and 13.

Online Learning Center

Students and instructors will find additional resources at www.mhhe.com/rourke12. For students, the site offers free access to current course-specific articles by leading authorities in the field, daily news feeds from a variety of media outlets including the

New York Times, interactive exercises including simulations, debates, research links, and chapter quizzes, chapter outlines, an interactive glossary, and interactive maps to enhance the classroom and learning experience. The password-protected instructor's edition of the site also contains chapter objectives, sample lectures, discussion questions, analytical exercises, and the Test Bank that provides approximately 1,500 multiple-choice and essay questions organized by chapter and degree of difficulty. A PowerPoint slide presentation is also included. All these items are available for easy download. Contact your local McGraw-Hill representative or McGraw-Hill Customer Service (1-800-338-3987) for a username and password.

John T. Rourke

To the Student

The world, familiar to us and unknown.
—William Shakespeare, *Henry V*

THE WORLD IS CHANGING at breathtaking speed! That reality is one of the most important things for you to understand about international politics. Yet I have found that most undergraduate students, having been born into this era of warp-speed change, consider it normal. It is not. Recorded history dates back over 30 centuries. A great deal of what we will discuss in this text has happened in the last century, even within your lifetime. But truly understanding this rate of change—maybe feeling the rate of change is a better way to put it—is hard without perspective.

There is an ever increasing number of centenarians, people who are age 100 or more. If you can, try to talk to one of these amazing people about how the world has changed in their lifetime. Many were born when Theodore Roosevelt was president of the United States. In other countries, an emperor ruled in China and a sultan headed the Ottoman Empire. Russia's czar, Germany's kaiser, and Austria-Hungary's emperor ruled much of Central Europe, and Edward VII reigned over the British Empire. Most of Africa and Asia were still colonies of European powers. The communist revolution would not occur until these centenarians were in their teens or later, and the Soviet Union would disappear within their lifetime. For me, communism and the cold war were the totality of my historical experience; for centenarians, they were mere interludes. For many who read this book they are not even memories, only matter learned about in history books.

If you think about events, trends, and technology in this way—in terms of what one person has seen and experienced—you can begin to grasp how fast they are moving. When centenarians were born people were basically earthbound or had just after 3,500 years of recorded history first taken wing when the first airplane flew in 1903. That first flight lasted just 12 seconds and went 120 feet. Within these centenarians' lifetimes, aviation rapidly advanced through transatlantic flights (1919), to jet planes (1939), to Soviet cosmonaut Yuri Gagarin becoming the first human in space (1961), to Neil Armstrong stepping onto the Moon's surface (1969). There are many other things to consider. Centenarians were in their forties before atomic weapons were invented; the world's population has about quadrupled during their lives. Centenarians are older than three-quarters of the countries that exist today. Televisions, computers, and some of the other technological innovations that affect us so profoundly now did not exist when centenarians were born.

One of the strong themes in this book is that challenges face the world and there are alternative approaches to addressing those challenges. Use centenarians to help you think about these issues. For example, it took all of human history—tens of thousands of years—to reach a world population of about 1.6 billion in the first decade of the 1900s when most centenarians were born. Since then and during their lifetimes we have added another 4.7 billion people. How much longer can such population growth continue before it overwhelms Earth's ability to provide food and water and to recycle personal and industrial waste? In this sense of contemplating the future by pondering the past, thinking about centenarians is really more about tomorrow than about yesterday or even today. When I talk about them, my thoughts are on our 21st century more than on their 19th and 20th centuries.

Using This Text

The text that follows is my attempt to introduce you to the complex and compelling study of international politics. Prefaces are often given scant attention, but they can be a valuable learning tool for you. They let you in on the author's conceptions, the mental pictures behind a text. What is the author's approach? What are the author's orientations and biases? Does the text have one or more basic themes? How is the text organized? In this preface I have addressed these issues. I hope you'll read it.

In writing this text I have tried to use straightforward prose and have assumed that students who take this course know little about international politics. To help you further, I have included an outline at the beginning of each chapter. Before you read the chapter, pay attention to its outline. It is axiomatic that if you know where you are going, you will find it a lot easier to get there! Additionally, I have written a numbered summary at the end of each chapter to help you quickly review the scope of the chapter. This, of course, is no substitute for carefully studying the chapter.

There are many figures, tables, maps, and photographs in this book. Pay close attention to them. You will find that they graphically represent many of the ideas presented in the text and will help you understand them. But if you really want to know all about something, you will have to read a lot more than just this book and to involve yourself in more than just the course for which it has been assigned. To make it easier for you to do this, I have chosen an "in-text" reference system that gives you citations as you read. Thus (Atkinson, 2006:509) refers to page 509 of the book or article written by (in this case, Professor Carol) Atkinson in 2006, which is listed alphabetically in the references at the end of the book. I have also noted studies that helped me think about and organize various topics and those that might be informative for you. I encourage you to utilize the references to advance your knowledge beyond the boundaries of this text. Explanations for terms set in **boldface** will be found in the glossary at the end of the text.

Some note should be made of this book's title, *International Politics on the World Stage,* and the Shakespearean quotations that begin each chapter and are used from time to time to highlight a point. The idea behind this motif is to convey some of the sweep and complexity of the world drama. No one who has ever read William Shakespeare can dismiss his masterpieces as easily understood or inconsequential. The events on the world stage are similar—complex, full of drama, sometimes hopeful, often tragic, and always riveting. But you, the reader, would be mistaken to assume that the play analogy means that, as a member of the audience, you can be content to sit back and watch the plot unfold. Quite the contrary—part of what makes the world drama so compelling is that the audience is seated onstage and is part of, as well as witness to, the action that is unfolding. And that is one reason why I have also quoted more recent world players. Shakespeare's plays are of the past; the world drama is ongoing. Furthermore, as in an improvisational play, you in the audience can become involved, and, given the consequences of a potentially tragic rather than a happy ending, you ought to become involved. If there is anything that this text proposes, it is that each of us is intimately affected by international politics and that we all have a responsibility and an ability to become shapers of the script. As we shall see, our play has alternative scripts, and what the next scene brings depends in part on us. There is wisdom, then, in Shakespeare's advice in *All's Well That Ends Well* that "Our remedies oft in ourselves do lie."

I am sincerely interested in getting feedback from the faculty members and students who use this text. My pretensions to perfection have long since been dashed, and your recommendations for additions, deletions, and changes in future editions will be appreciated and seriously considered. People do write me, and I write or call them back! You are encouraged to join this correspondence by writing to me at the Department of Political Science U1024, University of Connecticut, Storrs, CT 06269-1024 or sending me an e-mail at John.Rourke@uconn.edu. This book, just like the world, can be made better, but its improvement depends heavily on whether or not you are concerned enough to think and act.

John T. Rourke

Acknowledgments

I T IS A DIFFICULT task to keep this acknowledgment of those who have contributed to the text down to a reasonable length. There are many who have played an important part, and my debt to each of them is great. I have tried to make adjustments wherever possible. Some reviewers have pointed out specific concerns about matters of fact or interpretation, and a number of corrections were made. On a larger scale, this edition's organizational changes; its greater coverage of constructivism, postmodernism, and other critical approaches; and several other shifts in coverage are responses in part to their suggestions. Adding to the long list of those who have reviewed earlier editions and made this text better, I would like to also thank those who contributed to this edition:

Karen Adams
Louisiana State University

Craig Arceneux
California Polytechnic State University, San Luis Obispo

Desmond Arias
John Jay College of Criminal Justice, City University of New York

Dlynn Armstrong-Williams
North Georgia College & State University

Gawdat Bahgat
Indiana University of Pennsylvania

Mary Jane Burns
Idaho State University

Richard Byrne
Kirkwood Community College

Sophie Clavie
San Francisco State University

John A. C. Conybeare
University of Iowa

Katy Crossley-Frolick
DePaul University

Claire Cutler
University of Victoria

Robert Denemark
University of Delaware, Newark

Thomas Doleys
Kennesaw State University

Roxanne Doty
Arizona State University

Dennis Driggers
California State University, Fresno

Douglas Durasoff
Seattle Pacific University

Tahmineh Entessar
Webster University

Kevin S. Fridy
University of Florida, Gainesville

David Frolick
North Central College

Vilma Elisa Fuentes
Santa Fe Community College

Clifford E. Griffin
North Carolina State University, Raleigh

Gregory Hall
St. Mary's College of Maryland

Elizabeth Crump Hanson
University of Connecticut

Clinton Hewan
Northern Kentucky University

George Kent
University of Hawaii

Kent Kille
The College of Wooster

Jeffrey P. Krans
Keuka College

Marwan Kreidie
Villanova University

Timothy C. Lim
California State University, Los Angeles

Paul McCartney
Rutgers University

Daniel McIntosh
Slippery Rock University

Rajan Menon
Lehigh University

Allen Meyer
Mesa Community College

Layna Mosley
University of North Carolina, Chapel Hill

Mark J. Mullenbach
University of Central Arkansas

Todd Myers
Grossmont College

Steve Owen
Kirkwood Community College

Shannon Peterson
Utah State University, Logan

John Queen
Glendale Community College

G. Hossein Razi
University of Houston

J. Martin Rochester
University of Missouri–St. Louis

Karl Schonberg
St. Lawrence University

Wayne A. Selcher
Elizabethtown College

Rosemary Shinko
University of Connecticut, Stamford

Christopher D. Skubby
Lakeland Community College

Michael W. Sonnleitner
Portland Community College

Henry Steck
SUNY–Cortland

Stacy VanDeveer
University of New Hampshire

Kimberly Weir
University of Northern Kentucky

John Allen Williams
Loyola University

Robert E. Williams
Pepperdine University

Francesco R. Wong
City College of San Francisco

Michele Zebich-Knos
Kennesaw State University

I also owe a debt to each author listed in the references of this and the previous editions. The work that these scholars have done on specific subjects forms the intellectual building blocks that are a significant part of the final structure of this, or any, worthwhile introductory textbook. This text is also evolutionary, and I want to continue to express my appreciation to all those who read and commented on the previous editions. Additionally, I also want to thank the colleagues who have taken the time at International Studies Association meetings or other conferences to give me the benefit of their views. I have even, on occasion, taken off my name tag and helped the staff at the publisher's booth at professional meetings. The comments I have received in this anonymity have been sometimes encouraging, sometimes humbling, but always helpful.

Best of all, I have received many good suggestions from students. My own students have had to both read the text and listen to me, and their often obviously candid comments have helped the generations of students who will follow. My favorite was a sophomore who did not do well on his first exam and came to my office to lay blame at the door of the blankety-blank textbook. As we talked, he made some interesting, if pointed observations. It was also clear that he had not connected the author's

name on the front of the book with his professor. Boy, was he surprised when it finally dawned on him that he was grumping about the book to its author!

I owe special thanks to those who provided material for the Online Learning Center. Brian Urlacher of the University of Connecticut is responsible for revising the online Instructor's Manual and Test Bank to accompany *International Politics on the World Stage*. Brian shouldered the task of preparing, revising, and updating this instructor's tool for the twelfth edition with the utmost care and good nature. Another exciting feature of this text is the supplementary material and exercises for students that can be found in the Online Learning Center. I thank Jeff Golding for his meticulous updates and polish.

Then there is the staff of McGraw-Hill. McGraw-Hill's political science editors, Monica Eckman and Mark Georgiev, encouraged and supported me. More of a day-to-day mainstay is my general editor, Ava Suntoke. She has gently and expertly guided me through several editions, and I am continually delighted with her unusual combination of substantive expertise and editing expertise. Sheryl Rose, copyeditor, with her amazing eye for technical detail and substantive consistency, added to the process of ensuring accuracy. I also want to thank Brett Coker, Alison Meier, and the rest of the McGraw-Hill production staff for their diligence and for not threatening my life through innumerable changes.

One of the things I like best about this edition is "its look." Pamela Carley has assembled photographs and editorial cartoons that bring powerful visual life to the concepts I express in words. Andrei Pasternak did the striking interior and cover design. ICC Macmillan, India, performed the difficult but crucial task of composition and layout. Charles Vitelli drew the original cartoons in this book. He took my raw mental images and turned them into wonderful representations of the issues being discussed in the text. In the same area, Emma Ghiselli, John Waller, and Judy Waller did an extraordinary job with the exacting art of creating the text's many figures and maps. Thanks are also due to Alice and Will Thiede of Carto-Graphics for their standard of excellence in producing the maps in the book. I owe a great debt to those who have created such a visually attractive, educationally effective package for my words. To all of you:

I can no other answer make but thanks, thanks, and ever thanks.
—William Shakespeare, *Twelfth Night*

Contents in Brief

Contents

PART II   Political Orientations on the World Stage

CHAPTER 4   **Nationalism: The Traditional Orientation**   **101**

PART III   Organizational Structures of the Actors

CHAPTER 6   **National States: The Traditional Structure   166**

PART V   Pursuing Peace

CHAPTER 10   **National Security: The Traditional Road   305**

PART VI   Pursuing Prosperity

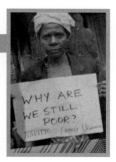

PART VII   Pursuing Human Rights and Environmental Viability

CHAPTER 14   **Preserving and Enhancing Human Rights and Dignity   451**

MAPS

A Brief Walkthrough of a Chapter in *International Politics on the World Stage*

JOHN ROURKE'S *International Politics on the World Stage* has an abundance of learning aids that help to enrich student understanding while enlivening the study of international relations. Engaging graphics and features prompt students to think critically about world events and concepts in international relations.

Chapter Opener Page

Shakespearean quotes and a photo set the stage by presenting the theme of the chapter.

The chapter structure is outlined on the opener page, providing an overview of the chapter coverage for the student.

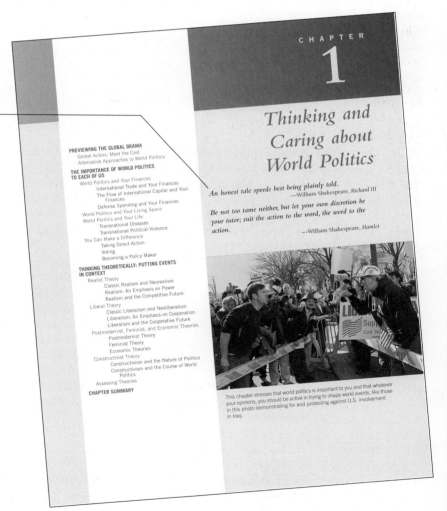

CHAPTER

1

Thinking and Caring about World Politics

An honest tale speeds best being plainly told.
—William Shakespeare, Richard III

Be not too tame neither, but let your own discretion be your tutor; suit the action to the word, the word to the action.
—William Shakespeare, Hamlet

This chapter stresses that world politics is important to you and that whatever your opinions, you should be active in trying to shape world events, like those in this photo demonstrating for and protesting against U.S. involvement in Iraq.

Boxes

Boxes provide students with opportunities to engage with the concepts in the text in a lively and interactive way. There are two types of boxes.

a. Debate the Policy Script boxes present students with the main points of a thought-provoking issue and ask them to decide on a course of action and to support their decision.

b. Get Involved boxes focus on student activism. They invite students to take action and become engaged with world issues.

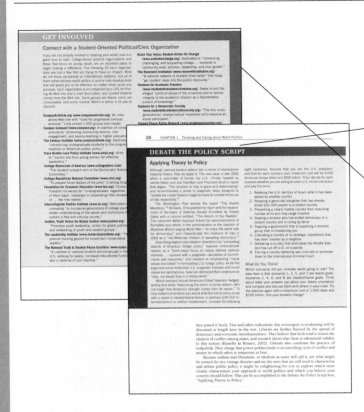

Figures

Exceptionally clear graphics with detailed captions allow students to grasp world events and trends at a glance.

Maps

Maps directly support the text discussions and provide students with the geographic context they need in order to gain a full understanding of the concepts in the text.

Tables

Up-to-date tables provide students with data in a succinct format, offering an excellent summary of complex topics.

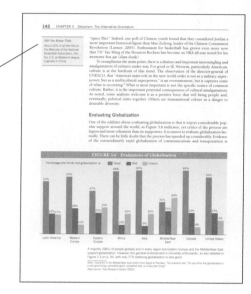

DYK

Did You Know clips provide a moment of diversion, giving students facts about the world today that are surprising, amusing, and informative.

Glossary

It is important for students to master the terminology of international relations, and this text helps them do so. Key terms are boldfaced in the text, listed for review at the end of the chapter, and defined in the glossary at the end of the book. The Online Learning Center has an interactive list of key terms for each chapter.

Chapter Summary

An excellent tool for chapter review is the numbered summary of main points at the end of the chapter.

Web Links

Web links to the Internet connect students to sites that are chosen to engage students in addition to containing more information on the topic being presented in the text.

---

40   CHAPTER 2   The Evolution of World Politics

rebirth and reform called the **Renaissance** (about 1350–1650). Many of the concepts that emerged, including scientific inquiry and personal freedom, undermined the authority of the Church.

> **Web Link**
> The text of the Treaty of Westphalia is available at www.yale.edu/lawweb/avalon/westphal.htm.

One significant outcome was the **Protestant Reformation**. Influenced by Renaissance thinking, Martin Luther rejected the Catholic Church as the necessary intermediary between people and God. In 1517 Luther proclaimed his belief that anyone could have an individual relationship with God. Within a few decades, nearly a quarter of the people of Western Europe became Protestants. The first great secular break with the Catholic Church occurred in England, where King Henry VIII (r. 1509–1547) rejected papal authority and established the Anglican Church. The Reformation also touched off political-religious struggles elsewhere in Europe. The ostensible issue was religious freedom, but there were also important political causes and consequences. When the century-long struggle between the imperial and Catholic Holy Roman Empire and the nationalist and Protestant ethnic groups ended with the **Treaty of Westphalia** (1648), centralized political power in Europe was over. The Holy Roman Empire had splintered into two rival Catholic monarchies (Austria and Spain); a number of Protestant entities (such as Holland and many German states) gained independence or autonomy. Yet other countries, such as Catholic France and Protestant England, were more secure in their independence. Therefore, many scholars regard 1648 as marking the births of the modern national state and of the world political system based on sovereign states as the primary political actors.

The Emergence of the Sovereign State

The breakdown of the feudal-universalistic system of governance did not, however, immediately make the **state** the uncontested, dominant political actor. Instead, the people of the Middle Ages experimented with several types of political organizations to see how well they would meet the security and economic needs of the time.

The Early State and Its Competitors   The revival of city-states, such as Venice, was one alternative scheme of political organization. Another was the formation of loosely confederated city-leagues based on common economic interests. The most famous of these mercantile alliances, the Hanseatic League, was founded in 1358 to protect commerce against piracy. It eventually included 70 northern European cities stretching from Bruges (in modern Belgium) to Novograd (in modern Russia) and became a major economic force.

What is important is that states, not city-states or city-leagues, became the new focus of political organization. The Hanseatic League ended in 1667. The fortunes of Venice and other city-states ebbed more slowly, but they eventually faded also. The failure of these experiments and the survival of the state occurred for identifiable, pragmatic reasons. Those are beyond our telling here, but the essential point is that in time "sovereign states displaced city-leagues and city-states . . . because their institutional logic gave them an advantage in mobilizing their societies' resources" (Spruyt, 1994:185). States were best equipped to conduct commerce, provide defense, and meet other needs.

Consequences of the Emergence of the State   The emergence and eventual triumph of the state as the dominant mode of governance had profound consequences for the international system. One of these was that states became the primary actors in the post-Westphalia international system. They continue in that starring role today. Therefore, much of the action on the world stage is about states and groups of states interacting with one another.

Key Terms   63

11. The pursuit of peace is also at something of a crossroads. The destructiveness of modern weaponry has made the quest for peace even more imperative. There are two overriding issues. One is how to respond to the challenge that asymmetrical warfare presents to traditional national defense strategies. The second is whether to seek overall security through the traditional approach of self-reliance or to place greater emphasis on international peacekeeping, arms control, and other alternative international security approaches.

12. The international economy is also changing in ways that have important implications for the 21st century. Economic interdependence has progressed rapidly. The transnational flow of trade, investment capital, and currencies has economically entwined all countries. There are, however, counterpressures, and countries have important choices to make in the near future. One is whether to continue down the newer path to economic integration or to halt that process and follow more traditional national economic policies. If the decision is to continue toward greater economic integration, then a second choice is how to regulate the global economy to deal with the legitimate concerns of those who are suspicious of or even outright opposed to greater globalization.

13. The effort to resolve the wide, and in many ways growing, gulf between the economic circumstances of the countries of the economically developed North and the less economically developed South is also a mounting issue in the new century.

14. A final set of issues that must be addressed in the new century involves the quality of life: human rights and the environment. Both issues have become the subject of much greater international awareness, action, progress, and interaction. Yet ending the abuses of human rights and protecting the environment are still distant goals.

For simulations, debates, and other interactive activities, a chapter quiz, Web links, and much more, visit **www.mhhe.com/rourke12/** and go to chapter 2. Or, while accessing the site, click on Course-Wide Content and view recent international relations articles in the *New York Times*.

KEY TERMS

anarchical political system	Eurowhite	multipolar system	Renaissance
appeasement policy	feudal system	Munich Conference	South
asymmetrical warfare	globalization	nationalism	sovereignty
balance of power	gross national product	newly industrializing	state
bipolar system	(GNP)	countries (NICs)	superpower
cold war	hegemonic power	North	sustainable development
containment doctrine	Holy Roman Empire	North Atlantic Treaty	Third World
détente	imperialism	Organization (NATO)	Treaty of Westphalia
East-West axis	industrial revolution	popular sovereignty	tribalism
economic	international system	power poles	weapons of mass
interdependence	less developed countries	Protestant Reformation	destruction (WMDs)
economically developed	(LDCs)	purchasing power	West
countries (EDCs)	limited unipolar system	parity (PPP)	westernization of the
ethnonational groups	McWorld	realpolitik	international system

OLC

Each chapter of the book has an Online Learning Center (OLC) organized by chapter. The OLC contains an abundance of learning tools, including quizzes and interactive exercises.

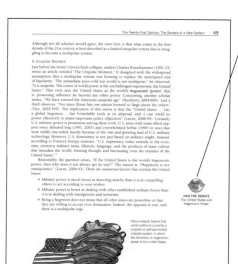

Web Site Icon

The interactive exercises on the OLC are tightly integrated with the text. Icons in the margins show students where there is a relevant activity on the OLC.

Web Site Exercise

Interactive simulations on the OLC allow students to step into a decision-making role using the concepts they learn in the text.

Web Site Exercise

Debate exercises on the OLC invite students to join the debate on controversial political, economic, and social topics.

Web Site Exercise

Interactive maps test and reinforce the geography students need to know in order to understand world politics.

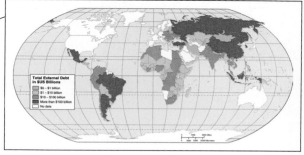

Thinking and Caring about World Politics

An honest tale speeds best being plainly told.
        —William Shakespeare, *Richard III*

*Be not too tame neither, but let your own discretion be
your tutor; suit the action to the word, the word to the
action.*

        —William Shakespeare, *Hamlet*

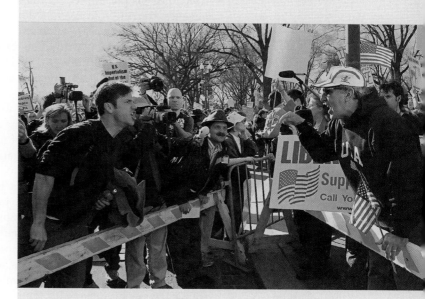

This chapter stresses that world politics is important to you and that whatever
your opinions, you should be active in trying to shape world events, like those
in this photo demonstrating for and protesting against U.S. involvement
in Iraq.

"Aᴌʟ ᴛʜᴇ ᴡᴏʀʟᴅ'ꜱ ᴀ ꜱᴛᴀɢᴇ, and all the men and women merely players," William Shakespeare (1564–1616) tells us in *As You Like It*. The Bard of Avon's words highlight the remarkable parallels between international relations and his masterful plays. Both have epic and complex plots. Their characters range from heroic to evil. The action is always dramatic and sometimes tragic. Justice sometimes prevails, but not always. Yet for all its complexity, the one constant in the action on the world stage is that it is riveting and a tale worth telling. It is to this epic story that we should now turn our attention.

PREVIEWING THE GLOBAL DRAMA

Whether you are watching a play, a movie, or a television program, getting into the story is easier if you already have a sense of what you are seeing from a playbill, movie review, or television guide. Similarly, it will help your journey through this book if you have some idea of the cast of characters you will meet and the basic outline of the script. So, before the curtain rises, here is a preview of the global drama that introduces the cast and the theme around which this text is organized.

Global Actors: Meet the Cast

Unlike cast members in a play, most of the actors in the world drama are organizations, not people. **States** (countries) are a type of organizational actor, and they have the starring role (Wendt, 2004). There are nearly 200 countries on the world stage. Like some theatrical stars, they can be self-absorbed and jealously guard their claim to fame, which for states is their **sovereignty**, the legal claim that there is no higher authority. It is this sovereign status that separates states from the other actors. Of course, sovereignty also means that the world drama has no director who can bring order to the interaction among the stars. This lack of central authority often leaves the actors in conflict with one another. Also, while all the states are legally equal, the reality is that some are bigger stars than others. The United States would certainly head the "A list" of top stars, with China and a few other countries also major players. Andorra, Vanuatu, and many other countries are usually consigned to bit parts.

Web Link

For up-to-date information about countries and related data, access the CIA's *World Factbook* at **https://www.cia.gov/cia/ publications/factbook/index.html.**

Joining the states onstage is a host of international organizations. The most prominent of these are the 300 or so **intergovernmental organizations (IGOs)** whose membership is made up of states. Some are global (the United Nations); others are regional (the European Union). Even more numerous are the transnational organizations. One type, **nongovernmental organizations (NGOs)**, has individuals as members. There are thousands of NGOs, and their concerns touch virtually every aspect of international politics ranging from the AIDS crisis (the International AIDS Society) to zero population growth (Population Connections). Multinational corporations (MNCs) are another type of transnational actor. The annual earnings of some of these companies rival the economic output of midsize states and dwarf most of the smaller ones. In a largely unregulated drama where money is an important source of power, MNCs can be important cast members.

Finally, some people are also important actors on the world stage. Usually individuals have an impact as decision makers, protesters, voters, or in some other role in a state or IGO. Sometimes, however, individuals play roles that transcend national and other institutional boundaries. Later in the book you will meet Jody Williams, a

MAP
World Countries

native of Putney, Vermont, who decided that land mines are evil. Along with others who felt the same way, she established an NGO to campaign against land mines, was responsible for an international treaty to ban them, and won the 1997 Nobel Peace Prize for her efforts.

Alternative Approaches to World Politics

This book is structured around the conviction that how the world is organized and conducts its international relations is in considerable flux. Long-dominant structures, ideas, and practices have all changed substantially and at an increasing rate during the last century or so. Traditionally, world politics has been a tumultuous drama centered on independent countries using their power for their self-interest and competing against other countries in a largely **anarchical international system**, one in which there is no central authority to set and enforce rules and resolve disputes. This remains the main thrust of world politics, but increasingly there is an alternative approach in evidence. Some of the differences that distinguish these two approaches are:

Dimension	Traditional Approach	Alternative Approach
Human organization	National societies	Global society
Interests	National/self-interests	Global/mutual interests
Interaction	Competition	Cooperation
Basis of safety	Self-protection	Collective security
Basis of prosperity	Self-help	Mutual assistance
Ultimate authority	Sovereign states	International organizations
Dispute resolution	Power prevails	Law prevails

The alternative approach may sound like academic "pie in the sky," but it is not. In the first place, it somewhat resembles how we as individuals interact with one another within countries. Certainly, we pursue our own interests in domestic systems, with considerable freedom to do so, and we partly rely on ourselves for our own safety and welfare. But in domestic systems, we individuals also recognize rules, are held accountable for obeying them, and have some sense of common identity, common good, and shared responsibility to achieve the common good and help struggling members of society.

Second, while the traditional approach continues to prevail, it is not as dominant as it once was. If a century ago a professor had written an international relations text predicting a world organization (the United Nations) with all countries as members, a legal community of 25 European countries (the European Union), the virtual disappearance of tariff restrictions under the World Trade Organization, tens of billions of dollars a year in economic aid from rich to poor countries, an International Criminal Court to try war crimes, or many of the other realities of today, that text, if printed at all, would have been consigned to the fiction section of the library.

What is even more important than what has changed is what the future holds. Clearly, the world is facing a series of critical choices related to the traditional and alternative approaches. Note carefully that it is not an either-or choice. The options are much more nuanced. They involve when and to what degree we intermix the traditional way world politics has been pursued for centuries and the newer, alternative approach that has been gaining some ground.

The international system includes many types of actors. Of these, states (or countries) are the most important. National boundaries are the most important source of political division in the world, and for most people nationalism is the strongest source of political identification.

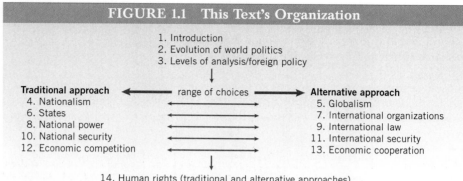

The organization of this text reflects our theme of comparing the traditional and still dominant competitive approach to world politics and an alternative cooperative approach that is increasingly evident. It is probable that the future will feature some blending of the two approaches. What their relative role will be is the question. For example, consider the range of choices along a continuum (scale) between relying solely on your own country's national security forces for protection or, at the other extreme, depending entirely on UN security forces for protection. If zero is one extreme (only national security) on the continuum of choices and 100 is the other extreme (only international security), it is arguable that the world was at zero a century ago and is at perhaps 10 to 15 now. Would you move the future marker back toward zero or further along the continuum toward 100?

Exploring the traditional and alternative approaches drives the structure of this text, as visualized in Figure 1.1. To begin, the first three chapters set the stage, so to speak, by discussing the importance of world politics and some basic theories of global politics (chapter 1), the evolution of and current instability in the world political system (chapter 2), and how foreign policy is made from the perspective of three levels of analysis—the system, state, and human levels (chapter 3).

After chapter 3, the theme of two approaches runs through the remaining chapters. Chapters 4 and 5 deal with divergent ways we define ourselves politically. The traditional orientation is nationalism (chapter 4), which focuses on the individual nation (such as Americans) and its self-governance in a state (such as the United States). Transnationalism (chapter 5), seeing yourself politically connected to others across borders, is the alternative approach. Chapters 6 and 7 deal with how we organize ourselves politically. Chapter 6 focuses on the traditional political unit, the state, and chapter 7 takes up international organizations, with particular emphasis on the European Union and the United Nations.

Chapters 8 and 9 explore different ways to conduct world politics. Chapter 8 covers the "might makes right" traditional approach of applying national power to diplomacy; chapter 9 examines the "right makes right" alternative road of international law and morality. The next pair of chapters take up physical security. One approach is the traditional emphasis on national security discussed in chapter 10. The other path, international security cooperation, is addressed in chapter 11.

Chapters 12 and 13 turn to international political economy. The commentary begins with chapter 12's examination of the traditional approach, national economic competition. Then chapter 13 offers the alternative, international economic cooperation. Departing from the alternative chapters scheme, chapters 14 on human rights and 15 on the environment look into current conditions and ways to improve them. Each chapter explores both the traditional policies and interactions of tension between states acting singularly and the alternative drive for international cooperation.

The text's organizing theme of two approaches and the choices we have to make brings us back to you, global politics, and that future. Tomorrow's course is not determined. It is for you to decide what should happen and, as best you can, to convert that conviction into what will happen.

THE IMPORTANCE OF WORLD POLITICS TO EACH OF US

Shakespeare's sage counsel in *As You Like It* that we are all players on the world stage extends to *The Merchant of Venice,* in which Antonio exclaims, "I hold the world [to be] . . . a stage where every man must play a part." Most Americans are not convinced of that wisdom, though. Only a small minority of them regularly follows foreign news or has much knowledge about world politics or geography. The terrorist attacks on September 11, 2001, increased Americans' interest in the world around them, but only a little. Prior to 9/11, 33% of Americans said they followed international news "most of the time." That share had improved only slightly to 39% in 2006.[1] Young adults, ages 18–24, have particularly low interest and knowledge about global affairs. One indication was a 2006 National Geographic survey finding that 63% of Americans in that age group could not find Iraq on a blank map, and 70% were unable to locate Afghanistan, despite the fact that U.S. troops were fighting in both countries.

It is important to note that this dearth of concern and information among Americans contrasts with the attitudes and knowledge levels found in most other economically advanced countries. As Figure 1.2 details, a study that presented 18–24-year-olds in nine countries with 56 questions about world geography and 8 questions about world affairs found that Americans finished last among the 8 developed countries and did only marginally better than young adults in Mexico, where educational opportunities are much more limited. One illustrative multiple-choice question about the size of the U.S. population revealed that only a scant 25% of Americans selected the correct answer, but, even worse, their score was lower than that of the respondents in any of the other 8 countries.[2]

Is this low level of information about or interest in world events justifiable? No, it is not! This text seldom tries to tell you what to think or do. But one message is stressed: The world drama is important and deserves our careful attention. Even more importantly, we do not have to content ourselves with being passive observers. Especially if you agree with Irish literary lion Oscar Wilde's (1854–1900) wry remark, "The world is a stage, but the play is badly cast," become an active player. You can make a difference! The script is not set. It is an improvisational play with lots of room for changing the story line.

Web Link

The National Geographic Society presents results of its 2006 survey of the geography knowledge of young Americans at **www.nationalgeographic.com/ roper2006/.**

FIGURE 1.2   National Difference in Knowledge of the World

Average test score

Swedes	70%
Italians	66%
Germans	64%
Japanese	59%
French	59%
British	52%
Canadians	51%
Americans	46%
Mexicans	39%

How much people know about the world around them varies from country to country. This figure shows the average score on a world affairs and geography test given to people aged 18 to 24 in nine countries. Note that Americans finished next to last, only somewhat ahead of Mexicans, who live in a poor country in which only about half of all youths graduate high school (compared to 90% in the United States).

Note: There were 10 questions on world affairs and 56 questions on geography. Two world affairs questions (one on the world's largest religion, the other on the euro) were factored out by the author for methodological reasons.
Data source: National Geographic–Roper 2002 Global Geographic Literacy Survey, November 2002. Calculations by author.

To help you think about trying to do so, you will find a number of "Debate the Policy Script" boxes in this text. Each asks you to evaluate an important policy issue and to formulate a position on it. To further highlight the importance of the world to you, let us turn to a number of ways, some dramatic, some mundane, in which international politics affects your economic well-being, your living space, and your very life.

World Politics and Your Finances

Web Link

The U.S. Energy Information Administration has good material about supply, demand, and prices for gasoline and other fuels at **www.eia.doe.gov/**.

World politics affects each of our personal economic conditions in many ways. Sometimes specific events are costly. In addition to the human toll of the 9/11 attacks, they cost the United States at least $81 billion in destroyed property, lost business earnings, lost wages, increased security expenditures, and other costs during just the four immediately following months. More routinely, the global economy impacts individuals in ever expanding ways as national economies become increasingly intertwined. Indeed, as we shall see, the ties between national and international affairs are so close that many social scientists now use the term **intermestic** to symbolize the merger of *inter*national and do*mestic* concerns. To illustrate the increasingly ubiquitous connections between your own personal financial condition and world politics, we will briefly explore just three of the many links: how international trade, international investment, and defense spending affect your finances.

International Trade and Your Finances

The global flow of goods (tangible items) and services (intangible items such as revenues from tourism, insurance, and banking) is important to your financial circumstances. One example is U.S. dependence on foreign petroleum. That reality was brought sharply into focus as crude oil prices rose more than 274%, from about $19 a barrel in January 2002 to over $71 a barrel in August 2006, driving up the prices of gasoline, heating oil, and other petroleum products to record highs in the United States. Thus, every time you pumped gas, you paid more thanks to the realities of the international system.

Trade also wins and loses jobs. There is a steadily increasing likelihood that international trade and your job are related. Exports create jobs. The United States is the world's largest exporter, providing other countries with $1.3 trillion worth of U.S. goods and services in 2005. Creating these exports employed some 18 million Americans, about 13% of the total U.S. workforce.

While exports create jobs, other jobs are lost to imports. Americans imported $2 trillion in goods and services in 2005. Many of the clothes, toys, electronics, and other items they bought were once produced in U.S. plants by American workers. Now most of these items are produced overseas by workers whose wages are

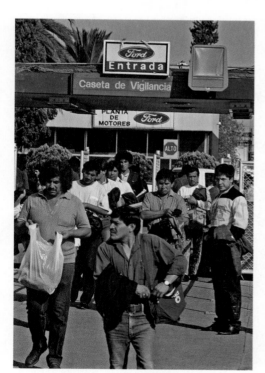

International trade affects jobs in every country. These workers leaving a Ford Motors plant in Cuautitlan, Mexico, are indicative of a shift in a significant percentage of U.S. manufacturing jobs to countries with lower wages. The plant employs 900 workers and makes pickup trucks for Mexico and for export to the United States.

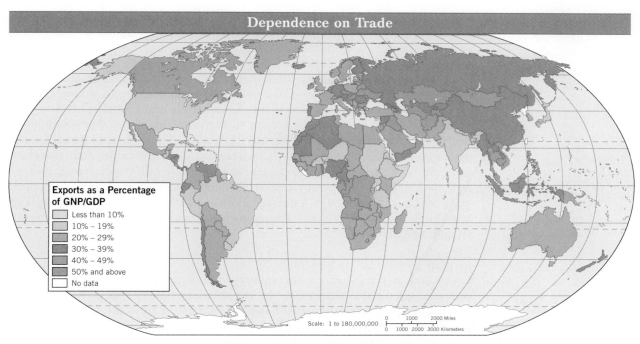

Dependence on Trade

Exports as a Percentage of GNP/GDP
- Less than 10%
- 10% – 19%
- 20% – 29%
- 30% – 39%
- 40% – 49%
- 50% and above
- No data

Scale: 1 to 180,000,000

All countries, even the most economically powerful ones, are becoming increasingly dependent on trade for their economic health. Whether you are an American or a Zimbabwean, there is a good chance that your job, the price you pay for goods you buy, and other factors in your economic well-being are dependent on global trade.

substantially lower. Jobs are also lost to service imports through "outsourcing" or "offshoring." Once, most of those who answered calls to the service help lines of U.S. computer companies were Americans. Now you will most likely get technical help for computer problems from a technician in Bangalore, India. In a different realm, Americans who have no or inadequate health insurance are increasingly outsourcing some of their medical care to internationally accredited foreign hospitals and physicians. A few procedures and their comparative costs are heart valve replacement, U.S.: $185,000, Singapore: $13,000; hip replacement, U.S.: $55,000, India: $9,000; and gastric bypass, U.S.: $55,000, Thailand: $15,000. There is no official data about the shift of service jobs overseas, but one recent study concludes that Americans are losing 90,000 business, professional, and technical jobs a year to outsourcing (Schultze, 2004).

Lost jobs are a serious matter, but before you cry "Buy American!" and demand barriers to limit foreign goods, it is important to realize that inexpensive foreign products improve your standard of living. For example, the United States annually imports more than $85 billion worth of clothes and footwear. What Americans pay for shirts, sneakers, and other things they wear would be much higher if the items were all made by American workers earning American wages.

The Flow of International Capital and Your Finances

The global flow of international finance affects you in more ways than you probably imagine. These are covered in greater detail in chapters 5 and 12, but to begin to see the impact of international capital we can look at **international investment capital,**

Did You Know That:

During 2006, the 591,050 foreign students enrolled in U.S. colleges contributed $14 billion to the U.S. economy. Foreign student expenditures are considered a U.S. service export.

MAP
Dependence on Trade

ANALYZE THE ISSUE
Finance

the flow of money in and out of a country to buy companies, stocks, bonds, real estate, and other assets. The amounts of money involved are immense. In 2006, for instance, Americans alone owned $10 trillion in foreign assets and foreigners owned $12.7 trillion in U.S. assets. One way that you may be affected is if you receive financial aid from your college. Schools generate part of their scholarship funds by investing their endowments in stocks and bonds, including foreign holdings. So the investment in these foreign assets and the dividends and capital gains that your college earns from them may be helping to pay your tuition. Another possibility is that you or someone in your family may be working for a company that is foreign owned. Sometimes foreign investors buy faltering U.S. companies and rejuvenate them, thus saving the jobs of their American workers. In other cases, foreign companies open new operations in the United States. For example, American workers make Nissan automobiles in Tennessee, Hondas in Ohio, Toyotas in Kentucky, and Mitsubishis in Illinois. Overall, foreign-owned firms in the United States employ 64 million Americans.

Defense Spending and Your Finances

Paying taxes to fund your country's military forces is yet another way that world politics affects you economically. U.S. defense spending, for example, totaled $536 billion during **fiscal year (FY)** 2006. This amount was 20% of the U.S. budget and equaled almost $1,800 per person in the United States.

There is a lively debate over whether defense spending is too high, too low, or about right, and that topic and other aspects of military security are examined in chapters 10 and 11. Whatever your position on the funding debate, though, it is clear that military forces are expensive and that to a considerable degree the military competes with domestic programs for funding. What the proper level of defense spending is and how it relates to other programs is just one area that you can influence as a voter and politically active citizen of your country. As you can see in Figure 1.3, countries set their spending priorities in very different ways.

Although there is no one-to-one relationship between reduced defense spending and increased higher education spending, it is worth thinking about what would be possible if U.S. budget priorities mirrored the average of the other three countries in Figure 1.3. That would add $358 billion to spending on U.S. schools and students. Just 25% of that extra money allocated to higher education would fund a $5,500 scholarship for each of the 16.5 million American students enrolled full-time in a U.S. college.

Be aware, though, that such a reallocation of defense spending, while great for college students, would harm the economic circumstances of other people. Nearly 6 million Americans are in the armed forces, work for the military as civilians, or work for a defense contractor. Many, perhaps most, of these people would lose their jobs. The ripple effect would economically damage the towns and cities where these defense workers are located and the businesses that serve them. It is for this reason, a former Defense Department official explains, that to a degree, "Both the administration and Congress . . . view defense as a federal jobs program."[3]

World Politics and Your Living Space

World politics affects more than your pocketbook. It also impacts the quality of the air you breathe, the water you drink, and other aspects of

Did You Know That:

Even limited military operations are very costly. Recent U.S. interventions and their costs are:

Grenada	1983	$76 million
Panama	1989	$164 million
Persian Gulf	1990–1991	$61 billion
Somalia	1992–1994	$675 million*
Haiti	1994–1995	$427 million
Bosnia	1996–	$1.3 billion*
Kosovo	1999–2000	$5.2 billion*
Afghanistan	2001–	$10 billion*
Iraq	2003–	$85 billion*

*first year of multiyear operation

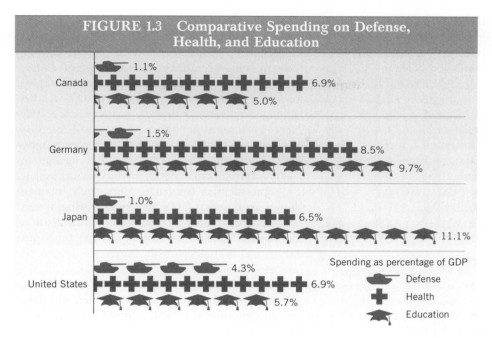

FIGURE 1.3   Comparative Spending on Defense, Health, and Education

To some extent, government defense spending involves a trade-off with domestic spending. This figure compares how much four wealthy countries spend in public funds on defense, health, and education as a percentage of their respective gross domestic products (GDPs). As evident, the United States spends 3.1% more of its wealth on defense than the average of the other countries. By the same standard, U.S. spending compared to the average of the other three is 0.4% lower for health and 2.9% lower for education. If U.S. budget priorities were the same as the average of Canada, Germany, and Japan, then U.S. defense expenditures in FY2005 would have been $388 billion less, health spending would have been $49 billion more, and spending on education would have increased $358 billion.

Data sources: SIPRI (2006), CIA (2006), OECD (2006).

the globe you inhabit. For one, the growth of the world's population and its pressure on resources threaten to change the quality of life as we know it. It took 100,000 years of human existence for the world population to finally reach 1 billion. Now, only a little more than 200 years later, there are 6.6 billion people because, as Figure 1.4 on p. 12 depicts, each additional billion people have been added in shorter and shorter periods of time. The growth rate has declined a bit, so that it will probably be 2012 before the world population reaches 7 billion. Still, this represents a tidal wave of new humans. In 2007, for example, the world added 77 million people, a number somewhat larger than the population of Egypt.

Among other concerns, Earth's expanding population presents serious environmental dangers. Burning oil and other fossil fuels to warm, transport, and otherwise provide for this mass of people annually creates more than 6 billion tons of carbon dioxide and other gas emissions. These, most scientists believe, are causing global warming. The year 2005 was the warmest since records were first kept in 1856, and 9 of the 10 warmest years occurred between 1996 and 2005.

Warmer temperatures may be welcome to some, but the overall ramifications are worrisome. Among other things, many scientists claim that global warming is melting the polar ice caps, thereby raising sea levels and threatening to flood coastal

ANALYZE THE ISSUE
The UN Population Fund

Web Link

The U.S. Census Bureau has national and global population clocks as well as other links to valuable related information at **www.census.gov/main/www/popclock.html.**

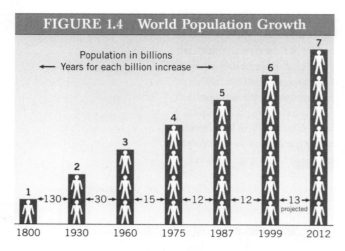

FIGURE 1.4 World Population Growth

From the time of the first humans, it took about 100,000 years for the world population to reach 1 billion in 1800. Another 130 years passed before there were 2 billion people. Now it takes only a little more than a decade for the population to expand yet another 1 billion people.

Data source: U.S. Census Bureau, UN Population Fund.

Web Link

Current and historical information on hurricanes is available from the U.S. National Hurricane Center at **www.nhc.noaa.gov/**.

areas of the world. Some Pacific island countries could even disappear under the rising seas. Additionally, many scientists believe that global warming is increasing the number and severity of damaging weather events such as heat waves, droughts, hurricanes, and other forms of destructive weather. Highlighting the view that such cataclysmic climate events are a political issue, a group called Scientists and Engineers for Change and Environment sponsored billboards criticizing President George W. Bush's environmental policy in Florida during the 2004 presidential campaign. One such billboard showed a photograph of a hurricane swirling toward Florida accompanied by the words, "Global warming equals worse hurricanes. George Bush just doesn't get it."[4] The horrific hurricane season the following year, including the devastation of New Orleans and the surrounding Gulf Coast area in August 2005 underscored the danger of global warming to those who believe it will bring environmental calamity.

Numerous other by-products of human activity also threaten our living space. The United Nations Environmental Programme (UNEP) reports that 10% of Earth's land has been or is in danger of "desertification" from overfarming and other harmful practices, nearly a billion people living in cities breathe dangerous levels of sulfur dioxide, and more than half the world's population could be facing critical water shortages by 2050. Certainly, world politics has not caused most environmental problems. However, we are unlikely to be able to stem, much less reverse, the degradation of the biosphere without global cooperation. As UNEP's director has put it, "We suffer from problems of planetary dimensions. They require global responses." Much more on this topic can be found in chapter 15, which details global warming and other threats to the environment, but also discusses the views of those who believe that such concerns are being overstated, and explores the politics of environmental regulation and remediation.

World Politics and Your Life

World politics affects not only how we live but in some cases whether we live at all. Disease and political violence are just two perils to your life that are connected to world politics.

Transnational Diseases

Politics may not directly cause diseases, but we are increasingly in need of global responses to counter health threats that ignore national borders. Some diseases are the result of environmental damage. By spewing chlorofluorocarbons (CFCs) and other chemicals into the air, we have significantly depleted Earth's ozone layer, which helps shield us from the sun's deadly ultraviolet rays. As a consequence, new cases of melanoma, the deadliest form of skin cancer, have skyrocketed. Among Americans, the chances of developing melanoma increased twenty-fold between

1960 and 2000. Annually, about 62,000 Americans are now diagnosed with melanoma, and almost 8,000 die from it. Certainly wearing sunscreen and taking other precautions will reduce your chances of becoming a skin cancer victim. But achieving that goal can also be greatly helped by international agreements, such as the UN-sponsored Montreal Protocol (1989). It mandates phasing out the use of CFCs and other ozone-attacking chemicals that were once used in such common items as air conditioners and deodorant sprays. Now, because of international cooperation, CFC concentrations in the atmosphere are declining, and the ozone layer is very gradually beginning to recover.

We also increasingly rely on global cooperation to prevent the spread of infectious diseases. Such diseases have always moved across borders, but modern transportation is now rapidly cutting the global travel time of many diseases as their human hosts jet from continent to continent. Since 1981 when the first cases of AIDS were identified in Africa, the disease has rapidly spread worldwide, and more than 34 million people are now HIV positive. AIDS is just one of several diseases that has emerged in recent years and rapidly claimed victims around the world. Figure 1.5 illustrates this point by tracing the increased incidence of West Nile virus in the United States. According to a top epidemiologist, the new number of infectious diseases and their ability to spread rapidly has made the period since "the 1970s without precedent in the history of the annals of medicine."[5] Of course each country acts to contain transnational diseases and treat their victims. However, it is far more effective to counter diseases where they first begin to appear than after they cross national borders, and it falls to the World Health Organization (WHO) to coordinate the global effort.

FIGURE 1.5   U.S. Cases of West Nile Virus

U.S. reported cases

Year	Cases
1999	62
2000	21
2001	66
2002	4,256
2003	9,862
2004	2,539
2005	3,000
2006	4,502

West Nile virus is one of several transnational diseases that have recently afflicted the United States. The disease is carried by birds and transmitted by mosquitoes and was first detected in Africa in 1937. After spreading slowly, West Nile virus first arrived in the United States in 1999. The U.S. mortality rate is 4%.

Note: The data for 2006 is estimated based on reported cases through October 2006. Data source: U.S. Centers for Disease Control.

Transnational Political Violence

War, terrorism, and other forms of transnational political violence are in many ways more threatening today than ever before (Horne, 2002). Until the 20th century, the vast majority of war deaths were soldiers. Civilian casualties began to rise drastically as military operations increasingly targeted noncombatants. Nearly as many civilians as soldiers were killed during World War II. Now more civilians than soldiers are killed. According to the UN, civilians accounted for more than 85% of everyone killed during wars in the 1980s and 1990s. In a nuclear war, military casualties would be a mere footnote to the overall death toll. And terrorists almost exclusively target civilians. In addition to military forces, terrorists also engage in international violence, as the attacks of September 11, 2001, underlined. Americans found that they were vulnerable to terrorism anywhere and at any moment in their daily lives. It must also be said that this unsettling reality has long been felt more acutely in other parts of the world that have been subjected to more frequent acts of international terrorism (Endgers & Sandler, 2006; Laquer, 2004).

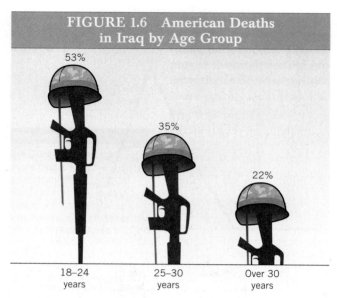

FIGURE 1.6   American Deaths in Iraq by Age Group

53%   18–24 years

35%   25–30 years

22%   Over 30 years

In Iraq, as in other wars, young adults make up a majority of the U.S. soldiers killed. More than half the young adults who have died in Iraq were age 18 to 24.

Note: The data is as of October 2006 when the death tally was 2,706.
Data source: U.S. Department of Defense.

War is a special concern for college-age adults because they are of prime military age. Of the American troops killed during the Vietnam War, 84% were aged 18 to 22. The average age of U.S. soldiers killed in the Iraq War beginning in 2003 is higher than it was in Vietnam, in part because U.S. forces in Iraq are part of an all-volunteer military, whereas many U.S. soldiers in Vietnam were draftees. Still, as Figure 1.6 shows, young adults bear the brunt of American casualties in Iraq.

It is also the case that military combat is a matter that increasingly affects women directly as well as men. In the United States and elsewhere, the types of combat units in which women are allowed to serve are expanding. As a result, many more women may fight and die in future wars. More than 200,000 women are on active duty with U.S. forces, and as late 2006, 61 American servicewomen had lost their lives in Iraq.

You Can Make a Difference

The next logical question is, "Can I make a difference?" Yes, you can! It is true that we cannot all be president or secretary of state, but we can take action and we can make our views known.

Taking Direct Action

One way to influence global relations is through various forms of direct action. In the United States, millions of individual student actions, ranging from burning draft cards, to massive and sometimes violent demonstrations, helped end American involvement in Vietnam. College students have also been at the forefront of demonstrations both for and against the war with and occupation of Iraq beginning in 2003 (Foyle, 2004). College students have also been active on numerous other issues related to foreign affairs. During 2006, for example, thousands of students at the University of Texas at Austin rallied on behalf of the rights of immigrants, and students at the University of California–Santa Cruz forced military recruiters off the campus. At the University of Washington, University of Vermont, University of California, and other colleges, campus chapters of the Students Taking Action Now: Darfur and other student groups persuaded their schools to sell all their stocks and bonds of companies that do business with the government of Sudan. Students on U.S. college campuses have also helped bring consumer pressure to bear on clothing and footwear companies that sell products manufactured in so-called sweatshops in Asia and elsewhere. These factories pay little, require employees to work long hours, and have poor safety records. Following their students' lead, 175 universities and colleges along with numerous human rights groups and Nike and other manufacturers united to form the Fair Labor Association, an organization working to help protect the rights of factory workers worldwide. The Get Involved box, "Connect with a Student-Oriented Political/Civic Organization," provides a starting place to increase your active presence on the world stage.

Web Link

You can find out if your school is a member of the Fair Labor Association by going to the FLA Web site at **www.fairlabor.org/.**

GET INVOLVED

Connect with a Student-Oriented Political/Civic Organization

If you are not already involved in shaping your world, now is a good time to start. College-based political organizations and those that focus on young adults are an excellent place to begin making a difference. The following 20 such organizations are but a few that are trying to have an impact. Most do not focus exclusively on international relations, but all of them either address world politics in part or help develop skills that will assist you to be effective no matter what cause you promote. Each organization is accompanied by a URL for finding its Web site and a brief description, and quoted material comes from the Web site. Some groups are liberal, some are conservative, and some, neutral. Which is which is for you to discover.

CampusActivism.org (www.campusactivism.org) An interactive Web site with "tools for progressive campus activists." Lists almost 1,500 groups and causes.

Campus Compact (www.compact.org) A coalition of college presidents "promoting community service, civic engagement, and service-learning in higher education."

The Century Institute (www.centuryinstitute.org) Dedicated to "introducing undergraduate students to the progressive tradition in American public policy."

Clare Boothe Luce Policy Institute (www.cblpi.org) Aims to "mentor and train young women for effective leadership."

College Democrats of America (www.collegedems.com) "The student outreach arm of the Democratic National Committee."

College Republican National Committee (www.crnc.org) "To prepare future leaders of the party" is among its goals.

Foundation for Economic Education (www.fee.org) Conducts Freedom University for "undergraduates, regardless of their major, interested in [expanding] their knowledge of . . . the free market."

Intercollegiate Studies Institute (www.isi.org) Dedicated to conveying "to successive generations of college youth a better understanding of the values and institutions that sustain a free and virtuous society."

JustAct: Youth Action for Global Justice (www.justact.org) "Promotes youth leadership, action for global justice, and networking of youth and student groups."

The Leadership Institute (www.leadershipinstitute.org) "The premier training ground for tomorrow's conservative leaders."

The National Youth & Student Peace Coalition (www.nyspc.org) "A coalition of national student activist groups in the U.S. working for peace, increased educational funding, and in defense of civil liberties."

Raise Your Voice: Student Action for Change (www.actionforchange.org) Dedicated to "connecting, challenging, and supporting college . . . students in community work, activism, leadership, and civic growth."

The Roosevelt Institution (www.rooseveltinstitution.org) "A national network of student think tanks" that helps "get student ideas into the public discourse."

Students for Academic Freedom (www.studentsforacademicfreedom.org) Seeks to end the alleged "political abuse of the university and to restore integrity to the academic mission as a disinterested pursuit of knowledge."

Students for a Democratic Society (www.studentsforademocraticsociety.org) "The first multi-generational, diverse radical movement with everyone an equal participant."

Student Peace Action Network (www.studentpeaceaction.org) "We organize for an end to physical, social and economic violence caused by U.S. militarism."

Student Public Interest Research Groups (www.studentpirgs.org) "Independent . . . student organizations that work to solve public interest problems related to the environment, consumer protection, and government reform."

United States Students Association (www.usstudents.org) "Works on building grassroots power among students to win concrete victories that expand access to education at the federal, state and campus level."

Young America's Foundation (www.students.yaf.org) "Committed to ensuring that increasing numbers of young Americans understand and are inspired by the ideas of individual freedom, a strong national defense, free enterprise, and traditional values."

Young Politicians of America (www.ypa.org) "A service-learning movement composed of young Americans aged 14–22 working together to revive political discourse and awareness by establishing nonpartisan civic clubs in high schools and colleges."

And all by itself:

Students for an Orwellian Society (www.studentsfororwell.org) An offbeat organization that promotes "the vision of a society based upon the principles of Ingsoc, first articulated by George Orwell in his prophetic novel, *1984.*"

Be Active

The only way to surely fail to shape politics to your liking is by being passive.

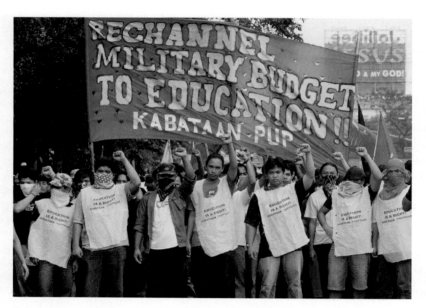

College students in many countries are an important political group. These Filipino students in Manila, for example, are protesting tuition hikes in 2007 and demanding that some of the money going to the Philippines military budget be redirected to educational funding.

Voting

Democracies provide opportunities to affect world politics through the ballot box. Voting for candidates is one of these. Leaders do not always follow campaign promises, but the person who gets elected usually does influence policy. During the 2004 U.S. presidential election, George Bush and John Kerry disagreed sharply over the degree to which the United States should act unilaterally in its foreign policy, on whether the war against Iraq was justified, on whether the U.S. should join global negotiations to reduce the emission of global warming gases, and on a range of other issues. The voters determined that it would be George Bush and not John Kerry who would guide U.S. foreign policy during 2005–2008 (Klinkner, 2006).

From a certain perspective, those who were disappointed with the results had cause to blame young adults for Kerry's defeat. As Figure 1.7 shows, young adults (age 18–24) favored Kerry over Bush by a substantial margin, in contrast to older American voters, who favored Bush. Yet, in the United States, as in most other countries, young adults are much less likely to vote than are older adults (Patterson, 2005; Phelps, 2004). This voting gap makes a difference, as the figure's caption discusses.

By 2006, however, the mood of the electorate had changed significantly, and that shift had a substantial impact on the composition of Congress and on U.S. policy in Iraq (Eichenberg, Stoll, & Lebo, 2006; Voeten & Brewer, 2006). The 2006 congressional elections became something of a referendum on Bush's leadership, especially in Iraq, and voter discontent helped the Democrats gain control of both houses of Congress for the first time in 12 years. As one analyst described it, "A lot of voters said, 'I'm going to vote Democratic.' They didn't even know the name of the Democrat, but they said, 'I'm going to vote Democratic because I don't like Bush, I don't like the war, I want to make a statement.'"[6]

Direct voting on international questions by referendum is also possible in some countries. In 2005, for example, voters in Luxembourg and Spain approved a proposed constitution for the European Union (EU), but French and Dutch voters rejected it, effectively blocking adoption (Hobol, 2006). Elsewhere in Europe during 2005 and 2006, Swiss voters agreed to increased openness of their job market to workers from EU countries but also tightened the rules for foreigners trying to claim political or humanitarian asylum in Switzerland. Even more significantly, the world's newest country came into being in 2006 when 55% of the electorate in Montenegro voted to declare independence from Serbia. Additionally in 2006, Panamanians approved a referendum measure allocating over $5 billion to expand and upgrade their interocean canal. The ability of citizens to make direct decisions about foreign policy is still not common, but it is becoming more so, and there is strong support in the United States, the countries of Europe, and other democracies for greater use of referendums and other such **direct democracy** techniques (Qvortrup, 2002).

Becoming a Policy Maker

It is also possible to become a policy maker by running for elective office or securing an appointment in an agency that deals with your country's foreign affairs. You can also work for the United Nations or one of the other important international organizations. It may take some time to work your way up through the ranks to a key position, but it is possible.

Studying political science can be a start on the path to becoming a policy maker. Secretary of State Condoleezza Rice holds both undergraduate and graduate degrees in political science. Other recent top U.S. policy makers with degrees in political science include President Bill Clinton, Speaker of the House Nancy Pelosi, Vice President Al Gore, Secretary of State Madeleine Albright, and Secretary of Defense Donald Rumsfeld. UN Secretary-General Ban Ki-moon and EU President José Manuel Barroso also have degrees in political science. Even if you remain a political scientist and do not become a policy maker, your teaching and research may influence those who will or who already hold official positions (Willinsky, 2006).

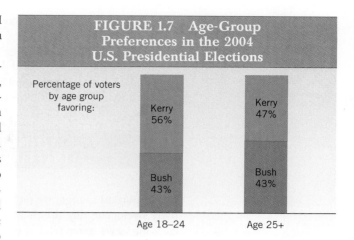

FIGURE 1.7 Age-Group Preferences in the 2004 U.S. Presidential Elections

Percentage of voters by age group favoring:

Age 18–24	Age 25+
Kerry 56%	Kerry 47%
Bush 43%	Bush 43%

American young adults (age 18–24) were more likely than older adults to favor John Kerry over George Bush for president in 2004. The same partisan pattern existed during the 2000 presidential election. Also in both elections, older adults were more likely to vote than were young adults. In 2004, for example, 62% of older adults, but only 42% of young adults, voted. These gaps in voting percentage and candidate preferences are important. Had young adults voted in 2000 and 2004 at the same rate as older adults, Al Gore would have won the 2000 election, and the 2004 race would have narrowed to the point where John Kerry might have won.

Note: The outcome in 2004 cannot be precisely calculated because of sampling error in the exit polls on which the data is based and other factors. Percentages do not add to 100 because of voter support of third-party candidates.
Data sources: Exit polls conducted for the Associated Press by Edison Media Research and Mitofsky International.

Some students of political science become top policy officials. Secretary of State Condoleezza Rice, seen here during graduation ceremonies at Stanford University, was an undergraduate and graduate student in political science, then taught the subject at Stanford and became its provost before joining the Bush administration.

The point is that you count—by voting, protesting, joining issue-oriented groups, donating money to causes you support, or even by having your thoughts recorded in a political poll. Few individual actions are dramatic, and by themselves few significantly change world politics, but the sum of many smaller actions can and does make a difference. Do not consider politics a spectator sport. It is more important than that. Treat politics as a participant—even a contact—sport.

THINKING THEORETICALLY: PUTTING EVENTS IN CONTEXT

It is important to organize our thinking about world events given their impact on our daily lives. The day this is being written, the front page of the *New York Times* is carrying news items related to suicide bombings in Afghanistan, U.S. foreign policy toward Israel, the impact of the Democrats' capture of Congress on U.S. policy in Iraq, Iran's alleged nuclear weapons program, and U.S.-Vietnam trade relations. Each of these stories relates to a unique issue; yet each is also part of a larger context. If you are not familiar with these issues or others that dominate the news as you read this book, then it is important to "catch up" on them by regularly following global events through the news media.

To get a better perspective of these and other stories, they should be put in both a historical and theoretical context. To help you with the historical context, chapter 2 provides a foundation for understanding world politics by laying out a brief history of the world system and its current trends. Good reporting in the news media will often include more immediate historical background.

Thinking theoretically is a second way to put things in their larger context. A **political theory** is an idea or connected set of ideas about why things happen and how events and trends relate to one another. Theory helps us see that trees are not just single plants but also part of a forest. Scholar James Rosenau (2004:327) advises that thinking theoretically

> is a technique that involves making a habit of asking a six-word question about anything we observe. . . . The six-word question seems quite simple at first glance. It is: "Of what is this an instance?" The "this" in the question is anything you observe (be it in world or personal affairs) and it is a powerful question because it forces you to find a larger category into which to locate that which you observe. That is, it compels you to move up the ladder and engage in the theoretical enterprise.

"Thinking theoretically" is a key to being able to understand how world events fit together.

There are many advantages to thinking theoretically. One is that it helps us build knowledge. If we confine ourselves to treating each event as unique, then our past and present are little more than a complex jumble of seemingly random events. By thinking theoretically, we look for patterns that help us understand more clearly what has occurred and, perhaps, to even predict what may occur. Second, thinking theoretically gives us a better chance of evaluating policy. One example is assessing the debate over whether the United States and other democracies should work to promote the democratization of the Middle East and elsewhere. Some insight can be found in chapter 6's exploration of "democratic peace theory," which is the idea that democratic states seldom if ever go to war with one another (Chernoff, 2004). If this theory is correct, then the path to world peace may be through world democratization. This would make promoting democracy not simply an altruistic ideal, but also a significant contribution to national security.

As you begin to think about events and to decide "of what is this an instance," do so expansively and do not worry for now whether your ideas seem controversial or even contradictory. Rosenau once ended up with 23 answers when he thought about one event and asked himself of what it was an instance. From such beginnings, you can test and refine your thinking to see what seems to hold up and what does not.

You will encounter discussions of various levels of political theory throughout this book, but a good place to begin is with a range of ideas that have been put forth to address the general study of international relations. To that end, we will proceed somewhat chronologically in the development of modern international relations theory by first taking two veteran theories: realism and liberalism. Then we will turn to postmodernist, feminist, and economic approaches to international politics. These are considered to be theories by some, part of larger theories by others, and critiques of realism and liberalism by others, but their classification is not as important as their contribution to the international relations theory debate beginning mostly in the 1970s. Finally, we will turn to constructivism, an analytical approach that in the view of many scholars emerged in the 1990s as a third macrotheory. Table 1.1 outlines the main points of realism, liberalism, and constructivism.

Before taking up the various schools of thought, four cautions are in order. First, none of these theories is truly comprehensive. Some scholars argue that even realism and liberalism are "best described as paradigm[s]," rather than full-scale theories

TABLE 1.1 Realism, Liberalism, and Constructivism			
Views/Emphasis	Realists/Neorealists	Liberals/Neoliberals	Constructivists
Human nature	Pessimistic: Humans self-interested and competitive	Optimistic: Humans capable of enlightened cooperation	Neutral/No assumption
Core concepts	Power, conflict	Cooperation, interdependence	Ideas, communications, language
Reality	Largely objective	Largely objective	Largely subjective
Politics stakes	Zero-sum	Non-zero-sum	Non-zero-sum
Conflict in system	Central and inevitable	Central but not inevitable	Central but not inevitable
International system	Anarchical	Anarchical, but growing order	Anarchical because assumed to be
Main cause of conflict	States pursuing conflicting self-interests	Lack of central processes to regulate competition	Assumptions of conflict and hostility
Best path to peace	Achieve balance of power	Increase interdependence, cooperation, and adherence to international law	Communicate to find common goals and ways to achieve them
Key organizations	States	IGOs, states	NGOs, IGOs, states
Morality	National interest is a state's moral imperative	Define and follow common moral standards	Morality is subjective
Policy prescriptions	Pursue self-interest, expand/preserve power	Cooperate to achieve mutual interests	Shape ideas and language to promote preferred reality

Did You Know That:

You can learn more about the U.S. college faculty in international relations in Susan Peterson, Michael J. Tierney, and Daniel Malinia, "Inside the Ivory Tower," *Foreign Policy* 51 (November/December 2005), pp. 58–64.

(Geller & Vasquez. 2004:1). Such controversies are not our focus here, so treat "theory," "paradigm," "approach," and other such words as synonymous.

Second, each theory has numerous variations because, "If you put four IR theorists in a room you will easily get ten different ways of organizing theory, and there will also be disagreement about which theories are relevant in the first place" (Jackson & Sørenson, 2003:34). There are, for instance, classical realists, neorealists, offensive realists, defensive realists, and other kinds of realists (Schmidt, 2004). We will briefly note some of these subdivisions but will mostly concentrate on the major premises of the basic theories.

Third, do not be fooled by the connotations of realism and liberalism. Realists do not necessarily see things as they "really" are. Also do not equate the use of "liberal" here with how it applies in domestic politics to left-of-center political parties. For example, President George W. Bush is a conservative in terms of American domestic politics, yet he has liberal leanings, such as wanting to promote democracy and free trade, in the international relations theory use of the term.

Fourth, focus on what each theory has to offer rather than whatever its shortcomings may be. Each of these approaches helps us to better understand world politics. Each also has its weaknesses. There are also considerable overlaps among theories (Snyder, 2005; Lebow, 2004).

Realist Theory

Realism is the view that world politics is driven by competitive self-interest. **Realists** therefore believe that the decisive dynamic among countries is a struggle for power in an effort by each to preserve or, preferably, improve its military security and economic welfare in competition with other countries. Furthermore, realists see this struggle for power as a **zero-sum game**, one in which a gain for one country is inevitably a loss for others. Realists are also prone to seeing humanity as inherently divided by national loyalty to countries or some other focus of political identity such as religion or culture.

Did You Know That:

The term *realpolitik*, power politics, was coined by Prussian/German Chancellor Otto von Bismarck in about 1870.

As an approach to international politics, realism can be traced to such ancient practitioners and thinkers as Sun Tzu (544–496 B.C.), the Chinese general and author of *The Art of War*; Thucydides (460–399 B.C.), a Greek historian and author of *The History of the Peloponnesian War*; and Kautilya (4th century B.C.), minister to the Mauryan emperor of India, who wrote in *Arthashastra*, "A king shall always endeavor to augment his own power." More recently, realism also marked the diplomacy of such statesmen as Otto von Bismarck (1815–1898), the Iron Chancellor, who engineered the unification of Germany under Prussia's control. For our purposes here, though, we will pick up the theory of realism when it emerged in the years surrounding World War II (1939–1945) as the dominant theory in the developing academic discipline of international relations scholarship.

Realist theory emerged partly as a reaction to the failure to preserve the peace after World War I (1914–1918). That horrific war shocked the conscience of many, who blamed the conflict on the realpolitik policies pursued by the major European powers. In response, an idealist movement developed. It advocated conducting global relations according to such lofty principles as cooperation, morality, and democracy. President Woodrow Wilson was a leading idealist. He argued, for example, that peace could only be restored and kept by "a partnership of democratic nations."[7] Wilson sought to bring that partnership into reality by helping found the League of Nations. The idealist vision also led to such initiatives as the

Kellogg-Briand Pact (1928), whose signatories pledged to renounce war "as an instrument of national policy."

The aggression of Germany and Japan, both signatories of the Kellogg-Briand Pact, persuaded many that idealism was not only naïve, but dangerous because it had led countries to abandon realpolitik, which might have steeled them to react more forcefully to such trends as the early stages of Germany's rearmament and, thus, might have prevented World War II. Among scholars, this view was taken up in writings of such scholars as British political scientist Edward H. Carr in *The Twenty Years Crisis 1919–1939* (1939) and even more notably in the work of the American scholar Hans Morgenthau, including his influential text, *Politics Among Nations* (1948). In it he argued (p. 13), "International politics, like all politics, is a struggle for power."

Classic Realism and Neorealism

As realist theory evolved, it split into two schools of thought based primarily on different views of the root cause of conflict. **Classic realism** is associated with Morgenthau and other realists who are pessimistic about human nature. They believe that political struggle among humans is probably inevitable because people have an inherent dark side. Therefore, classic realists believe that it is foolhardy to trust other countries and their people (Brewer, Gross, Aday, & Willnat, 2004). As one realist puts it, "The sad fact is that international politics has always been a ruthless and dangerous business and it is likely to remain that way" (Mearsheimer, 2001:2). Many realists trace their intellectual heritage to the English political philosopher Thomas Hobbes (1588–1679), who argued in *Leviathan* (1651) that humans have an inherent urge to dominate, which often causes them to "become enemies and . . . [to] endeavor to destroy or subdue one another." Similarly, Morgenthau (1945:17) described "the lust for power" in humans as an "ubiquitous empirical fact."

Neorealism also portrays politics as a struggle for power, but **neorealists** believe that the cause of conflict in the international system is its anarchic (unregulated) structure (James, 2002). As one neorealist puts it, the international system based on sovereign actors (states), which answer to no higher authority, is "anarchic, with no overarching authority providing security and order." The result of such a self-help system is that "each state must rely on its own resources to survive and flourish." But because "there is no authoritative, impartial method of settling these disputes—i.e. no world government—states are their own judges, juries, and hangmen, and often resort to force to achieve their security interests" (Zakaria, 1993:22).

The two schools of realism also disagree on how countries determine their foreign policies (Cozette, 2004). Classic realists believe a country should and usually does follow the dictates of power, but they do not believe that they always do so (Williams, 2005). Instead classic realists believe that national leaders can and do err by allowing morality, ideology, or anything else other than power realities to govern foreign policy. By contrast, neorealists pay little attention to the internal policy making in countries. This is because neorealists believe that countries are "rational actors" and therefore will react similarly and predictably to power realities in a given situation no matter who is in office. Because neorealists see states reacting predictably to power, these theorists are interested in ascertaining rules about how states will react in a given set of circumstances. Examples of how these rules work can be found in the discussion of the international system in chapter 3.

What unites both realists and neorealists is that they doubt whether there is any escape from conflict. Classical realists believe human nature is immutable, and neorealists are skeptical about the ability of interdependence or international organizations to promote cooperation (Sterling-Folker, 2002).

JOIN THE DEBATE
The Human Nature Divide

Realism: An Emphasis on Power

Realists contend that struggles between states to secure their frequently conflicting national interests are the main action on the world stage. Given this view, realists maintain that countries should and usually do base their foreign policy on the existence of what they see as a Darwinian world in which power is the key to the national survival of the fittest. In the words of one scholar, "In an environment as dangerous as anarchy," those who ignore realist principles will "ultimately not survive" (Sterling-Folker, 1997:18). From this perspective, realists define national interest mainly in terms of whatever enhances or preserves a state's security, its influence, and its military and economic power. For realists, then, might makes right—or at least it makes success.

With respect to justice and morality, Morgenthau reasoned that it is unconscionable for a state to follow policy based on such principles. He argued that "while the individual has a moral right to sacrifice himself" in defense of an abstract principle, "the state has no right to let its moral [views] . . . get in the way of successful political action, itself inspired by the moral principle of national survival" (Morgenthau, 1986:38). This does not mean that realists are amoral (Williams, 2004). Some argue that the highest moral duty of the state is to do good for its citizens. More moderately, other realists argue that surviving and prospering in a dangerous world requires that morality be weighed prudently against national interest. One scholar has summed up this realist rule of action with the maxim, "Do 'good' if the price is low" (Gray, 1994:8).

Realism and the Competitive Future

There are many implications to the realists' dark view of politics. One is that there is little hope for substantially reforming the anarchic international system. Morgenthau, for instance, argued that only a global government could permanently secure international peace and justice, but he concluded gloomily, "A world state cannot be established" (Speer, 1968:214). With meaningful change out of reach, realists advocate a pragmatic, realpolitik approach to world politics. One rule is to secure your own country's interests first and worry about the welfare of other countries second, if at all, on the assumption that other countries will not help you unless it is in their own interest. This makes realists wary of what they see as the self-sacrificing policies advocated by liberals (Goldsmith & Krasner, 2003). Such policies are not just foolish but dangerous, according to Morgenthau (1986:38), because countries that shun realpolitik will "fall victim to the power of others."

Second, realpolitik holds that countries should practice balance-of-power politics. This means to strive to achieve an equilibrium of power in the world in order to prevent any other country or coalition of countries from dominating the system. Methods for achieving this goal include building up your own strength, allying yourself with others, or dividing your opponents.

Third, realists argue that the best way to maintain the peace is to be powerful: "Peace through strength," as President Ronald Reagan was fond of saying. Showing his realist side, President George W. Bush takes a similar line, arguing, "We will build our defenses beyond challenge, lest weakness invite challenge."[8] Thus, realists believe that countries must be armed because the world is dangerous and reject the liberal counterargument that the world is dangerous because countries are so heavily armed. As Morgenthau put it about disarmament, "Take away their arms, and they will either fight with their bare fists or get themselves new arms with which to fight" (Speer, 1968:214).

It is incorrect to think that realists are militarists because they emphasize national power. For example, many realists opposed the U.S. invasion of Iraq in 2003 because they believed that it was not worth the cost and the loss of American lives, symbolized here by this funeral of a U.S. Marine, Lance Corporal Jose Gutierrez, the first American to die in the war.

Fourth, realists advise that a country should neither waste its power on peripheral goals nor pursue goals that it does not have the power to achieve. This frequently makes realists reluctant warriors, not warmongers, as they are sometimes portrayed. Morgenthau, for instance, criticized U.S. involvement in the war in Vietnam as a waste of resources in a tangential area. Many realist scholars also opposed the invasion of Iraq in 2003, arguing accurately that Iraq was not an immediate threat and, therefore, "Even if such a war goes well and has positive long-range consequences, it will still have been unnecessary. And if it goes badly—whether in the form of high U.S. casualties, significant civilian deaths, a heightened risk of terrorism, or increased hatred of the United States in the Arab and Islamic world—then its architects will have even more to answer for" (Mearsheimer & Walt, 2003:58). More generally, one realist scholar claims, "America's . . . realists [have] . . . warned of the dangers that a hegemonic United States would over-reach itself and, by asserting its power heavy-handedly, provoke opposition to it" (Layne, 2006:46).

Liberal Theory

Liberalism contends that people and the countries that represent them are capable of finding mutual interests and cooperating to achieve them, at least in part by working through international organizations and according to international law. **Liberals** reject the realists' contention that politics is inherently and exclusively a struggle for power. Liberals do not dismiss power as a factor, but they add morality, ideology, emotions (such as friendship and mutual identity), habits of cooperation, and even altruism as factors that influence the behavior of national leaders and the course of world politics. Liberalism also holds that international politics can be a **non-zero-sum game**, that it is possible to have win-win situations in which gains of one or more countries do not have to come at the expense of others. Liberals are also prone to think that all humans have a common bond that they can draw on to identify themselves beyond the narrow boundaries of their country or group and to identify and forge ties with people around the world.

Like realism, liberalism is not a new approach to world politics. Indeed, part of modern liberalism is resurrected idealism, although that label fell into disuse. Whatever its label, the approach includes such ideas as the notion that justice is a basic human right, which dates at least to Mesopotamia around 2500 B.C. (Altman, 2005). A sense of universalism has also long prompted efforts to organize internationally for peace. For one, French official Pierre Dubois proposed in *The Recovery of the Holy Land* (1306) that the Christian kingdoms create "a league of universal peace" to settle their disputes. Such views have persisted, with the idealism of President Woodrow Wilson and his drive to found the League of Nations a much more recent example.

Also like realism, the (re)emergence of liberalism was a reflection of the times. Realism, as noted, had gained strength among scholars during the alarming period between the outbreak of World War II and the depths of the cold war in the 1950s and 1960s. In the 1970s, however, the cold war began to thaw, the international landscape looked very different, and liberalism resurged. Reflecting the times, liberals made a number of claims. One was that, especially in a nuclear age, the assumptions of realism trapped the world into a mind-set of conflict that could literally destroy civilization. This concern prompted some scholars to pursue a "disciplined inquiry into the ways [that] values [such as peace and justice] can be realized" in global politics (Falk, 1986:16). Liberalism stressed the spread of democracy and the work being done on democratic peace theory. This idea, as detailed in chapter 6, contradicts the core realist assumption that all countries, democratic or not, would struggle with one another. Liberals also noted the expanding role of the UN, the growth of the European Union, and many other examples of global cooperation and charged that realism could not explain such changes (Nye & Keohane, 1970).

Classic Liberalism and Neoliberalism

Liberalism, like realism earlier, soon divided into two schools of thought. **Classic liberalism** is the older of the two and the direct descendent of idealism. Like classic realism, classic liberalism is based on its adherents' view of human nature. However, in contrast to the pessimism of classic realists, classic liberals are optimistic about human nature. In this sense, they trace their intellectual lineage to political philosophers such as Jean-Jacques Rousseau (1712–1778). He argued in *The Social Contract* (1762) that humans had joined together in civil societies because they found it easier to improve their existence through cooperation than competitive self-reliance. Contemporary liberals apply this notion to global society, and argue that people and their countries can better their existence by joining together to build a cooperative and peaceful global society.

　　Neoliberalism developed in the 1970s and 1980s somewhat parallel to neorealism. Neoliberals agree with neorealists that competition among sovereign states in an anarchical world system causes conflict. However, neoliberals contend that the system is not nearly an anarchical as neorealists claim. According to neoliberals, the system is marked by *complex interdependence*. This mean that countries are tied together through trade and many other economic, social, and other exchanges that both increase cooperation and limit conflict. Complex interdependence also promotes the increased use of international law and the creation of more and stronger international organizations to deal with the expanding ties among countries. In turn, the spread of international law and importance of international organizations progressively acts to reduce anarchy and, therefore, conflict in the system.

Liberalism: An Emphasis on Cooperation

Unlike realists, liberals do not believe that acquiring, preserving, and applying power must be or even always is the essence of international relations. Instead, liberals argue that foreign policy should be and sometimes is formulated according to the standards of cooperation and even altruism. This does not mean that liberals are never willing to use military force or other forms of coercion. Almost all liberals are willing to do so in self-defense or in response to overt international aggression. Many liberals would also use force, especially if authorized by the United Nations, to prevent or halt genocide and other gross violations of human rights. Beyond such cases, though, liberals differ. Some favor assertive liberalism, an approach that led Woodrow Wilson to send American troops to Europe in an effort to make the world safe for democracy and led George W. Bush to invade Iraq in part to foster democracy there. Proponents of more passive liberalism argue that using force is often counterproductive and that it also often leads to imperial domination even if the initial intentions were lofty (Morefield, 2004).

Whatever the exact coloration, liberalism has been evident in some post–cold war leaders. For example, President Bill Clinton asked Americans to support sending U.S. troops to Bosnia because "it is the right thing to do" to prevent the continued agony of "skeletal prisoners caged behind barbed wire fences, women and girls raped as a tool of war, [and] defenseless men and boys shot down in mass graves."[9] Even more recently and sounding much like Wilson's resolve to make the world safe for democracy, President Bush has pledged, "America will . . . support democratic movements . . . with the ultimate goal of ending tyranny in our world."[10]

Such views do not mean that Clinton, Bush, and others with liberal internationalist views do not also pursue realist policy. When, for example, Clinton sought the presidency in 1992, he condemned China as a tyrannical abuser of human rights and assailed President George H. W. Bush for his realpolitik approach to that country. As president, though, Clinton learned that he could not afford to overly antagonize a country as powerful as China, and he tempered his liberalism. Clinton had to admit near the end of his first term, "it would be fair to say that my policies with regard to China have been somewhat different from what I talked about in the [1992 presidential] campaign."[11]

Liberals also dismiss the realists' warning that pursuing ethical policy often works against the national interest. The wisest course, liberals contend, is for countries to recognize that their national interests and the common interests of the world are inextricably tied. For liberals, this means that improving global economic conditions, human rights, and democracy are very much in the national interest of the United States and other economically developed and democratic countries. This was the argument President Bush was making in 2005 when he told Americans, "In the long term, the peace we seek will only be achieved by eliminating the conditions that feed radicalism and ideologies of murder. If whole regions of the world remain in despair and grow in hatred, they will be the recruiting grounds for terror, and that terror will stalk America and other free nations for decades."[12]

Liberalism and the Cooperative Future

Liberals believe that humanity is struggling toward a more orderly and peaceful international system and can and must succeed in that goal. All theories recognize the importance of the state in world politics, but whereas realists focus almost exclusively on the state, liberals put a great deal of emphasis on the UN and other IGOs as both evidence and promoters of greater cooperation. Liberals are divided, however, over how far cooperation can and should go. Classic liberals believe that just as humans learned to form cooperative societies without giving up their individuality, so too can states learn to cooperate without surrendering their independence. These liberals believe that the growth of international economic interdependence and the spread of global culture will create a much greater spirit of cooperation among the world countries. Neoliberals are more dubious about a world in which countries retain full sovereignty. These analysts believe that countries will have to surrender some of their sovereignty to international organizations in order to promote greater cooperation and, if necessary, to enforce good behavior.

As for the future, liberals are encouraged by some recent trends. One of these is the willingness of countries to surrender some of their sovereignty to improve themselves. The EU, for instance, now exercises considerable economic and even political authority over its member-countries. Member-countries were not forced into the EU;

SURVEY
Identify Your Perspective on World Politics

DEBATE THE POLICY SCRIPT

Applying Theory to Policy

Although national leaders seldom talk in terms of international relations theory, they do apply it. This was clear in late 2006 when a committee of former top U.S. officials headed by James Baker and Lee Hamilton sent President Bush a report that began, "The situation in Iraq is grave and deteriorating" and recommended a series of pragmatic steps designed to "enable the United States to begin to move its combat forces out of Iraq responsibly."[1]

The *Washington Post* termed the report "The Realist Manifesto."[2] Similarly, *Time* greeted the report and the replacement of Secretary of Defense Donald Rumsfeld by Robert Gates with a column entitled, "The Return of the Realists." The columnist Walter Isaacson linked the neoconservatism of Rumsfeld and others in the administration to the idealism of Woodrow Wilson waging World War I "to make the world safe for democracy," and characterized the invasions of Iraq in 2003 as a "neo-Wilsonian mission of spreading democracy."[3]

Describing realism and idealism (liberalism) as "competing strands of American foreign policy," Isaacson characterized realism as a "hard-nosed focus on clearly defined national interests . . . pursued with a pragmatic calculation of commitments and resources," and idealism as emphasizing "moral values and ideals" in formulating U.S. foreign policy. As for the argument some make that U.S. pragmatic interests and moral values are synonymous, Isaacson dismissed that conjecture as "alas, not always true in a messy world."

Which standard should Americans follow? Isaacson hedged, writing that while "welcoming the return of some realism, let's not forget that America's strength comes from its values." To help determine whether you would write the future policy script with a realist or idealist/liberal theme, or perhaps both (full internationalism) or neither (isolationism), consider the following eight scenarios. Assume that you are the U.S. president, and that for each scenario your maximum cost will be 5,000 American troops killed and $500 billion. Then decide for each scenario whether you are willing to order U.S. forces into action and pay the price.

1. Retaking the U.S. territory of Guam after it has been seized by another country
2. Stopping a genocidal slaughter that has already killed 200,000 people in a distant country
3. Preventing a clearly hostile country from acquiring nuclear arms and long-range missiles
4. Ousting a dictator who has ended democracy in a distant country and is ruling by terror
5. Toppling a government that is supplying a terrorist group that is threatening you
6. Liberating a country of no strategic importance that has been invaded by a neighbor
7. Defeating a country that dominates the Middle East and has cut off U.S. oil supplies
8. Forcing a country harboring war criminals to surrender them to the International Criminal Court

What Do You Think?

Which scenarios did you consider worth going to war? The view here is that scenarios 1, 3, 5, and 7 are realist goals. Scenarios 2, 4, 6, and 8 are idealist/liberal goals. Think about what your answers say about your theory orientation and compare and discuss them with others in your class. Try the exercise again with a maximum cost of 1,000 dead and $100 billion. Did your answers change?

---

they joined it freely. This and other indications that sovereignty is weakening will be discussed at length later in the text. Liberals are further buoyed by the spread of democracy and economic interdependence. They believe that both tend to lessen the chances of conflict among states, and research shows that there is substantial validity to this notion (Kinsella & Russett, 2002). Liberals also condemn the practice of realpolitik. They charge that power politics leads to an unending cycle of conflict and misery in which safety is temporary at best.

Because realism and liberalism, or idealism as some still call it, are what might be termed the two vintage theories and are the ones that are still used to characterize and debate public policy, it might be enlightening for you to explore which more closely characterizes your approach to world politics and which you believe your country should follow. This can be accomplished in the Debate the Policy Script box, "Applying Theory to Policy."

Postmodernist, Feminist, and Economic Theories

Discontent with realist theory was not confined to those who fell into the liberal school of thought. At about the same time that the liberal challenge to realism was developing, some scholars were also beginning to apply postmodernist and feminist perspectives to criticize the state of international relations theory, especially realism. Additionally, there is a range of economic theories, some long existent, others more contemporary, which help us think theoretically about world politics.

Postmodernist Theory

At its core, **postmodernism** contends that what we take to be political reality is created by the ways that we think about it and by our discourse (writing, talking) about it. As such, postmodernists believe that much of what we assume to be real is merely mind-set that we have created by defining and communicating about things in a certain way. Similarly, our values, what we define as positive and negative, are mental constructs. In this sense, Shakespeare made a postmodern point in *Hamlet* when the Prince of Denmark mused, "there is nothing either good or bad, but thinking makes it so." For instance, postmodernists would dispute the conception of progress that defines scientific/technological modernity as good and seeks to impose it on people of traditional cultures.

Postmodernists are not some disconnected group who imagine that a warplane or the White House is only an illusion. But they would say that the need to have either of these, like many other political realities, is a matter of mind-set, in this case the result in part of defining yourself primarily as, say, an American who is distinct from other nationalities, as compared to defining yourself first and foremost as a human who has common links and interests with all other humans globally. From this starting point, postmodernists go on to explore ways to escape traditional thinking and create new ways of thinking, and thus new realities. To say that postmodernists advocate much greater creativity in "thinking outside of the box" hardly does them justice, but it does convey some sense of their approach.

This point about narrow thinking is the root of the postmodernist critique of realism and liberalism. Postmodernists charge that both theories perpetuate stale ways of conceiving how we organize and conduct ourselves by, for example, assuming the long-term continuance of national identities and the existence of the international system centered on independent countries. What postmodernists say is that these "realities" can be changed by thinking about and discussing ourselves and others in different ways. They believe that organizing ourselves politically around a geographically defined country is only an image in our mind reinforced by the way that we discuss politics. Postmodernists want to change political discourse so primary political identity could expand beyond nationalism to also include, for instance, being a North American, a woman, or simply a human.

As an example, most people define the concept of "national interest" to mean those things that benefit the country and its people in terms of gaining, increasing, and keeping wealth, military might, and status. Postmodernists reject such a meaning because, they contend, there is no such thing as an objective national interest. If that is true, we can change what it is by conceiving of national interest differently. It may be in American national interest to share more of America's wealth to uplift the multitude of abjectly poor people in the world, a policy that would arguably enhance Americans' sense of moral rectitude and their standing in the world. Indeed, postmodernists reject the validity of the "we" and "they" discourse in international politics that distinguishes between ethnonational groups.

Postmodernists even doubt the reality of the "metanarratives" (overarching stories) of history. The standard portrayal of the rise and fall of powerful states is based on the power struggles among them. Is that real? Perhaps the real story, as Karl Marx and Friedrich Engels suggested in the *Communist Manifesto* (1848), is that all history is defined by class struggle between the propertied class (the bourgeoisie) and the oppressed workers (the proletariat). Or maybe politics has been driven, as some feminist postmodernists suggest, by creating structures (such as states and organized religion) that have allowed men to oppress women in the supposed interest of protecting them. Because you have not heard such alternative stories, your instinct may be to dismiss them. But do not be so sure of what is fact and what is fiction.

One of the numerous postmodernist contributions is providing an alternative way to think about how to achieve peace. For example, they view states as linked to violence in many ways and are therefore suspicious of them. One charge is that states justify their existence and power by promoting a sense of danger. Postmodernists also believe that states focus on enhancing their own security as a structure, rather than in terms of their people. Moreover, states try to harness people to the state's purpose by creating nationalism as the exclusive political identity and by suppressing as muddled, even treasonous, attempts to create competing political identities. In short, according to one postmodernist, "It is force that holds the state together." Based on this view, to achieve peace, we must examine the relationship of violence to our current political structure and "encourage individuals to actively engage in politics" in order to change the discourse (Shinko, 2004).

Feminist Theory

Yet another critique of realism and liberalism is provided by feminist thought. Like all the theories and critiques we are exploring, feminism has many aspects and even its own internal disputes. To bridge these, we will adopt the strategy of one feminist author and use **feminism** "in its original meaning: the theory of, and the struggle for, equality for women" (Fraser, 1999:855). From this perspective, it is possible to highlight a number of common points in feminist thought about world politics. First, feminism argues that women have been left out of the process and even the conceptualization of world politics.

Feminist scholars maintain that the definition of what is relevant to the study of international relations is largely a product of the male point of view and ignores or underrepresents the role of women, their concerns, and their perspectives. Similarly, feminist scholars argue that to a significant degree male-dominated research has promoted methodologies that are not relevant to the questions posed by feminist scholars and to their perspective on knowledge (Tickner, 2005; Caprioli, 2004). In this sense, many feminists would agree with the postmodernists that mainline scholarship has presented a metanarrative of world politics that is not real. Instead it reflects just one set of perceptions (male, in this case). The overarching story from a feminist perspective would be very different.

Concepts such as peace and security are prime examples of how, according to feminists, men and women perceive issues differently. One feminist scholar suggests that "from the masculine perspective, peace for the most part has meant the absence of war" (Reardon, 1990:137). She terms this "negative peace." By contrast, Reardon (138) continues, women think more in terms of "positive peace," which includes "conditions of social justice, economic equity and ecological balance." Women, more than men, are apt to see international security as wider than just a military concept, as also including security from sexism, poverty, domestic violence, and other factors

SIMULATION
So Say the Mamas:
A Feminist World

that assail women. Women favor this more inclusive view of security because, according to another study, "the need for human security through development is critical to women whose lives often epitomize the insecurity and disparities that plague the world order" (Bunch & Carillo, 1998:230).

This inclusive view of violence is supported by women's experiences. "The most painful devaluation of women," according to one UN report, "is the physical and psychological violence that stalks them from cradle to grave" (UNDP, 1995:7). Fewer women than men may die or be wounded as soldiers, but women are at least as likely to be casualties in military and terrorist attacks on economic and population centers. Many women die from the starvation and disease that frequently accompany war, and yet others fall victim to widespread sexual abuse that occurs in some wars. During the early 1990s, the campaign against the Bosnians by the Serbs included an officially orchestrated campaign of sexual attack on many thousands of women and girls as young as 13 in an effort to terrorize the Bosnians. Sometimes even the supposed peacemakers may be sexual predators. A UN report in 2005 documented many cases of UN peacekeeping troops and officials in the Congo and elsewhere sometimes raping and more often coercing destitute women and girls as young as age 12 into "survival sex," swapping sex for as little as a dollar's worth of food or other necessities.[13] Among many other signs of endemic violence against women are the facts that (1) about 80% of the world's refugees are women and their children, (2) an estimated 100 million girls suffer genital mutilation, and (3) globally, the national incidence of women who have been the victim of abuse by an intimate partner averages 25% and ranges up to 58%.

Feminism is related to political identity in two ways (Croucher, 2003a). One is to create womanhood as a focus of women's sense of who they are politically. This does not mean that women are apt to try to forge an independent feminist state somewhere in the world, but it does mean that women may view their country and its policies through a heightened feminist consciousness. Second, the political identity of some women is influenced by their suspicion that states and other political structures are designed to maintain male dominance. This view, one feminist scholar writes, "strips the [state's] security core naked so that we can see its masculine-serving guises" (Sylvester, 1994:823).

Among other things, feminists believe that women should be equally active and as well represented among policy makers as men. The positive role that women play is captured in this photo of two of the many women who have won the Nobel Peace Prize, Northern Ireland's Betty Williams (1976) and Guatemala's Rigoberta Menchú Tum (1992). They were together in Guatemala City in 2006 during an event to motivate young adults to take a role in their world.

Economic Theories

Chapter 12, the first of two on the international political economy (IPE), includes a lengthy discussion of various theories related to its operation. Nevertheless, it is important to have some early sense of these approaches. **Economic nationalism** is closely related to realism and argues that countries do and should use their economic strength to increase national power and, in turn, use their national power to further build economic strength. **Economic internationalism,** by contrast, is akin to liberalism. Economic internationalists believe free economic interchange without political interference can bring prosperity to all countries.

Economic structuralism is the third major IPE approach. There are a number of variations to economic structuralist theory, but they all share the view that economics plays a key, perhaps dominant role in determining politics. All radical theorists also see the world divided by economic circumstance and believe that the wealthy (countries, corporations, societal classes) act in a self-interested way to keep poor countries and classes within societies impoverished and weak.

Being aware of the structuralist theories is particularly important at the beginning of this text in order to gain some perspective on matters taken up in other chapters, such as the yawning prosperity gap that exists between a few countries like the United States that are very wealthy and the many countries like Uganda that are excruciatingly poor (see Figure 2.4, p. 59). As evident in chapters 2, 5, 14, and elsewhere, economic structural theory is an important component of the critique of globalization. One charge is that globalization and its liberal agenda of lowering barriers to trade, investment, and other international economic exchanges has primarily served the interests of the United States and other wealthy countries by allowing them to further penetrate and dominate poorer countries. There is even an argument that when economic measures are not enough to preserve and expand the dominance of the core countries they will use force to further their ends. Casting globalization as a U.S. "project" designed to further American dominance, one critic writes, "The Iraq war should be seen as part of an intended endgame for a globalization project that . . . [serves] U.S. ambitions" (Schulzinger, 2006:16).

Constructivist Theory

As the realists and liberals battled it out intellectually, other scholars rejected all or parts of both theories and sought new ways of thinking. Among other influences, the views of postmodernist, feminist, and other scholars on the subjectivity of much of what we assume is real led in the mid-1980s to the formulation of constructivist theory (Jacobensen, 2003; Zehfuss, 2002). **Constructivism** views the course of international relations as an interactive process in which the ideas of and communications among "agents" (or actors: individuals, groups, and social structures, including states) serve to create "structures" (treaties, laws, international organizations, and other aspects of the international system). These structures, in turn, influence the ideas and communications of the agents. This definition, like constructivist theory itself, is very challenging to understand because, as an early constructivist scholar had noted in a reading entitled "World of Our Making," it takes "most readers into unfamiliar worlds" (Onuf, 2002:127).

Constructivism and the Nature of Politics

The title, "World of Our Making," is an apt description of the core beliefs of constructivists. Their view begins with a rejection of what they claim is the assumption by realists and liberals that most of the actors of world politics, such as states, and structures, such as the anarchistic international system, are a stable given. Constructivist read all such "knowledge" (it exists) as much more fluid than do realists and liberals. It is not that constructivists do not recognize that countries exist. It is that constructivists see them as primarily structures that are fluidly based on the willingness of agents (in this case citizens) to define themselves politically in terms of the state (national political identity) and behave in ways (fighting for it, paying taxes) that support it. Such political identities are mental pictures of who we are, and, as such, both they and the political structures that rest on them are more ethereal than you might assume. For example, in 1991 there was no doubt, even among constructivists, that the Soviet Union existed. It was the world's largest country with a complex governmental structure and a vast nuclear and conventional military inventory. Indeed, the Soviet Union was one of the world's two superpowers. Yet as the clock struck midnight on December 26, 2001, the Soviet Union disappeared. Why? That will be debated for a long time, but constructivists would argue that one factor was that the Soviet Union had been constructed in part in the minds of those within its borders. When they shifted their political identities to being Russians, Ukrainians, Kazaks, and other nationalities, rather than Soviets, these people "constructed" new sovereign states and "deconstructed" the Soviet Union, which was then disbanded by Russia and its other constituent republics.

Constructivists also differ from liberals and, especially, realists in what they see as the goals of the agents. Liberals and realists hold different views on how to best achieve goals, but they tend to see them in relatively concrete terms such as physical safety and material well-being. By contrast, constructivists believe that an important role is played by nonmaterial factors such ideology, morality, and other cultural outlooks and values. This stress on societal values makes constructivists place considerable emphasis on the internal political processes of countries and how those dynamics shape a country's perceptions of the world and interactions with it. Historians of American foreign policy, for example, have found a religious component in American culture that disposes it to see the "American way" as God given, which promotes a missionary zeal to carry its blessing to others. This messianic tendency in American culture helps explain from a constructivist point of view the determination to spread democracy to the Middle East and elsewhere. Factoring in values also helps understand policy choices.

Constructivism and the Course of World Politics

Because constructivism contends that to a great degree the world is what we make of it, most of its adherents do not share the pessimism of realists about the possibilities of escaping global competition and conflict. For instance, understanding that powerful countries may define their world role in different ways may help avoid confrontations. As this is being written in late 2006, the news includes an Associated Press story headlined, "Rice: U.S. Concerned about Rising China" that quotes Secretary of State Condoleezza Rice's worry about China's "outsized . . . military buildup." Realists would react with alarm, but constructivists would, among other things, look at China's history of strategic culture, which arguably has generally not sought to propel China militarily far beyond its borders (Lantis, 2005). Constructivists would worry that discussing China's military buildup as a threat might become a self-fulfilling prophecy, creating tensions between Washington and Beijing, escalating armaments by both sides, leading to yet higher tensions, more armaments, and so on. From this perspective, positive interactions with China might yield better results. Research indicates, for instance, that military-to-military contacts between U.S. military representatives and those of other countries are "positively and systematically associated with liberalizing trends" in those countries, a finding that "provides evidence that constructivist mechanisms do have observable effects, and that ideationally based processes play an important role in U.S. national security" (Atkinson, 2006:509).

Even more broadly for constructivists, the future rests on the ways in which we communicate (speak and write) and think about the world and our place in it. They believe that language calls things into existence. For them, choosing one label over another (foreigner, fellow human), then attaching certain values to that label (foreign = different, not my responsibility; fellow citizen = similar, my responsibility) is profoundly important politically because we act on the basis of what things mean to us (Tsygankov, 2003). Constructivists believe that we should reject traditional meanings because they have led to division and conflict. As one put it, "A path cannot be

SIMULATION
Multiple Choice Quiz

called a path without the people who walk it" (Simon, 1998:158). They do not believe that the anarchical condition of the international system forces states to take certain actions (like being armed). Instead, constructivists think that how we conceive of the lack of central authority is what determines interactions—"Anarchy is what states make of it" (Wendt, 1992:335). From this point of view, conflict is not the result of structural power politics. Rather, it stems from the discordant worldviews and the inability of people to communicate in ways that would allow them to construct a mutually beneficial vision and create structures to accomplish that vision. "Constructivism is about human consciousness and its role in international life . . . [and] rests on . . . the capacity and will of people to take a deliberate attitude towards the world and to lend it significance [by acting according to that attitude]," is how one constructivist put it (Ruggie, 1998:855). If values and perceptions change, then so too can relations, structural realities, and other aspects of the international system. Political identification can be among these changes. How we define ourselves and the values we place on that identification in relationship to others can, according to constructivists, reshape the structures by which we organize ourselves and the interactions among those structures.

Assessing Theories

"Good grief," you may be thinking, "with an avalanche of abstract theory I am having trouble connecting to reality." Do not be dismayed. That is not an unreasonable response to many pages of theory at the beginning of this text and your course. Moreover, as you progress further in this text and your course, and as you reflect on the outlines of the theories you have just encountered, they will begin to make more sense. They will also help you organize your thoughts about how to connect the actors, events, trends, and other aspects of the world drama that you will encounter.

As you continue thinking theoretically, here are a couple of suggestions that may help. One that was made at the beginning of the theory section but bears repeating is to avoid trying to "referee" the debate among the various schools of thought. Various well-educated, well-read scholars who have devoted their academic careers to studying theory profoundly disagree on which one is the best model of reality. You certainly may find one theory or another appeals to you, but for the present the best idea is to keep an open mind about all of them. Each has something important to say.

Also observe that many of the theories have both empirical (facts) and normative (values) aspects. Empirically, any good theory should provide insightful *description*. That is, it should be able to describe past and current events in a way that tells you of what they are an instance, to recall Rosenau's standard from earlier. Harder yet, but still a valid test of the empirical worth of a theory is how well it enables accurate *prediction*. Realists would probably predict diplomatic muscle flexing and perhaps even military action if, for example, two democracies are angrily disagreeing about each other's withdrawals from an oil field that lies under both their territories. Liberals would be more likely to predict that the democracies would not fight (democratic peace theory) and that, instead, they would negotiate a compromise or perhaps even submit the dispute to an intergovernmental organization such as the International Court of Justice. So one thing you can do to evaluate realism and idealism is to watch developing events, think about how realists and liberals would predict their outcome, and then see which proves more accurate.

Prescription is a third aspect of many theories. This involves policy advocacy, arguing what policy should be, rather than describing what it has been or is or predicting what it will be. Many realists, for instance, do not believe that countries always follow a self-interest course. Indeed, realists worry that their country may be persuaded by altruism, by ideological fervor, or by some other drive to pursue policies that are not in the national interest. Recall that realist Hans Morgenthau opposed the Vietnam War as a misuse of U.S. power and, more contemporarily, realist John Mearsheimer took essentially the same view of invading Iraq in 2003. Thus you can use theory to organize your views about what your country's foreign policy should be and, indeed, what the entire future course of world politics should be. If you do so from a solid grounding in theory, you will be far ahead of those who imagine that each event and situation is unique and not part of the ongoing drama on the world stage.

CHAPTER SUMMARY

PREVIEWING THE GLOBAL DRAMA

1. This book's primary message is captured by Shakespeare's line, "All the world's a stage, and all the men and women merely players." This means that we are all part of the world drama and are affected by it. It also means that we should try to play a role in determining the course of the dramatic events that affect our lives.

2. This text is organized to reflect the theme that the world system is evolving. Along the traditional path countries have pursued their national interests as far as their power permits within a largely anarchical international system. The alternative, evolving path would have states abandon their pursuit of short-term self-interest and take a more cooperative, globalist approach to world politics.

THE IMPORTANCE OF WORLD POLITICS TO EACH OF US

3. Economics is one way that we are all affected. The word *intermestic* has been coined to symbolize the merging of *inter*national and d*omestic* concerns, especially in the area of economics. Countries and their citizens have become increasingly interdependent.

4. Economically, trade both creates and causes the loss of jobs. International investment practices may affect your standard of living in such diverse ways as perhaps helping fund your college scholarship or creating employment for you or someone in your family. The global economy also supplies vital resources, such as oil. Exchange rates between different currencies affect the prices we pay for imported goods, the general rate of inflation, and our country's international trade balance.

5. Our country's role in the world also affects decisions about the allocation of budget funds. Some countries spend a great deal on military functions. Other countries spend relatively little on the military and devote almost all of their budget resources to domestic spending.

6. World politics also plays an important role in determining the condition of your living space. Politics, for the most part, has not created environmental degradation, but political cooperation almost certainly will be needed to halt and reverse the despoiling of the biosphere.

7. Your life may also be affected by world politics. You may be called on to serve in the military. Whether or not you are in the military, war can cost you your life.

8. There are many things any one of us can do, individually or in cooperation with others, to play a part in shaping the future of our world. Think, vote, protest, support, write letters, join organizations, make speeches, run for office—do something!

THINKING THEORETICALLY: PUTTING EVENTS IN CONTEXT

9. We improve our understanding of world politics by putting events within the context of theory to see patterns and make generalizations about the conduct of international affairs.

10. Realism, liberalism, constructivism, postmodernism, feminism and a variety of economic theories all help organize our ability to think theoretically.

11. Realism focuses on the self-interested promotion of the state and nation. Realists believe that power politics is the driving force behind international relations. Therefore, realists believe that both safety

and wisdom lie in promoting the national interest through the preservation and, if necessary, the application of the state's power.

12. Liberalism holds that humans are capable of cooperating out of enlightened common interests in an orderly, humane, and just world, and the world has moved significantly in that direction during the last century. Liberals also see the policy prescriptions of realists as dangerous.

13. Postmodernism criticizes existing theories, especially realism, for making unfounded assumptions about what is real. Feminism criticizes existing theories for ignoring the perceptions of women and their role in world politics. Nationalist, internationalist, and structuralist economic theories also provide insights into the course of world politics.

14. Constructivism contends that ideas, language, and communications created a subjective reality that we mistake for objective reality and that causes us to create structures that reinforce our perceptions.

15. For now, assess the theories by keeping an open mind, considering the insights each has to offer, and evaluating the descriptive, predictive, and prescriptive value of each.

For simulations, debates, and other interactive activities, a chapter quiz, Web links, and much more, visit **www.mhhe.com/rourke12/** and go to chapter 1. Or, while accessing the site, click on Course-Wide Content and view recent international relations articles in the *New York Times*.

KEY TERMS

anarchical international
  system
classic liberalism
classic realism
constructivism
direct democracy
economic internationalism

economic nationalism
economic structuralism
feminism
fiscal year (FY)
intergovernmental
  organizations (IGOs)
intermestic

liberalism
neoliberalism
neorealism
nongovernmental
  organizations (NGOs)
non-zero-sum game
political theory

postmodernism
realism
sovereignty
states
zero-sum game

The Evolution of World Politics

*I am amazed, methinks, and lose my way
Among the thorns and dangers of the world.*
—William Shakespeare, *King John*

*Whereof what's past is prologue, what to come,
In yours and my discharge.*
—William Shakespeare, *The Tempest*

This chapter's review of the evolution of world politics will help you to understand the current international system and to think about how it should operate in the future.

THIS CHAPTER HAS TWO PURPOSES. One is to establish a historical foundation for our analysis of international relations that emphasizes the themes and events you will encounter repeatedly in this book. Second, this chapter sketches the evolution of the current, rapidly evolving world political system. The concept of an **international system** represents the notion that (1) the world is more than just the sum of its parts, such as countries, (2) that world politics is more than just the sum of the individual interactions among those parts, and (3) that there are general patterns of interactions among the system's actors. The nature of the international system and its impact on world politics are further explored in chapter 3.

Be patient as you read this chapter. You will find that it often introduces a topic briefly and then hurries on to another point. "Wait a minute," you may think, "slow down and explain this better." Hang in there! Other chapters fill in the details.

THE EVOLVING WORLD SYSTEM: EARLY DEVELOPMENT

There have been numerous global and regional international systems, with some scholars dating them back to the southern Mesopotamian region of Babylon (in what is now Iraq) some 7,500 years ago. Modern politics is vastly different than it was, but that change has, for the most part, evolved slowly.

Ancient Greece and Rome

We can begin tracking the international system with a brief exploration of the era that included the Greek city-states (about 700 B.C. to 300 B.C.) and the rise of Rome in about 500 B.C. to its fall in A.D. 476. It was during this period that four of today's important political characteristics were first seen. Each of them subsequently almost disappeared, only to flourish more than a thousand years in the future.

Territorial State: Before the city-states, political organization was based on a ruler or on a cultural group, such as a tribe. Each controlled territory, but the political connection of those living in the territory was to the ruler or group, not to the territory itself. Other than the rulers, people had no sense of "owning" the territory. With the rise of the Greek city-states, territory as such defined a political entity. People in the city-states felt some permanent ownership of the land, and that connection became part of their political identity. As a result, the concept of citizenship first developed and laws began to specify who was and who was not a citizen. After 450 B.C. Athenian law granted citizenship (membership) in the territorially defined political unit. New entry into citizenship was possible only if both your parents were citizens or you had been legally approved through what may have been the world's first naturalization process. Overall, citizens may have made up only about a third of the population.

Sovereignty: Aristotle (384–322 B.C.), in his epic work, *Politics,* argued that supreme authority stemmed from a political unit's law and system of government, not just from its rulers or religion. Therefore, each Greek city-state *(polis)* considered itself to have **sovereignty** under its own law. This meant that it recognized no legitimate higher authority, either secular or religious.

Nationalism: The citizens of the Greek city-states identified strongly with the polis, making it the focus of political identity, as well as the place they lived. Or, as Aristotle commented, "Man is an animal of the polis." This state of mind was a precursor of nationalism, today's most important sense of political identity and one that interconnects people, government, and territory.

Democracy: Also in the Greek city-states, the people became the source of political authority for the first time in history. Athenians and others "did not think of themselves as subjects of a king. . . . Instead they were 'citizens' who were actively responsible for guiding their polis" (Sherman & Salisbury, 2004:56). This idea of citizen participation reached its zenith in Athens, where a democracy existed for approximately 150 years beginning about 500 B.C. Just about the time Athens was at its height, Rome was beginning to grow far to the west. Like Athens, it was a city-state that expanded into an empire, and then eventually declined and fell. Also like the Athenians, the Romans had a democracy until it was throttled by military dictatorship during the first century B.C. It would be incorrect to closely correlate the Greek and Roman political systems with modern ones. For example, Athenian democracy was limited to adult male Athenian citizens only, perhaps 15% of the people in the city, while women, slaves, and *metics* (resident foreigners) were excluded from participation. Still, the outlines of the modern state, sovereignty, nationalism, and democracy can all be traced to these ancient times.

After the Fall of Rome, A.D. 476 to 1700

Five centuries of Roman tyranny and empire obliterated most notions of democracy and nationalism. These ideas did not die, though. They merely lay moribund for a millennium awaiting the right historical circumstances to reemerge. During this extended period called the Middle Ages (to about 1500), political power in the West was wielded at two levels of authority—one universal, the other local.

Universal Authority in the Middle Ages

Governance during the Middle Ages rested in part on overarching authority that controlled territory and people but was defined by neither. There were religious and secular aspects to this universalistic authority.

Religious Authority   The Roman Catholic Church was one source of universalistic authority. It served as the integrating force in several ways. The Church provided a common language among intellectuals by keeping Latin alive. Christian doctrine underlay the developing concepts of rights, justice, and other political norms. Even kings were theoretically (and often substantially) subordinate to papal authority. To extend that, the pope in concert with various powerful monarchs sought to promote the idea of a universal Roman-Christian state. This goal led Pope Leo III to crown one Germanic king, Charlemagne, as "Emperor of the Romans" in 800. Similarly, Pope John XII bestowed Charlemagne's old title on another German king, Otto I, in 962, thereby legitimizing his control over what became known as the **Holy Roman Empire**.

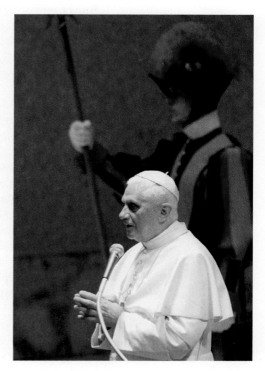

Political authority was once organized quite differently than it is now. One difference was the overarching secular as well as religious authority of the Roman Catholic Church and the pope. In an echo of this earlier status, a member of the Vatican's Swiss Guard stands behind Pope Benedict XVI. The now largely ceremonial unit was once a true fighting force and dates back to the sixteenth century.

Secular Authority   As the Middle Ages proceeded, the overarching authority of the Catholic Church was supplemented, and sometimes supplanted, by great multi-ethnic empires. Most of the people under the control of the Austro-Hungarian, British, Chinese, Dutch, French, German, Ottoman, Russian, Spanish, and other empires were not culturally related to the emperors and felt little loyalty to them. As for the monarchs, they claimed their authority came from God, and most of them did not feel a strong political identification with or an emotional attachment to the commoners. Many of these empires lasted into the 20th century, but they and the degree of macrolevel integration they provided were all eventually swept away by the rising tide of nationalism.

Local Authority in the Middle Ages

The local, microlevel of authority was called the **feudal system**. It was organized around principalities, dukedoms, baronies, and other such fiefdoms. Nobles ruled these, exercising near complete sovereignty over them. In theory, these nobles were vassals of a king or an emperor, but in fact they were usually autonomous and sometimes even more powerful than the monarch they supposedly served.

It is important to understand that the concepts of territory and political authority during the medieval period were much different from what they are now. Certainly monarchs and nobles controlled specific territories, but in theory they did not exercise sovereignty over them. Instead, God and God's Church gave monarchs the right to rule over certain lands, and, in turn, the kings subdivided their territory by granting dominion over parts of it to subordinate nobles. Thus the nature of the feudal system, in which vassals were theoretically subservient to kings and kings were theoretically subservient to emperors and popes, meant that sovereignty did not exist legally and often did not exist in fact. Commoners had little or no authority and were considered subjects, a concept closer to the status of property than to citizen.

By the 13th century the fabric of universalism and feudalism had begun to fray. During the next few centuries, "the international system went through a dramatic transformation in which the crosscutting jurisdictions of feudal lords, emperors, kings, and popes started to give way to territorially defined authorities" (Spruyt, 1994:1). The existing nonterritorially defined, hierarchical system was replaced by a system based on territorially defined states whose sovereignty made them equals legally.

The Decline of the Feudal System

Many forces of change in the Middle Ages eroded the feudal system. Of these, two stand out—military technology and economic expansion.

Military Technology   The introduction of gunpowder to European warfare in the mid-1300s and other changes in military capabilities diminished the ability of the smaller feudal fiefdoms to defend themselves. Inexpensive, little-trained commoners armed with rudimentary rifles could shoot highly trained, expensively armored knights, the epitome of the feudal warrior elite, off their horses. Relatively inexpensive cannons could readily demolish expensive castles, the centerpiece of feudal defense. These and other realities meant that static defenses of small territories needed to be replaced by a defense based on maneuver, which was best provided by a territorially larger unit, the state.

Economic Expansion   Europe's growing economy also undermined the feudal system. *Improved trade* was one factor that contributed to the economic expansion. The Mongol Empire's control of much of Asia and the Middle East in the late 13th century

States developed in part because of the need for political units larger than feudal baronies to facilitate the expansion of international trade. The theme of commerce is represented in this early map showing Niccolo and Maffeo Polo, father and uncle to Marco Polo, heading back in the late 1200s to Venice along the fabled "silk road" trade route that connected the Mediterranean region with China.

fostered the stability that trade needs to flourish. Expanded trade with Asia led Europeans to build larger ships, which, in turn, created even greater possibilities for trade. The journeys of Marco Polo of Venice to China and other lands between 1271 and 1295 were related to this new commercial activity. Later the search for new trade and trade routes led, among other things, to the journey of Christopher Columbus in 1492.

The beginning of *mass production* was a second factor driving economic expansion. Individual craftsmen began to give way to primitive factories. Full-scale industrialization did not take place for another 500 years, but the early stages of the industrial revolution were in place by the 1200s.

The growth of trade and manufacturing had important political consequences. First, it created a wealthy and powerful commercial class, the burghers, who increasingly dominated the expanding urban centers of trade and manufacturing. Second, the burghers became dissatisfied with the prevailing political system because they needed greater access to raw materials for their factories and markets for their products. This access was hampered by the impediments to commerce inherent in the maze of feudal entities. Third, the desire of the burghers to create larger political units to facilitate their commercial ventures made the monied business class natural allies with kings, who were constantly striving to increase their control over their feudal lords. The burghers and kings each had something the other needed. The kings could legitimately destroy the fiefdoms; the burghers could supply kings with money to pay for the soldiers and arms needed to overcome the nobles. The resulting alliance helped to create the modern state.

In sum, changing military technology made the feudal fiefdoms obsolete as a defensive unit, and changes in manufacturing and commerce left them obsolete as an economic unit. Safety and prosperity required larger units. States provided those.

The Decline of Universalistic Authority

At the same time that the micropolitical feudal system was decaying, the macropolitical claims of universalistic authority by the pope and the Holy Roman Emperor were being challenged by the growing power of the kings. This decline of papal authority and increase in royal power were reinforced by a period of cultural and intellectual

Web Link

The text of the Treaty of Westphalia is available at **www.yale.edu/lawweb/avalon/ westphal.htm.**

rebirth and reform called the **Renaissance** (about 1350–1650). Many of the concepts that emerged, including scientific inquiry and personal freedom, undermined the authority of the Church.

One significant outcome was the **Protestant Reformation**. Influenced by Renaissance thinking, Martin Luther rejected the Catholic Church as the necessary intermediary between people and God. In 1517 Luther proclaimed his belief that anyone could have an individual relationship with God. Within a few decades, nearly a quarter of the people of Western Europe became Protestants. The first great secular break with the Catholic Church occurred in England, where King Henry VIII (r. 1509–1547) rejected papal authority and established the Anglican Church. The Reformation also touched off political-religious struggles elsewhere in Europe. The ostensible issue was religious freedom, but there were also important political causes and consequences. When the century-long struggle between the imperial and Catholic Holy Roman Empire and the nationalist and Protestant ethnic groups ended with the **Treaty of Westphalia** (1648), centralized political power in Europe was over. The Holy Roman Empire had splintered into two rival Catholic monarchies (Austria and Spain); a number of Protestant entities (such as Holland and many German states) gained independence or autonomy. Yet other countries, such as Catholic France and Protestant England, were more secure in their independence. Therefore, many scholars regard 1648 as marking the births of the modern national state and of the world political system based on sovereign states as the primary political actors.

The Emergence of the Sovereign State

The breakdown of the feudal-universalistic system of governance did not, however, immediately make the **state** the uncontested, dominant political actor. Instead, the people of the Middle Ages experimented with several types of political organizations to see how well they would meet the security and economic needs of the time.

The Early State and Its Competitors   The revival of city-states, such as Venice, was one alternative scheme of political organization. Another was the formation of loosely confederated city-leagues based on common economic interests. The most famous of these mercantile alliances, the Hanseatic League, was founded in 1358 to protect commerce against piracy. It eventually included 70 northern European cities stretching from Bruges (in modern Belgium) to Novograd (in modern Russia) and became a major economic force.

What is important is that states, not city-states or city-leagues, became the new focus of political organization. The Hanseatic League ended in 1667. The fortunes of Venice and other city-states ebbed more slowly, but they eventually faded also. The failure of these experiments and the survival of the state occurred for identifiable, pragmatic reasons. Those are beyond our telling here, but the essential point is that in time "sovereign states displaced city-leagues and city-states . . . because their institutional logic gave them an advantage in mobilizing their societies' resources" (Spruyt, 1994:185). States were best equipped to conduct commerce, provide defense, and meet other needs.

Consequences of the Emergence of the State   The emergence and eventual triumph of the state as the dominant mode of governance had profound consequences for the international system. One of these was that states became the primary actors in the post-Westphalia international system. They continue in that starring role today. Therefore, much of the action on the world stage is about states and groups of states interacting with one another.

More subtly, the fact that states recognize no higher authority necessarily means that the international system has no central authority to maintain order and dispense justice. Therefore, international relations occur in an **anarchical political system**. This does not mean that the international system is a scene of unchecked chaos. There is an informal hierarchy based on power, with more powerful states often maintaining some semblance of order (Hobson, 2005). Moreover, the international system usually operates in a reasonable way. This occurs, however, mostly because countries find it in their interests to act according to expectations. When a state decides that it is in its interests to break the largely informal rules of the system, as Iraq did in 1990 when it invaded Kuwait, there is little to stop it except countervailing power.

The Eighteenth and Nineteenth Centuries

The emergence of the sovereign state as the primary actor marked a major shift in the international system. Following the Peace of Westphalia, national states continued to gather strength as monarchs such as Louis XIV of France (r. 1643–1715), Frederick II of Prussia (r. 1740–1786), and Peter the Great of Russia (r. 1682–1725) consolidated their kingdoms and even expanded them into empires. If anything, the pace of change quickened in the 18th and 19th centuries. Three themes stand out: the advent of popular sovereignty, the Westernization of the international system, and the zenith of the multipolar system.

Popular Sovereignty

In the early 18th century, most kings claimed to rule their realms by "divine right." *"L'état, c'est moi"* (I am the state), France's Louis XIV proclaimed. Perhaps, but in 1793 another French king, Louis XVI, lost his head over this presumption, and the people claimed the state for themselves under the doctrine of **popular sovereignty**.

The revival of popular sovereignty, which had lain dormant since the demise of Athenian democracy and the Roman republic, marked a major change in the notion of who owned the state and how it should be governed. Until this time, the prevailing belief was that kings ruled by divine right over both territory and people, who were subjects, not citizens. Understandably, the people had limited attachment to the state, since it was the king's, not theirs. The American (1776) and French (1789) revolutions challenged this philosophy. *Democracies* were established on the principle that ultimate political power rests with the people, not the monarch. Popular sovereignty also expanded the concept of *nationalism* to include mass identification with and participation in the affairs of the state. If the people owned the state, then they had both a greater emotional attachment to it and a greater responsibility to support it. One symbol of this change was that Napoleonic France

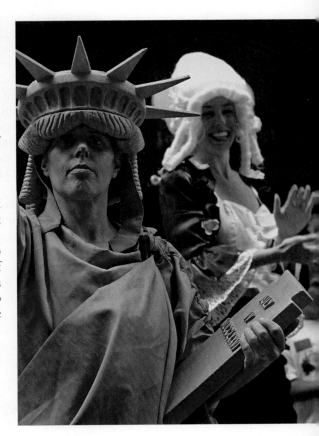

The American and French revolutions significantly advanced the emerging idea of popular sovereignty. The link between the two events is symbolized by these women dressed as the Statue of Liberty and Marie Antoinette, the queen toppled during the French Revolution. The women are at a party in New York City commemorating Bastille Day, July 14. On that day in 1789 a French mob stormed the Bastille Prison in Paris, beginning the revolution.

(1799–1815) was the first country to have a true patriotic draft that raised an army of a million strong.

From its beginnings in America and, particularly, in France, democratic nationalism spread throughout Europe and steadily undermined monarchical government and its concept of divine right. The collapse of the dynasties in China, Germany, Austria-Hungary, Russia, the Ottoman Empire, and elsewhere early in the 20th century marked the real end of strong monarchical government. Nationalism and popular sovereignty were also antithetical to empire. The large multiethnic and in some cases colonial empires that were prevalent in the early 1900s began to unravel in World War I. Then the British and French colonial empires fell apart in the midtwentieth century, and the last great multiethnic empire imploded in 1991 when the Soviet Union fragmented into 15 independent countries.

Westernization of the International System

The domination and shaping of the international system by the **West** was a second important characteristic of the 18th and 19th centuries. Somewhat earlier, the growth of European power had enabled Great Britain, France, and other European countries to thrust outward and take control of North and South America and some parts of Asia. The Arab, Aztec, Chinese, Incan, Mogul (Indian), Persian, and other non-European empires or dynasties began to decline and fall. The process accelerated in the 19th century, and Europeans came to dominate the globe and to see themselves "as forming an exclusive club enjoying rights superior to those of other political communities" (Bull & Watson, 1982:425). One reason for the **westernization of the international system** was the scientific and technological advances that sprang from the Renaissance in Europe. This sparked the **industrial revolution**, which began in the mid-1700s in Great Britain. During the next 150 years, industrialization spread rapidly but not globally. Instead, it was mostly a Western phenomenon, with the notable exception of Japan.

Industrialization and associated advances in weaponry and other technology had a profound impact on world politics. Europe gained strength compared with nonindustrialized Asia and Africa. Industrialization also promoted colonialism, because the manufacturing countries needed to expand resources and markets to fuel and fund their economies. Many industrialized countries also coveted colonies as a matter of prestige. The result was an era of Euro-American **imperialism** that stretched to all corners of the world. The fate of Africa is graphically displayed in the map on the facing page. **Eurowhites** similarly subjugated most Asian cultures. China, it should be noted, was never colonized, but after the 1840s it was divided into spheres of influence among the Western powers. Only Japan and Siam (now Thailand) remained truly sovereign. Joining the scramble for possession, Americans acquired Hawaii and Samoa in the 1890s. Victory in the Spanish-American War (1898) added Guam, Puerto Rico, and the Philippines. Additionally, U.S. military interventions in the Caribbean–Central American region became so frequent in following decades that the true sovereignty of those countries was questionable.

Even though these colonial empires were, for the most part, not long-lived, they still had a major and deleterious impact that continues to affect world politics. The imperialist subjugation of Asians, Africans, and others by Europeans and Americans set the stage for what became the division of the world into two spheres—one wealthy, one poor—that continue to exist.

The Growth of the Multipolar System

The 1700s and 1800s also saw the zenith of the **multipolar system**, which governed political relations among the globally dominant major European powers from the

The Colonization and Decolonization of Africa, 1878, 1914, 2005

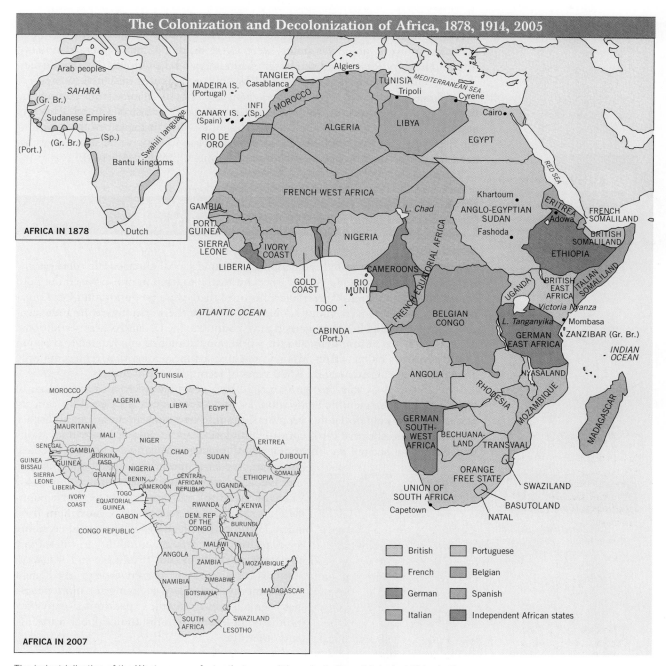

Legend:
- British
- French
- German
- Italian
- Portuguese
- Belgian
- Spanish
- Independent African states

The industrialization of the West was one factor that caused the colonization of Asia and Africa in the late 1800s and early 1900s. This map and its insets show that Africa was largely controlled by its indigenous peoples in 1878 (inset) but had by 1914 (larger map) become almost totally subjugated and divided into colonies by the European powers. Then, after World War II, the momentum shifted. Independence movements led to decolonization. Now there are no colonies left in Africa. Thus the West's domination of the world has weakened.

Source: Perry Marvin, Myra Chase, James R. Jacob, Margaret C. Jacob, and Theodore H. Von Laue. *Western Civilization: Ideas, Politics and Society,* Fourth Edition. Copyright 1992 by Houghton Mifflin Company. Adapted with permission.

Treaty of Westphalia in 1648 through the mid-twentieth century. In the century between the final defeat of Napoleon (1815) and the outbreak of World War I (1914), the major powers, or **power poles**, were Great Britain, France, Prussia/Germany, Austria-Hungary, Russia, and to a lesser extent Italy and the Ottoman Empire/Turkey.

The multipolar system was marked by shifting alliances designed to preserve the **balance of power** by preventing any single power or alliance from dominating Europe and, by extension, the world. Prime Minister Winston Churchill clearly enunciated Great Britain's balance-of-power politics when he explained that "for four hundred years the foreign policy of England has been to oppose the strongest, most aggressive, most dominating power on the Continent" (Walt, 1996:109).

THE EVOLVING WORLD SYSTEM: THE TWENTIETH CENTURY

The 20th century witnessed momentous and rapid global change. The *rapid pace of change* that continues today is an important theme to keep in mind. When the 20th century began monarchs ruled most countries; there were no important global organizations; and there were about 1.5 billion people in the world. By the time the century ended, elected officials governed most countries; the UN and other international organizations were prominent; and the world population had quadrupled to 6 billion people. All this happened in just one century, a time period that represents only about 3% of the approximately 3,500 years of recorded human history.

A great deal of this change is related to a seemingly ever-increasing pace of technological and scientific innovation, as evident in Figure 2.1. The 20th century saw the creation of television, computers, the Internet, nuclear energy, air and space travel, missiles, effective birth control, antibiotics, and a host of other innovations that benefit or bedevil us. Technology both creates and solves problems. Medical advances, for one, mean that many more babies survive and people live much longer, but those changes have also contributed to an explosive population growth. New technologies have also been a key factor in the expansion of the world economy by dramatically improving our ability to extract raw materials, turn them into products, and transport them to consumers. Here again, though, the benefit of an improved standard of living for most people has been offset by economic expansion's negative by-products: pollution, deforestation, global warming, and other ills.

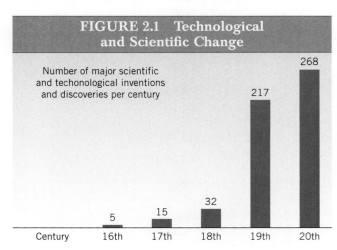

FIGURE 2.1 Technological and Scientific Change

Number of major scientific and techonological inventions and discoveries per century

The quickening pace of technological and scientific change has strongly affected human beings and their politics. This figure depicts the number of important discoveries and inventions since 1500. Fully 90% of them have occurred since 1800, with half in the 20th century alone.

Data source: World Almanac (2007).

The Eclipse of the Multipolar System

The pace of world political evolution began to speed up even more by the beginning of the 1900s. Democracy was rapidly eroding the legitimacy of monarchs. In 1900 there were still czars and kaisers; they would be gone in less than two decades. **Nationalism** increasingly undermined the foundations of multi-ethnic empires. World War I was a pivotal point.

Two empires, the Austro-Hungarian and Ottoman, were among the losers. From their rubble, countries such as Czechoslovakia, Poland, and Yugoslavia (re)emerged. Other countries like Jordan, Lebanon, Syria, and Palestine/Israel came under the mandate (oversight) of the League of Nations and finally became independent after World War II.

The Collapse of Europe as a Global Power Center

The causes of the demise of the European multipolar system by the mid-twentieth century are complex and subject to dispute. What is important, however, is that the system lost its ability to maintain a balance of power as the major powers coalesced into two rigid, nearly bipolar alliances that soon engaged in a death struggle. In World War I (1914–1918) the Central Powers included Germany, Austria-Hungary, and Turkey. The Allied Powers consisted of France, Russia, Great Britain, and Italy. After its defeat in the war, Germany was at first treated severely, but the **realpolitik** logic of a multipolar system led the British and French to let Germany rebuild its strength in the 1930s. That suited the British, who worried that France might once again dominate Europe and threaten them as it had under Napoleon. The seizure of power in Russia by Lenin's Bolsheviks in 1918 also prompted London and Paris to tolerate German revitalization. France was especially alarmed by the specter of Communist ideology combined with Russian military might and saw a rearmed Germany as a bulwark against the "Red menace." For the British and French, these balance-of-power maneuvers constituted a near-fatal mistake.

The grotesqueness of World War I was another reason why Great Britain and France did not seriously try to restrain resurgent Germany. The two victors had each lost almost an entire generation of young men. When Adolf Hitler came to power (1933) and rearmed his country, Great Britain and France vacillated timorously. The **Munich Conference** (1938) became synonymous with this lack of will. In that conference, Great Britain and France gave way to Hitler's demands for the annexation of part of Czechoslovakia based on the mistaken belief of British Prime Minister Neville Chamberlain and other leaders that an **appeasement policy** toward Germany would satisfy it and maintain the peace.

The Rise of Non-European Powers

Although Europe was center stage, important changes were occurring elsewhere. Almost all of the Western Hemisphere was made up of independent countries by 1900, and a few states in other areas also gained independence. Other existing states, especially Japan and the United States, began to play a more significant role and to undercut European domination of the international system. China began the century saddled with a decaying imperial government and foreign domination, but it overthrew its emperor in 1911 and started a long struggle to rid itself of foreign domination and to reestablish its role as a major power. Also during the first part of the century, the League of Nations was established, and many non-European countries became active in world diplomacy through membership in it. Thus, a shift was under way. The voices of Africa, Asia, and Latin America became stronger, and two non-European powers, the United States and Japan, readied themselves to take a starring role.

The Cold War and the Bipolar System

World War II (1939–1945) was a tragedy of huge proportions. It also finally destroyed the European-based multipolar structure. In its aftermath, a **bipolar system** dominated by the Union of Soviet Socialist Republics (USSR, Soviet Union) and the

Web Link

For a flavor of the Munich crisis in 1938, you can hear radio programming from the day that Neville Chamberlain explained to a happy British crowd his decision to appease Adolf Hitler at **http://archives.cbc.ca/IDD-1 -109-1257/1930s/1938/**.

United States soon formed. To those who experienced its intensity, the hostility between the two superpowers seemed to augur an unending future of bipolar confrontation and peril. As is often true, the view that the present will also be the future proved shortsighted. The bipolar era was brief. It began to gradually weaken in little more than a decade; by 1992 it was history.

The Rise and Decline of the Bipolar System

Web Link

See *Duck and Cover,* the movie produced by the U.S. government in the 1950s to teach children what to do in case of a nuclear attack, at **http://stream.state.gov/streamvol/ journals/fullversion.mov.**

World War II devastated most of the existing major actors. In their place, the United States emerged as a military and economic **superpower** and the leader of one power pole. Even though incredibly damaged, the Soviet Union emerged as the superpower leader of the other pole. The USSR never matched the United States economically, but the Soviets possessed a huge conventional armed force, a seemingly threatening ideology, and, by 1949, atomic weapons. The uneasy alliance that had existed between Washington and Moscow during World War II was soon replaced by overt hostility. Indeed, their rivalry divided much of the world into two antagonistic spheres in what became known as the **cold war**, a conflict with all but the shooting of a "hot war."

Historians still debate the causes of the cold war, but it is safe to say that varying economic and political interests and the power vacuum created by the collapse of the old balance-of-power structure created a bipolar system in which a great deal of world politics was centered on the confrontation between the two superpowers along the so-called **East-West axis**. The United States reacted to what it saw as a Soviet/communist threat with the **containment doctrine**, a policy of global opposition to the Soviet Union and other communist countries. To that end, Washington sponsored a number of regional alliances, most notably the **North Atlantic Treaty Organization** (NATO, established in 1949), which encircled the USSR, as evident in the map on the facing page. The Soviets responded in 1955 with the Warsaw Treaty Organization (or Warsaw Pact). Both sides also vied for power in the developing countries (known then as the **Third World**), and Soviet and American arms and money flowed to various governments and rebel groups in the ongoing communist-anticommunist contest. Yet despite the intense rivalry, a mutual fear of nuclear war deterred the superpowers from direct confrontations. The wisdom of avoiding eyeball-to-eyeball crises was evident in the Cuban missile crisis (1962), one of the few times the superpowers did directly confront each other. The scariest event of the cold war occurred when the Soviets began building nuclear missile sites in Cuba, and President John F. Kennedy risked nuclear war to force them out.

It is hard for those who did not experience the most intense part of the cold war in the 1950s and early 1960s to understand how scary a time it was. The fear among Americans about a possible nuclear attack by the Soviet Union is captured in this photo of a mother leading her two young children to their backyard nuclear fallout shelter in Sacramento, California, during a nuclear alert drill in 1961.

U.S.–Soviet Bipolarity

An Age of Bipolarity: The Cold War ca. 1970

- Soviet bloc
- U.S. and allies

The bipolar era was marked by mutual hostility and fear between the United States and its allies and the Soviet Union and other communist countries. Americans perceived Soviet-led communism to be threatening everywhere, and adopted the containment doctrine to counter it. The Soviets were equally alarmed by what seemed an encircling set of U.S.-led allies. This polar projection map depicts the world as something like the way Moscow saw it, with the communists (in red) alarmingly surrounded by the Western allies (in blue).

One outgrowth of the containment doctrine was the U.S. involvement in Vietnam. Vietnamese forces led by nationalist/communist Ho Chi Minh defeated France's colonial army in 1954 and achieved independence. But the country was divided between Ho's forces in the north and a nondemocratic, pro-Western government in the south. The struggle for a unified Vietnam soon resumed, and the United States intervened militarily in 1964. The war quickly became a trauma for Americans. Perhaps the most poignant domestic tragedy was the death in 1970 of four students at Kent State University during clashes between antiwar demonstrators and the Ohio National Guard. War-weariness finally led to a complete U.S. disengagement. Within a short time Ho's forces triumphed and Vietnam was unified in 1975.

Vietnam caused a number of important changes in American attitudes. One was increased resistance to the cold war urge to fight communism everywhere. Second, Americans saw more clearly that the bipolar system was crumbling, especially as relations between the Soviet Union and China deteriorated. Beginning approximately with the administrations of Soviet leader Leonid I. Brezhnev (1964–1982) and American President Richard M. Nixon (1969–1974), U.S.-Soviet relations began to improve, albeit fitfully. Nixon accurately assessed the changing balance of power,

Web Link

A site that focuses on the cold war with audio, video, and interactive elements is offered by CNN at **www.cnn.com/ specials/cold.war/.**

especially the rise of China, and he moved to improve relations through a policy of **détente** with Moscow and Beijing. They came to similar realpolitik conclusions about the changing power configuration of the international system and sought improved relations with Washington.

The End of the Bipolar System

During the 1970s and early 1980s, relations between Moscow and Washington continued to warm, fitfully at first, then more rapidly. Mikhail S. Gorbachev became the Soviet leader in 1985 and instituted a range of reforms designed to ease the Soviet Union's oppressive political system and to restructure its cumbersome bureaucratic and economic systems. While Gorbachev's goals were limited, he opened a Pandora's box for the communist Soviet Union and unleashed forces that were beyond his control.

Gorbachev also sought better relations with the West in an effort to reduce the USSR's burdensome military spending, to improve trade, and to accrue other economic benefits. Among other things, Gorbachev announced that the USSR would let Eastern Europeans follow their own domestic policies. They responded by moving quickly to escape Moscow's orbit. This was symbolized most dramatically in East Germany, where the communist government fell apart rapidly. East German guards withdrew from their posts along the Berlin Wall, which physically divided its city and symbolized the overall East-West split, and protesters and souvenir hunters soon tore most of the barrier down. East Germany dissolved itself in October 1990, and its territory was absorbed by West Germany into a newly reunified Germany. Other communist governments in the region also fell, and the Warsaw Pact dissolved in early 1991. It was hard to believe then, but the Soviet Union was next. It collapsed, and its constituent republics declared their independence. On December 25, 1991, Gorbachev resigned as president of a country that no longer existed. That evening, the red hammer-and-sickle Soviet flag was lowered for the last time from the Kremlin's spires and replaced by the red, white, and blue Russian flag. Few novelists could have created a story of such sweep and drama. The Soviet Union was no more.

Web Link

A site that has some interesting video clips of notable foreign policy speeches by U.S. presidents related to the cold war is in the April 2006 edition of the U.S. Department of State's electronic journal at **http://usinfo.state.gov/journals/journala.htm.**

THE TWENTY-FIRST CENTURY: THE GENESIS OF A NEW SYSTEM

"What's past is prologue," Shakespeare comments in *The Tempest*. That is as true for the real world of today and tomorrow as it was for the Bard's literary world of yesterday. One hopes that no future historian will write a history of the 21st century under the title *The Tempest*. Titles such as *As You Like It* or *All's Well That Ends Well* are more appealing possibilities for histories yet to be. It is we who will write the script for the history to come. As Shakespeare tells us in *Julius Caesar,* "It is not in the stars to hold our destiny but in ourselves." The sections that follow will help you determine your preferences for the future by examining the factors and trends that will benefit or beset the world "tomorrow, and tomorrow, and tomorrow," as Macbeth put it.

The Polar Power Structure in the Twenty-First Century

Few changes in the polar configuration of power have had as decisive a symbol as the collapse of the Soviet Union in 1991. Clearly the bipolar system is gone. What is not certain is how to characterize the current, still evolving system (Thompson, 2006).

Although not all scholars would agree, the view here is that what exists in the first decade of the 21st century is best described as a limited unipolar system that is struggling to become a multipolar system.

A Unipolar Moment

Just before the Soviet Union's final collapse, analyst Charles Krauthammer (1991:23) wrote an article entitled "The Unipolar Moment." It disagreed with the widespread assumption that a multipolar system was forming to replace the anticipated end of bipolarity. "The immediate post–cold war world is not multipolar," he observed. "It is unipolar. The center of world power is the unchallenged superpower, the United States." This view sees the United States as the world's **hegemonic power**, that is, possessing influence far beyond any other power. Concurring, another scholar writes, "We have entered the American unipolar age" (Ikenberry, 2004:609). And a third observes, "Not since Rome has one nation loomed so large above the others" (Nye, 2002:545). The implication of this status is that the "United States . . . [as] a global hegemon . . . has formidable tools at its disposal, and it can wield its power effectively to attain important policy objectives" (Layne, 2006:45). Certainly U.S. military power is prominent among these tools. U.S. arms with some allied support twice defeated Iraq (1991, 2003) and overwhelmed Serbia (1999) in wars that were wildly one-sided, mostly because of the vast and growing lead of U.S. military technology. However, U.S. dominance is not just based on military might. Instead, according to France's foreign minister, "U.S. supremacy today extends to the economy, currency, military areas, lifestyle, language, and the products of mass culture that inundate the world, forming thought and fascinating even the enemies of the United States."[1]

Reasonably, the question arises, "If the United States is the world's hegemonic power, then why does it not always get its way?" The reason is, "Hegemony is not omnipotence" (Layne, 2006:43). There are numerous factors that restrain the United States:

- Military power is much better at deterring attacks than it is at compelling others to act according to your wishes.
- Military power is better at dealing with other established military forces than it is at dealing with insurgencies and terrorism.
- Being a hegemon does not mean that all other states are powerless or that they are willing to accept your dominance. Indeed, the opposite is true, and there is a multipolar urge.

JOIN THE DEBATE
The United States and
Hegemonic Power

Many analysts believe that world politics is currently a unipolar or perhaps limited unipolar system, in which the dominant, or hegemonic, power is the United States.

The Multipolar Urge

In his poem, "Mending Wall," Robert Frost wrote about the seemingly inexorable forces of nature that topple stone walls. Wisely he observed:

> Something there is that doesn't love a wall,
> That wants it down.

Similarly, there is something in the balance-of-power nature of the international system that does not like unipolarity. U.S. dominance rankles many countries, whether they were allies, enemies, or neutrals in the cold war era (Layne, 2006a; Malone & Khong, 2003). In 2005 after a group of U.S. senators met in Paris with President Jacques Chirac, they told reporters that he had stressed his belief that the international system was multipolar and implied that France was one of the multiple power centers. Chirac "still doesn't like the idea of the unipolar world with the United States as top dog," Senator Joseph R. Biden, Jr. (D-DE) noted astutely.[2] Other countries' leaders have also noted their opposition to unipolarity. Among them, Russia's President Vladimir Putin has argued, "The world order can and should be multipolar," and Prime Minister Atal Behari Vajpayee of India spoke favorably of a "cooperative multipolar world order."[3]

MAP
European Colonization
1500–2000

These expressions of support for a multipolar world by the leaders of France, India, and Russia do not mean that they are anti-American, merely anti-unipolarity. The reason is that a world in which there is one dominant power, the United States in this case, is an international system in which all other countries are at least partly subordinate. We will see in chapter 3 that unipolarity arguably has some benefits, but it is a difficult state of affairs for any sovereign country (other than the single superpower, of course) to accept. In addition to this resistance, some critics charge that the United States is wandering into "hegemonic quicksand" by stubborn unilateralism and by squandering its power in Iraq and elsewhere in an ill-conceived pursuit of empire (Brzezinski, 2004:16). This view leads critics of U.S. policy to argue that to the extent that U.S. hegemonic power exists, the unipolar moment will soon pass (Cockburn & St. Clair, 2004; Mann, 2004).

Limited Unipolarity

There is no precise line where unipolarity begins and ends. This vague boundary is one reason why all analysts do not agree that the world is unipolar. Although unipolarity does not imply absolute power, the important challenges that exist to U.S. power lead some analysts to depict the current state of affairs as a **limited unipolar system**. The most important of the restraints on U.S. power result from the extensive degree to which the United States, like all countries, is intertwined with and reliant on other countries. For example, the U.S. war on terrorism will make little progress unless other countries cooperate in identifying and arresting terrorists within their borders and dismantling the financial networks on which terrorists often rely. Similarly, the U.S. economy may be the world's most powerful, but it depends heavily on favorable trade relationships with other countries for its prosperity. A third example involves the frequent U.S. need for diplomatic support. The simmering crisis with North Korea is likely to be resolved much more easily if the region's countries, especially China, cooperate with Washington in persuading Pyongyang to give up its nuclear weapons program. The point is that because the United States frequently benefits from the cooperation of others, it can only go so far in riding roughshod over their preferences on a range of issues (Patrick & Forman, 2002).

Currently, there are probably not too many issues on which a determined Washington cannot get its way. Almost by definition, a hegemonic power attempts to

DEBATE THE POLICY SCRIPT

Is Preemptive War Good Policy?

In "The National Security Strategy of the United States of America," a 2002 report to Congress, President George W. Bush argued that Americans were increasingly threatened by terrorism and weapons of mass destruction. To address these dangers, he announced that, "As a matter of common sense and self-defense, America will act against such emerging threats before they are fully formed. . . . [T]he only path to peace and security is the path of action." In essence, the president declared that the United States reserved the right to strike enemies before they attacked Americans.

Theory became reality when the United States invaded Iraq in 2003. Speaking to the nation, Bush argued that Iraq "threatens the peace with weapons of mass murder" and declared, "We will meet that threat now, with our [military forces] so that we do not have to meet it later with armies of firefighters and police and doctors on the streets of our cities."[1]

UN Secretary-General Kofi Annan was among those who disagreed with President Bush. Annan told the General Assembly that the idea of preemptive war "represents a fundamental challenge to the principles on which, however imperfectly, world peace and stability have rested for the last 58 years. My concern is that, if it were to be adopted, it could set precedents that resulted in a proliferation of the unilateral and lawless use of force, with or without justification."[2]

Preemptive war, hitting before you get hit, is controversial at both the practical and legal levels (Walzer, 2004). Pragmatically, striking enemies before they attack has clear benefits. However, liabilities also exist. What if you are wrong, and people die because of that? Another worry is that if you claim the right to preemptive war, others also have that right. It is important to ask yourself if world stability and security are enhanced or lessened by the universal application of the principle of legitimate preemptive war.

Legal controversy about preemptive war theory centers on the obligations of the United States and every other country that has signed the UN Charter, which is a binding treaty. Two articles in the Charter are especially relevant. Article 51 says that "nothing in the Charter" should be interpreted as denying a country "the inherent right of individual or collective self-defense if an armed attack occurs." Article 39 stipulates that except in self-defense, it is the UN Security Council that "shall determine the existence of any threat to the peace, breach of the peace, or act of aggression and . . . decide what measures shall be taken . . . to maintain or restore international peace and security."

Deciding about the wisdom of preemptive war is more than a "for-or-against" choice. Instead, you can be categorically for it, categorically against it, or favor preemptive war only in limited circumstances. If you favor the limited use option, then you also have to specify when preventive war is permissible and when it is not. Remember, the standard that you adopt as legitimate for your country also applies to every other country.

What Do You Think?

When, if ever, do threats justify war?

shape the international scene to its liking. The unipolar power does so with allies and other forms of multilateral support when possible, but it acts unilaterally when necessary. Trying to control events also implies being proactive, as least sometimes, rather than always responding to the initiative of others. These two standards of hegemony, willingness to exercise unilateral leadership and to act rather than react, were clearly evident in President George W. Bush's national security policy, and one aspect of that policy, preemptive war, is presented for your consideration in the Debate the Policy Script box, "Is Preemptive War Good Policy?" A suggestion is to ponder preemptive war in general terms and not to judge it solely by the course of the U.S. invasion and occupation of Iraq. Policy principle and policy execution are very different matters.

Future Polarity

Forecasting the future configuration of world power is difficult, beyond the safe-bet prediction that U.S. hegemony, like that of every other great power in history, will end. Certainly, as the statements by Chirac and others demonstrate, a great deal of the diplomatic strategy of many countries seeks to hasten the arrival of multipolarity. For example, many observers expressed the arguably reasonable suspicion that the

German and French opposition in 2003 to war with Iraq, which prevented the United States from getting UN Security Council support of the invasion, was based in part on a desire to assert their own authority in the system.

Particularly if U.S. policy is overly aggressive and unilateral, it could drive the next tier of powers, such as Russia and China, into alliance with one another and opposition to the United States. At the opposite extreme, if the United States drastically reduces its leadership role, then a multipolar system could quickly reemerge by default (Ikenberry, 2002; Bender, 2003). One view is that such a system will be state-centric and look and function much like the *traditional multipolar system* that existed in the 19th century (Mearsheimer, 2001). Another view is that the system is evolving toward becoming a *modified multipolar system*. Such a system would not look or operate like a traditional multipolar system because states and alliances are now being joined as important actors by regional and global international organizations, such as the European Union (EU) and the United Nations (UN). These new types of major actors could well change the dynamics of the international system in ways that are discussed in chapters 3 and 7.

Americans themselves are another major factor that will determine the future of U.S. hegemony and the shape of the international system. While the prospect of shaping the world appeals to many Americans and the United States gains many benefits from being a hegemonic power, there is also a price to be paid. One is the cost, including the massive amounts that the United States spends on national security. A related cost is the lives that are lost applying military power. A third cost stems from often being vilified. As discussed above, there is widespread antagonism toward hegemony. Even countries that benefit from the dominant state's power are restive to some degree. As such, some, although certainly not all, of the fear and anger that many countries and people express about the dominant power is not related to its policies but instead is a dynamic of a unipolar system reality that no hegemonic power has ever been beloved by the world it dominates.

The question is whether, to what degree, and how long Americans will be willing to accept the burdens as well as the benefits of hegemony. The middle course, being active in the world but emphasizing multilateral efforts, requires less effort, but it sometimes entails a willingness to forego pursuit of the goals that do not enjoy support of a substantial part of the international community. At the other extreme, isolationism, such as defending the United States and its territories from military and economic attack while letting events in the rest of the world take their course without a U.S. response, could be done at a small fraction of the annual U.S. defense budget. This would be especially true if the United States were willing to use all its power, including its nuclear arsenal, to deter and respond to an attack that had begun or was clearly imminent. Yet isolationism also might mean global realities that offend American values and that are inimical to long-term U.S. interests. To a substantial degree, which role the United States will play depends on what the American public wants or at least will tolerate. For now, as evident in Figure 2.2, a majority of Americans support playing an active role in world politics, but less than 20% want to play the part of the hegemonic

FIGURE 2.2   American Views on the U.S. Global Role

When asked what if any leadership role they want the United States to play, most people prefer shared leadership, with only small minorities wanting either to abandon leadership or to dominate the world.

Data source: Pew Research Center and Chicago Council on Foreign Relations poll, October 2005; data provided by The Roper Center for Public Opinion Research, University of Connecticut.

power. Therefore, presidents risk a politically dangerous backlash if they follow a policy that Americans feel overextends their country's global political involvement.

Other Power Changes in the Twenty-First Century

The shifts in the polar structure are not the only changes in power that will have important consequences during the coming century. Also of significance now is a growing shift of power away from the West, the challenges to the authority of the state in the international system, and changes in how we seek security.

The Weakening Western Orientation of the International System

Another ongoing change is the weakening of the dominant Western orientation of the international system as a result of the expansion of the number and power of non-Western states. The colonial empires established by the imperial Western powers collapsed after World War II, and in the ensuing years over 100 new countries have gained independence. The vast majority of these new countries are located in Africa, Asia, and other non-Western regions, as evident in the map below. A few, especially China, have achieved enough power to command center stage. Even the smaller non-Western countries have gained a stronger voice through their membership in international organizations. For example, non-Western countries now command a majority in the UN General Assembly, and in the Security Council the U.S. attempt in 2003 to gain support for war with Iraq failed because Washington was unable to persuade such Council members as Angola, Mexico, and Pakistan to support the U.S. position.

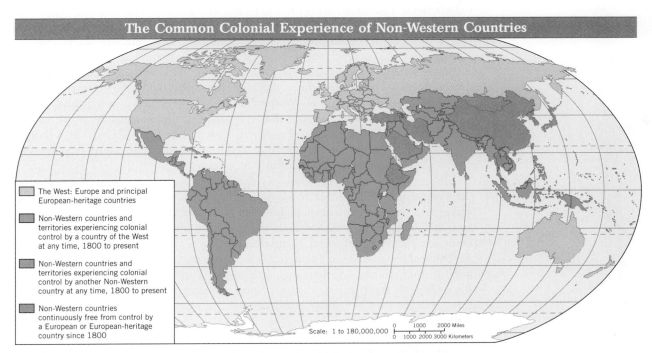

The Common Colonial Experience of Non-Western Countries

  The West: Europe and principal European-heritage countries

  Non-Western countries and territories experiencing colonial control by a country of the West at any time, 1800 to present

  Non-Western countries and territories experiencing colonial control by another Non-Western country at any time, 1800 to present

  Non-Western countries continuously free from control by a European or European-heritage country since 1800

Scale: 1 to 180,000,000

Most countries of the South share a past of having been direct or de facto colonies. With a few exceptions, the colonial power was a European country or the United States. There is a very short list of non-Western countries that did not come under control, and even most of those experienced outside domination. Much of China, for example, was divided into spheres of influence among European countries and Japan.

WEB POLL
What Does the Future
Hold for World Politics?

Web Link

A short version of Benjamin
Barber's "Jihad vs. McWorld"
can be read in article form
online at: **www.globalissues.org/
Geopolitics/WarOnTerror/
McWorld.asp.**

While the non-Western countries have many differences, they share several commonalities. Most struggle economically, are ethnically/racially not Eurowhite, and share a history of being colonies of or being dominated by Eurowhites. Furthermore, the value systems of many of these countries differ from Western values. Just one reason is that Eurowhite countries tend to base their values in major part on Judeo-Christian tradition, while other countries draw on the values of Islam, Confucianism, Hinduism, and other non-Western religions and philosophies.

It should not be surprising, then, that many of these new or newly empowered countries support changes in the international system. The result of all this is that the perspectives and demands of these countries are considerably changing the focus and tone of world political and economic debate.

Challenges to the Authority of the State

Along with the changing polar configuration and the rise of non-Western states, the 21st-century system is also being affected by the fact that states' starring role in the world drama has become somewhat less secure. This idea is captured by Benjamin Barber (1996) in his book, *Jihad vs. McWorld: How Globalism and Tribalism Are Reshaping the World.* He contends that the authority of states is being eroded by antithetical forces. Pushing in one direction, some forces (jihad or tribalism) are fragmenting states. Pushing on states in the other direction are forces to merge into an integrated world (McWorld) through a process called **globalization**. Barber (p. 4) worries that the first direction leads to the "grim prospect of a retribalization of large swaths of humankind by war and bloodshed: a threatened balkanization of nation-states in which culture is pitted against culture, people against people, tribe against tribe, a Jihad in the name of a hundred narrowly conceived [identifications and loyalties]." The other direction, Barber predicts, will meld "nations into one homogeneous global theme park, one McWorld tied together by communications, information, entertainment, and commerce." For now, Barber believes, "Caught between Babel and Disneyland, the planet is falling precipitously apart and coming reluctantly together at the very same moment." If this depiction is correct, it means that the world is moving back to something resembling the pre-Westphalian system of macroauthority and microauthority. Whereas that system's collapse resulted in the ascendancy of the middle level of authority (state power), the current system is being challenged by a reverse process of disintegration of the state into smaller units, and integration of states into more regional or universalistic wholes.

The Forces of McWorld   Many analysts believe that the political, economic, and social pressures that constitute the forces of **McWorld** are breaking down the importance and authority of states and moving the world toward a much higher degree of political, economic, and social integration.

Political integration, for example, is evident in the increasing number and importance of international organizations such as the World Trade Organization (WTO). When there are trade disputes, countries are no longer free to impose unilateral decisions. Instead, they are under heavy pressure to submit disputes to the WTO and to abide by its decisions.

Economic interdependence, the intertwining of national economies in the global economy, means that countries are increasingly less self-sufficient. This loss of economic control diminishes the general authority of a state. There is a lively debate over what this means for the future of states. One likely scenario is that advancing globalization will increasingly reduce the relevance of states, their ability to

This image of a Chinese heavy metal fan dancing at a performance of Sebastian Bach and his band during the Beijing Pop Festival in 2006 is not the rarity it once was, given the degree of cultural globalization that has occurred in recent decades.

unilaterally determine their course of action, and their practical, perhaps even legal, sovereignty, a possibility discussed in chapter 6.

Social integration is also well under way, in the view of many scholars. They believe that the world is being integrated— even homogenized—by rapid travel and communication and by the increased interchange of goods and services. People of different countries buy and sell each other's products at an ever-increasing rate; Cable News Network (CNN) is watched worldwide; the Internet provides almost instant global information and interpersonal interaction; English is becoming something of a lingua franca. At a less august level, it is possible to travel around the world dining only on Big Macs, fries, and shakes at the more than 31,000 McDonald's outlets in 119 countries that serve fast food to about 18 billion customers each year. In sum, there are indications that the world's people are moving toward living in a more culturally homogenized global village. This outward trend works to weaken inward-looking nationalism, the primary basis of identification with and loyalty to one's country.

There are numerous critics of globalization, and counterpressures exist, as we will discuss momentarily and even more in chapter 5. For all of these, though, globalization is a powerful trend that enjoys widespread support globally, as detailed in Figure 2.3 on p. 56. Therefore the most pressing question about globalization is how it should be shaped, not whether it should continue, which is almost certain.

The Forces of Tribalism   States are also being tested by and sometimes collapsing because of such pressures as erosive ethnic rivalries. Barber's main title refers to this as *jihad* (an Arabic word that means struggling to spread or defend the faith), but his other term, **tribalism**, better captures the process of disintegration.

Whatever the term, there has been an upsurge of states splintering and collapsing under the pressure of secessionist **ethnonational groups**. Most momentously, the Soviet Union dissolved into 15 independent countries in 1991, and some of them are ethnically unstable. The Chechen people, for instance, are engaged in a frequently bloody struggle to carve an independent Chechnya out of Russia. Similarly, Yugoslavia broke apart into four countries, and one of its new republics, Bosnia, itself collapsed in ethnic warfare. In 1998 an already diminished Yugoslavia further convulsed when ethnic Albanians, who are a majority in Kosovo Province, rebelled. What little was left of the old Yugoslavia split up yet again in 2006 when Montenegro declared independence, leaving Serbia as the last remnant of the Yugoslav federation. Additionally, if the plan formulated in 2007 by a UN special envoy for Kosovo moves forward, Kosovo will move decisively toward becoming the sixth sovereign phoenix rising from Yugoslavia's ashes.

Did You Know That:

Television is a major transnational force. One common reference point is CNN, which is now available in virtually every country on the world's 1.7 billion television sets.

FIGURE 2.3 Opinions on Globalization

Views of globalization in 45 countries

- Very good 17%
- Somewhat good 41%
- Unsure 24%
- Somewhat bad 13%
- Very bad 5%

Globalization enjoys majority support around the world, according to the results of a survey in 45 countries. However, support for globalization is guarded. Only 17% of the respondents said globalization was very good, while 41% characterized it as merely somewhat good and almost a quarter of those polled were unsure of globalization's impacts.

Note: Countries in the Middle/Near East stretch from Egypt to Pakistan. The question was: "Do you think that globalization is a very good thing, somewhat good, somewhat bad, or a very bad thing?"
Data source: Pew Research Center (2003).

Elsewhere, Somalia in the early 1990s fell into chaos among warring clans, and it remains a shell; Czechoslovakia split into two countries; East Timor declared its independence from Indonesia; Afghanistan struggles for stability among the rivalries of its numerous ethnonational groups; the Hutu massacre in 1994 of hundreds of thousands of Tutsis exposed the myth of a single Rwandan people; there is a sometimes violent Basque separatist movement in Spain; and, in an informal referendum among Kurds during the 2005 Iraqi national elections, 95% voted for an independent Kurdistan by circling the Kurdish flag on the ballot rather than the Iraqi one. Perhaps most distressingly, Sudan has been wracked since 2003 by violence between the country's Arab Muslims, who control the government, and black Muslims who live in the western area of Darfur. Over 200,000 people have died there, largely from attacks by a government-backed militia called the Janjaweed. The list could go on, but that is not necessary to stress the point that many states are troubled by ethnonational tensions.

Security in the Twenty-First Century

On the traditional path the world still follows, each state is responsible for its own protection and tries to maintain a military capable of defending its national interests. Other countries may aid a country that has been attacked but only if they find doing so is in their national interest. For example, the United States came to Kuwait's aid in 1991, but did so mostly because of oil. If Kuwait produced tropical fruit, it is unlikely that a half-million U.S. troops would have rushed to defend the world's banana supply from Iraqi aggression.

Self-reliance has its advantages, but there are also disadvantages. *Cost* is one. Even with the cold war over, cumulative world military expenditures between 1992 and 2005 came to nearly $11.4 trillion. Of these, the U.S. share was $4.4 trillion.

Uncertain effectiveness is the second drawback to the traditional approach to national security. Critics charge that "national security" is an oxymoron, given the fact that over 111 million people were killed in wars during the 20th century alone. This staggering total is almost 6 times more people than were killed in the 19th century and 16 times the number of people slain during the 18th century. Thus, even taking population growth into account, war is killing a greater percentage of humans each successive century. Most ominously, the advent of nuclear weapons means that the next major war could be humankind's final performance. Moreover, the possibility of such an apocalyptic scene being played out has been increased by the proliferation of **weapons of mass destruction (WMDs)** in the form of biological, chemical, nuclear, and radiological weapons, and by the spread of the missile technology to rapidly deliver these WMDs over long distances (Brown, 2003).

The limited ability of national forces alone to provide security was also highlighted by the terrorist attacks of September 11, 2001. The devastation raised global awareness of what has been termed **asymmetrical warfare**. As one analyst explained, "The notion of 'asymmetrical warfare' [involves] using unconventional tactics in

Did You Know That:

At $1.1 trillion, world military spending in 2005 was almost twice as much as the combined gross national products of the 47 poverty-stricken countries in sub-Saharan Africa and their 741 million people.

The front page of Melbourne's *Herald Sun* of October 10, 2006, shows its reaction to North Korea's test of a nuclear weapon the day before. Parts of Australia are within range of North Korea's missiles. Weapons of mass destruction and the missiles to deliver them bring into question the ability of countries to provide security for their citizens.

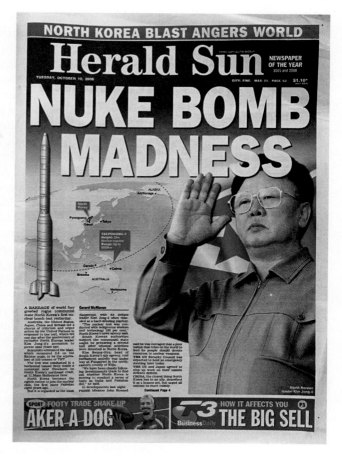

combat rather than using forces of comparable size and employing similar tactics in battle. Terrorism takes the concept of asymmetrical warfare to another level by not even engaging military forces in battle."[4] And if terrorists with conventional explosives and even airliners transformed into missiles were not scary enough, there is increasing concern about the possibility of terrorists acquiring WMDs.

Given the limited ability of the traditional approach to provide effective security, the world is beginning to try new paths toward safety, which chapter 11 details. *Arms control* is one approach by which the world is trying to limit weapons, war, and perhaps avert Armageddon. During the last decade alone, new or revised treaties have been concluded to deal with strategic nuclear weapons, chemical weapons, land mines, nuclear weapons proliferation, and several other weapons issues.

International security forces are another part of the alternative approach. UN peacekeeping forces provide the most prominent example. Prior to 1948 there had never been a peacekeeping force fielded by an international organization. In late 2006 there were 16 under way, with about 82,000 military and police personnel from 113 countries deployed. Such forces still have limited utility, but under different conditions they might offer an alternative to nationally based security.

The Bush administration came to office in 2001 with a skeptical view of international security cooperation, and that attitude was enhanced in 2003 when the Security Council refused to support the American and British resolution authorizing immediate force against Iraq. At least part of the inability of Washington to win support for action against Iraq was the disagreement of many countries and even many Americans with the idea of striking first. Where do you stand on this issue after considering the points raised in the earlier decision box, "Is Preemptive War Good Policy?"

Global Economics in the Twenty-First Century

There are a number of trends since World War II that will continue to affect the international system as this century evolves. Economic interdependence and economic disparity between the few wealthy countries and the many relatively poor ones are of particular note.

Economic Interdependence

One trend that has gained considerable momentum since World War II is the growth of **economic interdependence**. The trade in goods and services during 2006 exceeded

SIMULATION
You Be the Policy Maker: Who Should Be in Charge of Peacekeeping?

$14 trillion; Americans alone own more than $11.1 trillion in assets (companies, property, stock, bonds) located in other countries, and foreigners own more than $13.6 trillion in U.S. assets; the flow of currencies among countries now equals about $2 trillion every day. The impact of this increasingly free flow of trade, investment capital, and currencies across national borders is that countries have become so mutually dependent on one another for their prosperity that it is arguably misleading to talk of national economies in a singular sense.

To deal with interdependence, the world has created and strengthened a host of global and regional economic organizations. The leading global economic organizations are the World Bank, the International Monetary Fund (IMF), and the World Trade Organization (WTO). Among the numerous regional economic organizations are the Association of Southeast Asian Nations (ASEAN), the European Union (EU), and the Southern Common Market (Mercosur) in South America.

Before leaving our discussion of economic interdependence, we should note that the course of economic globalization is not smooth nor is its future certain. Trade and monetary tensions exist among countries. Many people oppose surrendering any of their country's sovereignty to the UN, the WTO, or any other international organization. Other people worry that free trade has allowed multinational corporations to escape effective regulation to the detriment of workers' rights, product safety, and the environment. Yet other critics agree with President Hugo Chávez of Venezuela, who condemns economic globalization as a "weapon of manipulation" used by the wealthy countries to keep poor countries in "the never-ending role of producers of wealth and recipients of leftovers."[5] These and other charges have sparked an upsurge of opposition to further interdependence and occasionally violent protests against it. There are, in short, significant choices to be made in how to order financial relations among countries.

Economic Disparity between North and South

A wide gulf in economic circumstances separates the small percentage of the world population who live in the few wealthy countries and the large majority of humanity that lives in the many much poorer countries. The terms *North* and *South* are used to designate the two economic spheres that divide the world. The **North** represents the wealthy and industrialized **economically developed countries (EDCs)**, which lie mainly in the Northern Hemisphere. By contrast, the **South** is composed of the **less developed countries (LDCs)**, the majority of which are near or in the Southern Hemisphere. This categorization does not mean that the world is divided precisely between wealthy and poor countries. Instead their economic circumstances range from general opulence (the United States) to unbelievable poverty (Bangladesh). There are a few countries, such as Portugal, grouped with the North that are far from rich. And there are some countries of the South, including a few petroleum exporting countries and such **newly industrializing countries (NICs)** as South Korea, that have a standard of living that exceeds some EDCs. Moreover, there are some wealthy people in LDCs and numerous poor people in EDCs. A somewhat more gradual economic classification of countries is used by the World Bank. It groups countries according to per capita **gross national product** (GNP, also called gross national income, GNI) into four groups. Categories of low income, lower middle income, higher middle income, and high income groups show that more than half the world's countries fall into the two lower ranges. The 2006 per capita GNP categories and number of countries in each group that year are shown in Table 2.1.

Whatever classification scheme is used, the core reality is that there is a huge economic disparity between North and South. In 2005, the per capita GNP of the

(continued on next page)

TABLE 2.1 Economic Classification of Countries		
World Bank income groups (2006)	Per capita GNP range	Number of countries
Low income	$825 or less	59
Lower middle income	$826–$3,255	53
Upper middle income	$3,256–$10,065	38
High income	$10,066 and up	42

Data source: World Bank online.

The World Bank's economic classifications indicate vast disparities in wealth among countries.

North was $35,131, which is 20 times (20:1) as much as the per capita wealth of the South, $1,746. Of course, many things are less expensive in LDCs than in EDCs, so another way to compare the data is by factoring in **purchasing power parity (PPP)**, a measure that adjusts for the cost of living in different countries. This approach narrows the spread, with the North's per capita GNP-PPP at $32,524 and the South's at $5,151. But this is still a ratio of more than 6 to 1 (6:1).

What makes these dry statistics important is that the yawning wealth gap, whether 20:1 or 6:1, has devastating implications for the LDCs. Their children are over 12 times more likely to die before age 5 than are children in the North. As Figure 2.4 shows, the people in countries of the North and those in the South live in virtually

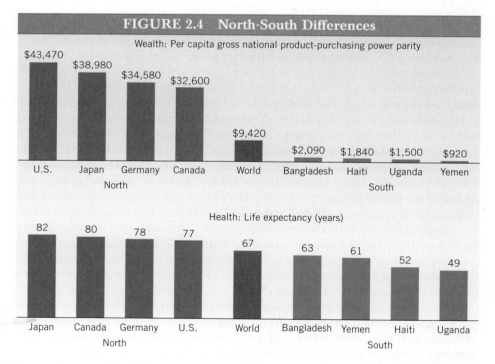

FIGURE 2.4   North-South Differences

Wealth: Per capita gross national product-purchasing power parity

U.S. $43,470; Japan $38,980; Germany $34,580; Canada $32,600 — North. World $9,420. Bangladesh $2,090; Haiti $1,840; Uganda $1,500; Yemen $920 — South.

Health: Life expectancy (years)

Japan 82; Canada 80; Germany 78; U.S. 77 — North. World 67. Bangladesh 63; Yemen 61; Haiti 52; Uganda 49 — South.

One way to measure the difference between the lives of people in the North and those in the South are per capita GNP-PPP wealth and life expectancy. By these, and many other standards, the people of the South are severely disadvantaged compared to those who live in the North. GNP-PPP is gross national product–purchasing power parity, that is, adjusted for living costs differences among countries.

Data source: World Bank online.

different worlds. The North is predominantly a place of reasonable economic security, literacy, and adequate health care. By contrast, the lives of the people of the South are often marked by poverty, illiteracy, rampant disease, and early death. One ramification of the weakening Western orientation of the international system discussed earlier is that this economic inequity is causing increased tension between the North and South. The LDCs are no longer willing to accept a world system in which wealth is so unevenly distributed.

Many people in the South blame much of their poverty on past colonial suppression and on what they believe to be continuing efforts by the EDCs to dominate the LDCs by keeping them economically and politically weak. Some in the North agree with this analysis. While such feelings do not justify terrorism, it is important to understand that the widespread grinding poverty among the LDCs is one of the factors that led to the rage behind the September 11, 2001, attacks on the United States. President Bush later indirectly acknowledged that by pledging to take such actions as doubling the size of the Peace Corps so that it could "join a new effort to encourage development and education and opportunity in the Islamic world," with the goal of "eliminating threats and containing resentment" in order to "seek a just and peaceful world beyond the war on terror."[6]

The point, whether or not you believe that the EDCs oppress the LDCs, is that choices must be made. One option for the wealthy countries is to ignore the vast difference in economic circumstances between themselves and the LDCs. The other option is to do more, much more, to help. Both options carry substantial costs.

SIMULATION
Systems of Political Power

ANALYZE THE ISSUE
The Group of 77

Quality of Life in the Twenty-First Century

The last few decades have spawned several changes involving the quality of human life that will continue to affect world politics in the new century and the choices we must face. Preserving human rights and the environment are two matters of particular note.

Human Rights

Violations of human rights have existed as far back into history as we can see. What is different is that the world is beginning to condemn human rights violations across borders and sometimes take action. International tribunals are trying individuals accused of war crimes and crimes against humanity in Sierra Leone, Rwanda, and the Balkans, and efforts are under way to constitute a new one to prosecute those committing atrocities in Darfur. Importantly, the reach of the law is extending to the highest levels. The former president of Yugoslavia, Slobodan Milosevic, was on trial for war crimes in the Balkans before he died in prison of heart failure in 2006, and Liberia's former President Charles Taylor has been charged with 650 counts of war crimes during his country's civil war and is in UN custody awaiting trial. Such prosecutions may become even more common now that the newly created (2003) permanent International Criminal Court (ICC) located in The Hague, the Netherlands, has begun to investigate alleged war crimes in several conflicts and has issued its first arrest warrants.

Demands for the protection of human rights are louder and stronger in numerous other areas. The rights of women are just one of these. Women have become increasingly active in defense of their rights around the world, and they have received support from many governments and international organizations. Women are "no longer guests on this planet. This planet belongs to us, too. A revolution has begun," Tanzanian diplomat Gertrude Mongella has proclaimed with considerable accuracy.[7]

It would be naïve to pretend that the end of human rights abuses is imminent or that progress has not been excruciatingly slow. Yet it would also be wrong not to recognize that there is movement. Leaders now regularly discuss human rights concerns; that was virtually unheard of not long ago. Sometimes, countries even take action based on another country's human rights record. Human rights conferences are no longer unnoticed, peripheral affairs. A significant number of human rights treaties have been signed by a majority of the world's countries. In sum, what was once mostly the domain of do-gooders has increasingly become the province of presidents and prime ministers.

The Environment

The mounting degradation of the biosphere is a by-product of the rapidly expanding world population and the technological changes that began with the industrial revolution. Considerable damage has been done to the world's land, air, and water by pollution, forest destruction, and other abuses. Additionally, many natural resources are disappearing. Among the many facets of repairing the damage and easing or at least halting these continued destructive practices, the greatest challenge is to achieve **sustainable development**. This requires achieving two seemingly contradictory goals: (a) continuing to develop economically while (b) simultaneously protecting the environment. Much needs to be done, but some progress is being made. Among other advances, the subject has shifted from the political periphery to presidential palaces. Many leaders now realize that their national interests are endangered by environmental degradation, as well as by military and economic threats. For example, a U.S. national security report concluded that environmental problems "compromise our national security," and warned of potentially "devastating threats if we fail to avert irreparable damage to regional ecosystems and the global environment. Other environmental issues, such as competition over scarce fresh water resources, are a potential threat to stability in several regions."[8]

The need to balance economic development and environmental protection is recognized by almost everyone, yet achieving sustainable development will not be easy. Among other challenges, the LDCs need extensive assistance to develop in an environmentally responsible way. UN officials have placed that cost as high as $125 billion a year, and the financial weakness of the South means that the only source for much of this funding is the North. One reason for the North to help, some observers argue, is because over the last 250 years it was and remains the source of a substantial majority of most pollutants, despite having less than one-fifth of the world population. "You can't have an environmentally healthy planet in a world that is socially unjust," Brazil's president noted.[9]

Although not everyone agrees with the social justice view, self-interest is a second arguable reason for the North to help the South. Pollution and the problems it spawns, like global warming caused by the buildup of carbon dioxide (CO_2) in the atmosphere, do not recognize national borders. To better understand the North's stake in LDC development and its impact on the environment, consider Figure 2.5. It shows that while the LDCs with about 85% of the world population still emit less CO_2 than do the

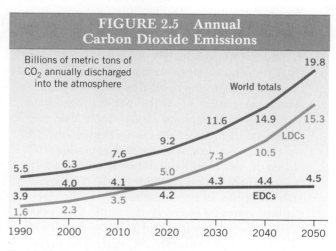

FIGURE 2.5   Annual Carbon Dioxide Emissions

Billions of metric tons of CO_2 annually discharged into the atmosphere

Historically, the economically developed countries (EDCs) have annually discharged most of the world's carbon dioxide (CO_2). However, the CO_2 emissions of less developed countries (LDCs) and their share of global CO_2 emission have both increased. If this trend continues, LDC emissions will surpass those of the EDCs in 2013 and spiral dangerously upward. The conundrum of sustainable development is how to encourage the LDCs to continue to develop their economies while simultaneously avoiding further increases in CO_2 emissions.

Note: A metric ton equals 2,204.6 pounds. There are two ways to calculate CO_2 emissions. The method used here by the U.S. government and others can be converted into the data reported by the World Bank and others using the other method by multiplying by 44/12. The reverse calculation is to divide by 3.6667.

Data source: World Bank; U.S. Department of Energy.

EDCs, this relationship is changing dramatically because of the efforts of the LDCs to upgrade their economies and their standards of living. If the changes that occurred between 1990 and 2000 continue, the LDCs will soon produce most of the CO_2 and world emissions will skyrocket to almost 73 billion metric tons in 2050. Even then, the LDCs will still be generating only 7.2 metric tons per capita, compared to 12.7 metric tons per capita in the EDCs.

CHAPTER SUMMARY

THE EVOLVING WORLD SYSTEM: EARLY DEVELOPMENT

1. This chapter has two primary goals. One is to establish a reference framework from which the historical examples used in this book can be understood in context. The second goal is to sketch the evolution of the current world political system.

2. The genesis of the modern world system can be traced to the classical civilizations of ancient Greece and Rome. Four important political concepts—the territorial state, sovereignty, nationalism, and democracy—have evolved from these ancient states.

3. Following the fall of the Roman Empire during the Middle Ages until 1500, governance rested in a universalistic authority on the one hand and a local, microlevel authority on the other.

4. The current world system began to develop around the 15th century, when modern states started to form due to a process marked by both integration and disintegration of earlier political authority. The Treaty of Westphalia (1648), more than any other event, demarcated the change between the old and the new systems. With the sovereign state at its center, the newly evolving system is anarchical.

5. Several changes occurred during the 1700s and 1800s that had an important impact on the international system. The emergence of the concept of popular sovereignty involved a shift in the idea of who legitimately controls the state. The divine right of kings gave way to the notion that political power does, or ought to, come from the people. During these two centuries, the system also became Westernized and the multipolar configuration reached its apogee.

THE EVOLVING WORLD SYSTEM: THE TWENTIETH CENTURY

6. The 20th century witnessed the most rapid evolution of the system. The multipolar system tottered, then fell. The bipolar system declined as other countries and transnational actors became more important, the expense of continuing confrontation strained American and Soviet budget resources, and the relative power of the two superpowers declined. The bipolar system ended in 1991 when the Soviet Union collapsed.

7. During the 20th century, nationalism also undermined the foundations of multiethnic empires. European contiguous empires, such as the Austro-Hungarian Empire, disintegrated. The colonial empires dominated by Great Britain, France, and other Eurowhite countries also dissolved.

THE TWENTY-FIRST CENTURY: THE GENESIS OF A NEW SYSTEM

8. There are numerous new trends, uncertainties, and choices to make as we enter the 21st century. One significant question is what will follow the bipolar system. For now a limited unipolar system exists, with the United States as the dominant power, but numerous forces are working to undermine U.S. power and move the system toward a more multipolar configuration. That could be a classic state-centric system or a modified multipolar system, in which global and regional international organizations, as well as states, play key roles.

9. Another shift in the international system is its weakening Western orientation. The number and strength of non-Western countries have grown substantially, and the strength of these states will almost certainly continue to grow in this century. These countries often have values that differ from those of the Western countries.

10. Challenges to the authority of the state represent a third shift in the international system, which has strong implications for the 21st century. There are both disintegrative internal challenges to the state and integrative external challenges.

11. The pursuit of peace is also at something of a cross-roads. The destructiveness of modern weaponry has made the quest for peace even more imperative. There are two overriding issues. One is how to respond to the challenge that asymmetrical warfare presents to traditional national defense strategies. The second is whether to seek overall security through the traditional approach of self-reliance or to place greater emphasis on international peacekeeping, arms control, and other alternative international security approaches.

12. The international economy is also changing in ways that have important implications for the 21st century. Economic interdependence has progressed rapidly. The transnational flow of trade, investment capital, and currencies has economically entwined all countries. There are, however, counterpressures, and countries have important choices to make in the near future. One is whether to continue down the newer path to economic integration or to halt that process and follow more traditional national economic policies. If the decision is to continue toward greater economic integration, then a second choice is how to regulate the global economy to deal with the legitimate concerns of those who are suspicious of or even outright opposed to greater globalization.

13. The effort to resolve the wide, and in many ways growing, gulf between the economic circumstances of the countries of the economically developed North and the less economically developed South is also a mounting issue in the new century.

14. A final set of issues that must be addressed in the new century involves the quality of life: human rights and the environment. Both issues have become the subject of much greater international awareness, action, progress, and interaction. Yet ending the abuses of human rights and protecting the environment are still distant goals.

For simulations, debates, and other interactive activities, a chapter quiz, Web links, and much more, visit **www.mhhe.com/rourke12/** and go to chapter 2. Or, while accessing the site, click on Course-Wide Content and view recent international relations articles in the *New York Times*.

KEY TERMS

anarchical political system
appeasement policy
asymmetrical warfare
balance of power
bipolar system
cold war
containment doctrine
détente
East-West axis
economic interdependence
economically developed countries (EDCs)
ethnonational groups

Eurowhite
feudal system
globalization
gross national product (GNP)
hegemonic power
Holy Roman Empire
imperialism
industrial revolution
international system
less developed countries (LDCs)
limited unipolar system
McWorld

multipolar system
Munich Conference
nationalism
newly industrializing countries (NICs)
North
North Atlantic Treaty Organization (NATO)
popular sovereignty
power poles
Protestant Reformation
purchasing power parity (PPP)
realpolitik

Renaissance
South
sovereignty
state
superpower
sustainable development
Third World
Treaty of Westphalia
tribalism
weapons of mass destruction (WMDs)
West
westernization of the international system

Levels of Analysis and Foreign Policy

Search, seek, find out; I'll warrant we'll unkennel the fox.
—William Shakespeare, *The Merry Wives of Windsor*

Dazzle mine eyes, or do I see three suns?
—William Shakespeare, *King Henry VI, Part 3*

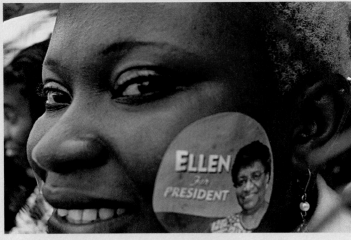

Women are playing a greater role in the politics of their countries and the world. This woman is at a first anniversary celebration of the January 2006 inauguration of Ellen Johnson Sirleaf as president of Liberia, the first woman to be elected to head an African country. President Sirleaf, who holds a master of public administration degree from Harvard, has helped stabilize the country. Indicative of her benign appearance and firm approach, she is widely called "Ma Ellen" and "the Iron Lady."

HAVING INTRODUCED THE GLOBAL DRAMA in chapter 1 and reviewed its history in chapter 2, it is time to turn our attention to what drives the action on the world stage. Much like the plot of a play, the course of world politics is the story of the motivations and calculations of the actors and how they put those into action. Because states have long been and remain the most powerful actors on the world stage, our focus here will be on how they make and carry out foreign policy. Therefore, most of what occurs in world politics is a dynamic story of states taking actions and other states reacting to them, either directly or indirectly through international organizations. States are certainly not the only global actors, though, and the roles and decision-making processes of individuals such as Osama bin Laden, international governmental organizations (IGOs) such as the UN, and international nongovernmental organizations (NGOs/transnational groups) such as Greenpeace are taken up in other chapters.

As the following pages will detail, the **foreign policy process** is very complex. Analysts untangle the intricacies by studying foreign policy making from three perspectives termed **levels of analysis**. These include (1) individual-level analysis—the impact of people as individuals or as a species on policy; (2) state-level analysis—how the organization and operation of a government affect policy; and (3) system-level analysis—the external realities and pressures that influence a country's policy.

INDIVIDUAL-LEVEL ANALYSIS

Individual-level analysis begins with the view that at the root it is people who make policy. Therefore, individual-level analysis involves understanding how the human **decision-making process**—people making decisions (as a species, in groups, and idiosyncratically)—leads to policy making.

Humans as a Species

The central question is this: How do basic human traits influence policy? To answer that, a first step is understanding that humans seldom if ever make a purely rational decision. For example, think about how you decided which college to attend. Surely you did not just flip a coin. But neither did you make a fully rational decision by considering all colleges worldwide and analyzing each according to cost, location, social atmosphere, class size, faculty qualifications, program requirements, job placement record, and other core considerations. Furthermore, and making your choice even less rational, it was almost certainly influenced by a range of emotions, such as how far away from home the school was and whether you wanted to be near, or perhaps far away from, your family, friends, or romantic partner. To make things even less rational, you probably had to make a decision without knowing some key factors of your college experience, such as who your dorm roommate would be.

It may be comforting to imagine that foreign policy decision making is fully rational, but the truth is that in many ways it does not differ greatly from your process in deciding which college to attend and many of the other important choices you make in life. They, like foreign policy decisions, are influenced by cognitive, emotional, psychological, and sometimes even biological factors, as well as by rational calculations.

Cognitive Factors

What you did in choosing your college and what national leaders do when deciding foreign policy is to engage in **cognitive decision making**. This means making decisions within the constraints of "bounded rationality." *External boundaries* include missing, erroneous, or unknowable information. To cite an example, President Bush and Prime Minister Blair had to decide whether to invade Iraq in March 2003 without knowing whether Saddam Hussein would respond with chemical or biological attacks on U.S. and British forces. *Internal boundaries* on rational decision making are the result of our human frailties—the limited physical stamina and intellectual capacity to study exceptionally complex issues. Whatever the "realities" were during the crisis leading up to the Iraq War in 2003, the universe of information available was far more than President Bush, Prime Minister Blair, President Saddam Hussein, or any human could absorb.

Needless to say, none of us likes to think that we are not fully rational, so we are apt to adopt one of a range of mental strategies for coping with our cognitive limits. As illustrations, three such strategies are seeking cognitive consistency, wishful thinking, and using heuristic devices.

Seeking Cognitive Consistency Decision makers tend to seek cognitive consistency by discounting ideas and information that contradict their existing views. The controversy about the snarl of information and misinformation about Iraq's abilities and intentions will continue for years, but it is informative to ask why top decision makers in London and Washington were willing to accept British intelligence that Baghdad was attempting to buy uranium from Africa and to ignore the substantial doubts expressed by the CIA. One reason is that the British finding "fit" with the existing negative images of Saddam Hussein and his intentions, whereas believing information that there was no nuclear program would have created uncomfortable cognitive inconsistency.

Wishful Thinking To self-justify our decisions, we humans often convince ourselves that our choice will succeed (Johnson, 2004). Given the overwhelming forces he faced, it is hard to understand why Saddam Hussein chose to fight rather than go safely into exile. The reason, according to some of his former aides, is that he believed he would survive in power. In the Iraqi dictator's mind, his military defeat in 1991 was only a tactical retreat. This wishful thinking was evident just before the 2003 war when a reporter pointed out that the forces facing him were even more powerful than those that had routed Iraq's army in the Persian Gulf War and asked, "Why would you think that you could prevail this time on the battlefield?" The Iraqi leader replied, "In 1991 Iraq was not defeated. In fact, our army withdrew from Kuwait according to a decision taken by us. . . . We withdrew our forces inside Iraq in order that we may be able to continue fighting inside our country." Extending his wishful thinking, Saddam Hussein assured the reporter, "If war is forced upon us, then Iraq will continue to be here. . . . [We] will not finish just like that, even though a huge power may want it to be like that."[1]

Using Heuristic Devices A third way humans deal with their cognitive limitations is by using **heuristic devices**. These are mental shortcuts that help us make decisions more easily by allowing us to skip the effort of gathering considerable information and analyzing it thoroughly.

Stereotypes are one type of heuristic device. For example, the willingness of the U.S. Department of Justice to countenance at least the limited torture of Muslim

Web Link

Excerpts from captured Iraqis about Saddam Hussein and Iraqi thinking before the Iraq War are included in a CIA report, *Comprehensive Report of the Special Advisor to the DCI on Iraq's WMD,* 30 September 2004, located at **https://www.cia.gov/ library/reports/general-reports-1/ iraq_wmd_2004/index.html.**

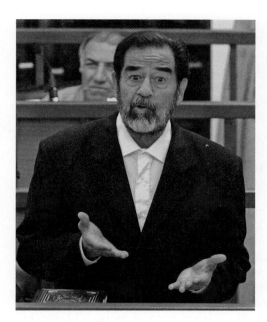

Wishful thinking is common in human decision making. Saddam Hussein seemed to believe that he would politically survive a war with the United States in 2003 just as he had in 1991. This may have increased his willingness to risk war. Wishful thinking cannot change reality. Saddam appears to have realized this by the time this photograph was taken of him during his trial for war crimes against his own people in the 1980s. Seven months after this photo was taken, Saddam was hanged by the Iraqi government for his crimes.

prisoners suspected of terrorism was arguably voiced in Attorney General John Ashcroft's stereotypic comment that "Islam is a religion in which God requires you to send your son to die for him. Christianity is a faith in which God sends His son to die for you."[2]

Analogies are another heuristic shortcut (Dyson & Preston, 2006; Breuning, 2003). We make comparisons between new situations or people and situations or people that we have earlier experienced or otherwise have learned about. One such mental connection that frequently figures in policy debates is the **Munich analogy**. This refers to the decision of France and Great Britain to appease Nazi Germany in 1938 when it threatened Czechoslovakia. World War II signified the failure of appeasement, and the "lesson" later leaders drew was that compromise with dictators only encourages them. The Munich analogy was clearly in the mind of Secretary of Defense Rumsfeld when he urged action against Iraq despite the lack of definitive evidence of Iraqi WMDs, by arguing, "Think of the prelude to World War II . . . [and] all the countries that said, 'Well, we don't have enough evidence.' . . . There were millions of people dead because of the miscalculations."[3] As the postwar attempt to democratize and stabilize Iraq went from bad to worse, opponents of the war used another analogy, Vietnam. When, for example, President Bush announced in early 2007 that he would "surge" 21,000 extra troops into Iraq, Senator Edward Kennedy (D-MA) warned, "The Department of Defense kept assuring us that each new escalation in Vietnam would be the last. Instead, each one led only to the next."[4] Figure 3.1 on page 68 shows how broadly the Vietnam analogy to Iraq resonated with Americans (Schuman & Corning, 2006).

Emotional Factors

Although it is comforting to imagine that decision makers are coolly rational, the reality is that they get depressed, sad, angry, and experience all the other human emotions. For example, President Jimmy Carter was irate when Iranian students studying in U.S. colleges picketed the White House in 1980 during the hostage crisis with Iran over its seizure of the U.S. embassy and its staff in Tehran. An incensed

SIMULATION
Heuristic Devices

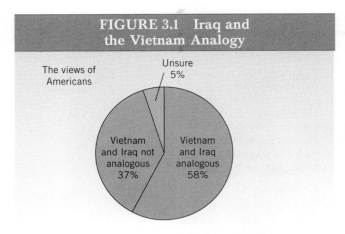

FIGURE 3.1 Iraq and the Vietnam Analogy

The views of Americans

Unsure 5%

Vietnam and Iraq not analogous 37%

Vietnam and Iraq analogous 58%

By 2006, most Americans saw the U.S. presence in Iraq as analogous to the U.S. entanglement in Vietnam (1964–1973). This analogy persuaded some people to advocate a quick U.S. withdrawal from Iraq. In other cases, the analogy strengthened the convictions of people already opposed to the U.S. military presence in Iraq.

Note: The question was: "Do you think the war in Iraq has turned into a situation like the United States faced in the Vietnam War, or don't you think so?"
Data source: CNN Poll, November, 2006; data provided by The Roper Center for Public Opinion Research, University of Connecticut.

Carter growled that he would like to "go out on the streets myself and take a swing at . . . those bastards" (Vandenbroucke, 1991:364). Carter could not go out on Pennsylvania Avenue and beat up protesters, but his anger and desperation to do something arguably led to his ill-advised and ill-fated attempt to rescue the hostages. Similarly, President Bush was outraged by the 9/11 terrorist attacks. "We're going to find out who did this," he told Vice President Cheney, "and we're going to kick their asses."[5]

Psychological Factors

Humans share a number of common psychological traits that also help explain why their feelings and decisions are usually less than fully rational. One such approach is **frustration-aggression theory**, which argues that individuals and even societies that are frustrated sometimes become aggressive.

"Why do they hate us?" President Bush rhetorically asked Congress soon after the 9/11 attacks.[6] "They hate our freedoms," was the answer the president supplied to his own question. Perhaps, but others put the source of rage in a very different light. Based on polling in nine Muslim countries, one analyst suggests that rather than a hatred for freedom, the reason for the widespread negative opinions among Muslims is that, "The people of Islamic countries have significant grievance with the West and the United States in particular" based on their view that the United States is "ruthless, aggressive, conceited, arrogant, easily provoked, [and biased against Muslims]."[7] It is not necessary to agree with Muslims, especially Arabs, to understand their sense of frustration over the lack of a Palestinian homeland, the underdevelopment that characterizes most of the Muslim countries, or the sense of being dominated and sometimes subjugated by the Christian-led West (Zunes, 2005). Nor does one have to agree that Muslims' anger justifies the violence that has sometimes occurred to pay heed to the old maxim that an "ounce of prevention is worth a pound of cure." Preventing terrorism surely includes building defenses and bringing terrorists to justice. Those are half-measures, though, and they will be much enhanced by addressing the root causes of terrorism rather than by simply waging war on the terrorists themselves.

Biological Factors

Although they are highly controversial, various biological theories provide yet another way to explain why human decisions fall short of being fully rational. One of the most important issues in human behavior is the degree to which human actions are based on animal instinct and other innate emotional and physical drives or based on socialization and intellect. With specific regard to politics, **biopolitics** examines the relationship between the physical nature and political behavior of humans. Biopolitics can be illustrated by examining two approaches: ethology and gender.

Ethology The comparison of animal and human behavior is called **ethology**. Konrad Lorenz (*On Aggression,* 1969), Desmond Morris (*The Naked Ape,* 1967), Robert Ardrey (*The Territorial Imperative,* 1961), and some other ethologists argue that like animals, humans behave in a way that is based partly on innate characteristics. Ardrey (pp. 12–14), for example, has written that "territoriality—the drive to gain, maintain, and defend the exclusive right to a piece of property—is an animal instinct" and that "if man is a part of the natural world, then he possesses as do all other species a genetic . . . territorial drive as one ancient animal foundation for that human conduct known as war."

It is clear that territorial disputes between neighboring countries are a common cause of war. As one study puts it, "empirical analyses consistently show that territorial issues . . . are more likely to escalate to war than would be expected by chance" (Vasquez & Henehan, 2001:123). To an outsider, some of these territorial clashes may seem rational, but others defy rational explanation. One inexplicable war was the 1998–2000 conflict between two desperately poor countries, Ethiopia and Eritrea, over tiny bits of territory along their border. The land was described in one press report as "a dusty terrain of termite mounds, goatherds, and bushes just tall enough for a camel to graze upon comfortably." It was, said one observer, "like two bald men fighting over a comb."[8] Even the leaders of the two countries could not explain why war was waged. "It's very difficult to easily find an answer," Eritrea's president admitted. "I was surprised, shocked, and puzzled," added Ethiopia's perplexed prime minister.[9]

Gender   A second biopolitical factor is the possibility that some differences in political behavior are related to gender. An adviser to President Lyndon Johnson has recalled that once when reporters asked him why the United States was waging war in Vietnam, the president "unzipped his fly, drew out his substantial organ, and declared, 'That is why.'"[10] Such earthy explanations by male leaders are far from rare in private, and they lead some scholars to wonder whether they represent a gender-based approach to politics or are merely gauche.

Political scientists are just beginning to examine whether gender makes a difference in political attitudes and actions. It is clear that a **gender opinion gap** exists between men and women on a range of issues. War and other forms of political violence is one of those. Polls among Americans going back as far as World War II have almost always found women less ready than men to resort to war or to continue war. For example, two-thirds of American men compared to half of American women supported going to war with Iraq in 2003.[11] This gender gap was again found internationally with, for instance, men in Australia, Canada, Great Britain, and Italy 10% to 15% more favorable toward war than their female counterparts. Indeed, cross-national polls have generally found that the gender gap on war is worldwide, as evident in Figure 3.2. Polls about attitudes toward other forms of political violence yield similar results. One survey that asked Muslims in 11 countries about suicide bombings found that 35% of the men, but only 31% of the women thought they were justified.[12]

Why do gender gaps exist? Are they inherently rooted in differences in male/female biological traits, or are they produced by differences in male and female socialization? The idea of gender, as distinct from sex, is based on the belief that all or most behavioral differences between men and women are based on learned role definitions. Thus sex is biology; gender is behavior. There are some, however, who argue that biology strongly controls behavior. One recent book, *Manliness,* argues that aggressive behavior is closely related to sex (Mansfield, 2006: 16, 64, 85, 206). The author contends that all humans can be aggressive, can exhibit the "bristling snappishness of a dog," but suggests that "the manly have this trait in excess." Furthermore, manliness includes a distinct sense of territoriality, a factor that can "connect aggression to defense of whatever is one's own." Such behaviors are apt to become national policy because more manly people (conceivably including women)

Web Link

To learn more about the parallels between the behavior of primates and humans, click the "Chimpanzee Central" link on the home page of the Jane Goodall Institute at **www.janegoodall.org/.**

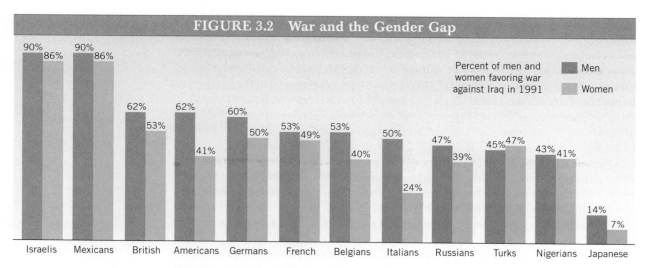

FIGURE 3.2 War and the Gender Gap

This figure shows the percentages of men and women in favor of using military force to expel Iraq from Kuwait in 1991. Notice that in all but one country, Turkey, more men than women favored using force. Also notice the variations among countries. Women cannot be described as antiwar, nor can men be characterized as pro-war because both men and women in some countries favored war and opposed it in others.

Note: The American response (Pew) was to a slightly different question than for all others (Wilcox, et al.) and is used here as generally representative only. Except for Americans, the poll was taken in each country's capital city. Respondents in the Soviet Union were therefore mostly Russian.

Data source: Wilcox, Hewitt, & Allsop (1996); Pew Research Center poll, January 1991.

are more likely to be leaders, given that **"The manly man is in control when control is difficult or contested"** (Kenneally, 2006).[13]

This view leads to the question of whether equal representation (or perhaps dominance) of women in foreign and defense policy making would change global politics. Concurring with Mansfield that men are particularly prone to bellicosity, Francis Fukuyama (1998:33) concludes that a world led by women "would be less prone to conflict and more conciliatory and cooperative than the one we inhabit now." Supporting this view, one recent study found that women tend to adopt more collaborative approaches to negotiation and conflict resolution, while men pursue more conflictual ones (Florea et al., 2003). Other studies, however, have found more mixed results about the potential impact of women decision makers and contend that a future world dominated by women "would not be as rosy as Fukuyama suggests" (Caprioli, 2000:271).

What do you think? Would the U.S. invasion of Iraq have occurred if Laura Bush, not her husband, George W., had been president of the United States; if the long-time head of Iraq had been Sajida Khairallah Telfah, not her husband, Saddam Hussein; and if most of the other top diplomatic and national security posts in the United States and Iraq had been held by women, not men?

JOIN THE DEBATE
Do Women Speak with a Different Voice?

Perceptions

There is an ancient philosophical debate over whether there is an objective world or whether everything is only what we perceive it to be. Whatever the answer to that debate may be, it is clear that we all view the world through perceptual lenses that distort reality at least to some degree. All the elements of individual-level analysis that we have been discussing, and others, help shape **perceptions**. Whatever their source, though, perceptions have a number of characteristics that influence global politics. To demonstrate this, we can take a look at four common characteristics of perceptions.

We tend to see opponents as more threatening than they may actually be. The nuclear programs of North Korea and Iran have alarmed many Americans. One survey found that 71% of Americans considered Iran a threat to regional stability and 77% saw North Korea in the same way. By contrast, in the other 20 countries surveyed, only 40% believed Iran to be a force for instability and just 47% perceived North Korea in that light.[14]

We tend to see the behavior of others as more planned and coordinated than our own. During the cold war, Americans and Soviets were mutually convinced that the other side was orchestrating a coordinated global campaign to subvert them. Perhaps more accurately, former Secretary of State Henry Kissinger (1979:1202) has described the two superpowers as behaving like "two heavily armed blind men feeling their way around a room, each believing himself in mortal peril from the other whom he assumes to have perfect vision." Each, according to Kissinger, "tends to ascribe to the other side a consistency, foresight, and coherence that its own experience belies."

We find it hard to understand why others dislike, mistrust, and fear us. President George W. Bush captured this overly positive sense of self during a press conference when he pronounced himself "amazed that there's such misunderstanding of what our country is about that people would hate us. . . . Like most Americans, I just can't believe it because I know how good we are."[15] Others are less sure of Americans' innate goodness. One recent survey found that 60% or more of poll respondents in countries as diverse as Indonesia, Nigeria, Turkey, and Russia thought that the United States posed a military threat to them.[16]

We and others tend to have similar images of one another. Between countries and even between leaders, it is common to find a **mirror-image perception**. This means that each side perceives the other in roughly similar terms. Figure 3.3 depicts this sense of mutual threat that exists between the United States and Muslim countries.

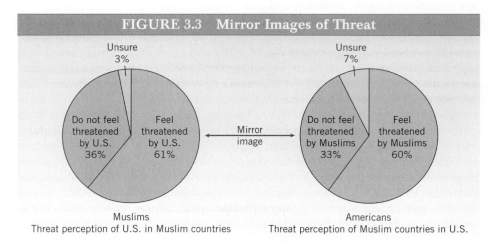

FIGURE 3.3   Mirror Images of Threat

Muslims
Threat perception of U.S. in Muslim countries

Americans
Threat perception of Muslim countries in U.S.

Americans and citizens of Muslim countries share a mirror image of hostility toward one another. Note the almost equal percentages of Americans who see Muslims as hostile and Muslims who see Americans as hostile.

Note: The question of Americans was, "Do you think the Muslim world considers itself at war with the United States?" The question in Muslim countries was, "How worried are you, if at all, that the U.S. could become a military threat to your country someday? Are you very worried, somewhat worried, not too worried, or not at all worried?"
Data source: Pew Research Center for the People and the Press (2003).

Organizational Behavior

Yet another common characteristic of humans is that they tend to think and act differently in collective settings than they do as individuals. This leads to a second approach to individual-level analysis, one that examines how people act in organizations. Two concepts, role behavior and group decision-making behavior, illustrate this approach.

Role Behavior

We all play a variety of **roles** based on our attitudes about the positions we have and the behaviors we adopt in them. For example, how you act when you are in class, on the job, or in a family situation varies depending in part on your role—on whether you are a professor or a student, a manager or a worker, a parent or a child.

Presidents and other policy makers also play roles. The script for a role is derived from a combination of *self-expectations* (how we expect ourselves to act) and *external expectations* (how others expect us to behave). For leaders, these latter expectations are transmitted by cues from advisers, critics, and public opinion. One common role expectation is that leaders be decisive. A leader who approaches a problem by saying, "I don't know what to do" or "We can't do anything" will be accused of weakness.

For example, President Bush was in Florida when the 9/11 attacks occurred, and the Secret Service wanted him to remain safely out of Washington, D.C., for a time. However, Bush's sense of his role as president soon prevailed, and he irritably told his chief of staff, "I want to go back [to Washington] ASAP." By 7:00 P.M. that evening he was back in the White House, and 90 minutes later he addressed the nation from the Oval Office. The president felt it was important to reassure the public by being visible at his post in the White House. "One of the things I wanted to do was to calm nerves," he later said. "I felt like I had a job as the commander in chief" to show the country "that I was safe . . . not me, George W., but me the president."[17]

Decision-Making Behavior within Organizations

When people give advice and make decisions within an organization, they not only have to consider what they think but also how their opinions and decisions will be viewed by others in the organization, especially its leaders. The calculation of how our views will "go over" tends to promote **groupthink**. This concept denotes pressure within organizations to achieve consensus by agreeing with the prevailing opinion, especially the view of the leader (Schafer & Crichlow, 2002).

The image of the devil's advocate pressing principled, unpopular views is appealing, but such individuals are rarities in organizations, in part because those who take this approach get forced out. Similarly, agencies that dissent can wind up with their budgets cut and their areas of responsibility diminished. In a case in point, Secretary of Defense Rumsfeld favored sending a relatively small force to invade and pacify Iraq in 2003. Disagreeing, General Eric Shinseki, head of the U.S. Army, told Congress that several hundred thousand troops would be needed. Rumsfeld, whose approach was summed up by another retired four-star general as "Do it my way or leave," forced Shinseki to retire.[18] According to another national security official at that time, Rumsfeld's actions "sent a very clear signal to the military leadership . . . [and] served to silence critics just at the point in time when, internal to the process, you most wanted critical judgment." History records that in time virtually everyone realized that, as one senator put it in 2007, "We never had enough troops to begin with. . . . General Shinseki was right."[19]

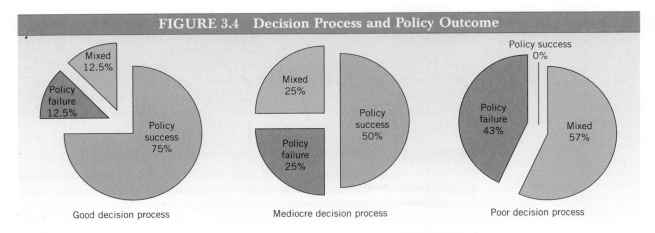

FIGURE 3.4 Decision Process and Policy Outcome

Good decision processes characterized by a lack of groupthink tend to result in better policy than mediocre and poor decision processes, which are respectively burdened with medium or high instances of groupthink. The research represented in this figure examined the decision making of various policies for evidence of groupthink and then asked experts to evaluate the success or failure of the resulting policy. As indicated, decisions with little or no evidence of groupthink worked well in the estimate of 75% of the experts, with another 12.5% each rating the policy a mixed outcome or a failure. By contrast, none of the experts judged any of the poor decision processes marked by significant groupthink to be a success.

Data source: Herek, Janis, & Huth (1987).

In some cases, not giving a leader unpleasant advice may even involve physical survival. One reason that Saddam Hussein miscalculated his chances of success was that his generals misled him about their ability to repel U.S. and British forces. The officers knew they could not withstand the allied onslaught, but they feared telling Saddam Hussein the truth. As one Iraqi general later explained, "We never provided true information as it is here on planet Earth. . . . Any commander who spoke the truth would lose his head."[20]

Even if a leader wants broad advice, getting it is sometimes difficult because groupthink tends to screen out those who "think outside the box." Anthony Lake, who served as national security adviser to President Clinton, recognized that "there is a danger that when people work well together" and are of the same mind, it can lead to "groupthink . . . [with] not enough options reaching the president."[21] That concern continues. As one adviser has commented about the flow of information in the Bush White House, "The president finds out what he wants to know, but he does not necessarily find out what he might need to know."[22]

Poor decisions are frequently the end result of groupthink. This characteristic is evident in Figure 3.4. Thus developing strategies to avoid such decision-making pathologies should improve the quality of the output (Mitchell, 2005).

Leaders and Their Individual Traits

Foreign policy making is much more likely than domestic policy making to be centered on a country's top leadership. Therefore, a third approach to individual-level analysis focuses on **idiosyncratic analysis**. This is the study of humans as individuals and how each leader's personal (idiosyncratic) characteristics help shape his or her decisions (Renshon & Larson, 2002). As one study puts it, "The goals, abilities,

ANALYZE THE ISSUE
The Cuban Missile Crisis

and foibles of individuals are crucial to the intentions, capabilities, and strategies of a state" (Byman & Pollack, 2001:111).

The fundamental question idiosyncratic analysis asks is how the personal traits of leaders affect their decisions. Why, for example, are older leaders more likely than younger ones to initiate and escalate military confrontations? (Horowitz, McDermott, & Stam, 2005). Five of the many possible factors to consider are personality, physical and mental health, ego and ambition, political history and personal experiences, and perceptions and operational reality.

Personality

When studying personality types and their impact on policy, scholars examine a leader's basic orientations toward self and toward others, behavioral patterns, and attitudes about such politically relevant concepts as authority (Dyson, 2006). There are numerous categorization schemes. The most well known places political personality along an active-passive scale and a positive-negative scale (Barber, 1985). Active leaders are policy innovators; passive leaders are reactors. Positive personalities have egos strong enough to enjoy (or at least accept) the contentious political environment; negative personalities are apt to feel burdened, even abused, by political criticism. Many scholars favor active-positive presidents, but all four types have drawbacks. Activists, for example, may take action in a situation when waiting or even doing nothing would be preferable. Reflecting on this, former Secretary of State Dean Rusk (1990:137) recalled, "We tended then—and now—to exaggerate the necessity to take action. Given time, many problems work themselves out or disappear."

Of recent U.S. presidents, Clinton has an active-positive personality. He reveled in the job and admitted to being "almost compulsively overactive" (Renshon, 1995:59). Scholars differ on President George W. Bush. One assessment is that he is an active-positive personality who "loves his job and is very energetic and focused" (DiIulio, 2003:3). Perhaps, but he is certainly less active than Clinton, and might even be positive-passive (Etheredge, 2001).

Whatever the best combination may be, active-negative is the worst. The more active a leader, the more criticism he or she encounters. Positive personalities take such criticism in stride, but negative personalities are prone to assume that opponents are enemies. This causes negative personalities to withdraw into an inner circle of subordinates who are supportive and who give an unreal, groupthink view of events and domestic and international opinion. Lyndon Johnson and Richard Nixon were both active-negative personalities who showed symptoms of delusion, struck out at their enemies, and generally developed bunker mentalities. Yet their active-negative personalities were but shadows of Saddam Hussein's. According to a postwar report to the CIA, Saddam's psychology was shaped powerfully by a deprived and violent childhood.[23] Reflecting that, he changed his original name, Hussein al-Takrit, by dropping al-Takrit (his birthplace) and adding Saddam, an Arabic word that means "one who confronts."

Physical and Mental Health

A leader's physical and mental health can be important factors in decision making. For example, Franklin Roosevelt was so ill from hypertension in 1945 that one historian concludes that he was "in no condition to govern the republic" (Farrell, 1998:xi). Among other impacts, some analysts believe that Roosevelt's weakness left him unable to resist Stalin's demands for Soviet domination of Eastern Europe when the two, along with British Prime Minister Winston Churchill, met at Yalta in February 1945, just two months before Roosevelt died from a massive stroke.

Occasionally leaders also suffer from psychological problems. Adolf Hitler was arguably unbalanced as a result of ailments that may have included advanced syphilis and by his huge intake of such medically prescribed drugs as barbiturates, cardiac stimulants, opiates, steroids, methamphetamine, and cocaine (Hayden, 2003). According to one analysis, "The precise effects of this pharmaceutical cocktail on Hitler's mental state [are] difficult to gauge. Suffice it to say, in the jargon of the street, Hitler was simultaneously taking coke and speed."[24] The drug combinations Hitler used offer one explanation for the bizarre manic-depressive cycle of his decision making late in the war.

Alcohol abuse can also lead to problems. Secretary of State Henry Kissinger once referred to President Richard Nixon as "my drunken friend," who among other events was once reportedly incapacitated during an international crisis with the Soviet Union (Schulzinger, 1989:178). More recently, an official in the Clinton administration has recalled that Russia's President Boris Yeltsin was often inebriated. Indeed, during the first summit meeting of the two presidents in 1994, Yeltsin arrived so drunk that he "could barely get off the plane." He continued to get "pretty roaring" at other times during the summit, and at one point was "staggering around in his underpants shouting for pizza." As for Yeltsin's decisions, the U.S. official terms them "sometimes . . . just wacko." As an illustration, the adviser relates that during the U.S.-led bombing campaign against Serbia in 1999, "Yeltsin, who was clearly in his cups, suggested that he and Clinton had to get together on an emergency basis, and . . . should meet on a submarine." Such images might have been grotesquely amusing had not the besotted Russian president controlled a huge nuclear arsenal.[25]

Web Link

For the personality of U.S. presidents and others and the suitability of your personality to achieve presidential greatness, visit the interactive Web site of the Foundation for the Study of Personality in History at **www.personalityinhistory.com/**.

Ego and Ambition

A leader's ego and personal ambitions can also influence policy. One thing that arguably drove Saddam Hussein was his grandiose vision of himself. According to one intelligence report, the Iraqi leader saw himself in "larger than life terms comparable to Nebuchadnezzar [the great Babylonian king, 605–563 B.C.] and Saladin [the Sultan of Egypt who in 1189 defeated the Christians during the Third Crusade]."

The ego of the first President Bush also may have influenced policy. He came to office in 1989 with a reputation for being wishy-washy, and *Newsweek* even ran a picture of him with a banner, "The Wimp Factor," on its cover. Arguably an ego-wounded Bush responded by being too tough. He soon invaded Panama, and the following year in the Persian Gulf crisis his fierce determination not to negotiate with Iraq left it little choice but to fight or capitulate. Certainly, it would be outrageous to claim that Bush decided on war only to assuage his ego. But it would be naïve to ignore the possible role of this factor. In fact, after defeating Panama and Iraq, the president displayed a prickly pride when he told reporters, "You're talking to the wimp . . . to the guy that had a cover of a national magazine . . . put that label on me. And now some that saw that we can react when the going gets tough maybe have withdrawn that allegation."[26]

Political History and Personal Experiences

Decision makers are also affected by their personal experiences. It is worth speculating how much the personal experiences of President Bush influenced his determination in 2003 to drive Saddam Hussein from power. It is clear that Bush is very close to his family (Greenstein, 2003; Helco, 2003). That connection, in the view of some, made him especially sensitive to the criticism of his father for not toppling the Iraqi dictator in 1991, and may have created in the younger Bush an urge to complete the business of his father (Wead, 2003).[27] Moreover, it is widely believed that Saddam

Hussein tried to have the first President Bush assassinated when he visited Kuwait in 1993. Nine years later, his son told a gathering, "There's no doubt [that Saddam Hussein] can't stand us. After all, this is the guy that tried to kill my dad at one time." White House officials quickly issued assurances that the president did not mean "to personalize" his campaign to depose the Iraqi dictator, but it is hard to totally discount the antipathy of a devoted son toward a man who "tried to kill my dad."[28]

Perceptions and Operational Reality

Decision makers' images of reality constitute a fifth idiosyncratic element that influences their approach to foreign policy. Although we have already examined human perceptions in this chapter, it is worth separately considering the perception of leaders here because of the central role they play in making policy. Whatever their source, the sum of a leader's perceptions creates his or her worldview (Hermann & Keller, 2004). One scholar who served on the staff of President George W. Bush has written, "By the time I left the White House . . . I was convinced . . . [that] the sitting president's 'world view'—'his primary, politically relevant beliefs, particularly his conceptions of social causality, human nature, and the central moral conflicts of the time'—probably explain as much or more about . . . foreign policy than any other single variable" (DiIulio, 2003:3).

Perceptions play a key role in policy because they form an **operational reality**. That is, policy makers tend to act based on perceptions, whether they are accurate or not. For example, research shows that supposedly "rogue states" are no more likely than any other country to start a war (Caprioli & Trumbore, 2005). Yet the operational reality of the perceptions among most ranking officials in the Bush administration was that one such rogue state, Iraq, one of the "axis of evil" in Bush's mind, had WMD capabilities and intended to develop them more fully. This was a key factor in the U.S.-led intervention. That those perceptions were wrong is an important question in its own right. But as far as the causes of the war itself are concerned, the operational reality (even though it differed from the objective reality) was determined by the belief of President Bush, Prime Minister Blair, and others that Saddam Hussein did have such weapons and that they presented a long-term threat.

A related perceptual phenomenon is called an **operational code** (Schafer & Walker, 2006). This idea describes how any given leader's worldview and "philosophical propensities for diagnosing" how world politics operates influence the "leader's . . . propensities for choosing" rewards, threats, force, and other methods of diplomacy as the best way to be successful (Walker, Schafer, & Young, 1998:176). President Bill Clinton's worldview saw the United States as operating in a complex, technology-driven, interconnected world, in which conflict was more likely to result from countries' internal conditions (such as poverty) than from traditional power rivalries between states. Among other things, this led Clinton to favor a multilateral approach to diplomacy, to often view the motives and actions of other countries in nuanced shades of gray, and to delve deeply into the intricacies of policy.

George W. Bush's operational code is very different. Whereas Clinton took a cerebral approach to policy, Bush has described himself as more a "gut" player than an intellectual (Daalder & Lindsay, 2003:7). Perhaps stemming from his profound religious convictions, Bush, more than Clinton, is apt to see the world in right-versus-wrong terms.[29] For him, not only were the terrorists who launched the 9/11 attacks analogous to the fascists of the 1930s, but countries suspected of abetting terrorism were part of an axis of evil. Compared to Clinton, this belief also makes Bush more disposed to see the world as a more inescapably dangerous place

A leader's sense of self can impact foreign policy. President George W. Bush arguably has a strong sense of obligation to reshape the United States and the world drawn from his family's tradition of public service. This 1950 photo shows Bush's grandfather, Senator Prescott Bush of Connecticut, as well as his father and future president, George H. W. Bush, who is holding the younger President Bush. Also shown are the senator's wife, Dorothy, and Barbara Bush, the current president's mother. Younger brother Jeb, now the governor of Florida, had not yet been born.

and to follow a unilateralist path in pursuit of what he believes to be right. Just as Woodrow Wilson's strong religious convictions helped shape his crusading desire to make the world safe for democracy, so too may Bush's religious fervor be an element in his missionary-like urge to make the world into a better place by promoting democracy, free enterprise, and generally what he might term the "American way" (Rhodes, 2003). As one analyst notes, "it is impossible to understand Bush's presidential character without fully appreciating his profoundly small 'd' democratic beliefs" (DiIulio, 2003:3).

Finally, some analysts believe that Bush draws a strong sense of duty to lead and sacrifice from the history of the Bush family's public service dating back several generations. For the president this sense of personal leadership translates into feeling responsible to use his position as the leader of what he sees as a great and good country to reshape the world. As one scholar has noted, for Bush, "With 9/11, the long-hidden mission, the purpose for everything that had gone before [in becoming president], seemed to snap into place. In the political ethos of the Bush family, the charge to keep was to behave with responsibility. The terrorist attack filled in the blank space as to what responsibility required in the new post–Cold War era. . . . The Bush Doctrine . . . was born" (Helco, 2003:20).

Policy as a Mix of Rational and Irrational Factors

After spending considerable time on the myriad emotional, perceptual, and other factors that detract from rationality, a balanced discussion requires us to stress here that while decisions are rarely fully rational, they are seldom totally irrational

(Mercer, 2005). Instead, it is best to see human decisions as a mix of rational and irrational inputs. This view of how individuals and groups make policy choices is called **poliheuristic theory**. This theory depicts decision making as a two-stage process (Kinne, 2005; Redd, 2005; Dacey & Carlson, 2004). During the first stage, decision makers use shortcuts to eliminate policy options that are unacceptable for irrational personal reasons. Poliheuristic theorists especially focus on reelection hopes and other domestic political considerations, but the shortcuts could include any of the other irrational factors we have been discussing. With the unacceptable choices discarded, "the process moves to a second stage, during which the decision maker uses more analytic processing in an attempt to minimize risks and maximize benefits" in a more rational way (Mintz, 2004:3). It is at this second stage that decision makers tend to set aside domestic politics and personal factors and concentrate on strategic, realpolitik considerations (James & Zhang, 2005; DeRouen Jr. & Sprecher, 2004).

For example, one recent study using poliheuristic theory looked at U.S. decision making during the hostage crisis with Iran. As noted above, there is ample evidence of nonrational factors in the decisions of President Carter and other top administration officials. The study concluded that "Carter ruled out alternatives" that had negative domestic political consequences, then "selected from the remaining alternatives according to its ability to simultaneously maximize net benefits with respect to military and strategic concerns" (Brulé, 2005:99).

STATE-LEVEL ANALYSIS

For all the importance of the human input, policy making is significantly influenced by the fact that it occurs within the context of a political structure. Countries are the most important of these structures. By analyzing the impact of structures on policy making, **state-level analysis** improves our understanding of policy. This level of analysis emphasizes the characteristics of states and how they make foreign policy choices and implement them (Hudson, 2005; Bueno de Mesquita, 2002). What is important from this perspective, then, is how a country's political structure and the political forces and subnational actors within the country cause its government to decide to adopt one or another foreign policy (Chittick & Pingel, 2002).

Making Foreign Policy: Type of Government, Situation, and Policy

Those who study how foreign policy is made over time in one country or comparatively in several countries soon realize there is no such thing as a single foreign policy process. Instead, how policy is made varies considerably.

Type of Government and the Foreign Policy Process

One variable that affects the foreign policy process is the type of government a country has. These types range along a scale that has absolute **authoritarian governments** on one end and unfettered **democratic governments** on the other. The more authoritarian a government is, the more likely it is that foreign policy will be centered in a narrow segment of the government, even in the hands of the president or whatever the leader is called. It is important to realize, though, that no government is absolutely under the thumb of any individual. States are too big and too complex for that to happen, and thus secondary leaders (such as foreign ministers), bureaucrats, interest groups, and other domestic elements play a role in even very authoritarian political systems.

At the other end of the scale, foreign policy making in democracies is much more open with inputs from legislators, the media, public opinion, and opposition parties, as well as those foreign policy–making actors that influence authoritarian government policy. President Bill Clinton signed the Comprehensive Test Ban Treaty on behalf of the United States, for example, but the Senate disagreed with his view and in 1999 refused to ratify it. Yet even in the most democratic state, foreign policy tends to be dominated by the country's top leadership.

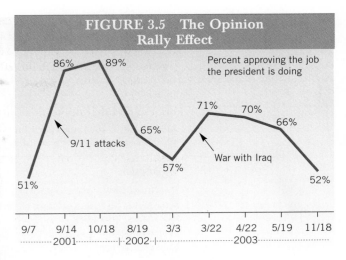

FIGURE 3.5   The Opinion Rally Effect

People usually rally behind their leader during times of crisis. Public approval of President Bush's performance in office skyrocketed 35% after the 9/11 attacks, then rose sharply again at the onset of the war with Iraq. Also note that the rally effect is fleeting, and the president's ratings soon declined after each peak.

Data source: CNN/*USAToday*/Gallup Polls found at Polling Report.com.

Type of Situation and the Foreign Policy Process

The policy-making process also varies within countries. Situation is one variable. For example, policy is made differently during crisis and noncrisis situations. A **crisis situation** occurs when decision makers are (1) surprised by an event, (2) feel threatened (especially militarily), and (3) believe that they have only a short time to react (Brecher & Wilkenfeld, 1997). The more intense each of the three factors is, the more acute the sense of crisis.

Whereas noncrisis situations often involve a broad array of domestic actors trying to shape policy, crisis policy making is likely to be dominated by the political leader and a small group of advisers. One reason this occurs involves the **rally effect.** This is the propensity of the public and other domestic political actors to support the leader during time of crisis. Figure 3.5 shows the impact of the rally effect on the popularity of President Bush at the time of the 9/11 attack and also at the onset of the Iraq War in 2003 (Hetherington & Nelson, 2003). A similar pattern was evident in Great Britain, the only major U.S. ally. There, support for the way Prime Minister Tony Blair was handling the crisis with Iraq rose from 48% before the war to 63% after it began.[30]

Type of Policy and the Foreign Policy Process

How foreign policy is decided also varies according to the nature of the **issue area** involved. Issues that have little immediate or obvious impact on Americans can be termed pure foreign policy. A narrow range of decision makers usually makes such decisions in the executive branch with little or no domestic opposition or even notice. For instance, President Bush consented to expanding the North Atlantic Treaty Organization (NATO) by adding seven new members (Bulgaria, Romania, Estonia, Latvia, Lithuania, Slovakia, and Slovenia) in 2004. Even though this substantially added to U.S. defense commitments by including countries that border Russia, the move was nearly invisible within the United States. The media made little mention of it, and pollsters did not even bother to ask the public what

The expansion of the North Atlantic Treaty Organization (NATO) eastward to the very borders of Russia has potentially great stakes for Americans because the NATO treaty pledges them to defend numerous small states that were once in the orbit of Moscow and even part of the former USSR. Yet as pure foreign policy issues, the rounds of expansion in 1999 and 2004 drew almost no notice and less dissent among the American people and members of Congress. By contrast, intermestic issues, such as trade, draw much greater public and legislative interest and activity.

it thought. Neither did the expansion arouse much interest in the Senate, which ratified it unanimously.

By contrast, foreign policy that has an immediate and obvious domestic impact on Americans is called **intermestic policy**. This type of policy is apt to foster substantial activity by legislators, interest groups, and other foreign policy–making actors and thereby diminish the ability of the executive leaders to fashion policy to their liking. Foreign trade is a classic example of an intermestic issue because it affects both international relations and the domestic economy in terms of jobs, prices, and other factors.

This domestic connection activates business, labor, and consumer groups who, in turn, bring Congress into the fray (Grossman & Helpma, 2002). Therefore national leaders, such as presidents, usually have much greater say over pure foreign policy than they do over intermestic policy. For example, in stark contrast to Bush's easy success in getting the NATO expansion ratified, he had to struggle mightily to persuade Congress to give him greater latitude (called *fast-track authority*) in negotiating trade treaties. Although his party controlled both houses of Congress, the president was only successful after a concerted effort that included personally going to Capitol Hill to lobby legislators and to offer inducements to gain support. Even then, the final vote in the House of Representatives was a razor-thin 215 to 212.

Making Foreign Policy: Political Culture

Each country's foreign policy tends to reflect its **political culture**. This concept represents a society's widely held, traditional values and its fundamental practices that are slow to change (Paquette, 2003; Jung, 2002). Leaders tend to formulate policies that are compatible with their society's political culture because the leaders share many or all of those values. Also, even if they do not share a particular value, leaders want to avoid the backlash that adopting policies counter to the political culture might cause. To analyze any country's political culture, you would look into such things as how a people feel about themselves and their country, how they view others, what role they think their country should play in the world, and what they see as moral behavior.

How Americans and Chinese feel about themselves and about projecting their values to others provide examples. Both Americans and Chinese are persuaded that their own cultures are superior. In Americans, this is called *American exceptionalism,* an attitude that, for instance, led 81% of Americans to agree in a poll that the spread of their values would have a positive effect on other parts of the world.[31] A similar sense of superiority among the Chinese is called *Sinocentrism.* This tendency of the Chinese to see themselves as the political and cultural center of the world is expressed, among other ways, in their word for their country: "Zhong Guó" means "middle place" and symbolizes the Chinese image of themselves.

Where Americans and Chinese differ is in their beliefs about trying to impose it on others. Americans are sometimes described as having a *missionary impulse,* that is, possessing a zeal to reshape the world in the American image. For example, it is this aspect of American political culture that has led the United States to try not only to defeat hostile regimes in Afghanistan, Iraq, and elsewhere, but additionally, to replace them with democratic governments. There is also evidence that the United States makes other decisions, such as foreign aid allocations, based in part on how closely countries adhere to American conceptions of human rights.

Chinese attitudes about projecting values are very different. Despite China's immense pride in its culture, there is no history of trying to impose it on others, even when China dominated much of the world that it knew. The orientation is based in part on Confucianism's tenet of leading by example rather than by forceful conversion. It also has to do with the Sinocentric attitude that the "barbarians" are not well suited to aspire to the heights of Chinese culture and are best left to themselves as much as possible. Among other current ramifications, this *nonmissionary attitude* makes it very hard for the Chinese to understand why Americans and some others try to insist that China adopt what it sees as foreign values and standards of behavior on human rights and other issues. Instead of taking these pressures at face value, the Chinese see them as interference or, worse, as part of a campaign to subvert them.

Foreign Policy–Making Actors

"Washington is like a Roman arena [in which] gladiators do battle," Secretary of State Henry Kissinger (1982:421) wrote. As his analogy implies, foreign policy making is not a calm, cerebral process. Instead it is a clash of ideas and a test of political power and skills to determine which of many policy proposals will prevail. The combatants of which Kissinger wrote are the **foreign policy–making actors**, including

One aspect of political culture that affects China's foreign policy is Sinocentrism, the tendency of the Chinese to see themselves and their country as the center of the political and cultural world. This self-image is represented by these Chinese characters. They are Zhong Guó, the Chinese name for their country, which translates as middle (Zhong, on the left) place (Guó, on the right).

Web Link

To support research about American political culture at the University of Pittsburgh, fill out the Web questionnaire at **www.pitt.edu/~redsox/polcul.html.**

political executives, bureaucracies, legislatures, political opponents, interest groups, and the people.

Heads of Government and Other Political Executives

In most countries, the executive branch is the most important part of the policy-making process. This is especially true in national security policy and foreign policy. The most powerful figure in the executive branch is usually the country's **head of government** (most commonly titled president, prime minister, or premier). A step below, but still of note, are the leader's cast of other **political executives**, such as ministers of foreign affairs (secretary of state) and ministers of defense (secretary of defense).

The degree to which the head of government dominates foreign policy is based on numerous factors. We have already touched on some of these, such as the type of government, the type of situation, and the type of policy. Three other important factors are the chief executive's formal powers, informal powers, and leadership capabilities.

Formal powers are the specific grants of authority that a country's constitution and its statutory (written) laws give to various offices and institutions. Most chief executives, for example, are the commander in chief of their country's armed forces. This gives them broad, often unilateral authority to use the military. Congress passed resolutions supporting President Bush's planned actions against Afghanistan in 2001 and Iraq in 2003, but he claimed the right to act without legislative support. Instead, the president claimed the authority to go to war "pursuant to my constitutional authority to conduct U.S. foreign relations as commander in chief and chief executive."[32] Such an assertion of unilateral authority dismays many Americans as undemocratic, and it is an issue for you to consider in the decision box, "Who Should Decide on War?"

Informal powers are a second source of authority for political executives. It is easier for people to identify with and look for leadership toward an individual than toward an institution, and this gives the president of the United States and other chief executives considerable prestige and political influence that cannot be found in the constitution or laws. For instance, more than any other political figure, the chief executive personifies the nation. This is especially true in world affairs and doubly so in crises where a president personifies the nation and embodies "we" in dealings with "them." The nation's focus on the chief executive also means that he or she is expected to lead. As one classic study of the U.S. presidency has put it, "Everybody now expects the man inside the White House to do something about everything" (Neustadt, 1990:7). Presidential prestige also means that they receive considerable more news media attention than any other political actor. One study found, for instance, that television networks devote almost 50% more time to covering the president than Congress (Graber, 2006).

Leadership capabilities are the third factor that helps determine how much authority a specific chief executive has. These capabilities include *administrative skills,* how well a president organizes and manages his or her immediate staff and the governments bureaucracy; *legislative skills,* the ability in a democratic system to win the support in the national legislature; *public persuasion* abilities, the ability to set forth a clear vision and to speak well and otherwise project a positive image that will win public support; and *intellectual capacity,* level of intelligence and ability to use it pragmatically to formulate policy. Measuring such qualities is very difficult, but Table 3.1 provides an interesting and undoubtedly controversial presentation and comparison of presidential intelligence and foreign policy success.

WEB POLL
Attitudes in Foreign Policy
Decision-Making

DEBATE THE POLICY SCRIPT

Who Should Decide on War?

Going to war is a country's most important decision. The question is, Who should make it? Article I of the Constitution empowers Congress "to declare war." Article II makes the president "commander in chief" of the military. These clauses reflect the belief of the Constitution's authors that presidents should "be able to repel [but] not commence war," as delegate Roger Sherman put it. The problem is where the line is between repelling an attack and commencing a war. President George W. Bush, for example, portrayed the Iraq War as preemptively repelling the threat of Iraqi weapons of mass destruction.

Historically, presidents have long used limited force without a congressional declaration of war or other resolution of support. But the frequency of such use and the size of the conflicts grew after World War II. Since Harry S. Truman, presidents have argued that they have almost limitless authority to use military force as they see fit. Signifying that, Truman waged the Korean War on his own authority.

Reacting to the unpopular war in Vietnam (which Congress had authorized), legislators enacted the War Powers Resolution (WPR, 1973) to try to rein in the president's self-claimed war power. The WPR specified limited circumstances when the president could use force unilaterally and required congressional consent in all other instances. The WPR has been largely ineffective. One reason is that Congress has never refused a presidential request that it authorize military action. Second, Congress has been unwilling to challenge presidents when they ignored the WPR and used the military unilaterally. Third, all presidents have rejected the WPR as

an unconstitutional restraint on their authority as commander in chief. For example, President George W. Bush welcomed resolutions of congressional support for action against Afghanistan (2001) and against Iraq (2003) as nice but not necessary, claiming that he was taking action solely "pursuant to my constitutional authority to conduct U.S. foreign relations as commander in chief and chief executive."[1] When in 2007 the Democrats as the newly elected majority in Congress sought to restrain the president from sending an additional 21,000 troops to Iraq, he rejected the ability of legislators to do so. "I'm the decision maker" about Iraq, he defiantly declared.[2] Fourth, the Supreme Court considers the issue a political one and has refused to hear challenges to the president's use of the military.

Think about amending the Constitution to clear up who should be able to make the decision to go to war. One option is a clause supporting current practice by explicitly giving the war power to the president. The second option is to explicitly bar presidents from using military force without congressional authorization except in cases of a direct, significant, and sustained attack on the United States, its territories, or its armed forces. A third option is specifying that except in the case of a significant and sustained attack, the president and Congress could only send U.S. forces into combat after approval by a majority of Americans voting in a national referendum.

What Do You Think?

How should the United States decide to wage war?

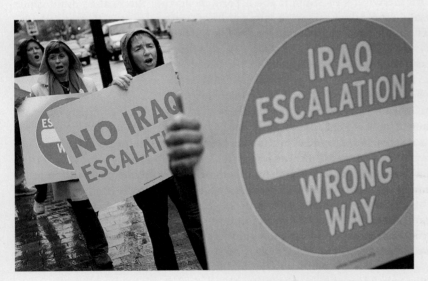

The debate in early 2007 over whether to send yet more troops to Iraq highlighted the question about who should have power to make such decisions. President Bush said he was the "decider" and increased troop levels even though doing so was opposed by a majority of Congress and a strong majority of the public, including these protesters. Does this seem proper democratic governance to you?

A high IQ is one trait that arguably makes a skilled leader. This table shows the estimated IQs of recent presidents. It also lists the ratings on a 1 to 100 basis that experts have given these presidents for their foreign policy. George W. Bush was not rated because he is still in office. The right column shows how each president ranks in IQ and policy success. How would you rank President George W. Bush's foreign policy compared to his eight immediate predecessors? How would you characterize the connection between IQ and success shown here?

TABLE 3.1	Presidential Intelligence		
President	Intelligence Quotient (IQ)	Foreign Policy Success (FPS)	IQ/FPS Rank
Kennedy	150.7	69.0	1/3
Johnson	127.8	40.7	7/8
Nixon	131.0	75.9	4/1
Ford	127.1	52.7	8/7
Carter	145.1	55.8	3/5
Reagan	130.0	68.6	6/4
Bush, G. H. W.	130.1	70.0	5/2
Clinton	148.8	54.3	2/6
Bush, G. W.	124.6	—	9/-

Note: The reported IQ scores are the average of the four estimated scores on the Stanford-Binet scale. A score of 100 is the average IQ; 120 is considered superior, and genius begins at 145.

Data sources: For international relations policy, C-SPAN Survey of Presidential Leadership at www.americanpresidents.org/survey/. For IQ, Simonton (2006), Table 1, p. 516.

For all the broad power to shape policy that chief executives have, their power is not unlimited even in authoritarian countries, and it is significantly restrained in democratic ones. Indeed, the spread of democracy and the increasingly intermestic nature of policy in an interdependent world mean that political leaders must often engage in a **two-level game** in which "each national leader plays both the international and domestic games simultaneously" (Trumbore, 1998:546). The strategy of a two-level game is based on the reality that to be successful, diplomats have to negotiate at the international level with representatives of other countries and at the domestic level with legislators, bureaucrats, interest groups, and the public in the diplomat's own country. The object is to produce a "win-win" agreement that satisfies both the international counterparts and the powerful domestic actors so that both are willing to support the accord. Reflecting this reality, one former U.S. official has recalled, "During my tenure as Special Trade Representative, I spent as much time negotiating with domestic constituents (both industry and labor) and members of the U.S. Congress as I did negotiating with our foreign trading partners" (Lindsay, 1994:292).

Bureaucracies

Every state, whatever its strength or type of government, is heavily influenced by its **bureaucracy**. The dividing line between decision makers and bureaucrats is often hazy, but we can say that bureaucrats are career governmental personnel, as distinguished from those who are political appointees or elected officials.

Although political leaders legally command the bureaucracy, they find it difficult to control the vast understructures of their governments. President Vladimir Putin of Russia and President George W. Bush candidly conceded that gap between legal and real authority during a joint press conference. The two presidents were optimistically expounding on a new spirit of U.S.-Russian cooperation when a reporter asked them if they could "say with certainty that your teams will act in the same spirit?" Amid knowing laughter, Bush replied, "It's a very good question you ask, because sometimes the intended [policy] doesn't necessarily get

SIMULATION
Utilizing Levels of Analysis

translated throughout the levels of government [because of] bureaucratic intransigence." President Putin agreed. "Of course, there is always a bureaucratic threat," he conceded.[33]

Bureaucrats sometimes do not agree with their country's foreign policy. Instead they may favor another policy option based on their general sense of their unit's mission. How any given policy will affect the organization is also an important factor in creating bureaucratic perspective. Often what a given bureaucracy will or will not favor makes intuitive sense. The military of any country will almost certainly oppose arms reductions or defense spending cuts because such policies reduce its resources and influence. But the stereotypical view of the military as always gung ho for war is not accurate (Gelpi & Feaver, 2002). Whether the area was Kosovo, Bosnia, Haiti, or elsewhere, the U.S. military has often been a reluctant warrior within the council of government, especially regarding the use of ground forces. A common view, expressed by then Chairman of the Joint Chiefs of Staff, General Colin Powell, is that "politicians start wars. Soldiers fight and die in them."[34]

Filtering information is one way that bureaucracies influence policy. Decision makers depend on staff for information, and what they are told depends on what subordinates choose, consciously or not, to pass on. This was illustrated after the Iraq War by the uproar over President Bush's assertion in his 2003 State of the Union message that Iraq "recently sought significant quantities of uranium from Africa." In reality, the statement was based on shaky British sources that the CIA doubted. Yet it wound up in the president's speech when his speechwriters used information from an intelligence report that cited the British report but buried the CIA's objections in a footnote.

This occurred in part because groupthink seemed to intimidate the CIA and prevent it from pushing more strongly a view that it assumed would not please the president. As Senator Pat Roberts (R-KS), chairman of the Senate Intelligence Committee, noted after hearings and reports on how the Iraq War began, "Groupthink caused the [intelligence] community to interpret ambiguous evidence such as the procurement of dual-use technology" to mean Iraq had an active weapons program. It is clear that this groupthink also extended to our allies.[35] Additionally, the dubious assertion about Iraq seeking uranium went unchallenged by the National Security Council (NSC) staff member who reviewed the speech despite an earlier telephone conversation with the CIA director, who said that the agency doubted that Iraq had sought uranium from Africa. The NSC official, who favored action against Iraq, later conceded, "I should have recalled . . . that there was controversy associated with the uranium issue," but many observers doubted that it was a mere oversight.[36]

Recommendations are another source of bureaucratic influence on foreign policy. Bureaucracies are the source of considerable expertise, which they use to push the agency's preferred position. One scholar, after analyzing bureaucratic recommendations in several countries, concluded that leaders often faced an "option funnel." This means that advisers narrow the range of options available to leaders by presenting to them only those options that the adviser's bureaucratic organization favors. This recommendation strategy, the analyst continued, "often decided what national leaders would do even before they considered a situation" (Legro, 1996:133).

Implementation is another powerful bureaucratic tool. There are a variety of ways that bureaucrats can influence policy by the way they carry it out. As the investigations into the 9/11 attacks have proceeded, it has become clear that the

ANALYZE THE ISSUE
Applying Levels of Analysis in the Wake of September 11 and the War in Iraq: The Bush Doctrine

This editorial drawing from Bulgaria depicts a common image of inept U.S. intelligence agencies supplying poor information about the possibility of weapons of mass destruction in Iraq and the possibilities of Iraq cooperation with al Qaeda terrorists prior to the U.S. invasion in 2003.

terrorists were able to carry them off in part because of flaws in the implementation of U.S. antiterrorist policy. Evidence shows that government agencies often failed to share information or otherwise cooperate, that they discounted the terrorist threat, and that they ignored information that pointed to an impending attack. For example, a congressional report indicates that an FBI agent warned in July 2001 that "an inordinate number of individuals of investigative interest" were taking flight training. Yet, the report noted, this alert "generated little or no interest" among FBI officials and was not passed on to the CIA or other relevant agencies. The following month the CIA's Counter-Terrorism Center warned in a report that "for every [al Qaeda operative] that we stop, an estimated 50 . . . slip through . . . undetected. . . . It is clear that [al Qaeda] is building up a worldwide infrastructure which will allow [it] to launch multiple and simultaneous attacks with little or no warning." The agency also predicted, "The attack will be spectacular and designed to inflict mass casualties against U.S. facilities or interests." These and numerous other signals went unheeded, however, leading the congressional committee to conclude that because government agencies "failed to capitalize" on available information, they had "missed opportunities to disrupt the September 11 plot and . . . to generate a heightened state of alert and thus harden the homeland against attack."[37]

Legislatures

In all countries, the foreign policy role of legislatures play a lesser role in making foreign policy than executive-branch decision makers and bureaucrats. This does not mean that all legislatures are powerless (Howell & Pevehouse, 2005; Scott & Carter, 2002; Leogrande, 2002). They are not, but their exact influence varies greatly among countries. Legislatures in nondemocratic systems generally rubber-stamp the decisions of the political leadership. China's National People's Congress, for example, does not play a significant role in foreign policy making.

Legislatures play a larger foreign policy role in democratic countries, but even in these states legislative authority is constrained by many factors. One of these is that chief executives usually have *extensive legal powers* in the realm of foreign policy. American presidents, for instance, are empowered by the U.S. Constitution to negotiate treaties, to extend diplomatic recognition to other countries, to appoint diplomatic and military personnel, to use U.S. forces as commander in chief, and to take numerous other actions with few or no checks by Congress or the courts. *Tradition* is a second factor that works to the advantage of chief executives in foreign policy making. The leadership has historically run foreign policy in virtually all countries, especially in time of war or other crises.

Third is the *belief that a unified national voice is important to a successful foreign policy.* This is particularly true during a crisis, when Congress, just like the public, tends to rally behind the president. This emotional response helped win support for a congressional resolution in late 2001 giving the president almost unchecked authority to use military forces against terrorism by votes of 98 to 0 in the Senate and 420 to 1 in the House of Representatives. Just 13 months later, by votes of 77 to 23 in the Senate and 296 to 133 in the House, Congress authorized military action against Iraq. Surely, many members agreed with the war, but at least some voted "aye" despite their misgivings because they agreed, as Senate Democratic leader Tom Daschle explained, commenting on his vote, that "it is important for America to speak with one voice."[38]

Fourth, *legislators tend to focus on domestic policy* because, accurately or not, most voters perceive it to be more important than foreign policy and make voting decisions based on this sense of priority. For this reason, legislators are apt to try to influence intermestic policy issues, such as trade, and are apt to be much less concerned with pure foreign policy issues, such as the membership of the NATO alliance.

By this logic, though, legislative activity is especially likely and important when a high-profile issue captures public attention and public opinion opposes the president's policy. Even more commonly, intermestic issues such as trade that directly affect constituents and interest groups spark legislative activity (Marshall & Prins, 2002). For instance, a study of 25 developed countries found that right-of-center parties, which are aligned with business, usually favor free trade, while left-of-center parties, which are supported by labor unions, lean toward protectionism (Milner & Judkins, 2004). Moreover, globalization is increasingly blurring the line between foreign and domestic affairs. As one member of the U.S. Congress put it, "Increasingly all foreign policy issues are becoming domestic issues. . . . [and] Congress is demanding to play a greater role."[39]

Interest Groups

Interest groups are private associations of people who have similar policy views and who pressure the government to adopt those views as policy. Traditionally, interest groups were generally considered to be less active and influential on foreign policy than on domestic policy issues. The increasingly intermestic nature of policy is changing that, and interest groups are becoming a more important part of the foreign policy–making process. We can see this by looking at several types of interest groups.

Cultural groups are one type. Many countries have ethnic, racial, religious, or other cultural groups that have emotional or political ties to another country. For instance, as a country made up mostly of **immigrants**, the United States is populated by many who maintain a level of identification with their African, Cuban, Irish, Mexican, Polish, and other heritages and who are active on behalf of policies that favor their ancestral homes. Religious groups are one type of cultural group that exercises influence in many countries. Conservative Protestant groups, for one, are influential in the administration of President George W. Bush because of his personal religious convictions and the important political support he receives from them. This connection among other domestic factors helps explain some of the president's unilateralist tendencies and reluctance to rely on the UN and other international organizations (Skidmore, 2005). As Bush told a friend after a meeting with the Christian Coalition, "Sovereignty. The issue is huge. The mere mention of [Secretary-General] Kofi Annan in the UN caused the crowd [the audience at the Christian Coalition meeting] to go into a veritable fit. The coalition wants America strong and wants the American flag flying overseas, not the pale blue of the UN."[40]

Economic groups are another prominent form of interest activity. As international trade increases, both sales overseas and competition from other countries are vital matters to many companies, their workers, and the communities in which they

---

Did You Know That:

The only U.S. legislator to vote against the U.S. declarations of war in both World War I and World War II was Jeannette Rankin (R-MT), the first woman elected to Congress.

live. They lobby their governments for favorable legislation and for support of their interests in other countries. In industrialized countries, for example, many labor unions oppose free trade treaties because increased imports tend to undercut domestic products and the workers who make them. U.S. unions were encouraged when a new Congress opened in 2007 with a majority of Democrats, who tend to support unions. One union cited "the American labor movement's strong opposition to globalization" because "labor unions have lost membership, and workers have had to offer give-backs to employers to retain the jobs that remain, in an era when labor and, indeed, manufacturing can be sourced abroad." With the Democrats in the majority, the unions anticipate that "provisions in future trade agreements will at least build barriers against their members being drowned in the tidal wave of new trade liberalization."[41]

Issue-oriented groups make up another category of interest group. Groups of this type are not based on any narrow socioeconomic category such as ethnicity or economics. Instead they draw their membership from people who have a common policy goal. The concerns of issue-oriented groups run the gamut from the very general to the specific and from liberal to conservative. Just one of the multitude of groups, the neoconservative Project for the New American Century, is an organization that during the later Clinton years included in its membership such soon-to-be Bush administration appointees as Secretary of Defense Rumsfeld and Deputy Secretary of Defense Paul Wolfowitz. It was this neoconservative (neocon) group that was the driving force behind the Bush Doctrine of preemptive war and its use in Iraq (Benn, 2004).

Transnational interest groups also deserve mention. Growing interdependence has increased the frequency of countries, international organizations, and private interest groups lobbying across borders. In 2005, there were over 1,800 lobbyists registered with the U.S. government as representing 589 foreign interest groups. Some represented national governments and others lobbied for subnational units such as the Province of Quebec in Canada. Yet other lobbyists registered as representatives of groups hoping to become national governments, including Tibet's exiled Dalai Lama, the Kurdish Regional Government of Iraq, and the Palestinian Authority. Other foreign registrants, reflecting a panoply of interests, included the Icelandic Tourist Board, Petroleos Mexicanos, the Euro-Asian Jewish Congress of Russia, and Volkswagen of Germany. Japanese interests (53 registrants) were the most heavily represented in Washington, followed by those of Mexico (29), Great Britain (27), and Canada (18).

The People

Like legislatures, the public plays a highly variable role in foreign policy. Public opinion is a marginal factor in authoritarian governments. In democracies, the role of the people is more complex (Everts & Isernia, 2001). On occasion, public opinion plays a key role. The United States got out of Vietnam in the 1970s in significant part because of the determined opposition of many Americans to continued involvement in that war. Yet even in democracies, the public usually plays only a limited role in determining foreign policy.

Public Interest in World Affairs   One reason for the public's limited role is that few citizens ordinarily pay much attention to international issues. During the 2004 and 2006 U.S. national elections, terrorism and Iraq were prominent issues. Worry about terrorism arguably secured President Bush's reelection in 2004, and voter discontent

Web Link

A semi-annual report on the Foreign Agents Registration Act is available through the U.S. Department of Justice at **www.usdoj.gov/criminal/fara/.**

with policy in Iraq was a factor in the Republicans losing control of both houses of Congress in 2006. Such elections were unusual, though. Normally, the public's political interest focuses on domestic issues. During the 2000 presidential election, for one, only 5% of voters identified a foreign policy matter as the most important issue to them. Moreover, even in most elections when foreign policy does play an important role, the majority of voters cite a domestic issue as the most important to their vote. In 2006, for example, 65% of people in one poll said "problems in the U.S." would be more important in their vote for Congress than "problems around the world." Only 17% took the opposite view, with another 17% saying both counted equally and 1% unsure.[42]

This is not to say that all of the public pays little heed to foreign policy all of the time. First, there is a segment of the public, the "attentive public," that regularly pays attention to world events. Second, crisis issues, such as the war with Iraq, and intermestic issues, such as trade, are apt to draw significantly greater public attention. Third, studies show that although the public is not versed in the details of policies, its basic instincts are neither disconnected from events nor unstable (Witko, 2003; Isernia, Juhasz, & Rattinger, 2002).

Channels of Public Opinion Influence on Foreign Policy   There are a few countries in which the public occasionally gets to decide a foreign policy issue directly through a national referendum. However, all democracies are basically republican forms of government in which policies and laws are made by elected officials and their appointees. Therefore, it is more common for public opinion to have an indirect democratic influence on policy through voting for officials and through the sensitivity of those officials to public attitudes.

Even if they cannot usually decide policy directly, voters do sometimes have a choice of candidates for national leadership positions who have different foreign policy goals and priorities (Fordham, 2002). During 2006, for instance, voters brought new chief executives or new legislative majorities into power in such countries as Canada, Chile, Italy, Mexico, Nicaragua, the Palestinian Territories, and Ukraine, as well as the United States. As in all national elections, many issues were involved, but, among other impacts, the election of a Hamas majority by the Palestinians raised tensions with Israel, the election in Ukraine brought a prime minister to power who favors greater connection with the West and fewer dealings with Russia, and the new center-left government in Italy soon withdrew the last Italian troops from Iraq.

Additionally, research shows that both elected and appointed officials are concerned with public opinion and that it often influences policy (Burstein, 2003; Heith, 2003; Reiter & Tillman, 2002). This is especially true when the public is clearly attentive to an issue (Knecht & Weatherford, 2006). One reason is that most decision makers in a democracy believe that public opinion is a legitimate factor that should be considered when determining which policy is to be adopted. Second, leaders also believe that policy is more apt to be successful if it is backed by public opinion. Third, decision makers are wary of public retribution in the next election if they ignore majority opinion. "I knew full well that if we could rally the American people behind a long and difficult chore, that our job would be easier," President Bush commented about ordering military action against Afghanistan in 2001. "I am a product of the Vietnam era," the president explained. "I remember presidents trying to wage wars that were very unpopular, and the nation split."[43] That image came to haunt Bush after the 2006 elections, and despite vowing to

TABLE 3.2 Opinions of U.S. Leaders and Public

Issues on Which Leaders and Public Agree			Issues on Which Leaders and Public Disagree		
The United States should:	Leaders Favoring	Public Favoring	The United States should:	Leaders Favoring	Public Favoring
Take active role in world	97%	67%	Make protecting American jobs a top goal	41%	78%
Play the role of global police force	18%	20%	Stress halting global flow of illegal drugs	46%	63%
Stress halting spread of nuclear weapons	87%	73%	Decrease legal immigration	10%	54%
Emphasize combating global terrorism	84%	71%	Make U.S. military superiority a top priority	37%	50%
Stress spreading democracy aboard	29%	14%	Make improving global environment a top goal	61%	47%
Make strengthening the UN a top goal	40%	38%	Do more to combat world hunger	67%	43%
Stress protecting U.S. business interests	22%	33%	Make helping poor countries a top goal	64%	18%
Be more willing to accept decisions of UN	78%	66%	Reduce U.S. military aid	40%	65%
Keep military bases in South Korea	71%	62%	Reduce U.S. economic aid	9%	64%
Keep military bases in Germany	54%	57%	Keep military bases in Saudi Arabia	25%	50%
Keep military bases in Japan	56%	52%	Keep military bases in Turkey	63%	46%
Bomb terrorist training camps and faculties	83%	83%	Keep military base at Guantánamo Bay, Cuba	47%	58%
Assassinate terrorist leaders	52%	68%	Use troops to defend S. Korea from N. Korea	82%	43%
Not torture suspected terrorists for information	88%	66%	Use troops to protect oil supply	36%	54%
Remain in NATO	66%	58%	Topple governments that support terrorism	38%	67%
Join Kyoto Protocol to cut CO_2 emissions	72%	71%	Use troops to protect Israel from Arabs	64%	43%
Give UN power to control global arms trade	55%	57%	Use troops to protect Taiwan from China	51%	33%
Participate in UN peacekeeping	84%	78%			
Wage preemptive war in some circumstances	71%	70%			
Use troops to halt genocide	86%	75%			
Ratify treaty to ban all nuclear weapons tests	85%	87%			
Ratify treaty to ban all land mines	80%	80%			
Use nuclear weapons only if attacked by them	57%	57%			

Notes: NATO is the North Atlantic Treaty Organization, UN is the United Nations, and CO_2 is carbon dioxide.
Data source: Chicago Council on Global Affairs (2004).

This table compares the opinions of U.S. political, social, and economic leaders and the American public. Usually the two groups agree, but they also often disagree, as the two lists show. Also look for more subtle differences. Whether the groups agree or not, the leaders are usually more internationalist than the public. Where the public is internationalist is on issues that directly and immediately affect Americans, such as protecting jobs from foreign competition.

"stay the course," the president clearly began to more flexibly look for a way to extricate the country from Iraq.

Web Link

Numerous foreign policy opinion analyses including surveys evaluating the opinions of U.S. global leaders and the foreign policy views of Americans and citizens from 17 countries can be found on the site of the Chicago Council on Global Affairs at **http://www.thechicagocouncil.org.**

Dimensions of Foreign Policy Opinion   Most polls only report overall public opinion on a topic, but it is important to realize that opinion is not split evenly across all segments of the public. One of these opinion splits, the gender gap, is discussed earlier in this chapter. Additionally, there is a **leader-citizen opinion gap** on some issues in the United States and other countries. This term represents the difference in the average opinions of those who are the leaders of government, business, the media, and other areas in a society and the general public. Table 3.2 lists a wide range of issues on which U.S. leaders and the American public agree and disagree.

SYSTEM-LEVEL ANALYSIS

Countries may be theoretically free to make any foreign policy decision they want, but as a practical matter, achieving a successful foreign policy requires that they make choices that are reasonable within the context of the realities of the international system. For example, Mexico's President Vicente Fox denounced as "disgraceful and shameful" the U.S. plan to build a wall along the two countries' border, and Mexico could exercise its sovereign authority and use force to try to prevent the barrier's construction.[44] However, doing so would be foolhardy because one fact of life in the international system is that the U.S. military power is vastly greater than that of Mexico. Thus, power realities in the international system dictate that Mexico would be wiser to attempt to use more moderate means in its effort to persuade the United States to abandon the notion that good fences make good neighbors.

System-level analysis focuses on the external restraints on foreign policy. This is a "top-down" approach to world politics that examines the social-economic-political-geographic characteristics of the system and how they influence the actions of countries and other actors (Moore & Lanoue, 2003). We can roughly divide the restraints on reasonable state behavior into those related to the system's structural characteristic, its power relationships, its economic realities, and its norms.

MAP
The Geopolitical World
at the Beginning
of the 21st Century

Structural Characteristics

All systems, whether it is the international system, your country's system, or the immediate, local system in your college international relations class, have identifiable structural characteristics. Two of particular relevance to our analysis here are how authority is organized in the international system and the scope and level of interaction among the actors in the system.

The Organization of Authority

The structure of authority for making and enforcing rules, for allocating assets, and for conducting other authoritative tasks in a system can range from hierarchical (vertical) to anarchical (horizontal). Most systems, like your class and your country, tend toward the hierarchical end of the spectrum. They have a **vertical authority structure** in which subordinate units are substantially regulated by higher levels of authority. Other systems are situated toward the **horizontal authority structure** end of the continuum. There are few, if any, higher authorities in such systems, and power is fragmented. The international system is a mostly horizontal authority structure. It is based on the sovereignty of states. *Sovereignty* means that countries are not legally answerable to any higher authority for their international or domestic conduct. As such, the international system is a **state-centric system** that is largely anarchic; it has no overarching authority to make rules, settle disputes, and provide protection.

WEB POLL
System-Level Analysis

The anarchical nature of the international system has numerous impacts on national policy. Consider defense spending, for instance. We debate whether it is too high, too low, or about right; but almost nobody suggests that we spend zero and eliminate our country's military entirely. To see why the anarchical international system pressures countries to have an army, ask yourself why all countries are armed and why few, if any, students bring guns to class. One reason is that states in the international system (unlike students in your college) depend on themselves for protection. If a state is threatened, there is no international 911 to call for help. Given this anarchical self-help system, it is predictable that states will be armed.

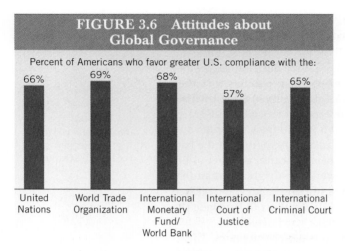

FIGURE 3.6   Attitudes about Global Governance

Percent of Americans who favor greater U.S. compliance with the:

- United Nations: 66%
- World Trade Organization: 69%
- International Monetary Fund/World Bank: 68%
- International Court of Justice: 57%
- International Criminal Court: 65%

Most Americans say they support increased U.S. compliance with a wide range of international organizations even if their decisions differ from U.S. policy preferences. However, questions about specific issues that go against current U.S. policy often bring a less internationalist response by Americans. For example, 65% of them want the United States to join the International Criminal Court, but only 37% are willing to have the ICC try American soldiers accused of war crimes if the U.S. government refuses to do so.

Data sources: Chicago Council on Global Affairs, *Global Views 2004: American Public Opinion and Foreign Policy* (Chicago: Chicago Council on Global Affairs, 2005) and Pew Global Attitudes Project Poll, January, 2003; data provided by The Roper Center for Public Opinion Research, University of Connecticut.

While the authority structure in the international system remains decidedly horizontal, change is under way. Many analysts believe that sovereignty is declining and that even the most powerful states are subject to a growing number of authoritative rules made by international organizations and by international law. Countries still resist and often even reject IGO governance, but increasingly they also comply with it. In 2006, for example, the World Trade Organization (WTO) ruled in favor of a U.S. allegation that the European Union (EU) was violating trade rules by using health regulations to bar the importation of genetically modified foods. That gladdened Washington, but it was disappointed in another ruling that year which upheld an EU complaint that U.S. tax breaks given to Boeing and other aircraft manufacturers were acting as a subsidy that gave Boeing an unfair advantage over Europe's Airbus under WTO rules. In both cases, as often occurs, the losing side grumbled mightily and hinted it might not comply, but history shows that countries do eventually change their practices when the WTO finds against them. Americans, like people in most countries, are sensitive about their sovereignty, yet they also are becoming more willing to accept the idea that their country should abide by IGO decisions, as Figure 3.6 indicates.

Scope, Level, and Intensity of Interactions

Another structural characteristic of any political system is the scope (range), frequency, and intensity (level) of interactions among the actors. In your class, for example, the scope of interactions between you and both your professor and most of your classmates (1) is probably limited to what happens in the course; (2) is not very intense; and (3) is confined to two or three hours of class time each week over a single semester.

At the international system level, the scope, frequency, and level of interaction among the actors is not only often much higher than in your class but has grown extensively during the last half century. Economic interdependence provides the most obvious example. Countries trade more products more often than they did not long ago, and each of them, even the powerful United States, is heavily dependent on others for sources of products that it needs and as markets for products that it sells. Without foreign oil, to pick one obvious illustration, U.S. transportation and industry would literally come to a halt. Without extensive exports, the U.S. economy would stagger because exported goods and services account for about 15% of the U.S. GNP.

Data about expanding trade does not, however, fully capture the degree to which the widening scope and intensifying level of global financial interactions are increasing transnational contacts at every level. For individuals, modern telecommunications and travel have made personal international interactions, once relatively rare, now commonplace. For example, between 1990 and 2005 the number of Americans traveling overseas increased 42% from 44.6 million to 63.5 million. During the same period, the number of foreign visitors to the United States jumped 25% from 39.4 million to 49.2 million. Communications are also expanding the scope, level, and intensity of communications. Satellite-transmitted television revolutionized communications. Most recently, al Jazeera, the Arab-based news network, has added an around-the-clock English-language broadcast. Trillions of phone calls, letters, and e-mail messages add to the globalization of human interactions, and the Internet ignores borders as it connects people and organizations around the world as if they were in the next room.

Power Relationships

Countries are restrained by the realities of power in the international system, much like individuals are limited by the distribution of power in more local systems. For instance, it is very probable that the distribution of power in your class is narrow. There is apt to be one major power, the professor, who decides on the class work, schedules exams, controls the discussion, and issues rewards or sanctions (grades). Sometimes students grumble about one or another aspect of a class, and they might even be right. But the power disparity between students and their professor makes open defiance exceptionally rare. Similarly, the conduct of the international system is heavily influenced by power considerations such as the number of powerful actors and the context of power.

SIMULATION
Rules of the Game

The Number of Powerful Actors

Historically, international systems have been defined in part by how many powerful actors each has (Wilkinson, 2004). Such an actor, called a **power pole**, can be (1) a single country or empire, (2) an alliance, or could be (3) a global IGO, such as the UN, or (4) a regional IGO, such as the EU.

These poles are particularly important to the realist approach and its concern with the balance of power. Sometimes the term is used to describe the existing distribution of power, as in, "the current balance of power greatly favors the United States." More classically, though, the theory of **balance-of-power politics** put forth by realists holds that: (1) all states are power seeking; (2) ultimately, a state or bloc will attempt to become hegemonic, that is, dominate the system; and (3) other states will attempt to block that dominance by increasing their own power and/or cooperating with other states in an antihegemonic effort.

Web Link

An online balance-of-power game can be played at **www.balance-of-power.ch/ main.html**.

Some scholars further believe that the number of power poles in existence at any one time helps determine how countries are likely to act. According to this view, it is possible to identify patterns or rules of the game for systems. Figure 3.7 displays four power configurations (unipolar, bipolar, tripolar, and multipolar) and ways in which the patterns of interaction arguably differ across them. Bear in mind that these rules indicate what actors are apt to try to do. The rules are neither ironclad nor do actors always succeed in implementing them.

As a sample of how these rules work, note that in a **unipolar system**, which exists in many ways today with the United States as the single pole, the **hegemonic power** tries to maintain control. From a system-level perspective, this impulse to power is not so much caused by the preexisting desires of the dominant power as by the pressure in the system to maintain stability and order. The argument is that "a unipolar system will be peaceful," but only so long as the hegemonic power acts like one (Wohlforth, 1999:23). This leads some scholars to worry that if the United States refuses to play the leading role in the world drama, then the system becomes unstable, leading to greater violence and other negative consequences (Lal, 2004).

FIGURE 3.7 The Dynamics of International Systems

Unipolar System

Traditional Hegemonic Dominance   World Federal System

One pole

Rules of the game are: (1) The central power establishes and enforces rules and dominates military and economic instruments. (2) The central power settles disputes between subordinate units. (3) The central power resists attempts by subordinate units to achieve independence or greater autonomy and may gradually attempt to lessen or eliminate the autonomy of subordinate units.

Bipolar System

Two poles

Acute hostility between the two poles is the central feature of a bipolar system. Thus primary rules are: (1) Try to eliminate the other bloc by undermining it if possible and by fighting it if necessary and if the risks are acceptable. (2) Increase power relative to the other bloc by such techniques as attempting to bring new members onto your bloc and by attempting to prevent others from joining the rival bloc.

Tripolar System

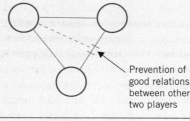

Prevention of good relations between other two players

Three poles

The rules of play in a triangular relationship are: (1) Optimally, try to have good relations with both other players or, minimally, try to avoid having hostile relations with both other players. (2) Try to prevent close cooperation between the other two players.

Multipolar System

Four or more poles

Rules of the game are: (1) Oppose any actor or alliance that threatens to become hegemonic. This is also the central principle of balance-of-power politics. (2) Optimally increase power and minimally preserve your power. Do so by negotiating if possible, by fighting if necessary. (3) Even if fighting, do not destabilize the system by destroying another major actor.

 Small Power   - - - - - - - - Short-Term or Potential Link

Large Power   ———————— Dominant and Lasting Link

The relationships that exist among the actors in a particular type of international system structure vary because of the number of powerful actors, the relative power of each, and the permitted interactions within the system. This figure displays potential international system structures and the basic rules that govern relationships within each system. After looking at these models, which one, if any, do you think best describes the contemporary international system?

Advocates of this view warn, "Critics of U.S. global dominance should pause and consider the alternative. If the United States retreats from its hegemonic role, who would supplant it? . . . Unfortunately, the alternative to a single superpower is not a multilateral utopia." What will occur, the argument continues, is a "power vacuum . . . an era of 'apolarity'," leading to "an anarchic new Dark Age: an era of waning empires and religious fanaticism; of endemic plunder and pillage in the world's forgotten regions; of economic stagnation and civilization's retreat into a few fortified enclaves" (Ferguson, 2004:32). This view is akin to Barber's (1996) image of tribalism, as discussed in chapter 2.

Needless to say, there is considerable debate over such views. Some scholars contend that a reduced U.S. presence in the world would not destabilize the system. Yet other analysts debate the motives behind and the implications of the United States conducting itself as the hegemonic power. Some condemn it as a destructive imperialistic impulse (Gitlin, 2003; Lobell, 2004). Speaking to an international conference in 2007, Russia's President Putin argued that the U.S. aggressive policy had made the world more dangerous than during the cold war. During that period of bipolar confrontation, Putin argued, there "was a fragile peace, a scary peace, but it was fairly reliable, as it turns out. Today it is less reliable."[45] Others argue that U.S. power is not only necessary for stability, but will also have other positive impacts such as spreading democracy (Kaplan 2004; Krauthammer, 2004). Amid all these sharply divergent views about the U.S. global role, though, there can be little doubt that changing the power equation changes the way a system operates.

The theory about the rules of the game in a unipolar system also suggests that lesser powers try to escape dominance. Arguably, that explains why many Europeans favor transforming the existing 60,000-soldier Eurocorps (with troops from Belgium, France, Germany, Luxembourg, and Spain) into a de facto EU army to rival or even to replace NATO, which the United States dominates. As former British Prime Minister Margaret Thatcher put it, "The real drive towards a separate European defense" is based on the unstated goal of "creating a single European superstate to rival America on the world stage."[46] The urge to escape the U.S. orbit also may help explain why France, Germany, Russia, and China were all opposed to U.S. action against Iraq in 2003. Certainly those countries objected to the war as such, but it was also a chance to resist the lead of the hegemonic power. In this context, it was not surprising that several European countries met soon after the Iraq War to discuss how to increase their military cooperation. "In order to have a balance, we have to have a strong Europe, as well as a strong U.S.," is how French President Jacques Chirac explained the purpose of the conference.[47] Moreover, surveys indicate that not only do Europeans agree that a stronger Europe to counterbalance U.S. power is desirable, so does a majority or plurality of people in most other countries surveyed on the question. The details are presented in Figure 3.8 on page 96. None of this means that any of these countries are implacably antagonistic toward the United States, only that Washington needs to exercise power carefully to avoid driving its former allies together with its former enemies in an anti-hegemony, not an anti-American, alliance (Carter, 2003).

The Context of Power

The United States is troubled by its massive trade deficit ($221 billion in 2006) with China, and there is pressure on the Bush administration to react strongly. U.S. manufacturers and unions assert that they are losing business and jobs to the flood of imports. Thus far, however, Washington has not pressed Beijing hard on the issue. One reason is that raising tariffs on Chinese goods and other decisive actions, which the United States has the power to do, would dramatically decrease China's willingness

FIGURE 3.8   Opinions on European and U.S. Power

Country	Positive	Neutral	Negative
Spain	81%	10%	9%
Germany	79%	11%	10%
Italy	76%	10%	14%
France	70%	8%	22%
Mexico	66%	26%	8%
China	66%	18%	16%
Great Britain	66%	8%	26%
South Africa	63%	12%	25%
Canada	63%	11%	26%
Australia	62%	15%	23%
Russia	60%	27%	13%
Lebanon	59%	27%	14%
Poland	58%	30%	12%
Argentina	57%	27%	16%
Indonesia	56%	22%	22%
Brazil	53%	19%	28%
South Korea	53%	7%	40%
Turkey	49%	32%	19%
Chile	48%	35%	17%
Japan	35%	52%	13%
India	35%	27%	38%
Philippines	35%	11%	54%
United States	34%	11%	55%

Opinions on Europe's power surpassing U.S. power

Positive   Neutral   Negative

"Uneasy lies the head that wears a crown," Shakespeare tells us in *Henry I, Part II*. This insight helps explain global attitudes toward the reigning hegemonic power, the United States. When people in 23 countries were asked whether it would be mainly a positive or negative development if "Europe becomes more influential than the United States in world affairs," a majority in 17 countries and a plurality in 2 others replied mainly positive. Only majorities of Americans and Filipinos thought the change would be negative, while people in India were closely divided and most Japanese were neutral.

Note: Unsure and all other answers other than positive or negative were coded as neutral here.
Data source: Program on International Policy Attitudes, 23 Nation Poll: "Who Will Lead the World?" April 2005.

to cooperate with the United States in other key areas. An example of these is North Korea's nuclear weapons program, a situation that could lead to the spread of nuclear weapons beyond North Korea to South Korea and Japan and even to war on the Korean Peninsula. China is one of the few countries with any influence in Pyongyang, and Beijing might respond to U.S. pressure to reduce the trade deficit by refusing to cooperate with Washington's efforts to persuade North Korea to end its nuclear program.

Economic Realities

System-level analysts contend that the economic realities of the international system help shape the choices that countries make. Again, this is the same in systems from the global to your local level. For example, a safe prediction is that after finishing your education you will get a job and spend most of the rest of your life working instead of pursuing whatever leisure activities you enjoy the most. You will almost certainly do that because the economic realities of your local system require money to get many of the things you want, and most of us need a job to get money. Similarly, the international system has economic facts of life that help shape behavior.

Interdependence is one of the economic facts of life that influences states' behavior. For example, many studies conclude that increasing economic interdependence promotes peace as countries become more familiar with one another and need each other for their mutual prosperity (Schneider, Barbieri, & Gleditsch, 2003). The ramifications of this on policy are evident by again turning to U.S.-China relations. It is tempting to advocate imposing tariff hikes and other sanctions on Beijing, and certainly that would stagger China's economy. But it would also damage Americans economically. Equivalent U.S.-made products would be much more expensive, thereby increasing the cost of living for the American consumer. Toys, electronic products, and many other things that Americans import from China might be in short supply or not available, at least until substitute sources could come on line. Many U.S. businesses and their stock- and bondholders might also suffer because they have invested heavily in setting up manufacturing plants in China that produce goods for the U.S. market. In short, the United States could decide to impose sanctions on China, but doing so would at least partly be the equivalent of Americans shooting themselves in their own economic foot.

Natural resource production and consumption patterns also influence the operation of the system. From this perspective, the U.S. military reaction to Iraq's attack on Kuwait in 1990 and its threat to the rest of the oil-rich Persian Gulf region was virtually foreordained by the importance of petroleum to the prosperity of the United States and its economic partners. As U.S. Secretary of State James A. Baker III explained to reporters, "The economic lifeline of the industrial world runs from the Gulf, and we cannot permit a dictator . . . to sit astride that economic lifeline."[48]

By contrast, U.S. officials repeatedly denied that petroleum was connected to the war in 2003. Secretary of Defense Rumsfeld, for one, asserted that the U.S. campaign against Iraq "has . . . literally nothing to do with oil."[49] Nevertheless, numerous analysts believe that it was an underlying factor. Some contend that Washington sought to ensure continued supplies at a stable price by adding control of Iraq to its already strong influence over Saudi Arabia, Kuwait, Qatar, and other oil-rich states in the region. The administration "believes you have to control resources in order to have access to them," argues Chas Freeman, a former U.S. ambassador to Saudi Arabia.[50] Other analysts believe that the motive behind U.S. policy was a power play. As one scholar put it, "Controlling Iraq is about oil as power, rather than oil as fuel. Control over the Persian Gulf translates into control over Europe, Japan, and China. It's having our hand on the spigot."[51]

There has also been speculation that the opposition of France, Russia, and some other countries to the U.S.-led invasion and their support for easing sanctions on Iraqi oil exports were in part oil related. The contention is that these countries were concerned with the contracts their oil companies had with Iraq to develop its oil production once sanctions were lifted, and they feared that those agreements would be abrogated and given to U.S. firms in the wake of a U.S. occupation of the country. As one U.S. oil expert put it before the war, "Most of these governments . . . have [a financial] interest in the current Iraqi government surviving. It's not trivial. . . . Once it's developed, the oil will be 2.5 million barrels [worth about $70 million] per day."[52]

MAP
Flows of Oil

Flows of Oil

Flows of Oil in Millions of Tons per Year
Lines are approximate proportional width.

World politics is strongly influenced by the reality in the international system that much of the world's petroleum is produced in the Middle East and consumed in North America, Europe, and Japan.

Norms

Like all the other factors we have been discussing, norms influence the actors in systems from the global level to the local level. Norms are one of the reasons that even on a very warm day you will almost certainly come to class wearing clothes rather than *au naturel*. In fact, norms make it reasonably predictable that most students will come to class not only dressed, but dressed similarly. Jeans, sweatshirts, sneakers or work boots, and baseball caps (often worn backwards) seem the most common "uniform."

Similarly, norms play a part in determining actions within the international system. It is hard for some to accept that norms exist in a world in which absolutely horrendous things sometimes happen. Moreover, it would be far too strong to say there is anything near a universally accepted standard of behavior. Yet it is the case that values do exist, are becoming a more important part of international conduct, and are becoming more uniformly global. During the war with Iraq in 2003, for example, one available U.S. option was "nuking" Iraq's main cities and military sites and killing most Iraqis. It surely would have ended the regime of Saddam Hussein, it would have been quick, and it would have cost many fewer American lives and dollars than the conventional attack and subsequent occupation. Yet the U.S. decision was to send troops to Iraq at great expense and at great risk, especially given the perceived threat of a chemical or biological attack on them. Why?

Norms were one reason for not using nuclear weapons. The global population would have been horrified, and Americans themselves might have risen up and removed President Bush from office. Indeed, the norm against using nuclear weapons, especially against a non-nuclear power, is so strong that only massive Iraqi use of chemical or biological weapons might have prompted such a response. Moreover, even during their conventional invasion, it is noteworthy that U.S. and U.K. military forces generally conducted operations in a way to keep civilian casualties much lower than they might otherwise have been. That reflected the growing norms in the world, including those of Americans, 75% of whom, according to one poll, believed there should be a "very high" or "high" priority on minimizing civilian casualties.[53]

It is easy to lose track of the main message in this long section on system-level analysis. So to recap our focus, system-level analysis looks for the way that the structure, power distribution, economic realities, and norms of the international system influence foreign policy. Indeed, we have seen that foreign policy making is much more complex than merely "what the president decides." Instead, foreign policy and by extension world politics are heavily influenced by numerous factors related to the traits of humans as individuals and as a species, to the complicated structure of government with its many important subnational actors, and to the context of the international system in which all countries operate.

CHAPTER SUMMARY

INDIVIDUAL-LEVEL ANALYSIS

1. Individual-level analysis is based on the view that it is people who make policy. It analyzes the policy-making process by examining how people (as a species, in groups, and individually) make decisions.

2. Individual-level analysis can be approached from three different perspectives. One is to examine fundamental human nature. The second is to study how people act in organizations. The third is to examine the motivations and actions of specific persons.

3. The human nature approach examines basic human characteristics, including the cognitive, psychological, emotional, and biological factors that influence decision making.

4. The organizational behavior approach studies such factors as role (how people act in their professional position) and group decision-making behavior, including groupthink.

5. The idiosyncratic behavior approach explores the factors that determine the perceptions, decisions, and actions of specific leaders. A leader's personality, physical and mental health, ego and ambitions, understanding of history, personal experiences, and perceptions are all factors.

6. The application of perceptions to policy can be explained by exploring operational reality and operational codes.

STATE-LEVEL ANALYSIS

7. State-level analysis assumes that since states are the most important international actors, world politics can be best understood by focusing on how foreign policy is influenced by the political structure of states, the policy-making actors within them, and the interactions among the policy actors.

8. Foreign policy is not formulated by a single decision-making process. Instead, the exact nature of that process changes according to a number of variables, including the type of political system, the type of situation, the type of issue, and the internal factors involved.

9. States are complex organizations, and their internal, or domestic, dynamics influence their international actions.

10. One set of internal factors centers on political culture: the fundamental, long-held beliefs of a nation.

11. Another set of internal factors centers on the policy-making impact of various foreign policy–making actors. These include political leaders, bureaucratic organizations, legislatures, political parties and opposition, interest groups, and the public. Each of these influences foreign policy, but their influence varies according to the type of government, the situation, and the policy at issue.

12. Usually, heads of government are the most powerful foreign policy–making actors. Bureaucratic organizations are normally the second most powerful actors.

SYSTEM-LEVEL ANALYSIS

13. To be successful, countries usually must make policy choices within the context of the realities of the international system. Therefore, system-level analysis examines how the realities of the international system influence foreign policy.

14. Many factors determine the nature of any given system. Systemic factors include its structural characteristics, power relationships, economic realities, and norms of behavior.

15. One structural characteristic is how authority is organized. The international system is horizontal, based on state sovereignty, and therefore it is anarchical. There are, however, relatively new centralizing forces that are changing the system toward a more vertical structure.

16. Another structural characteristic is a system's frequency, scope, and level of interaction. The current system is becoming increasingly interdependent, with a rising number of interactions across an expanding range of issues. Economic interdependence is especially significant.

17. When analyzing power relationships, an important factor is the number of poles in a system and how the pattern of international relations varies depending on how many power centers, or poles, a system has.

18. The current system most closely resembles either a unipolar system or limited unipolar system dominated by the United States.

19. The context of power is another system characteristic. One contextual factor is the applicability of power in a given situation.

20. Another aspect of the context is the intricate interrelationships among almost 200 countries and the need of even powerful countries for diplomatic reciprocity, the cooperation of others on a range of issues. It is therefore wise, before using power, to calculate the long-term impact of the attitudes of other countries.

21. Norms are the values that help determine patterns of behavior and create some degree of predictability in the system. The norms of the system are changing. Many newer countries, for instance, are challenging some of the current norms of the system, most of which are rooted in Western culture.

For simulations, debates, and other interactive activities, a chapter quiz, Web links, and much more, visit **www.mhhe.com/rourke12/** and go to chapter 3. Or, while accessing the site, click on Course-Related Headlines and view recent international relations articles in the *New York Times*.

KEY TERMS

authoritarian
  governments
balance-of-power politics
biopolitics
bureaucracy
cognitive decision
  making
crisis situation
decision-making process
democratic governments
ethology
foreign policy process

foreign policy–making
  actors
formal powers
frustration-aggression
  theory
gender opinion gap
groupthink
head of government
hegemonic power
heuristic devices
horizontal authority
  structure

idiosyncratic analysis
individual-level analysis
informal powers
interest groups
intermestic policy
issue area
leader-citizen opinion gap
leadership capabilities
levels of analysis
mirror-image perception
operational code
operational reality

poliheuristic theory
political culture
political executives
power pole
roles
state-centric system
state-level analysis
system-level analysis
two-level game
unipolar system
vertical authority
  structure

Nationalism: The Traditional Orientation

Who is here so vile that will not love his country?
—William Shakespeare, *Julius Caesar*

If he govern the country, you are bound to him indeed; but how honourable he is in that, I know not.
—William Shakespeare, *Pericles, Prince of Tyre*

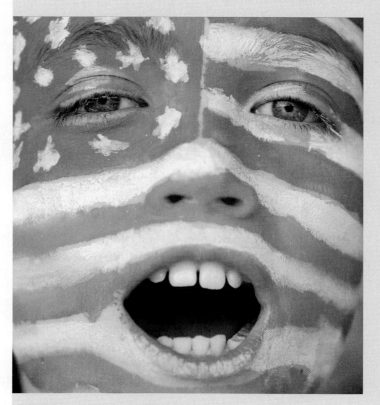

Nationalism, identifying politically first and foremost with your country, has long been and remains the most important political orientation of a majority of the people. This chapter explores the evolution of nationalism and its advantages and disadvantages.

ALIENS FASCINATE US. NOT THE ALIENS that immigration officials worry about, but the ones that come from other planets. Whether it is movies such as *Star Wars: Revenge of the Sith,* television such as the numerous Star Trek series, sci-fi novels, or comics, our entertainment media are filled with "others." These aliens can do more than amuse or scare us; they can teach us something. For instance, take E.T., the extraterrestrial being. Now, there was one strange-looking character. He—she?—had a squat body, no legs to speak of, a large shriveled head, saucer eyes, and a telescopic neck. And the color! Yes, E.T. was definitely weird. Not only that; there was presumably a whole planet full of E.T.s—all looking alike, waddling along, with their necks going up and down.

Or did they all look alike? They might have to us, but probably not to one another. Perhaps their planet had different countries, ethnic groups, and races of E.T.s. Maybe they had different-length necks, were varied shades of greenish-brown, and squeaked and hummed with different tonal qualities. It could even be that darker-green E.T.s with longer necks from the country of Urghor felt superior to lighter-green, short-necked E.T.s from faraway and little-known Sytica across the red Barovian Sea. If E.T. were a Sytican, would the Urghorans have responded to the plaintive call, "E.T. phone home"?

We can also wonder whether E.T. could tell Earthlings apart. Was he aware that some of his human protectors were boys and some were girls and that a racial and ethnic cross section of Americans chased him with equal-opportunity abandon? Maybe we all looked pretty much the same to E.T. If he had been on a biological specimen–gathering expedition, would he have collected a Canadian, a Nigerian, and a Laotian, or would he have considered them duplicates?

The point of this whimsy is to get us thinking about our world, how we group ourselves, and how we distinguish our group from others. This sense of how you are connected politically to others is called **political identity**. What we humans mostly do is to ignore our many and manifest similarities and perceptually divide ourselves into Americans, Chinese, Irish, Poles, and a host of other national "we-groups."

Web Link

You can participate in the Search for Extraterrestrial Intelligence (SETI) program at the University of California at Berkeley through its Web site at **http://setiathome .ssl.berkeley.edu/.**

UNDERSTANDING NATIONS, NATIONALISM, AND NATION-STATES

This chapter explores nationalism, which for more than five centuries has been, and continues to be, the most important way we identify ourselves politically. Nationalism's status as the key component of most people's political identity makes it one of the most important forces in traditional global politics. Despite its strength, however, nationalism is not as dominant a political identity as it once was. Indeed, some even doubt whether it will or should continue and predict or advocate various transnational alternative orientations. These alternatives are taken up in chapter 5, and their juxtaposition with the traditional nationalist orientation in this chapter represents one of this book's main themes: that the world must decide whether to continue to practice traditional world politics, to adopt a new approach to global affairs, or to blend traditional and new approaches and, if so, in what measure of each.

Nations, Nationalism, and Nation-States Defined

The world's political divisions rest in great part on three concepts: nation, nation-state, and nationalism. Understanding both the theory and reality of what they are and how they relate to one another is central to our analysis of international politics.

Nations

A **nation** is a people who (a) share demographic and cultural similarities, (b) possess a feeling of community (mutually identify as a group distinct from other groups), and (c) want to control themselves politically. As such, a nation is intangible; it exists because its members think it does. A state (country) is a tangible institution, but a nation is "a soul, a spiritual quality" (Renan, 1995:7). Americans, for one, are a nation; the institutional vehicle of their self-governance is their state, the United States.

Demographic and Cultural Similarities   The similarities that a people share help make them a nation. These similarities may be demographic characteristics (such as language, race, and religion), or they may be a common culture or shared historical experiences. It could be said that the American nation is the outcome of Valley Forge, World War II, Martin Luther King, McDonald's, MTV, the Super Bowl, Jennifer Lopez, the 9/11 terrorist attacks, and many other people, events, and processes that make up the American experience. Symbols such as the American flag, Uncle Sam, and the bald eagle reinforce nationalism (Kolstø, 2006; Geisler, 2005).

Feeling of Community   A second thing that helps define a nation is its feeling of community. Perception is the key here. Whatever its objective similarities, a group is not a nation unless it subjectively feels like one. Those within a group must perceive that they share similarities and are bound together by them. The central role of perceptions in defining a nation leads, perhaps inevitably, to a "we-group" defining itself not only by the similarities of its members but also in terms of how the members of the nation differ from others, the "they-groups." The group members' sense of feeling akin to one another and their sense of being different from others are highly subjective.

WEB POLL
International Identity

Desire to Be Politically Separate   The third element that defines a nation is its desire to be politically separate. What distinguishes a nation from an ethnic group is that a nation, unlike an ethnic group, desires to be self-governing or at least autonomous. In the United States there are many groups, such as Italian Americans, who share a common culture and have a sense of identification. They are ethnic groups, not nations, however, because they are not separatists. In nationally divided states (like Cyprus, with its majority Greek and minority Turkish communities), the minority nationalities refuse to concede the legitimacy of their being governed by the majority nationality.

It should be noted that the line between ethnic groups and nations is not always clear. In many countries there are ethnic groups that either teeter on the edge of having true nationalist (separatist) sentiments or that have some members who are nationalists and others who are not. In Canada, for instance, there is ongoing dissatisfaction among many French Canadians in the province of Quebec about their

Wanting to be politically separate is a key factor that distinguishes a nation from an ethnic group. This photo shows members of the Basque nation of Spain carrying a banner that reads, "New Basque Country" in their native language. Addressing the gathering on a huge screen in the background is Arnaldo Otegi. He leads Batasuna, the Basque party that advocates secession of the Basque region, which lies mostly in northern Spain and extends into France.

status in the Canadian state. Some Québécois favor separation; others do not. Once the prevailing opinion of the ethnic group perceives it to be distinct politically as well as culturally, then it becomes an **ethnonational group** (Conversi, 2002 & 2004).

Nationalism

The second aspect of the traditional political orientation is **nationalism**. It is the sense of political self that makes people feel patriotic about their country, connected to a we-group, and different from they-groups. It is hard to overstate the importance of nationalism to the structure and conduct of world politics. Nationalism is an **ideology**. Like all ideologies, nationalism is a set of related ideas that (1) establish values about what is good and bad, (2) direct adherents on how to act (patriotism), (3) link together those who adhere to the ideology, and (4) distinguish them from those who do not.

Specifically, nationalism connects individuals through links that are forged when people (1) "become sentimentally attached to the homeland," (2) "gain a sense of identity and self-esteem through their national identification," and (3) are "motivated to help their country" (Druckman, 1994:44). As an ideology, nationalism holds that the nation should be the primary political identity of individuals. Furthermore, nationalist ideology maintains that the paramount political loyalty of individuals should be patriotically extended to the nation-state, the political vehicle of the nation's self-governance. While most people have more than one political identity, nationalism almost always is their primary political orientation. For example, President Lyndon B. Johnson once said, "I am an American, a Texan, and a Democrat—in that order." Like Johnson, we emotionally rank our identities, and also like LBJ, most of us put our country first. Thus you probably see yourself first and foremost politically as a citizen of the United States or some other country. You might even be willing to fight and die for your country. Would you do the same for your hometown? Or Earth?

Web Link

A good source of additional information about nationalism is the Nationalism Project at **www.nationalismproject.org/.**

Nationalism is a learned form of political identity. None of these babies has a sense of loyalty to any of the countries represented by the flags on their blanket, but they soon will. As a result, even though they seem pretty much the same in this photo, each baby will come to see the others as different and perhaps even as hostile.

Nation-States

A third element of our traditional way of defining and organizing ourselves politically is the **nation-state**. This combines the idea of a nation with that of a state. A state, about which much more is said in chapter 6, is a country, a sovereign (independent) political organization with certain characteristics, such as territory, a population, and a government. Canada and China, for example, are states. Ideally, a nation-state is one in which virtually all of a nation is united within the boundaries of its own state, and the people of that state overwhelmingly identify with the nation. Few states even approach this ideal, as we shall see, but the image is a powerful force for both those nations seeking to found their own states and those states seeking national unity.

The Rise and Ascendancy of Nationalism

Nationalism is such a pervasive mindset in the world today that it is difficult to believe that it has not always existed. But it has not. Indeed, most scholars contend that nationalism is a relatively modern phenomenon. Certainly, there have always been cultures that defined people. It is also true that people have lived in one or another type of political unit as far back as we can see in history. As we shall find, though, what is relatively modern is the widespread sense among people that they have a personal attachment to the political unit, in this case their country, and are defined by the connection.

This reality that nationalism has not always existed is important because if something has not always been, it will not necessarily continue to be. As we shall see later in the chapter, nationalism has its pluses and minuses, and numerous observers believe that it is an outmoded, even dangerous, orientation that should be deemphasized. Understanding that nationalism is not an absolute also leads to a discussion of how it has evolved over time.

Early Nationalism

It is impossible to establish precisely when nationalism began to evolve (Smith, 2004). In the West, though, the fall of the universalistic Roman Empire set the stage. Under Rome something of common culture, language (Latin), and law prevailed, at least among the elite in the various parts of the empire. After Rome's collapse these common cultural and political ties deteriorated. Some sense of universality (such as the authority of the pope over kings and the use of Latin) survived in the Roman Catholic Church.

There were also various attempts to reestablish a Western empire. For example, the king of the Franks, Charlemagne (742–814), gained control over most of western and central Europe and in 800 was proclaimed by Pope Leo III to be *Imperatori Augustus,* a symbolic title reminiscent of the Roman emperors. This led to the concept of the Holy Roman Empire (HRE), which lasted in theory until 1806. Yet despite its pretentious title, the HRE never wielded the power of Rome and sometimes had little power at all.

As a result, the universality that had existed under Rome, and which the Church and the HRE tried to maintain, fragmented into different cultures. The use of Latin, a language spoken by all elites across Europe, declined, and the local languages that supplanted Latin divided the elites. This was but the first step in a process that eventually created a sense of divergent national identities among the upper classes. Beginning in 1517, the Protestant Reformation divided Western Christendom and further fragmented European culture.

The growth of nationalism became gradually intertwined with the development of states and with their synthesis, the nation-state. The history of states is reviewed in chapter 2, but we can say here that some of the earliest evidence of broad-based nationalism occurred in England at the time of King Henry VIII (1491–1547). His break with the centralizing authority of the Roman Catholic Church and his establishment of a national Anglican Church headed by the king were pivotal events. The conversion of English commoners to Anglicanism helped spread nationalism to the masses, as did the nationalist sentiments in popular literature. In an age when most people could not read, plays were an important vehicle of culture, and one scholar has characterized the works of William Shakespeare (1564–1616) as "propagandist plays about English history" (Hobsbawm, 1990:75). "This blessed plot, this earth, this realm, this England," Shakespeare has his King Richard II exult. In another play, *Henry VI,* Shakespeare notes the end of the authority of the pope in Rome over the king in London by having Queen Margaret proclaim, "God and King Henry govern England." This sounds commonplace today, but omitting mention of the authority of the papacy was radical stuff 450 years ago (Maley, 2003).

Ascendant Modern Nationalism

Modern nationalism began to emerge in the 1700s. Until that time, the link between the states and their inhabitants was very different than it is today. Most people were not emotionally connected to the state in which they lived. Instead, people were subjects who were ruled by a monarch anointed by God to govern (the divine right theory). This changed under the doctrine of **popular sovereignty**. It holds that people are not subjects, but citizens who have a stake in and are even owners (no matter how tangentially) of the state. Moreover, rulers governed by the consent of the people, at least in theory if often not in fact (Heater, 2004).

Until the late 1700s, popular sovereignty had been evolving slowly in Switzerland, England, and a few other places. Then it accelerated with the American Revolution (1776) and the French Revolution (1789). They dramatically advanced popular sovereignty by doing away with kings altogether and in their place proclaiming, in the words of the American Declaration of Independence, that governments derive their "just powers from the consent of the governed."

From these beginnings, the idea of popular sovereignty began to spread around the globe. Within 200 years of the American and French Revolutions, absolute monarchism, the most common form of governance from time immemorial, had virtually disappeared. Transnational ties among the elites also waned. When Great Britain's royal house of Stuart died out in 1714, it was still possible for the British to import a German nobleman to become King George I. Such a transplanted monarch or president would be virtually unthinkable today.

Nationalism's spread also dramatically changed the political map. An important factor was the associated concept of **self-determination**. This is the idea that every nation should be able to govern itself as it chooses. Following this notion, some nations that were divided among two or more political entities coalesced to create a single state. The formation of Germany and Italy in the 1860s and 1870s are examples. In other cases, national states were established on the ashes of empire. Indeed, a key change in the last 250 years has been the decline and death of vast multiethnic empires, as one after another has sunk under its own ponderous weight like a woolly mammoth in the La Brea tar pits. First, American colonists revolted against British colonial rule. Then the urge for self-determination contributed to the decline and fall of the Spanish empire in the 1800s, followed by the Austro-Hungarian and Ottoman empires in the late 19th century and early 20th century. In each case, many

Did You Know That:

National flags are relatively modern inventions that replaced flags of royal dynasties. The French tricolor, for example, dates only to 1794, when it replaced the white flag with the gold fleur-de-lis of the royal house of Bourbon.

of the nations that had existed within these empires established states. By the mid-twentieth century, nearly all of Europe and the Western Hemisphere had been divided into nation-states, and the colonies of Africa and Asia were beginning to demand independence. The British and French empires were similarly doomed by nationalist pressures within them and fell apart in the three decades after World War II. Finally, the last of the huge multiethnic empires, Russia/the Soviet Union, collapsed in 1991, with 15 nation-states emerging. Nationalism reigned virtually supreme around the world.

These developments were widely welcomed on two grounds. First, the idea of a nation implies equality for all members. Liberal philosophers such as Thomas Paine in *The Rights of Man* (1791) depicted the nation and democracy as inherently linked in the popularly governed nation-state. Supporters of nationalism also welcomed it as a destroyer of empires. Among other important expressions of this view is Article 55 of the United Nations Charter, which states that "the principle of . . . self-determination of peoples" is one of the "conditions of stability and well-being which are necessary for peaceful and friendly relations among nations." As we shall see later in the chapter, this support of self-determination is more controversial than it may seem.

Patterns of Nation-State Formation

As the history of nationalism suggests, nations, nationalism, and nation-states can come together in various patterns. Sometimes nations and nationalism precede states; sometimes states precede nations and nationalism; and at other times nations and nationalism evolve along with states.

Nations and Nationalism Precede Nation-States   The easiest form of **state building** occurs when a strong sense of cultural and political identity exists among a people, and the formation of the nation precedes that of the state. This process is called "unification nationalism" (Hechter, 2000:15). Europe was one place where nations generally came together first and only later coalesced into states. As noted, for example, Germans existed as a cultural people long before they established Germany in the 1860s and 1870s. In much the same way, the Italian peninsula was fragmented after the fall of the Roman Empire and remained that way until a resurgent sense of Italian cultural unity and its accompanying political movement unified most of the peninsula in a new country, Italy, in 1861. Similarly, on the other side of the world in Japan, increased nationalism helped end the political division of the Japanese islands among the *daimyo* (feudal nobles) during the Tokugawa Shogunate (1603–1867), and restored real power to what had been a figurehead emperor.

Nation-States Precede Nations and Nationalism   Another scenario is when the state is created first and then has to try to forge a sense of common national identity among the people and between them and the state. This state-building process is very difficult. Colonialism is one common cause of states coming into existence without a national core. For example, European powers artificially included people of different tribal and ethnic backgrounds within the borders of their African colonies (Larémont, 2005). When those colonies later became states, most lacked a single, cohesive nation in which to forge unity once independence had been achieved. Numerous problems resulted and persist. For example, Rwanda and Burundi are neighboring states in which Hutu and Tutsi people were thrown together by colonial boundaries that, with independence, became national boundaries, as depicted in the map of Africa on page 43. The difficulty is that the primary political identifications

One problem to be addressed in attempting to create a unified Iraq is building Iraqi nationalism. Among other obstacles are the nationalist sentiments of the Kurds, symbolized by this young Kurdish boy wearing a jacket bearing the proposed flag of an independent Kurdistan.

of these people have not become Rwandan or Burundian. They have remained Hutu or Tutsi, and that has led to repeated, sometimes horrific, violence.

The difficulties of building national identities and a stabilizing state have also beset the United States, and to a degree other involved countries, the UN, and regional organizations, in the aftermath of interventions in such places as Somalia and the Balkans in the 1990s and Afghanistan and Iraq more recently. Outside powers can find themselves "stuck" because they are neither able to create stable political situations that will allow them to withdraw nor willing to withdraw and permit a violent struggle for power to ensue (Etzioni, 2004; Fukuyama, 2004; Migdal, 2004).

Nations, Nationalism, and Nation-States Evolve Together Frequently nation-building and state-building are not locked in a strict sequential interaction, when one fully precedes the other. Sometimes they evolve together. This approximates what occurred in the United States, where the idea of being American and the unity of the state began in the 1700s and grew, despite a civil war, immigration inflows, racial and ethnic diversity, and other potentially divisive factors. Still, as late as 1861, the limitations of nationalism could be seen when Colonel Robert E. Lee declined President Abraham Lincoln's offer of the command of the United States Army and accepted command of the militia of his seceding home state, Virginia. The point is that American nationalism was not fully developed in 1776. As has happened elsewhere, living within a state over time allowed a diverse people to come together as a nation through a process of *e pluribus unum* (out of many, one), as the U.S. motto says.

NATIONALISM IN PRACTICE: ISSUES AND EVALUATION

The idea of a mutually identifying people coming together as a political nation to establish their own nation-state in order to govern themselves is an attractive one. Surely, it has brought benefits, but the reality of nationalism also has its dark side. As a first step toward evaluating the pros and cons of nationalism, it is important to understand how the theory and practice of nation-states differ.

Web Link

To explore ethnonational division in Europe, go to the site of the NGO Organization of European Minorities at **www.eurominority.org/version/eng/**.

Nation-States: More Myth Than Reality

Like most ideological images, the ideal nation-state is more myth than reality (Axtmann, 2004). The reason is that the territorial boundaries of nations and states often do not coincide. Instead, most states are not ethnically unified, and many nations are split by one or more national boundaries. This lack of "fit" between nations and states is a significant source of tension and conflict (Williams, 2003).

There are five basic patterns: (1) The first is the ideal model of one nation, one state. The other four are lack-of-fit patterns including (2) one state, multiple nations; (3) one nation, multiple states; (4) one nation, no state; and (5) multiple nations, multiple states.

One State, One Nation

Only about 10% of all countries approximate the ideal nation-state by both having a population that is 90% or more of one nation and also having 90% of that nation living within its borders. The United States is one such country. More than 99% of all Americans live in the United States, and there are no large ethnonational groups seeking independence or autonomy. There is some such sentiment among indigenous Americans, such as Native Hawaiians, but combined they make up only a bit more than 1% of the population. Moreover, Americans express high levels of national pride, patriotism, and other nationalistic sentiments (Smith & Kim, 2006). Indeed, as Figure 4.1 details, Americans not only have more national pride than people in almost any other country, but the level of that pride expressed by the dominant cultural group and minority groups is much closer than it is between the dominant and minority groups in many other countries.

One State, Multiple Nations

A far greater number of countries are **multinational states**, those in which more than one nation lies within a state. In fact, 30% of all states have no nation that constitutes a majority. The map on page 110 showing the degree of demographic unity of each country indicates racial and ethnic, as well as national, diversity. Most of these minority groups do not have separatist tendencies, but many do or could acquire them.

Canada is one of the many countries where national divisions exist. About one-fourth of Canada's 32 million people are ethnically French (French Canadians) who identify French as their "mother tongue" and first language (Francophones). The majority of this group resides in the province of Quebec, a political subdivision rather like (but politically more autonomous than) an American state. Quebec is very French; of the province's 7.2 million people, more than 80% are culturally French.

Many French Canadians have felt that their distinctive culture has been eroded in predominantly English-culture Canada. There has also been a feeling of economic and other forms of discrimination. The resulting nationalist sentiment spawned the separatist *Parti Québécois* and led to a series of efforts in the 1980s and 1990s to obtain autonomy, even independence, for the province. The most recent of these was a 1995 referendum on separation. The voters in Quebec rejected independence, but did so by only a razor-thin majority, with 50.6% voting *non* to sovereignty and 49.4% voting *oui*. The issue then receded somewhat, but it arose anew in late 2006

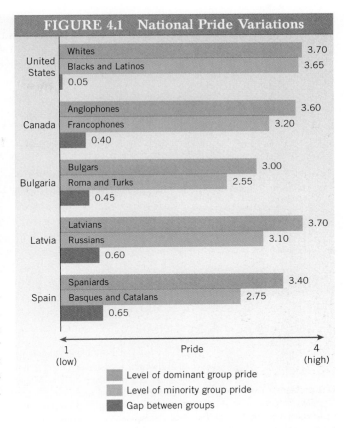

FIGURE 4.1   National Pride Variations

United States
- Whites — 3.70
- Blacks and Latinos — 3.65
- 0.05

Canada
- Anglophones — 3.60
- Francophones — 3.20
- 0.40

Bulgaria
- Bulgars — 3.00
- Roma and Turks — 2.55
- 0.45

Latvia
- Latvians — 3.70
- Russians — 3.10
- 0.60

Spain
- Spaniards — 3.40
- Basques and Catalans — 2.75
- 0.65

1 (low) — Pride — 4 (high)

- Level of dominant group pride
- Level of minority group pride
- Gap between groups

The United States comes closer than most countries to being a true nation-state. One indication is the relative levels of national pride expressed by members of each country's dominant cultural group and by members of its minority groups. As is normal, members of the dominant cultural group in every country expressed high national pride and also more national pride than did members of minority groups, which suffer discrimination. However, the gaps varied widely, with the smallest, a negligible 0.05, in the United States.

Note: In countries with more than one minority group, gap scores were averaged.
Data source: Dowley & Silver (2000), Table 5, p. 369.

MAP
Global Distribution
of Minority Groups

Global Distribution of Minority Groups

Minority Population
Percentage of the total population in groups other than the majority or plural population
- Less than 10%
- 10%–20%
- 21%–30%
- 31%–40%
- 41%–50%
- More than 50%

Very few states are ideal nation-states, ones where most of the people in the country are of one nation and where almost everyone of that nation lives within the country. Much more common are multinational states and multistate nations, as described in the text. Diversity within a state based on ethnicity, race, and religion is not necessarily divisive. Americans are fairly diverse, but most see themselves as Americans, whatever their demographic characteristics. In many other countries, though, diversity engenders separatist ethnonational groups and often leads to violence.

when separatist *Québécois* legislators in Canada's House of Commons (the dominant chamber) sought a declaration that it "recognizes that the *Québécois* form a nation." Prime Minister Stephen Harper responded by rhetorically asking and answering, "Do the *Québécois* form a nation within Canada? The answer is yes. Do the *Québécois* form an independent nation? The answer is no." Whether there will be a renewed concerted drive by Quebec to gain greater autonomy or even independence remains unclear, but at least one Canadian scholar commented, "This could become just as nasty as the last time around [1995]."[1]

Canada has avoided bloodshed over its national division, but many other multinational states have not. Some have suffered extraordinary violence. Rwanda, for one, is divided between two ethnonational groups, the minority (but politically dominant) Tutsi people and the majority Hutu people. In 1994 an orgy of killing decimated Rwanda when Hutus slaughtered some 800,000 Tutsis and their sympathizers over about 100 days and well over 1 million Tutsis and moderate Hutus fled for their lives to neighboring countries. Most recently, the violence in Iraq between Shiites and Sunnis and the quasi-autonomous status of the country's Kurds in their region in the north raise a question about Iraqi nationalism: How do many people living in Iraq see themselves first—as Iraqis or as a member of one of the religious/ethnonationalist groups?

One Nation, Multiple States

A **multistate nation** is another departure from the nation-state ideal. This type of misfit between nation and state occurs when a nation overlaps the borders of two or more states. Conflict between the states that share the nation is common (Woodwell, 2004).

One multistate nation pattern occurs when one nation dominates two or more states. The cold war created a number of such instances, including North and South Vietnam, North and South Korea, East and West Germany, and the two Yemens. The Irish in Ireland and Northern Ireland provide another possible example of a multistate nation, although the Scottish heritage of many of the Protestants in the North makes the existence of a single Irish nationality controversial. In any case, a single nation that dominates two states has an urge to unite itself by merging the two states. Often conflict over union occurs, as it did in Vietnam, Korea, Ireland, and Yemen. Today only Korea (and arguably Ireland) remain as examples of such a division.

Another multistate nation pattern is where a nation is a majority in one state and a minority in one or more other states. The 5.7 million Albanians provide a good example of this type of multistate nation. About 3.6 million of them live in Albania, where they form 95% of the population. Another 1.6 million Albanians live in and make up 90% of the population in Kosovo, a province of Serbia. Fighting broke out in 1997 when Albanian Kosovars asserted their autonomy. Serbia's brutal retaliatory campaign eventually sparked a U.S.-led NATO air war against Serbia in 1999 and the insertion of a NATO security force, Kosovo Force (KFOR), into the province, where it remains with about 17,000 troops. Fighting could erupt again, especially if the UN sponsors a referendum in Kosovo on independence. It would almost certainly win, but Serbia's foreign minister warns, "Serbia will not accept independence of Kosovo."[2] Yet another 500,000 Albanians live in Macedonia, where they constitute 25% of the country's population and are heavily concentrated in the parts of the country that border on Albania and Kosovo. Clashes between this group of Albanians and the Macedonian government during 2000 and 2001 also necessitated a NATO intervention, and a small force, now under EU control, remains.

Web Link

For a map showing the locations of ethnic Albanians in the Balkans and related commentary, visit the U.S. Institute for Peace site at **www.usip.org/pubs/specialreports/early/kosovomap.html**.

There are also multistate nations where a majority of the nation lives outside its associated state. Of about 26 million Azerbaijanis (Azeris), for example, only 28% of them live in Azerbaijan, located on the western shore of the Caspian Sea. Almost two-thirds of Azerbaijanis live in Iran, with the rest scattered throughout such nearby countries as Georgia, Russia, and Turkey. Conflict in cases where a nation dominates one state and has members in another state can occur in several situations. One is when the nation's associated state seeks to redress oppression of members of the nation living in another country. A second source of conflict is based on **irredentism**, a term based on the Italian word *irredenta* (unclaimed), and involves an effort by the nation's associated state to incorporate outlying members of the nation and their territory in another state.

One Nation, No State

A **stateless nation** is yet another pattern of misfit between state and nation. This occurs when a nation is a minority in one or more states, does not have a nation-state of its own, and wants one (Hossay, 2002). Two such stateless nations that have been much in the news in recent years are the Kurds and the Palestinians.

The Kurds   The Kurds are an ancient non-Arab people who are mostly Sunni Muslims. The most famous of all Kurds was Saladin, the great defender of Islam. He captured Jerusalem from the Christians (1187) and then defended it successfully against England's King Richard I (the Lion-Heart) and other invading Christians during the Third Crusade (1189–1192).

Estimates of the Kurdish population range between 14 million and 28 million. As the map below shows, the Kurds are spread among several states and have no country of their own. About half of them are in Turkey; Iran and Iraq each have another 20 to 25%; and smaller numbers reside in Armenia, Azerbaijan, and Syria. Sporadic and continuing attempts to establish an independent Kurdistan have caused conflicts with the countries in which the Kurds live. These disputes sometimes have involved outside countries. The United States and other countries protected the Kurds from attack by Saddam Hussein's regime in the UN-designated Kurdish Security Zone in northern Iraq from soon after the Persian Gulf War in 1991 until his fall in 2003 (Stansfield, 2005; McDowall, 2004).

Kurdish forces fought against the Iraqi army in 2003, thereby strengthening the autonomy they had enjoyed in the northern part of the country since 1991. What remains to be seen, and what worries Turkey and other neighbors of Iraq with Kurdish populations, is whether the Kurds in Iraq will be content to remain part of a reformed Iraq or will try to found an independent Kurdistan with irredentist claims on the Kurds in other countries. Under the American dominance of Iraq, its Kurds have participated in the national political process, but as that veered toward civil war and an American withdrawal, there have been ongoing and important indications of the Kurds' determination to remain at least autonomous in a post-occupation Iraq. Perhaps the clearest sign of the Kurds' long-term aspiration was the result of an informal referendum held in conjunction with the parliamentary election in 2005. Fully 98% of all Kurds voted for eventual independence. "The fact remains that we are two different nationalities in Iraq—we are Kurds and Arabs," one Kurdish leader noted.[3]

Any attempt to establish an independent Kurdistan in northern Iraq would almost certainly have significant international ramifications. For example, Turkey might intervene militarily because, as its prime minister explained, "Most Turks think, if there is a Kurdish state in northern Iraq, . . . our own Kurds will want to join with them, and, then, we will be losing Turkey's southeastern part, and, there will be a greater Kurdistan, and, Turkey will be losing its territory." As such, the prime minister warned, "Any attempt to set up a Kurdish state in northern Iraq would be considered by the Turkish state as a vital danger to Turkey. We would not let that happen. We would . . . do whatever we can . . . to kill it off."[4]

The Palestinians   The story of the Palestinians centers on the fact that they and another nation, the Jewish people, have long existed in the same area. The Jewish nation and its state, Israel, now control most of that territory; the Palestinians intend to reclaim enough of it to create their own state. The ancient dispute dates back many millennia to Abraham and his two sons: Isaac, who founded the Jewish nation, and Ishmael, the symbolic father of all Arabs. The historical ebb and flow in the region of Jews and Palestinians is cloudy and far too complex to unravel here, but we can pick up the story in 1920 when Palestine was governed by Great Britain. At that time, Palestinian Arabs were about 90% of the population.

In Europe, however, **Zionism** gathered strength in the 19th century. Zionism is the nationalist, not strictly religious, belief that Jews are a nation that should have an independent homeland. This belief and virulent anti-Semitism in Nazi Germany and elsewhere in Europe accelerated Jewish emigration to Palestine, swelling the Jewish population there from 56,000 in 1920 to 650,000 by 1948 (along with about 1 million Arabs). At that point, fighting for control erupted, the British withdrew, and Arab leaders rejected a UN plan to partition Palestine into a Jewish state and an Arab state. Israel won the ensuing war in 1948 and acquired some of the areas designated for the Arab state. About 500,000 Palestinians fled to refugee camps in Egyptian-controlled Gaza and elsewhere; another 400,000 came under the control of Jordan in an area called the West Bank (of the Jordan River), and 150,000 remained in the new state of Israel (Handelman, 2004).

Since then, Israel has fought and won three more wars with its Arab neighbors. In the 1967 war Israel captured considerable territory, including Gaza from Egypt and the West Bank (including East Jerusalem) from Jordan. Both these areas had major Palestinian populations. Victory, however, did not bring Israel peace or security. The key reason is the unresolved fate of the West Bank, which is central to Palestinians' quest for an independent homeland.

The struggle between Israelis and Palestinians for land, security, even survival has created an explosive situation that has defied resolution for over half a century. Surely, there have been times of progress. Most significantly, a majority of Israelis now grudgingly accept the idea that Palestinians should have their own state. And most Palestinians, with equal reluctance, now concede the permanent existence of Israel and that a Palestinian state will be largely confined to the West Bank. However, each time of hope for resolution has been followed by renewed violence.

At this writing in 2007, the cycle of occasional hope repeatedly slain by violence continues. A positive moment came after the death of longtime Palestinian president Yasser Arafat, when his replacement in early 2005 was the new, popularly elected leader Mahmoud Abbas. He strongly denounced terrorist tactics and tried to constrain Palestinian militants. Israel responded with a number of conciliatory moves. Raising hopes further, Abbas and Prime Minister Ariel Sharon of Israel met in the first Israeli-Palestinian summit since 2000 and agreed to cease all violence against one another. Israel then withdrew its forces from Gaza, leaving it entirely in Palestinian hands.

Soon, however, hope again faded. Prime Minister Sharon was felled by a debilitating stroke in early 2006 and was succeeded by Ehud Olmert, who shared Sharon's views but did not have his stature as a war hero, nor Sharon's ability to overcome domestic opposition to accommodation with the Palestinians. For their part, the Palestinians added their own blow to hope in 2006 by electing a parliament dominated by members of Hamas, a radical group with terrorist ties, and making one of the group's members the Palestinian prime minister. A few months later, Palestinian militants attacked an Israeli border post, killing two soldiers and capturing one, which led Israel to send its forces back into Gaza. That was soon followed by a major clash and associated regional conflict. Members of Hezbollah,

Israel and Its Neighbors

MEDITERRANEAN SEA

LEBANON

SYRIA

Nahariyyah
Acre
Haifa
Sea of Galilee
Nazareth

ISRAEL

Nabulus
Tel Aviv-Jaffa
Lod
WEST BANK
Jordan River
Ramallah   Amman
Ashdod
Jerusalem   Jericho
Ashkelon
Bethlehem
Gaza
Hebron   DEAD SEA

Beersheba

Dimona

GAZA STRIP
NEGEV DESERT   JORDAN

☐ Area gained by Israel in 1949
☐ Area occupied by Israel since 1967
☐ Area under total Palestinian control
☐ Areas of joint control

EGYPT

Elat

Did You Know That:

Hamas has two meanings. It translates from Arabic as "zeal," and it is also an Arabic acronym for Harakat al-Muqawama al-Islamiya, Islamic Resistance Movement.

another militant group, launched guerrilla attacks against Israel from positions in Lebanon, and Israel retaliated with a full-scale military assault on much of Lebanon. Israeli forces later withdrew from Lebanon and Gaza, but the region was left more unstable than in many years. Polls show that most Palestinians and Israelis want peace, but also that they are divided on the very difficult issues between them (Nabulsi, 2004). Just a few of these are the status of Jerusalem (which both claim as their rightful capital), the Palestinians' claimed "right of return" to Israel to reclaim their land, the future of Jewish settlements in the West Bank, and the legitimacy of the security fence that Israel is building in part on lands claimed by the Palestinians. It may come to pass that Palestinians and Israelis will eventually coexist peacefully in neighboring sovereign states, but such an outcome remains problematic and distant at best.

Multiple Nations, Multiple States

Still another misfit pattern that falls short of the ideal nation-state occurs when several states and several nations overlap. This complex configuration is common and is illustrated by Afghanistan, Russia, and their respective neighboring countries.

Afghanistan and Neighboring Countries Afghanistan, the countries around it, and their ethnonational groups illustrate the volatile mix created by overlapping borders among nations and states. Afghanistan exists as a legal state, but it teeters on the edge of being a **failed state**, a country so fragmented that it cannot be said to exist as a unified political or national entity. Symbolizing the ethnonational complexity within Afghanistan and the links that many of its groups have to nearby nations and countries, the word *Afghan* was coined over 1,000 years ago from an ancient Turkic word meaning "between." While there have been brief periods of some unity in the face of invaders or under strong rulers, the sense of being an Afghan has been much less central to the political identification of most people in the country than their ethnic identification. Afghanistan's ethnic groups (and their percentage of the population) include the Pashtuns (42%), Tajiks (27%), Hazaras (9%), and Uzbeks (9%), with smaller groups making up the remaining 13%.

Extending the focus outward to the neighboring countries further complicates the ethnonational tangle. To begin, there are 10 million Pashtuns in Afghanistan and another 18 million in neighboring, Punjabi-dominated Pakistan. Together this stateless Pashtun nation has some aspirations to found its own state, Pashtunistan. Further to the north are the Tajiks, the Uzbeks, and a small number of Turkmen, who are linked respectively to their ethnic brethren in the neighboring countries of Tajikistan, Uzbekistan, and Turkmenistan. Then there are the Hazaras, who claim descent from Genghis Khan and the Mongols and harbor some dreams about an independent Hazarajat. These groups speak some 34 different languages and dialects.

One ramification of this is that the United States has found that it was far easier to take over the country in 2001 and oust the Taliban regime than to create a viable, united Afghani state. The central problem, as one expert put it, is that "You don't have a functioning state [in Afghanistan]. There is no sense of nationhood. . . . Blood [kinship] is much more important."[5] Although Afghanistan now has an elected national government and a North Atlantic Treaty Organization (NATO) force remains in the country to try to maintain its unity, there is still a persistent and recently resurgent effort by the Pashtun-dominated Taliban to regain power.

Russia and Neighboring Countries Czarist Russia and its successor state, the Soviet Union, were a multiethnic empire that dissolved in 1991 into Russia and 14 other former Soviet republics (FSRs). This left a hodge-podge of nations and states that frequently resembles a *matryoshka,* the classic nested Russian folk art doll in which each doll has a smaller one inside. For example, in addition to living in their own nation-state, Russians make up 10% or more of the populations of seven other FSRs (Belarus, Estonia, Kazakhstan, Kyrgyzstan, Latvia, Moldova, and Ukraine).

Russia itself is predominantly Russian, but it has some restive ethnonational groups, especially the Chechens. The approximately 1 million mostly Muslim Chechens live in the northern Caucasus region just west of the Caspian Sea. Chechnya (or the Chechen Republic) encompasses about 6,000 square miles (a bit larger than Connecticut). Imperial Russia began a campaign in 1783 and eventually conquered the territory, but the Chechens' ongoing resistance was so strong that one Russian military governor warned there would be "no peace as long as a single Chechen remains alive."[6]

During World War II, Moscow deported the entire Chechen population to Siberia in the east because Soviet dictator Josef Stalin suspected the Chechens might assist the invading Germans in return for independence. More than one-third of all Chechens died during their time in Siberia, but they were unbowed. They were allowed to return

What was once the Soviet Union (USSR) remains a hodgepodge of nations and states. One of these nations, the Soviet republic of Georgia, reemerged when the USSR collapsed in 1991, but within it are the South Ossetians, who themselves want independence. This photograph shows a nervous Georgian soldier and local residents reacting to heavy fighting between Georgian and separatist forces.

to their native land in the mid-1950s but remained restive. Once the USSR dissolved, their quest for self-rule redoubled. Amid ferocious fighting that left 100,000 dead, the Chechens achieved autonomy in 1996, then lost it in 2000 when Russian arms again overran them. The struggle continues, however, with sporadic, often brutal fighting in Chechnya and occasional Chechen terrorist attacks in Russia. The most ghastly of these occurred in the Russian town of Beslan, where Chechen terrorists seized an elementary school in 2004. During the ensuing siege, 330 people, mostly Russian schoolchildren, were killed. For now, Russia maintains a tenuous hold on Chechnya, but current Russians leaders, like czars and commissars before them, are finding it daunting to subdue a people whose national anthem asserts in part:

> Never will we appear submissive before anyone,
> Death or Freedom—we can choose only one way. . . .
> We were born at night, when the she-wolf whelped.
> God, Nation, and the Native land.

Many of the other FSRs also have complicated ethnonational compositions. As noted above, Uzbeks and Tajiks not only live in Uzbekistan and Tajikistan, respectively, they also live in Afghanistan. To further complicate matters, numerous Tajiks live in Uzbekistan, and many Uzbeks live in Tajikistan. Numerous separatist movements also exist in the European FSRs, including those in the South Ossetia and Abkhazia regions of Georgia, the so-called Transdniester Republic within Moldova, and the Nagorno-Karabakh enclave in Azerbaijan. Each has seen fighting that could spread and bring neighboring countries into conflict. This possibility led President

Traian Băsescu of nearby Romania to describe the tensions as "transnational threats" to European stability. "We cannot leave the countries of this region as victims of European history, as unstable borderlands outside Eastern Europe," Băsescu warned.[7]

Positive and Negative Aspects of Nationalism

Nationalism has been a positive force, but it has also brought despair and destruction to the world. During an address to the UN General Assembly, Pope John Paul II spoke of these two nationalisms. One was *positive nationalism*, which the pontiff defined as the "proper love of one's country . . . [and] the respect which is due to every [other] culture and every nation."[8] The other was *negative nationalism*, "an unhealthy form of nationalism which teaches contempt for other nations or cultures . . . [and] seeks to advance the well-being of one's own nation at the expense of others."

Positive Nationalism

Most scholars agree that in its philosophical and historical genesis, nationalism was a positive force. It continues to have a number of possible beneficial effects and many defenders (Conway, 2004, Wiebe, 2002).

Nationalism promotes democracy. In the view of one scholar, "Nationalism is the major form in which democratic consciousness expresses itself in the modern world" (O'Leary, 1997:222). The logic is that nationalism, at least in so far as it is rooted in the notion of popular sovereignty, promotes the idea that political power legitimately resides with the people and that governors exercise that power only as the agents of the people. The democratic nationalism that helped spur the American Revolution has spread globally, especially since World War II, increasing the proportion of the world's countries that are fully democratic from 28% in 1950 to 46% in 2005.

Nationalism discourages imperialism. During the past 100 years alone, nationalism has played a key role in the demise of the contiguous Austro-Hungarian, Ottoman, and Russian empires and of all or most of the colonial empires controlled by the countries of Europe and the United States. Among these colonies, East Timor gained independence most recently. It was one of the last remnants of the moribund Portuguese empire when its people declared independence in 1975. Freedom was stillborn, however, when Indonesia bloodily annexed East Timor. For the East Timorese, though, Indonesian overlords were no more acceptable than European ones, and their continuing campaign for self-determination as well as considerable international pressure finally persuaded Indonesia to allow a referendum on independence in 1998. Seventy-nine percent of the East Timorese voted for independence. Indonesia's military tried to keep control by arming a horde of thugs who killed thousands of East Timorese, but security was achieved when Australia and the United Nations intervened militarily. The UN created a transitional administration for East Timor, then turned the government over to a fully independent East Timor in 2002.

Nationalism has also strengthened the resolve of other countries and their nation(s) to resist foreign domination. A century ago, the establishment of a colonial government controlled by the victorious power might have followed a conflict such as the Iraq War of 2003. Certainly the initial postwar government in Baghdad was heavily influenced by the Americans, but it was clear that real power would eventually have to be turned over to Iraqis. Global norms and even American public opinion would have reacted too strongly against a colonial takeover. Moreover, Iraqis would have been violently opposed. Although 2006 found Iraqis divided internally on many issues, one thing that united them was their desire to have U.S. and other

One of the positive aspects of nationalism is that it fortifies a people to resist foreign domination. Outsiders long controlled much of China, but the Chinese identity remained strong, and China has reemerged as a proud and fully independent country. A manifestation of this strong nationalism are these faces sculpted in the earth in Hehnan Province as part of a patriotic art performance. About 3,000 people took part, shouting patriotic slogans as they gathered around the design.

coalition forces out of their country in the near future. A poll in late 2006 found that more than three-fourths of all Iraqis suspected that the United States was planning to build permanent bases in Iraq, and 71% of Iraqis wanted the foreign forces out of their country within a year.[9]

Nationalism allows for economic development. Colonies and minority nations within states have often been shortchanged economically. Many countries in Africa and elsewhere are still struggling to overcome a colonial legacy in which the colonial power siphoned off resources for its own betterment and did little to build the economic infrastructure of the colony. This pattern also occurred in theoretically integrated multiethnic empires, such as the Soviet Union. There, the six predominantly Muslim FSRs (Azerbaijan, Kazakhstan, Kyrgyzstan, Tajikistan, Turkmenistan, and Uzbekistan) were neglected under Russian/Soviet control and still have an average per capita gross domestic product (GDP) that is only one-third of Russia's and a child mortality rate that is more than quadruple that of Russia. It is certain that these new countries face years of economic hardship, but, from their perspective, at least their efforts will be devoted to their own betterment.

Nationalism allows diversity and experimentation. Democracy, for instance, was an experiment in America in 1776 that might not have occurred in a one-world system dominated by monarchs. Diversity also allows different cultures to maintain their own values. Some analysts argue that regional or world political organization might lead to an amalgamation of cultures or, worse, to cultural imperialism, the suppression of the cultural uniqueness of the weak by the strong. For good or ill, as chapter 5 details, the world is coming closer together culturally. However, nationalism embodied in sovereign states at least helps ensure that whatever acculturation occurs will generally be adopted willingly by the people rather than dictated by an outside power.

Negative Nationalism

For all its contributions, nationalism also has a dark side. "Militant nationalism is on the rise," Bill Clinton cautioned early in his presidency. He warned that it is "transforming the healthy pride of nations, tribes, religious, and ethnic groups into

FIGURE 4.2   Ethnonational Violence

Ethnonational violent conflict rose steadily after 1950 and peaked in the mid-1990s. It has declined since then because many conflicts have ended—sometimes peacefully, sometimes with the final defeat of one group by another—and fewer new conflicts have broken out. Still, ethnonational fighting remains much more common than other forms of internal conflict or wars between countries. Whether the drop-off in violence represents a long-term shift or a short-term aberration remains to be seen.

Note: The author's interpretations of the data differ in a few instances from the classifications on the source.
Data source: "Major Episodes of Political Violence: 1946–2006," data compiled by Monty G. Marshall, Center for Systemic Peace.

cancerous prejudice, eating away at states and leaving their people addicted to the political painkillers of violence and demagoguery."[10] Illustrating this, Figure 4.2 shows that the number of ongoing ethnonational conflicts over self-determination rose steadily from 4 in 1956 to 41 in 1990. Then the number declined steadily to 22 in 2004. Perhaps ethnonational conflict will continue to decline, but it is too early to tell (Fearon & Laitin, 2003). Unfortunately, whatever the number of conflicts, the intensity and magnitude of ethnonational conflicts remain high. Moreover, these internal conflicts can become internationalized given the evidence that "states suffering from ethnic rebellions are more likely to use force and to use force first when involved in international disputes than states without similar insurgency problems" (Trumbore, 2003:183).

Although it has a number of aspects, the troubling face of nationalism begins with how nations relate to one another. By definition, nationalism is feeling a kinship with the other "like" people who make up the nation. Differentiating ourselves from others is not intrinsically bad, but it is only a small step from the salutary effects of positively valuing our we-group to the negative effects of nationalism. Because we identify with our we-group, we tend to consider the they-group as apart from us. This lack of identification with others often leads to a reluctance to help others, exclusionism, exceptionalism and xenophobia, internal oppression, and external aggression.

Reluctance to Help Others   Our nationalist sense of difference and separateness limits our sense of responsibility—even our human caring—for the "theys." Most of us not only want to help others in our we-group, but we feel we have a duty to do so through national social welfare budgets and other methods. Internationally, most of us feel much less responsible. Horrendous conditions and events that occur in other countries often evoke little notice relative to the outraged reaction that would be

JOIN THE DEBATE
Can Nationalism Go Too Far?
The Case of U.S. Minutemen

forthcoming if they happened in our own country. In the region of sub-Saharan Africa, for example, only 41% of the people live to age 55, compared to 80% of Americans. And the chances of an infant in sub-Saharan Africa perishing before his or her first birthday are 15 times greater than the risk to American babies.

If most Americans began dying before retirement age or if the death rate of American babies skyrocketed, there would be an outburst of national anguish among Americans, and vast financial resources would flow to increase adult longevity and decrease the infant mortality rate. Yet, the U.S. government's response to the equivalent human tragedy in sub-Saharan Africa is largely limited to sending about $4 billion in economic and humanitarian aid—bilateral (to individual countries) and multilateral (through international organizations)—to the region. This comes to just over $5 per person in sub-Saharan Africa or about $13 per American. Is this enough? Most Americans think so. A poll found that 64% of them thought their country was spending too much on foreign aid. Only 8% thought it too little.[11] In part, that is because, on average, Americans think that 31% of the federal budget goes to foreign aid.[12] The actual percentage is about 1% for all foreign aid, with about 0.7% for economic assistance. Ironically, the average respondent thought foreign aid should be cut to 19% of the federal budget, which would actually be a monumental increase. None of this means that Americans are uncharitable. Instead it means that, like people in other countries, Americans have a much greater sense of responsibility for people in their own country than for people in other countries. Therefore, most people contend, government aid should go primarily toward addressing needs "at home" rather than abroad.

Exclusionism   Each year, millions of people are forced or seek to flee from their homes due to political violence, poverty, and other forces beyond their control. Indeed, as chapter 14 details, refugees are a global problem. The we-they basis of nationalism creates a near-universal resistance of "them" coming to "our" country. A survey of people in 40 countries found that on average 76% of them wanted to further their country's limits on immigration, as detailed in Figure 4.3. A strong majority of Americans (81%) and Canadians (69%) felt that way, even though most of them come from immigrant stock. Opinion in the two countries with the smallest percentage of people favoring more restrictions, Japan (43%) and South Korea (37%), ironically may reflect the fact that both countries already have stringent immigration restrictions and very few immigrants.

Exceptionalism and Xenophobia   Valuing one's nation is a positive aspect of nationalism, but it too often leads to feeling superior to others or even fearing and hating them. **Xenophobia** is one destructive way in which some people relate to they-groups. This emotion involves disliking or fearing other nationalities. **Exceptionalism**, the belief that your nation is better than others, is less virulent but still troubling. A global survey taken in 43 countries found that a majority of people in 39 of them "completely" or "mostly" agreed with the statement,

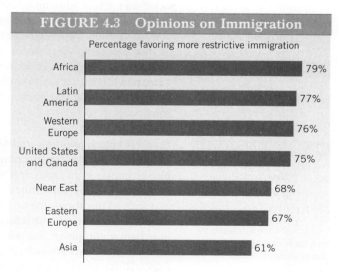

FIGURE 4.3   Opinions on Immigration

Percentage favoring more restrictive immigration

Region	Percentage
Africa	79%
Latin America	77%
Western Europe	76%
United States and Canada	75%
Near East	68%
Eastern Europe	67%
Asia	61%

Most people around the world are reluctant to admit immigrants to their country because of the "we-they" differentiation between their nation and others. Globally, 72% of those polled felt that way, with a majority of respondents in every region favoring tighter restrictions on immigration.

Note: The average was based on averaging the 42 countries involved in the poll, not the regions.

Data source: Pew Research Center (2002).

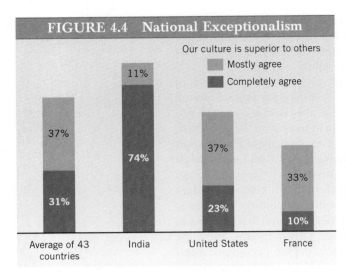

FIGURE 4.4   National Exceptionalism

Our culture is superior to others

Mostly agree

Completely agree

- Average of 43 countries: 37% / 31%
- India: 11% / 74%
- United States: 37% / 23%
- France: 33% / 10%

Exceptionalism, feeling superior culturally or in other ways to others, is one negative aspect of nationalism. As evident here, exceptionalism is common. Indeed, a majority of people in 39 of the 43 countries surveyed agreed that, "Our people are not perfect, but our culture is superior to others." Contrary to stereotypes the French were least exceptionalistic, and Americans were a bit below average. Indians were the most exceptionalistic.

Data source: Pew Research Center (2003).

Web Link

The impact of the Battle of Kosovo (1389) on the Serbs' sense of oppression is captured in the heroic painting *The Maiden of Kosovo* and the epic poem of the same title, both available at: **www.kosovo.net/history/dorich _kosovo/kosovo16.htm/.**

"Our people are not perfect, but our culture is superior to others." Overall, 68% of people felt this way. Indians were the most exceptionalistic, and, defying a common stereotype, the French were least exceptionalistic. The view of people in these two countries and others is shown in Figure 4.4. Some critics charge that among other recent instances, the Wilsonian impulse to advance democracy in the world that helped persuade the Bush administration to invade Iraq is an example of the exceptionalist urge to reshape the world in your own image (Lieven, 2004).

Xenophobia and exceptionalism often lead to conflict (Marx, 2003; Wimmer, 2002). This reality moved Voltaire to lament in 1764 that "it is sad that being a good patriot often means being the enemy of the rest of mankind."[13] Feelings of hatred between groups are especially powerful if there is a history of conflict or oppression. Past injuries inflicted "by another ethnic group [are] remembered mythically as though the past were the present."[14] Understanding the intensity that xenophobia can reach helps explain much of what has happened in the Balkans since the early 1990s. An emotional catalyst for Serbs centers on the Battle of Kosovo in 1389. In it, the Ottoman Turks defeated Serbia's Prince Lazar, thus beginning five centuries of Muslim domination. The battle, according to one commentary, is "venerated among the Serbs in the same way Texans remember the Alamo." Adds Serb historian Dejan Medakovic, "Our morals, ethics, mythology were created at that moment, when we were overrun by the Turks. Kosovo . . . has permeated the Serbian people."[15] The festering mythic wound of 1389 for the predominately Christian Orthodox Serbs spilled its poison through their so-called ethnic cleansing attacks on Bosnian Muslims in the early 1990s, then on Kosovar Muslims later in the decade.

Cultural Discrimination and Oppression   In those states with a dominant ethnonational group and one or more minority groups, the dominant group almost always has political, economic, and social advantages over the other(s). At its extreme, dominant groups sometimes violently suppress minority groups or even attempt genocide. This aptly characterizes the Serbs' ethnic cleansing frenzy in Bosnia and Kosovo, the genocidal attacks on the Tutsis by the Hutus in Rwanda, and the recent murderous campaign against black Christian and black Muslim groups by Arab Muslims in Sudan. An even more horrific example occurred in Nazi Germany, where Adolf Hitler preached in *Mein Kampf* that pure Germans were an "Aryan nation" that epitomized human development (Eastwell, 2006). By contrast, Russians and other Slavic people were considered marginal humans to be kept as virtual and expendable slaves in segregated and degrading conditions. Jews and Gypsies were "nonpeople" and "racial vermin" to be exterminated, along with the insane and homosexuals.

Even in less dire circumstances, when the oppression of minorities is limited to economic and social deprivation, conflict often occurs. Almost inevitably, the disadvantaged groups become restive. However, their complaints often get little positive response because, as UN Secretary-General Kofi Annan pointed out, the social and economic inequality of minority groups "tends to be reflected in unequal access to political power that too often forecloses paths to peaceful change."[16] Not surprisingly, oppressed groups then take direct action if they are unable to resolve their grievances through the legal or political processes. In more fortunate countries, these take the form of protest marches, economic boycotts, and other peaceful tactics. The strategy followed by American blacks led by the Reverend Martin Luther King during the 1960s serves as an example. Other countries are less fortunate, and many of the numerous ethnonational wars represented in Figure 4.2 have been the result of frustrated minority groups taking up arms when less violent avenues of action led nowhere.

Imperialism   Negative nationalism can lead to external aggression based on the belief that it is acceptable to conquer or otherwise incorporate other nations. Russian/Soviet history provides an example. The country was a classic multiethnic empire built on territories seized by centuries of czarist Russian expansion and furthered by Soviet arms. From its beginning 500 years ago as the 15,000-square-mile Duchy of Moscovy (half the size of Maine), Russia/the USSR grew to be the world's largest country. This expansion is shown in the map below. Many of those territories were

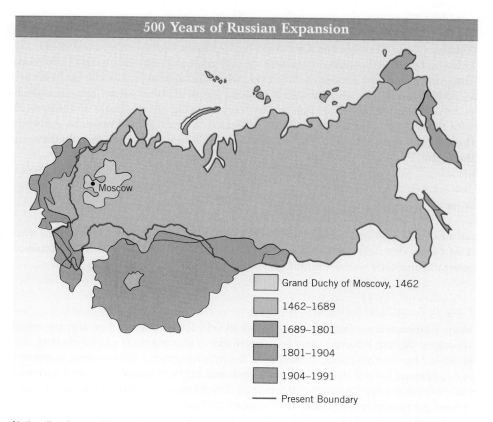

500 Years of Russian Expansion

- Grand Duchy of Moscovy, 1462
- 1462–1689
- 1689–1801
- 1801–1904
- 1904–1991
- —— Present Boundary

Nationalism has positive and negative effects, and both are illustrated in the history of Russia. Among the negative effects, nationalism often prompts expansionism. The Grand Duchy of Moscovy was about half the size of Maine when it was founded in about 1480. It expanded under Russian czars and then Soviet commissars to become what was the world's largest country.

lost in 1991 when the Soviet Union fragmented, and Russia's weakened position precludes any determined attempt to reassert its earlier domination of its neighbors. Indeed, old-fashioned imperialism may have become too costly economically and diplomatically to pursue in the future.

Yet it may be well to remember the warning of Karl Marx (1818–1883) that "the policy of Russia is changeless. Its methods, its tactics, its maneuvers may change, but the polar star of its policy—world domination—is a fixed star."[17] Indications that Marx may have been right continue (Bugajski, 2004). For example, Russia's parliament, the Duma, has passed resolutions asserting that the dissolution of the Soviet Union (and, by inference, the independence of the FSRs) was illegal and welcoming secessionist areas from other FSRs to (re)join Russia. "What Russian deputies did reveals their neo-imperialistic ambitions," a diplomat from a neighboring FSR worried.[18]

Russian ambitions were also evident in 2004, when in Ukraine's presidential election, President Putin supported the fraudulent election of Russian-leaning candidate Viktor Yanukovych over Western-leaning Viktor Yushchenko. Massive protests by Yushchenko supporters and pressure from the West forced Putin to stand aside as new, internationally monitored elections were called, and Yushchenko won a resounding victory. Russia is also meddling in several other FSRs, by supporting Russian nationals in the breakaway region of Transdniester in Moldova and also assisting separatist movements in the South Ossetia and Abkhazia regions of Georgia. President Putin has not been willing so far to be overt, but in 2006, the Duma's deputy speaker argued, "We should immediately establish diplomatic relations with Abkhazia, South Ossetia and Transdniester."[19] Russia has also supported Alexander Lukashenko, the dictatorial president of Belarus, based on his interest in eventually uniting the two countries. However, when Lukashenko wavered on that path in 2006, President Putin retaliated by ending the delivery of subsidized natural gas in an effort to impoverish Belarus to force it back on the path of integration with Russia. "Raising gas prices . . . is equivalent to breaking off relations entirely," Lukashenko warned Putin. "We will survive, but you will lose the last ally [among the FSRs]."[20]

Self-Determination as a Goal

An additional gap between the ideal and reality of nationalism is related to the wisdom of self-determination as a goal (Danspeckgruber, 2002). As with nationalism generally, there are positive and negative aspects of self-determination.

Positive Aspects of Self-Determination

Many observers have lauded the principle of self-determination. For one, President Woodrow Wilson believed that "self-determinism is not a mere phrase. It is an imperative principle of action."[21] Moreover, the origins of many nation-states are rooted in the demand for self-determination of their nation. For example, the Declaration of Independence begins with the proclaimed determination of Americans to "assume among the powers of the earth, the separate and equal station to which the laws of nature and of nature's God entitle them."

Certainly, there are numerous reasons to support self-determination. In addition to the benefits of nationalism noted earlier, self-determination ends many of the abuses that stem from ethnic oppression. If all ethnic groups were allowed to peacefully found their own sovereign units or join those of their ethnic brethren, then the tragedies of Bosnia, Chechnya, East Timor, Kosovo, Rwanda, Sudan, and many other strife-torn peoples and countries would not have occurred.

Concerns about Self-Determination

The principle of self-determination becomes more problematic in practice. The core problem is that there are thousands of ethnic groups worldwide. Each has the potential to develop a national consciousness and to seek independence or autonomy. If the principle of self-determination is valid, then what would the world be like if each of these groups was able to establish its own sovereign state? Before dismissing such an idea as absurd, recall that political scientists widely recognize the existence of Barber's (1996) tribalism tendency: the urge to break away from current political arrangements and, often, to form into smaller units. To do so involves several potential problems.

Untangling Groups   Untangling groups is one challenge presented by self-determination. Various nations are intermingled in many places. Bosnia is such a place; Bosnian Muslims, Croats, and Serbs often lived in the same cities, on the same streets, in the same apartment buildings. How does one disentangle these groups and assign them territory when each wants to declare its independence or to join with its ethnic kin in an existing country?

A second problem that the principle of self-determination raises is the prospect of dissolving existing states, ranging from Canada (Quebec), through Great Britain (Scotland and Wales), to Spain (Basque region and Catalonia). Americans also need to ponder this problem. They have long advocated the theory of a right of self-determination. One has to wonder, however, how Wilson would have applied this principle to national minorities in the United States. Should, for example, the principle of self-determination mean that Americans support those native Hawaiians who claim correctly that they were subjugated by Americans a century ago and who want to reestablish an independent Hawaii?

In other places, creating ethnically homogeneous states would have multiple complexities. To create nation-states out of the various ethnonational groups in Afghanistan would require disentangling many places where the groups overlap. It would also include some groups joining neighboring countries such as Tajikistan and Uzbekistan. But then what would happen to the Tajiks who live in Uzbekistan and the Uzbeks who live in Tajikistan? And in the case of the Pashtuns, a Pashtunistan would have to be created by pieces taken out of Pakistan and Iran, as well as Afghanistan.

Microstates   A third problem of self-determination relates to the rapidly growing number of independent countries, many of which have a marginal ability to survive on their own. Is it wise to allow the formation of **microstates**, countries with tiny populations, territories, and/or economies? Such countries have long existed, with Andorra, Monaco, and San Marino serving as examples. But in recent years, as colonialism has become discredited, many more of these microstates have become established. The problems microstates create are detailed in chapter 6. We can say here, though, that about one-third of the world's countries have populations smaller than that of Los Angeles, California, and about 10% have less land than that city. Such countries often cannot defend themselves, cannot economically

ANALYZE THE ISSUE
Taiwan

sustain themselves, or both. This incapacity to perform one or both of two basic obligations of a state—to provide for the security and the economic welfare of its citizens—undermines such states' reason for being, increases economic burdens on the rest of the world, and creates potentially unstable power vacuums (Klabbers, 2006).

International Instability   Allowing current states to fragment could also decrease regional and even world stability. The concern about microstates has already been discussed. Another type of threat to international stability related to self-determination was set in motion by the U.S. invasion of Iraq in 2003. Among other consequences, toppling Saddam Hussein increased the potential for a dismembered Iraq. It is divided among the majority Shiite Muslims, Sunni Muslims (who dominated under Saddam Hussein), and Kurds. As noted earlier, most Kurds' ultimate goal is an independent Kurdistan. Trying to achieve that goal, however, would almost certainly meet with violent resistance from what remained of Iraq. Moreover, Baghdad might find a ready ally in Turkey, which fears losing its own Kurdish region to an emergent Kurdistan. Yet another concern about a fragmented Iraq is that its Shiite-dominated eastern region might fall within the orbit of Shiite Iran. Additionally, a weakened Iraq would no longer be an effective buffer separating Iran from Saudi Arabia and the other oil-rich Arab states that lie to the south of Iraq along the western shore of the Persian Gulf. U.S. and other foreign troops kept Iraq from atomizing after Saddam's downfall, but once they are gone, as they will be relatively soon, the prospect of a truly united Iraq is grim.

Deciding about Self-Determination   Existing countries face important choices when deciding whether to recognize new countries. Among other things, as new countries come into existence, the global community, through its commitments to the United Nations and to the integrity of the international system, acquires some obligation to assist them in the face of external aggression. Similarly, new and impoverished states add pressure on already inadequate international economic assistance through donor countries and international organizations. Furthermore, recognizing secessionist movements as new states arguably encourages yet more ethnonational groups to seek independence.

Given that there is a large array of ethnonational groups with aspirations to self-determination that believe their goals are just as legitimate as were American goals in 1776, the issue is whether to support them at all, or if not, which ones and why? Some commentators advocate broad support of self-determination, which one analyst calls "the most powerful idea in the contemporary world" (Lind, 1994:88). Others reply that "self-determination movements . . . have largely exhausted their legitimacy. . . . It is time to withdraw moral approval from most of the movements and see them for what they mainly are—destructive" (Etzioni, 1993:21; Dahbour, 2003). Between these two ends of the spectrum of opinion, many seek a set of standards by which to judge whether or not a claim to the right of secession is legitimate. One such standard is whether a minority people is being discriminated against by a majority population. Simple viability is another standard. It asks whether a potential state has the human and economic resources to function independently. Whatever the standard, though, it is certain that applying the principle of self-determination is difficult in a complex world. How would you write the script for self-determination in the future? That is the question asked in the debate box, "Should There Be a Limit to Self-Determination?"

DEBATE THE POLICY SCRIPT

Should There Be a Limit to Self-Determination?

Self-determination is one concept that is hard to oppose. After all, the United States and most other countries were born amid nationalistic assertions of a claimed right to self-determination. Since then, President Woodrow Wilson and other U.S. leaders have also lauded the importance of the principle of self-determination.

Despite its appeal in the abstract, self-determination becomes more problematic when faced with some realities. Take Tokelau, for instance. This self-administering territory of New Zealand lies about halfway between New Zealand and Hawaii. It is made up of three small atolls that together measure 3.9 square miles, about one-fiftieth the size of Tulsa, Oklahoma. Tokelau's population numbers 1,396 and its highest point is about 50 feet above sea level. It has neither farmable land nor commercially valuable natural resources. Tokelau's largest source of income is the $4 million in annual aid it receives from New Zealand.

Although there are no charges that the Tokelauans' human rights are being abused, there are those who decry the fact that the islands were taken by colonial Great Britain in 1889 and turned over to New Zealand to administer in 1925. Such sentiments led to a UN-sponsored referendum in which the Tokelauans could decide on whether to join the world's other 193 sovereign states. An independent Tokelau would be the world's second-smallest and least-populated state, larger only than the Holy See (the Vatican; population, 932; area, 0.17 of a square mile).

On February 16, 2006, Tokelauans voted. They favored independence by a 349-to-232 majority, but that 60% yes vote fell 30 votes short of the two-thirds majority required for independence under the terms of the referendum. Independence advocates were dismayed but remained determined, and it is likely that the UN will soon ask for a new vote.

What Do You Think?

Should entities like Tokelau become sovereign states? It and 15 other "non-self-governing territories," such as the Falkland Islands, Gibraltar, Guam, and Pitcairn, are on the UN's list for potential decolonization, and there are numerous other territories with relatively small populations and economies that also arguably have as good a claim to independence as Tokelau does. What, if anything, should be the criteria for self-determination?

The idea of self-determination argues that the South Pacific people of Tokelau should be independent if they wish. Yet there are pragmatic questions about whether the 1,400 people and their three tiny atolls should be able to join the ranks of sovereign states. One of Tokelau's limitations is that it has no ports or airports, and most cargo coming into Tokelau has to be unloaded from ships beyond the reefs, then brought ashore in small boats, as seen here.

NATIONALISM AND THE FUTURE

People have almost certainly always identified with one or another group, be it based on family, extended clan, religion, or some other basis. However, nationalism, the particular form of political identification that welds a mutually identifying people, their territory, and self-governance, is much more recent. Some scholars find traces of nationalism extending back to ancient times, but there is little disagreement that nationalism has only been an important political idea for about the past 500 years and that it did not reach its current ascendancy as a source of primary political identification until the 19th and 20th centuries.

What of the future, though? Since nationalism has not always been, it is not immutable. It could weaken or even disappear as our dominant sense of political identification. In addition to recognizing this possibility, we should ask ourselves how we would evaluate the persistence or demise of nationalism. Would that be positive or negative?

The Recent Past and Present of Nationalism

Nationalism continues to thrive and dominate our political consciousness in most ways. Yet, doubts about nationalism have increased in some circles. It has weakened somewhat, and there are those who predict and/or advocate its further diminution or even its extinction as the primary focus of political identification.

The Predicted Demise of Nationalism

World War II changed the thinking of many people about nationalism. They blamed fascism and other forms of virulently aggressive nationalism for the war itself, and for the other horrors of the period. Moreover, critics argued that the second global war in 30 years demonstrated that the state system based on national antagonism was not only outdated, but dangerous. The advent of weapons of mass destruction added urgency to the case, making "the nation and the nation-state . . . anachronisms in the atomic age."[22] As a counterpoint, the establishment of the United Nations in 1945 symbolized the desire to progress from competitive, often conflictive nationalism toward cooperative globalism.

The thrust of this thinking led numerous scholars to predict the imminent demise of the national state or, at least, its gradual withering away. As it turned out, such retirement announcements and obituaries proved reminiscent of the day in 1897 when an astonished Mark Twain read in the paper that he had died. Reasonably sure that he was still alive, Twain hastened to assure the world: "The reports of my death are greatly exaggerated." Similarly, one scholar notes that contrary to predictions of nationalism's impending extinction, "this infuriatingly persistent anomaly . . . refused to go away" (Wiebe, 2001:2). Instead, nationalism gained strength as a world force.

SIMULATION
The Future of the State:
Will Nationalism Survive?

Persistent Nationalism

The continued strength of nationalism is unquestionable. Insistence on national self-determination has almost tripled the number of states in existence since World War II. For most of this time, the primary force behind the surge of nationalism was the anti-imperialist independence movements in Africa, Asia, and elsewhere. More recently, nationalism has reasserted itself in Europe. Germany reemerged when West Germany and East Germany reunited. More commonly, existing states disintegrated. Czechoslovakia became two states and Yugoslavia eventually dissolved into six countries. Even more momentously, another 15 came into being when the last great multiethnic empire, the vast realm of Russia, then the USSR, atomized. Except for East Timor, Eritrea, Namibia, and Palau, all of the states that have achieved independence since 1989 are in Eastern Europe or are FSRs. There are also nationalist stirrings—in some cases demands—among the Scots, Irish, and Welsh in Great Britain; the Basques and Catalans in Spain; and among other ethnonational groups elsewhere in Europe.

Another sign of persistent nationalism is the continuing attachment of people to their countries (Gijsberts, Hagendoorn, & Scheepers, 2004). As detailed in Figure 4.5, one cross-national survey found that a strong majority of all people said they would rather be a citizen of their own country than any other. Somewhat unexpectedly, the strength of nationalist sentiment was not closely connected to a country's economic circumstances. For example, among those in relatively poor countries, 88% of both Bulgarians and Filipinos felt that way. By contrast, only 50% of the relatively wealthy Dutch shared that view (Mayda & Rodrik, 2005). Asking people if they would move to another country yields similar results. One such poll found that only 18% of those in relatively poor India would do so, while 38% of those in comparatively well-off Great Britain would.[23]

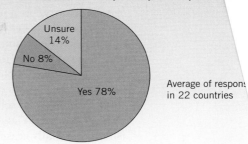

FIGURE 4.5   Nationalist Sentiment

I would rather be a citizen of my country than any other

Unsure 14%

No 8%

Yes 78%

Average of responses in 22 countries

Nationalism makes most people feel attached to their country. One survey found that a large majority of the people polled in 22 countries worldwide felt that way. Only a small percentage was ambivalent; even fewer people were emotionally unattached to their country.

Data source: International Social Survey Program, National Identity Study, 2003/2004; Mayda & Rodrick (2005), Table 12, p. 1425.

The Future of Nationalism

It may seem contradictory, but the continuing strength of nationalism does not necessarily mean that those who earlier predicted its demise were wrong. Perhaps they were only premature. This possibility is raised by numerous signs that nationalism is waning and that states are weakening. Therefore, a critical question is whether nationalism will significantly weaken or even die out.

The answer is unclear. The existence of divergent political identities based on community, language, religion, and other cultural differences extend as far back into time as we can see (Smith, 2004, 2005). From a biblical perspective, there may have been a single people at the time of Adam and Eve and their immediate descendants. But later in the first book of the Bible, God divides them after they attempt to build the Tower of Babel up to the heavens. To defeat that pretentious plan, God creates different languages to complicate communication. "Behold," God commands, "the people is one, and they have all one language. . . . [L]et us go down, and there confound their language, that they may not understand one another's speech" (Genesis 11:6–7).

Whether this tale is taken literally or symbolically, the point is that diverse cultural identities are ancient and, some analysts would say, important—perhaps inherent—human traits, stemming from the urge to have the psychological security of belonging to a we-group (Hammond & Axelrod, 2006). It may be, for example, that being a member of a nation both "enables an individual to find a place . . . in the world [in] which he or she lives" and also to find "redemption from personal oblivion" through a sense of being part of "an uninterrupted chain of being"

MAP
World Languages

Did You Know That:

There are 6,809 languages spoken in the world. That is a decline of 306 since 1600, with another 500 or so currently in danger of extinction.

(Tamir, 1995:432). Yet it must also be said that group identification and nationalism are not synonymous. The sense of sovereignty attached to cultural identification is relatively modern. "Nationalism and nations have not been permanent features of human history," as one scholar puts it (O'Leary, 1997:221). Therefore, nationalism, having not always existed, will not necessarily always be the world's principal form of political orientation.

What does the future hold? One view is that nationalism will continue as the main source of political identification. "Given that globalization has done little to diminish the nation's political [and] ideological . . . appeal—and in many cases has invigorated it," one scholar writes, "we are stuck with the nation—politically, academically, practically, and theoretically" (Croucher, 2003:21). Others expect nationalism to eventually cease to be an important political phenomenon. The most common view among political scientists is a middle position that holds that nationalism will persist for the foreseeable future as a key sense of the political identification of most people but that it will not enjoy the unrivaled center stage presence it has had for several hundred years.

Also unclear is what would follow if state-centric nationalism were to die out. One possibility is that it will be replaced by culture, religion, or some other demographic characteristic as the primary sense of political self. Alternatively, a sense of global nationalism could emerge based on the similarities among all humans and their common experiences, needs, and goals. One such scholar envisages "a nation coextensive with humanity" that would then come together in a "United States of the World" (Greenfeld, 1992:7).

What can we conclude? Will nationalism persist "until the last syllable of recorded time," to borrow words from Shakespeare's *Macbeth*? More importantly, should it, given its benefits and drawbacks? You can help supply the answer to these questions because the script for tomorrow's drama on the world stage has yet to be written.

ANALYZE THE ISSUE
Nationalism: A Melting Pot?

CHAPTER SUMMARY

UNDERSTANDING NATIONS, NATIONALISM, AND NATION-STATES

1. Nationalism is one of the most important factors in international politics. It defines where we put our primary political loyalty, and that is in the nation-state. Today the world is divided and defined by nationalism and nation-states.

2. Nations, nation-states, and nationalism are all key concepts that must be carefully defined and clearly differentiated and understood.

3. The political focus on nationalism has evolved and become ascendant over the last five centuries.

NATIONALISM IN PRACTICE: ISSUES AND EVALUATION

4. There are differences between the theory of nationalism and its application. To evaluate nationalism objectively, these must be considered.

5. One issue is that the ideal nation-state is more myth than reality. In practice the boundaries of nations and the borders of states are seldom congruent.

6. Another issue is negative aspects, as well as positive aspects of nationalism.

7. The problems associated with nationalism also raise issues about self-determination and the question of whether this liberal ideal is always wise in the real world.

NATIONALISM AND THE FUTURE

8. After World War II, some predicted an end to nationalism, but they were wrong. Today nationalism is stronger, and the independence of Afro-Asian countries, the former Soviet republics, and other states has made it even more inclusive.

9. In a world of transnational global forces and problems, many condemn nationalism as outmoded and perilous. Some even predict its decline and demise.

Such predictions are, however, highly speculative, and nationalism will remain a key element and a powerful force in the foreseeable future.

For simulations, debates, and other interactive activities, a chapter quiz, Web links, and much more, visit **www.mhhe.com/rourke12/** and go to chapter 4. Or, while accessing the site, click on Course-Related Headlines and view recent international relations articles in the *New York Times*.

KEY TERMS

ethnonational group
exceptionalism
failed state
ideology
irredentism

microstate
multinational states
multistate nation
nation
nationalism

nation-state
political identity
popular sovereignty
self-determination
state building

stateless nation
xenophobia
Zionism

Globalism: The Alternative Orientation

What wouldst thou do with the world,
. . . if it lay in thy power?

—William Shakespeare, *Timon of Athens*

Why, here's a change indeed in the commonwealth!
What shall become of me?

—William Shakespeare, *Measure for Measure*

When Rudyard Kipling predicted in 1889 that "East is East, and West is West, and never the twain shall meet," he could not have foreseen the degree to which this chapter's subject matter, globalization and transnationalism, would prove him wrong. Now you and this Cambodian Buddhist monk could e-mail one another, swap computer files, or use your ability to communicate globally to form a transnational group to promote your common interests.

MOST OF US USUALLY THINK OF THE WORLD in terms of its parts, such as different countries and peoples. Nationalism and its message of primary political loyalty to and concern with our nation and our state is the core political concept associated with this view of a divided world. Indeed, this orientation is so familiar that most people find it difficult to imagine alternatives. There are, though, and this chapter challenges our traditional view and explores such alternatives by focusing on three closely related concepts: globalism, globalization, and transnationalism.

Globalism is the view that the world is more than just its parts, that it is also a whole, one which has many commonalities and connections that cut across political borders, national identities, and cultural differences. **Globalization** is the process of expanding globalism and denotes the increasing integration of economics, communications, and culture across national boundaries. As such, globalism is the world's "underlying basic network," while globalization refers to the "dynamic shrinking" of the factors that divide the world economically and socially (Nye, 2002:1).

Transnationalism is the most "personal" of our three main concepts here. It focuses on the identity of and contacts among individuals and groups acting in a private (nongovernmental) capacity. Thus, transnationalism is primarily concerned with **civil society**, a concept that includes all the cultural, social, economic, and other activities of individuals and groups that are beyond direct government control. More specifically, transnationalism denotes a range of cross-border political identities and signifies social, economic, and political links among people and private organizations across national borders. Many of these regional and global links serve to promote or intensify a common sense of identity among people, and these ties can form the basis of political self-identification that in some cases can rival or supplant nationalism. Religion, for example, often transcends political borders and identities. As with nationalism, transnationalism has its positive and negative sides. It can promote cooperation, but it can sometimes pit groups against one another.

All three of these phenomena have long existed, but they have been gaining strength in recent decades. Therefore, human interaction and political identification are moving beyond traditional national boundaries and creating myriad regional and global links. Keep your mind open to the possibilities of these different ways of connecting yourself to the political world even if they seem far-fetched. Bear in mind that in Shakespeare's time people believed, as he had a character exclaim in

This drawing captures the intermeshing of the world's economy, communications, transportation, and many other functions in the globalization process.

The Taming of the Shrew, "He that is giddy thinks the world turns round." To simplify the complex changes that are occurring, it is possible to divide them into two related trends: globalization and transnationalism.

GLOBALISM

Although the notion of globalism is becoming more familiar and gaining wider acceptance in recent decades, it is not a new idea. Indeed, the idea has ancient origins. Globalist thought in Western culture can be traced to Stoicism, a philosophy that flourished in ancient Greece and Rome from 300 B.C. to A.D. 200. The Stoics saw themselves as part of humanity, not as members of one or another smaller political community. As such, Stoics were cosmopolitan, a word derived from combining the Greek words *cosmos* (world) and *polis* (city). One of those with a sense of being a global citizen was the Roman emperor Marcus Aurelius, who wrote in *Meditations,* "my . . . country, so far as I am [the emperor], is Rome, but so far as I am a man, it is the world."

Other ancient, non-Western great philosophical traditions contain teachings that are similar to the cosmopolitan thrust of Stoicism. Philosophies such as Confucianism and religions such as Buddhism and Hinduism all contain transnational elements. For example, Siddhartha Gautama (ca. 563–483 B.C.), who became known as the Buddha, urged that we adopt a universal perspective. "Whatsoever, after due examination and analysis, you find to be conducive to the good, the benefit, the welfare of all beings," he taught, "that doctrine believe and cling to, and take it as your guide."

Although Stoicism declined, the concept of transcending local political identity remained alive over the centuries. During the Middle Ages, the Roman Catholic Church was a globalist force. As one study notes, "The pope's temporal rule in Vatican City reminds twenty-first-century observers" of the Roman Catholic Church's early "notion of political unity" with its "roots in medieval Christendom and papal claims of universal temporal authority" (Nelsen & Guth, 2003:4).

Still later, globalist thought was evident in the philosophy of Thomas Paine and other revolutionaries of the late 18th century. Americans remember Paine as a patriot of their revolution, but that is an ill-fitting description. Indeed, Paine's primary political identification was not as an American. Instead, he described himself as a "citizen of the world" and was dubious about countries because they "limited citizenship to the soil, like vegetation." Paine's writing helped galvanize Americans during their struggle for independence, but he wrote in *The Rights of Man* (1779) that he would have played "the same part in any other country [if] the same circumstances [had] arisen."[1] Putting this view into practice, Paine also supported the French Revolution, which he saw as continuing the work of its American counterpart and leading a "march [of liberty] on the horizon of the world. . . . [that nothing] can arrest" (Fitzsimons, 1995:579). That transnational march, Paine predicted, would lead to free trade and to an international congress to resolve differences among states. Thus today's globalization would have neither surprised nor dismayed Paine.

During the same era, the philosopher Immanuel Kant took the idea of international cooperation for peace even further. He wrote in *Idea for a Universal History from a Cosmopolitan Point of View* (1784) that countries should abandon their "lawless state of savagery and enter a federation of people in which every state could expect to derive its security and rights . . . from a united power and the law-governed decisions of a united will." The thinking of nineteenth-century German communist philosophers Friedrich Engels and Karl Marx also contained strong transnational elements.

They believed that all human divisions were based on economic class and that the state was a tool of the wealthy bourgeoisie to oppress the proletariat. Therefore, *The Communist Manifesto* (1848) explained, "Workingmen have no country." Moreover, Engels predicted that once the proletariat prevailed, "the state would lose its purpose as the "special repressive force" of the bourgeoisie and, being "superfluous," would "die out of itself."

Marxist thought has declined dramatically, while globalist thought has persisted and strengthened in recent decades. It is, for example, a key component in idealism/classic liberalism, a school of thought that is part of the overall liberal approach to analyzing world politics. This is discussed in extensive detail in chapter 1 and can be reviewed there. That chapter also explores constructivism and postmodernism, schools of thought with which globalism and the related idea of transnationalism are also often, if not necessarily, associated. Each of these theories emphasizes that nationalism is not preordained and conflict is not inevitable. Instead both stress that we have considerable latitude to determine how we conceive of ourselves and our ties with others. This includes the possibility of conceiving human beings as more similar than different, of primarily identifying politically with the world and humankind rather than with a country and ethnonational group, and seeing self-interest and long-term global interests as synonymous rather than conflictive.

GLOBALIZATION

Globalism and its advance through globalization may seem fairly abstract concepts, but in reality they are everyday phenomena for each of us. The morning activities of your author include working on the chapter you are now reading and preparing lecture notes for a class. Globalization permeates these activities. My computer keyboard was made in Thailand, the mouse came from China, the monitor was produced in South Korea, and the CD I use to back up my files was manufactured in Taiwan. Both my phone and desk calculator are from Malaysia. During my work today I have connected with Web sites in more than a half-dozen countries. My morning newspaper's top stories include President Bush's decision to "surge" 21,000 more American troops into Iraq, the ongoing sectarian strife in that country, preliminary indications that global warming made 2006 the warmest year on record, and passage by the House of Representatives of most of the 9/11 Commission's recommendations for new programs to protect Americans against terrorism. Getting back to my immediate activities, this book will be produced in the United States, but there is a good chance the paper started as a tree in Canada, and my editor is originally from India. The shirt I am wearing is from Mauritius, my shoes were made in China, and my sweater began its existence in Ireland. The car I drove to the office today was assembled in Mexico and propelled by fuel probably imported from Venezuela, Nigeria, or another foreign source. My class this afternoon has students from a variety of countries beyond the United States, and my graduate assistant is Israeli. If you think about it, globalization is probably entwined with your daily existence as much as it is with mine.

SIMULATION
Transnational Personal Inventory

Factors Accelerating Globalization

To a degree, globalization is ancient. It has been under way since the first isolated tribes and other groups of humans began to trade and otherwise interact with one another. Yet from another perspective, globalization is primarily a modern phenomenon

FIGURE 5.1 Global Trade, 1929–1938

Annual global trade: US$ billions

$32.7

$26.1

$18.7

$16.0

$11.9

$12.6 $12.4 $12.2 $13.0 $14.1

1929 1930 1931 1932 1933 1934 1935 1936 1937 1938

Increasingly restrictive trade policies of many countries in the 1920s were followed by a collapse of global trade, which sank 64% between 1929 and 1934. Many analysts believe that the Great Depression helped foster fascism and, in turn, World War II. Economic globalization is partly a result of policy instituted after World War II to promote freer economic interchange in order to minimize chances of a recurrence of global economic turmoil and subsequent war.

Data source: Dallin (1945).

because the speed with which globalization has progressed has increased greatly during the past two hundred years or so and even more extraordinarily since World War II. The modern acceleration of globalization is the product of two factors: technological change and government policy.

Technological advances have rapidly expanded the speed with which merchandise, money, people, information, and ideas move over long distances. Certainly people, money, culture, and knowledge have flowed across political borders since ancient times. What is different, though, is the speed at which globalization is now proceeding. As discussed in chapter 2 (see Figure 2.1, p. 44), about 90% of history's significant technological advances have occurred since 1800, and the rate of discovery and invention has been accelerating during that time. Be it the Internet, jet travel, or some other advance, a great deal of this technological innovation is moving the world away from the national orientation that has dominated for several centuries and toward a growing global connectedness. "It's a Flat World, After All," the title of an article by a veteran journalist telling "a tale of [globalized] technology and geoeconomics that is fundamentally reshaping our lives," is a bit overdrawn, but it captures the importance of globalization.[2]

Government policy is a second factor that has promoted globalization, especially on the economic front. After World War I, countries increasingly tried to protect their economies from foreign competition by instituting trade restrictions in the form of high tariffs and by impeding the free exchange of currencies. In hindsight, policy makers concluded this approach had been disastrous. Much of Europe struggled economically during the 1920s, then collapsed at the end of the decade. Between 1929 and 1932 industrial production in Europe fell 50% and unemployment shot up to 22%. The U.S. stock market crashed in 1929, and the American economy soon imploded, as did the economies of Japan and other countries. Global trade plummeted, as evident in Figure 5.1, and the world sank into the Great Depression. During the 1920s, fascist dictator Benito Mussolini had seized power in downtrodden Italy, and during the Great Depression, Adolf Hitler and other fascist dictators rose to power in Germany, Japan, Spain, and elsewhere. World War II soon followed, exacting a horrific price. Many observers argued that the restrictive economic policies after World War I had created the economic desperation that allowed fascism to take hold, which, in turn, led to World War II.

Based on their analysis of the causes of World War II, policy makers planning for the postwar period focused in part on preventing a reoccurrence of global conflict. On the economic front, the United States led the effort to create the General Agreement on Tariffs and Trade (GATT), a treaty and an organization of the same name (later renamed the World Trade Organization, WTO) meant to eventually eliminate the trade barriers that were blamed for World War II. Policy makers also established the International Monetary Fund (IMF). Such belief in and government support for globalization remain powerful factors today. Among other reasons to note this is that the role of government in promoting globalization tends to undercut the argument expressed by President Bill Clinton that "Globalization is not something we can hold off or turn off . . . it is the economic equivalent of a force of nature—like wind or water."[3] Countries, especially acting collectively, can shape, restrain, or even reverse many aspects of globalization by increasing economic barriers, by restricting travel and interfering with transnational communications, and by other policies designed to make national borders less permeable.

Globalization of Transportation and Communications

Globalization could not exist to the degree it does without the technological ability to transport products and people rapidly and in large numbers across great distances. Similarly, globalization is dependent on the technology that permits us to transmit images, data, the written word, and sound easily and rapidly all over the world.

FIGURE 5.2 Global Travel

Millions of international travelers annually

25 — 1950
69 — 1960
166 — 1970
278 — 1980
441 — 1990
681 — 2000
806 — 2005

Modern transportation has promoted globalization by helping to increase the number of international travelers.

Data source: World Tourism Organization.

Global Transportation

Modern transportation carries people and their products across national borders in volume and at a speed unimaginable not very long ago. Oceangoing transport provides a good example. The most famous merchant vessel of the mid-1800s was the *Flying Cloud* (1851–1874), a 229-foot-long sailing ship. Now the oceans are being plied by such modern megaships as the tanker *Jahre Viking,* which at 1,504 feet long is so large that crew members often use bicycles on board to travel from one point to another. The immense ship carries more than a half-million tons of cargo, 900 times the capacity of the *Flying Cloud.* Yet the *Jahre Viking* is but one of the vast world merchant fleet of almost 28,000 freighters and tankers with a combined capacity of over 733 million tons of goods. These behemoths not only carry more cargo, but they have also expanded trade by reducing seagoing transportation costs to a small fraction of what they were a century ago. In 2006, for example, it cost only about three cents per gallon to transport oil from the Middle East to the United States.

Advances in transportation have been important in moving people as well as goods. When the first English settlers traveled from the British Isles to what would be Jamestown, Virginia, in 1607, the only way to make the trip was by ship, and the voyage took almost five months. International travel is almost routine today, with hundreds of millions of travelers moving between countries within a few hours each year as Figure 5.2 indicates.

Global Communications

It is almost impossible to overstate the impact that modern communications have had on international relations. In only a century and a half, communications have made spectacular advances, beginning with the telegraph, followed by photography, radio, the ability to film events, telephones, photocopying, television, satellite communications, faxes, and now computer-based Internet contacts and information through e-mail and the World Wide Web.

The Growth of Communications Capabilities The flow of these communications is too massive to calculate precisely, but if the growth of international telephone calls is any indication, we are increasingly able to "reach out and touch someone"

WEB POLL
How Globalized Are You?

Did You Know That:

The per-minute price of a call from New York City to London has dropped from $74.89 in 1900, to $1.32 in 1990, to as little as 5 cents today using a prepaid phone card.

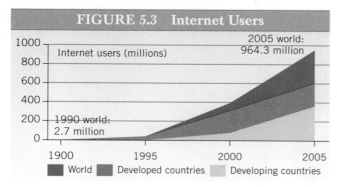

FIGURE 5.3   Internet Users

The growth of the Internet is a true communications revolution. In just 15 years, as shown here, the number of people using the Internet grew 36,988% from 2.7 million users to 964.3 million users. Most users are still in the economically developed countries, but as evident, use is also rising rapidly in the economically less developed countries.

Data sources: International Telecommunications Union, *World Telecommunications Indicators Data Base 2006;* World Bank, World Development Indicators, 2007.

internationally, as the AT&T advertising slogan went. One indication is that the total annual minutes of international telephone use more than tripled between 1991 and 2005 from 40 billion to 140 billion.

The technological revolution in communications has also meant that more and more people around the globe are getting their news from the same sources. The most obvious example is CNN, which now reaches virtually every country in the world and broadcasts in nine languages. And while CNN carries something of an American perspective to the rest of the world, non-U.S. news networks are bringing foreign news perspectives to Americans. Al Jazeera, which translates as "The (Arabian) Peninsula," is based in Qatar and began operations in 1996 as the first Arabic language television news network. Since then it has become well known around the world for its broadcasts of, among other things, video and audio tapes of Osama bin Laden from his hiding place. In 2006 Al Jazeera added broadcasts in English originating in the United States, and the news agency also has Internet news sites in both Arabic and English, which, it claims, get more than 160 million hits a year, making it the most visited Arabic language Web site and among the top 200 most visited sites worldwide.

Not only are almost instantaneous news and information available over the Internet, but the number of people using the Internet is growing exponentially. Between 1990 and 2004, the share of the world population using the Internet soared from only 0.5% to 14%, and the number of total users is approaching 1 billion, as Figure 5.3 indicates. Internet access is still more readily available in the economically developed countries, where 54% of the population uses it, but use in the less developed countries has grown to nearly 7%. Furthermore, today's Internet users are not only able to access the Web, they can use it to communicate with one another via e-mail and create Web sites for themselves or their groups to share information and to promote their causes globally.

Web Link

For an Arab perspective on world events, go to the Web site of Al Jazeera at **http://english .aljazeera.net.**

The Impact of Globalized Communications   The communications revolution, with its ongoing spread of global access to information and interactive communications, is of immense importance. One impact is "democratic internationalism." Transnational communications have provided citizens from different countries with the ability to espouse causes of nearly every imaginable type, to exchange views, to organize across national borders, and to undertake political action (Schmitz, 2004). As discussed later in this chapter, transnational groups are flourishing and having an important impact on policy at the international level through the UN and other international organizations and on the national level through the pressure brought on governments by the groups' national chapters.

Modern communications have also enabled people to seek alternative information and opinions from what is normally available to them. For example, Arabs in the Middle East can get an American perspective on the news by accessing CNN, and Americans an Arab view of the world on Al Jazeera.

A third effect of global communications is to undermine authoritarian governments. The rapid mass communications that are taken for granted in the industrialized democracies are still greeted with suspicion by authoritarian governments. China tries to control the Web by using technology to monitor and block dissident communications and by imposing fines and imprisonment on those who the government claims endanger national security by transmitting dissident information and opinions. In the end, though, Beijing's efforts are probably doomed to failure. "The more they [Chinese authorities] do to block it, the more people want to get online," says dissident Liu Xiaobo. "People in China now understand a lot more about what's going on than . . . in the '70s and '80s. Then, the only contact we had with the outside world was through meeting the very occasional foreigner or somehow getting hold of a foreign paper or magazine." According to Liu, "That's why in China these days you can see all kinds of organizations and activities springing up, moving the country towards real change."[4]

Economic Globalization

Economic interchange across borders is bringing the world together and creating economic **interdependence** in many ways. The intensifying reality of economic interchange and interdependence is detailed in chapters 1, 2, and 12, but several of the basic points related to trade, investments, and monetary relations are important here.

Trade

International trade has expanded exponentially, increasing from $53 billion in exports in 1948 to almost $14.5 trillion ($14,500 billion) in 2006. Trade can be divided into two parts. **Merchandise trade** is the more familiar. It consists of goods—tangible items—including primary goods (raw materials) and manufactured goods. **Services trade** is less well known but also important. Services include things people do for one another. When U.S. insurance companies earn premiums for insuring foreign assets or people, when American movies earn royalties abroad, when U.S. trucks carry goods in Mexico or Canada, the revenue they generate constitutes the export of U.S. services. Whatever their nature, services are a major source of income for countries, amounting to more than 20% of all international trade.

Several factors have spurred increased trade. First, *improved production technology* has increased the supply of goods. The industrial revolution, which began in eighteenth-century Europe, led to mass manufacturing. As production rates sped up, manufacturers increasingly had to seek markets for their burgeoning supply of goods farther away and even across national borders. This, in turn, created an *increased demand for raw material and synthetic resources* to supply the factories. *Materialism* is a third factor that accounts for increased trade. The rise in the world's standard of living, especially in the industrialized countries, has expanded international trade as people have sought more material goods and improved services. A fourth factor is *improved transportation*. As discussed above, it has increased our ability to carry the growing supply of materials and manufactured goods and to meet the demand for them. Also as noted earlier, *government policy* seeking to reduce barriers to international economic interchanges is a fifth factor that has promoted trade.

Whatever the causes, the impacts of increased trade are profound. Much of what we consume comes from abroad. In 2005, for example, the $2 trillion in U.S. imports accounted for 23% of the $8.7 trillion that American individuals and companies spent on goods and services. Therefore the price and availability of foreign goods and services is a key determinant of our standard of living and cost of living. Much of a country's gross domestic product (GDP), the value of what is produced within its borders, also goes into trade. As such, exports provide jobs for workers and other

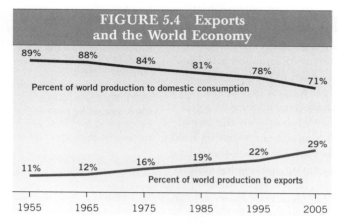

FIGURE 5.4   Exports and the World Economy

What a country produces (its gross domestic production, GDP) is either consumed domestically (within the country) or exported to other countries. This figure shows that from 1955 through 2005, total world exports as a share of the combined GDPs of world countries rose from 11% to 29%. Conversely, countries' consumption of their own products fell from 89% to 71%. The increasing importance of exports to economic prosperity is an indication of economic globalization.

Data source: World Bank online.

important benefits to a country. Moreover, the importance of trade as a stimulus to productivity is steadily increasing, a change evident in Figure 5.4.

International Investment

Trade has not been the only form of international economic activity that has grown rapidly. A parallel globalization of international investment has created increased financial interdependence among countries. For example, Americans had $10 trillion in investments, property, stocks, bonds, and other assets abroad in 2006, making not only individual investors but also the health of the entire U.S. economy dependent to a degree on the state of the world economy. Conversely, foreigners had a $12.7 trillion stake in the United States, and the ebb and flow of those funds into the country are also a central factor in Americans' prosperity, or lack of it. Two types of foreign assets are particularly important: **foreign direct investment (FDI)**, which involves buying real estate, setting up a new company, or buying enough stock to control an existing company in another country, and **foreign portfolio investment (FPI)**, buying stocks and bonds on a smaller scale that does not involve controlling companies or owning real estate. Such investments have long existed, but they have accelerated greatly in recent decades.

Because it involves ownership control, FDI is the more important of the two major types of investment. For the most part, the world's **multinational corporations (MNCs)**, also called transnational corporations (TNCs), account for the lion's share of the global FDI. MNCs are businesses that operate in more than one country. MNC operations can involve sales outlets, mines and other natural resource–extraction processes, farms and ranches, manufacturing plants, or offices that supply banking and other services. MNCs date back at least to the Dutch East India Company in 1602, but it was not until after World War II that they began to expand in number and size at a rapid pace. Now over 75,000 MNCs with 660,000 foreign subsidiaries exist, and they pack enormous economic muscle. Their annual revenues (gross corporate product, GCP) provide one good measure. The top 500 MNCs alone had a collective GCP of $18.9 trillion in 2005. This equaled an astounding 42% of the world's collective GNP ($45 trillion) for that year. The amount of money these MNCs invest each year is immense and, as Table 5.1 shows, growing by every measure.

Monetary Exchange

Global increases in travel, trade, investment, and other activities have necessarily meant that larger amounts of money are exchanging hands across national borders. Currently, as much as $2.5 trillion worth of currencies are exchanged daily into other currencies. To accommodate the globalization of money, there has been a parallel globalization of financial services, such as banking. In recent decades, banks have grown from hometown to national to multinational enterprises and have expanded their operations beyond traditional banking to include many financial services such as issuing credit cards, providing venture capital, offering insurance, and maintaining brokerage houses and other investment functions. There are now dozens of

TABLE 5.1 Foreign Direct Investment Growth				
Measure/Year	FDI Assets	Gross Annual FDI	Net Annual FDI	FDI Assets as a Share of World GDP
1990	$1.8 trillion	$218.7 billion	$201.4 billion	8.5%
2005	$10.1 trillion	$916.3 billion	$646.9 billion	22.7%
Increase	461%	419%	221%	167%

Data source: UNCTAD, *World Investment Report, 2006.*

Foreign direct investment (FDI) has grown in size and importance as part of the globalization process. This table shows four measures of FDI and each one's increase between 1990 and 2005. These four are the value of all FDI assets held worldwide, the total amount of new money invested annually, the net amount invested (new investments minus sale of old investments), and how the total FDI assets compare to the world's annual GDP. This range of data indicates that foreign investors own more and more of the productive assets of almost all countries.

banks with assets over $1 billion, and 11 of them each command assets over $1 trillion. The largest of these is Great Britain's Barclays ($1.6 trillion). It employs 118,000 people, and in addition to its extensive operations in the United Kingdom, Barclays has 1,542 branches in 59 other countries; holds $111 billion in foreign bonds; has direct financial dealings with over 15 million clients, including foreign governments, institutions, businesses, and individuals; administers 65 of the 100 largest pension plans worldwide; and operates 150 investment funds worth $240 billion trading on 10 different stock exchanges. In size and global reach, Barclays is followed closely by U.S.-based Citigroup ($1.5 trillion) and Japan's Mizuho Financial Group ($1.3 trillion). Controlling enormous sums of money in such a variety of financial services gives these multinational banks considerable power over the international flow of capital through their traditional banking services, such as making loans, and their many other financial services. For example, American banks have almost $700 billion in foreign assets (such as overseas loans) and about $1 trillion in foreign liabilities (such as foreign deposits in the banks).

Cultural Globalization

Much of the early development of different languages, customs, and other diverse aspects of world cultures resulted from the isolation of groups of people from one another. It is not surprising, then, that a degree of cultural amalgamation has occurred as improved transportation and communication have brought people of various societies into ever more frequent contact. Analyzing the blurring of cultural differences inevitably includes a great deal about fast food, basketball, rock music, and other such aspects of pop culture, but they do not trivialize the subject. Instead, a long-standing "bottom-up" line of political theory argues that the world's people can build on commonplace interactions and increasing cultural commonalities that engender familiarity with and confidence in one another to create a global civil society that might evolve into a global nation. Some nations emerged from civil societies and, as discussed in chapter 4, carved out their own nation-states. By the same process, if transnational civil societies develop, then regional and even global schemes of governance could conceivably form and supplement or supplant the territorial state. Scholars who examine this bottom-up process of transnational integration look for evidence in such factors as the flow of communications and commerce between countries and the spread across borders of what people wear, eat, and do for recreation.

While it is premature to talk of a world culture, and indeed that may never come, there is significant evidence of cultural amalgamation in the world. The leaders of China once wore "Mao suits"; now they wear Western-style business suits. When dressing informally, people in Shanghai, Lagos, and Mexico City are more apt to wear jeans, T-shirts, and sneakers than their country's traditional dress. Young people everywhere listen to the same music, with, for example "My Love" by Justin Timberlake on the top 10 charts in Brazil, China, Ireland, Israel, Russia, Turkey, South Africa, and many other countries in addition to the United States in 2006. And whatever it means to our gastronomic future, Big Macs, fries, and milk shakes are consumed around the world.

Before looking further at the evidence of cultural amalgamation, one caution is in order. You will see that a great deal of what is becoming world culture is Western, especially American, in its origins. That does not imply that Western culture is superior; its impact is a function of the economic and political strength of Western Europe and the United States. Nor does the preponderance of Western culture in the integration process mean that the flow is one way. American culture, for example, is influenced by many "foreign imports," ranging from fajitas, through soccer, to acupuncture.

Language

One of the most important aspects of converging culture is English, which is becoming the common language of business, diplomacy, communications, and even culture. President Hamid Karzai of Afghanistan and many other leaders of countries or international organizations can converse in English. Indeed, a number of them, including

Web Link

To find out what movies people in other countries are watching and what music they are listening to, visit the box office and music charts at **http://allcharts.org/**.

Cultural globalization is evident in these Chinese performers dressed in Santa suits during a Christmas celebration in Shaanxi Province, China. Some disapprove of such activities, though, and a group of college students published a letter warning against adopting the trappings of foreign cultures.

UN Secretary-General Ban Ki-moon of South Korea, learned or improved their English while enrolled at U.S. universities. A bit more slowly, English is spreading among common citizens around the world. This is evident in differences among various age groups. Among Europeans, for instance, 89% of all school children now have English instruction.

Modern communications are one factor driving the spread of English. There have been notable advances, such as the ability to search in nearly 100 languages through Google, in making the Web more accessible to non-English speakers, but the vast majority of what is available on the Internet has been and remains in English. As the Webmaster at one site in Russia comments, "It is far easier for a Russian . . . to download the works of Dostoyevsky translated in English to read than it is for him to get [it] in his own language." Business needs also promote the global growth of English. The U.S. status as the world's economic powerhouse makes it far more common for foreign businesspeople to learn the language of Americans than it is for Americans to learn other languages. A report issued by the Japanese government declared that "achieving world-class excellence demands that all Japanese acquire a working knowledge of English."[5] The use of English will probably continue to expand throughout the world because, as Figure 5.5 indicates, a majority of people in every region in the world believe that their children are more likely to prosper if they learn English.

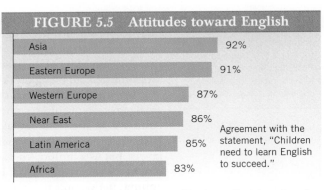

FIGURE 5.5 Attitudes toward English

Asia	92%
Eastern Europe	91%
Western Europe	87%
Near East	86%
Latin America	85%
Africa	83%

Agreement with the statement, "Children need to learn English to succeed."

The growth of English as the language of business, the Internet, and other aspects of global communications is likely to spur the continued increase in the number of English speakers. Strong majorities of people in every world region believe that it is important for their children to learn English in order to succeed in the modern world.

Note: The Near East is broader than the Middle East and stretches from Egypt to Pakistan.
Data source: Pew Research Center (2003).

Consumer Products

The interchange of popular consumer goods is another major factor in narrowing cultural gaps. American movies are popular throughout much of the world. In Japan, for example, the top drawing film in 2006 was *Pirates of the Caribbean 2*. Moreover, foreign distribution is vital to the U.S. film industry, which earns 61% of its revenue overseas. By contrast, foreign films account for just 3% of the U.S. market. American television programming is also widespread, but unlike movies, it is a declining part of most foreign television markets. However, jeans, logo-bearing T-shirts, and other American-style dress trends are nearly ubiquitous globally, and burgers, fried chicken, and other types of fast food further spread common culture.

China provides just one example of the degree to which diverse cultures have succumbed to many things American. Children in China pester their parents to take them to see Mi Loushu (Mickey Mouse) at the Hong Kong Disneyland. Kentucky Fried Chicken has over 1,700 outlets in China and McDonald's has 800, even though at $0.60, a *jishi hanbao* (cheeseburger) is pricey for most Chinese workers. Chinese musical tastes are also changing, and the Web site of the Hard Rock Café in Beijing advises that the city is "the capital of rock 'n' roll" (*gun shi*). Finally after a fast-food meal and a night of *gun shi*, the revelers can get some rest at one of the many hotels in China operated by Hilton and other Western chains. While at the hotel relaxing, patrons can turn on television and watch CNN in English or change channels to watch MTV-China or catch a National Basketball Association (NBA) game. Finding one will be easy, because all Chinese stations carry NBA games. During the 1990s, the Chinese were enthralled with Chicago Bulls great Michael Jordan, whom they called "space flier." Indeed, one poll of Chinese youth found that they considered Jordan a more important historical figure than Mao Zedong, leader of the Chinese Communist Revolution (Larmer, 2005). Enthusiasm for basketball has grown even more now that 7'6" Yao Ming of the Houston Rockets has become an NBA all-star noted for his awesome *kou qui* (slam dunk).

To reemphasize the main point, there is a distinct and important intermingling and amalgamation of cultures under way. For good or ill, Western, particularly American, culture is at the forefront of this trend. The observation of the director-general of UNESCO, that "America's main role in the new world order is not as a military super-power, but as a multicultural superpower," is an overstatement, but it captures some of what is occurring.[6] What is most important is not the specific source of common culture. Rather, it is the important potential consequences of cultural amalgamation. As noted, some analysts welcome it as a positive force that will bring people and, eventually, political units together. Others see transnational culture as a danger to desirable diversity.

Evaluating Globalization

One of the oddities about evaluating globalization is that it enjoys considerable popular support around the world, as Figure 5.6 indicates, yet critics of the process are legion and more vehement than its supporters. It is easiest to evaluate globalization factually. There can be little doubt that the process has speeded up considerably. Evidence of the extraordinarily rapid globalization of communications and transportation is

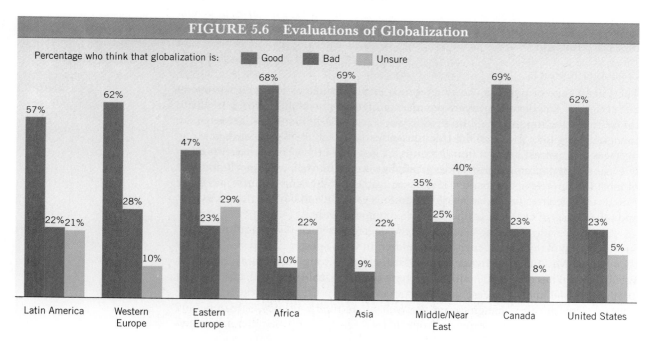

FIGURE 5.6   Evaluations of Globalization

A majority (58%) of people globally and in every region but Eastern Europe and the Middle/Near East support globalization. However, this general endorsement is not wildly enthusiastic, as also detailed in Figure 2.3 on p. 56, with only 17% believing globalization is very good.

Note: Countries in the Middle/Near East stretch from Egypt to Pakistan. The question was: "Do you think that globalization is a very good thing, somewhat good, somewhat bad, or a very bad thing?"
Data source: Pew Research Center (2003).

beyond dispute. The economic data is also clear. Measured by trade, investment, monetary flow, and every other standard, economic globalization has advanced quickly and far. Cultural globalization is harder to measure, but anyone who has traveled internationally for several decades will attest to how much more common the use of English, Western-style dress, fast-food restaurants serving burgers and fries, and many other aspects of a spreading common culture have become. Evaluating globalization qualitatively, deciding whether it is a positive or negative trend, is much more difficult.

Arguments for Economic Globalization

As noted earlier, economic globalization speeded up after World War II because it was promoted by American and other policy makers who believed in the causal sequence: reducing fewer international economic restrictions would $\longrightarrow$ increase prosperity, thereby $\longrightarrow$ decreasing a source of potential conflict among countries. Many policy makers, scholars, and others continue to believe in the validity of this causal sequence and to promote globalization based on it. They also see additional links between globalization and peace. One thought is that globalization increases prosperity and that democracy is more likely in prosperous countries. Since democratic peace theory contends that democracies seldom if ever fight with one another, then a positive sequence is: globalization $\longrightarrow$ greater prosperity $\longrightarrow$ more democracies $\longrightarrow$ fewer wars. Yet another argument is that globalization creates interdependent economies, which make it difficult and economically self-destructive to fight wars. This second positive linkage sequence is: globalization $\longrightarrow$ increased interdependence $\longrightarrow$ fewer wars.

Just as some policy makers and scholars see positive links between economic globalization and peace, some analysts believe that as globalization creates more personal interaction, cultural interchange, and amalgamation among people, it makes others seem less alien and threatening, and the resulting familiarity enhances peace. Thus, in a third positive sequence: globalization $\longrightarrow$ increased cross-cultural contacts and amalgamation $\longrightarrow$ a decreased sense of difference among nations $\longrightarrow$ less conflict. Whatever the precise sequence of the links, President Bill Clinton was expressing his belief in the general globalization $\longrightarrow$ peace concept when he told Congress, "These are the challenges we have to meet so that we can lead the world toward peace and freedom in an era of globalization."[7] Numerous scholars also link globalization to peace, arguing in one case, "The United States and other major powers can best discourage conflict by promoting greater global economic ties" (Gartzke & Li, 2003:285). It is important to note, however, that not everyone agrees that globalization promotes peace or, even if it does, that it is a positive process. Therefore there are concerns about both economic and cultural globalization.

Concerns about Economic Globalization

Analyzing the impact of economic globalization is a complex undertaking that takes up a great deal of chapter 13. However, an overview of the arguments found there merit inclusion here. One aspect relates to the causal arguments linking prosperity directly to peace or indirectly through democratization to peace. While there is substantial evidence supporting these contentions, there are analysts who doubt them, either entirely or in part.

A second and broader concern about economic globalization relates to how benefits are distributed. The basic arguments that critics make is that the benefits are not distributed anywhere near equally, with the wealthy benefiting and the poor gaining little or nothing and sometimes even becoming worse off, at least relatively. The answer depends to a degree on which numbers are stressed. Since 1945 world prosperity has

Globalization has many opponents, particularly those who feel threatened by it. One such individual is this South Korean rice farmer, who is trying to stop a train carrying rice imported from the United States. His flag bears the slogan, "No import of rice, block FTA [the free trade agreement] between U.S. and South Korea."

grown overall. The economically developed countries (EDCs) led by the United States have done exceptionally well, and conditions in the less developed countries (LDCs) have improved overall. Many of them have made great strides and while not truly prosperous are not generally poor either. Yet there are still a billion people worldwide living in extreme poverty on the equivalent of a dollar or two a day, and many countries remain desperately poor. Moreover, the gap between the per capita wealth of the EDCs and LDCs has expanded. In 1980, for every 1 dollar of wealth generated per person in the LDCs, the EDCs produced 14 dollars per capita. In 2005 that 1:14 gap had grown to 1:20.

At the extreme, some contend that poverty persists and the wealth gap has grown because globalization is a tool used by the EDCs to exploit the LDCs by pressuring them to open their economies to penetration and domination by EDCs. A related view is that even within the EDCs, the wealthy are using globalization to increase their wealth by using the financial power of the multinational corporations (MNCs) they control to escape regulations protecting the environment, workers, and consumers by either moving operations to a permissive country or pressuring governments to ease or end regulations. Those who see globalization as a process that is making the rich richer by exploiting both poor countries and the poor within wealthy countries advocate radical change in global economic trends and policy. A less dire interpretation of the causes of the expanding wealth gap and other unsatisfactory trends and conditions is that many LDCs do not have an adequate economic base to compete openly in the global market. From this perspective, the prescription is reform of the globalization process by giving more economic assistance to LDCs, by regulating international working conditions, by creating global environmental codes, and by instituting a wide variety of other reforms that will create a more equitable globalization process internationally and within countries.

Concerns about Cultural Globalization

Those who object to cultural globalization condemn it for undermining the world's rich tapestry of cultural diversity and potentially producing a less vibrant monoculture that one scholar has described as the "eternal yawn of McWorld" (Barber, 1996:vi). The alternative perspective is, "We should not fear that globalism will lead to homogenization. Instead, it will expose us to the differences that surround us" (Nye, 2002:1).

What do people around the world think of cultural amalgamation? The answer has several parts (Edwards, 2006). One is that most people welcome the availability of foreign culture. A worldwide survey in 45 countries found that 77% thought that having foreign products available was good, and 61% felt that way about foreign movies and other entertainment media. However, a second part of the answer is that few people are unreservedly positive about importing foreign culture. When asked about foreign entertainment media, for instance, only 30% thought it was "very good," and another 31% said it was merely "somewhat good." A third part of the answer is that many people have conflicting views, as shown in Figure 5.7, with a strong majority of people around the world arguing simultaneously that cultural imports are good and that their way of life is threatened and needs protection from outside influences.

FIGURE 5.7 Opinions on Cultural Globalization

Cultural imports are bad	Traditional way of life being lost	Way of life needs protection from foreign influences
Unsure 3% / Yes 28% / No 69%	Unsure 3% / No 26% / Yes 71%	Unsure 4% / No 34% / Yes 62%

People are ambivalent about cultural globalization. In each of these three pie charts, the "pro-globalization" answer is in green, the "anti-globalization" answer in red, and "unsure" is in yellow. In the left chart, 69% of the respondents in 45 countries took a pro-globalization stance, saying they saw imported products, movies, and other entertainment media as positive. Yet in the second and third charts, majorities took anti-globalization stances, with 71% saying that their traditional way of life was being lost and 62% wanting that way of life to be protected. There was little variation among geographic regions on all these questions, with a majority of people in each region taking the pro-globalization position on cultural imports and the anti-globalization position on "way of life" issues.

Data source: Pew Research Center (2003).

A fourth part of public reaction to cultural imports relates to the demographic patterns. Age makes a difference, with older people usually more averse to cultural imports than younger people. In the West African country of Senegal, for example, 76% of young adults (age 18 to 29) favor cultural imports; only 47% of adults aged 50 and over support that view. By contrast, geography and the relative wealth of countries generally do not make a great deal of difference in the responses to various questions about cultural imports, although Muslim countries, especially those in the Middle East, are somewhat more resistant than other groups of countries.

A final note about cultural imports is that countries sometimes try to restrict them either because governments want to whip up nationalist feeling or are responding to the demands of nationalist groups. France and China provide two examples. At least 90% of the French favor popular culture imports and believe their children should learn English. Yet the government of France has strongly resisted the encroachment of foreign culture. President Jacques Chirac warned that the spread of English poses a "major risk for humanity." The government requires the exclusive use of French in teaching, business, and government, and pressures the entertainment industry to feature French-language movies and music. Such measures have not worked well. For example, the new James Bond movie, *Casino Royale,* and other English-language movies led the box-office revenue in France during the final weeks of 2006.

Like their French counterparts, 90% of China's people also view cultural imports favorably. Yet dissenters worry about the loss of Chinese traditional culture. The end of 2006, for instance, saw a campaign on the government-controlled *China Daily* Web site that warned, "Western culture has been changing from a breeze and a drizzle into a wild wind and a heavy storm. This is vividly embodied in the rising popularity of Christmas," the site lamented, and it urged "our countrymen to be cautious about Christmas, to wake from their collective cultural coma and give Chinese culture the dominant role." Not everyone agreed. "It might not be a bad thing for traditional Chinese culture to make some changes under Western influence. There should be competition among different cultures," one posting on a Blog site objected. "It is not necessary to boycott Western culture. You just can't," was another post.[8]

TRANSNATIONALISM

Transnationalism springs from two sources. Globalization is one. Economic interdependence, mass communications, rapid travel, and other modern factors are fostering transnationalism by intertwining the lives of people around the world and promoting a much higher level of transnational contacts. Human thought is the second source of transnationalism. "I think, therefore I am," philosopher René Descartes argued in *Discourse on Method* (1637). The ability to think abstractly allows humans to imagine—to see themselves beyond what they have experienced and to define how they wish to be connected to people, ideas, and institutions. Transnationalism, indeed any political sense, is based on this abstract self-awareness.

Transnationalism has both action and identification elements. On the action dimension, transnationalism is the process of people working together as individuals and collectively in private groups across borders with other individuals and groups to accomplish a common purpose. On the other dimension, transnationalism provides alternatives to nationalism as a source of **political identity**. This concept refers to how we see ourselves connected as individuals to ideologies (such as communism), religion (such as Islam), demographic characteristics (such as ethnicity or gender), region (such as Europe), or virtually any other perceived common bond. We will speculate on the future of transnationalism later in the chapter, but it is important to say here that most people will not abandon nationalism in the foreseeable future. It is also important to see, however, that things are changing, and that at least some people are shifting some or all of their political identification away from their nationalist identity and toward one or more other identities.

As our discussion of transnationalism proceeds, you will see that it has the potential to significantly restructure the international system and its conduct. Some aspects of transnationalism tend to undermine nationalism and, by extension, the state. For example, some citizens of the European Union identify as Europeans, instead of simply as French, German, or some other nationality. In other cases, transnational identification and organization help change attitudes and policies around the world related to a specific area of concern. This will be illustrated by examining the global women's movement.

You will also see that transnationalism is neither an inherent force for peace nor for discord. Some aspects of transnationalism promote greater global interdependence and harmony and, as such, are very much in accord with the vision of the liberal school of political thought discussed in chapter 1. Yet globalization has also spurred a transnationalist antiglobalization movement that believes the process is destructive (O'Neill, 2004). Yet another, and in this case, dire image of transnationalism envisions a world divided and in conflict along cultural lines. Those who see transnationalism in this light tend to be realists, many of whom would strengthen the national state as a bulwark against the dangers of hostile transnational alignments. To explore transnationalism, we will first survey transnational organizations, then turn our attention to regional transnationalism, cultural transnationalism, religious transnationalism, and transnational movements before looking at the future of transnationalism.

Transnational Organizations

One indication of the increased strength of transnationalism is the phenomenal growth in the number and activities of transnational organizations called **nongovernmental organizations (NGOs)**. These are organizations that operate across national boundaries, that have a membership composed of private individuals, and that do not answer to any government. Two other types of transnational organizations that fall within the definitional boundaries of NGOs but are usually treated separately are terrorist groups and transnational corporations (multinational corporations). These are treated in greater detail in chapters 10 and 12 respectively.

The Growth of NGOs

Between 1900 and 2005, the number of NGOs grew from 69 to over 11,400, as Figure 5.8 shows. Note that by far the greatest growth spurt has occurred since 1975 in parallel to rapidly advancing globalization. Of these, more than 2,000 hold consultative status with the United Nations, up from 928 such groups in 1992 and 222 such groups in 1952. These groups have a highly diverse range of interests that include peace, human rights, the environment, and virtually every other public concern.

The increasing number of NGOs and their diverse range of interests and activities reflect globalization in several ways (Reimann, 2006). First, there is a growing awareness that many issues are partly or wholly transnational. For instance, one country's discharge of atmospheric gases that attack Earth's vital ozone layer increases the rate of skin cancer globally, not just in the country that emitted the gases. Similarly, many women believe that the status of women in any one country is linked to the treatment of women everywhere. Second, NGOs have flourished because advances in transportation and communication have made transnational contacts easy, rapid, and inexpensive. Third, the growth of NGOs reflects disenchantment with existing political organizations based in or dominated by states in an age of globalization and transnational problems. As a result, people are seeking new ways to work with one another beyond traditional government-to-government diplomacy.

The Activities of NGOs

In essence, NGOs are organized interest groups that operate singly or in combination with one another to promote their causes. In the realm of environmental politics, for example, there are such groups as Friends of the Earth International, headquartered in the Netherlands. It coordinates a transnational effort to protect the environment and also serves as a link among 5,000 Friends of the Earth member-groups in 70 countries. Just like more domestically oriented interest groups, NGOs promote their goals by such techniques as attempting to raise public awareness and support for their causes and by providing information, argumentation, and electoral backing to policy makers in national governments and intergovernmental organizations (IGOs, international organizations in which the members are states).

FIGURE 5.8 Growth of International Nongovernmental Organizations

One indication of the growth of transnational activity is the sharp increase in the number of transnational nongovernmental organizations (NGOs), especially since 1975.

Data source: Union of International Associations.

Web Link

The wide range of NGO concerns is evident in the list of UN-accredited NGOs on the Web site of the Conference of Non-Governmental Organizations at **www.ngocongo.org/**.

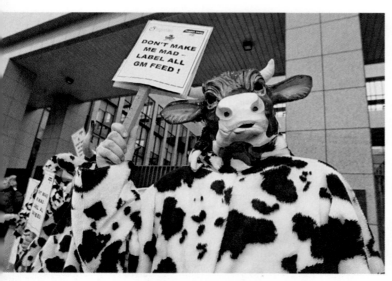

Groups of private citizens working together in nongovernmental organizations (NGO) have become an important part of world politics. Friends of the Earth are one prominent environmental NGO, and some of its members are shown here demonstrating in front of the European Union headquarters in Brussels, Belgium. They are demanding that any meat from animals raised on genetically modified (GM) feed be labeled as such when it is sold.

On the domestic front, for example, government agencies often work with NGOs to accomplish goals and sometimes even seek their support to obtain funds and other types of support. Speaking before the U.S. Conference of Catholic Bishops in 2006, the head of the U.S. Agency for International Development (USAID) stressed that the "the U.S. government and NGO community together must use their comparative advantages . . . in combating poverty." He also urged the clerics and their "NGO colleagues" to "lobby the Hill [Congress] for increases in foreign assistance."[9]

NGOs also play a role in the international policy-making processes of the UN and other IGOs, who have long sought out relationships with NGOs; these ties have expanded greatly over time. In 1948, there were 40 NGOs that had official "consultative status" status with the UN. That number passed 1,000 in 1996 and stood at 2,870 in 2006. NGOs are also active through their participation in multinational conferences convened by the United Nations and other IGOs to address global problems. Since the early 1990s, all such conferences have two parts. One is the official conference that includes delegates from governments. The second is the parallel NGO conference. The largest such dual conference was the 2002 World Conference on Sustainable Development in Johannesburg, South Africa, drawing some 41,000 delegates from more than 6,600 NGOs to its parallel meeting.

International conferences are both the result of the work done by NGOs and a vehicle that promotes their role by enhancing their visibility and by serving as a place where they can create **transnational advocacy networks (TANs)**. These are groups of NGOs and IGOs that share an interest in a specific aspect of global society (Park, 2005; Betsill & Bulkeley, 2004; Rodrigues, 2004). For example, the effort to protect the environment combines the efforts of a TAN comprising national government agencies such as the U.S. Environmental Protection Agency, NGOs such as Greenpeace, and IGOs such as the United Nations Environment Programme. Another key role for NGOs is to provide a way for individuals to become involved in and have an impact on global events. Some pointers on how you can take advantage of that opportunity are provided in the participation box, "Join an NGO."

ANALYZE THE ISSUE
UN Conference for Nongovernmental Organizations

The Impact of NGOs

It is hard to measure the impact of NGOs or any other single factor on policy making, but there is evidence that NGOs are gaining recognition as legitimate actors and are playing an increased role in the policy process. One measure is funding. The amount of aid flowing through NGOs to economically less developed countries (LDCs) increased from $1 billion in 1970 to approaching $10 billion today. Historically, NGOs have received most of their funds from their members. More recently, some governments and IGOs have begun to channel some of their aid funds through NGOs. For example, USAID directs some of its funding through a number of NGOs and also gives funds to strengthen NGOs themselves in order to allow them to bring about economic development, democratization, and other desired changes.

Did You Know That:

An opinion survey in 43 countries found that 74% of all respondents evaluated the role of NGOs positively. Only 13% thought poorly of NGOs, with 13% unsure.

GET INVOLVED

Join an NGO

Are you happy with the way that everything, absolutely everything, is going in the world? If you are not, then do something about it!

Each of us has an opportunity to play a part in world affairs by joining one of the multitude of nongovernmental organizations (NGOs). There is almost certainly one and probably several of these voluntary groups that address any transnational issue that you are interested in from almost any policy perspective that you have.

Be Active!

To seek out a group to your liking, visit the Web site of the UN Department of Public Information/Non-Governmental

Organizations at **www.un.org/dpi/ngosection/index.asp**. Particularly helpful is the information accessed through the hyperlink "UN System Focal Points." Also worthwhile is the information provided by the NGO Unit of the Department of Economic and Social Affairs at **www.un.org/esa/coordination/ngo/.** A listing of all the NGOs that have consultative status with the UN Economic and Social Council is located at **www.un.org/esa/coordination/ngo/pdf/INF_List.pdf**.

Global issues–UN system partnership

Africa	Development Cooperation	Food	Labor	Statistics
Aging	Disabilities, Persons with	Governance	Law of the Sea and Antarctica	Sustainable Development
Agriculture	Disarmament	Health	Least Developed Countries	Terrorism
AIDS	Drug Control and Crime Prevention	Human Rights	Millennium Assembly	Trade and Development
Atomic Energy	Education	Human Settlements	Question of Palestine	Volunteerism
Children	Elections	Humanitarian Affairs	Peace and Security	Water
Climate Change	Energy	Indigenous People	Population	Women
Culture	Environment	Information Communications Technology	Refugees	Youth
Decolonization	Family	Intellectual Property	Social Development	
Demining	Financing, International	International Law	Outer Space	

NGOs have also helped move some of their causes to the center of the political stage by increasing public information and demanding action. According to a former British diplomat, "You used to have a nice, cozy relationship [between states]. Now you have more figures on the stage. . . . This adds to the pace and complexity of diplomacy."[10] For example, 50 years ago, the environment received little political attention. Now it is an important issue that generates world conferences (such as those in Rio in 1992 and Johannesburg in 2002); it is a frequent topic of conversation among heads of government, and the subject of numerous international agreements.

Transnational NGOs and their national chapters also individually and collectively bring pressure on governments. In the United States, for example, the League of Conservation Voters lobbies legislators and agency officials and takes such public relations steps as maintaining a "scorecard" that rates the voting record of members of Congress on the environment. It should also be noted that some forms of NGO activity can be destructive and, therefore, illegitimate in the view of most. For example, al Qaeda and many other terrorist groups are transnational organizations.

Regional Transnationalism

Chapter 7 on international organizations examines the European Union (EU) as an example of a regional organization. The EU has evolved since its genesis soon after World War II to the point now where there is advanced economic integration. Although at a slower rate, political integration has also proceeded. These changes are beginning to affect how Europeans define their political identity (Caporaso, 2005). Even if there is no doubt that nationalism continues to dominate, there is also a sense of other identifications taking some hold. Among Europeans, 40% define themselves only as citizens of their country. Another 44% define themselves as citizens of their country first and Europeans second. Even more transnationally identified, 8% feel more European than national, and 4% perceive themselves as exclusively European (with 3% unsure).[11] Thus while nationalism reigns supreme, it is notable that one out of every eight people in the EU has transferred his or her traditional national identification to a primary or exclusive sense of being European and that 60% of EU citizens have some sense of political identification with it, even if it is secondary.

There are other indications that political identification with the EU may increase. One is the higher percentage of people (18%) with a primary or exclusive European identity in the six countries that in 1958 founded what became the EU than in the newer member-countries. Also, there is a stronger European identification (15%) among younger Europeans (age 15 to 24), with support dropping off with age to only 8% among Europeans aged 55 or more.

There is no other area of the globe with a regional organization that even approaches the economic, much less the political integration of the EU. Thus, to date any sense of regional political identity is almost exclusively confined to Europe. But in the 1950s, Europe's Common Market was just beginning, and it was limited to trade, much as several regional organizations such as the North American Free Trade Agreement (NAFTA, which links Canada, Mexico, and the United States) are today. What has evolved in Europe could occur elsewhere.

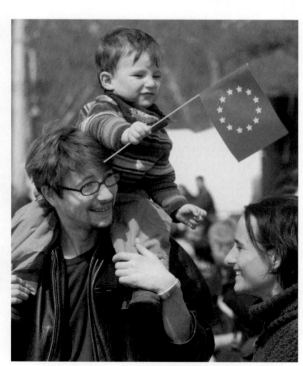

Although only a small minority of Europeans identify with the European Union today, that sense may increase as children who do not remember pre-EU times grow up. Perhaps when this Hungarian child holding an EU flag grows up, he and many of his contemporaries will consider themselves European first and Hungarian, British, French, or some other nationality second.

Cultural Transnationalism

There is considerable scholarship that demonstrates how greater intercultural familiarity reduces stereotyping, suspicion, fear, and other divisive factors that promote domestic and international conflict. Therefore, the familiarity with different cultures that globalization brings and even the blending of cultures holds the prospect of reducing conflict in the world.

A darker view is that cultural transnationalism will lead to a "**clash of civilizations.**" The best-known proponent of this view is Samuel P. Huntington's theory (1993, 1996). Like many analysts, Huntington (1993:22–26) believes that nationalism will "weaken . . . as a source of identity." What will happen next is the key to his controversial thesis. He believes that new cultural identifications will emerge that will "fill this gap" and countries will align themselves in "seven or eight cultural blocs," including "Western, Confucian, Japanese, Islamic, Hindu, Slavic-Orthodox, Latin American, and possibly African." These blocs, Huntington further predicts, will become "the fundamental source of conflict" as "different civilizations" engage in "prolonged and . . . violent conflicts."

Most Western scholars reject Huntington's theory (Henderson, 2004). However, it seems more plausible in other parts of the world. Additionally, some research has found evidence of increasing intercivilizational clash since World War II, although it has mostly involved the West and Islam (Tusicisny, 2004). As a result, whatever the perspective may be from the United States or other Western, largely Christian-heritage countries, there is considerable suspicion among Muslims that a concerted campaign is under way to undermine their religion and its cultural traits. It is important to note that the view of such actions as anti-Islam or, at least, reflecting cultural insensitivity is not confined to Muslims. Just before his death, Richard Nixon wrote of the long delay before the West intervened to stop the slaughter of Muslims in Bosnia, "It is an awkward but unavoidable truth that had the [mostly Muslim] citizens of Sarajevo [the capital of Bosnia] been predominantly Christian or Jewish, the civilized world would not have permitted [the atrocities that occurred]."[12]

As discussed later in the chapter, there is a history of conflict between Christendom and Islam that goes back more than a millennium, and to some Muslims current policy by the U.S.-led West is an extension of that conflict. Muslims making that case might point, among other things, to their perceptions of the following U.S. and/or European policies:

- Inaction while Christian Serbs slaughtered Bosnian Muslims (1992–1995)
- Exclusion of Muslim Turkey from the mostly Christian EU
- Opposition to Iraq or Iran getting nuclear weapons while ignoring Israeli nuclear weapons
- Two invasions of Iraq and one of Afghanistan and the long-term presence of Western troops in both countries
- Sanctions on Iraq after 1991 that lasted longer than those on Germany after 1945
- Lack of sanctions on largely Christian Russia for its often brutal campaign against the Muslim Chechens
- Support of Israel

Whether or not such actions reflect a bias against Islam or at least cultural insensitivity, it is important to see that they are perceived to be true by many Muslims. A survey taken of Muslims in 14 countries in Africa, Asia, and the Middle East found that nearly half felt their religion to be in danger. This perception has arguably fostered the greater sense of solidarity that a strong majority of Muslims also expressed in the survey.[13] These findings are detailed in Figure 5.9 on p. 152.

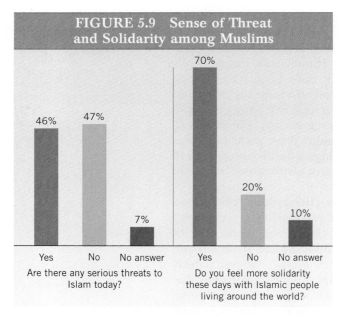

Whatever the cause, about half of all Muslims believe that their religion is under attack. This sense of threat is especially high in the Middle East, where 78% perceived serious threats. Perhaps as part of a defensive reaction, 70% of Muslims indicated that they are currently feeling greater solidarity with other Muslims around the world. Indeed, these feelings were expressed before the U.S. invasion of Iraq in 2003 and were almost certainly intensified by that action and the ensuing occupation.

Note: The survey was conducted in 2002 among Muslims in Jordan, Lebanon, Pakistan, Turkey, Uzbekistan, Bangladesh, Indonesia, Ghana, Ivory Coast, Mali, Nigeria, Senegal, Tanzania, and Uganda.

Data source: The Pew Research Center for People and the Press, "Views of a Changing World" (June 2003).

MAP
World Religions

Transnational Religion

Most of the world's great religions have a strong transnational element. It is particularly apt to exist when a religion, which is a basis of spiritual identity, becomes a source of political identity among its members. When religion and political identities become intertwined, members of a religion may take a number of political actions. One is to try to conform the laws and the foreign policy of their country to their religious values. A second is to provide political support for the causes of coreligionists in other countries. This sense of support is why, for example, Jews from around the world are likely to support Israel and Muslims everywhere are apt to support the Palestinians. Religion also helps explain why Osama bin Laden, a Saudi, was able to recruit Muslims from Egypt, Pakistan, Chechnya, and elsewhere, including the United States and Europe, to the ranks of al Qaeda and to find a base for the organization in Afghanistan.

Religion and World Politics

"You're constantly blindsided if you consider religion neutral or outside world politics," cautions one international relations scholar.[14] It is wise counsel because religion plays many roles in world politics (Shah & Toft, 2006; Fox & Sandler, 2004). Often, it is a force for peace, justice, and humanitarian concern (Johnston, 2003). It is also true, though, that religion has been and continues to be a factor in many bloody wars, conflicts, and other forms of political violence (Fox, 2004). For example, religion is an element of the conflict between mostly Jewish Israelis and the mostly Muslim Arabs. Religion is also part of what divides Pakistan and India, each of which has nuclear weapons, giving rise to what some people believe is the world's most dangerous situation.

Religion also causes or exacerbates conflict within countries. What was Yugoslavia disintegrated partly along religious lines into Catholic Croats, Muslim Bosnians, and Eastern Orthodox Serbs. More recently, religion plays a role in the deadly cultural divide between Serbs and Muslim Albanians in Yugoslavia's Kosovo Province. Conflict can also occur within a religion, as demonstrated by the horrific violence in Iraq between Sunni and Shiite Muslims and even between factions of Shiites.

Organized religion also plays a range of positive roles as a transnational actor. Among Christians, the World Evangelical Alliance, founded in 1846, is an early example of a Protestant NGO. Even older, the Roman Catholic Church is by far the largest and most influential religion-based NGO. The Vatican itself is a state, and the pope is a secular as well as a spiritual leader. The political influence of Roman Catholicism, however, extends far beyond the Vatican. During the cold war, for instance, the Church worked successfully to weaken communism's hold on Poland and other mostly Roman Catholic countries in Eastern Europe. Soon after the Soviet Union collapsed in 1991, its last president, Mikhail S. Gorbachev, wrote, "Everything that happened in Eastern

Europe in these last few years would have been impossible without the presence of the pope and without the important role—including the political role—that he played on the world stage."[15]

The Strength of Religious Fundamentalism

One aspect of religion that has gained strength in many areas of the world is **fundamentalism** (religious traditionalism). Indeed, one study reports, "The world as a whole now has more people with traditional religious views than ever before—and they constitute a growing proportion of the world's population" (Norris & Inglehart, 2004:1). As used here, a fundamentalist/traditionalist is someone who holds conservative religious values and wishes to incorporate those values into national law. Some fundamentalists also have a primary political identity with their religion, not their nation-state. This perspective promotes political cooperation among coreligionists across borders; it may also mean driving out people of another or no faith or suppressing their freedoms within borders.

There is considerable debate over whether the rise of fundamentalism is a series of isolated events or related to a larger global trend. Advocates of the latter view believe that at least part of the increase in the political stridency of religion is based on a resistance to the cultural amalgamation that fundamentalist traditionalists believe is undermining the values on which their religion is based. Religiosity is also heightened among those in "vulnerable populations" who are or who see themselves "facing personal survival-threatening risks" from war, poverty, or other causes (Norris & Inglehart, 2004:4). Whatever its source, a sense of siege increases people's awareness of their religious identity and their solidarity with their coreligionists across national borders. It is strongest in poorer countries, but also affects wealthier ones. What makes the increase in fundamentalism important to world politics is that political conservatism, religious fundamentalism, and avid nationalism often become intertwined in volatile ways.

India and Pakistan   Relations between India and Pakistan provide a prime example of the impact of religion on politics. The two countries were part of British India until 1947, when they were partitioned into Hindu-dominated India and Muslim-dominated Pakistan amid horrific religious conflict that left hundreds of thousands of people dead. Since then a volatile mix of religion and nationalism has beset relations between the two countries and led to three wars and numerous other military clashes. As it has been since 1947, the most perilous flashpoint is the border province of Kashmir, which is part of India but whose population is mostly Muslim.

Two things make the future of the region especially worrisome. One is that nuclear war became a horrendous possibility when India and Pakistan both tested nuclear weapons in 1998. Both countries also have missiles capable of raining nuclear warheads down on each other's cities. The second source of danger is a strong element of religious fundamentalism. In Pakistan it is part of the increase in religious traditionalism throughout the Muslim world as discussed elsewhere in this chapter. India has also seen a rise of nationalist religious traditionalism, politically represented by the Bharatiya Janata Party (BJP), which was founded in 1980 as a Hindu nationalist party. Many members wish to create *Hindutva*, a theocratic Hindu India, or even *Akhand Bharat* (Old India), a mythical concept of a unified Indian subcontinent under Hindu Indian leadership. National elections in 1998 put the BJP in control of India's government. Within months it conducted India's first nuclear weapons tests and in the following several years there were several clashes with Pakistan in the Kashmir region. Certainly the nuclear weapons program in India had long been under development, and the usual charges and countercharges were exchanged between India and Pakistan over responsibility for their clashes, but it is also the case that the BJP brought a more muscular, religious-nationalist lean to Indian foreign policy. The BJP lost power as a result of the 2004 elections, but remains the second-largest party in India's parliament. Thus it is too soon to know whether the fundamentalist appeal of the BJP has weakened among India's voters or whether the BJP will return to power in the 2009 elections.

Israel   Religious traditionalism also influences politics in Israel, where its ultra-orthodox Jewish groups tend to favor a hard-line stance with the Palestinians, no compromise on the status of Jerusalem, and the continuation of Jewish settlements in the West Bank. Indeed, this political faction claims that the West Bank and the Golan Heights are part of the ancient land given in perpetuity to the Jewish nation by God. Whether the policy ramifications are domestic or international, "the issue," according to an Israeli scholar, "is whether Israel will shape a way of life according to Western, democratic concepts, or one infected by Middle Eastern fundamentalism and theocratic impulse." Others dismiss such concerns. "We're not going to make a second Iran in the Middle East," a rabbi who also heads a religion-oriented political party assures listeners.[16]

The United States   Whatever U.S. constitutional doctrine may be, separation of church and state in the United States has never been a complete political reality. Religion has long played a role in U.S. foreign policy. Moreover, many observers contend that religion has been an especially important factor during the presidency of George W. Bush, with Evangelical Christians and other traditionalist Protestants gaining a greater policy voice. Many analysts point to the emphasis on spreading democracy and other aspects of the American way by word if possible and by the sword if necessary as rooted in a religious missionary impulse (Arnold, 2004). Typically, Bush once declared, "The liberty we prize is not America's gift to the world, it is God's gift to humanity."[17] Washington has "exported" conservative religious "family values" as part of U.S. policy in ways such as withholding funds from international agencies that provide abortion assistance (Kline, 2004). Some analysts also link Bush's very strong support of Israel to the strength of the Evangelicals. A survey that asked Americans whether U.S. policy should favor Israel over the Palestinians found that among religious groups, Evangelicals (52%) were second only to Jews (75%) in saying "yes."[18] One reason for this view, explains Evangelical minister Pat Robertson, is, "We believe that the emergence of a Jewish state is in the land promised by God to Abraham."[19]

To understand the Evangelicals' influence on policy, one scholar writes, "it is important to recognize that the rise of the religious right as a political force in the United States is a relatively recent phenomenon that emerged as part of a . . . strategy by [leaders] in the Republican Party who—while not fundamentalist Christians themselves—recognized the need to enlist the support of this key segment of the U.S. population in order to achieve political power" (Zunes, 2004:1). Of course, not all the connections between religion and politics in the United States or any other country are rooted in traditionalist beliefs. Opposition to war, pressure to advance the cause of global human rights, demands that wealthy countries do more to help poorer ones, and many other examples of policy advocacy are centered in more mainline religious beliefs and organizations. That raises the question of whether religion should play a strong role in foreign policy and world politics.

For all connections between religion and global politics that we have been discussing, none has been more in the news than the role of Islam. Therefore, let us turn our attention to a detailed look at Islam because of its current importance on the world stage and because its history and tenets are too often unknown or misrepresented in the Western world.

Islam and the World

Islam is a monotheistic religion founded by Muhammad (ca. 570–632). The word *Islam* means "submission" to God (Allah), and *Muslim* means "one who submits." Muslims believe that Muhammad was a prophet who received Allah's teachings in a vision. These divine instructions constitute the Koran (or Qur'an), meaning "recitation."

It is the political application of Islam by Muslims that interests us here. A traditional Islamic concept is the *ummah*, the idea of a Muslim community that is unified spiritually, culturally, and politically. Muhammad was the first leader of the ummah. Muslims distinguish between Muslim-held lands, *dar al-Islam* (the domain of Islam), and non-Muslim lands, *dar al-harb* (the domain of unbelief). One tenet of Islam is the *jihad*, "struggle" carried on in the name of Allah by *mujahedin*. It is important to stress that jihad can mean spreading Islam or defending the faith peacefully and does not necessarily mean armed struggle any more than the noted hymn that begins "Onward, Christian Soldiers, Marching as to War" implies Christian militancy. This reality has too often been lost in false stereotypes of Islam as intrinsically violent. Certainly, there are militant Muslims. But virtually every religion is afflicted by fanatics who distort its meaning and commit unimaginable atrocities in its name.

The political ramifications of Islam are important because there are over 1 billion Muslims worldwide and they make up a majority in many countries, as demonstrated by the map below. Additionally, Muslims constitute an important political force in countries where they are not the majority population, such as the Philippines. Overall,

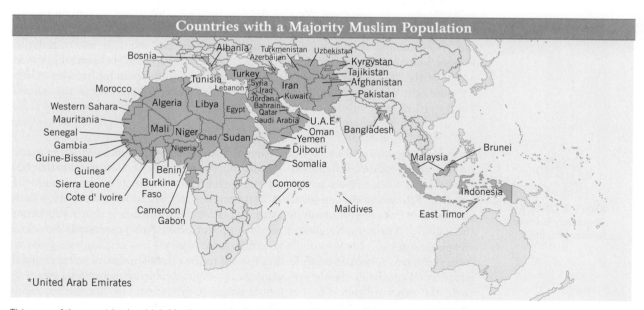

Countries with a Majority Muslim Population

*United Arab Emirates

This map of the countries in which Muslims constitute a majority of the population illustrates that Islam is not confined to the Arab states in the Middle East. In fact, most Muslims are not Arabs. The largest predominantly Muslim state is Indonesia, where 88% of the country's 238 million people are Muslims. The people of Pakistan, Bangladesh, Nigeria, and Iran, the next four most populous predominantly Muslim countries, are also not Arabs.

MAP
Countries with a Majority
Muslim Population

only about one of every four Muslims is an Arab, and the world's largest Muslim community (204 million) is in Indonesia, where it constitutes 88% of the population.

The Political Heritage of Muslims

Muslim attitudes toward the non-Muslim world are shaped by three historical elements. A *triumphant beginning* is the first. During Islam's early period, it experienced rapid religious and political expansion by peaceful conversion and violent conquest. At its farthest, Muslim domination encompassed the Middle East, North Africa, southwestern Asia to the Ganges River, Spain, and central Europe to just south of Vienna.

Conflict with Christian powers, especially those of Europe, is a second element of the Muslim political heritage. Eight crusades were launched by Europe's Catholic kings against Muslims between 1195 and 1270, and other lesser expeditions lasted into the 1400s. Muslims also clashed for hundreds of years with Christianity's Orthodox emperors of Byzantium and later with the Orthodox czars of Russia.

The domination of Muslims by others is the third key historical element of Muslims' political heritage. After about the year 1500, Muslim secular strength declined, and by the late 1800s a variety of European powers had come to dominate many Muslim areas. The last vestige of Muslim power was eclipsed when the Ottoman Empire collapsed after World War I, and the British and the French became the colonial overlords of the Middle East. As a result, most Muslim countries, whatever their location, share an experience of recent colonial domination by mostly European, Christian-heritage powers. During the last half century, direct political domination ended with the collapse of colonialism. New countries came into being; others moved from autonomy to full independence.

Yet there is a strong sense among many Muslims that Western dominance, led by the United States, has continued through alleged neocolonialist practices such as protecting authoritarian pro-Western regimes in Saudi Arabia and Kuwait and using military force to smite Muslim countries that defy U.S. demands to support its interests. For example, a poll in Turkey asking about the possible U.S. use of force to remove Saddam Hussein from power found that a majority (53%) believed that it was a part of the "U.S.'s war against Muslim countries that it sees as unfriendly." Only 34% thought Washington's policy had to do with a desire for stability in the Middle East, and 13% were unsure or refused to answer.[20]

Islam and Nationalism

JOIN THE DEBATE
Can Democracy Succeed in
Islamic Countries?

There are elements of contemporary Islam that support unification by creating a true ummah. After centuries of outside domination, the people in the region that stretches from Gabon to Indonesia have begun to reclaim their heritage in what might be called a "Muslim pride" movement. This includes Islamic solidarity efforts, which have ranged from coordination in protecting Islamic holy places, through support of the Palestine Liberation Organization, to support of Pakistan's possession of nuclear weapons. Among Arab Muslims, the common tie of Islam has helped promote Pan-Arab sentiment. This Pan-Arab feeling has led to the establishment of some regional cooperation (the Arab League, for example) and even attempts to merge countries. For these and other reasons, a majority of Muslims in predominantly Muslim countries identify more strongly with their religion than their country. This focus is different from Christians in mostly Christian countries as Figure 5.10 demonstrates.

Nevertheless, it is very unlikely that Muslims will reestablish the ummah in the foreseeable future. Nationalism is one factor that will prevent this (Telhami & Barnett, 2002). Many Muslim countries have sharp differences and vie with one another for

FIGURE 5.10   Christians, Muslims, and Nationalism

Are you first a citizen of your country or first a member of your religion?

Muslims in 5 mostly Muslim countries
- Other answers 18%
- Country 22%
- Religion 60%

Christians in 6 mostly Christian countries
- Other answers 14%
- Religion 24%
- Country 62%

Nationalism is more important than religion to people's self-identification among Christians in mostly Christian Western countries, but religion provides a stronger sense of identity in mostly Muslim countries.

Note: The six mostly Christian countries were France, Germany, Russia, Spain, the United Kingdom, and the United States. The five mostly Muslim countries were Egypt, Indonesia, Jordan, Pakistan, and Turkey. "Other answers" included refusal to answer, unsure, both equally, and others.

Data source: Pew Research Center, "Conflicting Views in a Divided World," 2006.

regional influence. Iraq and Iran, for example, fought an eight-year-long war in the 1980s that claimed at least 1 million lives. Further solidifying nationalism, there are major ethnic differences within Islam. Culturally, Indonesians are no more like Syrians than are Canadians. Even neighboring Muslim countries can be quite diverse. Most Iranians, for example, are ethnic Persians who speak Farsi; Iraqis are ethnic Arabs who speak Arabic. Furthermore, there is a strong sense of patriotic pride in many Muslim countries. This nationalism is particularly strong when faced by an outside influence, as the United States found out in postwar Iraq. Whatever their views of the departed Saddam Hussein, a substantial percentage of Iraqis chafed at the idea of an extended American presence in their country.

Islam and the Non-Islamic World

The political history of Muslims influences their attitudes toward the outside world, especially the West. First, many Muslims see the United States as the most recent of a long line of threatening Euro-Christian heritage powers. Muslims also see the struggle with Israel and what they perceive as U.S. bias toward Israel as part of a long, ongoing history of attempted Western domination of their region. "There is a deep feeling that when it comes to the Arabs, it's always very harsh treatment, and when it comes to the Israelis, it's easy," notes an Egyptian analyst.[21]

Opinion polls confirm the degree to which these feelings are held widely among Muslims. Even before the U.S.-led invasion of Iraq, a poll of nine Muslim countries found that only 22% of the respondents had a favorable opinion of the United States, and just 12% of Muslims thought the West respects Islamic values. As for the question of Israel and the Palestinians, 84% of Muslims said that the United States favors Israel over the Palestinians. Even a plurality (47%) of Israelis agreed that U.S. policy favors them, with 38% characterizing U.S. policy as balanced, 11% saying it favors the Palestinians, and 4% unsure.[22] Not surprisingly, Muslim views of the West in general and the United States in particular were even more negative after the invasion of Iraq in 2003.

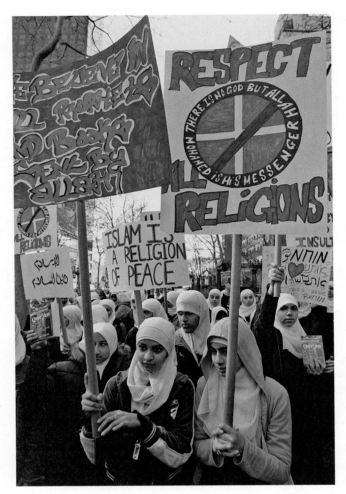

One factor in the widespread anger among Muslims toward the West is the feeling that Americans, Europeans, and others do not respect Islam. These young Muslim women are outside the Danish consulate in New York City protesting a cartoon published in a Danish newspaper. It depicted the prophet Muhammad wearing a bomb-shaped keffiyeh (Muslim men's headdress) with an ignited fuse.

Americans also held a negative mirror image of Muslims. Only 24% of the Americans polled held a favorable opinion of Muslim countries, while 41% expressed an unfavorable view. The poll also found that most Americans have little respect for Muslim culture, with about two-thirds of Americans saying Muslim countries would be better off if they adopted U.S. and Western values.[23] In another mirror image, as depicted in Figure 3.3 on page 71, most Americans felt threatened by Muslims and most Muslims felt threatened by Americans.

Islamic Sectarianism

Religion is not always a source of Islamic unity; sectarian splits within Islam have sometimes caused conflict. The most important division separates the majority Sunnis and the Shiite minority. The issues between the two sects involve doctrinal matters beyond our scope of inquiry. What is important here is that the sometimes quiescent Sunni-Shiite rivalry was reignited in 1979 when the Ayatollah Ruhollah Khomeini led fundamentalist Shiites to power in Iran. One result was Iran's grueling war with Iraq (1980–1988). There were territorial and other nationalistic causes behind the war, but Khomeini's determination to overthrow the Sunni-dominated regime of Saddam Hussein was also a factor.

Sunni-Shiite strife has also spelled continuing tragedy for Afghanistan. For example, there have been frequent charges that Iran is supporting the Shiite Hazara ethnonational group's resistance to the control of the Sunni-dominated central government in Kabul. Even more pointedly, events in Iraq show the interrelationship of sectarian and national forces. The downfall of Saddam Hussein, a Sunni, has opened the way for the country's majority Shiites to dominate the new government. Many Sunnis fear that change, and what was primarily an insurgency against the U.S. presence in Iraq increasingly in 2005 and after became a civil war with Sunnis and Shiites ethnically cleansing areas they controlled and committing daily atrocities against one another. There are also worries that Shiite-dominated Iran might try to gain influence in Iraq through its Shiite majority. Yet the possibility of that happening is severely constrained by the fact that Iraqis are Arab, Iranians are Persians, and historically the two groups have often clashed. Symbolic of this, Saddam Hussein warned Iraqis to continue to fight the Persians as he stood on the gallows in 2007. Adding to the complexity, most Iraqi Kurds are Sunnis, but they have their own variations on Islam that differ from Iraq's Arab Sunnis.

The tensions in Iraq are also being felt regionally as Saudi Arabia, Jordan, and some other predominantly Sunni countries have become uneasy with what they see as the growing influence of Shiite Iran. For example the Jordanian newspaper *Ad-Dustour* ran a story in 2007 warning of a conspiracy to spread Shiism from India to Egypt by, among other things, assassinating "prominent Sunni figures." Some Arabs see the sectarian split as "the most dangerous problem now in the region." Others dismiss it as only marginal, and there is also considerable sentiment that its existence is part of an outside effort to divide and defeat Islam. When reporters asked one Egyptian at a tea stand about the split, his reply was, "There's a proverb that says, 'Divide and conquer.' Sunnis and Shiites—they're not both Muslims? . . . In whose interest is it to divide them?" The answer he supplied to his own question: "It's in the West's interest. And at the head of it is America and Israel."[24]

Web Link

To learn more about the complex religious makeup of Iraq, visit the "Muslim, Islam, and Iraq" site created by Professor Alan Godlas of the University of Georgia at **www.uga.edu/islam/iraq.html**.

Islamic Traditionalism and Secularism

A second point of division within Islam separates Muslim traditionalists and secularists. Traditionalist (fundamentalist) Muslims want to preserve or, in some cases, resurrect their cultural traditions. Many of these, such as banning alcohol and having women cover their faces in public, have been weakened under the influence of Western culture. Fundamentalists also want to establish legal systems based on the *shari'ah* (the law of the Koran) rather than on Western legal precepts. Some traditionalists even want to reestablish the *ummah* by creating a unified political community of Muslims governed by Islamic law. Secularists, by comparison, believe that within Islam there can be many Muslim states and that religious and secular law should be kept separate.

Whatever may be theologically correct, the fact is that since the early 1990s traditionalist Muslim movements have gained strength in many Muslim countries. One reason this may be occurring is that Muslims are especially worried about spreading mostly Western culture. An indication is that 80% of people in mostly Muslim countries feel that their culture needs protection, compared to 62 percent of people globally (see Figure 5.7, p. 145). This sense of cultural threat makes many Muslims welcome the influence of Islam and its traditional values, as Figure 5.11 shows. Yet that does not mean that most Muslims favor the triumph of traditionalism, as the figure also shows.

What does all this mean about the possible existence of a "green peril," a term that relates to the traditional association of the color green with Muslims? The first answer is that it is equally wrong to ignore the role of religion in politics and to make dire and misleading predictions based on the false assumption of pan-Muslim solidarity. For example, it is probable that much of the strong sense of Muslim solidarity that exists is a defensive reaction prompted by the perception of many Muslims that their religion is being threatened. People who feel threatened by a common enemy often unite in opposition to that antagonist. In particular, there are numerous indications that the issue of the Palestinians and the U.S. support of Israel is a key element in the opinion of Muslims, especially Arabs, toward the United States. Given that, a peaceful solution that addresses the needs and rights of both Jews and Arabs in the region will benefit not only those two groups, but the United States and the rest of the world as well. Perhaps the best lesson to draw is that religion is a significant factor in international relations. Like any set of coherent ideas, religion helps define who is on

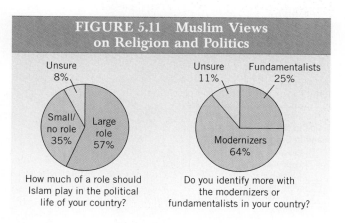

FIGURE 5.11   Muslim Views on Religion and Politics

Unsure 8%
Small/ no role 35%
Large role 57%

How much of a role should Islam play in the political life of your country?

Unsure 11%
Fundamentalists 25%
Modernizers 64%

Do you identify more with the modernizers or fundamentalists in your country?

Polls show that most Muslims welcome significant religious influence in their country's politics, as the left pie chart shows. That does not necessarily mean that most Muslims would welcome dominance by religious traditionalists in their country. Of those Muslims who believe that there is a struggle between secular modernizers and religious fundamentalists in their country, almost two-thirds identify more closely with the modernizers, as shown in the right pie chart.

Data source: Pew Research Center, "Views of a Changing World" (2003) for the left pie chart and "Conflicting Views in a Divided World" (2006) for the right pie chart.

which side and thus often plays a powerful role in shaping the perceptions of political leaders and the actions of the countries they command.

Transnational Movements

A wide range of transnational movements focus on one or another general aspect of the human condition. They can even influence people's political identity, although they do not carry the possibility of people abandoning their national loyalties in the same way that regional and some other forms of transnationalism do. Some of these movements focus on specific issues, such as the transnational environmental movement. Others are organized around demographic groups. Representing this latter type, the women's movement provides an excellent case study of the organization and operation of transnational movements.

Women in the World

Women worldwide have had and continue to have fewer economic, political, and social opportunities than men. Progress has been made, but no country has yet to achieve socioeconomic or political gender equality. The map below shows the current state of affairs, and the most obvious variable is that the gap between men and women is generally greater in less developed countries (LDCs) than in economically developed countries (EDCs). Culture also plays a role, with many of the countries with the most inequality in the predominantly Muslim areas stretching from the Northwest coast of Africa east through Pakistan.

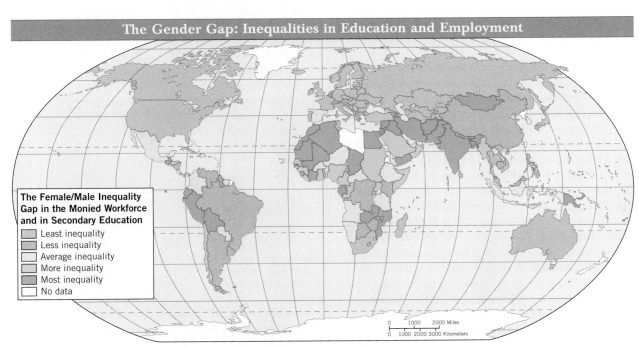

The Gender Gap: Inequalities in Education and Employment

The Female/Male Inequality Gap in the Monied Workforce and in Secondary Education

- Least inequality
- Less inequality
- Average inequality
- More inequality
- Most inequality
- No data

The day may come when one end of a scale of male/female equality is labeled "equal." That time has not arrived yet. This map classifies countries on a scale of relative inequality, ranging from least inequality to most inequality. All societies are held back by legally or socially restricting the educational and work opportunities of females, who make up half the population. While every country does this, the less developed countries, those that need "people power" the most, tend to be the most restrictive and to waste more of the talents of their women.

The status of women is detailed in chapter 14's section on human rights, but for now consider the following barrage of facts: Women constitute 70% of the world's poor and 64% of the world's illiterate adults. They occupy only about 1 in 7 of the world's managerial and administrative jobs and constitute less than 40% of the world's professional and technical workers. Worldwide, women are much less likely to have access to paid employment, and the average woman who does have a job earns only about half of what the average man does. As noted earlier, women are much more likely than men to be refugees, the victims of domestic violence, and the targets of organized sexual assault during conflicts. A recent survey of 35 cities globally found that 2.2% of the women reported having been the victim of a sexual assault.[25] With such crimes often going unreported, the real percentage is almost surely substantially higher.

Such economic, social, and political deprivations of women are not new. What has changed is the ability of women around the world to see their common status through transnational communication and transportation. Also new is the increased determination of women and the men who support the cause of gender equality to work together through transnational NGOs to address these issues. As one UN report points out, "Moving toward gender equality is not a technocratic goal—it is a political process."[26] The global women's movement is the driving force in this political process.

MAP
The Gender Gap:
Inequalities in Education
and Employment

Goals of the Transnational Women's Movement

Transformation is a term that captures the goals of the transnational women's movement. Chapter 6 takes up the role of women as national leaders, but we can say here that despite making up half the world population, women are only a small minority of the world's heads of government, national cabinet ministers, and national legislators. International organizations are no less gender skewed. No woman has ever headed the UN, the International Monetary Fund (IMF), the World Trade Organization (WTO), or the World Bank; and women occupy only about 15% of the senior management positions in the leading IGOs. Like male political leaders, some females have been successful in office; others have not. Yet, as the longtime (1980–1996) president of Iceland, Vigdis Finnbogadottir, has remarked, the stereotype remains that "women are not competitive enough or women do not understand economics." "If you do something wrong," she warned other women at a conference, "you will be attacked with the strongest weapon—mockery."[27]

Advocates of women's political activism see their goal as more than simply a drive for power. For them, increased power for women is also a way to change policy based on their view that, overall, women have different values than men on a variety of issues. While history demonstrates that women leaders can and have used military force, it is also the case, as discussed in chapter 3, that women have been generally less inclined than men to advocate force. Research also indicates that countries with higher percentages of women in their national legislatures are less likely than more male-dominated states to commit human rights abuses (Melander, 2005). Furthermore, there is evidence that women place more emphasis on international social and economic programs than do men, who are apt to stress international security programs.[28]

The transnational women's movement additionally addresses the normative issue of how to improve the lot of women—and everyone else—in the international system. As such, the concern extends beyond sexism's deleterious effect on women to include the impact of discrimination on the entire society. Feminists point out correctly that keeping women illiterate retards the entire economic and social development of a society. It is not a coincidence, for example, that the percentage of women in the paid workforce is lowest in those countries where the gap between male and female literacy is the highest. Educating these illiterate women would increase the number of ways that they could contribute to their countries' economic and social growth. Beyond this, there is a correlation between the educational level of women and their percentage of the wage-earning workforce, on the one hand, and restrained population growth, on the other. In other words, one good path to population control is creating a society of fully educated men and women who are employed equally in wage-earning occupations.

Organization of the Transnational Women's Movement

Web Link

One excellent site related to the global women's movement is the UN's WomenWatch at **www.un.org/womenwatch/**.

Women have been and are politically active in a large number of organizations that focus all or in part on women's issues. These organizations and their members interact transnationally at many levels ranging from the Internet through global conferences. For instance, women can now find out more about their common concerns through the Internet. Collectively, women are now frequently gathering in such global forums as the UN Conference on Population and Development (UNCPD) held in Cairo (1994), the **World Conference on Women (WCW)** in Beijing (1995), and the **Beijing + 5 Conference** that convened in New York City (2000). Beyond the substantive proceedings, such conferences also facilitate transnational contacts among women. Parma Khastgir, a Supreme Court justice in India and a delegate to the 1995 WCW, stressed this contribution, noting that "what appealed to me most [about the WCW] was that people overcame their ethnic barriers and were able to discuss universal problems. They showed solidarity."[29] Even more importantly, women draw on their contacts and experiences through NGOs to promote and influence national and international policy (Jutta, 2003). A good example is Shirin Ebadi, an Iranian woman who has applied her energy and legal skills to bettering the rights of women and children in her country and globally. These efforts earned Ebadi the Nobel Peace Prize in 2003. Her work to empower Iranian women, one study concludes, has increased their "support for the international norms . . . , as well as their desire to change archaic Islamic laws, [which] will nudge . . . [Iran] along the path of globalization more so than ever before" (Monshipouri, 2004:11).

It is difficult to measure the precise impact that transnational communications among women is having through individual interactions, world and regional conferences, and the mass media (Shaheed, 1999). There is evidence, however, that cultural differences among women relating to their roles are narrowing (Inglehart & Norris, 2003). To a significant degree, for example, the "feminist revolution" that began in the United States, Canada, and Western Europe in the 1960s and 1970s affected women not only in those countries, but also as Figure 5.12 shows, seems to have spread to and influenced women in more traditional countries. Overall, then, it is possible to say the process of globalization is having a positive impact on the status of women (Gray, Kittilson, & Sandholtz, 2006).

FIGURE 5.12   Women Legislators

Women's share of national legislative seats

3.0% 7.5% 8.1% 10.9% 12.0% 11.6% 17.0%

1945   1955   1965   1975   1985   1995   2006

One indication that the feminist movement has made strides globally is the increase in the percentage of seats that women hold in the world's national legislatures.

Data source: Inter-Parliamentary Union.

Advances of Women in Politics

Another standard by which to judge the impact of the transnational feminist movement is the advancement of women in politics. "Never before have so many women held so much power," writes one scholar.

"The growing participation and representation of women in politics is one of the most remarkable developments of the late-twentieth century" (Jaquette, 1997:23).

Both these statements are certainly factual, but it is also the case that progress is slow, and that women remain a political minority part of both national and international governance. The changes within national governments, which are detailed in chapter 6, parallel the uphill climb of women to political power in international organizations. The UN Charter pledges equal opportunity for men and women. The reality a half century after the charter was adopted is that women remain seriously underrepresented among the UN's professional staff positions, its top leadership posts, and the ambassadors who head their countries' delegation. "We are a collection of all the world's chauvinisms," one UN staff member has commented bluntly.[30] Still, progress is being made. Most notably at the UN, Canadian diplomat Louise Fréchette served as deputy secretary-general (1998–2006), and she was followed in 2007 by Asha-Rose Migiro, former foreign affairs minister

Women have assumed top leadership positions in many international organizations as well as national governments. The woman at the center of this photograph is Asha-Rose Migiro, who was then serving as Tanzanian foreign affairs minister. Well-wishers are cheering her in early 2007 soon after the announcement that newly named UN Secretary-General Ban Ki-moon had appointed her deputy secretary-general, the second highest UN post.

of Tanzania. Migiro and six other women make up one-third of the 32 members of the UN's Senior Management Group, the secretary-general's Cabinet. Thus, things are changing, although 33% of the senior managers is not half. Former UN executive Nafis Sadik has recalled that in the 1970s when she first came to work at the UN, "Western men saw me as an Asian woman; very decorative, but I couldn't possibly have any ideas."[31] When she retired in 2000 after 13 years as head of UNFPA, no one any longer saw Executive Director Sadik as an adornment.

The accomplishments of these women have been, of course, personal. Many of the other advances of women have been made through national efforts. It is also the case, however, that the progress of women almost everywhere has been facilitated by and, in turn, has contributed to the transnational feminist movement. Women have begun to think of themselves politically not as only American, or Canadian, or Zimbabwean women, but as women with a transnational identity and ties. This is both transforming national politics and weakening the hold of nationalism.

ANALYZE THE ISSUE
UN Women Watch: Transnational Women's Movements and the Case of Gender Mainstreaming

The Future of Transnationalism

It is impossible to predict how far transnationalism will progress. It is not inconceivable that a century from now humans will share a common culture and perhaps even a common government. That is, however, far from certain. There are those who doubt that the trend of today toward transculturalism will continue into the future. Some analysts believe, for example, that English will cease to be the common language of the Internet as more and more non-English-speaking people gain access. "Be careful of turning astute observations about the current state of the Web into implications for the future," one observer cautions wisely.[32]

Moreover, nationalism is proving to be a very resilient barrier to globalization and to transnational movements. For example, it is true to some degree that a transnational identity has evolved among Europeans in connection with the EU. Yet those with that new political identity remain a small minority that is dwarfed by the percentage of people living in the EU countries who retain their traditional loyalty to the nation-state.

Thus we can say that the world is changing and even that it has been changing during recent decades at a rapid pace relative to the normal rate of change throughout history. If anyone 50 or 60 years ago had predicted that globalization and transnationalism would progress as far as they have by the middle of the first decade of the 21st century, critics would have called that person hopelessly befuddled. So what has occurred is remarkable. That does not mean, however, that the transnational trend will continue.

CHAPTER SUMMARY

GLOBALISM

1. Globalism is the view that the world is more than just the sum of its parts, and it focuses on the common heritage that all humans share regardless of the part of the world they come from. It is an ancient viewpoint, evident in ancient Greece, and expressed by philosophers and thinkers through the ages.

GLOBALIZATION

2. Globalization is the process of the integration of communications and transportation, national economies, and human cultures across national boundaries. Transnationalism includes a range of loyalties, activities, and other phenomena that connect humans across nations and national boundaries. This chapter explores the bases and evidence of how globalization has furthered transnationalism in the world.

3. Globalization is an ancient process but has speeded up considerably due to government policies that promote it and due to technological change.

4. The world has become much more interdependent and interconnected through transportation and communications globalization, economic globalization, and cultural globalization. This globalization has spurred transnationalism.

TRANSNATIONALISM

5. The lineage of transnational thought extends in Western culture back to the Stoics of ancient Greece and Rome and to Buddhism in Eastern culture. Transnational thought is evident today in many aspects of postmodernism, constructivism, and feminism.

6. Evidence of the recent advance of transnationalism is provided by the rapid growth, in number and range of activities, of transnational nongovernmental organizations.

7. Regional transnationalism, so far evident only in Europe, could lead to the growth of political identification with regions, rather than nation-states.

8. Many observers believe that cultural transnationalism will lead to greater harmony in the world. There are other analysts, however, who think that we are not moving toward a common culture but, instead, toward a future in which people will identify with and politically organize themselves around one or another of several antagonistic cultures or so-called civilizations.

9. Most religions have a strong transnational element. Some religions assert universalistic claims; other religions create an urge to unite all the members of that religion across countries.

10. Religion has played many roles in world politics, both positive and negative. The current rise in religious fundamentalism in many areas of the world is worrisome.

11. To understand the role of religion in world politics, a case study of Islam discusses the global impact of a transnational religion.

12. An important modern trend in international relations is the growth of transnational movements and organizations that are concerned with global issues. This includes the transnational women's movement and its associated organizations.

13. Although women's attitudes and emphases may vary, the transnational women's movement shares a similar philosophy and goals. These center on the idea that women around the world should

cooperate to promote gender equality and to transform the way we think about and conduct politics at every level, including the international level.

14. Feminists, both women and the men who support gender equity, are pursuing numerous projects and making progress. The fourth World Conference on Women and its follow-up Beijing + 5 Conference are examples of activity in this area.

15. For all the transnational change that has taken place, there is resistance to it. Nationalism remains a powerful, resilient force, and it still dominates people's political identification.

For simulations, debates, and other interactive activities, a chapter quiz, Web links, and much more, visit **www.mhhe.com/rourke12/** and go to chapter 5. Or, while accessing the site, click on Course-Related Headlines and view recent international relations articles in the *New York Times*.

KEY TERMS

Beijing + 5 Conference
civil society
clash of civilizations
foreign direct investment (FDI)

foreign portfolio investment (FPI)
fundamentalism
globalism
globalization
interdependence

merchandise trade
multinational corporations (MNCs)
nongovernmental organizations (NGOs)
political identity

services trade
transnational advocacy networks (TANs)
transnationalism
World Conference on Women (WCW)

National States: The Traditional Structure

For the whole state, I would put mine armour on.
—William Shakespeare, *Coriolanus*

Something is rotten in the state of Denmark.
—William Shakespeare, *Hamlet*

These three jovial fellows may look like everyday tourists, but in fact they are leaders of three of the world's most powerful states at an international meeting in Hanoi, Vietnam. The men, from left to right, are China's President Hu Jintao, Russian President Vladimir Putin, and U.S. President George Bush. This chapter takes up the political nature and role of the state, the traditional and still most important political actor on the world stage.

H OW WE SHOULD GOVERN ourselves is the subject of this and the next chapter. Each examines one way we can politically organize the world stage. This chapter focuses on the traditional path that we have been following for several centuries. Organizationally, it features the state (nation-state, national state) as the overwhelmingly dominant political actor. In particular, this chapter looks at the nature of the state as a political unit, and the implications of its past, present, and possible future as the central actor in the international system.

For all their importance, states have not always existed (Opello & Rosow, 2004). Humans have organized themselves in cities, leagues, empires, and other political structures at various times in history. In fact the state is actually a relatively recent organizational innovation. As chapter 2 discusses, states began to emerge late in the Middle Ages (ca. 500–1350). One part of that evolution occurred when European rulers expanded their political authority by breaking away from the secular domination of the Holy Roman Empire and the theological authority of the pope. The second phase occurred as kings subjugated feudal estates and other small entities within their realms. Indeed, as evident in the accompanying map, most current states are less than 100 years old. These facts—that the state as a form of governance has a beginning and that most states are relatively young—are important because they underscore the possibility that we may not always govern ourselves exclusively through states. Hard as it is to imagine, there are other ways of politically organizing ourselves and our world.

If we choose not to continue to govern ourselves through states or, more likely, if the role of the state diminishes, then what? Chapter 7 provides possible answers by taking up the United Nations, the European Union, and other global and regional organizations as alternatives to the sovereign state or as co-governors with the state in an increasingly globalized world.

MAP
Sovereign States:
Duration of Independence

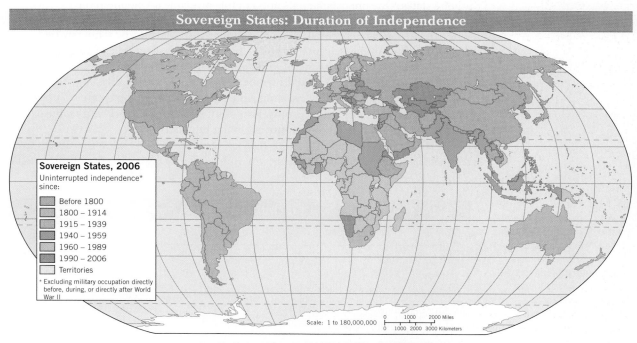

Sovereign States: Duration of Independence

Sovereign States, 2006
Uninterrupted independence*
since:

- Before 1800
- 1800 – 1914
- 1915 – 1939
- 1940 – 1959
- 1960 – 1989
- 1990 – 2006
- Territories

* Excluding military occupation directly before, during, or directly after World War II

Scale: 1 to 180,000,000

0   1000   2000 Miles
0   1000 2000 3000 Kilometers

This map gives you an opportunity to see the geographic dimensions of the recent rapid growth in the number of countries. Notice that Asia and Africa have seen the most change. Most of the countries that now exist on those continents were colonies of a European country in 1940.

THE NATURE AND PURPOSE OF THE STATE

Countries dominate our governance so completely that we seldom question their status. That is a mistake, because to evaluate states it is vital to know what they are and what they are meant to do.

The State Defined

States are units of governance that exercise legal authority over specific territory and the people in it and that recognize no legitimate external higher authority. As chapter 4 on nationalism notes, states are also at the center of the political identity of most people. When Olympic champions step atop the ceremonial stand to receive their gold medal, their country's flag is raised and its national anthem is played. Furthermore, states are the most powerful of all political actors. Some huge companies approach or even exceed the wealth of some poorer countries, but no individual, company, group, or international organization has anywhere near the coercive power wielded by most states. Whatever their other individual differences, states share all or most of six characteristics: sovereignty, territory, population, diplomatic recognition, internal organization, and domestic support.

Sovereignty

The most important political characteristic of a state is **sovereignty**, which means having supreme legal authority. Applied to states it means that they have the exclusive legal right to govern the territory and people within their borders and do not recognize the legal legitimacy of any outside authority. Sovereignty also denotes legal equality among states. One important application of this principle is evident in the UN General Assembly and many other international assemblies, where each member-state has one vote. Are all states really equal, though? Compare San Marino and China in Table 6.1. San Marino lies entirely within Italy and is the world's oldest republic, dating back to the fourth century A.D. After years of self-imposed nonparticipation, the San Marinese in 1992 sought and were granted membership in the UN with the same representation in the General Assembly as China and every other sovereign state. "The fact of sitting around the table with the most important states in the world is a reaffirmation of sovereignty," explained the country's foreign minister.[1]

It is important to note that *sovereignty,* a legal and theoretical term, differs from *independence,* a political and applied term. Independence means freedom from outside

The legal concept of sovereign equality is evident in the equal votes of San Marino and China in the UN General Assembly. Very different are the more tangible measures of equality, such as the two countries' territories, populations, economic production, and military personnel.

TABLE 6.1 San Marino and China: Sovereign Equals			
	San Marino	China	Ratio
Territory (sq. mi.)	24	3,705,400	1:154,392
Population	29,251	1,313,973,713	1:44,921
Gross domestic product (US$ millions)	880	2,455,900	1:2,790
Military personnel	0	2,225,000	1:∞
Vote in UN General Assembly	1	1	1:1

Note: ∞ = infinity
Data sources: World Bank (2007), CIA (2007).

control, and in an ideal, law-abiding world, sovereignty and independence would be synonymous. In the real world, however, where power is important, independence is not absolute. Sometimes a small country is so dominated by a powerful neighbor that its independence is dubious at best. Especially in terms of their foreign and defense policies, legally sovereign countries such as Bhutan (dominated by India), the Marshall Islands (dominated by the United States), and Monaco (dominated by France) can be described as having only circumscribed independence.

Territory

A second characteristic of a state is territory. It would seem obvious that a state must have physical boundaries, and most states do. On closer examination, though, the question of territory becomes more complex. There are numerous international disputes over borders; territorial boundaries can expand, contract, or shift dramatically; and it is even possible to have a state without territory. Many states recognize what they call Palestine as sovereign, and the Palestinians do exercise varying degrees of autonomous control over Gaza (a region between Israel and Egypt) and parts of the West Bank (a region between Israel and Jordan). Nevertheless, these areas can hardly be construed as territory over which the Palestinians exercise sovereign authority. Pakistan provides an example of another limit on the idea of a state's territorial authority. Northwestern Pakistan is controlled by Pashtuns, an ethnonational group that is also the largest group in neighboring Afghanistan. Pakistan's Punjabi-dominated government exercises only limited authority over the border region and its well-armed Pashtuns, and that is one reason that Osama bin Laden has been able to hide there since 2001 and that the Taliban, Pashtun Muslim fundamentalists who governed Afghanistan until overthrown by U.S. troops in 2001, have recently been able to stage a campaign to regain control of that country.

Population

People are an obvious requirement for any state, but populations vary greatly from the 932 inhabitants of the Holy See (the Vatican) to China's approximately 1.3 billion people. Increasingly less clear in the shifting loyalties of the evolving international system is exactly where the population of a country begins and ends. Citizenship has become a bit more fluid than it was not long ago. For example, a citizen of one European Union (EU) country who resides in another EU country can now vote in local elections and even hold local office in the country in which he or she resides. Also a growing number of countries, now more than 90, recognize dual citizenship, being a citizen of two countries. For example, Mexico recently amended its laws to allow Mexicans who have emigrated to the United States and have become U.S. citizens to retain their Mexican citizenship, vote in that country's presidential election, and even have their children who are born in the United States claim dual citizenship.

Diplomatic Recognition

Statehood rests on both a claim to that status and its recognition by existing states. How many countries must grant recognition before statehood is achieved is a more difficult matter. When Israel declared its independence in 1948, the United States and the Soviet Union quickly recognized the country. Its Arab neighbors did not extend recognition and instead attacked what they considered to be Zionist invaders. Was Israel a state at that point? It certainly seems so, because which countries, as well as how many of them, extend recognition is important.

Yet a lack of recognition, even by a majority of other countries, does not necessarily mean a state does not exist. Most countries' diplomatic recognition of the

---

Web Link

Maps of the world's individual countries and other territorial units are available at **http://www.theodora.com/maps/**.

Did You Know That:

The United States allows dual citizenship. The estimated number of Americans with dual citizenship varies greatly from 500,000 to 5.5 million.

GET INVOLVED

The Future of Tibet

Tibet is almost twice the size of Texas and sits 15,000 feet high in the Himalayas. There are about 2.5 million Tibetans in their homeland, and nearly as many in adjacent areas in China and northern India. The spiritual leader of Tibetan Buddhism and the former secular leader of Tibet is the fourteenth Dalai Lama, who was born Lhamo Dhondrub and enthroned in 1940 when he was just five years old. Tibet was independent from the 800s to the 1300s. It then came under Mongol rule for over 300 years, but exercised considerable autonomy under its theocratic leader, who in 1577 was designated as the Dalai Lama (lama of all within the seas) by the Mongols. That autonomy ended when the Chinese emperor launched an invasion and in 1751 established his suzerainty over Tibet. A new era of independence began when imperial China collapsed in 1911 until Chinese forces again seized control in 1950. At first, the Dalai Lama remained in Tibet and exercised some authority. Then in 1959 the Tibetans revolted against China. They were crushed, and the Dalai Lama and his supporters fled south to India.

Now the status of Tibet is disputed. China claims it is a province. Most Tibetans and many others maintain that their homeland is an occupied state. The Chinese government has offered its ethnic Chinese population various incentives to move to Tibet in an attempt to dilute the Tibetan-heritage population and bring Tibet culturally closer to other Chinese provinces. As part of this effort, in 2006 China opened its newest rail line connecting Lhasa, the capital of Tibet, to China's Qinghai Province. The high-tech engineering feat, the world's highest rail line, crosses the "roof of the world" at altitudes reaching 16,640 feet. Although China claims the link will promote trade and prosperity in the impoverished state, Tibetans fear that the accessibility is yet another threat to their unique culture, making it easier for China to assert control over Tibet.

The Dalai Lama is a charismatic figure who is Tibet's chief diplomat. He tirelessly campaigns for his people's political rights, while opposing violence to achieve them. These traits have earned the Dalai Lama access to world leaders and widespread support by many individuals, including such celebrities as actor Richard Gere. Not even the Dalai Lama, however, has been able to win support from any of the world's governments for Tibetan autonomy, much less independence. Thus for now, China has the upper hand. Certainly the attitudes of other states reflect China's growing power, but it is also true that no country established relations with Tibet between 1911 and 1959, when China was much weaker.

Be Active!

While near-term change in Tibet's status is unlikely, nothing is certain. So get involved if you support the Tibetan cause. There are numerous groups on college campuses and elsewhere that would welcome your support. A starting place is to visit the Web site of the Tibet government in exile at **www.tibet.com/**. There, the "How You Can Help Tibet" hyperlink offers suggestions and also provides further links to supportive groups such as Students for a Free Tibet (**www.studentsforafreetibet .org/**). No known citizen groups support Beijing's position, but you can find out more about it and establish contacts if you wish through the China Tibet Information Center at **http://en.tibet.cn/**.

---

communist government of Mao Zedong in China came slowly after it took power in 1949. U.S. recognition was withheld until 1979. Did that mean that the rechristened People's Republic of China did not exist for a time? Clearly the answer is no because the political stand that the legitimate government of China was the defeated nationalists who had fled to Taiwan was an obvious fiction from the beginning.

The issue of recognition remains a matter of serious international concern. Taiwan is for all practical purposes an independent country, with more than two dozen countries recognizing it as such. Yet Taiwan itself does not claim independence from China, and thus is a *de facto* (in fact) but not *de jure* (in law) state. Tibet provides another example in the region of what might be called a state-in-waiting, as the participation box "The Future of Tibet" explains above.

Another contemporary issue involves the Palestinians. Almost 100 countries including China and India recognize the Palestinian National Authority (PNA) as the government of the Palestinian nation. The PNA is also a member or an observer in several international organizations, including the United Nations. The UN Security Council passed a resolution in 2002 calling for a separate Palestinian state, and the

United States and many other countries now also support the eventual creation of a Palestinian state as part of an overall Israeli-Palestinian agreement. Moreover, U.S. interest in that goal increased in 2007 because of Washington's view that resolving the Palestine issue increased the chances for a successful end to the U.S. intervention in Iraq. This hope led to Secretary of State Condoleezza Rice calling on Israeli and Palestinian leaders to meet with her to "accelerate the . . . move to a Palestinian state."[2] Yet amid all the diplomatic maneuvering, it is clear that an independent Palestine does not exist and that any claim that the PNA is the government of a sovereign state is more a matter of legal nuance than practical reality.

While the connection between statehood and diplomatic recognition is imprecise, it is an important factor for several reasons. One is that only states can fully participate in the international system. For example, the PNA holds a seat in the UN General Assembly but cannot vote. This is roughly analogous to Puerto Rico having only a nonvoting member of the U.S. House of Representatives. External recognition is also important because states are generally the only entities that can legally do such things as sell government bonds and buy heavy weapons internationally. Israel's chances of survival in 1948 were enhanced when recognition allowed the Israelis to raise money and purchase armaments in Europe, the United States, and elsewhere. Also, it would be difficult for any aspirant to statehood to survive for long without recognition. Economic problems resulting from the inability to establish trade relations are just one example of the difficulties that would arise. Taiwan's prosperity shows that survival while in diplomatic limbo is not impossible, but it is such an oddity that it does not disprove the general rule.

Internal Organization

States must normally have some level of political and economic structure. Most states have a government, but statehood continues during periods of severe turmoil, even anarchy. Afghanistan, Liberia, Sierra Leone, Somalia, and some other existing states have dissolved into chaos during the last decade or so. Yet none of these chaotic states has ceased to exist legally. Each, for instance, continued to sit as a sovereign equal, with an equal vote, in the UN General Assembly. Some of these disordered states have been restored to a modicum of order, but not all of them. For example, Somalia has not had a functioning government since the early 1990s. For most of the time the Transitional Federal Government (TFG) of Somalia was located in Kenya because it lacked the power to meet in safety in Mogadishu, the country's capital. Meanwhile, real control of Somalia was divided among various warring clans. They, in turn, were defeated by fundamentalist Muslims called the Islamic Courts in 2006. Then in early 2007, the forlorn TFG staged an assisted comeback when Ethiopian troops, supported by U.S. air strikes, drove the fundamentalists from power. Defeating the fundamentalists did not, however, mean empowering the TFG, and most observers gave it little chance of taking effective control of the country.

Some countries lack one or more of the characteristics that define a state. Internal organization is one such characteristic, and Somalia is among the existing countries that have little or no internal structure or cohesion. This 2007 photo of an armed insurgent in the Somali capital, Mogadishu, depicts the disarray. The anarchy sometimes forces the Somali government to flee to neighboring Kenya.

The earlier, multinational state of Yugoslavia collapsed because it did not command the internal loyalty of most of its people. Yugoslavia atomized into six countries, and many Kosovars want to secede and establish a seventh country.

Domestic Support

The final characteristic of a state is domestic support. In its most positive form, a state's population is loyal to it and grants it legitimacy: the willing acceptance of the authority to govern. At its most passive, the population grudgingly accepts the reality of a government's power to govern. For all the coercive power that states usually possess, it is difficult for any state to survive without at least the passive acquiescence of its people. The dissolution of Czechoslovakia, the Soviet Union, and Yugoslavia are illustrations of multinational states collapsing in the face of the separatist impulses of disaffected nationalities. One of the challenges facing postwar Iraq is whether it will be possible to create sufficient domestic support for any government among the badly divided Shiites, Sunnis, and Kurds, all of whom, in turn, have their own internal divisions.

States and Semistates

As is evident from the foregoing discussion of the characteristics of a state, what is or is not a state is not an absolute. Because a state's existence is more a political than a legal matter, there is a significant gray area. Thus there are political entities that well meet all the criteria and are indisputably states. Brazil, Canada, China, France, Egypt, and most of the existing 193 countries serve as examples. It is also clear though, that in the gray area there are a number of what might be termed semistates, those that have many but not indisputably all the characteristics of a state. Semistates can be divided into two groups.

Embryonic states constitute the first group. Such political entities have many or even most of the characteristics of a state, yet they are not generally accorded the status of a full-fledged state. No country truly imagines that the Palestinians control a sovereign state, yet many countries recognize it as such for political reasons. By the same political token, Taiwan functions in most ways like a state, but China's power keeps it in a legal limbo. And no matter what the Tibetans and their Dalai Lama say and no matter what anyone's sympathies may be, Tibet is not and has never been recognized as a sovereign state by any government.

Failed states make up the second group. These are existing states, but they have lost one or more of the characteristics that define a state. They remain legally sovereign entities by default because nothing else can be easily done with them and because other states are reluctant to acknowledge that a state can die due to such causes as lack of internal support; absent or incompetent internal organization; or the lack of real independence, as distinct from legal sovereignty.

One gauge of the number of failed states and states under stress is available in a study conducted by a research institute in 2007. They evaluated 175 countries for stability using 12 criteria and rating each country from 1 (very stabilizing) to 10 (very destabilizing). With a possible range from 12 (absolutely stable) to 120 (absolutely chaotic), 12 countries led by Sudan (113.7) scored 100 or above and might reasonable constitute the failed state category. Another 20 scored in the exceptionally stressed 90s. Scoring 17.1, Norway was the most stable country, with the United States at a fairly stable 33.6. Categories of the rankings of states throughout the world are presented in the map on page 173.

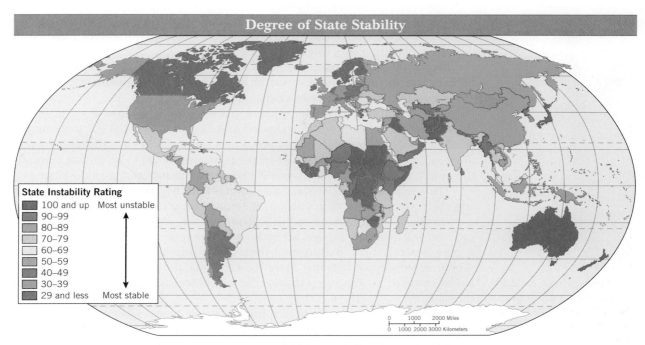

Degree of State Stability

State Instability Rating

- 100 and up Most unstable
- 90–99
- 80–89
- 70–79
- 60–69
- 50–59
- 40–49
- 30–39
- 29 and less Most stable

States range widely in their degree of stability. This map categorizes states according to the stability score of each for 2007. The scores reflect 12 social, economic, and political indicators calculated for each country by the Fund for Peace. About 18% of the countries fall into the very unstable 100+ and 90–99 categories, about 15 are very stable and score under 40, and the rest of the countries fall in between, with the median score at 76.

Purposes of the State

Have you ever stopped to think about why we humans organize ourselves into political units with governments? After all, governments are expensive and they tell us what we must and must not do. Yet, despite this, humans have subjected themselves to governance as far back in history as we can see.

Although political philosophers have disagreed over why humans create societies and establish governments, *individual betterment* is a common theme among them (Baradat, 2003). For example, this theme is evident in the writing of such classical theorists as Thomas Hobbes (1588–1679) and John Locke (1632–1704). Each contended that people had once lived as individuals or in family groups in a **state of nature**. Communities of unrelated individuals did not exist, and people possessed individual sovereignty, that is, they did not grant authority (legitimate power) to anyone or anything (a government) beyond their families to regulate their behavior. They also argued that people eventually found this highly decentralized existence unsatisfactory. Therefore, the theory continues, it was the desire to improve their lives that prompted individuals and families to join together in societies, to surrender much of their sovereignty, and to create governments to conduct the society's affairs. All this was based on an implicit understanding called a **social contract** that specified the purposes of governments and the limitations on them.

Hobbes and Locke disagreed about what persuaded people to abandon the state of nature and merge into societies. Hobbes said it was fear, arguing that life without government was so dangerous that people created strong governments to provide protection. Taking a more positive view, Locke contended that people joined together in societies because they realized that they could improve their lives more easily through cooperation than by individual effort alone.

Among other places, the ideas of Hobbes and Locke are clearly evident in the fundamental documents of the American Revolution and the United States. The idea in the Declaration of Independence that people had a right to "life, liberty, and the pursuit of happiness," and "that to secure these rights, governments are instituted among men," is drawn closely from Locke. And the preamble to the U.S. Constitution combines Hobbes's emphasis on protection and Locke's focus on individual advancement in its words that the purpose of the new government is to "insure domestic tranquility, provide for the common defense, [and] promote the general welfare."

The key point about Hobbes and Locke is that they agreed that political units and their governments were instruments created for a utilitarian purpose and that governments were legitimate and should survive only as long as they fulfilled their practical mission and did not abuse their power under the social contract. This approach is called the **instrumental theory of government**. The idea, as President Woodrow Wilson put it, is that "government should not be made an end in itself; it is a means only. . . . The state exists for the sake of society, not society for the sake of the state."[3]

How does this discussion of the purpose of government relate to world politics? The connection is that having a sense of what states and their governments are meant to do is necessary in order to evaluate how well they are operating. Being able to judge how well states are working will help you analyze the arguments at the end of this chapter about whether we should continue to govern ourselves principally through states.

HOW STATES ARE GOVERNED

Having explored the nature and purpose of states, our next task is to look at the state as our primary political organization. Chapter 1 points out that the quasi-anarchical nature of the international system stems from the fact that the sovereign state is the key actor in the system. Chapter 3 examines how states make foreign policy. Here we explore differing theories of governance and discuss national interests.

How states are governed has a number of ramifications for world politics. These implications relate to such questions as whether some types of government are more warlike than others, whether some are more successful in their foreign policies than others, and whether it is wise to promote a specific form of governance, much as the United States is pledged to foster democracy around the world.

We can begin to address these questions by dividing theories of governance into two broad categories. One includes *authoritarian governments*, those that allow little or no participation in decision making by individuals and groups outside the upper reaches of the government. The second category includes *democratic governments*, those that allow citizens to broadly and meaningfully participate in the political process. As with many things we discuss, the line between authoritarian and democratic is not precise. Instead, using broad and meaningful participation as the standard, there is a scale that runs from one-person rule to full, direct democracy (or even, according to some, to anarchism). The map on the facing page provides one way to order types of government, with the countries in shades of green being generally democratic and the countries in other colors being generally authoritarian.

MAP
Political Systems

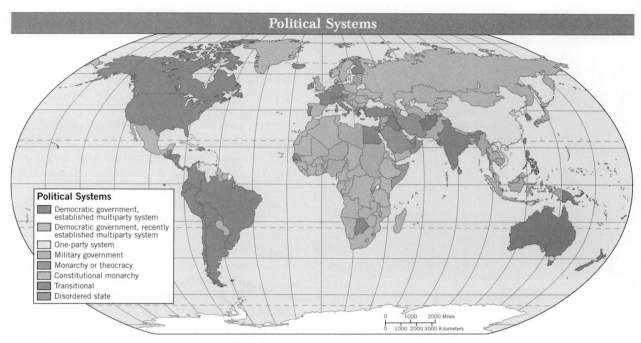

Political Systems

Political Systems
- Democratic government, established multiparty system
- Democratic government, recently established multiparty system
- One-party system
- Military government
- Monarchy or theocracy
- Constitutional monarchy
- Transitional
- Disordered state

0   1000   2000 Miles
0   1000 2000 3000 Kilometers

The democratization of the world's countries, which began symbolically with the American (1776) and French (1789) Revolutions, progressed slowly for 150 years, then accelerated after World War II. Now, as this map indicates, the majority of countries are full-fledged or quasi-democracies. Because of different criteria, this map takes a narrower view of what a "failed" or "disordered" state is than does the previous map depicting state stability.

Authoritarian Government

Throughout history, the most common form of governance was for an individual or group to exercise control over people with little or no concern about whether they consented to it or agreed with the ruler's policies. This approach has included many garden-variety dictatorships that sprang from an urge to power by an individual or a group rather than from any overarching theory of how societies are best governed. Yet there are a number of rationales supporting **authoritarianism**, rule from above.

One of the oldest forms of nondemocratic governance is **theocracy**, rule by spiritual leaders. Today, it has virtually disappeared, and the Holy See (the Vatican) is the world's only pure theocracy. Additionally, theocratic elements remain in the popular, if not the legal, status of Japan's emperor, Thailand's king, and (most strongly) Tibet's exiled Dalai Lama. Iran's government is also partly theocratic. Moreover, Islamic religious law (the *shari'ah*) plays a strong role along with secular law in a number of Muslim countries. Furthermore, the increased strength of religious fundamentalism in many places means that it is not unthinkable that a rejuvenation of theocracy might occur.

Arguments for secular authoritarianism are also ancient. For example, the Greek philosopher Plato (ca. 428 B.C.–347 B.C.), in his famous work, *Republic,* dismissed democracy as "full of . . . disorder and dispensing a sort of quality of equals and unequals alike." He contended that the common citizenry trying to direct the state would be analogous to sailors on a ship "quarrelling over the control of the helm; each thinks he ought to be steering the vessel, though he has never learned

ANALYZE THE ISSUE
Measuring Freedom

There are few theocracies, religious-based governments, in the world today, but Iran is close to being one. Many key decisions must be approved by the country's religious leader, Ayatollah Sayyid Ali Khamenei. The realities of political power in Iran are caught in this photograph of Iran's President Mahmoud Ahmadinejad kissing the hand of the ayatollah during the president's inauguration ceremony in Tehran.

navigation . . . ; what is more, they assert that navigation is a thing that cannot be taught at all, and are ready to tear in pieces anyone who says it can." Plato's conclusion was that ships needed strong captains and crews that took orders and that "all those who need to be governed should seek out the man who can govern them."

Monarchism is one form of secular authoritarianism, although the theory that God had granted kings the divine right to govern contained a touch of theocracy. This system of governance through hereditary rulers has declined considerably. There are only a few strong monarchs (such as Saudi Arabia's king) scattered among a larger number of constitutional monarchies that severely restrict the monarch's power.

Communism as applied by Vladimir Lenin and his successors in the USSR, by Mao Zedong in China, and by other Communist leaders elsewhere, also falls within the spectrum of authoritarian governance. Karl Marx expected a "dictatorship of the proletariat" over the bourgeoisie during a transitional socialist period between capitalism and communism. Lenin institutionalized this view by centralizing power in the hands of the Communist Party, which in turn was dominated by the Politburo and its head. Party control over all aspects of society became so strong that its critics labeled it totalitarianism. Communism peaked in the later part of the 20th century when communist governments controlled the Soviet Union, China, the countries of Eastern Europe, and other countries whose combined populations equaled about 30% of the world population. Since then it has faltered badly, remaining the system of government only in China, Cuba, North Korea, and Vietnam. Nevertheless, Communist parties remain active in many countries and have been the dominant party in Moldova since 2001. Communists also played a substantial role in the recent overthrow of Nepal's king, and party members made up 25% of the interim parliament seated in early 2007 pending national elections.

Yet another authoritarian political philosophy is **fascism**. The term is often used incorrectly to describe almost anyone far to the right. More accurately, the tenets of fascism espoused by Benito Mussolini of Italy, Adolf Hitler of Germany, and other fascists include (1) rejecting rationality and relying on emotion to govern; (2) believing (especially for Nazis) in the superiority of some groups and the inferiority of others; (3) subjugating countries of "inferior" people; (4) rejecting individual rights in favor of a "corporatist" view that people are "workers" in the state; (5) demanding that economic activity support the corporatist state; (6) viewing the state as a living thing (the organic state theory); (7) believing that the individual's highest expression is in the people (*volk* in German); and (8) believing that the highest expression of the *volk* (and, by extension, the individual) is in the leader (*führer* in German, *duce* in Italian), who rules as a totalitarian dictator.

Fascism is of contemporary interest because it is again astir in a variety of countries (Ignazi & Kesselman, 2004). The term *fascist* is so tainted by history that few admit to being fascist. That does not, however, diminish the worry, expressed by an official of the UN Commission on Human Rights, that "neo-fascism and neo-Nazism are gaining ground in many countries—especially in Europe."[4] There neofascist parties have won seats, sometimes several of them, in many national parliaments and in that of the European Union. No fascist has become a head of government, but in the 2002 French presidential elections, Jean-Marie Le Pen, leader of the ultra–right wing National Front Party, received 17% of the vote and finished second among 16 candidates. Le Pen advocates xenophobic, anti-immigrant policies and has dismissed the extermination of 6 million Jews and others in the Holocaust as a mere "detail of history."[5] In the 2007 elections, Le Pen's support sagged somewhat, but he did receive 10% of the popular vote.

Xenophobia and other traits of fascism have received a particular boost from concerns about terrorism and an associated negative focus on Muslims, who make up a significant part of the population in several European countries. Typical of this view, the leader of Belgium's Vlaams Belang (Flemish Interest Party) asserts, "We can't allow that [Muslims] come to our country, that they come to Europe, and they keep their own culture, their own religion—Islamic religion—which is not always compatible with our way of life, our culture."[6] In usually liberal Denmark, *Islamists and Nativists* was the best-selling book in late 2006. Its thrust, according to its authors, is to "compare Islamism to Nazism and communism because they are all three of them a totalitarian ideology." In a third of many possible examples, increased right-wing violence in Germany prompted its government in 2007 to launch a $25 million program, "Youth for Diversity, Tolerance, Democracy—Against Right-Wing Extremism, Racism and Anti-Semitism," meant according to a senior official to send a "clear signal to extremists who want to undermine the values of our society."[7] Thus, in the early 21st century, it is possible to give only a mixed report on the prospects for the end of authoritarian government. The number of authoritarian governments has declined considerably, yet retrograde political philosophies are far from extinct.

Democratic Government

Democracies (from the Greek word *demos,* meaning "citizenry") date back to about 500 B.C. and the ancient Greek city-states. For more than 2,000 years, however, democracy existed only sporadically and usually in isolated locations. The gradual rise of English democracy, then the American and French Revolutions in the late 18th century, changed democracy from a mere curiosity to an important national and transnational political idea. Still, the spread of democracy continued slowly. Then during the past few decades, the pace of democratization picked up considerably, as Figure 6.1 shows.

Democracy, at minimum, is a system of government that extends two types of rights to citizens. The first type is a range of *political rights,* such as voting freely and frequently for competitive candidates who have different policy views and who, if elected, will have an important impact on policy making. The second is a range of *civil liberties,* such as freedom of expression and association and equality before the law, that are important to free government. Note that our definition of democracy contained the words "at

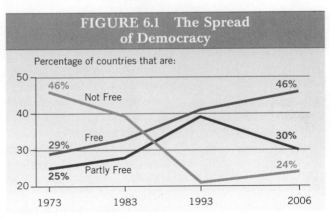

FIGURE 6.1   The Spread of Democracy

Percentage of countries that are:

The worldwide spread of democracy is evident in the upward trend from 29% of all countries being free, as Freedom House terms it, in 1973 to 46% being free in 2006. Meanwhile the percentage of not free countries in 2006 was about half of what it was 33 years earlier.

Data source: Freedom House.

minimum." This caveat reflects the fact that there is debate over some of the attributes of democracy and over the precise line between which countries are and are not democracies. In particular it is important to see that there are no ideal, 100% democracies. Even those countries that by consensus are classified as democratic could be more democratic.

Process versus Outcome

One dimension of the debate over how complete any country's democracy is relates to the relative importance of process versus outcome. Almost everyone agrees that democracy requires a free process. If citizens have free speech, periodically get to choose among competing candidates, and follow other such procedures, then by this standard there is a **procedural democracy**. Stressing procedure to evaluate the extent of democracy is particularly evident in Western thought.

More controversial is the belief that a free process is only part of what defines a democracy, and that real democracy is also characterized by substantive fairness and equality. This notion is called **substantive democracy**. Proponents of this standard contend that a country is not fully democratic if, despite meeting procedural requisites, it produces a perpetual socioeconomic underclass based on race, ethnicity, gender, or some other factor. Such a system, they contend, has two flaws. First, it denies the most important element of democracy—the substantive human right to equality—even if the government adheres to the procedural motions of democracy. Second, the contest is not fair. Any system in which citizens have vastly different economic circumstances is inherently undemocratic because wealthy individuals, groups, and corporations can spend much more than the poor to influence the political process in their favor.

Degree of Participation

Breadth and depth of participation are other standards by which to judge a democracy. Political participation should be open to virtually all citizens, although some limits, such as a minimum voting age, are acceptable. Societal barriers that limit participation must be taken into account, because these can be as important as legal restrictions. There are many groups that could be used to illustrate legal and societal limits, but women will serve to make the point.

Full participation for women is one aspect of democracy that has lagged during its evolution. They did not win the right to vote in national elections until 1893 in New Zealand. Now, almost all countries allow women to vote, although there are some exceptions such as Saudi Arabia. Access to political office for women has come even more slowly. It has only been a century since the world's first elected female national legislators took their seats in Finland's parliament in 1907. Other than monarchs, no woman served as the head of her country until the middle of the 20th century. As former Norwegian

Democracy is a relative term, and how democratic a country is rests partly on the degree to which all its citizens can participate equally in politics. One advance of democracy in recent decades has been the slow but steady advance of women in terms of both their presence in government and the positions they hold. Representing this progress is Germany's first woman leader, Chancellor Angela Merkel, seen here reviewing troops during her visit to China in 2006.

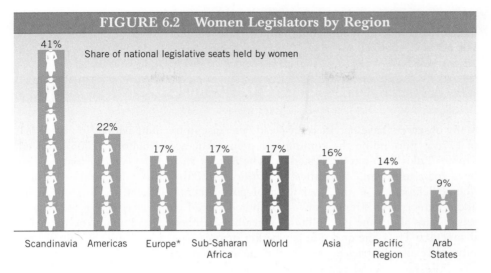

FIGURE 6.2 Women Legislators by Region

Share of national legislative seats held by women

Scandinavia	Americas	Europe*	Sub-Saharan Africa	World	Asia	Pacific Region	Arab States
41%	22%	17%	17%	17%	16%	14%	9%

Since the first women took their seats in a national parliament in Finland in 1907, the percentage of national legislative seats held by women has progressed slowly to 17% in late 2006. At that time, women held the largest share of seats, 48%, in Sweden. Kyrgyzstan and 11 other countries had no women in their parliaments. The United States fell below the world average with women comprising 16.1% of the 109th Congress (2005–2007) and 16.3% of the 110th Congress (2007–2009).

*Europe excluding Scandinavia.
Data source: Inter-Parliamentary Union.

prime minister Gro Harlem Brundtland commented dryly, "I was the first woman in 1,000 years [to head Norway's government]. Things are evolving gradually."[8] Giving truth to that observation, women in early 2007 were only about 5% of the world's heads of government (presidents or prime ministers of their countries), 8% of all cabinet ministers, 9% of all judges, and 17% of the national legislators. Such numbers represent progress compared, for example, to the 3% of the national legislative seats held by women in 1945. Yet even 17% falls far short of equal—50%. Moreover, the overall figures do not reveal that women have an even smaller political presence in some regions, as Figure 6.2 indicates.

By implication, the figure also indicates that since (a) most of the legal barriers to women being elected to parliaments have ended, but (b) that women are still vastly underrepresented, that (c) barriers continue to exist but are mostly societal. Perhaps the most important of these is the chauvinism that exists widely just below the surface. One glimpse of this came in 2006 after a joint press conference held by Russia's President Vladimir Putin and Israel's Prime Minister Ehud Olmert. Not realizing the microphone was still on, Putin told Olmert that Israeli President Moshe Katsav, who had been accused of sexual assault, had "turned out to be quite a powerful man. He raped 10 women. I never expected it from him. He surprised all of us. We all envy him."[9]

Whatever the cause, the proportionate representation for women or any other demographic group is important to the democratic process because underrepresented groups, such as women, often have opinions on issues that differ from overrepresented groups, such as men. As noted in chapter 3, for example, statistics show that women around the world are usually less bellicose than are men of their country.

Did You Know That:

In 1920 the United States became the 28th country out of about 60 in existence at that time to guarantee women the right to vote.

Did You Know That:

U.S. Secretary of State Condoleezza Rice, an avid fan of the Cleveland Browns of the National Football League, says her "dream job" is NFL commissioner.

Given this, some analysts believe that increased female participation through a more inclusive democratic model could reduce global conflict.

THE FUTURE OF DEMOCRACY

Web Link

One place to get involved in promoting democracy is through the Carter Center, whose Web site is located at **www.cartercenter.org.**

Many observers have heralded the steady increase in freedom evident in Figure 6.1, p. 177, as portending the coming of a democratic age (Diamond, 2003). Indeed, Francis Fukuyama has suggested in "The End of History?" (1989:3) that we may have come to the end of political evolution, with "the universalization of Western liberal democracy as the final form of government." Others are less optimistic about democracy's strength or its continued spread (Inglehart, 2003). Such views raise issues about the possibility of spreading democracy and about the impact of democracy. Thus one question is whether democracy will continue to spread until ultimately all countries are free and none are even only partly free, much less not free. The second and related question is whether to passively allow the future spread—or perhaps retreat—of democracy within countries to take its own course or to actively try to promote democracy where it does not exist and to protect it where it does.

If the active approach is chosen, then a number of subsidiary issues arise. One is whether democracy is always possible, at least in the short term.

The Possibilities of Spreading Democracy

One issue related to the spread of democracy is whether, at least in the short term, it is always possible. In most of the West, where democracy has existed the longest and seems the most stable, it has evolved slowly and often fitfully over centuries. More recently, other parts of the world have experienced increased degrees of democratization, but the likelihood that any single country can or will adopt democratic values and practices may be limited by internal factors, such as the country's educational and economic level and the attitudes its people have about democracy.

Democracy and Economic Development

It is clear that there is a strong relationship between democracy and economic development. This is evident in Figure 6.3, which shows that the wealthier a country is, the more likely it is to be a democracy, and the poorer a country is, the more likely it is to be authoritarian. The issue is something of a chicken-and-egg argument. If democracy promotes development, then it is wise to press poor countries to democratize. Among those who take this view, the recipient of the 1998 Nobel Prize in economics

FIGURE 6.3   Prosperity and Democracy

Economic development and democracy are related as evident in this figure, which divides countries into economic groups based on per capita GDP and indicates the percentage of each group that is politically free, partly free, or not free. Notice that the greatest percentage of free countries and the lowest percentages of partly free and not free countries are in the high-income countries. Moreover, all the partly free or not free high-income countries are Arab oil states. Without these, 100% of the high-income countries would be free.

Note: The income groups are from the World Bank for 2005: high income: $10,066 or more; upper middle income: $3,256–$10,065; lower middle income: $826–$3,255; low income: $825 or less. Political classifications by Freedom House.
Data sources: Freedom House (2006), World Bank (2007). Calculations by author.

contends that democracy promotes economic growth by pressing leaders to invest their countries' capital in education, consumer products, and other areas that will build economic strength and stimulate production, instead of in military spending and other less productive economic paths (Sen, 1999).

Others believe that economic development is a necessary precursor for democracy, contending that people need to have a certain sense of economic well-being before they can spare the energy to participate in a democratic system. Leaders of economically disadvantaged countries often argue that their struggle to feed, clothe, and otherwise attend to the needs of their people does not allow the "luxury" of Western-style democracy, with its incessant political bickering and its attention to the individual.

Proponents of the development-first approach also note that educational levels parallel development and that an educated populace is necessary for a strong democracy. From this perspective, attempting to promote full-fledged democracy in countries with poor economic and educational conditions may be doomed to failure. Doing so may even prove counterproductive by destabilizing a country to the point that it collapses into violence and loses any ground it has gained toward both democracy and economic development. From this perspective, in one scholar's succinct phraseology, "Democracy can be bad for you" (Hobsbawm, 2001:25).

Attitudes about Democracy

To have a democracy, it is also necessary for most of a country's people to want one. When people around the world are asked in the abstract whether they favor having a democracy, majorities almost everywhere say that they do. This is even true among Muslims, even though some commentators argue that Islam and democracy are incompatible. A survey of Muslims in nine countries found that 62% said democracy could work in their country, compared to 30% who rejected democracy as a "Western idea," and 8% who were unsure.[10] Yet there are also many indications that democratic principles are not firmly held by people in many countries. For example, as Figure 6.4 illustrates, support for democracy ebbs from its abstract levels if you ask people whether they would prefer having a democracy or a strong economy or whether a democracy or a strong leader is best suited to solve their county's problems. Such responses lead one scholar to conclude that while "today almost everyone gives lip service to democracy . . . when one probes deeper, one finds disturbing evidence that mass support is not as nearly solid [as one would hope]" (Inglehart, 2003:52).

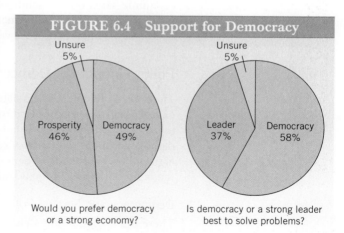

FIGURE 6.4   Support for Democracy

Would you prefer democracy or a strong economy?

Is democracy or a strong leader best to solve problems?

According to a poll of people in over 40 countries, strong majorities favor democracy for their country almost everywhere. However, other types of questions, as shown in the two pie charts, find lower levels of support for democracy. The left pie indicates that if they had to choose, almost as many people would rather have their country prosperous than a democracy. The right pie shows that a substantial minority of people think a strong leader can address their country's problems better than a democratic form of government.

Data source: Pew Research Center (2003).

Exporting Democracy

Another error would be to assume that the United States or any other country can easily or consistently export democracy successfully to other countries. Certainly, there are reasons to promote democracy. Altruism is one. Freedom is better than repression. Spreading democracy may also have more applied benefits. In the next section we will take up democratic peace theory, whose argument is that

WEB POLL
McDonald's or Democracy?

democratic countries seldom if ever go to war with one another. If that is true, then a fully democratic world would be a peaceful one.

There are also problems with the idea of promoting democracy. One is that some low-income countries may not be ready to adopt democracy and may even have their economic development hindered, according to some analysts. A second problem is that, as we noted earlier, there are different standards of democracy. Those emphasized by Americans, the British, and others tend to favor individualism and procedural democracy. Others disagree and take a more communitarian and substantive view of democracy. Arguing this view in a speech, President Hugo Chávez of Venezuela drew strong applause in the UN General Assembly during a 2006 speech when, referring to Americans, he charged, "They say they want to impose a democratic model. But that's their democratic model. It's the false democracy of elites."[11] Further supporting this perspective, a survey taken in 16 countries found that 50% of all respondents did not like American-style democracy, compared to 41% who liked it and 9% who were uncertain.[12] Additionally, trying to export democracy, particularly by force, can cause people in the target country to resist (Bueno de Mesquita & Downs, 2006). Studies do not find a high rate of success when a country tries to democratize another by military force, and only somewhat better results when UN forces are involved (Pickering & Peceny, 2006).

A third limitation on democratizing other countries can be the willingness of people in the exporting country to support the endeavor. About 90% of Americans think that spreading democracy should be at least a somewhat important U.S. foreign policy goal, but most are willing to go only so far to accomplish that. A poll in 2005 found that to promote democracy a majority of Americans were willing to support projects such as giving technical and educational help, sending election monitors, and extending economic aid to countries striving to achieve democracy. But a majority opposed channeling funds to dissidents in authoritarian countries or imposing economic sanctions or sending troops to install or preserve a democratic government. Additionally, 68% of Americans preferred working through the UN to promote democracy, compared to 25% who favored unilateral U.S. efforts.[13]

Policy Impacts of Democracy

The spread of democracy to date and the prospect of it becoming the global standard of acceptable governance lead to questions about what that does and what that would mean for world politics. To address this, we can examine the connection between democracy and foreign policy success, the impact of a greater role for women in foreign policy as a result of democratization, and what the spread of democracy portends for both international and domestic security.

Democracy and Foreign Policy Success

There is a long-standing debate over whether one form or another of government is more successful in foreign affairs, especially war. The noted French observer Alexis de Tocqueville argued in *Democracy in America* (1835) that "it is most especially in the conduct of foreign relations that democratic governments appear to me to be decidedly inferior to governments carried on upon different principles." The drawbacks, Tocqueville wrote, are that democracies tend "to obey the impulse of passion rather than the suggestions of prudence" and also that "a democratic people is less capable of sustained effort than another."

Recent scholarship disputes this view. In fact, some studies find that democracies are more successful than autocracies, at least in war (Ajin, 2004; Biddle & Long,

2004). One study found that democracies have won about 75% of the wars they have fought since 1815 and concluded, "It appears that democratic nations not only might enjoy the good life of peace, prosperity, and freedom; they can also defend themselves against outside threats from tyrants and despots" (Reiter & Stam, 2002:2). Yet other research finds that those wars that democracies do initiate are "uniformly shorter and less costly than wars initiated by nondemocracies" (Filson & Werner, 2004:296).

Democracy and International Security

Another compelling connection between democracy and world politics relates to **democratic peace theory** (Owen, 2004). It is associated with German philosopher Immanuel Kant, who argued in *Perpetual Peace* (1795) that the spread of democracy to all countries would eliminate war. Kant reasoned that a democratic peace would occur because "if the consent of the citizens is required in order to decide that war should be declared . . . , nothing is more natural than that they would be very cautious in commencing such a poor game, decreeing for themselves all the calamities of war." Modern scholarship tends to confirm the idea that democracies seldom if ever take up arms against one another (Doyle, 2005; Kinsella, 2005; Halperin, Siegle, & Weinstein, 2004). Indeed, this view is accepted by many scholars "as 'the closest thing to an empirical law' in world politics" that exists (Henderson, 1999:482).

Several caveats about democratic peace theory should be noted. First, democracies do go to war, although only with autocracies. The easy example is the United States, which is both a leading democracy and the country that has most often been at war since 1945. Second, not all scholars agree with democratic peace theory (Rosato, 2005). For example, some analysts are skeptical that the absence of war between democracies is anything more than a historical anomaly that may not persist in the future (Henderson, 2002). Future history may prove democratic peace theory wrong. For now, though, there is broad, albeit not complete, agreement among scholars that democracies have more peaceful relations with each other than do democracies with authoritarian states or authoritarian states with one another. From this perspective, even if a world in which all countries were democratic did not produce perpetual peace, as Kant thought it would, it might produce preponderant peace and, thus, should be promoted.

This theory debate has serious implications for day-to-day world politics. President Bush has asserted, and some scholars agree, that increasing democracy in the Middle East would make that region less conflict-prone and would ease terrorism (Hafez, 2004). Another matter of great current concern is whether democracy will survive in Russia. President Putin has instituted numerous changes in recent years that have alarmed many as threats to the continuance of Russian democracy (Fish, 2005; Herspring, 2004). If Moscow does sink once again into authoritarianism, and if democratic peace theory is correct, then the potential for conflict between Russia and the democratic West will increase.

Many observers fear, as this cartoon indicates, that President Vladimir Putin is dismantling democracy in Russia. If that is true, and if democratic peace theory is also valid, then the end of democracy in Russia could mean a revival of hostility with the United States and with the democratic countries of Europe and elsewhere.

Democracy and Domestic Security

Views on the impact of democracy on a country's domestic policy range widely. Some research has found little impact on, for example, reducing child mortality and other measures of domestic welfare and safety (Ross, 2006). Other observers contend that the transition from authoritarian to democratic government can produce very negative domestic side effects. It can unleash previously suppressed domestic intergroup hatreds (Mann, 2004). Furthermore, this domestic conflict can spill over into the international sphere. It is possible to argue, for example, that the turmoil that engulfed what was once Yugoslavia was a result of the end of the authoritarian control of the communist government. Once that control was relaxed, the multiple ethnonational rivalries that had been dormant soon erupted into bloody conflict. Similar patterns can be seen in several African countries, in the former Soviet Union, and elsewhere in cases where independence or the coming of democracy has unleashed bloody ethnic clashes.

To this contention, supporters of global democratization respond that in the long run democracies commit less violence against their citizens than do authoritarian governments (Davenport, 2004). Another counterargument is that any bloodshed that the transition to democracy brings pales when compared to the brutality inflicted by authoritarian regimes. One study of "democide," the killing of unarmed residents by governments, demonstrates that the degree to which a government is totalitarian "largely accounts for the magnitude and intensity of genocide and mass murder" committed by that government. Therefore, the study reasons, "the best assurances against democide are democratic openness, political competition, leaders responsible to their people and limited government. In other words, power kills, and absolute power kills absolutely" (Rummel, 1995:25).

STATES AND THE FUTURE

Because sovereign, territorially defined states have not always existed, as chapter 2 details, it is only logical that they will not necessarily persist in the future. It is unlikely that states will vanish as important political actors in the foreseeable future, but it is also unlikely that states will dominate governance in the future as much as they have for the past five centuries. The question then is what role they will and should play. The future of the state is one of the most hotly debated topics among scholars of international relations. As one analyst explains, "Central to [our] future is the uncertain degree to which the sovereign state can adapt its behavior and role to a series of deterritorializing forces associated with markets, transnational social forces, cyberspace, demographic and environmental pressures, and urbanism" (Falk, 1999:35). As you ponder your verdict about states, recall the discussion above about the purpose of government and apply your own conclusions about what governments should do to your evaluation of the success or failure of the state as the continued dominant model of governance.

The State: Changing Status

In many ways, states remain alive and well on the world stage. One sign of health is their increasing number. As Figure 6.5 depicts, there are now more than twice as many countries as there were in the middle of the 20th century. Additionally, and as noted frequently, states remain the most important and powerful type of international actor. Some of them, especially the United States, are truly formidable. Much of what underpins states, such as nationalism, also remains strong. Yet all is not well for the preeminent position of states. This is evident in the rise of rivals to the state's dominance of governance and in the weakening of the doctrine of sovereignty.

Limits to State Governance

Chapter 1's introduction of the cast of actors in the global drama notes that joining states on the stage is an increasing number of intergovernmental organizations (IGOs) such as the United Nations and World Trade Organization (WTO) at the global level and the European Union (EU) and Organization of American States (OAS) at the regional level. There are now eight times as many of these NGOs as there were a century ago. Some of them, like the UN, have a wide range of functions. Others, including the WTO, are more specialized. One link among many NGOs is that to some degree they help govern the international system. All the countries that have joined an NGO agree to support certain principles and to act in certain ways. To some extent, some IGOs also have the ability to enact new rules that members are legally obliged to follow. When there are disputes over whether members are living up to their obligations, some IGOs have judicial-like processes to resolve the dispute. Trade disagreements are now much more likely to be fought with lawyers during a hearing at the WTO than with gunboats.

Another phenomenon that grew rapidly in number during the last century was multilateral treaties, some of which have been ratified by nearly all the world's countries. For instance, 185 of the world's 193 countries have legally agreed to abide by the Convention on the Elimination of All Forms of Discrimination against Women (CEDAW, 1980). Most of the multilateral treaties are lawmaking treaties that bind ratifying countries to follow the pacts' clauses. Some of these treaties even arguably bind states that have not ratified them. For one, a series of multilateral treaties dating as far back as 1864 and collectively called the Geneva Conventions govern many aspects of the conduct of war. Those who commit war crimes in violations of these treaties may well find themselves answerable to the International Criminal Court or some other international tribunal whether or not the accused's country is a party to the conventions.

It would be naïve to imagine that IGOs can wield the authority that is at the command of most states or that multilateral treaties and other aspects of international law are not only often ignored but violated with impunity by states. But it would also be missing an important change in the way that the world is governed to imagine that IGOs and multilateral treaties are not an increasingly important factor in determining the conduct of states and even private organizations and individuals. This shift in governance is detailed in the chapters on the alternative approach to world politics, especially chapter 7 on IGOs and chapter 9 on international law.

The Weakening of State Sovereignty

A second key change in the status of countries is the weakening of the doctrine of state sovereignty. The long-standing notion that a state is answerable to no other authority higher than itself is on the wane. One aspect of this, as noted, is that ever so slowly, countries are taking on obligations to conduct themselves internationally

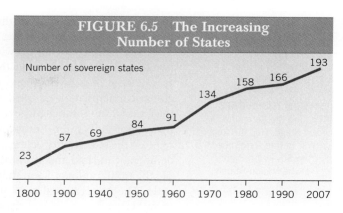

FIGURE 6.5 The Increasing Number of States

Number of sovereign states

23 — 57 — 69 — 84 — 91 — 134 — 158 — 166 — 193

1800 1900 1940 1950 1960 1970 1980 1990 2007

This figure charts the rapid growth in the number of countries. From the beginning of the sovereign state system about 500 years ago, it took until 1940 for there to be 69 states. In less than 70 years since then, the number of states has nearly tripled.

by the rules and decisions of the WTO and other IGOs and the terms of the Geneva Conventions and other treaties.

JOIN THE DEBATE
Casting the Actors for the World Stage: Has the Recent War in Iraq Reinforced the Sovereign Rights of the Nation-State?

Even what countries do within their own borders is no longer beyond international oversight. For example, the world community is beginning to reject sovereignty as a defense of a government's mistreatment of its citizens. During the early 1990s, global condemnation coupled with economic and other forms of sanctions forced the Eurowhite-dominated government of South Africa to end the apartheid system that oppressed its non-European-heritage citizens, especially its blacks. The UN also rejected the sovereignty defense when in 1994 it condemned the military overthrow of democracy in Haiti and authorized UN members to form a multinational force to topple the military junta. Soon thereafter, a U.S.-led force sent the generals packing into exile. The international community in the late 1990s demanded that the Yugoslav [now Serbian] government cease its brutal attacks on rebellious Albanians in Kosovo, even though that province is clearly part of Yugoslavia. When diplomacy and sanctions failed, NATO warplanes went into action. The Serbs were driven from Kosovo, and the province was occupied by a multinational force. Two years later, more recently, the UN authorized the use of force to topple the government of Afghanistan when it did not comply with demands that it surrender accused al Qaeda terrorists. Even more recently, the UN Security Council has demanded that Sudan halt the killing of people in Darfur by Janjaweed militia and that it turn over war criminals to the International Criminal Court (ICC) in The Hague, the Netherlands. Sudan's parliament has condemned the UN resolution, which it said was devoid of "any basis for justice and objectivity and violates the principle of national sovereignty."[14] Expressing the opposite and prevailing global view, the UN secretary-general praised the resolution as lifting "the veil of impunity that has allowed human rights crimes in Darfur to continue unchecked."[15]

A related and dramatic demonstration of the diminution of sovereignty is the trial of two presidents for international crimes. One was Slobodan Milosevic, the former president (1989–2000) of Yugoslavia who was tried by a UN-authorized tribunal located in the Netherlands for war crimes he allegedly abetted during the 1990s in Bosnia, Croatia, and Kosovo. Given the evidence, Milosevic would have almost certainly been convicted and sentenced to life in prison had he not died of heart failure in 2006. Similarly, Charles Taylor is currently on trial by another special tribunal, also located in the Netherlands, for international crimes he committed before and during his time as president of Liberia (1997–2003).

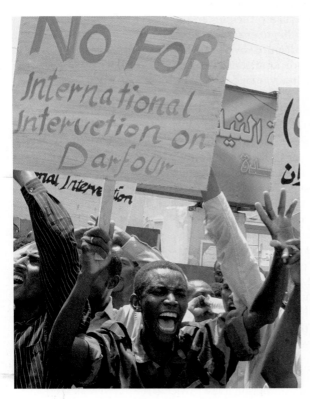

These Sudanese are protesting in their capital, Khartoum, against the international pressure on their government to allow a strong UN peacekeeping force to enter the war-torn Sudanese region of Darfur. They claim this would constitute a violation of Sudan's sovereignty. Most of the international community disagreed that sovereignty could serve to shield Sudan from outside intervention, and in 2007 Khartoum agreed to the entry of an enhanced UN force.

What should we make of these restraints on internal sovereignty in South Africa, Haiti, Yugoslavia, Afghanistan, and Sudan? It would be naïve to imagine they mean that in the foreseeable future the world community will regularly ignore sovereignty to take a stand against racism or authoritarianism whenever and wherever they occur. It would be equally wrong, however, not to recognize that the actions against racial oppression, military coups, ethnic cleansing, and neofascism were important steps away from the doctrine of unlimited state sovereignty.

The State: The Indictment

Some people view the diminution of sovereignty and other indications that states are weakening as a good thing. They contend that states are obsolete and/or destructive. Others contend that states are an appropriate and viable focus of governance and reject attacks on the state as unwise and even unpatriotic. You would be wise as you consider the arguments for and against the state to be wary of being overly influenced by your loyalty to your country and letting that lead you to reject the antistate points out of hand. Remember that states, like all units of government, should be considered utilitarian objects meant to protect and promote the common good. If states are not doing that, it is not treason to seek change. As the Declaration of Independence counseled, "Governments are instituted among men" to promote their "life, liberty, and pursuit of happiness," and, "Whenever any form of government becomes destructive [or incapable] of these ends, it is the right of the people to alter or to abolish it, and to institute a new government" in a form that "to them shall seem mostly likely to effect their safety and happiness."

States Are Obsolete

The argument that states are obsolete begins with the premise that they were created as a form of government hundreds of years ago to meet security, economic, and other specific utilitarian needs and to replace the feudal system and other forms of political organization that no longer worked effectively. Critics charge that states are obsolete because, first, they no longer meet their utilitarian responsibilities very well and, second, because states often pursue foreign policies that do not reflect the interest or wishes or their citizens.

States Are No Longer Utilitarian Those who believe that states will and/or should play a diminished role in the future point to a number of areas where they say countries are not adequately performing the tasks they were created to do. This charge is leveled against all states, but it is particularly applied to the many states created in the past half century that have some or all of the following limitations: small territories, small populations, and few prospects for economic viability. Timor-Leste, a recently independent country (2002), provides an example. Its population (about 950,000) is similar to that of Montana, the 44th least populous U.S. state, and Timor's territory (5,794 sq. mi.) is larger than only three U.S. states: Connecticut, Delaware, and Rhode Island. "Impoverished" understates Timor's economic distress. Its $570 per capita GNP, one of the lowest in the world, is 1/73rd of the U.S. per capita GNP. Most Americans would smile at the thought of, say, an independent Arizona joining the ranks of sovereign states on the world stage. Yet it or any other U.S. state would be a more viable state than East Timor is. That country is something of an extreme case, but on a broader basis, an independent Arizona would be well into the middle ranks of countries in terms of population and territory and would be a leader in terms of its economic size, as Figure 6.6 shows.

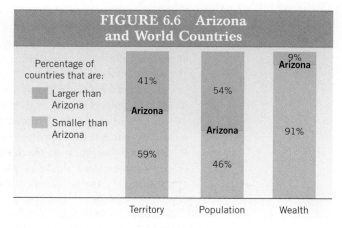

FIGURE 6.6 Arizona and World Countries

Percentage of countries that are:
- Larger than Arizona
- Smaller than Arizona

Territory: 41% (Arizona), 59%
Population: 54%, Arizona 46%
Wealth: 9% Arizona, 91%

Arizona's viability as an independent country would be questionable, yet that U.S. state has a territory that is larger than 59% of the world's countries and a population larger than 46% of them. Although not especially wealthy by U.S. standards, Arizona's per capita income compared to the per capita national incomes of the world's countries would make Arizonans wealthier than the people in 91% of all countries. The small size, population, and economic base (and sometimes all three) of many world countries casts doubt on the future of the sovereign state as the central actor in the international system.

Data sources: CIA (2007), World Bank (2007), U.S. Bureau of Economic Analysis (2007).

Providing physical safety is one key role of states. Yet their ability to protect their citizens is limited, and it has been getting worse since the signing of the Treaty of Westphalia (1648), the symbolic beginning of the state system. From then to now, almost 600 wars have occurred, killing over 140 million people. Moreover, the number of victims has risen rapidly through the centuries as we have "improved" our ability to kill one another. Indeed, 75% of all the people killed in wars during the last 500 years died in the 20th century. What is worse, science and technology have now created nuclear, chemical, radiological, and biological weapons of mass destruction (WMDs), against which there is little or no defense. Such weapons are possessed by states, but in time terrorists will also acquire at least some forms of rudimentary WMDs. Therefore, the question is: Can states provide their people with reasonable safety in a world beset by WMDs and terrorists?

Providing economic prosperity is a second key role that states are supposed to play. The same type of questions asked about safety apply to the economic functions of a state. The tidal wave of trade and capital that moves across national borders means that states are increasingly less able to provide for the prosperity of their residents. For example, jobs are won or lost depending on a variety of factors, such as where transnational corporations decide to set up manufacturing, choices over which national governments have little or no control.

Providing for the general welfare is a third key role of states. Health is one such concern, and states as independent entities are finding themselves increasingly unable to contain the spread of disease in an era when people and products that may carry the threat of disease with them move quickly and in massive numbers around the globe. AIDS is the most obvious example, and in the past few decades it has spread around the world and has killed about 28 million people. Other epidemics loom menacingly. Currently there is great concern that avian flu, which has killed some people in Asia, could rapidly spread globally with disastrous consequences. The World Health Organization (WHO) estimates that avian flu could infect as much as 30 percent of the world's population. One WHO official estimates that conservatively such a pandemic would kill between 2 million and 7 million people, and, "The maximum range is more . . . maybe 20 [million] to 50 million people."[16]

Whether it is AIDS, avian flu, or another microbial enemy, the reality, according to a U.S. physician, is that "today, in 30 hours, you can literally travel to the other side of the world. And likewise, while you are there, you can pick up a germ or a microorganism that may not exist on this side of the globe and within 30 hours you can have that back in the United States."[17] National borders provide increasingly scant protection against these globally transportable diseases, which, if they are to be contained, must be attacked through an international effort.

States Do Not Pursue the Interests of Their People

Most states are huge enterprises that have authority over many millions of people and in two cases (China and India) over more than a billion of them. The issue is whether such mega-organizations are closely connected enough to their people to operate in their interests. This criticism touches on domestic as well as foreign policy, but for our purposes we will concentrate on national interest in world politics.

Critics of **national interest** as a guide for foreign policy advance a number of objections. One is that there is no such thing as an objective national interest. Critics say that what is in the national interest is totally subjective and defining it tends to be the province of every country's dominant political class, its **power elite**, rather than its citizens. This accounts for the frequent policy differences between what a country's leaders and its common citizens support, as detailed in chapter 3's discussion of the leader-citizen opinion gap. It is also the case that a determined individual leader can decide that a course of action is in the national interest even when an overwhelming majority of the country's citizens disagree. As evident in Figure 6.7, that is what occurred in 2007 when President Bush decided to send more troops to Iraq.

A second objection is that using national interest as a basis of policy incorrectly assumes that there is a common interest. The contention here is that every society is a collection of diverse subgroups, many of which have differing interests. Furthermore, the concept of national interest inherently includes the assumption that if a collective interest can be determined, then that interest supersedes the interests of subgroups and individuals. Writing from the feminist perspective, for example, one scholar has noted that "the presumption of a similarity of interests between the sexes is an assumption" that cannot be taken for granted because "a growing body of scholarly work argues that . . . the political attitudes of men and women differ significantly" (Brandes, 1994:21).

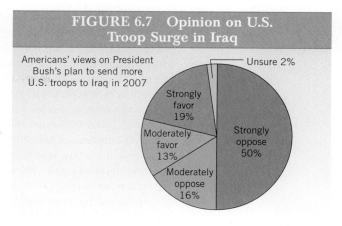

FIGURE 6.7   Opinion on U.S. Troop Surge in Iraq

Americans' views on President Bush's plan to send more U.S. troops to Iraq in 2007

- Unsure 2%
- Strongly favor 19%
- Moderately favor 13%
- Moderately oppose 16%
- Strongly oppose 50%

President Bush announced in January 2007 that he was dispatching additional troops to Iraq. A poll the next day found that two-thirds of Americans opposed the idea, with half of all respondents adamantly against it. Most members of Congress also opposed the plan. Yet there was only one person whose view of the national interest counted in this case, and that was President Bush. Such instances raise questions about the suitability of countries as representatives of the interests of their citizens.

Data source: CNN poll, January 11, 2007; data provided by The Roper Center for Public Opinion Research, University of Connecticut.

Critics of the state system argue it would be far better to explore other ways of defining interests. *Global interests* are one alternative to national interest. Proponents of this standard do not reject national interest as such. Instead, they say that in the long run, a more enlightened view of interests is that all states will be more secure and more prosperous if the more fortunate ones help the others to also achieve peace and prosperity. That is essentially the point that Han Seung-soo, president of the UN General Assembly, made when he commented that particularly "in the wake of September 11" it is imperative to recognize "that development, peace, and security are inseparable," because the poorest countries are "the breeding ground for violence and despair."[18]

Individual interests are another alternative to national interest. Virtually all individuals are rightly concerned with their own welfare. In his inaugural address, President John F. Kennedy called on Americans to "ask not what your country can do for you—ask what you can do for your country." Maybe Kennedy had it backwards. Your country is arguably there to serve you, not the other way around, and what is good for your country or your nation may not be what is good for you. Considering your individual interests might seem very narrow-minded, but it also can be liberating because it can free you from attaching your policy preference to what is good for a collective (your nation) or an organization (your state). It is appropriate to ask, then, whether your individual interests, your nation's interests, your country's interests, and your world's interests are the same, mutually exclusive, or a mixed bag of congruencies and divergences. Only you, of course, can determine where your interests lie and what policies you support or oppose.

States Are Destructive

Pursuing the national interest is the essence of what a sovereign state does and what its citizens expect it to do. Critics castigate this emphasis on the national interest as inherently self-serving and inevitably leading to conflict and inequity. As France's foreign minister observed recently, the world should no longer act as if "we are . . . in prehistoric times when whoever had the biggest club would try to knock the other guy out so he could steal his mammoth skin."[19] The logic is simple. If countries pursue their national interests and those objectives are incompatible, then one likely possibility is that they will clash. Another possibility is that the interest of whichever state is the more powerful will prevail. That is, power, not justice, will win. Certainly, countries often negotiate and compromise. But in an anarchical international system that emphasizes self-interest and self-help, the chances of a peaceful and equitable resolution are less than in a hierarchical domestic system that restrains the contending actors and offers institutions (such as courts) that can decide disputes if negotiation fails.

Critics of the state system further contend that whatever the wins and losses are for states, the most likely losers are average citizens. Much more than leaders, the citizenry bear the brunt of war, economic sanctions, and other diplomatic tools states use in conflict with one another. To make matters worse, states often inflict violence and otherwise abuse the human rights of the very people they are supposed to protect. Estimates vary considerably about the number of people killed by governments oppressing their own people, but at least 80 million people died as a result of tyranny and genocide. At least another 50 million people perished from famine caused by the politically inspired programs of their government, with deaths in two communist states, the USSR and China, leading the list. What is clear is that more people died from such domestic causes than died during international and traditional civil wars combined.

A third argument is that states are destructive because they are unstable. As detailed in chapter 4, most states are a mélange of ethnonational groups rather than ideal nation-states. This ethnonational mix leads to conflict between groups that can drag outside countries into the fighting. Instability in other states comes from their grinding poverty. Whatever the cause, the result is numerous weak and even failed states, and these are the source of many of the problems the world faces (Fearon & Laitin, 2004; Fukuyama, 2004).

The State: The Defense

While those who predict or advocate the diminishment or demise of the state as a primary political organization make a strong argument, it is hardly an open-and-shut case against the state (Paul, Ikenberry, & Hall, 2004). First, as noted, nationalism has proven resilient, and its political vehicle, the state, still has many resources at its disposal. Moreover, the number of states has increased significantly. These facts undermine the assertion about the substantial weakening, much less the disappearance, of states as sovereign actors (Lentner, 2004). It is also the case, one scholar argues, that while globalization is decreasing the importance of borders as information, money, goods, services, and people flow increasing across them, "States are responding to globalization by attempting to restore meaning to national borders, not as barriers to entry, but as boundaries demarcating distinct political communities" (Goff, 2000:533).

Second, states may be able to adjust to the new realities by learning to cooperate and live in peace with other countries. Analysts who hold this view point to the increasing creation of and membership in numerous IGOs, like the WTO, as evidence that states are willing to give up some of their sovereignty in return for the benefits provided by free trade and other transnational interactions.

Third, states are arguably being strengthened as increasingly complex domestic and international systems create new demands for services. "Empirical evidence demonstrates that the roles of the state are changing rather than diminishing," according to two scholars. "The state remains crucially involved in a wide range of problems," they continue, and "in each of these areas, specific initiatives may make state policies more efficient . . . as the roles of the nation-state continue to evolve" (Turner & Corbacho, 2000:118–119). One indication that states are not withering on the vine is found in Figure 6.8, which shows that in recent decades states have increased their importance in the world economy.

Fourth, sovereignty has always been a relative, not an absolute, principle and a dynamic, rather than static, concept. States and their leaders have long violated the principle when it suited their interests. Most of the examples of diminished sovereignty have occurred when stronger states or coalitions of states imposed their will on weaker states. For this reason smaller states are often suspicious that interventions, even those sponsored by the UN, are an imperialist wolf dressed in humanitarian sheep's clothing. More powerful states, the contention continues, retain all their sovereignty or can and sometimes do withdraw from agreements to follow the decisions of IGOs. The United States, for instance, has refused to surrender any of its sovereign authority by joining the International Criminal Court (ICC), which would allow U.S. troops and citizens to be potentially prosecuted for war crimes by the international tribunal. This stance was also evident after the International Court of Justice (ICJ) ruled against the United States in a case involving its treatment of foreign nationals accused of crimes within the country. In response, the White House announced in 2005 that the United States was withdrawing from the part of the ICJ treaty giving that court jurisdiction over such disputes.

Fifth, sovereign states may prove to be better than the other forms of political organization. States do provide some level of defense, and some states have been relatively effective at shielding their citizens from the ravages of war. Sometimes that is a matter of power, as is true for the United States. But in other cases, it is related to geography, diplomatic skill, or a simple resolution not to take sides under almost any circumstances. Sweden and Switzerland, for example, managed to avoid becoming involved in any war, including either world war, during the 20th century.

Sixth, it is yet to be proven that IGOs provide an effective alternative to the state. Peacekeeping by the United Nations and other IGOs has had successes, but also notable failures. The WTO and other economic IGOs are under attack for benefiting rich countries, corporations, and individuals at the expense of less developed countries, small businesses, and workers. It may well be, as we will discuss in the next chapter, that IGOs can prove to be more effective and just instruments of governance as they evolve. That remains an open question, though.

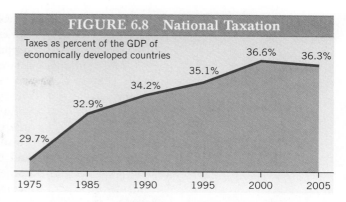

FIGURE 6.8   National Taxation

Taxes as percent of the GDP of economically developed countries

29.7% — 32.9% — 34.2% — 35.1% — 36.6% — 36.3%

1975   1985   1990   1995   2000   2005

The view that states have become less important and will decline further is arguably contradicted by their continued and in some ways increasing status as the world's most significant economic organizations. This figure shows tax revenues collected by governments of the mostly industrialized countries in the Organization of Economic Cooperation and Development (OECD). From 1975 through 2000, government taxes (and, not shown, government expenditures) accounted for a steadily increasing share of the GDPs of the OECD countries. Although the chart seems to indicate that a decline began in 2000, that is misleading. The downturn lasted only through 2003 (35.8%) before increasing from that point in 2004 and again in 2005. As a point of reference, each 0.1% increase in the OECD tax rate equals about $31.5 billion in revenue. Total OECD tax revenues in 2005 were about $11.4 trillion.

Data source: OECD (2007).

The state as the central unit of human governance has proven very resilient, despite all its shortcomings. States remain the most powerful political actors globally, and they are still the focus of most people's political loyalties. This strength and focus is captured in this image of Turkish army helicopters with flags flying and special forces soldiers dangling from ropes during the country's Republic Day parade, October 29.

SIMULATION
The Future of the State:
Will Nationalism Survive?

Seventh, realists doubt that self-interest and conflict can ever be substantially eliminated from the system and support the state as a necessary guardian of the national interest. Former U.S. Secretary of State Henry Kissinger (1994:37), for one, warns against what he sees as Americans' "distrust of [U.S.] power, a preference for multilateral solutions and a reluctance to think in terms of national interest. All these impulses," Kissinger believes, "inhibit a realistic response to a world of multiple power centers and diverse conflicts."[20] Realpolitik nationalists further contend that we live in a Darwinian political world, where people who do not promote their own interests will fall prey to those who do. Nationalists further worry about alternative schemes of global governance. One such critic of globalism notes that in intellectual circles "anyone who is skeptical about international commitments today is apt to be dismissed as an isolationist crank." Nevertheless, he continues, globalization should be approached with great caution because "it holds out the prospect of an even more chaotic set of authorities, presiding over an even more chaotic world, at a greater remove from the issues that concern us here in the United States" (Rabkin, 1994:41, 47).

The State: The Verdict

For now, the jury is still out on whether states will and should continue to dominate the political system and be the principal focus of political identity. States continue to exercise great political strength and most of them retain the loyalty of most of their citizens. Yet it is also true that the state exists in a rapidly changing political environment that is creating great pressures, whether they are those of Barber's (1995) tribalism or McWorld. The only certainty is that it would be an error to assume that the state-based system is invulnerable to change. There is wisdom in the observation, "History sides with no one. . . . [The] lesson to be drawn [from the rise and evolution of states] is that all institutions are susceptible to challenges." Therefore, the sustainability of states depends in substantial part on whether they provide "efficient responses to such challenges" (Spruyt, 1994:185).

Where does this leave the future of sovereign states in the early 21st century? Most political scientists take a middle ground, recognizing the decline in the importance of states, but not predicting their demise in the foreseeable future (Holsti, 2004; Sørensen, 2004). As one puts it, "Although the system of sovereign states is likely to continue [for now] as the dominant structure in world politics, the content of world politics is changing" (Keohane & Nye, 1999:118). A policy choice for all of us is how much we want it to change and in what direction: further along the alternative path or back along the traditional path of world politics.

CHAPTER SUMMARY

THE NATURE AND PURPOSE OF THE STATE

1. States are the most important political actors. States as political organizations have these defining characteristics: sovereignty, territory, population, diplomatic recognition, internal organization, and domestic support.

2. There are various theories about why humans formed themselves into political units with governments. These theories give insight into what the purpose of these units is and, therefore, what people should expect from them.

HOW STATES ARE GOVERNED

3. Monarchism, theocracy, communism applied politically, and fascism are four forms of authoritarian governance. The percentage of countries ruled by authoritarian regimes has declined, but dictatorial governments are still common.

4. Democracy is a complex concept. Different sets of standards serve as a basis to determine the degree to which a political system is democratic.

THE FUTURE OF DEMOCRACY

5. There are disputes over when it is possible or advisable to press all countries to quickly adopt democratic forms of government.

6. Economic development, the attitudes of the people in the potential democratizing country, and the pros and cons of trying to export democracy all play a role in determining whether democracy can be promoted.

7. The numerous possible policy implications for democratization include whether democracy is well suited for successful foreign policy, whether democracies wage war on one another, and whether democracies are less likely than authoritarian government to victimize their own citizens.

STATES AND THE FUTURE

8. The future of the state is a hotly debated topic among scholars of international relations.

9. Some analysts predict the demise of states as principal actors, claiming that states are obsolete and destructive.

10. Other analysts of nationalism contend that the state is durable and has many resources at its disposal. These analysts doubt that states will weaken substantially or disappear as sovereign actors.

11. The final verdict among many scholars is that states will continue to exist but they will play a diminishing role in the future.

For simulations, debates, and other interactive activities, a chapter quiz, Web links, and much more, visit **www.mhhe.com/rourke12/** and go to chapter 6. Or, while accessing the site, click on Course-Related Headlines and view recent international relations articles in the *New York Times*.

KEY TERMS

authoritarianism	fascism	national interest	sovereignty
communism	instrumental theory of	power elite	state of nature
democracy	government	procedural democracy	substantive democracy
democratic peace theory	monarchism	social contract	theocracy

Intergovernmental Organizations: Alternative Governance

Friendly counsel cuts off many foes.
—William Shakespeare, *Henry VI, Part 1*

You peers, continue this united league.
—William Shakespeare, *King Richard III*

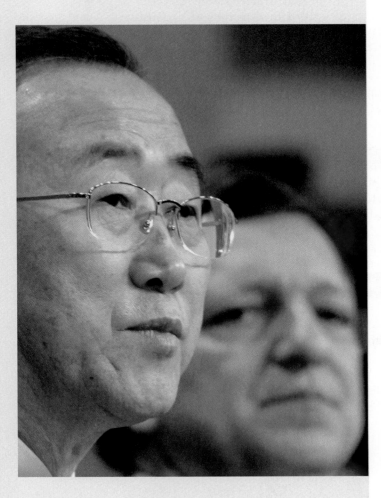

International organizations provide an alternative to governance, a role traditionally reserved exclusively for the sovereign state. UN Secretary-General Ban Ki-moon in the foreground and European Commission President José Manuel Barroso symbolize the authority of the global and regional IGOs that are the focus of this chapter.

ALTHOUGH THE STATE IS and has long been the primary actor in the international system, it is not the only one. **Intergovernmental organizations (IGOs)** are another type of international actor. This type of international organization has countries as its members. Thus IGOs are distinct from the private-membership nongovernmental organizations (NGOs) detailed in chapter 5. More importantly, IGOs provide an alternative to some of the traditional authority of sovereign states to govern themselves domestically and to determine the course of events in the state-based system. Critics of this system say that it is inadequate to meet the challenges of a globalizing world, and it is violence-prone because of its emphasis on self-interested states operating in an anarchical international system. From this perspective, a better approach would be to pay heed to Shakespeare's counsel, in *Henry VI, Part 3,* to "Now join your hands, and with your hands your hearts" by empowering IGOs to increasingly regulate the behavior of states in an effort to reduce violence and provide a platform to address world problems. To assess this possibility, this chapter focuses on two IGOs, the United Nations (UN) and the European Union (EU). Before taking them up, though, an overview of IGOs is in order.

AN OVERVIEW OF INTERGOVERNMENTAL ORGANIZATIONS

There is considerable diversity among IGOs. Some of them, such as the UN, have many members; others, like Africa's Economic Community of the Great Lakes Countries, with three members, are quite small. Another way to classify IGOs is by function. There are multipurpose IGOs such as the UN and EU that address a wide range of issues, and more specialized IGOs like the Arab Monetary Fund with very limited functions. Additionally, there are both global IGOs like the World Bank and regional IGOs like the African Union. Table 7.1 on page 196 presents a range of IGOs.

A History of IGOs

Examples of IGOs may be found far back in history. What was arguably the first rudimentary IGO was established in 478 B.C. when the Greek city-states established the Delian League to create a unified response to the threat from Persia. Although mostly an alliance, the League had two IGO characteristics. First, it was permanent and supposed to last until "ingots of iron, thrown into the sea, rose again." Second, the League had an assembly of representatives appointed by the city-states to decide policy. Although Athens dominated, the assembly was a precursor of such current structures as the UN General Assembly.

MAP
Post–Cold War
International Alliances

Theories of IGO Formation

The intellectual roots of IGOs extend back into history and include the early globalist concept of a common humanity discussed in chapter 5. One stream of this view focused on establishing IGOs to promote peace. Early examples include the proposal of French official Pierre Dubois in *The Recovery of the Holy Land* (1306) for the creation of a "league of universal peace" to settle disputes among members; *Le Nouveau Cynée* (1623) in which French writer Émeric Crucé called for creating permanent courts of arbitration to settle international disputes; and German philosopher Immanuel Kant's advocacy in *Perpetual Peace* (1795) of founding a "league of peace . . . to make an end of all wars forever."

TABLE 7.1 Select Intergovernmental Organizations				
Organization	Mission	Members	Headquarters	Chief Officer
League of Arab States	Political, cultural, and economic cooperation	22	Egypt	Egyptian
Association of Southeast Asian Nations	Economic and other forms of cooperation	10	Indonesia	Singaporean
European Union	Multipurpose	25	Belgium	Portuguese
International Atomic Energy Agency	Peaceful use of nuclear energy	143	Austria	Egyptian
International Cocoa Organization	Cocoa production and trade	40	Great Britain	Dutch
International Criminal Police Organization	Investigation of global crime	186	France	American
International Monetary Fund	Currency cooperation and stability	184	United States	Spanish
International Whaling Commission	Regulation of whaling	72	Great Britain	American
North Atlantic Treaty Organization	Military security	26	Belgium	Dutch
Office International des Epizooties	Animal health	167	France	French
Organization of Petroleum Exporting Countries	Oil production and prices	12	Austria	Libyan
United Nations	Multipurpose	192	United States	South Korean
World Bank	Economic development	185	United States	American
World Trade Organization	Free economic interchange	150	Switzerland	French

There are nearly 300 intergovernmental organizations (IGOs), and they perform a wide variety of functions. Some sense of the range of IGO activities and their global, regional, or specialized membership basis can be gained from this selection. As you can see, membership ranges from near universal to only a few countries, and the functions of IGOs range from the UN's broad range of missions to the single purpose of the International Cocoa Organization.

Similar visions have also prompted calls for regional organizations. In a glimmer of what would eventually be the European Union, the Abbé de Saint-Pierre's *Projet de paix perpetuelle* (*Project for Perpetual Peace*, 1713) proposed establishing a league of European countries to not only ensure peace but also prosperity through economic integration (Bohas, 2003). Expanding on such ideas in 1943, French diplomat Jean Monnet, who was a driving force during the early days of European integration in the 1950s, declared, "There will be no peace in Europe if the states rebuild themselves [after World War II] on the basis of national sovereignty, with its implications of prestige politics and economic protection." Furthermore, Monnet argued, "The countries of Europe are not strong enough individually to be able to guarantee prosperity and social development for their peoples. The states of Europe must . . . form a federation or a European entity that would make them into a common economic unit."[1] Such thoughts of regional unity have not been confined to Europe. To cite just one example, Simón Bolívar, the liberator of much of South America from Spanish colonialism, envisioned a South and Central American federation and initiated the first hemispheric conference, the Congress of Panama (1826), to try to further that goal. Whether thinking globally or regionally, the common bond that unites these visionaries is their belief that IGOs could be a force for peace and other positive goals. However, on the question of how to best achieve their goal, those who promote IGO formation are split into two schools of thought.

One of these, **functionalism**, springs from the idea that the way to global cooperation is through a "bottom-up," evolutionary approach that begins with limited, pragmatic cooperation on narrow, nonpolitical issues. One such issue was how to deliver the mail internationally. To solve that problem, countries cooperated to found the Universal Postal Union in 1874. Plato's description of "necessity" as "the mother of invention" in *The Republic* (ca. 380 B.C.) might well serve as a motto for modern functionalists.

Functionalists support their view about how global cooperation is being achieved by pointing to the thousands of IGOs, multilateral treaties, NGOs, and other vehicles that have been pragmatically put in place to deal with specific international concerns. Functionalists further hold that by cooperating in specific, usually nonpolitical areas like delivering mail, countries and people can learn to trust one another in disarmament and other such politically sensitive areas. Each such instance of cooperation serves as a building block to achieve broader cooperation on more and more politically sensitive issues along the path to comprehensive cooperation or even global government.

Neofunctionalism is the second school of thought. This "top-down" approach to solving world problems rejects the idea that global cooperation and the IGOs that go with it necessarily need to evolve from cooperation through IGOs that deal with functional issues, like delivering mail, and progressively build up to cooperation and IGOs related to security and other critical political issues.

Functionalist theory argues that each successful example of cooperation in an international governmental organization (IGO) serves as a building block, giving countries confidence to further expand the authority of IGOs to address even more complex and sensitive world problems.

Instead, neofunctionalists believe that if you create IGOs and give them the resources and the authority they need to address central global problems, then in time countries and their people will learn to trust and govern through these IGOs and possibly even shift their primary sense of political identity and allegiance to them (Schmitter, 2005). In a sense, neofunctionalism was a theme in the 1989 Kevin Costner movie, *Field of Dreams*. Its mantra, "If you build it, he will come," urged Ray Kinsella (Costner) not wait to build a baseball park in Iowa until it was needed. Instead, it told Kinsella to build a stadium, and his father and others would come to it. It is not that neofunctionalists do not recognize or value IGOs that serve a functional role. Rather, neofunctionalists are skeptical about the functionalist belief that nonpolitical cooperation can, by itself, lead eventually to full political cooperation and to the elimination of international conflict and self-interested state action. Among other things, neofunctionalists also worry that the functionalists' evolutionary approach will not move quickly enough to head off many of the world's looming problems.

The Growth of IGOs

Whatever the theory about IGO formation, and despite such occasional examples as the Delian League, IGOs are primarily a modern phenomenon. By the 1800s, a few IGOs were beginning to come into existence to deal with specific transnational matters. The six-member Central Commission for the Navigation of the Rhine, established in 1815, is the oldest surviving IGO, and the International Telegraphic (now Telecommunications) Union (1865) is the oldest surviving IGO with global membership. Still, there were only six IGOs established during the 1800s.

The rate of IGO creation began to grow slowly during the first part of the 1900s. The turn of the century saw the formation of the **Hague system**, the first IGO dedicated to curbing warfare. It was named for two conferences held at The Hague, the Netherlands, in 1899 and 1907. The goals were to limit weapons, to establish procedures to arbitrate and mediate international disputes, and to otherwise avoid or mitigate warfare. The second of these was more comprehensive, with 44 European, North American, and Latin American states participating. Organizationally, it included a limited general assembly and a judicial system. A third Hague Conference was scheduled to meet in 1915, but it never took place because of the outbreak of World War I (1914–1918).

After the war, the Versailles Peace Conference (1919) sought to establish a postwar order by, among other things, creating the **League of Nations**. It had a more developed organizational structure than that of the Hague system. Although intended mainly as a peacekeeping organization, the League also had some elements aimed at social and economic cooperation. Once again, unfortunately, peace did not prevail, and the League died in the rubble of World War II (1939–1945).

However the core idea behind the Hague system and the League of Nations did not perish, and more than 50 countries met at the end of the war and established the **United Nations (UN)** in 1945. Like the League, the UN was founded mainly to maintain peace, but it was also charged with improving humankind's social and economic situation. Abiding by this mandate, the UN has increasingly become involved in a broad range of issues that encompasses almost all the world's concerns. The years surrounding the formation of the UN also saw a rapid growth in the number of all types of IGOs. The pace was especially fast in the 1960s and 1970s when there was rapid decolonization. The many new countries of Africa and Asia and other regions, joined by already independent countries seeking to improve conditions and their leverage in the international system, created an array of new, most commonly regional IGOs. Since then, the rate at which new IGOs are being created has declined, although it is still faster than at any time since before the 1960s. This growth pattern is evident in Figure 7.1. Not evident in that figure is the overall number of IGOs, which peaked at 365 in 1984 after the growth spate in the 1960s and 1970s and has since declined to 246 in 2005. Almost all of the IGOs that were disbanded or fell into disuse were regional and proved to be duplicative of other existing or new IGOs.

Reasons for Growth

Both functionalist and neofunctionalist concepts have played an important role in IGO growth. Whatever the immediate impetus for founding an IGO, they have all been created because states have realized that through IGOs, countries "are able to achieve goals that they cannot accomplish [alone]" (Abbot & Snidal, 1998:29). We can note six causes for this expansion.

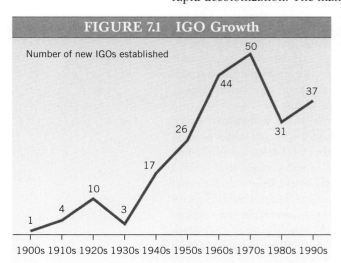

FIGURE 7.1 IGO Growth

Number of new IGOs established

1900s 1910s 1920s 1930s 1940s 1950s 1960s 1970s 1980s 1990s

The growing presence of intergovernmental organizations (IGOs) in the international system is evident in the increased number of new IGOs founded during each decade of the 20th century.

Note: Data includes only the UIA's "conventional IGOs," those with at least three member-countries and a permanent, functioning organizational structure.
Data source: Union of International Associations.

1. *Increased international contact.* The revolutions in communications and transportation technologies have brought the states of the world into much closer contact. These interchanges need organizational structures in order to become routine and regulated. The International Telegraphic Union, founded over a century ago, has been joined in more modern times by the International Mobile Satellite Organization (IMMARSAT, 1979) and many others.

2. *Increased global interdependence.* The International Monetary Fund (IMF) and the World Bank are just two examples of IGOs that have been created to address international economic issues that are beyond the control of individual countries. Regional trade and monetary organizations, cartels, and, to a degree, multinational corporations are other examples.

3. *The expansion of transnational problems.* Some issues that affect many states require solutions that are increasingly beyond the resources of any single state to address. One such issue (and its associated IGO) is transnational crime (International Criminal Police Organization, Interpol). Continuing global problems in health, food, human rights, and other areas have also spurred the organization of IGOs.

4. *The failure of the current state-centered system to provide security.* This factor in IGO expansion is not only about the failure to prevent recurrent wars, including World Wars I and II. The inability of the traditional approach to provide security is also evident in its general failure to restrain the development and use of weapons capable of killing more and more people quickly. The first Hague Convention worried about such (then modern) horrors as explosive projectiles dropped from balloons. Fifteen years later, World War I was under way. Machine guns, tanks, warplanes, and poison gas first came into general and widespread use, leaving almost 9 million dead. Two decades later, World War II and its even more terrible weapons claimed the lives of 58 million soldiers and civilians from military action and another 10 million or more civilians during the Holocaust and other atrocities. Then in 1945 the atomic age dawned with the prospect of the death toll reaching the millions in minutes rather than years. The twin realities of continued warfare and ever more lethal weapons convinced many that peace is not safe in the hands of nation-states. The United Nations is the latest attempt to organize globally for the preservation of peace, but many regional organizations such as the African Union are also involved in mediation and other forms of crisis intervention and in fielding peacekeeping forces.

5. *The efforts of small states to gain strength through joint action.* The concentration of military and economic power in a handful of countries has led less powerful actors to cooperate in an attempt to influence events. For example, less developed countries (LDCs) have formed such IGOs as the 116-member Nonaligned Movement (NAM) and the Group of 77 (G-77), now with 131 member-countries, to promote economic development. One of their strategies is to use their "joint negotiating capacity" to press the economically developed countries (EDCs) to increase development aid, reduce barriers to LDC exports, and take other steps favorable to the LDCs.[2] This factor was a key reason for the sharp increase in the number of IGOs founded in the 1960s and 1970s.

6. *The successes of IGOs.* The sixth reason for IGO expansion is that as countries have learned that they can sometimes work together internationally, they have created additional IGOs to help address an ever greater range of transnational issues.

MAP
Transportation Patterns

Web Link

The Web site of the International Criminal Police Organization, or INTERPOL, is at **www.interpol.int/**.

Roles That IGOs Play

Given the expanding number of IGOs, we should consider what they do and what we want them to do (Muldoon, 2003). It is possible to arrange the current and potential future roles of IGOs along a scale that measures how close each is along the continuum ranging from the traditional approach to the alternative approach to world politics. Starting at the traditional end of the scale and moving toward the alternative end, the four possible roles are: interactive arena, creator and center of cooperation, independent international actor, and supranational organization.

Interactive Arena

The most common function of IGOs is to provide an interactive arena in which member-states pursue their individual national interests. This approach is rarely stated openly, but it is obvious in the struggles within the UN and other IGOs, where countries and blocs of countries vigorously wage political struggles (Thompson, 2006; Foot, MacFarlane, & Mastanudo, 2003). The view that the UN should be an arena for countries to advance their interests was expressed recently by the chairman of the U.S. Senate Committee on Foreign Relations, who asserted that the "core diplomatic mission" of the new U.S. ambassador to the UN should be "securing greater international support for the national security and foreign policy objectives of the United States."[3]

Of course, that view is also held by other countries and can lead them to oppose U.S. initiatives for similar self-interested reasons (Voeten, 2004). For example, during the maneuvering in the UN Security Council in 2003 over Iraq, France and Russia (both of which have a veto in the Security Council) along with Germany were at the forefront of resisting the U.S. efforts to win UN support for military action against Iraq. In addition to their views on Iraq as such, these countries also used the crisis to demonstrate their diplomatic independence and to try to rein in what they saw as an arrogant, overly aggressive United States. This was evident in the comment of French President Jacques Chirac, "France considers itself one of the friends of the Americans, not necessarily one of its sycophants. And when we have something to say, we say it."[4] Similarly, a Russian analyst noted that his country's leaders "do not want to see the United Nations downgraded or the advent of a world order based on U.S. hegemony."[5]

The use of IGOs as an interactive arena does, however, also have advantages. One is based on the theory that international integration can advance even when IGOs are the arena for self-interested national interaction. The reasoning is that even when realpolitik is the starting point, the process that occurs in an IGO fosters the habit of cooperation and

SIMULATION
Searching for International Organizations: Roles and Resources

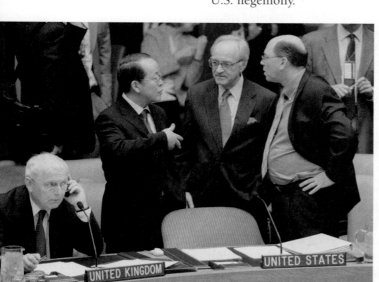

One role of the UN and other IGOs is to serve as an interactive arena in which countries promote their interests. This photograph shows diplomats negotiating before a Security Council meeting in 2007 to vote on sanctions against Iran. The British Ambassador to the UN, Emyr Jones Parry, left, speaks on a telephone while U.S. Ambassador Alejandro Daniel Wolff, right, and Chinese Ambassador Wang Guangya, second from right, negotiate with French Ambassador Jean-Marc de la Sablière. The United States and Great Britain have been much more willing to press for strong sanctions against Iran than either France or, especially, China.

compromise. Another advantage is that it is sometimes politically easier to take action if an IGO has authorized it. For example, there was considerable consensus behind military action against Iraq in 1991 (unlike what occurred in 2003), and taking action under UN auspices in the earlier conflict made it easier for Muslim countries and some others to participate in an invasion conducted primarily by Christian-heritage powers (the United States, Great Britain, and France). Third, debate and diplomatic maneuvering may even provide a forum for diplomatic struggle, which, as an alternative to the battlefield, helps promote the resolution of disputes without violence. As Winston Churchill put it once, "To jaw-jaw is better than to war-war."[6]

Center of Cooperation

A second IGO role is to promote and facilitate cooperation among states and other international actors. Secretary-General Kofi Annan observed correctly that the UN's "member-states face a wide range of new and unprecedented threats and challenges. Many of these transcend borders and are beyond the power of any single nation to address on its own."[7] Therefore, countries have found it increasingly necessary to cooperate to address physical security, the environment, the economy, and a range of other concerns. The Council of the Baltic Sea States, the International Civil Aviation Organization, and a host of other IGOs were all established to address specific needs and, through their operations, to promote further cooperation.

When cooperation develops in a number of related areas, then *regime theory* argues that the specific points of cooperation become connected with one another in more complex forms of interdependence called an international **regime**. This term is not a single organization. Instead, regime is a collective noun that designates a complex of norms, rules, processes, and organizations that, in sum, have evolved to help to govern the behavior of states and other international actors in an area of international concern.

One such area is the use and protection of international bodies of water and the corresponding regime that has evolved for oceans and seas (Heasley, 2003). Figure 7.2 depicts this regime's array of organizations, rules, and norms that promote international cooperation in a broad area of maritime regulation, including navigation, pollution, seabed mining, and fisheries. The UN Convention on the Law of the Sea (1994) proclaims that the oceans and seabed are a "common heritage of mankind," to be shared according to "a just and equitable economic order." To that end, the treaty provides increased international regulation of mining and other uses of the oceans' floors and empowers the International Seabed Authority to help advance the treaty's goals. On a related front, the International Maritime Organization has helped create safeguards against oil spills in the seas, which have declined dramatically since the early 1970s. The International Whaling Commission, the Convention on the Preservation and Protection of Fur Seals, and other efforts have begun the process of protecting marine life and conserving resources. The Montreal Guidelines on Land-Based Pollution suggest ways to prevent fertilizer and other land-based pollutants from running off into rivers and bays and then into the oceans. Countries have expanded their conservation zones to regulate fishing. The South Pacific Forum has limited the use of drift nets that indiscriminately catch and kill marine life. NGOs such as Greenpeace have pressed to protect the world seas. Dolphins are killed less frequently because many consumers buy only those cans of tuna that display the "dolphin safe" logo. It is not necessary to extend this list of multilateral law-making treaties, IGOs, NGOs, national efforts, and other programs that regulate the use of the seas to make the point that in combination they are part of an expanding network that constitutes a developing regime of the oceans and seas.

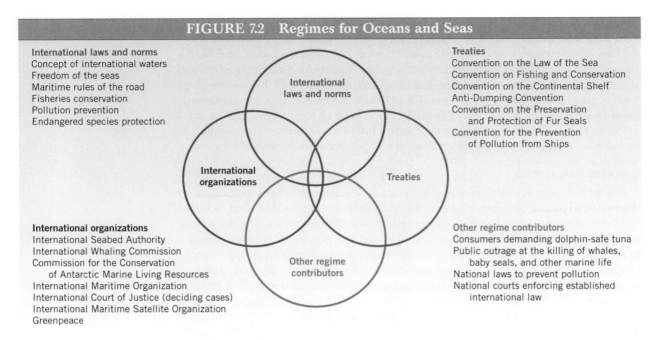

FIGURE 7.2   Regimes for Oceans and Seas

International laws and norms
Concept of international waters
Freedom of the seas
Maritime rules of the road
Fisheries conservation
Pollution prevention
Endangered species protection

International organizations
International Seabed Authority
International Whaling Commission
Commission for the Conservation
   of Antarctic Marine Living Resources
International Maritime Organization
International Court of Justice (deciding cases)
International Maritime Satellite Organization
Greenpeace

Treaties
Convention on the Law of the Sea
Convention on Fishing and Conservation
Convention on the Continental Shelf
Anti-Dumping Convention
Convention on the Preservation
   and Protection of Fur Seals
Convention for the Prevention
   of Pollution from Ships

Other regime contributors
Consumers demanding dolphin-safe tuna
Public outrage at the killing of whales,
   baby seals, and other marine life
National laws to prevent pollution
National courts enforcing established
   international law

The concept of an international regime represents the nexus of a range of rules, actors, and other contributors that regulate a particular area of concern. This figure shows some of the elements of the expanding regime for oceans and seas.

Note: Entries are only a sample of all possibilities.

Independent International Actor

The third IGO role is that of an independent international actor (Haftel & Thompson, 2006; Barnett & Finnemore, 2004). This role is located toward the alternative end of the traditional–alternative scale of IGO activities. Technically, what any IGO does is controlled by the wishes and votes of its members. In reality, many IGOs develop strong, relatively permanent administrative staffs.

     These individuals often identify with the organization and try to increase its authority and role. Global expectations—such as "the UN should do something"—add to the authority and reach of IGOs. As a result, one scholar contends, IGOs have a "strong measure of autonomy from their member-states," and are "especially likely to act on their own initiative if states are indifferent to a situation." Indeed, IGOs "may act, at least obliquely, against the perceived interests of member-states, even against the interests of important states" (Ferguson, 2005:332). Thus, an IGO may be a force unto itself, more than the sum of its (member-country) parts. Sometimes this independence is controversial, as we shall see in the discussions of the UN and EU that follow. In other cases, a degree of organizational independence is intended and established in the charters of various IGOs, such as the International Court of Justice (ICJ).

Supranational Organization

Some people believe that the world is moving and should continue to move toward a more established form of international government (Tabb, 2004). "The very complexity of the current international scene," one scholar writes, "makes a fair and effective system of world governance more necessary than ever" (Hoffmann, 2003:27).

This model envisions a fourth role for IGOs, that of a **supranational organization** with legal authority that overrides the sovereignty of its members.

Some IGOs already possess a degree of limited supranationalism in specialized areas because many states in practice accept some IGO authority in the realm of "everyday global governance" (Slaughter, 2003:83). For example, countries now regularly give way when the World Trade Organization (WTO) rules that one of their laws or policies contravene the WTO's underlying treaty, the General Agreement on Tariffs and Trade (GATT). Even greater supranational authority is exercised on a regional level by the European Union. It not only has most of the structure of a full-scale government, but it makes policy, has courts, receives taxes, and in many other, if still limited, ways functions like a government of Europe.

A major question for the future is whether and how far to extend the supranational authority of IGOs and how to structure such powerful new actors. On the dimension of governance, supranational IGOs could range from *single-purpose* IGOs that govern one narrow area, through *multipurpose* IGOs that exercise authority in a number of related areas, to *general-purpose* IGOs that exercise power in a broad range of areas. Geographically, the possibilities range from *regional* IGOs, to *multicontinental* IGOs with members from many regions, to *global* IGOs with most or all of the world's states as members.

Ultimately limited supranationalism might evolve into **regional governments** or a **world government**. The powers of any such global or regional government also range along a scale based on the degree of power-sharing between the central government and the subunits, as depicted in Figure 7.3. **Unitary government** is at the end of the scale where the central government has all or most of the power and the subordinate units have little or none. In such a system, countries would be nonsovereign subunits that serve only administrative purposes. A less centralized alternative would be a **federation**, or federal government, one in which the central authority and the member-units each have substantial authority. The United States and Canada are both federal structures, with Canada's 10 provinces having greater authority than the 50 U.S. states. A **confederation** is the least centralized of the three arrangements. In

FIGURE 7.3   Power-Sharing Models of Governance

Whether at the national, regional, or global level, governments share power between the central government and territorial government in a variety of ways. In countries, territorial units are commonly termed states or provinces. In a global or regional government, countries would be the territorial unit. This figure shows the scale of possible power-sharing relationships. At one end of the scale, a league, the central government has little more than symbolic authority, and most power remains with the territorial units. At the other end of the scale, a unitary government, the central government monopolizes power and the territorial units perform only administrative functions. The most centralized international government organization today, the European Union, is a confederation.

a confederal government, the central government has quite limited powers, while the members retain all or most of their sovereign authority. The least centralized model, and one that borders on not being a government at all, is a **league**, an arrangement in which the centralized government is mostly symbolic and has little if any functional authority.

Arguments for Expanding Supranational Authority The arguments for greater global government begin with the criticism of the current state-based system detailed in chapter 6 (Volgy & Bailin, 2003; Wendt, 2004). The World Federalist Movement (WFM), for one, argues, "Ours is a planet in crisis, suffering grave problems unable to be managed by nations acting separately in an ungoverned world." Given this perspective, the WFM calls for founding "world institutions . . . [with] actual and sufficient authority to make and enforce law in their given jurisdictions."[8] It should be noted that the WFM and most others who favor greater global governance do not advocate the abolition of state sovereignty and the creation of an all-powerful world government. More common are calls for a federal structure, with countries retaining sovereignty over their internal affairs.

Web Link

The Web site of the World Federalist Movement is **www.wfm.org/**.

Arguments against Expanding Supranational Authority Critics of greater global governance raise numerous objections (Coates, 2005). First, they argue that there are practical barriers. Their assumption is that nationalism has too strong a hold and that neither political leaders nor masses would be willing to surrender substantial sovereignty to a universal body. Are we ready to "pledge allegiance to the United States of the World"? Second, critics of the world government movement pose political objections. They worry about the concentration of power that would be necessary to enforce international law and to address the world's monumental economic and social problems. A third doubt is whether any such government, even given unprecedented power, could succeed in solving world problems any better than states can. Fourth, some skeptics further argue that centralization would inevitably diminish desirable cultural diversity and political experimentation in the world. A fifth criticism of the world government worries about preserving democracy. With power concentrated in a central international government and little countervailing power left to countries, the seizure of the world government by authoritative forces might, in a stroke, roll back hundreds of years of democratic evolution.

The idea of regional government answers some of the objections to global government. Regions would still have to bring heterogeneous peoples together and overcome nationalism, but that would be an easier task than addressing even greater global heterogeneity. Moreover, regional governments would allow for greater cultural diversity and political experimentation than would a global government. To this skeptics reply that at best regional government is the lesser of two evils compared to global government. Opponents also contend that creating regional governments would simply shift the axis of conflict from among states to among regions. Indeed, in the novel *Nineteen Eighty-Four*, George Orwell predicted in 1949 that the future would find world political control exercised by

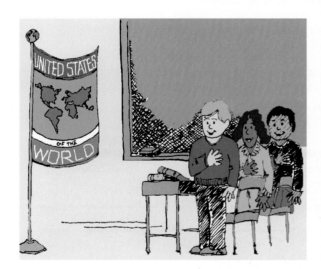

Historically our primary political loyalty has slowly shifted from smaller units such as tribes and village to larger units, especially countries. Some people believe this trend should continue and that a world government should be established. This image of children pledging allegiance to the flag of the United States of the World may seem strange, but a global government is not inconceivable.

three regional governments (Oceania, Eurasia, and Eastasia) all perpetually at war with one another. Making matters worse, democracy was a memory. Oceania was ruled by the totalitarian iron hand of "Big Brother," and the other two megaregions were also presumably subject to authoritarian discipline. It is not hard to project the EU as the core of Eurasia, a U.S.-centered Oceania, and an Eastasia built around China. So while Orwell's vision did not come to pass by 1984, opponents of regional or global government might contend that perhaps he should have entitled the book *Twenty Eighty-Four.*

Web Link

For more on the view that U.S. sovereignty is at risk, visit the Web site of U.S. Representative Ron Paul (R-TX) at **http://www. house.gov/paul/** and browse the index of his weekly column, "Texas Straight Talk."

GLOBAL IGOs: FOCUS ON THE UNITED NATIONS

Of the growing range and importance of activities of IGOs at the global level, the United Nations' activities are by far the most notable. Therefore, this section focuses on the UN as a generalized study of the operation of IGOs and as a specific study of that key institution. We look at issues related to membership and voting in the UN, its executive leadership, its administration and finance, and its activities. Figure 7.4 provides an overview of the UN's structure.

Membership and Voting

At root, every IGO is an international organization whose membership is made up of two or more countries. Therefore, one key determinant of how an IGO operates is how its membership is structured, who is or is not a member and why, and how various organizational factors and voting procedures help determine the influence of each member in the organization. It is, for example, impossible to grasp how the

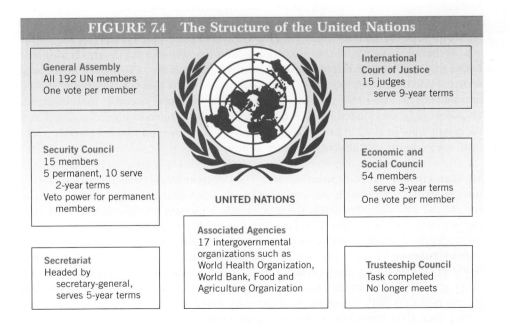

FIGURE 7.4   The Structure of the United Nations

General Assembly
All 192 UN members
One vote per member

International Court of Justice
15 judges
    serve 9-year terms

Security Council
15 members
5 permanent, 10 serve
    2-year terms
Veto power for permanent
    members

Economic and Social Council
54 members
    serve 3-year terms
One vote per member

UNITED NATIONS

Secretariat
Headed by
    secretary-general,
    serves 5-year terms

Associated Agencies
17 intergovernmental
organizations such as
World Health Organization,
World Bank, Food and
Agriculture Organization

Trusteeship Council
Task completed
No longer meets

The United Nations is a complex organization. It has six major organs and 17 associated agencies.

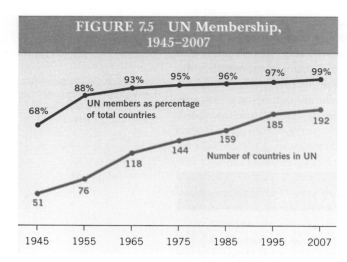

FIGURE 7.5 UN Membership, 1945–2007

UN members as percentage of total countries: 68%, 88%, 93%, 95%, 96%, 97%, 99%

Number of countries in UN: 51, 76, 118, 144, 159, 185, 192

1945   1955   1965   1975   1985   1995   2007

Membership in the UN has almost quadrupled since 1945. The primary reason has been the creation of new states, but there has also been a growing expectation that the UN should have universal membership.

Data sources: UN at www.un.org/overview/unmember.html. Various historical sources for number of states.

UN works without being aware that 5 of its members possess a **veto** in the Security Council and the other 187 do not.

Membership Issues

There is a range of membership issues related to IGOs. Some concern membership in the overall organization and others concern membership in the various substructures within IGOs.

General Membership Issues   Theoretically, membership in the UN and most other IGOs is open to any state that is both within the geographic and functional scope of that organization and also subscribes to its principles and practices. In reality, politics is sometimes an additional standard. Today with the exception of the Holy See (the Vatican), the UN has universal membership, as Figure 7.5 shows, but that was not always the case.

Standards for admitting new members are a point of occasional controversy. One instance occurred in 1998 when the General Assembly voted overwhelmingly to give Palestinians what amounts to an informal associate membership. They cannot vote, but they can take part in debates in the UN and perform other functions undertaken by states.

Successor state status can also sometimes be a political issue. When the UN recognized Russia as the successor state to the Soviet Union, it meant, among other things, that Russia inherited the USSR's permanent seat and veto on the Security Council. Taking the opposite approach, the UN in 1992 refused to recognize the Serbian-dominated government in Belgrade as the successor to Yugoslavia once that country broke apart. Instead, the General Assembly required Yugoslavia to (re)apply for admission, which was finally (re)granted in 2000.

Withdrawal, suspension, or expulsion is another membership issue. Nationalist China (Taiwan) was, in effect, ejected from the UN when the "China seat" was transferred to the mainland. In a move close to expulsion, the General Assembly refused between 1974 and 1991 to seat South Africa's delegate because that country's apartheid policies violated the UN Charter. The refusal to recognize Yugoslavia as a successor state in 1992 began what was, in effect, an expulsion that lasted eight years until a less oppressive government gained power.

Membership Issues in IGO Substructures   Not every internal decision-making structure in an IGO necessarily has representatives from each member-country. At the core of the UN and other IGOs there is usually a **plenary representative body** that includes all members. The **UN General Assembly (UNGA)** is the UN's plenary organ. Such assemblies normally have broad authority within their organizations and are supposedly the most powerful elements of their organizations. In practice, however, the assembly may be secondary to the administrative structure or some other part of the organization. A second type of representative body is a **limited membership council**. Based on the theory that smaller groups can operate more efficiently than large assemblies, there are many councils that have representatives only from some parent organization's membership. For example, the UN's Economic and Social Council (ECOSOC) has representatives from 54 members, elected by the General Assembly for three-year terms based on a plan of geographical representation. Membership is also sometimes limited on the theory that some members have a greater concern or capacity in a particular area. The **UN Security Council (UNSC)** has five permanent members (the P5: China, France, Russia, the United Kingdom, and the United States). These five were the leading victorious powers at the end of World War II and were thought to have a special peacekeeping role to play. Additionally, with the idea of keeping membership limited to improve efficiency, the total UNSC membership was set at 15, with the 10 nonpermanent members chosen by the UNGA for two-year terms. The emphasis on the powerful role of the P5 on the Security Council should not be read as meaning that the other 10 seats have little consequence. While secondary to the P5, the rotating seats are important and much sought after. Not only do these nonpermanent members share the limelight in a key decision-making body, but some of them receive increased foreign aid and other incentives from the United States and perhaps other big powers in order to win their cooperation (Kuziemko & Werker, 2006). Also indicative of the importance of the 10 nonpermanent seats, the maneuvering in 2006 to elect 5 new members including the "Latin American" seat being vacated by Argentina turned into a struggle between the United States, which backed Guatemala, and Venezuela, whose president is a persistent critic of the United States. After 47 votes in the UNGA, neither side could prevail, and in a compromise, Panama was named the region's new representative on the Council.

Controversy over Membership on the Security Council   The combination of the P5's permanent Security Council membership and veto is a simmering issue in the UN. There are several sources of discontent. *Lack of democracy* is one line of criticism. Expressing this view, Zambia's president argued that the council "can no longer be maintained like the sanctuary of the Holy of Holies with only the original members acting as high priests, deciding on issues for the rest of the world who cannot be admitted."[9] *Geographic and demographic imbalance* is another source of discontent. Geographically, Europe and North America have four of five permanent seats, and those four permanent members are also countries of predominantly Eurowhite and Christian heritage. Yet other critics charge that the permanent members are an *inaccurate reflection of power realities.* As the German mission to the UN puts it, "The Security Council as it stands does not reflect today's world which has changed dramatically since 1945."[10] From this perspective, Germany, India, Japan, and some other powerful countries have begun to press for permanent seats for themselves.

In recent years there have been a number of proposals to expand the membership of the UNSC and, in some cases, to increase the number of permanent members. Some reform proposals have sought to give the new members a veto; even more proposals have called for the elimination of the veto power of the permanent members. Most countries in the UN favor reform, yet none has been possible because of the two nearly insurmountable hurdles to amending the UN Charter and altering the composition of the UNSC. First, Charter amendments require the endorsement of two-thirds of the Security Council, and the P5 are not especially open to diluting their influence by adding more permanent members, by giving new permanent members a veto, and, least of all, by eliminating the veto altogether. Specific rivalries also influence the P5. China, for instance, would be reluctant to see either of its two great Asian power rivals, Japan or India, get a permanent seat. Beijing also complains that Japan has not apologized adequately for its aggression and atrocities during World War II. The second hurdle for a Charter revision is to also get a two-thirds vote

JOIN THE DEBATE
Changing Permanent Membership and the Almighty Veto Power in the Security Council: How Can Reform Strengthen the UN Security Council?

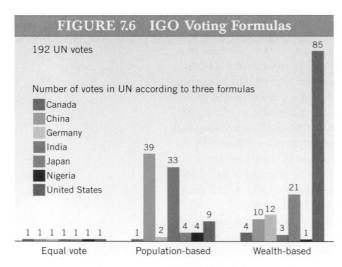

FIGURE 7.6   IGO Voting Formulas

192 UN votes

Number of votes in UN according to three formulas

- Canada
- China
- Germany
- India
- Japan
- Nigeria
- United States

Equal vote   Population-based   Wealth-based

To see the impact of various voting formulas, imagine that the UN allocated the 192 votes in the General Assembly based on equality, population, and wealth. Voting power would vary widely. Compare the United States and China, for example. Equality would give both one vote. In a population-based system, China would have 39 of 192 votes; the United States would have 9. A system based on wealth—gross national product—would have 85 U.S. votes and only 10 votes for China. Are any of these formulas fair? What would be a fair formula?

Data sources: World Bank online and author's calculations.

WEB POLL
The Place of Democratic
Governance in International
Organizations

of the UNGA. There, agreement on any new voting formula would be difficult, given the sensitivities of the 192 countries. For example, the proposal that India have a permanent seat alarms Pakistan, whose UN representative has characterized the idea as "an undisguised grab for power and privilege."[11]

Voting Issues

One of the difficult issues that any IGO faces is its formula for allocating votes. Three formulas used in at least one of the major IGOs are majority voting, weighted voting, and unanimity voting. The implications of various voting formulas are evident in Figure 7.6.

Majority voting is the most common formula used in IGOs. This system has two main components: (1) Each member casts one equal vote based on the concept of sovereign equality, and (2) the issue is carried by a simple majority (50% plus one vote), reflecting the democratic notion that the will of the majority should prevail. The UNGA and most other UN bodies operate on this principle. A variation is **supermajority voting**. This requires more than a simple majority to pass measures. A two-thirds vote is most common, and some of the supermajority formulas, like the one used by the Council of the European Union, can be quite complex.

The objection to equal voting power is that it does not reflect some standards of reality. Should Costa Rica, with no army, cast an equal vote with the powerful United States? Should San Marino, with a population of thousands, cast the same vote as China, with its more than 1.3 billion people? It might be noted, for example, that in the UNGA, two-thirds of the votes are wielded by 128 states whose combined populations are less than 15% of the world's population. By contrast, the 11 countries with populations over 100 million combine for 61% of the world's population, yet they have just 6% of the available votes in the General Assembly.

Weighted voting allocates unequal voting power on the basis of a formula. Two possible criteria are population and wealth. As detailed later, the European Parliament provides an example of an international representative body based in part on population. Voting in the World Bank and the International Monetary Fund is based on member contributions. The United States alone commands about 17% of the votes in the IMF, and it and a handful of other top economically developed countries (EDCs) have majority control, yet combine for little more than 10% of the world population. By contrast, China and India, which combined have 37% of the world's population, together have less than 6% of the IMF votes. This "wealth-weighted" voting is especially offensive to LDCs, which contend that it perpetuates the system of imperial domination by the industrialized countries.

Unanimity voting constitutes a fourth scheme. It requires unanimous consent, although sometimes an abstention does not block agreement. The Organization for Economic Cooperation and Development (OECD) and some other IGOs operate on that principle. Unanimity preserves the concept of sovereignty but can easily lead to stalemate. In a related formula, as noted, the rules of the UNSC allow any of the five permanent members to veto proposals. Taking exception to this arrangement, a Venezuelan diplomat described the **veto** as "an antidemocratic practice . . . not in accordance with the principle of the sovereign equality of states."[12] Vetoes were cast frequently during the cold war, mostly by the Soviet Union, as Figure 7.7 shows. More recently, the number of vetoes has dropped sharply, with the United States casting 71% of them between 1996 and 2007.

Although the use of the veto has declined dramatically, the power remains important. First, vetoes are still sometimes cast. In 2006, for example, the United States vetoed a resolution calling on Israeli forces to withdraw from Gaza on the grounds that the resolution ignored the provocation—the kidnapping of two Israeli soldiers. Second and more commonly, the threat of a veto can persuade countries not to press an initiative. For example, the United States and Great Britain did not push for Security Council authorization to take military action against Iraq in 2003 because it was clear that even if majority support could be gathered, France and Russia would exercise their veto power. In 2006, the race for secretary-general was finally decided in an informal vote in the Security Council. Voting was anonymous, but the votes of the P5 were coded distinctly, and every candidate but Ban Ki-moon received at least one "discourage" vote from a member with a veto. Recognizing reality, the other candidates all withdrew, and the Council soon nominated Ban. The veto can also be a diplomatic tool. The United States, for instance, has successfully pressured the UN to exempt U.S. troops serving as UN peacekeepers from the jurisdiction of the International Criminal Court by threatening to veto all UN peacekeeping operations.

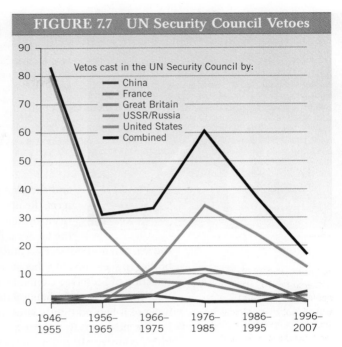

FIGURE 7.7   UN Security Council Vetoes

Vetos cast in the UN Security Council by:
- China
- France
- Great Britain
- USSR/Russia
- United States
- Combined

The use of the veto in the UN Security Council has changed over the years. In the first two decades of the cold war, Russia cast the vast majority of vetoes, and accounts for 47% of the 261 vetoes in UN history. In more recent years, U.S. vetoes have become more common, but the overall number of vetoes has declined sharply.

Source: Global Policy Forum.

Leadership

It is difficult for any organization to function without a single administrative leader, and virtually all IGOs have a chief executive officer (CEO). The UN's administrative structure is called the **Secretariat**, and the secretary-general is the CEO. The UN secretary-general and the heads of many other IGOs are more than mere administrators; they are important diplomatic figures in their own right.

The Selection of IGO Leaders

One indication that IGOs are important players on the world stage is the often intense struggle among member-countries over who will head various IGOs. Clearly, the selection process would not engender so much sound and fury if it were not important.

Selecting the UN Secretary-General   Formally the process of selecting a secretary-general involves the Security Council nominating one or more candidates for the post

One sign of the importance of the UN and other IGOs is the spirited contest that countries wage over who will lead these IGOs. South Korea's Ban Ki-moon became the UN's new secretary-general in 2007, but only after prevailing over several other candidates. The contest was marked by multiple ballots and considerable negotiations among Security Council members. Finishing second was a UN diplomat from India, Under-Secretary-General for Communications and Public Information Shashi Tharoor, seen here addressing an audience at the UN in 2007. He was reportedly opposed by the United States as too liberal and by China, which did not want to see someone from regional rival India holding the prestigious position.

and the General Assembly then electing that official for a five-year term. Reality is less democratic than theory. In practice the Security Council controls the choice by submitting only one name to the General Assembly. Moreover, each of the permanent members, the P5, can and does veto candidates, and still other possible contenders do not even bother to seek the office because of known opposition from one or more of the P5. The selection of Secretary-General Ban Ki-moon in 2006 seemed somewhat less contentious than that of his immediate predecessors, but there was still considerably maneuvering, most of it behind tightly shut diplomatic doors. Initially, there were seven candidates for the position. By tradition the name of each had been put forward by his or her home country, although a number of them, such as Undersecretary-General for Communications and Public Information Shashi Tharoor of India, were self-activated candidates who had lobbied their country's government for support. Six of the seven candidates were from Asia (Afghanistan, Jordan, India, South Korea, Thailand, Sri Lanka). The seventh, Vaira Vike-Freiberga of Latvia, the only woman in the race, had no real chance because of the informal rotation of the secretary-generalship among regions. It had been 25 years since the last Asian secretary-general, U Thant of Burma, had served, making it time for an Asian to once again take up that post.

The campaigning of the various candidates involved their meeting diplomatic representatives of various influential countries, members of the Security Council, and especially the P5. At least some of the home governments also seemed to have tried to advance their national's interests. Stories surfaced, for example, that South Korea was trying to win the support of Security Council member Tanzania for Ban by increasing its aid to Africa, including a new grant of $18 million for an educational program in Tanzania. Ban also sought to improve his chances by meeting France's informal requirement that a secretary-general must speak French. He took a crash course in French during his candidacy and despite only modest progress, seemed to have earned a pass from France after reportedly promising to continue his lessons. Ban seemed to admit both to his poor French and to his commitment to improve when, after being asked a question in French at a news conference, he replied, "I have taken French lessons over the last few months. I . . . will continue to study it. [Today, though], I would prefer to speak in English."[13]

After several months of indecisive straw polls in the Security Council, Ban and Tharoor finally emerged as the front-runners. Then Ban won the day in a final straw vote in October when he received 14 "encourage" votes, zero "discourage" votes, and 1 "no opinion" vote. Critically, he was the only candidate who did not receive a "discourage" vote from a P5 member, the equivalent of a veto. Runner-up Tharoor had 10 encourage votes, 2 no opinion votes, and 3 discourage votes, one of which was fatally from a P5 member. Most speculation about which country had vetoed Tharoor focused on the United States and its reported concern about his somewhat leftist political leanings. But there were also those who thought China had cast the veto because it did not want to see Asian rival India receive the prestige of having one of its citizens serve as secretary-general. In the end, Ban won more because he did not evoke opposition than because he engendered strong support. That may not be the optimum standard for appointing the head of the world's leading IGO. As one commentary put it, "It would help if the next secretary-general was a brilliant, compelling leader. But to actually be chosen for the job, the candidate must be a person who offends no one."[14]

Selecting CEOs of other IGOs   Sharp struggles over who will lead an IGO are not confined to the UN. For example, there have been spirited contests during changes in leadership at the WTO. In 1999 the focus was a determined effort by the LDCs to break the EDC's monopoly on the top jobs in the leading financial IGOs. The result was a compromise: An EDC national, Mike Moore of New Zealand, was selected with the understanding that in 2002 he would step down in favor of Thailand's Supachai Panitchpakdi, who would serve until 2005. By contrast, the selection of the WTO's current (2005–2009) director-general, Pascal Lamy of France, was relatively smooth. Like the earlier WTO selection, the LDC challenge was also evident in the selection of the IMF head, when many non-Western countries backed Egyptian Mohamed El-Erian. Eventually the unbroken tradition of a European holding that position was preserved with the selection of Rodrigo de Rato y Figaredo of Spain, but it was one more instance of what promises to be an ongoing struggle of non-Western countries to play a greater role in the direction of IGOs and, indeed, the course of world politics. The basic point is that the jostling among countries, blocs, and regions to appoint one of their own or someone of their liking to the top jobs indicates how important these IGOs are.

The Role of IGO Leaders

An issue that swirls around IGO executives is their proper role. The role orientations of the UN secretary-general and other IGO leaders can range from activism to restraint (Kille & Scully, 2003). For the most part, the documents that established IGOs anticipated a restrained role. In the UN Charter, for example, the Secretariat is the last major organ discussed. That placement indicates the document's drafters intended a limited, largely administrative role for the secretary-general. That has not, however, been the history of the office.

Former UN Secretaries-General   Whatever was intended, the first two secretaries-general, Trygve Lie of Norway (1946–1953) and Dag Hammarskjöld of Sweden (1953–1961), were activists who steadily expanded the role of their office. Hammarskjöld argued that he had a "responsibility" to act to uphold the peace "irrespective of the views and wishes of the various member governments" (Archer, 1983:148). Hammarskjöld's approach was epitomized during the civil war that followed the independence of the Belgian Congo in 1960. The secretary-general aggressively used UN military forces to try to restore peace. It is somehow sadly fitting that he died in the area when his plane crashed after reportedly being shot down by one of the warring factions.

The Soviets were so upset at the activist and what they saw as a pro-Western stance of Hammarskjöld that they pressed for successors with more restrained conceptions of the role of secretary-general. Over time, however, secretaries-general have once again tended toward activism. The sixth secretary-general, Egypt's Boutros Boutros-Ghali (1992–1996), believed that "if one word above all is to characterize the role of the secretary-general, it is independence. The holder of this office must never be seen as acting out of fear or in an attempt to curry favor with one state or groups of states."[15] Just as Hammarskjöld's activism had led him into disfavor, so too did Boutros-Ghali's views, and his bid for a second term was denied by a U.S. veto.

Since most secretaries-general have served two terms, Africans argued it was still their turn, and sub-Saharan Africans were particularly intent on having one of their number recognized. After extensive maneuvering, the final choice was Kofi Annan, a career UN diplomat from Ghana. He had a reputation as a capable and moderate diplomat and administrator, and his personal history (a B.A. degree in economics from Macalaster College in St. Paul, Minnesota, an M.A. in management from MIT) helped assuage Washington's concern that a secretary-general from black Africa might prove too radical.

During his first term, Annan proved himself more assertive than many predicted the career bureaucrat would be, but his smoothly diplomatic approach avoided confrontations with Washington and other major capitals, and he was easily reappointed for a second term beginning in 2002. His second term was more contentious, however, with Iraq becoming a major point of contention between his leadership at the UN and the Bush administration in Washington. Annan angered the White House by condemning the U.S. invasion of Iraq as "a fundamental challenge to the principles on which, however imperfectly, world peace and stability have rested for the last 58 years."[16]

Toward the end of what most consider a laudable tenure as secretary-general, Annan's stewardship was marred by revelations of corruption in the oil-for-food program for Iraq that operated from 1996 to 2003. Established to allow Iraq to sell oil and use the receipts to buy food, medicine, and other humanitarian supplies under UN supervision, the program became corrupt, with the UN's program administrator getting bribes from firms for allowing them to purchase Iraq's oil and for ignoring Iraqi diversion of billions of dollars in receipts to prohibited uses. As for suspicions about Annan himself, a UN investigation headed by Paul Volcker, former head of the U.S. Federal Reserve Board, concluded, "There is no evidence . . . [that the program] was subject to any . . . improper influence of the secretary-general."[17] Annan was also dogged, as other recent secretaries-general have been, by criticism of the UN bureaucracy, an issue taken up below.

The Current UN Secretary-General   Ban Ki-moon took office as the eighth UN secretary-general on January 1, 2007. At the time he was chosen, the 62-year-old Ban was South Korea's minister of foreign affairs and trade. Among his numerous connections with the United States, Ban served in South Korea's embassy in Washington, D.C., and in 1985 he earned a master's degree in public administration from Harvard University. Indeed, Ban recalls a pivotal event that "helped to inspire a life of public service" occurred "in 1962, [when] as an 18-year-old boy from rural Korea, I came to Washington for the first time . . . [and] was one of a group of lucky teenagers invited to the White House to meet President Kennedy."[18]

Like his two immediate predecessors, Ban was selected in part because of his reputation as a quiet diplomat, one not expected to assertively promote the role of the UN as an autonomous force in world politics. However, neither Boutros Boutros-Ghali nor Kofi Annan complied with that expectation. What Ban's record will be in the long run remains unclear. He says of himself, "I may look soft from the outside, but I have inner strength when it's really necessary."[19]

The United States especially wants Ban to do two things. One is to reform the UN's administration, as discussed below. Ban has pledged to do that. As one diplomat put it, the new secretary-general wants "to make the [UN] hum like an electronics factory in Seoul. There are worse fates for the place than to be like Daewoo, I suppose."[20] Washington also hopes that Ban will be more accommodating to U.S. desires than were Boutros-Ghali or Annan. It remains too early to tell, but Washington will be disappointed once again if Ban's start is any indication. Two weeks after taking office, he traveled to Washington to meet with the president and other top officials. At the top of their agenda was persuading Ban to support greater UN involvement in Iraq, thereby relieving some of the pressure on the Bush administration. As Annan had, Ban rejected this proposal on the grounds that the United States could not make a mess in violation of UN procedures and then expect the UN to help clean things up. Ban also renewed his predecessor's call for the United States to live up to its treaty obligations and reverse its unilateral reduction of funding for the UN. To add to Washington's dismay, he also called on it to close the prison on the U.S. naval base at Guantánamo Bay, Cuba, where alleged terrorists have been held since 2001.

However Ban's leadership at the UN develops, the debate over the proper role of top officials in other IGOs will continue. The controversy is part of a struggle between the traditional approach versus the alternative approach to world politics. Traditionally, national states have sought to control IGOs and their leaders. As IGOs and their leaders have grown stronger, however, they have more often struck out independently down the alternative path. As Kofi Annan commented, all secretaries-general have carried out their traditional duties as chief administrative officer, but they have also to one degree or another assumed another, alternative role, one that Kofi Annan described as "an instrument of the larger interest, beyond national rivalries and regional concerns."[21] Presidents and prime ministers have found, as a U.S. diplomat comments, that "you can't put the secretary-general back in the closet when it's inconvenient."[22]

Web Link

If your college does not have one, you can help start a model UN program. Information is available on the Web site of the UN's Model UN Headquarters at **www.un.org/cyberschoolbus/ modelun/links_6.asp.**

Administration and Finance

No organization can be successful unless it is well organized and efficient and also receives the staffing and budget resources it needs to accomplish its missions. So it is with the UN, and such matters as staff and finances are important to the function of the UN and other IGOs, even if they do not often capture the headlines.

Administration

The secretary-general appoints the other principal officials of the Secretariat. However, in doing so, he must be sensitive to the desires of the dominant powers and also must pay attention to the geographic and, increasingly, to the gender composition of the Secretariat staff. Controversies have occasionally arisen over these distributions, but in recent years the focus of criticism has been the size and effectiveness of the staffs of the UN headquarters in New York and its regional offices (Geneva, Nairobi, and Vienna). In this way, the UN is like many other IGOs and, indeed, national governments, with allegedly bloated, inefficient, and unresponsive bureaucracies that have made them a lightning rod for discontent with member-governments.

Administrative Reform Over its existence, critics of the United Nations, especially those in the United States, have regularly charged that it cost too much, employed too many people, and managed its affairs poorly. Defenders of the UN reply that many of these charges reflect animus toward the UN rather than a balanced evaluation. As a commentary in the *Asia Times* put it recently, "unrelenting conservative attacks on the UN were never about 'mismanagement, waste and corruption' . . . [They were] always about policies and the temerity of the organization and its officials in defiantly holding onto policies that differed from Washington's."[23] There is an element of truth to this accusation, but even defenders of the UN have agreed that the operation of the organization needed to be improved. Soon after he became secretary-general, Annan reported to the General Assembly that, to a degree, "over the course of the past half century certain . . . [UN] organizational features have . . . become fragmented, duplicative, and rigid."[24] To address these issues, many administrative changes were instituted, the UN's regular budget increases have been modest, and the UN's staff member numbers have remained static despite significantly increased peacekeeping operations. There remains, however, considerable discontent in the U.S. government and elsewhere over the administrative efficiency of the UN, and, as noted, part of the support of the United States and some other countries for the appointment of Secretary-General Ban was based on his pledge to continue to reshape the UN administrative structures and processes.

Gender diversification has been another notable reform. The UN has a relatively good record compared to most countries for increasing the percentage of management positions held by women. They now occupy more than 40% of the professional posts, up 11% since 1991. And among the most senior UN positions, women fill a third of the jobs.

Putting Charges of Maladministration in Perspective   As with almost any government bureaucracy, it is possible to find horror stories about the size and activities of IGO staffs. The oil-for-food program scandal and the evidence of sexual abuse of supposedly protected persons by UN peacekeeping troops and personnel that swept over the UN like a tsunami in 2004 are recent and particularly disturbing examples (Pilch, 2005). But the charges that the UN and its associated agencies are corrupt and a bureaucratic swamp need to be put in perspective.

One way to gain insight about the size of the UN staff is to compare it to government employment in the United States. Between 1997 and 2007, there was nearly identical growth in the number of UN employees (+11.3%) and the U.S. federal, state, and local government workforce (+10.8%). The Secretariat's staff (16,324), which deals with a world population of 6.4 billion people, is about the same as the staff of San Antonio, Texas, which has 1.9 million people. The entire staff (57,988, excluding peacekeeping forces) of the UN and its associated agencies is only slightly larger than the number (52,200) of municipal employees of Los Angeles, California.

When evaluating UN administration it is important to acknowledge its flaws. There have been times of poor leadership and scandal at UN headquarters and in its various agencies. In the most recent of these, Secretary-General Annan was at least naïve in not ensuring better oversight of the oil-for-food program. Similarly, it is possible to find instances of ineptitude, wasted money, overstaffing, and other problems in the UN bureaucracy. However, it also important to recognize that all these problems occur in national governments, including the U.S. government. The basic point is that the standards one applies to the leaders of countries and those of IGOs should not differ. Nor should reactions to bureaucratic blundering. Within countries, problems may lead to the abolition of a particular agency, but the thrust is reform, not destruction of the entire government. From this perspective, it is more reasonable to address problems at the UN through reform rather than disbanding it.

In the same vein, it is important to see that reforming any large organization is difficult and usually a slow process. But the task is especially difficult in the UN where the secretary-general has 192 bosses, each with self-interested views of bureaucratic arrangements and all squabbling among themselves as to what is superfluous and what is vital. In 2006, for instance, the secretary-general proposed a plan to create several panels of countries to oversee UN finances, rather than leaving that task to the large, often unwieldy General Assembly. Many poor countries suspected, with some reason, that the proposal was meant to give additional financial control to the wealthier countries that contribute most of the UN's budget. "We should always remember that we are all equal partners in this organization, regardless of . . . how much we contribute to the budget of the organization," Egypt's ambassador asserted. With poor countries forming an overwhelming majority in the General Assembly, the proposal never moved forward, a fate that the British ambassador termed "destructive, a setback for the reform effort."[25] Reflecting such roadblocks, the U.S. General Accountability Office found that 70% of the reforms that the secretary-general had initiated and could implement on his own authority had proceeded, but only 44% of 32 reforms needing member-country approval had made significant progress.[26] The implication of this data is that when members complain about the UN's operation, they might look to themselves as barriers to change.

Finance

All IGOs face the problem of obtaining sufficient funds to conduct their operations. National governments must also address this issue, but they have the power to impose and legally collect taxes. By contrast, IGOs have very little authority to compel member-countries to support them.

The United Nations budget system is complex. For the UN in its narrowest organizational sense, there are two budgets: the *regular budget* for operating the UN's headquarters, its organs, and major administrative units, and the *peacekeeping budget* to meet those expenses. Looking at the UN system in a broader sense also includes the *specialized agencies budgets* and the *voluntary contributions budgets* of the agencies and various other UN associated programs. The agencies raise some funds based on assessments on members, but they and some other UN programs rely for most of their funding on voluntary contributions of countries and private groups and individuals. UN spending through these budgets has increased considerably, but as evident in Figure 7.8, the lion's share of that increase has been caused by a sharp increase in funds for peacekeeping operations and money going to various UN socioeconomic programs, rather than to the central administration, as is sometimes charged. These four budgets and some special budget categories, such as funding international tribunals, brought the total UN budget for 2006 to $19.8 billion.

To pay for its regular and peacekeeping operations, the UN depends almost entirely on assessments it levies on member-countries. By ratifying the UN Charter and joining the UN, members accept a legal obligation to pay these assessments and may have their voting privilege in the General Assembly suspended if they fall behind by more than a year. The amount each country is supposed to pay is determined by a complicated equation formulated by the General Assembly based on national wealth. As a result, nine countries each have assessments of 2% or more of the budget. They and their percentages of the regular budget are: the United States (22.0%), Japan (19.5%), Germany (8.7%), Great Britain (6.1%), France (6.0%), Italy (4.9%), Canada (2.8%), Spain (2.5%), and China (2.1%). At the other end of the financial scale, about 25% of UN members are assessed at the minimum level, 0.001%. The assessment level for the specialized agencies is the same as for the regular budget. Because of their special responsibility (and their special privilege, the veto), permanent

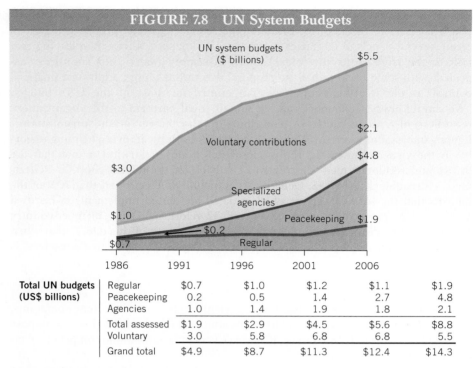

FIGURE 7.8 UN System Budgets

Total UN budgets (US$ billions)		1986	1991	1996	2001	2006
	Regular	$0.7	$1.0	$1.2	$1.1	$1.9
	Peacekeeping	0.2	0.5	1.4	2.7	4.8
	Agencies	1.0	1.4	1.9	1.8	2.1
	Total assessed	$1.9	$2.9	$4.5	$5.6	$8.8
	Voluntary	3.0	5.8	6.8	6.8	5.5
	Grand total	$4.9	$8.7	$11.3	$12.4	$14.3

At the core of the UN financial system are the UN assessed regular and peacekeeping budgets. To these can be added the assessed contributions that countries incur when they join one of the 12 autonomous specialized agencies, such as the World Health Organization. Yet another layer could be the voluntary contributions made to the specialized agencies and to numerous other UN programs, such as the UN Children's Fund. Notice that the regular, mostly administrative budget has grown relatively slowly. By contrast, the bulk in the increased funding of the UN and its specialized agencies has been programmatic: going either to peacekeeping or to socioeconomic programs.

Data sources: Global Policy Forum online; budgets of UN and agencies.

UNSC members pay a somewhat higher assessment for peacekeeping, with the U.S. share at 25%. The assessment scheme is criticized by some on the grounds that while the 9 countries with assessments of 2% or higher collectively pay almost 75% of the UN budget, they cast just 5% of the votes in the UNGA.

Such numbers are something of a fiction, however, because some countries do not pay their assessment. Member-states were in arrears on the regular and peace-keeping budgets by $3.3 billion in late 2006. As a result, the UN's financial situation is always precarious at the very time it is being asked to do more and more to provide protection and help meet other humanitarian and social needs. "It is," a frustrated Boutros-Ghali observed, "as though the town fire department were being dispatched to put out fires raging in several places at once while a collection was being taken to raise money for the fire-fighting equipment."[27] The analogy between the UN's budget and firefighting is hardly hyperbole. During 2006, the public safety (police and fire departments) budget of New York City was larger than the UN peacekeeping budget.

Just as it determines many things in this world, U.S. policy toward the UN's budget is a key to its financial stability. Some Americans think that their country overpays;

DEBATE THE POLICY SCRIPT

Santa or Scrooge? The United States and the UN Budget

From one perspective, Americans may feel like Santa Claus for their support of the United Nations. After all, the United States is just 1 of 192 UN members, yet it is assessed 22% of the UN's core budget and 25% of its peacekeeping budget. The United States also contributes to the budgets of the UN specialized agencies. For 2005 U.S. funding was about $530 million for the core budget, about $550 million for the peacekeeping budget, and about $900 million for the agencies, for a total just under $2 billion.

Two billion dollars sounds like a lot, but it is less extravagant from other perspectives. One is that total U.S. funding came to only about $10.26 per American. That is about 4% of what the average American spends each year going to the movies. In another context, only $1 out of every $1,200 dollars in the U.S. budget ($2.4 trillion) for 2005 went to supporting the UN. Focusing on security, Washington spends more every 15 hours on its military forces than it did for the entire year on UN peacekeeping.

Ratcheting down the image of Santa Claus even more, and perhaps even casting Americans as Scrooge, is the fact that the United States is also the UN's biggest debtor. In early 2005, Washington owed $1.4 billion to the UN, accounting for 37% of all UN arrearages. This debt persists even after the United States in 2002 pressured the UN into reducing the U.S.

assessments from 25% to 22% for the core budget and from 30% to 25% for the peacekeeping budget.

Most Americans think that their government should pay its debt. A 2002 poll that asked them whether they favored or opposed U.S. payment of its UN debt found 58% in favor, 32% opposed, and 10% unsure.[1] As for the annual payments, a 2003 survey found that 11% of Americans wanted to increase UN funding, 50% wanted to keep it the same, 37% wanted to decrease it, and 2% were uncertain.[2] How Americans would feel today about funding is unclear. On the one hand, the oil-for-food scandal and other frustrations have undercut American support of the UN. A 2005 poll showed considerable disenchantment among Americans with the UN. Yet the same survey recorded only 13% of its respondents as favoring a U.S. withdrawal from the UN, and almost 65% saying that the UN plays "a necessary role in the world today."[3]

What Do You Think?

How would you rewrite the script for the U.S. approach to the UN budget? Would you quickly pay off the U.S. debt or ignore it? How about the level of funding—should Santa Claus give less? Should Scrooge give more? Or is U.S. funding of the UN about right?

others see the United States as a penurious piker. The debate box, "Santa or Scrooge? The United States and the UN Budget" asks you to sort out this controversy and decide the future of U.S. funding of the United Nations.

Activities of the UN and Other IGOs

The most important aspects of any international organization are what it does, how well this corresponds to the functions we wish it to perform, and how well it is performing its roles. The following pages will begin to explore these aspects by examining the scope of IGO activity, with emphasis on the UN. Much of this discussion will only begin to touch on these activities, which receive more attention in other chapters.

Activities Promoting Peace and Security

The opening words of the UN Charter dedicate the organization to saving "succeeding generations from the scourge of war, which . . . has brought untold sorrow to mankind." The UN attempts to fulfill this goal in numerous ways.

Creating norms against violence is one. Countries that sign the charter pledge to accept the principle "that armed force shall not be used, save in the common interest" and further agree to "refrain in their international relations from the threat or the use of force except in self-defense." Reaffirming the charter's ideas, the UN (and other IGOs) condemned Iraq's invasion of Kuwait in 1990, Serbian aggression

Web Link

You can watch a wide range of UN activities, such as press conferences and Security Council meetings, at the UN Webcast site at **http://www.un .org/webcast/index.asp.**

against its neighbors, and other such actions. These denunciations and the slowly developing norm against aggression have not halted violence, but they have created an increasing onus on countries that strike the first blow. When, for example, the United States acted unilaterally in 1989 to depose the regime of Panama's strongman General Manuel Noriega, the UN and the OAS condemned Washington's action. Five years later, when the United States toppled the regime in Haiti, Washington took care to win UN support for its action. Of course, norms do not always restrain countries, as the U.S.-led invasion of Iraq in 2003 demonstrates. Yet the efforts of U.S. and British diplomats to get a supportive UN resolution underlined the existence of the norm. Moreover, the angry reaction in many parts of the globe to the Anglo-American preemptive action and the postwar difficulties during the occupation may, in the long run, actually serve to reinforce the norm.

Providing a debate alternative is a second peace-enhancing role for the UN and some other IGOs. Research shows that membership in IGOs tends to lessen interstate military conflict (Chan, 2004). One reason is that IGOs serve as a forum in which members publicly air their points of view and privately negotiate their differences. The UN thus acts like a safety valve, or perhaps a soundstage where the world drama can be played out without the dire consequences that could occur if another "shooting locale" were chosen. This grand-debate approach to peace involves denouncing your opponents, defending your actions, trying to influence world opinion, and winning symbolic victories.

Intervening diplomatically to assist and encourage countries to settle their disputes peacefully is another security role that IGOs play. IGOs engage in such steps as providing a neutral setting for opposing parties to negotiate, mediating to broker a settlement between opposing parties, and even deciding issues between disputants in such forums as the International Court of Justice.

Promoting arms control and disarmament is another IGO security function. The International Atomic Energy Agency, a specialized agency, focuses on the nonproliferation of nuclear weapons. The UN also sponsors numerous conferences on weapons and conflict and has also played an important role in the genesis of the Chemical Weapons Convention and other arms control agreements.

Imposing sanctions is a more forceful step to pressure countries that have attacked their neighbors or otherwise violated international law. As we will see in chapter 12, sanctions are controversial and often do not work, but they are also sometimes effective and they additionally serve as an important symbol of the views of the international community.

SIMULATION
The Work of
the United Nations

Peacekeeping is the best-known way that the UN and some other IGOs promote peace and security. This function is extensively covered in chapter 11, but a few preliminary facts are appropriate here. Through early 2007, the United Nations had mounted 61 peacekeeping operations, and they have utilized military and police personnel from most of the world's countries. These operations ranged from very lightly armed observer missions, through police forces, to full-fledged military forces. Never before have international forces been so active as they are now. The number of UN peacekeeping operations has risen markedly in the post–cold war era, as shown in Figure 7.9. As of December 2006 there were 16 UN peacekeeping forces of varying sizes in the field at

FIGURE 7.9 UN Peacekeeping Operations

Number of UN peacekeeping operations under way

The end of the cold war standoff between the United States and Soviet Union in the Security Council has freed the UN to conduct many more peacekeeping operations since then.

Data source: UN Department of Peacekeeping.

locations throughout the world, with about 81,000 troops and police from 114 countries deployed. Fortunately, UN peacekeeping forces have suffered relatively few casualties, but almost 2,300 have died in world service. For these sacrifices and contributions to world order, the UN peacekeeping forces were awarded the 1988 Nobel Peace Prize.

Social, Economic, Environmental, and Other Activities

In addition to maintaining and restoring the peace, IGOs engage in a wide variety of other activities. During its early years, the UN's emphasis was on security, a concern that has not abated but has been joined by social, economic, environmental, and other nonmilitary security issues. This shift has been a result of the ebb and eventual end of the cold war, the growing number of LDCs since the 1960s, realization that the environment is in danger, and changing global values that have brought an increased focus on human and political rights. "Peacekeeping operations claim the headlines," Secretary-General Annan observed astutely, "but by far the lion's share of our budget and personnel are devoted to the lower-profile work of . . . helping countries to create jobs and raise standards of living; delivering relief aid to victims of famine, war, and natural disasters; protecting refugees; promoting literacy; and fighting disease. To most people around the world, this is the face of the United Nations."[28] Recent examples of this effort include the UN program to supply emergency relief to people in the embattled region of Darfur in Sudan and the refugees from there who have fled to neighboring countries.

It would be impossible to list here, much less fully describe, the broad range of endeavors in which the UN and other IGOs are involved. Suffice it to say that they cover most of the issues that humans address at all levels of government. Many of these activities will be highlighted in subsequent chapters, so this discussion is limited to a few of the programs and successes of the UN and other IGOs.

Promoting *economic development* is an important role, with the United Nations Development Programme (UNDP), the World Bank, and a significant number of other global and regional IGOs working to improve the economic well-being of those who are deprived because of their location in an LDC, their gender, or some other cause. The UNDP alone has a budget of about $1 billion and is the conduit of about another $3 billion in foreign aid from individual countries in support of thousands of projects globally. The UN Development Fund for Women (UNIFEM) focuses on improving the lives of women in LDCs.

Advocating human rights is a closely related IGO function. Beginning with the Universal Declaration of Human Rights in 1948, the UN has actively promoted dozens of agreements on political, civil, economic, social, and cultural rights. The UN Commission on Human Rights has used its power of investigation and its ability to issue reports to expose abuses of human rights and to create pressure on the abusers by highlighting and condemning their transgressions. In an associated area, the International Labour Organization (ILO) leads the global effort to free the estimated 250 million children who are forced to work instead of being sent to school, to end the sexual predation of children that is big business in some parts of the world, and to eliminate other abuses that debase the meaning of childhood.

Advancing international law and norms is another important role of the UN and other IGOs (Coate & Fomerand, 2004). For example, international courts associated with IGOs help establish legal precedent. IGOs also sponsor multinational treaties, which may establish the assumption of law. Over 300 such treaties have been negotiated through the UN's auspices. As one scholar sees the norm-building function of IGOs, "The procedures and rules of international institutions create information structures.

Peacekeeping is the best-known UN activity, but the UN also addresses a broad range of other needs of the world. One is providing food to starving and dislocated persons, a mission in evidence in this photograph of two men in the Darfur region of Sudan with a World Food Program grain sack.

They determine what principles are acceptable as a basis for reducing conflicts and whether governmental actions are legitimate or illegitimate. Consequently, they help shape actors' expectations" (Keohane, 1998:91).

Improving the quality of human existence has many aspects. More than 30 million refugees from war, famine, and other dangers have been fed, given shelter, and otherwise assisted through the UN High Commissioner for Refugees. A wide variety of IGOs also devote their energies to such concerns as health, nutrition, and literacy. For example, UNICEF, WHO, and other agencies have undertaken a $150 million program to develop a multi-immunization vaccine. This vaccine program is designed to double the estimated 2 million children who now annually survive because of such international medical assistance. The Food and Agriculture Organization (FAO) has launched a program to identify, preserve, and strengthen through new genetic techniques those domestic animals that might prove especially beneficial to LDCs. Western breeds of pigs, for example, usually produce only about 10 piglets per litter; the Taihu pig of China manages 15 to 20. The FAO hopes to use the latter and other appropriate animals to increase protein availability in the LDCs.

Guarding the environment is one of the newer roles of IGOs. Beginning with the UN Conference on Environment and Development (dubbed the Earth Summit) in 1992, the UN has sponsored several global meetings on the environment. These have resulted in the initiation of programs that will slow down, stop, or begin to reverse the degradation of the environment. IGOs are increasingly also requiring that environmental impact statements accompany requests for economic development aid and in some cases are refusing to finance projects that have unacceptable negative impacts on the biosphere.

Encouraging independence through self-determination has long been a role of IGOs. The UN Trusteeship Council once monitored numerous colonial dependencies, but the wave of independence in recent decades steadily lessened its number of charges. When in October 1994 Palau gained its independence from the United States, the last trust territory was free. Therefore, the Trusteeship Council's mission was fulfilled and, while it continues to exist technically, it no longer meets.

Evaluating Global IGOs

The UN has existed for only a little more than 60 years. Most other IGOs are even younger. Have they succeeded? There are good and dubious standards to use when evaluating an IGO.

Fulfillment of ultimate goals is one dubious standard. Article 1 of the UN Charter sets out lofty goals such as maintaining peace and security and solving economic, social, cultural, and humanitarian problems. Clearly, the world is still beset by violent conflicts and by ongoing economic and social misery. Thus, from the perspective of meeting ultimate goals, it is easy to be skeptical about what the UN and other IGOs have accomplished. One has to ask, however, whether the meeting of ultimate goals is a reasonable standard. There is, according to one diplomat, a sense that "failure was built into [the UN] by an extraordinary orgy of exaggerated expectations."[29]

Acquiescence to your goals is another dubious standard. The United Nations is decidedly not meant to consistently help advance the policy goals of any individual country, especially if those goals clash with others. As the world's dominant power and the UN's largest contributor, the United States has been frequently frustrated with its inability to bend the UN to its wishes. President Bush was especially harsh after the UN refused to support the invasion of Iraq in 2003. Acknowledging the UN's stress with the United States, Secretary-General Ban traveled to Washington soon after taking office to try to mend fences. "But," he told an audience, "let me be clear: a constructive partnership between the U.S. and the UN . . . should not advance at the expense of others. Every one of our member-states has the right to be heard, whatever the size of its population or its pocketbook." Moreover, Ban continued, people around the world "in whose name the United Nations was founded, have the right to expect a UN which serves the needs of people everywhere. That is, after all, the only kind of UN they will respect."[30]

What is possible is a better standard by which to evaluate the UN and other IGOs. Insofar as the UN does not meet our expectations, we need to ask whether it is a flaw of the organization or the product of the unwillingness of member-states to live up to the standards that countries accept when they ratify the charter.

Just as President Bush and others castigated the UN for not supporting the war with Iraq, others berated the UN for not stopping the U.S. invasion. Reflecting on his decade as secretary-general, Kofi Annan told an audience, "The worst moment, of course, was the Iraq war, which, as an organization, we couldn't stop. I really did everything I could to try to see if we could stop it."[31] But of course, there was nothing he could do given UN resources. At a less dramatic level, simply paying their assessments regularly and on time is another thing more countries could do. In the end, the UN will also work better if countries try to make it effective. It is a truism, as Kofi Annan put it, that there is a "troubling asymmetry between what the member-states want of the [UN] and what they actually allow it to be."[32]

Progress is a second reasonable standard by which to evaluate the UN and other IGOs. Is the world better off for their presence? That is the standard Kofi Annan appealed for when he urged, "Judge us rightly . . . by the relief and refuge that we provide to the poor, to the hungry, the sick and threatened: the peoples of the world whom the United Nations exists to serve."[33] Between its 50th and 60th anniversaries, the United Nations surpassed all previous marks in terms of numbers of simultaneous peacekeeping missions, peacekeeping troops deployed, and other international security efforts. The Millennium Development Goals (MDGs) that the members of the UN unanimously adopted in 2000 for attainment by 2015 "have become the principal global scorecard for development," and the record shows that while much remains to be done, much has been accomplished by the UN to address the world's social, economic, and environmental problems. The UN kicked off the 21st century by sponsoring a series of global conferences on issues such as racism (Durban, 2001), aging (Madrid, 2002), sustainable development (Johannesburg, 2002), financing for development (Monterrey, 2002), small islands (Mauritius, 2005),

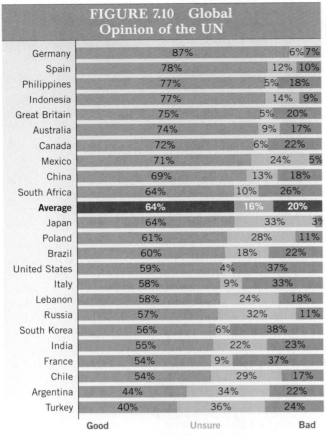

FIGURE 7.10 Global Opinion of the UN

Country	Good	Unsure	Bad
Germany	87%	6%	7%
Spain	78%	12%	10%
Philippines	77%	5%	18%
Indonesia	77%	14%	9%
Great Britain	75%	5%	20%
Australia	74%	9%	17%
Canada	72%	6%	22%
Mexico	71%	24%	5%
China	69%	13%	18%
South Africa	64%	10%	26%
Average	**64%**	**16%**	**20%**
Japan	64%	33%	3%
Poland	61%	28%	11%
Brazil	60%	18%	22%
United States	59%	4%	37%
Italy	58%	9%	33%
Lebanon	58%	24%	18%
Russia	57%	32%	11%
South Korea	56%	6%	38%
India	55%	22%	23%
France	54%	9%	37%
Chile	54%	29%	17%
Argentina	44%	34%	22%
Turkey	40%	36%	24%

Would a more powerful UN be a mostly good or mostly bad thing?

One indication of the generally favorable attitudes toward the United Nations worldwide was evident in a survey in 23 countries that asked people whether they thought it would be "mainly positive or mainly negative" for the UN to become "significantly more powerful in world affairs." A majority in all but two countries saw the possibility as a good thing.

Data source: BBC World Service Poll, March 2005; data supplied by the Program on International Policy Attitudes.

and the information society (Tunis, 2005). Such conferences and other planning efforts have not been all talk and no action. One MDG goal was to reduce the child (under age 5) mortality rate in the LDCs by two-thirds by 2015, from its 1990 level (10.3%). By 2004, that rate was down to 8.6%, good progress toward the 2015 goal of 6.9%.

World opinion is a third good standard. There is an old saw about not being able to fool all the people all of the time, and the UN earns good marks from the average person around the world. One survey of people in 43 countries found that 67% said the UN was having a good impact on their country. Only 20% saw a negative impact, with 13% unsure. A related question to test attitudes is to ask whether people want the UN to play an even more prominent role than it does. Another survey did that, and it showed, as detailed in Figure 7.10, most people do.

Whether alternatives exist is a fourth solid standard by which to evaluate the UN and other IGOs. John Bolton, the U.S. ambassador to the UN (2005–2006), once caustically commented that if 10 of the UN headquarter's 38 floors were eliminated "it wouldn't make a bit of difference."[34] Even if Bolton's opinion that "there's no such thing" as a well-functioning UN was correct, one must ask, If not the UN and other international organizations, then what? Can the warring, uncaring world continue unchanged in the face of nuclear weapons, persistent poverty, an exploding population, periodic mass starvation, continued widespread human rights violations, resource depletion, and environmental degradation? Somehow the world has survived these plagues, but one of the realities that this book hopes to make clear is that we are hurtling toward our destiny at an ever-increasing, now exponential speed. In a rapidly changing system, doing things the old way may be inadequate and may even take us down a road that, although familiar, will lead the world to cataclysm. At the very least, as Secretary of State Madeleine Albright noted, "The United Nations gives the good guys—the peace-makers, the freedom fighters, the people who believe in human rights, those committed to human development—an organized vehicle for achieving gains."[35]

This returns us to the question, If not the UN, then what? There may be considerable truth in the view of the British ambassador to the UN that "it's the UN, with all its warts, or it's the law of the jungle."[36] It is through this jungle that the road more familiar has passed, and following it into the future may bring what Shakespeare was perhaps imagining when he wrote in *Hamlet* of a tale that would "harrow up thy soul, [and] freeze thy young blood."

REGIONAL IGOs: FOCUS ON THE EUROPEAN UNION

Even more than has been true for global IGOs, the growth of regional IGOs has been striking. Prior to World War II there were no prominent regional IGOs. Now there are many, and they comprise about 75% of all IGOs. Most are specialized, with regional economic IGOs, such as the Arab Cooperation Council, the most numerous. Other regional IGOs are general purpose and deal with a range of issues. Examples are the African Union (AU, formerly the Organization of African Unity, OAU) and the Organization of American States (OAS).

Another noteworthy development regarding regional IGOs is that some of them are transitioning from specialized to general-purpose organizations. The Association of Southeast Asian Nations (ASEAN) was founded in 1967 to promote regional economic cooperation. More recently, though, ASEAN has begun to take on a greater political tinge, and, in particular, may serve as a political and defensive counterweight to China in the region. The Economic Community of West African States (ECOWAS) has also expanded its roles. It was created in 1975 to facilitate economic interchange, but it has since established a parliament and a human rights court. ECOWAS has also taken on regional security responsibilities and intervened in civil wars raging in the Ivory Coast, Liberia, and Sierra Leone. Beyond any of these examples of regional IGOs, the best example of regionalism is Europe. There, the European Union, with its 27 member-countries, has not only moved toward full economic integration, it has also achieved considerable political cooperation.

The Origins and Evolution of the European Union

The **European Union (EU)** has evolved through several stages and names. "What's in a name?" you might ask, echoing Shakespeare's heroine in *Romeo and Juliet*. As she discovered, the names Capulet and Montague proved important. So too, the name changes leading up to the current EU are important in the tale they tell.

Economic Integration

The EU's genesis began in 1952 when Belgium, France, (West) Germany, Italy, Luxembourg, and the Netherlands created a common market for coal, iron, and steel products, called the European Coal and Steel Community (ECSC). Its success prompted the six countries to sign the Treaty of Rome on March 25, 1957, which established the **European Economic Community (EEC)** to facilitate trade in many additional areas and the European Atomic Energy Community (EURATOM) to coordinate matters in that realm (Dinan, 2004).

Continued economic success led the six countries to found an overarching organization, the **European Communities (EC)**, in 1967. Each of the three preexisting organizations became subordinate parts of the EC. Then in 1993 a new name, the European Union, was adopted to denote both the existing advanced degree of integration and the EU's goal of becoming a single economic entity.

Even more significant was the adoption of a single currency, the euro, by most of the EU's members in 2002 (Martin & Ross, 2004). As the financial transactions among the EU's countries rapidly grew, it became clear that continually converting currencies from one to another made little sense. Therefore in the early 1990s, the EU agreed to move toward a common currency. Once the new currency was ready for launch, only those countries that met certain criteria for sound governmental financial management (such as limited inflation and budget deficits) could adopt the euro. With a few exceptions, all countries are required to move toward that point and to adopt the euro. In 2002 it went into general circulation in countries using it, while their traditional currencies ceased to be legal tender. As of the EU's 50th birthday in 2007, 13 of the EU countries were using the euro, and a number of small, non-EU countries, such as Monaco, had also adopted it. Of the older EU members, Great Britain, Denmark, and Sweden still do not use the euro for various reasons. Of the countries that have joined the EU since 2004, Slovenia already uses the euro, and the rest of the newer members are slated to transition to the euro once they achieve the required benchmarks of financial stability.

Creating the euro was important both economically and politically. Economically, it has tied the EU members even closer together by eliminating one of the hallmarks of an independent economy, a national currency. Adding to the economic importance of adopting a common currency that may well one day overspread an entire continent, there is great political symbolism in the replacement of Germany's Deutsche Mark, France's franc, Italy's lira, and other countries' national currencies with a common currency.

Adding to the EU's momentum provided by its new currency, 10 new members joined it in 2004 and 2 more in 2007, bringing the total to 27, as detailed in Figure 7.11.

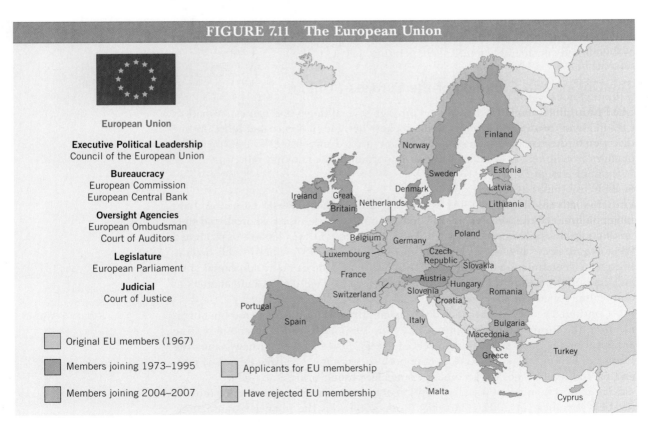

FIGURE 7.11   The European Union

European Union

Executive Political Leadership
Council of the European Union

Bureaucracy
European Commission
European Central Bank

Oversight Agencies
European Ombudsman
Court of Auditors

Legislature
European Parliament

Judicial
Court of Justice

Original EU members (1967)

Members joining 1973–1995

Members joining 2004–2007

Applicants for EU membership

Have rejected EU membership

The world's most integrated regional organization is the European Union. It has expanded from the six original countries that established the European Economic Community in 1958 to 27 countries today. The EU's focus is primarily economic, but it has become increasingly integrated on matters of the environment, human rights, and other policy areas.

Three more countries have applied for EU membership, and the eventual, if not quite stated, goal of the EU is to encompass all the region's countries (Poole & Baun, 2004). In the words of one top EU official, "There will be no such things as 'in countries' and 'out countries'; rather there will be 'ins' and 'pre-ins.'"[37]

For about 30 years, European integration focused on economics. Members of the EC grew ever more interdependent as economic barriers were eliminated. Over the years, the EC members moved toward economic integration and empowering the EC by such steps as abolishing all tariffs on manufactured goods among themselves, establishing a common external tariff, bargaining collectively through the EC with other countries in trade negotiations, and creating a revenue source for the EC by giving it a share of each country's value-added tax (VAT, similar to a sales tax) and money raised by tariffs on imported goods. Making official what was already under way, the EC members agreed to the Single European Act (SEA) of 1987, which committed the EC to becoming a fully integrated economic unit.

Political Integration

There comes a point where economic integration cannot continue without also taking steps toward political integration. This occurs because it is impossible to reach full economic integration among sovereign states whose domestic and foreign political policies are sometimes in conflict. Moreover, as the people unite economically, it is easier to think of becoming one politically.

Having reached this point by the 1990s, the EC's members moved forward by agreeing to the far-reaching Treaty on European Union (1993). Also known as the **Maastricht Treaty**, it laid the foundation for increased political integration. As one step in that direction, European citizenship was expanded. People can now travel on either an EU or a national passport, and citizens of any EU country can vote in local and European Parliament elections in another EU country in which they live. The Maastricht Treaty called for the EU to act increasingly as a political unit by eventually creating a common foreign and defense policy and a common internal policy relating to such issues as crime, terrorism, and immigration. Gradually, such ideas have moved toward reality. For example, the EU and the United States exchange ambassadors. Moving even further, the Treaty of Amsterdam (1999) strengthened EU political integration by such steps as enhancing the powers of the president of the EU Commission and the European Parliament (EP). Four years later, the Treaty of Nice (2003) set the stage for further expansion of the EU's membership by detailing political arrangements—such as the distribution of seats or votes in the EP—that would occur as new member-countries join the EU.

The EU has also taken on the symbols of a state. It has a flag and has adopted the *European Anthem.* The anthem has no words in recognition of the EU's linguistic diversity. However, its melody, the "Ode to Joy" movement of Ludwig van Beethoven's Ninth Symphony (1823), was chosen because it refers to Friedrich von Schiller's poem, "Ode to Joy" (1785), which expresses hope for a time when "All men become brothers." This view is also evident in the EU's motto, "United in diversity." Adding substance to symbolism, the EU has also voted to create a European constitution, an undertaking that we will explore in a later section (Cowles & Dinan, 2004).

Web Link

You can hear the European Anthem at: **http://europa.eu./ abc/symbols/anthem/index _en.htm.**

Governance of the European Union

The EU's organizational structure is complex, but a brief look at it helps illustrate the extent to which a regional government exists. As an IGO, the governance structure of the EU is not exactly a government, but it is arguably moving in that direction and it shares most of the institutional characteristics of a government. Moreover, like a government, the structure and the authority of the various EU units play an important part in determining how policy is made (Meunier, 2000). Figure 7.11 gives a brief overview of this structure. The EU's government can be divided for analysis into its political leadership, bureaucracy, legislature, judiciary, and other review agencies.

Political Leadership

Political decision making is centered in the **Council of the European Union**, formerly called the Council of Ministers. It meets often with ministers of member-countries (such as finance ministers) in attendance. The Council meets twice a year as a gathering of the prime ministers and other heads of government, and on its own authority, or along with the European Parliament, it decides on the most important policy directions for the EU, including the direction of its Common Foreign and Security Policy. Assisting the Council is an administrative staff called the General Secretariat headed by the Secretary-General of the Council. This post has become increasingly important in recent years, with its incumbent (Spain's Javier Solana since 2004) speaking for the Council in international relations and exercising other visible and key roles.

Most Council sessions are held in Brussels, Belgium, the principal site of the EU administrative element. Decisions are made by three voting plans. Routine procedural decisions require a *majority vote*. A weighted-vote plan termed a *qualified majority vote* is used for most decisions. Under this plan, there are 345 votes, with four countries (France, Germany, Great Britain, and Italy) each having 29 votes, and the votes of the other 23 members ranging from 27 (Spain and Poland) to 3 (Malta). Voting procedures are complex, but a qualified majority means meeting three standards: (a) a majority (14) of countries, (b) 255 or more votes, and (c) the votes of countries that represent at least 62% of the EU's population. A third voting plan, *a unanimous vote*, is required for votes on taxation, defense, foreign affairs, and a few other matters. The advantage of the voting rules is that the qualified majority and unanimous vote plans require a high degree of consensus in Europe before the EU can adopt policies that one or more of its members oppose. This check has made moving forward along the economic and political integration tracks easier because the sense of sovereignty that EU members retain seems less threatened. The downside of the Council of Ministers' voting rules is that the supermajorities required for most votes make it very difficult to move forward on controversial issues and promotes stalemate.

Bureaucracy

The EU's bureaucracy is organized under the **European Commission**, which administers policy adopted by the Council and the Parliament and can also propose legislation to those branches. There are 27 commissioners, one from each country, who serve five-year terms and act as a cabinet for the EU. One of the commissioners is selected by the Council of the European Union to be **President of the Commission**. This official serves as the EU's administrative head and is the overall director of the EU bureaucracy headquartered in Brussels. Each of the remaining 26 commissioners head a ministry overseeing one or another functional areas. This practice of having a minister from each country has arguably led to an overly large commission and a fragmented bureaucratic structure, including a ministry of multilingualism, as the number of EU members has grown.

Counterbalancing the commission's fragmentation, the post of president has evolved into one of the most significant in the EU. A great deal of that evolution can also be attributed to Jacques Delors, a French national who served as president from

1985 through 1994 and who became known as "Mr. Europe" because of his strong advocacy of European integration. Delors and his staff created a core structure, informally referred to as "Eurocracy," which has a European point of view, rather than a national orientation. As of 2007, the Commission's president was José Manuel Barroso of Portugal.

One of many indications of the importance of the Commission, as well as the political integration of Europe, is the emergence of an ever larger, more active, and more powerful EU infrastructure. The EU's administrative staff has about quadrupled since 1970 to about 25,000 today. The annual number of EU regulations, decisions, and directives from one or the other EU body has risen from 345 in 1970 to over 600. The EU's 2007 budget was about $164 billion. About 70% of this comes from member-countries contributing 0.73% of their respective gross national products (GNP, also called gross national income), with the remaining 30% coming about evenly from EU tariff revenues and the value added tax (VAT), a type of sales tax.

As occurs in the United States and every other country, the bureaucracy in the EU is a lightning rod for much of any dissatisfaction that exists with the government. Typical of the criticism, the British newspaper *Daily Mail* charged in 2007 that "Brussels bureaucrats have produced so many [regulations]—many of them completely unnecessary—that the paperwork weighs more than a ton, the same as a whale or rhinoceros," and if laid out in a line "would be over 120 miles long."[38] Commenting further on the reported 667,000 pages of administrative regulations instituted since 1957, the newspaper derisively noted, among other things, a requirement that teachers "assess how noisy school children can be"; a "Working at Height Directive" that made it so difficult to use ladders on a job that "one priest had to pay an expert £1,300 [about $2,500] to change a light bulb in his church"; a "50-page-long directive on the use of condoms"; and a 24-page directive on work boot safety.

Some sense of the importance of the EU in the lives of Europeans is captured in this photograph of farmers demonstrating in Brussels, the EU's "capital," about a plan by the EU to cut price supports for sugar. The SOS banner on top reads, "The European Commission exterminates us." The name on the cuff of the fist is that of Franz Fischler, the EU commissioner of agriculture. The plant on the Spanish flag is a sugar beet.

Oversight Agencies

The EU has two unusual regulatory oversight structures. One of these is the **European Ombudsman**, who is appointed by the European Parliament. EU residents or organizations who believe they are being treated unfairly by EU authorities can ask the office of the ombudsman to investigate. If it feels that an injustice has been done, the office can recommend remedial action to EU agencies and can also make recommendations to the European Parliament for legislative action.

A second oversight institution is the **Court of Auditors**. Each member-country has one member on the Court, which directs a staff that oversees the EU budget to ensure that it is legally implemented, adheres to established policy, and is soundly managed. The Court has no independent corrective authority, but it can make recommendations to the Council and the Parliament.

Legislature

The **European Parliament (EP)** serves as the EU's legislative branch and meets in Strasbourg, France. It has 785 members who are elected to five-year terms, apportioned among the EU's 27 countries on a modified population basis. The most populous country (Germany) has 99 seats; the least populous country (Malta) has 5 seats. Delegates to the assemblies of most IGOs are appointed by their government, but members of the EP are elected by voters in their respective countries (Scully & Farrell, 2003). Furthermore, instead of organizing themselves within the EP by country, the representatives have tended to group themselves by political persuasion. As it stood in early 2007, the center-right coalition, the European People's Party, was the largest of 8 blocs with 35% of the seats, followed by the mildly left Socialists Group with 27% of the seats. The remaining seats were divided among six other groups, ranging from the centrist Alliance of Liberals and Democrats (14%) to far-left and far-right blocs, each with approximately 5% of the seats. Reflecting Europe's propensity to elect more women to office than any other world region (see chapter 5), females made up a third of the EP membership.

The EP's role began as a mostly advisory authority, but it has grown. It now has "co-decision" legislative authority with the Council of the European Union on the EU budget and a significant range of other policy matters. Parliamentarians also confirm the members of the European Commission and its president. Demonstrating the import of that authority, the EP refused to confirm any of the list of commissioners submitted in 2004 by the new President of the Commission, José Manuel Barroso, until he replaced Italy's Rocco Buttiglione as the EU's Commissioner for Justice, Freedom, and Security. Legislators objected to his comments that homosexuality is a "sin" and that the purpose of families is "to allow women to have children and to have the protection of a male who takes care of them."[39] The EP also can veto some regulations issued by it (Maurer, 2003). In one recent example, members voted nearly unanimously to block a rule that would have made it easier to patent software. The commission claimed the rules would better protect innovations; the parliamentarians believed that the rules would have blocked new innovators from entering the software field.

Judiciary

The **Court of Justice** is the main element of the judicial branch of the EU. The 27-judge court—one justice from each EU county—sits in Luxembourg and hears cases brought by member-states or other EU institutions and sometimes acts as a court of appeals for decisions of lower EU courts. Only rarely does the full court hear a case. Instead, almost 90% of the cases are heard by 3- or 5-judge panels. This allows the court to deal with a much higher number of cases (400 to 500 a year) than the U.S. Supreme Court (about 75 cases a year).

Did You Know That:

The 2007 EU budget ($164 billion) is larger than the budgets of all but 16 of the world's countries.

Did You Know That:

Alessandra Mussolini, granddaughter of Italian dictator Benito Mussolini, is a member of the European Parliament's far-right bloc, the Identity, Tradition, and Sovereignty Group.

The combined treaties of the EU are often considered its collective "constitution" in lieu of a formal constitution. Like the EU's other institutions, the courts have gained authority over time. They can strike down both EU laws and regulations and those of member-countries that violate the basic EU treaties. In 2006, for example, the Court invalidated an EU-U.S. agreement made soon after 9/11 by which the EU was giving American officials 34 items of personal information about any passenger leaving on a flight to the United States. The European Parliament had objected that the EU Commission lacked a legal basis to make such an agreement, and the court agreed. Another bit of evidence of the mounting influence of the court is that its workload became so heavy that in 1989 the EU created a new, lower court, the Court of First Instance, which hears cases related to the EU brought by corporations and individuals.

ANALYZE THE ISSUE
The Future Direction of the European Union

The Future of the EU

Part of the story of the EU is its rapid evolution, beginning with the formation of the ECSC in 1952. Within just a few decades, much of Europe had been transformed from a continent marked by perpetual rivalry and frequent war to a continent largely at peace, with a high degree of economic integration, and with the beginning of significant political integration as well. In the grand sweep of human history, the approximately 50 years in which all this happened was a proverbial blink of the eye. Heartened by their unbroken string of successes moving European integration forward, EU leaders turned their focus to taking the next logical integrative step, writing and adopting an EU constitution.

Campaign for a Constitution

Drafting the constitution began in 2002 when a convention chaired by former French President Valery Giscard d'Estaing met to write it. The resulting document was completed in 2004. Its details are complex, but it was designed to considerably strengthen the EU institutions, to give the EU greater authority in areas such as immigration, to extend the rights of EU citizens, to make passing of laws easier for the Council, and to create some new posts, such as a fixed-term (instead of rotating) president of the Council of the Europe Union and a foreign minister in order to strengthen the EU's executive branch. In sum, it would have moved the EU further toward the centralization of authority on the scale of the division of power in Figure 7.3 on page 203.

To take effect, however, the constitution required ratification by the member-states, with each able to decide its own ratification process (Gilbert, 2004; Calleo, 2003). Fifteen members opted to have their parliaments alone consider the issue. The other 10 states chose either a binding or nonbinding referendum as part of that process.

Initially, prospects for the adoption of the constitution seemed good. It enjoyed strong support among the most established leaders in Europe. Not only did the heads of every EU country sign it, but in January 2005 the EP endorsed it by a vote of 500 to 137, with 40 abstentions. Moreover, early polls also indicated solid public support, including a proconstitution majority in every country except Great Britain. The ratification process also began smoothly in November 2004 when Lithuania's parliament consented to the constitution by a lopsided 84 votes in favor and a mere 4 against. Parliaments in eight other countries added their ratifications by equally one-sided votes in the months that followed. And in the first referendum test, 77% of Spanish voters approved the document.

However, as the dates for referendums in a number of countries drew closer and as the debate over the constitution heated up and put the issues in sharper focus,

The possibility of predominantly Muslim Turkey becoming a member of the European Union was one factor that led voters in France and the Netherlands to reject the EU's constitution. Now Turkey's hopes of joining the EU are even dimmer than before.

opinion in some countries began to turn negative. France was especially worrisome because of its size and importance to the EU and because French voters had approved the Maastricht Treaty by only a slim 2% margin in 1994. President Jacques Chirac went on television to urge a yes vote, but his appeal was unsuccessful, and 55% of French voters cast a no ballot. A few days later, the Dutch also defeated ratification, with 62% voting against it. No single factor could be attributed to the French or Dutch rejection votes (Brouard & Tiberj, 2006; Milner, 2006; Stefanova, 2006).

A postreferendum poll in France found that among those who voted no, about half voiced an economic concern, such as fear that jobs would be lost to new, lower-wage member-countries in Eastern Europe, or to workers from those countries traveling to France. Another common reason among no voters was seeing their vote as a rejection of President Chirac's leadership. Much less common were objections to the basic idea of the EU or further integration, such as opposition to Turkey's potential membership, loss of sovereignty, oppositions to the EU per se, and opposition to "a United States of Europe."[40] Dutch no voters were much more diverse in what caused their decision. The most common answers were lack of information (32%), loss of sovereignty, and voting no to reject the current Dutch government. In contrast to France, economic concern seemed to play only a minor role.[41]

Some of the negative sentiment had to do with domestic discontent with the French and Dutch governments that were supporting ratification. Still, the votes also signaled popular discontent with the simultaneous "wide and deep" pace of EU evolution. Voters were unsettled with the rapid pace of wider expansion in the number of EU member-countries at the same time the constitution called for even deeper EU political integration. For example, EU economic growth has lagged in recent years, unemployment is much higher than in the United States or Japan, and Western European workers worried that they would be competing for jobs. Polls also showed discontent with what voters saw as the EU burgeoning bureaucracy and budget and concerns that they were losing control of their country to the EU. Among other points, voters were worried that EU rules would force them to accept increased numbers of immigrants from North Africa and elsewhere. The strong anti-immigrant tide in Europe, increased anti-Muslim sentiments, and the prospect of Muslim Turkey joining the EU also added to the no vote.

Reflecting on the EU's Future

In the aftermath of the double body blow to the EU constitution, some supportive leaders put on a brave front and urged the process to go on with France, Holland, and any other country that said no being given a second chance to say yes. But reality soon set in, and EU leaders suspended the adoption process for a "period of reflection" (Hooghe & Marks, 2006). When that period ends is uncertain, but there are signs that Europe's leaders will once again try to convince the citizenry to endorse greater integration through an EU constitution. In 2007, for example, German Chancellor Angela Merkel declared in a speech to the European Parliament that, "It is in the interest of Europe, its member-states and its citizens to bring this process [adoption of a constitution] to a successful conclusion. A collapse in that process would be a historic failure. We must give a soul to Europe."[42] In addition to their belief that the EU has promoted peace and prosperity in Europe, many of the continent's leaders also are intent on reviving the growth and integration of the EU because of the looming shadow of a hegemonic United States (Hassler, 2004). Expressing that sentiment in 2005, President Chirac urged French voters to ratify the EU constitution as a way of avoiding an "Anglo-Saxon, Atlanticist Europe . . . dominated by America." Chirac warned, "We [cannot] defend our interests alone. We can only defend them collectively, and if Europe is united. . . . Otherwise, we'll be swept away."[43]

Whether Chancellor Merkel and others who favor further integration and expansion of the EU can persuade the EU public to follow them remains unclear. Most Europeans have a positive view of the EU and in the abstract believe that its expansion has been positive. However, a majority of Europeans also worry that further expansion will hurt their country's employment situation. Moreover, while Merkel and many European leaders believe in a neofunctionalist, top-down approach that will increase European integration by creating constitutions and institutions that tie Europeans together, the public tends to be more functionalist, favoring a bottom-up approach that stresses creating common economic and cultural conditions before taking legal steps. This sense is evident in Figure 7.12.

Each step toward integration encounters increasingly tougher barriers as political sovereignty and other traditional orientations are lessened (Gilbert, 2003). Making the change in people's minds from being German, French, or some other nationality toward increasingly identifying as European is crucial. Yet it has only just begun and must overcome many centuries of tradition, therefore facing an uncertain future (Hermann, Risse, & Brewer, 2004). It could be that Europe's leaders will be able to ease the concerns of voters over such matters as loss of sovereignty, jobs, and immigration and quickly move the EU further. That seems improbable in the current climate in Europe, but then the rapid growth and integration of the EU to date once seemed improbable and

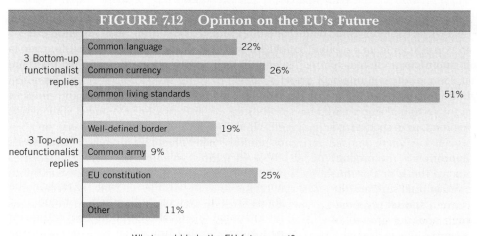

FIGURE 7.12   Opinion on the EU's Future

3 Bottom-up functionalist replies
- Common language — 22%
- Common currency — 26%
- Common living standards — 51%

3 Top-down neofunctionalist replies
- Well-defined border — 19%
- Common army — 9%
- EU constitution — 25%

Other — 11%

What would help the EU future most?

The drive to expand the European Union and increase its economic and political integration has been accomplished by European leaders often using a top-down, neofunctionalist approach of creating institutions and laws with the belief that social and other forms of integration would follow. The resistance of the EU public to this approach alone was evident in the rejection of the EU constitution in 2005. This figure shows that when asked what one or two things would help the EU's future most, the public is more likely to favor the bottom-up approach (achieving a common language, having the euro be the common currency throughout the EU, and achieving a common standard of living) than the top-down approach (establishing a well-defined border, creating a common EU army, and adopting an EU constitution).

Note: Respondents could give up to two answers, and averaged 1.6, so percentages exceed 100.
Data source: EU Barometer, The Future of Europe, May 2006.

it happened. It could be that Valéry Giscard d'Estaing will be proven correct in his prediction that rejection of the constitution might mean "the gradual falling apart of the European Union."[44] But that seems improbable also. Perhaps what is most likely, then, is that an extended period of "settling" will be required after rather rapid change in the EU before the public will be comfortable with once again moving forward boldly. All that is certain, though, about the future of the EU is that the stakes are high, and progress of the EU toward true federation will be difficult.

At a much more preliminary level, the questions, issues, and factors regarding the future of the EU are either the same or similar to those that related to how we will govern the international system at large in the decades and centuries to come. In this way, the evolution of the EU is noteworthy beyond the immediate issue of Europe's future. The EU also serves as something of a test case to see if humans who have found that the way they had been conducting themselves politically for centuries is not working well can overcome tradition and inertia and establish a new form of governance at a regional or perhaps even global level. Whatever the choices Europeans and everyone make in the future about their governance, there is wisdom in Shakespeare's *Julius Caesar* that is worth pondering. The playwright counsels us:

> There is a tide in the affairs of men
> Which, taken at the flood, leads on to fortune;
> Omitted, all the voyage of their life
> Is bound in shallows and in miseries.

CHAPTER SUMMARY

AN OVERVIEW OF INTERGOVERNMENTAL ORGANIZATIONS

1. One sign of the changing international system is the rapid rise over the last century in the number of intergovernmental organizations (IGOs). There are many classifications of international organizations, including global, regional, and specialized IGOs.

2. Current international organization is the product of three lines of development: the idea that humans should live in peace and mutual support, the idea that the big powers have a special responsibility for maintaining order, and the growth of specialized international organizations to deal with narrow nonpolitical issues.

3. The rapid growth of all types of international organizations stems from increased international contact among states and people, increased economic interdependence, the growing importance of transnational issues and political movements, the inadequacy of the state-centered system for dealing with world problems, small states attempting to gain strength by joining together, and successful IGOs providing role models for new organizations.

4. There are significant differences among views on the best role for international organizations. Four existing and possible roles of IGOs are: providing an interactive arena, acting as a center for cooperation among states, evolving into an independent national actor, and becoming a supranational organization.

5. Some observers argue that international organizations are best suited to promoting cooperation among states rather than trying to replace the state-centered system. Still others contend that international organizations should concentrate on performing limited functional activities with the hope of building a habit of cooperation and trust that can later be built upon. Finally, many view international organizations as vehicles that should be manipulated to gain national political goals.

6. Some observers favor moving toward a system of supranational organization, in which some form of world government, or perhaps regional governments, would replace or substantially modify the present state-centered system.

GLOBAL IGOs: FOCUS ON THE UNITED NATIONS

7. The United Nations provides an example of the development, structure, and roles of a global IGO.

8. There are several important issues related to the structure of international organizations. One group of questions relates to membership and criteria for membership.

9. Voting schemes to be used in such bodies are another important issue. Current international organizations use a variety of voting schemes that include majority voting, weighted voting, and unanimity voting.

10. Another group of questions concerns the administration of international organizations, including the role of the political leaders and the size and efficiency of IGO bureaucracies. The source of IGO revenue and the size of IGO budgets are a related concern.

11. International organizations have many roles. Peacekeeping is one important role. Others include creating norms against violence, providing a debate alternative, intervening diplomatically, imposing sanctions, and promoting arms control and disarmament.

12. The UN and other international organizations perform other, varied functions: they promote international law, promote arms control, better the human condition, promote self-government, and further international cooperation.

13. However one defines the best purpose of international organization, it is important to have realistic standards of evaluation. The most fruitful standard is judging an organization by what is possible, rather than setting inevitably frustrating ideal goals.

REGIONAL IGOs: FOCUS ON THE EUROPEAN UNION

14. The EU provides an example of the development, structure, and roles of a regional IGO. The EU has evolved considerably along the path of economic integration and is by far the most integrated regional organization.

15. The movement toward political integration is more recent and is proving more difficult than economic integration. The French and Dutch rejections of the proposed EU constitution were a significant setback in the process of EU expansion and integration. It is unclear, though, whether the negative votes would only cause a pause in EU progress toward becoming a United States of Europe or augured a stalling or even reversal of the trend of recent decades toward integration.

For simulations, debates, and other interactive activities, a chapter quiz, Web links, and much more, visit **www.mhhe.com/rourke12/** and go to chapter 7. Or, while accessing the site, click on Course-Related Headlines and view recent international relations articles in the *New York Times*.

KEY TERMS

confederation
Council of the European Union
Court of Auditors
Court of Justice
European Commission
European Communities (EC)
European Economic Community (EEC)
European Ombudsman

European Parliament (EP)
European Union (EU)
federation
functionalism
Hague system
Intergovernmental organizations (IGOs)
league
League of Nations
limited membership council

Maastricht Treaty
majority voting
neofunctionalism
plenary representative body
President of the Commission
regime
regional government
Secretariat
supermajority voting

supranational organization
UN General Assembly (UNGA)
UN Security Council (UNSC)
unanimity voting
unitary government
United Nations (UN)
veto
weighted voting
world government

National Power and Statecraft: The Traditional Approach

Then, everything includes itself in power,
Power into will, will into appetite.
> —William Shakespeare, *Troilus and Cressida*

Bid me discourse, I will enchant thine ear.
> —William Shakespeare, "Venus and Adonis"

Power is a multifaceted concept. This photograph taken in Shanghai, China, displays the exhortation, "Strengthen National Power, Build a Solid National Defense." You will find in this chapter that a country's power and its diplomatic success do not just grow out of the barrel of a gun. Indeed, some argue that military power is increasingly less significant as a factor that determines a country's national power and foreign policy success.

Traditionally, the state has been at the center of the international system, and each state's pursuit of its self-defined national interests has been the central dynamic of world politics. This process, how states pursue their national interests, is the focus of this chapter.

National capabilities are the first thing we will explore. Each state's ability to achieve its goals is based in substantial part on a range of capabilities. These are particularly important when the goals of two or more states clash, and the story line of the global drama is often about whose interests prevail and whose do not. But capabilities, such as the ability to skillfully articulate goals and persuade others that the goals are mutually beneficial, are even important in noncompetitive situations. **Power** is the term we will use here to represent the sum of a country's capabilities. Because power in common usage carries the connotation of "hit-over-the head" or "make you" capabilities, it is very important to stress that power as used here is more than that. As we will explore later in the following pages, power can be based on positive persuasion as well as negative coercion. Indeed, power has many forms. Military muscle, wealth, and some others are fairly obvious and tangible. Others such as national will power and diplomatic skills are much less obvious and intangible.

Applying national capabilities in the pursuit of the national interest is our second topic. **Foreign policy** includes not just the international goals that a country has, but how countries use their national capabilities to achieve those goals. A great deal of discussion in chapter 3 focuses on how foreign policy is made. Here the emphasis will be on how it is carried out. **Statecraft** is the term often used to encapsulate how a country applies its national capabilities to achieve its foreign policy goals. As one scholar has defined it, statecraft:

> refers to the use of policy instruments to satisfy the core objectives of nation-states in the international system. . . . Statecraft is most usefully thought of in broad and multidimensional terms. It involves the application and interplay of multiple instruments—military, economic, diplomatic, and informational—to achieve the multiple objectives of states, including national security, economic prosperity, and political prestige and influence. (Mastanduno, 1988:826)

Before moving on to our exploration of power and the implementation of foreign policy, note that in the context of this book's theme—the traditional and alternative approaches to world politics—this chapter looks at the traditional ways of establishing which policies will prevail in the world. Usually that is determined by which country or coalition has the greater capabilities. The alternative approach, discussed in chapter 9, involves the establishment of international law and norms of justice to regulate the conduct of international relations. Chapter 9 also examines the role of international courts in trying to ensure that the rule of law limits destructive behavior by states and individuals. That way who is right, rather than who is mightiest, has a better chance of prevailing.

THE COMPLEX NATURE OF POWER

Power is an elusive concept. Its multifaceted characteristics make it hard to precisely describe or measure. As former Harvard University dean and top U.S. national security official Joseph Nye (2000:55) puts it, power "is like the weather. Everyone talks about it, but few understand it."

Characteristics of Power

One of the many reasons that it is so challenging to get a handle on power is that it has many characteristics, some of which seem almost contradictory. It is both an asset and a goal, hard and soft, absolute and relative, objective and subjective, and a function of both capabilities and will. Additionally, power is situational.

Power as an Asset and Goal

One source of confusion in discussions about power is that it is both an asset and a goal. Our discussion of power so far has generally treated it as an *asset* that can be applied to help countries achieve goals. In this sense, power is akin to money as a sort of political currency that can be used to acquire things. Money buys things; power causes things to happen. There are, of course, differences between money and power. One is that political power is less liquid than money; it is harder to convert into things that you want. A second difference is that power, unlike money, has no standard measurement. Therefore it is much harder to be precise about how much power any country has, as we shall see in our section on measuring power.

Power is also a goal because in a world of often conflicting goals among countries it is only prudent to seek, acquire, or preserve sufficient power to pursue your national goals. Here again, the analogy between power and money has merit. We all expend money as an asset, yet we also seek to acquire money and to build up a reserve against both anticipated needs and contingencies.

The duality of power as an asset and goal creates a debate over whether more is always better. Some people believe that countries can become fixated on acquiring power, especially military power, beyond what is prudently needed to meet possible exigencies. This, critics say, is unwise because power is expensive, it creates a temptation to use it, and it spawns insecurity in others. Critics of recent U.S. foreign policy see its massive arms spending and its misadventure in Iraq as a case in point.

To such charges, realists warn that not being willing to pay the price today to guard against future and unknown dangers leaves states vulnerable (Schweller, 2004). Realists also dismiss the concern about having too much power and say that the real danger is unwise use of the power you have by wasting it on marginal goals. A third realist caution is against a country being too reluctant to expend its power to advance its national interests. Former Secretary of State Henry Kissinger, for one, portrays Americans as sometimes too-reluctant warriors and believes that "American leadership [needs] to articulate for their public a concept of the national interest and explain how that interest is served . . . by the maintenance of the balance of power" through a forceful U.S. presence on the world stage.[1]

Hard and Soft Power

As noted earlier, the most common image of power involves the ability to make someone else do something or suffer the consequences. Often called **hard power**, this type of power rests on negative incentives (threats, "sticks") and on positive incentives (inducements, "carrots"). There is also **soft power**, the ability to persuade others to follow your lead by being an attractive example. As one scholar puts it, "A country may obtain the outcome it wants in world politics because other countries—admiring its values, emulating its example, aspiring to its level of prosperity and openness—want to follow it" (Nye, 2004:5).

The value of these two forms of power is the source of much debate. Hard power is easier to appreciate because it is easier to see that certain coercive measures or positive incentives have been used and to observe the result. Realists are also apt to dismiss the concept of soft power, arguing that countries follow other countries' lead if they share the same interests, not out of altruistic sentiments such as admiration.

Rebutting this, those who believe that soft power can be potent point, as an example, to the negative impact they say the Iraq War has had on U.S. soft power by greatly diminishing the U.S. image abroad. Citing poll results, such as those in Figure 8.1, showing that opinion about the United States has plummeted almost everywhere in the past several years, one analyst worries that "the United States' soft power—its ability to attract others by the legitimacy of U.S. policies and the values that underlie them—is in decline as a result" (Nye, 2004a:16). One reason this is a concern, according to this view, is because the United States needs the cooperation of other countries to combat terrorism and many other problems, but "When the United States becomes so unpopular that being pro-American is a kiss of death in other countries' domestic politics, foreign political leaders are unlikely to make helpful concessions, reducing U.S. leverage in international affairs." To such commentary, those who are skeptical of the importance of soft power might echo the words of President Bush, who professed his "respect [for] the values, judgment, and interests of our friends and partners," but also asserted, "We will be prepared to act apart" if necessary and "will not allow . . . disagreements [with allies] to obscure our determination to secure . . . our fundamental interests and values."[2]

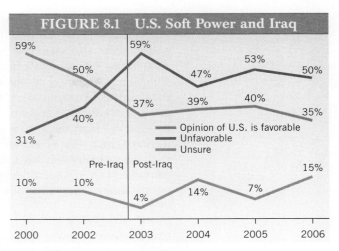

FIGURE 8.1 U.S. Soft Power and Iraq

Polls in six countries indicate that after the U.S. invasion of Iraq in March 2003 there was an increase in the share of people who viewed the United States unfavorably and a similar decline in the U.S. favorable rating. The shifts between 2000 and 2002 may be related to the fact that by the summer of 2002 when the poll was taken, there were already strong reports of a U.S. readiness to act against Iraq. This decline in U.S. prestige arguably undercut U.S. "soft power" and the willingness of other governments to cooperate with Washington.

Note: The question was, "Please tell me if you have a very favorable, somewhat favorable, somewhat unfavorable or very unfavorable opinion of the United States." The six countries were France, Germany, Great Britain, Pakistan, Turkey, and Russia. Pew reported the favorable data only for 2000; the two other data points for that year are estimated.

Data source: Pew Research Center for the People and the Press (2000, 2003, 2006).

Absolute and Relative Power

By one standard, power that indisputably exists and can be potentially used is **absolute power**. An example is the approximately 5,000 nuclear warheads and bombs that are deployed on about 1,000 U.S. missiles and bombers. They indisputably exist, will have a specific impact if used, and in theory can be used by a president without any legal check on the ability to authorize their deployment.

Whatever the theory may be, however, power does not usually exist in a vacuum. Since power is about the ability to persuade or make another actor do or not do something, calculating power is of limited use except to measure it against the power of the other side. When assessing capabilities, then, **relative power**, or the comparative power of national actors, must be considered. We cannot, for example, say that China is powerful unless we specify in comparison to whom. Whatever Beijing's power resources may be, China's relative power compared to another major power, such as Japan, is less than is China's relative power compared to a smaller neighbor, such as Vietnam.

A related issue is whether power is a **zero-sum game**. If a gain in power of one actor inevitably means a loss of power for other actors, the game is zero-sum. If an actor can gain power without the power of other actors being diminished, then the game is **non-zero-sum**. Realists tend to see power as zero-sum; idealists usually portray

Web Link

You can play a zero-sum game and a variety of other political strategy games such as "Free Rider" and "Prisoner's Dilemma" online at **www.egwald.com/operationsresearch/gameintroduction.php.**

it as non-zero-sum, that is, gains do not necessarily come at the expense of others. Without delving too far into this controversy, we can say that the relative nature of power implies that sometimes, especially between antagonists, power approaches zero-sum. When China's Asian rival India tested nuclear weapons in 1998, it decreased China's relative power compared to India and arguably reduced China's influence in the countries to its southwest. More broadly, though, only the most cynical would see power as absolutely zero-sum. As some of the world's less developed countries (LDCs) have moved from the low-income category to lower-middle- or even upper-middle-income status, their economic strength has increased. Yet it would be hard to make the case that this decreased the economic strength of the economically developed countries (EDCs). Indeed, the progress of the LDCs has arguably benefited the EDCs by, for instance, providing new investment opportunities and new markets.

Power as Capacity and Will

Every country's power is determined substantially by its power assets: its military and economic strength, its leadership, the size and talents of its population, and numerous other factors. Together these make up a country's **power capacity**, its potential for exercising international power. By themselves, though, substantial power assets are not enough to create a powerful global presence. They give a country the capacity to exercise power, but to be effective they must be supplemented by a **will to power**. This is a country's willingness to use its capacity, to turn potential power into applied power. Japan offers a current example.

Economically Japan is the world's second most powerful country, with an annual GNP that is second only to that of the United States and larger than that of China, France, and Great Britain combined. Japan's 127 million well-trained people are also a significant asset. With little fanfare, Japan has also amassed a very well-equipped military force supported by an annual military budget of over $41 billion. Yet for all of this, Japan's global influence has been limited by its post–World War II reluctance to assert itself. Symbolically, the Japanese constitution forbids the "use of force as a means of settling international disputes." More importantly, the Japanese have been unwilling to take an assertive stand, much less use their forces, to promote their views.

This attitude has begun to change (Szechenyi, 2006). Polls show a growing sense of national pride in Japan, and recent prime ministers have found it politically wise to annually visit the Yasukuni Shrine, which honors Japan's troops killed in World War II. Japan has also very slowly begun to deploy military units abroad. They now participate in UN peacekeeping missions, and Tokyo deployed 600 noncombatant troops (engineering and medical units) to Iraq in 2003. Additionally, the Japanese navy is readying its first helicopter-carrier ship and intensifying commando training, both moves that will add to the country's ability to project its power further from

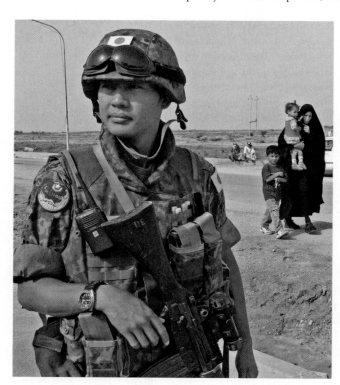

Having the will to use the power you possess is an important power factor. Japan has a strong military force but its people have been unwilling to use it because of their experience in World War II. This reluctance to use force is beginning to change, and Japan has taken a number of tentative steps toward a more assertive foreign policy. It has deployed its troops, including this Japanese soldier in Iraq, to support the U.S.-led mission there.

its shores. This worries some of Japan's neighbors, especially when combined with recent renewed claims by Japan to islands and territorial waters lost to or in dispute with China, Russia, and South Korea since World War II. Yet another sign of growing Japanese assertiveness is the country's campaign for a permanent seat on the UN Security Council. "Japan is changing," the U.S. ambassador there recently commented. "I think Japan has decided, 'We're a great, big country, we're the second-largest economy in the world, and we probably have the second-largest navy in the Pacific. We want a seat on the Security Council. We want a role to play in the international arena.' I think all those changes are at work and will continue." Confirming that impression, Japan's foreign minister told reporters, "There are expectations that Japan play a greater role in dealing with international conflicts. And I believe that Japan must do so."[3] All this portends a Japan that will increasingly convert its power capacity into applied power and play a stronger role.

Objective and Subjective Power

Just as a country's power is influenced by its willingness to use its assets, so too it is influenced by what other countries perceive to be those assets and the intent to use them. **Objective power** consists of assets that you possess and that you are willing to use. As such, objective power is a major factor in determining whose interests prevail, as Iraq found out in 2003 in its war with the U.S.-led coalition forces.

Subjective power is also important. A common assertion is that a country will damage its reputation for strength and tempt future aggression if it does not display unity, abandons a commitment, or backs down in a crisis (Foster, 2006). One aspect of this that has been an issue for the United States in recent decades relates to the belief that, as one French general put it, Americans want "zero-dead wars."[4] The view that American public opinion will not tolerate many U.S. casualties was formed amid the U.S. reluctance to commit ground forces in the aftermath of the frustrating Vietnam War and has been intensified in the mind of some by the U.S. withdrawal in the face of relatively minor casualties in Lebanon (1983) and Somalia (1993), and the U.S. decision to use air power exclusively, but not troops, to defeat Yugoslavia during the Kosovo crisis in 1999 (Koch & Gartner, 2005; Smith, 2005; Vasquez, 2005). Those who doubt American resolve in the face of casualties also point to the reaction to approximately 3,200 U.S. troops that died in the first four years of the Iraq War and occupation. While every death in every war is sad, it is also the case that in the overall history of military actions, U.S. casualties in Iraq have been relatively light. By one measure, far more Americans were killed on a single day at Pearl Harbor (4,498) in 1941 or on D-Day (4,900) in 1944. By another standard, the 3,200 death toll in Iraq pales beside the more than 67,000 Americans who died at the hands of drunk drivers during the same period. Yet this slaughter draws much less attention than does Iraq.

Because it is difficult to measure reputation, judging its impact is challenging. Some scholars conclude that concern over reputation is overdrawn, but that does not negate the case that a country's power is to a degree based on others' perceptions of its current or potential power or its reputation for being willing (or not willing) to use it and that the perception that a country is not currently powerful can tempt another country. It is arguable, for example, that Saddam Hussein's willingness in 1991 and 2003 to risk war with the United States was based in part on his perception that Americans would not tolerate the cost and casualties necessary to invade Iraq and topple him. As Saddam put it prior to the first war, "The nature of American society makes it impossible for the United States to bear tens of

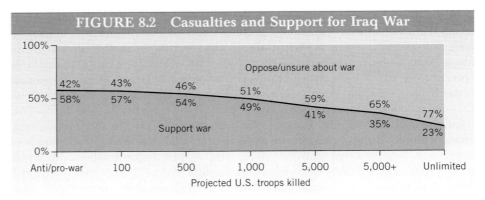

FIGURE 8.2 Casualties and Support for Iraq War

Before the Iraq War began in 2003, one poll asked Americans if they would support a decision by the president to launch a ground attack against Saddam Hussein. Most (58%) said yes; 35% said no, and 7% were unsure. Remember that in 2003, most Americans thought Iraq had weapons of mass destruction and was cooperating with terrorists. The poll then presented war supporters with a range of potential U.S. casualties. As this figure shows, American support for an attack went down as the possible U.S. deaths went up. By 1,000 deaths, support had dropped below 50%. Does this show a prudent public or a weak public unwilling to accept military casualties to achieve U.S. policy goals?

Data source: Los Angeles Times poll, December 2002; data provided by The Roper Center for Public Opinion Research, University of Connecticut.

thousands of casualties."[5] Figure 8.2 examines U.S. support for the 2003 Iraq War in light of projected mounting casualties and asks what you think the data says about Americans.

Situational Power

A country's power varies according to the situation, or context, in which it is being applied. A country's **situational power** is often less than the total inventory of its capabilities. Military power provides a good example. During the last weeks of March and first weeks of April 2003, American and British forces faced those of Iraq in a classic conventional war situation. In that context, the conflict was one-sided with the U.S./U.K. forces quickly destroying and dispersing those of Iraq. During the postwar period, the conflict situation changed when forces opposed to the U.S./U.K. presence in the country began to use guerrilla warfare and terrorist tactics. Soon, more U.S. soldiers had died in the "postwar" period than during the war, and U.S. policy was in considerable disarray even though the American forces in Iraq were as numerous as the ones that had so easily toppled the regime of Saddam Hussein. The difference was that in the very different situation after "victory," a great deal of the U.S. high-tech weapons inventory, its heavy armored vehicles, and its air power were of no use in countering the resistance tactics in Iraq.

SIMULATION
Winning Wars Isn't Simple

Measuring Power

It would be a very good thing if it were possible to measure power precisely. One reason is that countries sometimes wind up in wars because they miscalculate their own power or that of their opponent. To a degree that is what happened to the United States following its invasion of Iraq in 2003. The equation of comparing U.S. military power to Iraqi military power was relatively easy. The United States was immensely more powerful, and that was demonstrated by the ease with which U.S. forces

Most aspects of national power are relevant in only some situations. During the invasion of Iraq in 2003, U.S. tanks helped rout Iraq's poorly equipped military. In the subsequent occupation phase that featured terrorist attacks and guerrilla fighting, often in urban areas filled with noncombatants, this column of U.S. tanks and other weapons systems had very limited relevance to the struggle.

defeated Iraq's armed forces. That was only part of the equation, though, and U.S. leaders miscalculated both the strength of the long-term resistance to U.S. occupation forces and the power of existing U.S. forces in Iraq to deal with those attacks. Unfortunately, power is very difficult to measure, both because of the difficulty in quantifying many of its aspects and because it is highly changeable.

Quantification Difficulties

At a general level, it is possible to measure or at least estimate power. There can be no doubt, for example, that China is more powerful than Mongolia. Beyond such broad judgments, there is no widely accepted formula for measuring power. It is easy enough to measure such tangible factors as per capita GNP or number of soldiers. But it is harder to assign weights to each to establish their relative importance to one another when constructing a power formula. Even harder is measuring and giving relative weights to intangible factors such as the diplomatic skill of a country's leaders or its soft-power ability to lead by example. These difficulties were illustrated by a study that reviewed four attempts by various scholars to devise formulas to measure national power during the cold war (Taber, 1989). The four often came to dramatically different conclusions because of different methods of measuring power. Two studies rated the Soviet Union the most powerful. One each rated the United States and China most powerful. One ranked China only seventh. Brazil ranked number three in one study, and India ranked number four in another study; yet two studies did not place either country in the top ten. The list need not go on to make the point that different formulas for measuring power yielded very different results.

Power Dynamics

Power is also difficult to measure because it is in constant flux. Economies prosper or lag, arms are modernized or become outmoded, resources are discovered or are depleted, and populations rally behind or lose faith in their governments.

Web Link

View an online version of a recent attempt to measure national power at **www.rand.org/publications/MR/MR1110/.**

ANALYZE THE ISSUE
Measuring a Country's Power

No superpower from Rome, through imperial Britain, to the Soviet Union has maintained its status permanently. Each eventually declined and some even vanished, as did the USSR. To take their place, other countries have risen from humble beginnings to the rank of major power, as did the United States. Still others, like China today, may reemerge from a period of eclipse and strive to recapture their lost status (Tammen et al., 2002).

There are numerous reasons why power is so fluid. One theory of system-level analysis is that *power cycles* occur over a period of a few decades, or even as much as a century (Tessman & Chan, 2004). The cycles are demarcated by great-power or "systemic" wars, such as the two world wars, that reflect strains or power shifts within the system and act as political earthquakes, altering the system by destroying the major power status of declining powers and elevating rising powers to pole status. Then the process of power decay and formation begins anew. *Balance-of-power politics* is another system-level cause of change as countries form alliances and take other actions to avoid being dominated.

From a state-level-of-analysis perspective, several factors account for the rise or fall of a country's power. One involves the *sources of power.* The advent of nuclear weapons some 60 years ago instantly elevated the status of countries that possess them. *Internal conditions* also affect an actor's power. The Soviet Union collapsed in part because it no longer commanded the loyalty of most of its citizens. Most Americans are patriotic, but the country cannot remain a superpower if its people are unwilling to bear the cost of being a leader in the international system. That does not mean the United States should lead, only that it cannot remain dominant unless it accepts the burdens, as well as the benefits of leadership.

SIMULATION
Creating Your Own
International Power Index

THE FOUNDATION OF NATIONAL POWER

Although it is common to think of national power in terms of military might and wealth, those elements of power rest substantially on a more basic foundation. The elements of that foundation include national geography, the quality of the population, the quality of the government, and the country's technological infrastructure. In the following sections, we will analyze these basic elements. The first element focuses on the core of the national state. That core can be roughly divided into three parts: national geography, people, and government.

National Geography

Shakespeare's King Henry VI proclaimed:

> Let us be backed with God and with the seas
> Which He hath given for fence impregnable, . . .
> In them and in ourselves our safety lies.

Whether or not God has ever aided England, King Henry's soliloquy reminds us that the English Channel has helped save Great Britain from Napoleon, Hitler, and every other threat from Europe for nine centuries. Geography counts.

Location can be an advantage or a disadvantage. Spain was able to avoid involvement in either world war partly because of its relative isolation from the rest of Europe. Poland, sandwiched between Germany and Russia, and Korea, stuck between China and Japan, each has a distinctly unfortunate location. The Israelis would almost certainly be better off if their promised land were somewhere—almost anywhere—else.

And the Kuwaitis probably would not mind moving either, provided they could take their oil fields with them. Location also impacts relative power. The weight of China's army as a power factor is different in Beijing's relations with the United States and Russia because Russia and China share a border, while the vast Pacific Ocean separates China and the United States.

Topography—a country's mountains, rivers, and plains—is also important. The Alps form a barrier that has helped protect Switzerland from its larger European neighbors and spared the Swiss the ravages of both world wars. Throughout history, Afghanistan's rugged mountains have bedeviled invaders, including since 2001 U.S. and other NATO troops trying to eliminate al Qaeda and Taliban forces. Topography can also work against a country. For example, the southern and eastern two-thirds of Iraq is a broad plain that provided a relatively easy invasion avenue for the mechanized U.S. and British forces in 2003. The Tigris and Euphrates river systems and the associated swampy areas provided some topographical defenses, but too few to make a difference.

Size is an important geographic factor. Bigger is often better. The immense expanse of Russia, for example, has repeatedly saved it from conquest. Although sometimes overwhelmed at first, the Russian armies have been able to retreat into the interior and buy time in exchange for geography while regrouping. By contrast, Israel's small size gives it no room to retreat.

Climate can also play a power role. The tropical climate of Vietnam, with its monsoon rains and its dense vegetation, made it difficult for the Americans to use much of their superior weaponry. At the other extreme, the bone-chilling Russian winter has allied itself with Russia's geographic size to form a formidable defensive force that decimated Napoleon's soldiers in the winter of 1812–1813 and the German army during World War II. In fact the Russian winter has proved so formidable that Czar Nicholas I commented, "Russia has two generals we can trust, General January and General February."

People

A second element of the national core is a country's human characteristics. Tangible demographic subcategories include number of people, age distribution, and such quantitative factors as health and education. There are also intangible population factors such as morale.

Population

As is true for geographic size, the size of a country's population can be a positive or a negative factor. Because a large population supplies military personnel and industrial workers, sheer numbers of people are a positive power factor. It is unlikely, for instance, that Tonga (pop. 115,000) will ever achieve great-power status. A large population may be disadvantageous, however, if it is not in balance with resources. India, with 1.1 billion people, has the world's second-largest population, yet because of the country's poverty ($720 per capita GNP), it must spend much of its energy and resources merely feeding its people.

Age Distribution

It is an advantage for a country to have a large percentage of its population in the economically productive years (15–64 by international reporting standards). Some countries with booming populations have a heavy percentage of children who must be supported. In other countries with limited life expectancy, many people die before they complete their productive years. Finally, some countries are "aging," with a geriatric population segment that consumes more resources than it produces (Longman, 2004).

Did You Know That:

Mexico's President Porfirio Díaz (1886–1911) once lamented, "Poor Mexico, so far from God, so close to the United States."

Web Link

You can find the current and projected age distribution (population pyramid) of countries and territories around the world on the U.S. Census Bureau Web site at **www.census.gov/ipc/www/idbpyr.html.**

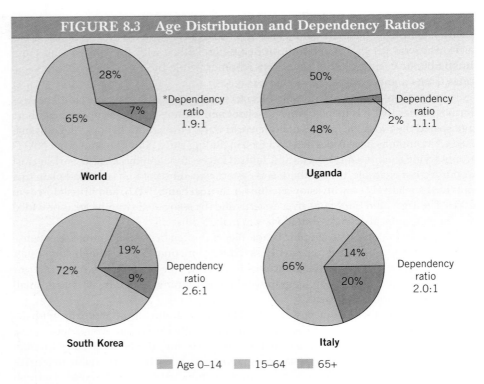

FIGURE 8.3   Age Distribution and Dependency Ratios

Most less developed countries (LDCs), like Uganda, are disadvantaged because their population has a high percentage of children. These children consume resources for their education and general care that they will only begin to "repay" the system in terms of productivity and taxes when they become adults. A high percentage of senior citizens, as in Italy, is also economically suboptimal. South Korea has good age distribution with 72% in the "working years."

*Dependency ratio is a World Bank calculation of the ratio of the working-age population (ages 15–64) to the dependent population (age 14 and younger plus age 65 and older). Generally, the higher the ratio, the more economically advantaged a country is.

Data source: CIA online.

MAP
Employment by
Economic Activity

Worldwide, 28% of Earth's population was less than 15 years old in 2006; 7% was 65 or over; 65% was in the working-age years (15–64). Figure 8.3 shows the age distributions of several countries, which you should compare. The figure also shows the dependency ratio of young and old people combined compared to the working-age population. Many analysts would contend that South Korea is relatively advantaged by its large working-age population, while Uganda, with numerous children, and Italy, with a high percentage of senior citizens, are relatively disadvantaged.

Whereas growing populations and high ratios of children were once the main population worries, there is now growing concern in some places about low birthrates, zero or even a negative population growth, and **demographic graying**, that is, a growing proportion of the population is of retirement age. A negative aspect is that a relatively large retirement-age population slows down per capita GDP growth because of a relative scarcity of workers. A growing geriatric population also challenges a country's ability to pay the cost of providing pensions and other services to retired citizens. Demographic graying is already pronounced in the economically developed countries and is projected to increase. By 2050, for instance, 33% of Japan's population and 30% of Europe's will be age 65 and older. The U.S. age distribution is still relatively

DEBATE THE POLICY SCRIPT

Is Immigration a Solution to Demographic Graying?

Japan and Europe are facing a problem that could undermine their economic vitality and international power. They are graying demographically, with a growing percentage of their populations aged 65 or older. Increased longevity is one cause. Life expectancy in the EDCs is now 78 years, up 9% since 1975. Decreased fertility rates (the average number of children a woman will have) are the second cause of graying. In Western Europe and Japan, the rate is now 1.4, far below the replacement rate (about 2.1) needed to keep the population from declining and to produce younger adults to offset the older adults reaching retirement age.

A graying population is a double-barreled problem. One threat is that with relatively fewer children being born, the supply of future adults is waning. A relatively smaller workforce will cause labor shortages, a dropoff in consumer spending, and other problems that will harm economic growth. The second threat is that governments will struggle to pay for retirement, health care, and other programs that support senior citizens.

The United States is graying also, but less markedly than most EDCs. Whereas 30% of the population in Europe will be 65 or older in 2050, only 21% of Americans will be 65+ by mid-century. Immigration is the most important reason for the relative U.S. advantage. U.S. immigration has risen substantially and now averages about 1 million immigrants a year. The share of the U.S. population that is foreign-born grew from 6% in 1980 to 11% in 2000. Europe once provided most immigrants. Now most come from Latin America and Asia.

Immigrants help keep the percentage of the U.S. working-age population higher than in most other EDCs. Currently, 59% of all foreign-born Americans are between ages 25 and 54, whereas only 42% of native-born Americans are in that age group. Immigrants are also the reason that the U.S. fertility rate (2.1) is actually up since 1980 (1.8). Whites (2.0) and African Americans (2.1) are at about the replacement rate, but Asian Americans (2.3) and Hispanics (2.9) are above it. Thus it is these groups that are disproportionately producing the children of today and the adult workers of tomorrow.

Another thing many EDCs share is a heated debate about immigration policy. A 2005 survey of Americans found that 41% agreed with the statement, "Immigration adds to our character and strengthens the United States because it brings diversity, new workers, and new creative talent to this country." But 48% differed, saying, "Immigration detracts from our character and weakens the United States because it puts too many burdens on government services, causes language barriers, and creates housing problems." Another 10% said "both" or "it depends," and 1% were unsure.[1] Reflecting this division, another poll found that 33% of its respondents wanted to keep immigration at its current level, 14% wanted to increase it, 49% wanted to decrease it, and 4% were unsure.[2]

What Do You Think?

Should immigration continue at its current level, be increased, or be cut? If you favor an increase or decrease, by how much?

---

good: 0–14 (20%), 15–64 (67%), and 65+ (13%). But Americans are also graying, and the retirement-age population is projected to rise to 21% in 2050.

So far, demographic graying is mostly confined to the EDCs, but it is beginning to also affect LDCs, especially China. Its one-child-per-couple policy instituted to restrain population growth coupled with increasing longevity means that senior citizens will rapidly increase as a share of China's population from 8% now to 25% by 2050. Graying will steadily increase the daunting costs of providing health care, housing, and other social services for the elderly. Furthermore, as global aging progresses, a smaller percentage of the population will be between 15 and 64 "doing the work, paying the taxes, saving for the future, and raising the next generation" (Peterson, 2001:3). How to address this problem is a major policy challenge for the United States and other EDCs, and one possible solution is presented for your consideration in the decision box, "Is Immigration a Solution to Demographic Graying?"

Education

An educated population is important to national power. *Quantity of education* is one factor, and it is a source of weakness for the LDCs, especially the poorest ones. Although education has improved substantially in low-income countries over the last 15 years or so, with the primary school completion rate up +9%, it is still only

JOIN THE DEBATE
The Foreign Student Program in the United States: Does It Serve U.S. National Interests?

FIGURE 8.4 Comparative Educational Achievement

Country	Achievement level
Japan	629
South Korea	624
Finland	620
Australia	589
Average	500
United States	496
Poland	432
Portugal	383
Greece	382
Mexico	283

National power rests in part on a well-educated populace. For Americans, this is something of a concern. The data in this figure is drawn from the overall scores amassed by 15-year-old students in 26 mostly developed countries for skills in reading, mathematics, and science. The results here are for the four countries with the highest and lowest scores, the United States, and the average of the 26 countries. As evident, American students finished below average, well below the leading countries, and not that far ahead of some relatively poor countries, such as Poland.

Note: The actual scores were reduced by 1000 to better highlight comparative data. That is, for example, the score for Japan was actually 1629.
Data source: Organization for Economic Development and Cooperation, *Education at a Glance*, 2005.

75%. In the United States it is 93%. Beyond primary school, the data become progressively worse. Less than half of children in low-income countries go to high school, and only about 9% get any post-secondary technical or college education and can serve as the nucleus of the educated workforce a modern economy needs. Moreover, in a circular problem, the lack of opportunity in many of the poorest LDCs creates a "brain drain," as its professionals emigrate to seek a better life.

Quality of education is also important. For example, 84% of Americans over age 24 have graduated high school, 27% have a college degree. Furthermore, the country spends a greater percentage of its wealth on education than all but a handful of countries. Yet there is evidence that the U.S. educational system is not adequately preparing students to meet the requirements of the modern world. It may be that the basic 3 Rs—reading, 'riting, and 'rithmetic—that once served to train a workforce will no longer suffice in the 21st century. Instead, the requirements will be more like the 3 Cs—computers, calculus, and communications. Another problem may be that American students during their four years of high school spend an average of only about half as much time on core subjects as do students in Japan, France, and Germany. An additional difficulty may be discipline in American schools. Students in the United States, for instance, are six times more likely to encounter discipline problems in the classroom than Japanese students.[6] Whatever the cause, a recent study in 26 mostly developed countries measuring the mathematic, scientific, and reading skills of 15-year-olds showed that American students finished 14th overall and below average in each of the three areas of study. Figure 8.4 depicts some of the results.

Yet another way to break down general educational statistics is to see how well a country trains various segments of its population. Most countries limit their power potential by underutilizing major elements of their population. For example, sexism limits the possible contribution of women in virtually all countries. In Bangladesh, for instance, a male teenager is almost twice as likely as a female teenager to be enrolled in secondary school. Racial, ethnic, and other bases of discrimination add to this failure to maximize a population's potential. The fact that among adults over age 24 in the United States just 18% of African Americans and 13% of Latinos, compared to 30% of whites, have completed college means that the potential of a significant number of these disadvantaged people has been lost to the country.

Health

Poor health can also sap a country's power. Providing an example, Russia is experiencing a health crisis among its men due to widespread alcoholism and smoking. Drug addiction is also on the rise. Two-thirds of all adult Russian males smoke (2.5 times the U.S. rate), and the lung cancer death rate is twice that of the United States. To make

Web Link

Health-related data for countries can be found on the World Health Organization Web site at **www.who.int/countries/en/.**

matters worse, about 60% of all Russian men are alcohol abusers, with the average Russian male drinking a quart of vodka every two days, supplemented by other alcohol. "Sobriety is no longer the moral norm in Russia," says one health official there.[7]

The effect is lethal. Longevity for Russian males has declined to less than 59 years (compared to 73 years for Russian women). Widespread bootlegging adds to the problem, with 17,000 Russians dying in 2006 from unsafe homemade vodka and other spirits. Alcoholism threatens Russia's national strength in several ways. If current trends continue, the country's population could drop by a third in the next two decades. There are also immense economic consequences, including lost productivity and the costs of providing medical treatment and supporting abandoned families. Another issue relates to Russia's military strength. Officers complain that most potential military recruits are so wasted from alcohol and drugs that they cannot withstand basic training. Overall, the internal health crisis has replaced any possible external enemy as "the clearest possible threat to national security," according to one Russian study.[8]

Attitudes

The beliefs and orientations of a country's population on a number of dimensions affect national power. For example, countries such as the United States, China, and Japan whose people have a reasonably unified national identity are in a stronger position than are countries with deep ethnonational divisions, as chapter 4 details. Similarly, countries in which morale is low because of economic or other difficulties are disadvantaged. Low national morale can lead to civil unrest and even topple governments. The end of the USSR in 1991 provides an example of the impact of both ethnonational divi-

Russia's power is being undermined by epidemic alcoholism, especially among its men. The health crisis in Russia is presented with irony in this image of an inebriated Russian holding himself upright only by grasping the statue of a drunken man in the city of Krasnoyarsk.

sion and low morale. As the country's economic system went from bad to worse, the populace was increasingly disheartened. By 1990, 90% believed that the country's economic situation was dire, and 57% had no confidence in the future. This profound pessimism led to an almost total collapse of support for the government of Soviet President Mikhail Gorbachev and, indeed, the country's political system. Accelerating Soviet difficulties, the ethnonational identities of Ukrainians, Kazaks, Latvians, and the other nationalities reasserted themselves. Soon the Soviet Union imploded amid a vacuum of public support.

Government

A third power element associated with the national core is the quality of the government. *Administrative effectiveness* is one aspect. It involves whether a state has a well-organized and effective administrative structure to utilize its power potential fully.

Did You Know That:

Vodka has long undermined Russia's power. In 1373 the Russians lost a battle to the Tartars reportedly because the czar's forces were too inebriated to fight. The defeated Russians were thrown into a nearby river, which was then dubbed the Reka Pianaya, the Drunk River.

For example, U.S. power has been undoubtedly undermined by problems in the country's intelligence agencies. Intelligence failures led, among other things, to the expenditure of vast amounts of U.S. power in a war with and occupation of Iraq, launched primarily to destroy weapons of mass destruction that in fact did not exist. Reflecting that, a presidential commission bemoaned what it called "one of the most . . . damaging intelligence failures in recent American history." As for the cause of the catastrophe, the commission concluded:

> This failure was in large part the result of analytical shortcomings; intelligence analysts were too wedded to their assumptions about Saddam's intentions. But it was also a failure on the part of [the intelligence agencies]. . . . [They] collected precious little intelligence for the analysts to analyze, and much of what they did collect was either worthless or misleading.[9]

Leadership ability is a second aspect of government that adds or detracts from a country's power. As chapter 3 indicates, leadership is a mix of administrative, political, and public relations skills. Like other intangible power assets, **leadership capabilities** are hard to measure, yet they clearly make a difference. Table 3.1, p. 84, provides an estimate of the foreign policy leadership of recent U.S. presidents.

National Infrastructure

National power also rests on a country's infrastructure, which might be roughly equated with the skeleton of a human body or to a building's foundation and its framing or girders. To examine the infrastructure of the state as an element of national power, the following sections will discuss technological sophistication, transportation systems, and information and communications capabilities. Each of these factors is related to a country's power capacity.

Overall technological availability and sophistication is at the heart of this element of power. Think about how monumentally wrong Charles H. Duell, commissioner of the U.S. Office of Patents, was when he declared in 1899, "Everything that can be invented has been invented." To the contrary, most of the technology that undergirds a great deal of contemporary national power has been invented since Duell's short-sighted assessment. Air conditioning modifies the impact of weather, computers revolutionize business and education, robotics speed industry, synthetic fertilizers expand agriculture, new drilling techniques allow for undersea oil exploration, microwaves speed information, and lasers bring the military to the edge of the Star Wars era. Thus, technology is an overarching factor and will be discussed as part of the tangible elements of power.

One source of U.S. strength is the considerable money that its government, corporations, and universities spend on research and development (R&D). Indeed, investment in basic research is an essential element in "the scientific balance of power."[10] During 2005 the United States was the global leader, spending $285 billion, far ahead of the three next largest spenders on R&D: Japan ($114 billion), China ($85 billion), and Germany ($57 billion). Another good measure of technological sophistication and capability is computing capacity. Needless to say, business, education, science, and other key elements of national power depend on computers, and, as Figure 8.5 shows, there is a vast disparity in national capabilities.

Transportation systems are a second and more specific part of the national infrastructure. The ability to move people, raw materials, finished products, and sometimes the military throughout its territory is another part of a country's power equation and is heavily dependent on technology. For example, one of the major hurdles that Russia must overcome to invigorate its economy is its relatively limited and decrepit

FIGURE 8.5 Computing Capacity

Computers per 1,000 people

749 | 587 | 561 | 132 | 130 | 108 | 105 | 41 | 7

U.S. Japan Germany Russia **World** Mexico Brazil China Nigeria

Computer capacity is an indication of the strength of a country's technological infrastructure. As evident here, there is a huge gap, called the "global digital divide," among countries in computing power.

Data source: World Bank online.

transportation systems. As one standard, for every 1,000 square miles of its land territory, the United States has 14 times as many miles of paved roads and four times as many miles of railroad track than does Russia. Inadequate transportation systems are also a problem for LDCs.

Information and communications systems are yet another part of the national technological infrastructure, and capabilities in these areas are becoming increasingly important to national power. Satellites and computers have accelerated the revolution begun with radio and television. Photocopying machines, then fax machines, and now the Internet have dramatically changed communications. Enhanced communications technology increases the ability of a society to communicate within itself and remain cohesive. It also increases efficiency and effectiveness in industry, finance, and the military. Here again, the gaps among countries are wide. For example, U.S. annual per capita expenditures on information and communications ($3,595) are more than 54 times that of China ($66). On a per capita basis, there are 2.3 times more cell phone subscribers and 8.6 times more people with access to the Internet in the United States than in China.

MILITARY POWER

For good or ill, military power is an asset that sometimes determines whether a country will prevail or not in its pursuit of its foreign policy goals. Therefore, it is appropriate to consider the nature of military power that provides the sword for policy makers to wield.

Measuring Military Power

Some aspects of military power, such as numbers of weapons and troops, are easy to count. Other factors, including training, equipment quality, and military morale, are much harder to quantify. A third set of factors, such as military and civilian leadership, are almost impossible to measure precisely.

FIGURE 8.6 U.S. and China's Military Spending

Unadjusted   Adjusted for purchasing power parity

Measuring defense spending by amount is tricky. The left pie chart shows that in unadjusted spending, the United States annually spends over 12 times as much on its military than does China. When spending is adjusted for the relative cost of living in the two countries (purchasing power parity: PPP), however, the spending gap shrinks from about 12:1 to about 3:1. Neither measure is satisfactory by itself. For instance, using PPP helps adjust for the relative cost of pay and other personnel costs. But PPP is less relevant for fuel costs, since both U.S. and Chinese forces depend in part on imported petroleum, which costs both countries the same.

Note: Chinese military spending official reports are understated. The figures here are the author's estimates based on the sources listed below.
Data sources: CIA, SIPRI, and the ISSI, all online.

Military Spending

Defense spending is one of the largest categories in most countries' budgets, and there can be little doubt that the level of spending has some impact on military capabilities. U.S. expenditures ($498 billion in 2006) far exceed those of any other country, and there are relatively few scenarios in which the armed forces of any other country could defeat U.S. forces in a conventional war.

Yet none of the ways defense spending is commonly reported is wholly satisfactory. *Amount*, either total spending or on a per capita basis, can be misleading because of what the money can buy in different countries. An entry-level American soldier's monthly base pay is $1,300 a month; a similar Chinese soldier makes $40. Figure 8.6 compares the military spending of China and the United States in unadjusted currencies and in terms of the purchasing power parity (PPP), an adjustment for the different cost of living in the two countries. *Economic burden*—defense spending as a percentage of a country's GNP—can also be deceptive. Israel spends about 9% of its GNP on defense, much higher than the world average of 2.5%, but Israel's expenditures must also be analyzed in terms of the monumental threats it faces.

Weapons

Comparison of two countries' or alliances' military might are often focused on number of weapons. Quantity is certainly an important consideration. Knowing that the United States had 16,000 tanks and Iraq had 1,900 tanks prior to their war in 2003 is one indication of the relative power of the two countries' armored forces. Had the potential combatants been the United States and Russia or China, Moscow's 21,000 tanks or Beijing's 11,000 tanks would have made for a much different military situation.

Numbers are only part of the military weapons equation, however, with quality at least equally important. Even if the U.S. and Iraqi tank forces had had equal numbers,

SIMULATION
What Would You Spend
for Security?

Web Link

The Federation of American Scientists maintains an excellent site with details about American military weaponry at **www.fas.org/man/index.html.** Other countries' systems can be explored by keying "rest of world" in the Search function.

Iraq's aging Soviet-export tanks would have been no match for U.S. main battle tanks, which are capable of maneuvering at nearly highway speeds, using thermal sights and computerized targeting, firing shells coated with depleted uranium that can destroy almost any armored opponent, and clad in depleted uranium armor capable of repelling the shells fired by Iraqi tanks.

For all the advantages of sophisticated weapons, there are drawbacks. An F-22, one of the newest U.S. fighters, is a technological marvel that can defeat any other fighter. Each costs $150 million, though, compared to a less excellent, but still good Russian-built SU-30 fighter, which is available for export at $37 million each. Second, high-tech weapons are often also more difficult to operate and repair. Third, the effectiveness of military hardware is very situational. Therefore, a country's military systems need to be appropriate to the challenges they will face. American tanks were very effective during the short conventional warfare phase of the Iraq war; U.S. tanks were only marginally relevant to fighting the insurgency that followed.

Personnel

As with weapons, a number of quantitative and qualitative factors determine the capabilities of a country's military personnel. *Number of troops,* both total and compared to an opponent, is one factor. Generally, size matters. For example, China (2.3 million troops), India (1.7 million), the United States (1.5 million) and Russia (1.0 million) all have enough troops to play a major regional and even global role. By contrast, Belize, with about 1,000 troops, has very little military muscle to use as a diplomatic asset. Like spending, though, sheer numbers of troops must be measured against the scope of their deployments and reasonable estimates of their potential use. For example, the large U.S. force becomes less dominant when its global commitments are considered. Indeed, U.S. forces have been stretched thin by their deployment in Iraq, requiring an extensive, long-term call-up of reserve units.

Recruit quality is a second factor impacting personnel. To build a good military, a country must be able to recruit intelligent, healthy, reliable enlisted troops and officers. Standards for U.S. recruits have traditionally been high, but the strain of the Iraq War created some cause for concern. The U.S. Army has experienced problems in recruiting enough soldiers, falling 17% below the target of 80,000 recruits in 2005. To a degree shortfalls have been overcome by lowering the educational and moral standards for recruits. Between 2003 and 2006, for example, the number of waivers given for a criminal background jumped 65%, and reached 11% of all Army recruits in 2006.

Training is a third personnel factor. Good training significantly improves the quality of a country's military force. This is especially true given the complicated nature of many of today's high-tech weapons. For instance, considerable flight time is critical for fighter pilots because of the complex weapons systems they use. Yet providing practice is costly, and significant differences in training exist. The countries of the North Atlantic Treaty Organization (NATO) generally meet the alliance's standard of providing fighter pilots with 180 to 200 hours of inflight training annually. Because of Russia's struggling economy, its pilots reportedly receive only about 20 hours a year in the air to hone their skills.

Morale is a fourth variable in measuring military personnel. Russian soldiers fought with amazing valor amid horrific conditions during World War II. Yet in more recent times, the morale of Russia's soldiers has been sapped by poor pay, housing, equipment, and training and by the widespread image of corruption and incompetence among officers (Hespring, 2006). In the aftermath of the collapse of Iraq's army in 2003, some Russian military experts were worried that a similar fate might await Russia's army in a war. "Go on the street and ask who is ready to defend the motherland, and you will

MAP
Size of Armed Forces

Did You Know That:

The world's smallest army is the Vatican's 110-man Swiss Guard. The original force was formed from Swiss mercenaries who had defended Pope Clement VII during the sacking of Rome in 1527 by, oddly, Charles V, the Holy Roman Emperor.

immediately see unpleasant parallels," fretted one Russian military expert. "The outcome of a war depends on the army's morale."[11]

Leadership is a fifth personnel variable. U.S. and British forces would have surely defeated the Iraqi military in 2003, but Saddam Hussein's practice of placing those most loyal to him, rather than the best officers, in command of his country's armed forces accelerated the rapid collapse of Iraq's army. Saddam did this, according to one Iraqi colonel, because "he was afraid the regular army might rise up against him." However, when war came, another Iraqi officer explained, the result was, "there was no coordination between [the generals]—they hate[d] each other."[12]

Military Power: Debating How Much

Given the importance of military power as an instrument of foreign policy, a common assumption is that more is better. This is not necessarily so because there are dangers associated with overemphasizing military power. These perils include insecurity, temptation, and expense.

Military power creates insecurity. One result of amassing power is the "spiral of insecurity." Efforts by one country to increase its power to achieve security are frequently perceived by other states as a threat. They then seek to balance power, which the first country sees as threatening, causing it to acquire even more power, and so on ad infinitum, in an escalating spiral. As chapter 11's discussion of disarmament details, arms races are not automatic. Still, the interaction of one country's power and other countries' insecurity is an important factor in world politics.

Military power creates temptation. A second peril of amassing excess military power is the temptation to use it in a situation that is peripheral to the national interest (Fordham, 2004). The United States went to war in Vietnam despite the fact that President Lyndon Johnson derided it as a "raggedy-ass fourth-rate country." One reason Americans intervened in Vietnam was because of a so-called arrogance of power. Had U.S. military power been more modest, the United States might have emphasized diplomacy or maybe even acquiesced to the reunification of North and South Vietnam. One can never be sure, but it is certain that it is hard to shoot someone if you do not own a gun.

This drawing of Uncle Sam reaching beyond his grasp illustrates the view that U.S. power is declining because of "imperial overstretch," whereby a country spends so much on military power that it neglects other important aspects of power such as education, health, and renewing its infrastructure.

Military power is expensive. A third problem with amassing military power is that it is very expensive. In addition to short-term budget pressure, there is a longer-range concern related to high military spending. Some analysts argue that it saps national economic strength. One scholar who studied the decline of great powers between 1500 and the 1980s formulated an **imperial overstretch thesis** to explain their degeneration (Kennedy, 1988). He argued the former superpowers spent so much on military power that, ironically, they weakened their strength by siphoning off resources that should have been devoted to maintaining and improving the country's infrastructure. Kennedy's study did not include the Soviet Union, but it is arguable that the collapse of the USSR followed the pattern of overspending on the military while starving the country's economic core. Declinists warn that the United States is similarly guilty of imperial overstretch and could go the way of other great powers that rose, dominated, then declined. "America is marching in the well-trod footsteps of virtually all of the imperial powers of the modern age," one such analyst writes (Snyder, 2002:2).

The imperial overstretch thesis has many critics (Levey & Brown, 2005). Some argue that far more danger is posed by a "lax Americana" than by any effort to create a "pax Americana." The reasoning, as detailed in chapter 3, is that a U.S. failure to exercise leadership as the hegemon puts the international system in danger of falling into disorder.[13] Similarly, critics of the declinist thesis warn that cuts in U.S. defense

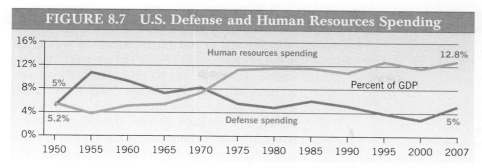

FIGURE 8.7 U.S. Defense and Human Resources Spending

Some argue that U.S. defense spending is too high and saps the national economy by diverting funds that could be better spent to strengthen the national infrastructure. Those who dispute this point out that defense spending has generally declined as a share of the U.S. GDP since the early cold war years, and that despite the upturn under President Bush in recent years, it was at the same level in 2007 as in 1950. These analysts contend that the real problem with the U.S. budget is increased outlays on human resources, such as health and income security, which grew from 5.2% of the GDP in 1950 to 12.8% in 2007.

Notes: Human resource spending includes education, health, Medicare, income security, Social Security, and veterans' benefits. In 2007, education and veterans' benefits combined were less than 1% of human resource spending. The author added 0.08% of GDP to defense spending for 2007 to reflect the Bush administration's supplemental budget requests for Iraq and Afghanistan not included in the regular budget.

Data sources: U.S. Budget, FY2008 and author's calculations.

spending are shortsighted. One study that reviewed the sharp cuts in U.S. military spending at various points since World War II concluded, "In each case the savings proved only temporary, as declining defense budgets eroded military readiness and necessitated a rush to rearm in the face of new dangers abroad" (Thies, 1998:176).

Finally, those who disagree with the declinists point out that U.S. defense spending measured in terms of U.S. wealth is not at a dangerous level and in fact has declined during the decades the United States has been a superpower. Indeed, some advance a **social overstretch thesis**, arguing that it is out of control social spending, not military spending, that saps national economies. According to one such view, "Whether in the form of bread and circuses in the ancient world or medical care for the lower classes and social security for the aged in the modern world," it is social welfare spending that has undermined national economies (Gilpin, 1981:164). Figure 8.7 compares U.S. defense and social welfare spending.

ECONOMIC POWER

Countries not only adopt foreign policies to increase their economic strength, they also use their economic power to pursue a wide range of both economic and noneconomic foreign policy goals. The determinants of national power include financial position, natural resources, industrial output, and agricultural output.

Financial Position

The center of any country's economic power is its basic financial position. Numerous factors make up a country's financial position, and we can analyze these and how they add or detract from economic power by examining the United States.

FIGURE 8.8 U.S. Foreign Debt

Percentage of federal public debt held by foreigners

To finance its budget deficits, the U.S. government borrows money, partly by selling bonds. The debt owed to those holding U.S. bonds grew from $261 billion in 1965 to $4.8 trillion in 2006. Increasingly, as this figure shows, that debt is held abroad, creating vulnerabilities for the U.S. economy. One is that the U.S. government paid $83 billion in interest to its foreign debt holders in 2006.

Data source: U.S. Federal Budget, FY2007.

Overall size of the economy is one factor, and bigger is better. At almost $13 trillion, the U.S. GNP is immense: the world's largest, twice the size of the next largest country (Japan), and equal to 29% of the world's combined GDP. *Per capita size of the economy* is also important. China has the world's fourth largest GNP overall but ranks 110th among countries on a per capita GNP basis. *Exports of goods and services,* which bring in earnings, also contribute to financial strength. Here again the U.S. position is good, with its over $1.2 trillion in annual exports slightly more than the next largest country (Germany) and equal to almost 11% of all exports. *International investments,* which also bring in revenue, are a third positive area, with Americans having more than $10 trillion in foreign investments, far more than any other country.

Yet despite its size, the U.S. economy, like the biblical Goliath, has worrisome vulnerabilities. Most of the U.S. weaknesses are associated with lack of financial discipline. *Budget deficits* are one weakness. The U.S. government had a budget deficit for 50 of the 58 years during the period FY1950–FY2008. One result of chronic deficit spending is that the U.S. government has had to increasingly borrow money from foreigners to finance the debt, as Figure 8.8 shows. This leaves the country vulnerable to external financial pressure. *Net trade* is a second weakness and indication of lack of financial discipline. Americans import far more than they export, and have rung up a **net trade** (exports minus imports) deficit during all but two years since 1971. The $764 billion trade deficit for 2006 was the largest ever, and far bigger than any other country's. Balance of payments is a third U.S. problem area. The enormous net trade deficit and other flows of money out of the country have made for a huge U.S. deficit in its **balance of payments for current accounts**, a measure that represents the entire flow of money into and out of a country's economy except funds for investments. Since its last surplus in 1989, the United States has amassed ever-larger balance-of-payments deficits, both in dollars and as a percentage of the country's GNP. The $791 billion deficit in 2005 equaled a very worrisome 5.7% of the U.S. GNP. Thus far, the immense U.S. economy has been able to absorb these negative trends in U.S. budget, trade, and balance-of-payments deficits, but even the financially mightiest of countries must eventually balance its accounts or face severe financial problems.

Web Link

An excellent source for details of the current U.S. balance of payments and other data on the U.S. position in the international economy is the Web site of the U.S. Bureau of Economic Analysis at **www.bea.gov/**.

Natural Resources

The possession, or lack, of energy, mineral, and other natural resources has become an increasingly important power factor as industrialization and technology have advanced. Natural resources affect power in three related ways: (1) The greater a country's self-sufficiency in vital natural resources, the greater its power. (2) Conversely, the greater a country's dependency on foreign sources for vital natural resources, the less its power. (3) The greater a country's surplus (over domestic use) of vital resources needed by other countries, the greater its power.

The key here is not just how much of a given resource a country has and how much it extracts for use each year; it is production compared to consumption. Oil is the most obvious example, and is illustrated in Figure 8.9. For countries with large reserves,

Did You Know That:

Americans, who make up about 5% of the world population, consume about 25% of its petroleum.

FIGURE 8.9   Petroleum Resources and Use

Share of world petroleum
- Reserves
- Production
- Consumption

Saudi Arabia — 22.0%, 13.5%, 2.3%
Iran — 11.5%, 5.1%, 2.0%
Russia — 6.2%, 12.1%, 3.4%
China — 1.3%, 4.6%, 8.5%
United States — 2.4%, 8.0%, 24.6%
European Union — 1.5%, 6.2%, 19.1%
Japan — 0%, 0%, 6.4%

Every country's power is affected by how much of various economically vital natural resources it has (reserves), how much of each it produces, and how much of each it consumes. Oil is a vital resource, and of the countries here, Saudi Arabia, Iran, and Russia are in relatively powerful positions because each has large reserves and uses much less than it produces. China, the United States, the European Union, and Japan are relatively vulnerable because each has small or no reserves of oil and consumes far more than it produces.

Note: Data on reserves does not include deposits in tar sands and oil shale.
Data sources: BP, *Statistical Review of World Energy 2006*, online, and author's calculations for the EU.

high production, and low consumption, the so-called black gold has been a major source of revenue. For example, Saudi Arabia's oil exports totaled about $206 billion during 2006. Oil has also increased the global political power and significance of Saudi Arabia and other such oil-surplus countries. By contrast, the United States has only limited reserves and despite pumping them at a high rate still uses far more petroleum than it produces. The resulting need for vast quantities of imported petroleum makes the country vulnerable to disruptions in the flow of oil that it needs to maintain prosperity and fuel its military. Second, when international instability or other factors drive up energy prices, as has happened in recent years, the cost to Americans increases, the economy can lag, and the trade deficit goes up. During 2006 alone, the United States imported about $325 billion in oil, an amount roughly half that year's trade deficit.

Industrial Output

Even if a country is bountifully supplied with natural resources, its power is limited unless it can convert those assets into industrial goods. On a global basis, industrial production is highly concentrated. For instance, just five countries (China, Japan, Russia, the United States, and South Korea) produce a majority of the world's steel. Vehicle production is another indication of industrial concentration, as indicated in Figure 8.10. It shows that in 2004 the three biggest vehicle manufacturers (Germany, Japan, and the United States) made 44% of the global total.

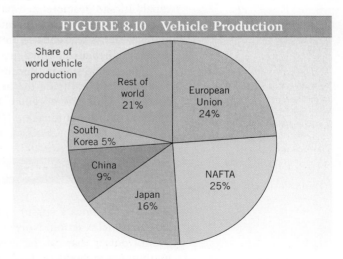

FIGURE 8.10   Vehicle Production

Share of world vehicle production

- European Union 24%
- NAFTA 25%
- Japan 16%
- China 9%
- South Korea 5%
- Rest of world 21%

Global industry is highly concentrated. The countries of the North American Free Trade Association (NAFTA: Canada, Mexico, and the United States) and the European Union each produce about a fourth of the world's cars, trucks, and buses each year, and along with Japan, China, and South Korea make four out of every five vehicles. The United States (18%) is the largest producer in NAFTA; Germany (9%) is the largest in the EU. About 66.5 million vehicles were produced in 2006.

Data source: International Organization of Motor Vehicle Manufacturers.

Those 3 plus the other 7 countries that make up the top 10 vehicle producers accounted for 78% of world production. About 85% of the world's countries (including all those in Africa) produce no, or only a negligible number of, vehicles.

Agricultural Output

A country's agricultural capacity adds or detracts from its economic power. Self-sufficiency varies widely in the world. The United States not only meets its own needs, it also earns money from agricultural exports. With agricultural exports exceeding imports by about a 10-to-1 ratio in 2006, the U.S. net trade surplus came to approximately $50 billion. Other countries are less fortunate. Some have to use their economic resources to import food. Sub-Saharan Africa is in particularly desperate shape. Senegal, for one, needs to import machinery, fuel, and other products necessary to diversify and industrialize its economy, yet it must spend 28% of its limited import funds to buy food.

Another significant agricultural factor is the percentage of its economic resources that a country must expend to feed its people. Countries are relatively disadvantaged if they have larger percentages of their workforce engaged in agriculture, and thus not available for the manufacturing and service sectors. For example, over half of China's workforce is in agriculture compared to only 2% of all U.S. workers. A country is also challenged if it has to spend a significant part of its economic effort (measured as a percentage of GDP) to feed its people. Here again, China is relatively disadvantaged by having to devote 15% of its GDP to farming, compared to just 2% for the United States. A major problem for China and similar countries is that they are inefficient because they have so little farm machinery. As one measure, Americans have almost three times the number of tractors per square mile of farmland than do the Chinese.

Now that we have explored national capabilities, we can turn to foreign policy implementation, to how countries seek to utilize their resources, skills, and other capabilities to promote their national interests. A first step is to reiterate that power is a very sophisticated concept, including but also extending well beyond military might and wealth. As we shall see presently, these two factors often have little or nothing to do with whether a country succeeds or fails in advancing its foreign policy goals.

The second step in this introduction to implementing foreign policy is to take up statecraft by identifying the **instruments of foreign policy**, the tools that countries use to implement their policy. There are four instruments: military, economic, diplomatic, and informational.

THE MILITARY INSTRUMENT

War is sometimes a spasm of violence begun by an irrational leader or set off by an emotional reaction. Normally, however, a country's military assets are part of its overall power that can be used directly or indirectly to help the country achieve its diplomatic goals. As German strategist Carl von Clausewitz argued in *On War* (1833): "War is not merely a political act, but also a political instrument, a continuation of political relations, a carrying out of the same by other means." Used wisely, force remains a tool of diplomacy. Even UN Secretary-General Kofi Annan had to concede, "You can do a lot with diplomacy, but of course you can do a lot more with diplomacy backed up by firmness and force."[14] Chapter 10 includes an extended examination of the use of violence in the international system, but it is appropriate here to briefly review violence as a national policy instrument. This mostly involves the military, but it can also involve assassinations and other covert forms of violence.

Applying Force from Intimidation to Attack

Military power may be applied in several escalating ways. These range from serving as a diplomatic backdrop, through threats, to using military forces to defeat an opponent (Slantchev, 2005; Cimballa, 2002; Nathan, 2002). It also should be noted that the options provided by the five levels of violence form a multiple menu. That is, they are often exercised concurrently.

The very existence of significant military power establishes a *diplomatic backdrop* that influences other countries. Military strength not only deters opponents, it also influences friends and neutrals. One reason the United States has been, and remains, a leader of the West is because massive U.S. conventional and nuclear military power creates a psychological assumption in others that Washington will play a strong role. This reality led one U.S. ambassador to China to put a photograph of a U.S. aircraft carrier on his office wall with the caption, "90,000 tons of diplomacy."[15]

Overt threats are the next step up the escalation ladder. That is what President Bush did in his address on March 17, 2003, when he declared, "Saddam Hussein and his sons must leave Iraq within 48 hours. Their refusal to do so will result in military conflict, commenced at a time of our choosing."

Indirect and covert intervention is a further escalation and includes the use of any of a number of techniques to apply military power while avoiding a commitment of your armed forces to direct combat. One example is supplying arms or providing training and advisers to another government or to a rebel force. Another is conducting covert operations using special military forces, intelligence agents, or mercenaries in another country to conduct clandestine operations.

Limited demonstrations are well up the escalatory ladder. These involve overtly wielding restrained conventional force to intimidate or harass rather than defeat an opponent. On two occasions (1993 and 1996), for example, the United States attacked Iraqi military installations with cruise missiles in retaliation for Baghdad's attempt to assassinate former President Bush, then to pressure Iraq to end military operations against the Kurds in the northern part of Iraq.

Direct action is the most violent application of a country's military assets. It involves using full-scale force to attempt to defeat an opponent. Within this context, the level of violence can range from highly constrained conventional conflict, as occurred in Iraq in 2003, to unrestricted nuclear war.

The Effectiveness of Force

Deciding to use force is the most fateful decision that a country can make. People will almost certainly die, the cost of war and reconstruction is high, and victory is never assured. German Chancellor Theobald von Bethmann-Hollweg was wise when he warned as Europe teetered on the edge of World War I in 1914, "If the iron dice roll, may God help us." Given these realities, we should explore the effectiveness of force by looking at measurements of and conditions for success.

Measurement

Cost/benefit analysis is one way to measure the effectiveness of force. War is very expensive. There is no accurate count of the deaths in the Iraq War, but in the initial

Did You Know That:

King Frederick the Great of Prussia (1712–1786), once commented, "Diplomacy without arms is like music without instruments."

military invasion and the following occupation through early 2007, 3,400 U.S. and coalition troops died and 23,400 were wounded. About 90% of these have been Americans. Between 20,000 and 45,000 Iraqi soldiers and at least 2,500 civilians died during the invasion, and the estimated number of Iraqis to have died during the occupation either directly or indirectly from the violence and destruction range from 50,000 to 600,000. As far as financial costs, U.S. spending on the war and subsequent occupation was approaching the $400 billion mark in early 2007. The cost to Great Britain and other intervening countries and the destruction in Iraq easily push the total cost of the war past the $1 trillion mark. Most Americans would say that the war has not been worth the cost, but what goal would be? Answering that is difficult because while the decision for war, to trade lives and treasure for a political goal, is often made, it is impossible to arrive at any objective standards that can equate the goal sought and the price to be paid even if you could accurately calculate it before taking action.

Goal attainment is the second way to judge the effectiveness of force. Generally, the decision for war is not irrational because leaders usually calculate, accurately or not, their probability of successfully achieving their goals. This calculation is called the "expected utility" of war. By the utilitarian standard, war does sometimes work. From 1495 to 1991, great powers won 60% of the wars they started (Wang & Ray, 1994). Moreover, the success rate went up from 59% through 1799 to 75% between 1800 and 1991. During the first three centuries (1495–1799), the initiators won 59% of the wars they fought. But during the last two centuries (1800–1991), the success rate increased, with the initiators winning 75% of the wars. Leaders often miscalculate, as Saddam Hussein did in 1990 and again in 2003, and start or risk a war they ultimately lose. Also, it is sometimes hard to evaluate whether goals were attained. If the U.S. goal in 2003 was to defeat Iraq and topple Saddam Hussein, it certainly succeeded. However, to the extent the goal was to destroy Iraq's weapons of mass destruction (WMDs), the invasion was a failure since they did not exist. Finally, to the degree that the goal was to bring democracy to Iraq, the verdict is still out about whether Iraq's future will be one of democracy or an internal bloodbath as various religious factions fight for power, but the prospects are grim at best.

Conditions for Success

The next question, then, is: When does force succeed and when does it fail to accomplish its goals? There is no precise answer, but it is possible to synthesize the findings of a variety of studies and the views of military practitioners to arrive at some rudimentary rules for the successful use of military force, especially in cases of intervention when a country has not been directly attacked.[16] Note that these criteria do not guarantee success. They only improve the chances. With that caveat in mind, a country improves its chances of success during an intervention when military force is:

1. Used in areas where it has a clearly defined, preferably long-standing, and previously demonstrated commitment.
2. Supported firmly and publicly by most of the country's leaders.
3. Supported strongly by public opinion.
4. Utilized to defeat other military forces, not to control political events.
5. Applied early and decisively, not after extended threatening and slow escalation.
6. Meant to achieve clear goals and does not change or try to exceed them.

Web Link

An up-to-date calculation of the ongoing cost of the Iraq war and occupation for the United States is available at **http://costofwar.com/**.

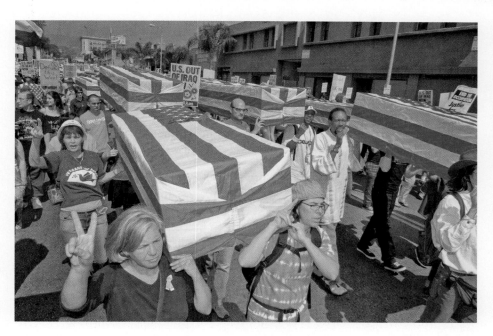

Many analysts believe that a country's ability to use military force successfully is determined in part by strong support of the action by public opinion. The U.S. invasion and occupation of Iraq were not very popular among Americans to begin with, and public opinion and support dropped off steadily once U.S. casualties began to mount. This further diminishes any chances of success for the occupation.

THE ECONOMIC INSTRUMENT

Although economic power cannot be as easily wielded as military power, countries with considerable economic power have a potent policy instrument in their ability to use trade, aid, and other economic means to achieve national foreign policy ends. Chapters 11 and 12 focus on economics and include in-depth discussions of trade, aid and other aspects of the international political economy. That material supplements the somewhat narrower discussion of incentives and sanctions as economic instruments for foreign policy.

Economic Incentives

States regularly offer economic incentives to induce other states to act in a desired way. Incentives include providing foreign aid, giving direct loans or credits, guaranteeing loans by commercial sources, reducing tariffs and other trade barriers, selling or licensing the sale of sensitive technology, and a variety of other techniques. Sometimes incentives are meant to achieve an economic goal, but more often specific offers (as distinct from, say, general foreign aid) are aimed at achieving a political goal. For example, the efforts by the EU to persuade Iran to give up its alleged nuclear weapons development program and the similar effort by the United States and other countries to convince North Korea to give up its program both involve the offer of energy aid and significant other economic incentives. One study finds incentives more effective with authoritarian than democratic countries (Lai & Morey, 2006).

Some foreign aid is given multilaterally through the World Bank and other intergovernmental organizations (IGOs), but the United States and most other aid donors give funds directly to other countries. About 80% of all U.S. foreign aid is bilateral. Much of it has a political focus. Indeed, about 40% of U.S. aid is military aid.

Following the 9/11 attacks, the Bush administration focused aid heavily in support of the war on terror. In 2006, Iraq was the top U.S. aid recipient, with Afghanistan, Pakistan, and the moderate Arab regimes in Egypt and Jordan also among the top ten recipients. U.S. concerns about the Islamic extremists in Somalia, Sudan, and elsewhere in the northeastern African "horn" region also put Ethiopia among the top ten recipients. That paid off when Ethiopian forces invaded Somalia in late 2006 and ousted the Islamic fundamentalist regime that dominated Mogadishu and most of the rest of the country. A few other U.S. strategic interests were also evident in the distribution of aid. Concern about illegal drugs led Colombia to be a top-10 aid recipient.

It is important to note that the political use of aid is not confined to the United States. It is somewhat ironic that China, which once loudly criticized aid from the West to less developed countries (LDCs) as imperialist, became itself subject to that charge once it began to give limited aid. There has been considerable criticism of Beijing, for example, because of its aid to and general support of Sudan, despite the Sudanese government's horrific ethnic cleansing campaign in Darfur. China claims it opposes outside interventions in other countries' domestic affairs, but critics tie China's support to its considerable interests in Sudan's oil fields. Elsewhere in Africa, China's aid has been tied to easier access for Chinese goods and other benefits, leading South Africa's President Thabo Mbeki to rebuke China for seeking for itself "a replication of that colonial relationship" that once existed "between Europe and its African possessions a century ago."[17]

Economic Sanctions

Web Link

Current UN sanctions are available at **www.un.org/sc/committees/**; current U.S. sanctions are listed at **www.treas.gov/offices/enforcement/ofac/programs/index.shtml.**

Countries can also use their economic power in a negative way by applying sanctions. The use of **economic sanctions** dates back to at least 432 B.C. when the city-state of Athens embargoed all trade with another city-state, Megara, an ally of Sparta, which was a bitter rival of Athens. Despite being ancient, though, sanctions were uncommon until fairly recently (Elliot & Oegg, 2002). Increased use has occurred, in part, because countries are more willing to ignore sovereignty and impose penalties on oppressive governments, because economic interdependence makes target countries more vulnerable to sanctions, and because they are an alternative to war. For example, the United States imposed sanctions on Syria in 2004 because of its alleged support for terrorism, its occupation of Lebanon, and its chemical weapons program. Overall, in 2006 the U.S. government had economic sanctions ranging from full economic embargoes (no trade) to more limited restrictions in place against Belarus, Burma (Myanmar), Cuba, Iran, Ivory Coast, North Korea, Serbia, Sudan, and Zimbabwe. It should be noted that sanctions can be imposed by international organizations as well as by individual countries. During its history, the UN has used sanctions against numerous countries, with restriction in place against 10 countries in early 2007.

The Effectiveness of Sanctions

Whether imposed unilaterally or multilaterally through the UN or some other IGO, economic sanctions have two purposes. One is to register symbolic disapproval. This may not have a practical impact, but there is something to be said about refusing to have normal economic relations with a country that has committed aggression, is engaged in ethnic cleansing, or is otherwise morally deficient. The second use of economic sanctions is to attempt to change a target country's behavior. In this more applied use, the effectiveness of sanctions is mixed (Druary & Li, 2006; Marinov,

2005). Sometimes they can be effective. For example, the sanctions first imposed on Libya in the early 1990s almost certainly played a role in its 2003 agreement to end its program of building weapons of mass destruction and to allow inspections by the International Atomic Energy Agency and other international agencies. Usually, though, sanctions fail to accomplish their goal, with success-rate estimates ranging from 5% to 33% (Elliott & Oegg, 2002). Thus while scholars disagree on the exact success rate, "something of a conventional wisdom has emerged," one writes, "suggesting that, while sanctions may serve domestic political or symbolic purposes, they are not particularly effective at inducing target states to change their behavior" (Morgan, 2005:1).

Studies also indicate that sanctions are most likely to be effective in certain circumstances (Lacy & Niou, 2004). These include instances when (1) there is strong multilateral cooperation; (2) the target is politically unstable and/or economically weak; (3) those imposing the sanctions are strong economically; the targeted country has substantial trade with the targeting countries; (4) sanctions are put into effect quickly and decisively to maximize psychological impact; and (5) the targeting countries are not themselves harmed significantly by the cost of maintaining the sanctions. Within this list, it is most important to note the first criterion: multilateral cooperation. Unilateral sanctions, those imposed by one country against another, have a very slim chance of success. The United States has had various sanctions in place against Cuba since 1960 in an effort to topple the leftist regime of Fidel Castro. Yet as of 2007, Castro was still in power and, indeed, was the world's longest serving political leader. Reports of serious ill health make it unlikely that Castro will remain as president another 48 years, but it is far more likely that time and nature will remove him from power than will the United States.

The Drawbacks of Sanctions

Countries that apply sanctions must be wary of their potential negative impact on unintended victims. One such difficulty is that sanctions may harm economic interests other than those of the intended target. The UN sanctions imposed on Iraqi oil exports between 1991 and 2003 cost Jordan and Turkey many millions of dollars annually by way of lost revenues. Both countries would have earned revenues for the use of pipelines that run from Iraq through them and on to ports from which the oil is shipped. Economic interests in the targeting country can also be harmed. For instance, U.S. sanctions barring trade with other countries reduced American exports by about $15 billion a year. That is a tiny part of the U.S. economy, but, as one study notes, "the costs of sanctions are never spread evenly" across the economy. For example, the analysis continues, "the long-standing U.S. embargo on Cuba arguably has a much larger impact on Florida than on other states" (Hufbauer & Oegg, 2003:8).

A third criticism of sanctions is that they are often the tool used by EDCs to continue their dominance of LDCs. Of the 71 incidents of sanctions applied during the 1970s and 1980s, 49 of the cases (69%) involved EDCs placing sanctions on LDCs (Rothgeb, 1993). A fourth charge against sanctions is that they may constitute a rogue action in the view of many countries that do not support them. For the 15th consecutive year and by a vote of 183 to 4, the UN General Assembly in 2006 condemned the unilateral U.S. sanctions against Cuba. A fifth criticism is that sanctions often harm the innocent. Taking this view, President Fidel Castro of Cuba has called them "noiseless atomic bombs" that "cause the death of men, women, and children."[18] Iraq provides a good example of Castro's point. There, the UN sanctions that remained in place with strong U.S. support between 1991 and 2003 had a devastating impact on the Iraqi population, especially its children. There is a debate

JOIN THE DEBATE
Are Sanctions against Cuba
Still in the Best Interests
of the United States?

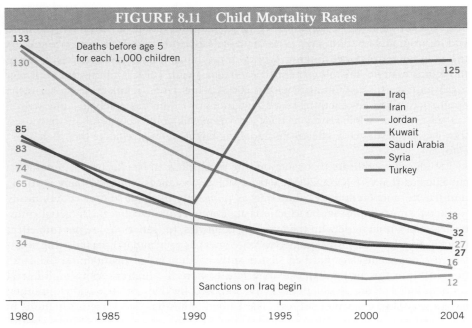

FIGURE 8.11 Child Mortality Rates

Throughout the Persian Gulf region, the child mortality rate for Iraq and all its neighbors declined steadily from 1980 to 1990. Then UN sanctions were placed on Iraq. From that point, the child mortality rate for Iraq shot upward alarmingly, while the rate for all its neighbors continued to decline. In 2004, the number of children per 1,000 dying in Iraq before they reached age 5 was 125 (or 12.5%). This was more than three times the rate of the next highest country in the region (Iran, 38), and 51% higher than Iraq's own rate in 1980 (83). Such data casts doubt in the minds of some about the morality of economic sanctions.

Data sources: World Bank online, UNICEF online.

over whether the sanctions themselves should be blamed or whether the fault lies with Saddam Hussein for diverting funds that should have been spent on food and medicine for the civilian population. Whatever the resolution of that argument, the net result, according to various studies by the UN, Harvard University's School of Public Health, and others, was that during the sanctions period over 1 million Iraqi children than would normally be expected were malnourished and upward of 500,000 died. This deleterious effect is evident in Figure 8.11, which compares the child mortality rate in Iraq to that of its neighbors.

THE DIPLOMATIC INSTRUMENT

National diplomacy is a complex game of maneuvering in which a country tries to get other countries or international organizations to do what it wants them to do. While diplomacy is often portrayed by an image of somber negotiations over highly polished wooden tables in ornate rooms, it is much more than that. Modern diplomacy is a far-ranging communications process including many channels in addition to ambassadors and other such diplomats (Starkey, Boyer, & Wilkenfeld, 2005; Steiner, 2004). Additionally diplomacy is not only about words. Although it is presented here as an individual instrument of foreign policy, the reality is that diplomacy is conducted along the scale of methods ranging from the overt use of economic and military muscle, through the argumentation of skilled diplomats who have little power other than their own abilities to support their country's goals. Moreover, diplomacy involves building up a reserve of good will and respect, soft power, that can be drawn upon in future negotiations or even confrontation to try to maintain allies, help assuage opponents, and otherwise achieve a positive result.

The Context of Diplomacy

Before taking up the conduct of diplomacy, it is important to understand the global context in which it operates. Diplomacy is an ancient art, dating back at least to the time of the great Babylonian emperor, Hammurabi (1792–1750 B.C.). But while treaties, ambassadors, and some other parts of modern diplomatic practice also have long histories, diplomacy has changed dramatically because of the evolving context of world politics. The early 20th century serves as a benchmark in the transition to modern-era diplomacy. In this evolving new context, the "old diplomacy" did not vanish, but it changed substantially. The eclipse of colonialism, advances in travel and communications, the spread of democracy, and other factors have all played a role in changing the context of diplomacy.

Multilateral Diplomacy

Although there were a few exceptions, the normal form of negotiation prior to 1900 was **bilateral diplomacy**, direct negotiations between two countries. The use of **multilateral diplomacy**, conferences involving a number of nations, has expanded greatly since then. More than any event, the founding of the League of Nations in 1920 marked this change, and there are now about 250 permanent world and regional intergovernmental organizations (IGOs). Conferences to address specific issues and treaties are also more apt to be multilateral. Before 1900, the United States attended an average of one multilateral conference per year. Now, the United States is a member of scores of international organizations and American diplomats participate daily in multilateral negotiations. For example, the effort to persuade North Korea to give up its nuclear weapons program has been conducted through the Six Party talks hosted by China and also include Japan, North Korea, Russia, South Korea, and the United States.

One reason that multilateral diplomacy has increased is that modern technology allows faster and more frequent contacts among countries. Second, many global concerns, such as the environment, cannot be solved by any one country or through traditional bilateral diplomacy alone. Instead, global cooperation and solutions are required. Third, diplomacy through multilateral organizations is attractive to smaller countries as a method of influencing world politics beyond their individual power.

Fourth, there is the growing expectation of **multilateralism**, the notion that important international actions, especially those using military force, will be taken within the framework of a multilateral organization such as the United Nations. The contrasting approach is **unilateralism**. This occurs when a single country, perhaps leading a small coalition of other countries, takes action without the approval of an IGO. Recent wars against Iraq illustrate the two approaches. Prior to the Persian Gulf War (1991) the first President Bush secured the authority of the UN to oust Iraq from Kuwait, and the U.S.-led invasion included military support from 33 countries. In 2003, President Bush sent troops into Iraq without the UN's imprimatur and with substantial military support only from Great Britain and token support from 3 other countries.

SIMULATION
An Adventure in Diplomacy

Many political leaders within the United States and internationally have strongly criticized what they see as the arrogant and heavy-handed unilateralism of the second President Bush. Not atypically, one condemnation of Bush's foreign policy blasts unilateralism as a "flagrant disregard for . . . cooperation," and also "foolhardy [because] it makes of one [country] a clear aggressor, a likely target of retaliation, and liable to bear the full brunt of paying for the operation, both in personnel and money" (Seigfried, 2006:20). Others have taken the opposite view, though, arguing against what is "short-term popular, but long-term unwise. . . . trust[ing] U.S. security to the goodwill of international organizations" (Rubin, 2006:3). From a different perspective, a recent review of the general scholarly commentary against unilateralism argues that it has been mostly based on views of the policies, such as the Iraq War, themselves and not on the actual process of unilateralism. That review concludes, "Unless and until" better research is done, "scholarly grounds for a general stance against U.S. unilateralism on the basis of its purported international costs do not exist" (Brooks & Wohlforth. 2005:524).

Leader-to-Leader Diplomacy

It was once rare for monarchs and other leaders to meet or otherwise communicate directly with one another. Now modern transportation and communications have made direct exchanges common. President Bush departed on his first foreign visit only 27 days after his inauguration in 2001, and during his first six years made 36 trips and visited 58 countries. Additionally during that time, he received visits from 2,190 heads of government or foreign ministers representing 80 countries. Beyond such face-to-face encounters, presidential telephone calls to foreign leaders are a common occurrence.

There are *advantages* to face-to-face meetings. Sometimes they have high symbolic value. Richard Nixon's visit to China in 1972 to meet Chairman Mao Zedong signaled an epic shift in U.S. policy. Another advantage is that leaders sometimes make dramatic breakthroughs. The 1978 Camp David Accords, which began the process of normalizing Egyptian-Israeli relations after decades of hostility and three wars, were produced after President Jimmy Carter, Egyptian President Anwar Sadat, and Israeli Prime Minister Menachem Begin isolated themselves at the presidential retreat in Maryland. A third advantage of leader-to-leader diplomacy is that it can facilitate communications and smooth relations. The first President Bush believed that "The best diplomacy starts with getting to know each other" and that "If [another leader] knows the heartbeat a little bit from talking [with me], there's less apt to be misunderstanding."[19]

Sometimes personal warmth grows between two leaders that can be helpful. George W. Bush learned during his friendly conversations with Junichiro Koizumi that the Japanese prime minister is a huge fan of rock 'n' roll and especially Elvis Presley. So when Koizumi visited the United States in 2006, Bush presented him with a vintage jukebox complete with 1950s and 1960s rock 'n' roll records and then escorted him to visit Graceland in Tennessee. There, when Bush urged Koizumi to sing some of his favorite Elvis tunes, the prime minister warbled a few bars of "Love Me Tender," then crooned, "Wise men say, 'Only fools rush in'," which is also pretty good diplomatic advice.

Disadvantages also exist in leader-to-leader diplomacy. One is that there are numerous instances when leaders have made and reached what each thought was a mutual agreement, only to find to their dismay that they had misunderstood each other. A second problem is that while leaders can disavow mistakes made by lower-ranking officials, a leader's commitments, even if not wise, cannot be easily retracted.

Did You Know That:

Bill Clinton is the most traveled U.S. president, having made 54 trips to 133 countries and being abroad for 229 of his 2,922 days in office.

"When presidents become negotiators no escape routes are left," former Secretary of State Henry Kissinger warns (1979:12). "Concessions are irrevocable without dishonor." Additionally, poor personal chemistry can damage relations between leaders. For example, relations between President G. W. Bush and German Chancellor Gerhard Schröder turned sour in 2002 over their opposing views, "The personal relationship is not just damaged, it is broken, and I fear beyond repair," lamented a German official. "That is regrettable because personal trust in the negotiating parties is important for political cooperation."[20]

Democratized Diplomacy

Few countries were democracies before the 20th century, and in that context conducting diplomacy and agreeing to treaties and other international obligations were almost exclusively within the monarch's realm of authority. "*L'état, c'est moi*" (I am the state), Louis XIV supposedly proclaimed with some justification. Executive leaders still dominate the foreign policy–making process, but it is no longer their exclusive domain. Instead, **democratized diplomacy** is the norm, with legislatures, interest groups, and public opinion all playing a greater role.

Indeed, the importance of domestic politics in foreign policy making has given rise to **two-level game theory**. This holds that to be successful a country's diplomats must find a solution that is acceptable to both the other country at the international level and, at the domestic level, to the political actors (legislators, public opinion, interest groups) in the diplomat's own country (Tarar, 2005). From this perspective, the diplomatic setting exists at the domestic as well as at the international level, and is influenced by the interplay of the two levels when leaders try to pursue policies that satisfy the actors at both levels. During the several tense times over the future of Taiwan, for instance, U.S. and Chinese leaders not only have had to find points of agreement between themselves, they also have had to fend off domestic forces in their respective countries pushing to escalate the crisis. As China's president put it, "Any leader who lets this [Taiwan's independence] pass would be overthrown."[21]

Parliamentary Diplomacy

Another part of the modern diplomatic context is **parliamentary diplomacy**. This includes debate and voting in IGOs as a supplement to negotiation and compromise. The maneuvering involved in parliamentary diplomacy was strongly evident in the UN during the U.S. campaign to win Security Council approval for an invasion of Iraq in 2003. That required the backing of 9 of the Council's 15 members, including a "yes" vote or an abstention from each of the 5 veto-wielding permanent members. Washington's strategy, according to one U.S. diplomat, was to "win backing like you would in Congress—going after votes one by one by one." Tactics reportedly included offering a variety of economic incentives such as access to lucrative contracts to rebuild postwar Iraq. As one U.S. diplomat conceded, "We'll put it to them simply: Do you want to be part of reconstruction and all that means—or leave it to us?"[22] In the end, Washington was certain that France and perhaps Russia would veto the U.S./U.K. resolution, which probably did not even have 9 votes. To avoid an embarrassing defeat, the British ambassador to the UN announced that Washington and London "have agreed that we will not pursue a vote."[23]

Open Diplomacy

Secrecy was once the norm in diplomacy, with negotiations and sometimes even treaties concluded in secret. Seeking change, Woodrow Wilson called for "open covenants, openly arrived at" in his Fourteen Points. He got his wish and in the context of expanded democracy since his time, the norm is **open diplomacy**, with negotiations and the contents of international agreements widely reported and documented. While this change is important to the principle of democratic government, it does have its disadvantages. Public negotiations are difficult. Disclosure of your bargaining strategy compromises your ability to win concessions. Public negotiations are also more likely to lead diplomats to posture for public consumption. Concessions may be difficult to make amid popular criticism. Perhaps the most critical negotiations in all history possibly prevented a nuclear war when the United States secretly agreed to never seek to overthrow Fidel Castro in return for Soviet withdrawal of their nuclear weapons from Cuba during the 1962 Cuban missile crisis. In sum, it is difficult to negotiate (or to play chess) with someone kibitzing over your shoulder. Indeed, domestic opposition to dealing with an adversary may be so intense that it may be impossible to negotiate at all.

Diplomacy as a Communications Process

As a communications process, diplomacy involves (1) communicating to one or more countries or other actors what your concerns, general goals, and specific objectives are, and (2) persuading the other actors to support or comply with your objectives. Such communications are not carried out solely by designated diplomats, such as ambassadors. Instead there are multiple channels that range from a country's president or prime minister down through the government structure and sometimes even involve private citizens. We shall also see that diplomatic communications can include actions as well as words. Whatever the specifics, the diplomatic communication process is carried out through negotiation and signaling.

Negotiations occur when two or more parties communicate with one another, either directly or indirectly through an intermediary. It is very difficult to accomplish anything unless the different sides are talking directly or at least indirectly through an intermediary. As U.S. Secretary of State Colin Powell once put it, diplomacy is about seeking solutions, and "what will get us there are political discussions and the sooner we can get them the better."[24]

Most diplomatic communications are part of an exchange of views, but they can sometimes be one-sided. When, in 1972, South Vietnam resisted the U.S.-negotiated settlement with North Vietnam, President Richard Nixon cabled President Nguyen Van Thieu that "all military and economic aid will be cut off . . . if an agreement is not reached" and that "I have . . . irrevocably decided to proceed . . . to sign [the agreement]. I will do so, if necessary, alone [and] explain that your government obstructs peace." "Brutality is nothing," Nixon told an aide. "You have never seen it if this son-of-a-bitch doesn't go along, believe me" (Kissinger, 1979:1420, 1469). Thieu went along.

Signaling entails saying or doing something with the intent of sending a message to another government. When leaders make bellicose or conciliatory speeches, when military forces are deployed or even used, when trade privileges are granted or sanctions invoked, or when diplomatic recognition is extended or relations are broken, these actions are, or at least should be, signals of attitude and intent to another country.

Signals can be quite direct and, indeed, sometimes leaders signal one another through the open airwaves rather than through diplomatic channels. That is what was occurring in 2006 when Vice President Richard Cheney publicly warned, "The Iranian regime needs to know that if it stays on its present course [toward developing nuclear weapons], the international community is prepared to impose meaningful consequences." Adding to the threat, Cheney did not forswear the use of military force, instead noting, "For our part, the United States is keeping all options on the table. We will not allow Iran to have a nuclear weapon."[25]

Less direct signaling was evident in the U.S. invasion of Afghanistan after the 9/11 terror attacks. Certainly that was meant to attack al Qaeda and the Taliban government, but it was also a signal to others. "Let's hit them hard," Bush told the chairman of the Joint Chiefs of Staff when he directed the general to send ground troops as well as warplanes and missiles against Afghanistan. "We want to signal this is a change from the past," the president explained. "We want to cause other countries like Syria and Iran to change their views [about supporting terrorism]."[26]

Conducting Diplomacy

Skilled diplomacy is more art than science. To be effective, diplomats must tailor their approach to the situation and the opponent. Still, there are some basic rules of good diplomacy, and it is also wise to understand the implications of various choices diplomats make about the channel, level, visibility, type of inducement, degree of precision, method of communication, and extent of linkage that they will use.

Web Link

An online diplomatic game, Diplomatic Pouch, is available at **www.diplom.org/index.py.**

General Rules of Effective Diplomacy

Delineating the methods of diplomatic communications is far easier than utilizing them effectively. There is no set formula that will ensure success, but unless you are willing to quickly escalate a conflict, some basic rules of effective diplomacy are:

- *Be realistic.* Have goals that match what you can and are willing to do to achieve them. Getting North Korea to unilaterally give up its nuclear weapons might have been ideal, but the United States did not have the power to do that short of a first-strike nuclear attack. Therefore offering North Korea economic incentives in 2007 in return for beginning to shut down its capacity to make new weapons was an achievable goal.

- *Be careful about what you say.* Many observers feel that North Korea's decision to test a nuclear weapon in 2006 may have been a defensive reaction that can be traced to 2002 when President Bush called North Korea one of the "axis of evil" countries and 2003 when he ordered the invasion of Iraq, another of the axis of evil countries.

- *Seek common ground.* Focus first on common interests, perhaps avoiding war, and work toward achieving them. Research indicates, for instance, that peace treaties reached through common accord are much more durable than those imposed on one or more belligerents (Werner & Yuen, 2005).

- *Be flexible.* Generally be willing to compromise or to give way for an offsetting concession on everything other than the most vital points.

- *Understand the other side.* Try to find out what your opponents really want and also appreciate their perspective even if you do not agree with it. There was good diplomatic advice in the Elvis Presley song, "Walk a Mile in My Shoes," which urged in part: "Before you abuse, criticize, and accuse / . . . walk a mile in my shoes."

- *Appreciate the other side's domestic constraints.* Remember that they, like you, have domestic political problems that, again just like you, push them to engage in two-level diplomacy. It is impossible to be realistic about negotiations in the Middle East unless you understand that whatever concessions moderate Palestinian and Israeli leaders might be willing to make are apt to be violently opposed by each side's hardliners.

■ *Be patient.* Being overly anxious may result in unwise concessions or to deadlines that, if not met, can lead to an escalation of conflict. Throughout the negotiations with North Korea, which were frustrating and included many setbacks, the Bush administration wisely avoided time lines.

■ *Leave avenues of retreat open.* The adage that rats will fight if trapped in a corner often applies to countries. Therefore, it is usually wise to leave yourself and your opponent an "out." Ultimatums, especially public ones, often lead to war. Whatever its other merits, President Bush's demand that in 2002 Saddam Hussein leave Iraq in 24 hours or face war left no room for him to maneuver. War followed.

Direct or Indirect Negotiations

One issue that diplomats face is whether to negotiate directly with each other or indirectly through an intermediary. *Direct negotiations* have the advantage of avoiding the misinterpretations that an intermediary third party might cause. As in the old game of "Gossip," messages can become garbled. Direct negotiations are also quicker. An additional plus is that they can act as a symbol.

Indirect negotiations may also be advisable. Direct contact symbolizes a level of legitimacy that a country may not wish to convey. For example, the Bush administration has resisted talking directly and bilaterally to Iran because that would have handed a diplomatic victory to a country that the United States has not recognized since 1980 when it allowed a mob to seize the U.S. embassy in Tehran and hold 52 American diplomats hostage for 444 days. Yet Washington has not closed the diplomatic doors completely, and has kept a range of unofficial contacts with Iran alive. Among these have been recent exchanges through Iran's UN Ambassador Javad Zarif. He is considered a moderate by Iranian standards and holds a B.A. and M.A. in international relations from San Francisco State University and a Ph.D. in international law and policy from the Graduate School of International Studies, University of Denver, the same program where Secretary of State Condoleezza Rice earned her doctorate.

High-Level or Low-Level Diplomacy

Who should communicate is another important choice in the conduct of diplomacy. Should high- or low-level diplomats be sent to a conference, should positions be announced at a high level, perhaps by the head of government, or by a lower level official?

High-level diplomacy has its advantages. Verbal and written statements by heads of government are noted seriously in other capitals. It was major news during the diplomatic maneuvering over North Korea's nuclear program in 2003 when President Bush took the occasion of a trip to Asia for an international conference to declare publicly, "I've said as plainly as I can say that we have no intention of invading North Korea" and that there might be a way "to say exactly what I said publicly on paper."[27] This move, in turn, caused a shift in North Korea's position from demanding a formal treaty to a more flexible willingness to meet with the United States and other countries to explore the president's intimated readiness to sign some document pledging nonaggression.

Low-level diplomacy is a wiser move at other times. Communications at a low level avoid overreaction and maintain flexibility. Dire threats can be issued as "trial balloons" by cabinet officers or generals and then, if later thought unwise, disavowed by higher political officers. During the ongoing tensions over Taiwan, the principal leaders generally have used lower level officials to make military threats. For example,

China's military newspaper, *Liberation Army Daily,* was far enough removed from official policy makers to warn provocatively that China would "spare no effort in a blood-soaked battle" if Taiwan declared independence.[28] From a position safely distant from the pinnacle of U.S. authority in the Oval Office, a mid-level Defense Department official growled back that China would face "incalculable consequences" if it attacked Taiwan.[29]

Using Coercion or Rewards

Yet another diplomatic choice is whether to brandish coercive sticks or proffer tempting carrots. To induce an opponent to react as you wish, is it better to offer rewards or to threaten punishment? **Coercive diplomacy** can be effective when you have the power, will, and credibility to back it up (Lake, 2005). At one point when China became particularly alarmed about Taiwan's intentions, Beijing conducted military "training" operations near Taiwan. This demonstration of military might included, among other things, firing six nuclear warhead–capable missiles into the seas off Taiwan's coast. For its part, the United States responded to the implied Chinese threat by sending a major naval flotilla, centered around the carriers USS *Nimitz* and USS *Independence,* into the waters off Taiwan.

There are also drawbacks to coercive diplomacy. If your threat does not work, you face an unhappy choice. Not carrying out your threats implies weakness that may well embolden the opponent and perhaps future opponents in crises to come. Yet putting one's military might and money where one's mouth is costs lives and dollars and is not necessarily successful either. Even if coercion does work, it may entail a long-term commitment that was not originally planned or desired. The U.S. ensnarement in Iraq after a quick military victory in 2003 serves as a case in point.

There are many times when *offers of rewards* may be a more powerful inducement than coercion. One song in the movie *Mary Poppins* includes the wisdom that "a spoonful of sugar helps the medicine go down," and an increase in aid, a trade concession, or some other tangible or symbolic reward may induce agreement. At the heart of the 2007 breakthrough in negotiations over North Korea's nuclear arms program was an offer by the United States and others to provide Pyongyang with about $400,000 million in fuel and other forms of economic aid.

Often, the best diplomacy mixes carrots and sticks. As one U.S. State Department official commented, it is difficult to apply a "scientific cookie-cutter approach" that works consistently. "Sometimes it's the carrot, and sometimes it's the stick," he said, adding that the right mixture varies from situation to situation. "You can slice and dice this any way you want. Hopefully, you know, the sausage machine produces something that's halfway coherent at the end."[30]

Economic sanctions and other diplomatic sticks helped topple the regime of Slobodan Milosevic in October 2000. The new government refused, however, to turn him over for trial by the war crimes tribunal sitting in The Hague. What seemingly turned the trick was proffering an exceptionally attractive bunch of carrots to Belgrade. In an unspoken but obvious deal, the Yugoslav government extradited Milosevic in June 2001, and within hours the

It is not clear whether the Filipino editorial artists who drew this image of North Korean leader Kim Jong Il approved or disapproved of the aid package that helped persuade North Korea to halt its nuclear arms program. However, there can be no doubt that economic incentives were part of the diplomatic maneuvering that moved the Six Party talks to success.

United States, the European Union, and other donor countries and organizations (such as the World Bank) that were meeting in Brussels pledged $1.28 billion in aid to the country.

Being Precise or Intentionally Vague

Most diplomatic experts stress the importance of being precise when communicating. There are times, however, when purposeful vagueness may be in order. *Precision* in both written and verbal communications is usually advantageous because it helps avoid misunderstandings. Being precise can also indicate true commitment, especially if it comes from the national leader.

Vagueness may sometimes be a better strategy. Being vague may paper over irreconcilable differences. Lack of precision can also allow a country to retreat if necessary. A degree of ambiguity was one hallmark of legislation passed by China's parliament in 2005 that authorized the use of force against Taiwan if "major events" move the island toward independence or if "possibilities for peaceful reunification are completely exhausted." Since China's leaders do not need permission from the rubber-stamp parliament, the act was meant as a strong signal to Taiwan. Still, it left the leadership room to maneuver by not defining what a major event was or what would constitute the exhaustion of the possibilities for peaceful reunification. Adding to the statute's mixed message, Chinese Premier Wen Jiabao held a press conference soon after it was enacted and focused his remarks on other provisions of the law that call for more economic and cultural exchanges with Taiwan. "This is a law for advancing peaceful reunification. It is not targeted at the people of Taiwan, nor is it a war bill," Wen reassured his listeners with one breath, then, with another added a bit more ominously, "Only by checking and opposing Taiwan's independence forces will peace emerge in the Taiwan Strait."[31]

Communicating by Word or Deed

Diplomacy utilizes both words and actions to communicate. *Oral and written communications,* either delivered directly or through public statements, can be good diplomatic strategy. Washington has repeatedly assured Beijing that U.S. policy does not favor an independent Taiwan and will not support a unilateral Taiwanese declaration of independence. Such communications have helped ease China's fears and thus its reactions to pro-independence leanings in Taiwan's government. Verbal threatening signals also have their place. Secretary of State Rice was clearly trying to put pressure on North Korea to resume talks when during a 2005 trip to South Korea she told reporters, "We need to resolve this issue. It cannot go on forever" and that if Pyongyang refused to end its nuclear weapons program through negotiations, "Then we will have to find other means to do it."[32] What that meant, ranging from economic sanctions to military force, she left unclear.

Signaling by action is often more dramatic than verbal signaling and it has its uses. When Secretary of State Rice visited South Korea in 2005, she signaled U.S. determination to defend that country by becoming the highest-ranking American official to ever visit Command Post Tango, a bunker built into a mountain that would serve as the command center during a war with North Korea. There are drawbacks to such physical signals, though, because it is harder to retreat from them than from words. When the Soviets threatened to blockade Berlin in 1961, President John F. Kennedy took the risky step of going there and publicly proclaiming himself a symbolic citizen of the threatened city. *"Ich bin ein Berliner,"* Kennedy's words rang out. By putting his personal honor on the line, Kennedy persuaded the Soviets to back down. He also gave Germans on both sides of the Berlin Wall a good chuckle by making a minor grammatical error. *"Ich bin Berliner"* (I am a Berliner) is what he meant to say. Inadvertently adding *"ein"* changed the meaning of *Berliner* to refer to a jelly doughnut locally called a *berliner.* This left the leader of the free world actually declaring, "I am a jelly doughnut."[33]

Linking Issues or Treating Them Separately

A persistent dispute is whether a country should deal with other countries on an issue-by-issue basis or link issues together as a basis for a general orientation toward the other country. Advocates of *linking issues* argue that it is inappropriate to have normal relations on some matters with regimes that are hostile and repressive. Those who favor *treating issues separately* claim that doing so allows progress on some issues and keeps channels of communications and influence open.

Critics of the Bush administration have charged that its professed commitment to promoting democracy is hypocritical. Among other things, they point to Bush's continued good relations with Russia despite the increased restrictions on democracy under the Putin government and the brutal campaign against the Chechen independence movement. From the administration's point of view, linking Russia's internal policies to U.S. relations with that country on a range of other matters would be foolhardy. One top U.S. official explained that while "the issue about the democracy and freedom agenda is at the center of the president's foreign policy," it was also the case that "there's a lot more to our relationship with Russia than just this discussion [about democracy]."[34]

Cuba has been another matter, though, and the delinkage of issues has not extended to that country. A number of U.S. measures, including the Helms-Burton Act (1996), have instituted economic sanctions on Cuba and foreign companies doing business with Cuba in an attempt to weaken the government of President Fidel Castro. President Bush increased those in 2004, imposing additional sanctions as a "strategy that says, 'We're not waiting for the day of Cuban freedom, we are working for the day of freedom in Cuba.'"[35] What is unclear is why delinking is good policy toward Russia and not toward Cuba.

Maximizing or Minimizing a Dispute

Diplomats face a choice over whether to put a confrontation in a broad or narrow context. *Maximizing a dispute* by invoking national survival, world peace, or some other major principle may be advantageous because doing so increases credibility. At one point, China maximized the stakes of the Taiwan issue when its premier publicly depicted the matter as a "core principle" involving China's "territorial integrity."[36] The drawback of maximizing a dispute is that it makes it very hard to back away from confrontation if a settlement is not reached. President Bush maximized the stakes of the crisis with Iraq. Speaking before the UN General Assembly he declared that the world was being "challenged . . . by outlaw groups and regimes that accept no law of morality and have no limit to their violent ambitions," and he singled out Iraq's "weapons of mass murder" as the single greatest global threat.[37] By doing so, the president signaled U.S. resolve, but he also painted himself into something of a corner. Given the dire picture he painted, he arguably would have appeared weak internationally and also been politically vulnerable domestically unless the Iraqis totally capitulated to U.S. demands or were defeated in a war to remove the threat (which, ironically, did not exist).

Minimizing a dispute may work positively to avoid overreactions. In contrast to its rhetoric about Iraq, the Bush administration sought to cool the atmosphere regarding North Korea by, among other things, refusing to call it a crisis. Describing it as the "C-word," one U.S. official said, "We are not thinking in those terms," and the administration labeled the North Korean decision to restart its nuclear facility as merely "regrettable," rather than using a more heated term. Some observers applauded the U.S. restraint, but others criticized it as weakness in the face of a threat. From this perspective, Bush's choice of "regrettable" was "the kind of word you use when the soup isn't very good before dinner."[38]

THE INFORMATIONAL INSTRUMENT

Traditional diplomacy primarily involves interacting on a government-to-government basis with another country. The information instrument involves communicating specific information and general images beyond another country's leaders to a much wider array of politically important forces, such as public opinion, in an effort to influence it. Sometimes this information is knowingly false and falls into such categories as disinformation and propaganda. At other times, the information is highly selective and reflects the bias of the transmitter. U.S. government–produced images of American activity in Iraq tend to focus on rebuilding, on the decimation of civilians by car bombs and other terrorist devices, and other themes that support U.S. objectives. By contrast, Al-Zawraa TV, which is run by a former Saddam Hussein official and beamed from Damascus, Syria, by satellite throughout the Middle East, concentrates on images of civilians injured by American military actions, attacks on U.S. forces by insurgents, and other anti-American scenarios. Whether false, biased, partly true, or completely true, the information instrument is part of an effort to win over "the hearts and minds" of the public, as the phrase popularized during the Vietnam War goes.

Such efforts are not new. Information and the ability to convey specific pieces of it and general images to others has always been a powerful instrument of foreign policy. During the thirteenth century, for example, the Mongols under Genghis Khan and his successors followed a policy in which they slaughtered most of the population in cities that refused to surrender, but spared most of the population in cities that surrendered without a fight. In either case, some of the survivors were sent ahead to other cities to carry the information about the different fates of those cities that resisted and lost and those that gave way immediately. Resistance became increasingly rare.

What has changed about informational campaigns is their frequency. This shift has occurred for two reasons. One is the spread of democracy. As noted earlier, more and more countries have become democracies. This means that how the media, public opinion, interest groups, and legislators react to other countries and to events is much more important than it once was in the foreign policy–making process. The

Public diplomacy, which attempts to reach beyond leaders and influence public opinion, is the purpose of this billboard in Ulan Bator, the capital of Mongolia. It promotes democracy and U.S.-Mongolian friendship.

second reason that it is important to reach beyond other countries' leaders to try to influence the wider domestic structure is the communications revolution. Radio, then television, and now the Internet place countries, their leaders, and their policies increasingly on display before the world. The communications revolution also allows governments to communicate much more easily with a worldwide audience.

As a result, international relations are also increasingly conducted through **public diplomacy**. This is the process of creating an image that enhances a country's ability to achieve diplomatic success by increasing its soft power. Highlighting the idea behind public diplomacy, UN Secretary-General Kofi Annan commented, "If I can't get the support of governments, then I'll get the support of the people. People move governments."[39]

In addition to traditional propaganda, public diplomacy includes shaping what leaders and other top diplomats say and do to play to public opinion abroad and otherwise conducting diplomacy in part as a public relations campaign. One scholar's concept of public diplomacy envisions a "theater of power" that is a "metaphor for the repertoire of visual and symbolic tools used by statesmen and diplomats." As players in the theater of power, leaders "must be sensitive to the impression they make on observers. . . . They surely [are] subject to the same sort of 'dramatic,' if not aesthetic, criticism of other kinds of public performances" (Cohen, 1987:i–ii).

Public diplomacy is practiced in all phases of a country's foreign policy effort. When President Bush traveled to Russia in May 2005 to join in ceremonies marking the 60th anniversary of VE Day (May 8, 1945), the end of World War II in Europe, he was careful to also schedule visits to two former Soviet republics, Latvia and Georgia, to demonstrate continued U.S. support of the countries against any outside interference, especially by their former overlord, Moscow. Among other things, Bush underlined that point by placing a wreath at a monument in Riga honoring those who died fighting for Latvian independence.

Governments also use a variety of agencies and other organizations to project their image. The United States, for one, operates or sponsors the Voice of America, Radio Free Europe/Radio Liberty, and Radio Martí. The U.S. Information Agency also produces Worldnet, a television service available globally, provides Web sites, and has other modern communications capabilities. Other efforts are contracted to private public relations firms. In one such effort in 2002 and 2003, the United States ran a $15 million television campaign in several Arab countries. Called "Shared Values," the media effort was meant to convince viewers that Americans were tolerant of Muslims and their beliefs and practices. In one spot, an Arab American female schoolteacher explained, "I wear a *hijab* (head covering) in the classroom where I teach. I have never had a child who thought it was weird or anything like that."[40] Evidence surfaced in 2005 that the U.S. government was also paying freelance reporters to "place" stories favorable to the United States in newspapers in the Middle East and elsewhere. More broadly, all U.S. diplomats abroad are expected to be part of the image effort. This was highlighted in a 2006 message from U.S. Undersecretary of State for Public Diplomacy Karen Hughes to all U.S. diplomatic posts spelling out "Karen's Rules" for dealing with the media, including:

> Rule #1: Think Advocacy. I want all of you to think of yourselves as advocates for America's story each day. . . . I want you out speaking to the press, on television interviews preparing and executing a media strategy, and providing our points on issues. As President Bush and Secretary Rice have stated, public diplomacy is the job of every [diplomat]. We want you out there on television, in the news, and on the radio a couple of times a week and certainly on major news stations in your country and region.[41]

ANALYZE THE ISSUE
Multitrack Diplomacy

CHAPTER SUMMARY

THE COMPLEX NATURE OF POWER

1. National power is the sum of a country's capabilities to successfully implement its foreign policy, especially when those policies are opposed by other states or need the cooperation of other states.

2. Measuring power assets is especially difficult. The efforts to do so have not been very successful, but they do help us see many of the complexities of analyzing the characteristics of power. These characteristics include the facts that power is dynamic; both objective and subjective, relative, and situational; and a country's will to power expresses its determination to apply power assets.

THE FOUNDATION OF NATIONAL POWER

3. National power rests on a foundation that includes the country's geography, people, government, and infrastructure.

4. The national infrastructure consists of a country's technological sophistication, its transportation system, and its information and communications capabilities.

MILITARY POWER

5. Military power is both tangible and intangible. Tangible elements of power, such as tanks, are relatively easy to visualize and measure. Intangible elements of military power, such as morale and reputation, are much more difficult to operationalize.

6. More military power is not always better. It creates the temptation to use it, it makes others insecure, and it is costly.

ECONOMIC POWER

7. Economic power is based on financial position, natural resources, industrial output, and agricultural output.

THE MILITARY INSTRUMENT

8. Force can be used in a range of ways that extend from serving as an unspoken backdrop to negotiations to all-out war.

9. Measuring the effectiveness of force is easier in terms of goal attainment than on a cost/benefit basis.

10. Using force is always very risky, but there are some standards that improve the chance of success.

THE ECONOMIC INSTRUMENT

11. Economic power can be applied through a variety of economic incentives, such as foreign aid, and economic sanctions, such as trade embargos.

THE DIPLOMATIC INSTRUMENT

12. Modern diplomacy occurs in a context including multilateral diplomacy, parliamentary maneuvering, democratized diplomacy, open diplomacy, and leader-to-leader interactions and communications.

13. Diplomacy is a communication process including transmitting information and intentions and persuasion.

14. There are some general rules for conducting effective diplomacy and also a series of options including whether contacts should be direct or indirect, what level of contact they should involve, what rewards or coercion should be offered, how precise or vague messages should be, whether to communicate by message or deed, whether issues should be linked or dealt with separately, and the wisdom of maximizing or minimizing a dispute.

THE INFORMATIONAL INSTRUMENT

15. Conveying information beyond other governments to their citizens has become increasingly important with the advance of democracy and rapid communications. Public diplomacy is a major part of a country's foreign policy activity.

For simulations, debates, and other interactive activities, a chapter quiz, Web links, and much more, visit **www.mhhe.com/rourke12/** and go to chapter 8. Or, while accessing the site, click on Course-Related Headlines and view recent international relations articles in the *New York Times*.

KEY TERMS

absolute power
balance of payments for
   current accounts
bilateral diplomacy
coercive diplomacy
democratized diplomacy
demographic graying
economic sanctions
foreign policy

hard power
imperial overstretch
   thesis
instruments of foreign
   policy
leadership capabilities
multilateral diplomacy
multilateralism
net trade

non-zero-sum
objective power
open diplomacy
parliamentary diplomacy
power
power capacity
public diplomacy
relative power
situational power

social overstretch thesis
soft power
statecraft
subjective power
two-level game theory
unilateralism
will to power
zero-sum game

International Law and Justice: An Alternative Approach

Which is the wiser here, Justice or Iniquity?
—William Shakespeare, *Measure for Measure*

The law hath not been dead, though it hath slept.
—William Shakespeare, *Hamlet*

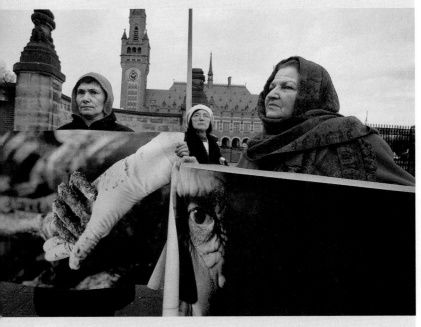

It is easy to disparage the idea of international law in a world of violence where might often means success. As this chapter discusses, however, the law is gradually playing a greater role. These Bosnian women are demonstrating outside the International Court of Justice in The Hague, the Netherlands, where the world court was hearing a case brought against Serbia. Bosnia accused Serbia of genocide against Bosnian Muslims and Croats during the implosion of Yugoslavia in the 1990s. Many were dismayed when in 2007 the ICJ dismissed the case, but it is important that such cases are beginning to be tried in court.

THIS CHAPTER FOCUSES ON international law and justice in the conduct of world politics as an alternative to the power-based diplomatic pursuit of self-interest discussed in chapter 8. It would be naïve to ignore the reality that most global actors emphasize their own interests. However, this is also true in domestic systems. What is different between global and domestic systems is not so much the motives of the actors as the fact that domestic systems place greater restraints on the pursuit of self-interest than the international system does (Joyner, 2005).

Legal systems are one thing that restrains the power-based pursuit of self-interest in a domestic system. Certainly, powerful individuals and groups have advantages in every domestic system. Rules are broken and the guilty, especially if they can afford a high-priced attorney, sometimes escape punishment. Still, laws in the United States cannot overtly discriminate under the "equal protection" clause of the Fourteenth Amendment to the Constitution; for example, an attorney is provided to indigent defendants in criminal cases. Thus, the law somewhat evens the playing field.

Justice is a second restraint on power in domestic systems. What is just and what is legal are not always the same. Justice involves what is "right" here, not just what is legal. Whether the word is *just, moral, ethical,* or *fair,* there is a greater sense in domestic systems than there is in the international system that justice should prevail, that the ends do not always justify the means, and that those who violate the norms should suffer penalties. Surely, there is no domestic system in which everyone acts justly (Amstutz, 2005). Yet the sense of justice that citizens in stable domestic systems have does influence their behavior.

This means that since it is possible to restrain power politics in the domestic system by the creation of legal systems and through a greater emphasis on what is moral and fair, then it is theoretically possible to use the same standards to curb the unbridled pursuit of interests in the international system. Accomplishing that will require major changes in attitudes and practices, but it can be done.

FUNDAMENTALS OF INTERNATIONAL LAW AND JUSTICE

What actors may and may not legitimately do is based in both international and domestic law systems on a combination of expectations, rules, and practices that help govern behavior. We will explore the fundamentals of these legal systems and moral codes by looking first at the primitive nature, growth, and current status of international law; then by turning to issues of justice.

The Primitive Nature of International Law

All legal systems, domestic or international, evolve. Each advances from a primitive level to more sophisticated levels. As such, any legal system can be placed on an evolutionary scale ranging from primitive to modern. Note that modern does not mean finished; people in the future may consider our current legal systems to be rudimentary. This concept of a *primitive but evolving legal system* is important to understanding international law.

The current international legal system falls toward the primitive end of the evolutionary scale of legal systems. First, it does not have a formal rule-making (legislative) process as more sophisticated systems do. Instead, codes of behavior are derived from custom or from explicit agreements among actors. Second, there is little or

Web Link

Some anthropologists study the development of law as part of the evolution of political systems. More on this focus can be found on the Web site of the Association for Political and Legal Anthropology at **www.aaanet.org/apla/.**

The injustices of war and other aspects of international relations led the Dutch jurist and statesman Hugo Grotius (1583–1645) to formulate rules to govern conflict and other interactions among states. This effort earned him the title "father of international law."

no established authority to judge or punish violations of law. Primitive societies, domestic or international, have no police or courts. They rely on self-help techniques ranging from negotiation to violence and occasionally on mediation to resolve disputes. Viewing international law as a primitive legal system helps us to understand that international law does exist, even if it is not as developed as we might wish. Also, we can see that international society and its law may evolve to a higher order, as have domestic systems.

The Growth of International Law

International law has its beginnings in the origin of states and their need to regulate their relations. Gradually, elements of ancient Jewish, Greek, and Roman custom and practice combined with newer Christian concepts to form the beginning of an international system of law. A number of theorists were also important to the genesis of international law. The most famous of these was Holland's Hugo Grotius (1583–1645), the first scholar of international law who wrote *De Jure Belli et Pacis* (On the Law of War and Peace). Grotius and others advanced ideas about the sources of international law, its role in regulating the relations of states, and its application to war and other specific circumstances. From this base, international law evolved slowly over the intervening centuries, as the interactions between the states grew and as the needs and expectations of the international community became more sophisticated.

During the last century or so, concern with international law has grown rapidly. Globalization has significantly expanded the need for rules to govern functional areas such as trade, finance, travel, and communications. Similarly, our awareness of our ability to destroy ourselves and our environment, and of the suffering of victims of human rights abuses, has led to lawmaking treaties on such subjects as genocide, nuclear testing, use of the oceans, and human rights. Even the most political of all activities, war and other aspects of national security, have increasingly become the subject of international law. Aggressive war, for example, is outside the pale of the law. The UN's authorization of sanctions and then force against Iraq after that country invaded Kuwait in 1990 reflected that. So did the UN's refusal to support what most countries saw as an unjustified U.S.-led invasion of Iraq in 2003.

The Practice of International Law

Those who discount international law contend that it exists only in theory, not in practice. As evidence, they cite war, human rights violations, and other largely unpunished examples of "lawlessness." What this argument misses is that international law is effective in many areas despite many holes in its coverage. There is substantial evidence in the behavior of states that they "do accept international law as law, and, even more significant, in the vast majority of instances they . . . obey it" (Joyner, 2000:243). Furthermore, the fact that the law is not *always* followed does not disprove its existence. There is, after all, a substantial crime rate in the United States and most other countries, but that does not mean they are lawless.

International law is *most effective* in governing the rapidly expanding range of transnational **functional relations**. These involve "low politics," a term that designates such things as trade, diplomatic rules, and communications. International law is *least effective* when applied to "high-politics" issues such as national security relations. When vital interests are involved, governments still regularly bend or even ignore international law. Yet it is also the case that the law and standards of justice sometimes do influence strategic political decisions. Both international law and world values, for instance, are strongly opposed to states resorting unilaterally to war except in immediate self-defense. Violations such as Iraq's invasion of Kuwait still occur, but they are met with mounting global condemnation and even counterforce. Now even countries as powerful as the United States regularly seek UN authorization to act in cases such as Afghanistan in 2001 and Iraq in 2003, when not long ago they would have acted on their own initiative. It is true that the United States and Great Britain ultimately went ahead in 2003 without UN support, but that does not disprove the existence of the norm against unilateral war. Indeed, the widespread condemnation of the invasion shows the norm does exist, and the ability of the United States to ignore the norm demonstrates that power often continues to trump international law and justice.

The Fundamentals of International Justice

Concepts of just behavior stem from religious beliefs, from secular ideologies or philosophies, from the standard of equity (what is fair), or from common practice. We will see in our discussion of roots of international law that what a society considers just behavior sometimes becomes law. At other times, legal standards that are considered just are gradually adopted by a society. Insofar as just behavior remains an imperative of conscience rather than law, we can consider justice in a broad sense. Distinctions can be made between moral, ethical, equitable, and humanitarian standards and behavior, but the four individually and in sum equate to justice.

It would be wrong—given recurring war, gnawing human deprivation, persistent human rights violations, and debilitating environmental abuse—to imagine that justice is a predominant global force. Yet it would also be erroneous to use these ills to argue that law and justice do not play a role. Instead, the conduct of most countries is a balance between what is ideal and what is pragmatic. Moreover, there is a growing body of ethical norms that help determine the nature of the international system. Progress is slow and inconsistent, but it exists. American and British forces did not drop nuclear weapons on Iraq in 2003, even though doing so arguably could have saved time, money, and the lives of American and British troops. Many countries give foreign aid to less developed countries. National leaders, not just philosophers and clergy, regularly discuss and sometimes even make decisions based on human rights. Thus the reality is that world politics operates to a degree within the context of international law and justice.

Web Link

A good entry point for more information on international law and international courts is through the UN at **http://www.un.org/law/**.

THE INTERNATIONAL LEGAL SYSTEM

International law, like any legal system, is based on four critical considerations: the philosophical roots of law, how laws are made, when and why the law is obeyed (adherence), and how legal disputes are decided (adjudication).

The Philosophical Roots of Law

Where does law originate? There are three major schools of thought. Two of these are rooted in sources external to the practices of human society. The third holds that the law reflects the internal desires and conduct of each society. A key implication of law being external to society is that there exists a standard of law that governs all humans, whether or not they accept it or abide by it. By contrast, if law is derived from society and, as is the case, there are many human societies (nations), then there is (a) no single law and (b) no basis for asserting the moral superiority of one system of law and values over another.

The first external law view is the **ideological/theological school of law**, which holds that law is derived from an overarching ideology or theology. For instance, a substantial part of contemporary international legal theory can be traced back to Christian doctrine such as the writings of Saint Augustine and Saint Thomas Aquinas on the law of war. There are also long-standing elements of law and scholarship in Islamic, Buddhist, and other religious traditions that serve as a foundation for just international conduct.

The **naturalist school of law** advances the other set of ideas about an external source. This approach contends that humans, by nature, have certain rights and obligations. English philosopher John Locke argued in *Two Treatises of Government* (1690) that there is "a law of nature" that "teaches all mankind, who will but consult it, that all [people] being equal and independent [in the state of nature], no one ought to harm another in his life, health, liberty, or possessions." Since countries are collectives of individuals, and the world community is a collective of states and individuals, natural law's rights and obligations also apply to the global stage and form the basis for international law.

The third view of the roots of law focuses on the customs and practices of society. This is the **positivist school of law**, which advocates that law reflects society and the way people want that society to operate. Therefore, according to positivist principles, law is and ought to be the product of the codification or formalization of a society's standards.

Each of these schools has detractors as well as advocates. Those who reject the idea of external sources of law contend that standards based on ideology or theology are undemocratic because the law is decided and interpreted by either religious officials or, for ideologies, by dogmatists such as Communist Party officials. As for natural law, critics charge that it is vague and also puts so much emphasis on individualism that it almost precludes any sense of communitarian welfare. For example, Locke argued that people had a right to their property. If it is true that a person's property is protected by natural law, then, among other things, it is a human rights violation to take an individual's property through taxes levied by the government without the individual's explicit agreement. Critics condemn the positivist approach as amoral and sometimes immoral, in that it may legitimize immoral, albeit common, beliefs and behavior of a society as a whole or of its dominant class. These critics would say, for instance, that slavery was once widespread and widely accepted, but it was never moral or lawful, by the standards of either divine principle or natural law.

ANALYZE THE ISSUE
Law and Justice: Finding Its Place in the Current International System

How International Law Is Made

Countries usually make domestic law through a constitution (constitutional law), by a legislative body (statutory law), or through statutorily authorized rule making by government agencies and officials (decrees, regulation). In practice, law is also established through judicial decisions (interpretation), which set guidelines (precedent) for later decisions by the courts. Less influential sources of law are custom (common law) and what is fair (equity). Compared to its domestic equivalent, modern international lawmaking is much more decentralized. There are, according to the Statute of the International Court of Justice, four sources of law: international treaties, international custom, the general principles of law, and judicial decisions and scholarly legal writing. Some students of international law tentatively add a fifth source: resolutions and other pronouncements of the UN General Assembly. These five rely primarily on the positivist approach but, like domestic law, include elements of both external and internal sources of law.

International treaties are the primary source of international law (Simmons & Hopkins, 2005). A primary advantage of treaties is that they **codify**, or write down, the law. Agreements between states are binding according to the doctrine of ***pacta sunt servanda*** (treaties are to be served/carried out). All treaties are binding on those countries that are party to them (have signed and ratified or otherwise given their legal consent). Moreover, it is possible to argue that some treaties are also applicable to nonsignatories. When a large number of states agree to a principle, it begins to take on system-wide legitimacy. The Convention on the Prevention and Punishment of the Crime of Genocide (1948), for example, has been ratified by 140 countries. Therefore, genocide is arguably a crime under international law, and that standard is binding on all states whether or not they are party to the treaty. Now people are being tried, convicted, and sentenced for genocide, whether or not their country ratified the antigenocide treaty.

International custom is the second most important source of international law. The old, and now supplanted, rule that territorial waters extend three miles from the shore grew from the distance a cannon could fire. If you were outside the range of land-based artillery, then you were in international waters. Maritime rules of the road and diplomatic practice are two other important areas of law that grew out of custom. Sometimes, long-standing custom is eventually codified in treaties. An example is the Vienna Convention on Diplomatic Relations of 1961, which codified many existing rules of diplomatic standing and practice.

International custom is also found in domestic legal practices and standards that are common to most states. Such commonalities help determine international law and are sometimes applied by a country's courts to domestic as well as international law cases. In one recent example, the U.S. Supreme Court ruled in *Roper v. Simmons* (2005) that executing individuals for crimes committed as a juvenile violated the Constitution's ban on "cruel and unusual punishments." To demonstrate the punishment was "unusual" the court pointed to "the stark reality that the United States is the only country in the world" to execute people for crimes committed as a child and also noted "the overwhelming weight of international opinion against the juvenile death penalty." Some hailed the court's decision as an advance for

> **Did You Know That:**
>
> The word *genocide* was coined by Raphael Lemkin in *Axis Rule in Occupied Europe* (1944) and is derived from the Greek word *genos* (race, tribe) and the Latin suffix *cide* (to kill).

One source of international law is what is customary among the states. Sometimes, in turn, a country's courts apply such standards to its own system. This occurred when the U.S. Supreme Court ruled in *Roper v. Simmons* (2005) that executing an individual for crimes committed as a juvenile violated the Constitution's ban on "cruel and unusual punishments." In the ruling, the justices cited the fact that world custom did not allow such executions. Many people hailed the decision, but others, including the artist who drew this editorial cartoon, were appalled that the Supreme Court would be influenced by world opinion and practice. Should U.S. courts look abroad or stick strictly to U.S. law and opinions?

human rights. Others condemned it as a violation of U.S. sovereignty. One such critique charged that "globalization has [spawned] a variety of 'global networks,' including. . . . a transnational class of judicial . . . elites who are increasingly freed from the constraints of territoriality, national sovereignty, and domestic political constituencies, and whose judicial . . . decisions reflect a deterritorialized, 'cosmopolitan' moral sensibility" (Delahunty & Yoo, 2005:329).

General principles of law are a third source of international law. The ancient Roman concept of *jus gentium* (the law of peoples) is the basis of these principles, and the International Court of Justice (ICJ) depicts them as "the general principles of law recognized by civilized nations." Such language serves to incorporate "external" sources of law, such as the idea that freedom from unprovoked attack is an inherent human right, into international law. More than any other standard, it is for violating basic human rights principles that former president of Liberia Charles Taylor was arraigned in 2002 before an international tribunal in the Netherlands. Some charges against Taylor are for violating specific treaties such as the Geneva Conventions. But the indictment was also based on *jus gentium,* including such "crimes against humanity" as abetting "sexual slavery and any other form of sexual violence" and "other serious violations of international humanitarian law" including "conscripting or enlisting children under the age of 15 years into armed forces or groups."

Judicial decisions and scholarly writing also add to the law. In many domestic systems, legal interpretations by courts set precedent according to the doctrine of *stare decisis* (let the decision stand). This doctrine is specifically rejected in Article 59 of the Statute of the International Court of Justice, but in practice judges on both domestic and international courts cite other legal decisions in justifying their own rulings (Slaughter, 2003). Judicial review, deciding whether a government law or action is constitutional, is another possible role of international judicial bodies. Many domestic courts have this authority, and a few international courts also have it. The European Union's Court of Justice (commonly called the European Court of Justice, ECJ) can review decisions of the EU political and bureaucratic decision makers for compliance with EU law and to a degree can also review decisions of EU member-states by the same standard. Similarly, the European Court of Human Rights (ECHR), which was established in 1959 under Europe's Convention for the Protection of Human Rights and Fundamental Freedoms (1953) has some judicial review authority over the 46 countries in Europe that adhere to it. In a recent case, the Salvation Army brought suit against the city of Moscow, which refused to let the charitable organization operate on the grounds that its members wore uniforms and had ranks and, therefore, were members of a "paramilitary organization." Russian courts upheld the city's stance, but the ECHR rejected it in a 2006 decision. Russia's foreign minister angrily charged, "We consider some rulings of the European Court to be politicized," but then added, "Despite the fact that we do not agree with certain rulings of the court in principle, we do comply with them."[1]

International representative assemblies are arguably a fifth source of international law. Compared to the generally recognized preceding four sources of international law, the idea that laws can come from the UN General Assembly or any other international representative assembly is much more controversial. Clearly, to date, international law is not statutory. The General Assembly cannot legislate international law the way that a national legislature does. Yet, UN members are bound by treaty to abide by some of the decisions of the General Assembly and the Security Council, which makes these bodies quasi-legislative. Some scholars contend that resolutions approved by overwhelming majorities of the General Assembly constitute international law because such votes reflect international custom and/or the general principles of law. We may, then, be seeing the beginnings of legislated international law, but, at best, it is in its genesis. Certainly, UN resolutions and mandates often are not followed, but some would argue that this means that the law is being violated rather than that the law does not exist.

Multiple, reinforcing sources, while not a separate source of law, are perhaps the strongest foundation for international law. The prohibition of torture provides an example. There are numerous multilateral treaties that bar torture. Among them, the Convention against Torture and Other Cruel, Inhuman or Degrading Treatment or Punishment (1984) has been ratified by 75% of the world's countries. Various judicial decisions have found that torture violates the specific treaties and the general principles of law, and some individuals have been jailed for ordering or tolerating torture. The UN General Assembly has repeatedly and by lopsided margins condemned torture, and, as Figure 9.1 indicates, most people in most countries oppose torture. Whatever the view of an individual or a country, it is safe to say that torture violates international law.

Adherence to the Law

Adherence to the law is a third essential element of any legal system. As Figure 9.2 represents, people obey the law because of a mixture of voluntary and coerced compliance, and they enforce the law through a mixture of enforcement by central authorities and enforcement through self-help.

Compliance with the Law

Obedience to the law in any legal system—whether it is international or domestic, primitive or sophisticated—is based on a mix of voluntary compliance and coercion. *Voluntary compliance* occurs when the subjects obey the law because they accept its legitimacy, that is, people abide by rules because they accept the political authority that made the rules and/or agree with the rules themselves. *Coercion* is the process of gaining compliance through threats of violence, imprisonment, economic sanction, or other punishment.

Any society's legal system can be placed somewhere along the compliance scale between complete reliance on voluntary compliance and complete reliance on coercion. Voluntary compliance is usually more important, but there are wide variations among societies. Americans tend to obey the law voluntarily; in Myanmar (Burma) obedience to the laws of the country's military junta is primarily a function of force.

Compliance with international law is mostly voluntary rather than based on coercion. Pragmatic legitimacy is the key to international voluntary compliance. Countries recognize the need for a system that is made predictable by adherence to laws. Therefore they follow the law because it is in their interest that other countries

FIGURE 9.1   Opinions on Torture

Country	No torture	Unsure	Some torture
Italy	81%	5%	14%
France	75%	6%	19%
Australia	75%	3%	22%
Canada	74%	4%	22%
United Kingdom	72%	4%	24%
Germany	71%	8%	21%
South Korea	66%	3%	31%
Spain	65%	19%	16%
Egypt	65%	10%	25%
Chile	62%	16%	22%
Turkey	62%	14%	24%
Poland	62%	11%	27%
Brazil	61%	7%	32%
Average	**59%**	**12%**	**29%**
United States	58%	6%	36%
Philippines	56%	4%	40%
Iraq	55%	3%	42%
Ukraine	54%	17%	29%
Kenya	53%	9%	38%
Indonesia	51%	9%	40%
Mexico	50%	14%	36%
China	49%	14%	37%
Nigeria	49%	12%	39%
Israel	48%	9%	43%
Russia	43%	20%	37%
India	23%	45%	32%

Percent favoring: ■ No torture   ■ Unsure   ■ Some torture

World public opinion helps to establish international custom and general principles of law, which are sources of international law. Whether it is permissible to torture suspected terrorists and others for information has been widely debated since 9/11. A majority of the people in 18 of the 24 countries shown here and a majority of people overall oppose torture. There was no country in which a majority favored torture, and only 29% worldwide did so.

Data source: BBC World Service Poll, 2006; data courtesy of World Public Opinion.

FIGURE 9.2 Factors in Adherence to the Law

Enforcement by central authorities

United States (domestic)   Myanmar (domestic)

Voluntary compliance ←—————————————————→ Compliance through coercion

21st century world society   Pre-21st century world society

Enforcement through self-help

Two crucial factors in international law are how the law is enforced and what encourages compliance. These factors differ over time and for different societies.

follow it (Goldsmith & Posner, 2005; von Stein, 2005). For this reason, functional international law governing day-to-day relations between states has expanded. Legitimacy based on norms is less well established, but it has also grown. Aggression, violation of human rights, and other unacceptable practices still occur, but they increasingly meet with widespread condemnation. Unilateral military action is, for example, becoming ever more difficult for a country to launch without meeting severe criticism. Such events continue to occur, as the U.S.-led invasion of Iraq in 2003 indicates. But they occur much less often than they once did. Moreover, even countries determined to go to war will almost always make a concerted effort to gain international authorization, as the diplomacy leading up to the 2003 war again shows. Also, failure to win support subjects a country, no matter how just it thinks its cause, to extensive international criticism, which, as noted, was amply evident in global reactions to the 2003 war against Iraq. A very powerful country like the United States can ignore international opposition in the short run, but there may be a price to pay later. Washington found this out after the war when it mostly failed in its effort to get other countries to share the financial and military burden of occupying and rebuilding Iraq.

Enforcement of the Law

In all legal systems, enforcement relies on a combination of *enforcement through self-help* and *enforcement by central authorities*. Primitive societies begin by relying primarily on self-help to enforce laws and norms, then gradually develop central enforcement authorities. Advanced legal systems, like those found in stable countries, rely mostly on formal law enforcement organizations (usually the police) and sanctions (fines, prison) to compel compliance with the law. Still, even advanced legal systems recognize the legitimacy of such self-help doctrines as self-defense.

As a primitive society, the global community continues to focus on self-help for enforcement, and neither law enforcement organizations nor sanctions are well developed at the international level. Yet there is observable movement along the evolutionary path toward a more centralized system. For example, war criminals were punished after World War II. More recently, indictments have been handed down for war crimes in Bosnia and elsewhere, and some of the accused have been tried, convicted, and imprisoned. Economic and diplomatic sanctions are becoming more frequent and are sometimes successful, as discussed in chapter 8. Armed enforcement by central authorities is even less common and rudimentary. The UN-authorized military action against Iraq in 1991 and the NATO intervention in Kosovo in 1999 were more akin to an Old West sheriff authorizing posses to chase the outlaws than true police actions, but they did represent a step toward enforcement of international law by central authorities.

Adjudication of the Law

How a political system resolves disputes between its actors is a fourth element along the primitive-to-modern evolutionary scale. As primitive legal systems develop, the method of settling disputes evolves from (1) primary reliance on bargaining between adversaries, through (2) mediation/conciliation by neutral parties, to (3) **adjudication** (and the closely related process of arbitration) by neutral parties. The international system of law is in the early stages of this developmental process and is just now developing the institutions and attitudes necessary for adjudication.

International Courts

There are a number of international courts in the world today. Their genesis extends back less than a century to the Permanent Court of International Arbitration established by the Hague Conference at the turn of the century. In 1922 the Permanent Court of International Justice (PCIJ) was created as part of the League of Nations, and in 1946 the current **International Court of Justice (ICJ)**, which is associated with the UN, evolved from the PCIJ. The ICJ, or so-called World Court, sits in The Hague, the Netherlands, and consists of 15 judges, who are elected to nine-year terms through a complex voting system in the UN. By tradition, each of the five permanent members of the UN Security Council has one judge on the ICJ, and the others are elected to provide regional representation, as is evident in the accompanying map.

MAP
The International Court of Justice (ICJ)

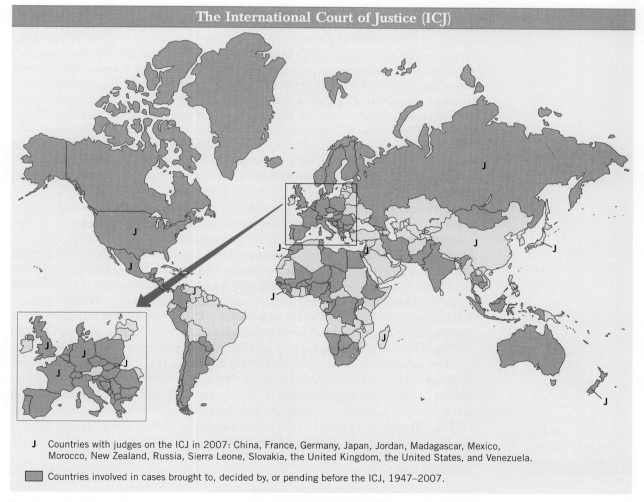

The International Court of Justice (ICJ)

J   Countries with judges on the ICJ in 2007: China, France, Germany, Japan, Jordan, Madagascar, Mexico, Morocco, New Zealand, Russia, Sierra Leone, Slovakia, the United Kingdom, the United States, and Venezuela.

Countries involved in cases brought to, decided by, or pending before the ICJ, 1947–2007.

The International Court of Justice (ICJ), which sits in The Hague, the Netherlands, draws both its judges and its caseload from around the world. This map shows the home countries of the ICJ's 15 judges in 2007, and the 84 countries that have been a party in cases before the ICJ between 1947 and 2007.

In addition to the ICJ, there are a few regional courts of varying authority and levels of activity: Europe's Court of Justice (ECJ) and European Court of Human Rights (ECHR), the Inter-American Court of Human Rights, the Central American Court of Justice, and the Community Tribunal of the Economic Community of West African States. None of these has the authority of domestic courts, but like the ICJ, the regional courts are gaining more credibility.

Jurisdiction of International Courts

Although the creation of international tribunals during this century indicates progress, the concept of sovereignty remains a potent barrier to adjudication. The authority of the ICJ extends in theory to all international legal disputes. Cases come before the ICJ in two ways. One is when states submit legal disputes that arise between them and other states. The second is when one of the organs or agencies of the UN asks the ICJ for an advisory opinion.

From 1946 through 2005, the court has averaged only about two new cases annually. Although this number has increased slightly in recent years, it remains relatively low, given the ICJ's broad jurisdiction and the number of issues facing the world and its countries. More than any other factor, the gap between the court's theoretical and actual roles is a matter of the willingness of states to submit to its jurisdiction, to litigate cases before it, and to abide by its decisions. Although all UN member-countries are technically parties to the ICJ statute, they must also sign the so-called *optional clause* agreeing to be subject to the compulsory jurisdiction of the ICJ. About two-thirds of all countries have not done so, and others that once were adherents to the optional clause have withdrawn their consent. For example, when Nicaragua filed a case in 1984 with the ICJ charging that U.S. support of the Contra rebels and its mining of Nicaraguan harbors violated international law, the United States argued that the charges were political and, therefore, that the court had no jurisdiction. When the ICJ ruled that it did have jurisdiction in the case, the United States withdrew U.S. consent to the optional clause.

It should be noted that nonadherence to the optional clause does not entirely exempt a country from ICJ jurisdiction. It is common for treaties to have a clause that commits the signatories to submit disputes arising under the treaty to the ICJ. One such treaty that has brought two suits against the United States in the ICJ in recent years is the Vienna Convention on Consular Relations (1963). In it the signatories, including the United States, agree to settle disputes arising from the treaty in the ICJ. The treaty permits countries to assist their citizens who have been accused of serious crimes in another country. Mexico in 2003 brought a case to the ICJ contending that various U.S. states were violating the treaty in several death penalty cases by not allowing German and Mexican consular officials access to 51 accused or condemned individuals.

The jurisdiction of the regional courts is determined by the charter under which each was founded. Of all the regional courts, the ECJ has the broadest jurisdiction. It can both review a wide range of actions by the EU executive and legislative institutions, and it can also determine whether the laws and actions of member-countries violate EU law. The caseload of the ECJ, shown in Figure 9.3 p. 285, is one mark of its substantial jurisdiction and growing importance.

Effectiveness of International Courts

There are some important limits on the impact of the ICJ and other international courts. The *jurisdictional limits* just discussed are one restraint. *Lack of enforcement* is a second impediment to the effectiveness of international courts. All courts rely heavily on the willingness of those within their jurisdiction to comply voluntarily or, when that fails, on a powerful executive branch to enforce court decrees. Effective domestic

SIMULATION
The World Court: Creating a
Trial for the Classroom

courts have these supports. By contrast, countries are often reluctant to follow the decisions of international courts, which, unlike the courts in most countries, are not backed up by an executive branch with powerful enforcement authority.

The International Court of Justice   The ICJ has only limited effectiveness. The UN Secretariat, which is the ICJ executive branch, does not have the authority or power to enforce ICJ rulings. This allows countries to sometimes ignore ICJ rulings. In *United States of America v. Mexico* (2003), for example, the ICJ upheld Mexico's claim that the United States was violating the Vienna Convention on Consular Relations (1963) by not ensuring that U.S. states allow arrested Mexican nationals to contact their country's diplomatic representatives. The ICJ directed the United States to do so and to provide relief to the prisoners who had been denied their treaty rights. The United States had ratified the convention in 1969, but the Bush administration responded to the ICJ ruling by announcing it was withdrawing U.S. consent to the treaty provision allowing the ICJ to decide cases under the treaty. Many legal experts doubted whether such presidential authority existed, but the Supreme Court inferentially upheld it by refusing to hear a case asking for enforcement on the ICJ decision.

Fortunately for global peace and justice, not all ICJ cases end this way. The ICJ sometimes does play a valuable role. Its rulings help define and advance international law. Furthermore, the court can contribute by giving countries a way, short of war, to settle a dispute once diplomacy has failed. The current ICJ case filed in 2004 by Bulgaria against Ukraine over their maritime border in the Black Sea provides a good example. More important than the details of the dispute is the fact that unlike many

FIGURE 9.3   EU Court of Justice Cases

Average annual number of new cases

504
428
347
152
48
20

1953–1959   1960s   1970s   1980s   1990s   2000–2005

One measure of the importance of the European Court of Justice is its workload. It has increased steadily as indicated in this figure showing the average number of new cases filed annually with the ECJ. The court has jurisdiction over EU legislative and executive actions as well as over some laws passed by EU member-countries.

Data source: European Court Annual Report, 2005.

Although the jurisdiction and impact of the ICJ are limited, the court still makes an important contribution by providing countries with an alternative other than war to settle disputes. This picture shows Nicaraguan troops getting ready to patrol the San Juan River area, which is in dispute with Costa Rica. In the past, countries might have used force to settle the issue. In this case, Costa Rica filed suit in the ICJ, and the case will probably be argued in 2007 or 2008.

disagreements throughout history over land and maritime borders that have resulted in war, the existence of the ICJ provides Bulgaria and Ukraine a way to come to a peaceful resolution.

ICJ advisory opinions also help resolve issues between IGOs and may even help establish general international law. In separate actions, the UN General Assembly and the World Health Organization each asked the ICJ to rule on the legality of using nuclear weapons. The court ruled in 1996 that "the threat or use of nuclear weapons would generally be contrary to the rules of international law applicable in armed conflict," except arguably "in an extreme circumstance of self-defense, in which the very survival of a state would be at stake." Among other impacts, the ICJ's ruling puts any leader considering the use of nuclear weapons except in extremis on notice that he or she could wind up the defendant in some future war crimes trial.

Regional Courts   Like the ICJ, this group of courts has struggled to make an impact. The two European regional courts, the ECJ and ECHR, have been by far the most effective of the regional courts.

The ECJ is particularly notable for the number of cases it hears (466 in 2005) and its authority to make decisions and to have those rulings followed in areas that were once clearly within the sovereign realm of states. As Figure 9.4 shows, the rulings of the ECJ have tended to promote EU integration by finding for plaintiffs who argue that the policy of one or another member-country violates EU law. In one example, the court ruled in 2001 that Germany was discriminating against women by barring them from serving in combat positions in the military. Soon thereafter, Germany changed its policy and its armed forces began to train women for combat. An important pending decision relates to Microsoft Corporation's appeal of a decision by the EU Commission fining the software giant $613 million for monopolistic practices such as bundling Media Player and other programs with its Windows operating system. That ruling will have a major financial impact on Microsoft and, by extension, on both the U.S. stock market and possibly the way that software is sold all over the world.

FIGURE 9.4   EU Court of Justice Decisions

Ruled for country
4%

Ruled against country
96%

The European Union's Court of Justice has promoted EU integration by usually ruling for plaintiffs who bring a case against their home country claiming that one of its laws or policies clashes with EU law. Of 136 ECJ rulings in 2005 on complaints that an EU member-country had failed to meet its obligations under EU law, the court found for the plaintiff and against the country in 131 cases, dismissing the complaint in only 5 cases.

Data source: Court of Justice Annual Report, 2006.

Evaluating Judicial Effectiveness   Given the limitations on the effectiveness of the ICJ and most regional courts, it is tempting to write them off as having little more than symbolic value. Such a judgment would be in error. Whatever the outcome of a specific case, there is evidence that countries are gradually becoming more willing to utilize the ICJ, the ECJ, and other international courts and to accept their decisions. The map of the ICJ's justices and cases on page 285 shows that countries around the world have justices on the court and almost half are or have been a party to its cases. Now more than 60 countries, including Canada, India, and the United Kingdom, adhere to the optional clause giving the ICJ compulsory jurisdiction over their international legal disputes. In sum, it is true that the international judicial system is still primitive, but each of the over 160 opinions issued by the PCIJ and the ICJ since 1922 is one more than the zero instances of international adjudication in previous centuries.

APPLYING INTERNATIONAL LAW AND JUSTICE

Law and justice are easy to support in the abstract, but it is much more difficult to agree on how to apply them. To examine this, we will look at issues of cultural perspective, issues of applying international law and standards of justice equally to states and individuals, and issues of pragmatism.

Law and Justice in a Multicultural World

As the international legal system evolves and expands to incorporate diverse peoples, one problem is the "fit" between differing culturally based concepts of law and justice. Most of international law and many of the prevailing ideas about justice that influence world politics are based on the concepts and practices of the West. This is a result of U.S. and European dominance, though, and does not mean that Western concepts are superior to those held in other parts of the world. Now, in a changing international system, Africans, Asians, Latin Americans, and other non-Westerners are questioning and sometimes rejecting law based on Western culture.

Law and Cultural Perspectives

Western and non-Western precepts of law and justice differ on numerous points. The *Western view* of law is based on principles designed to protect the long-dominant power of this bloc of states. Order is a primary point, as is sovereignty. Closely related is the theory of property, which holds that individuals (and states) have a "right" to accumulate and maintain property (wealth). This is a major philosophical underpinning of capitalism. Western law also relies heavily on the process and substance of law rather than on equity. Thus, there is an emphasis on courts and what the law is rather than on what is fair. One current controversy that touches on both property rights and "law versus fairness" involves patents held by Western pharmaceutical firms and the desire of less developed countries (LDCs) to produce low-cost generic equivalents. Patent drugs can cost 50 times more than generic equivalents, and the LDCs argue that it is unfair, whatever patent law may be, for the poor to suffer untreated because they cannot afford drugs that, in essence, are only available to wealthy individuals and countries. Additionally, LDCs worry that in the face of a quickly moving pandemic, the economically developed countries will keep most of a limited supply of drugs for themselves. One current dispute focuses on Indonesia and avian influenza. Drug research teams need samples of the latest strains of bird flu that have occurred to develop drugs to defeat the constantly mutating virus. Indonesian authorities have been refusing to supply samples, however, until they receive assurances that they will receive enough vaccine from the EDCs to fight bird flu if it begins to spread rapidly among humans. Many in the EDCs condemned Indonesia's stance, but it struck a positive chord in many LDCs. Commented one official of Thailand's Ministry of Health, "The Indonesian health minister is wise, and sending a strong message that, unless developing countries which are at the epicenter of the pandemic can be assured access to potential pandemic flu vaccines, they should not cooperate by sending out the viruses to [help develop the vaccines]."[2]

The *non-Western view* of international law is influenced by the different cultural heritage of non-Western states, by the recent independence of those states, and by

Web Link

Those interested in a career in international law or other applied aspects would do well to check out the Web site of the American Society of International Law at **www.asil.org/.**

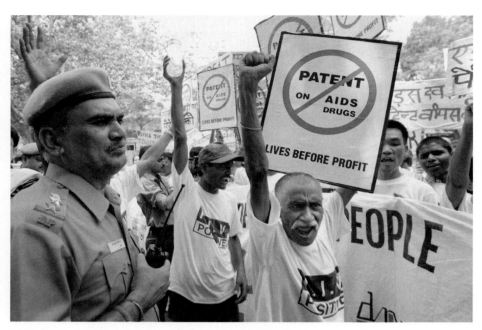

Much of international law, which is based on Western concepts, sometimes clashes with the views of justice held elsewhere. In less developed countries many believe that the high prices of U.S. patented medicines are unjust because they are unaffordable and therefore they should not be protected under international law. For example, these HIV-positive/AIDS victims in India are demonstrating against a patent held by U.S.-based Gilead Sciences Inc. for the AIDS drug Tenofovir Disoproxil Fumarate. The per-patient annual cost is close to $5,000. Gilead asserts that it offers the drug at $208 a year per patient to poor countries, but Doctors Without Borders claims that few of these countries actually get the drug.

the history of exploitation their people have often suffered at the hands of the West. These states claim that since they had little or no role in determining the rules that govern the international system, they are not necessarily bound by preexisting agreements, principles, or practices. Instead, they support sovereignty and reject aspects of international law that they claim are imperialistic abridgments of that principle. They insist on noninterference, which, for example, was one reason that many LDCs opposed the American and British intervention in Iraq in 2003. Whatever their sympathies with the plight of the Iraqis under Saddam Hussein, and whatever the LDCs' views of whether or not he posed an international danger, they are concerned that they could be the target of a future intervention. These states are keenly aware that such interventions are only launched against weaker countries and that the more powerful economically developed countries are, in effect, exempt from intervention no matter what the issue (Farer, 2003; Lang, 2003).

The LDCs also reject weighted voting schemes that favor the rich and powerful, such as those in the UN Security Council, the World Bank, and the International Monetary Fund. Emphasizing equity over the substance and process of law, for LDCs, the important standard is justice, especially in terms of what they consider to be the unjust maldistribution of wealth in the world that leaves a few countries wealthy and most countries poor. A final note about multiculturalism and its interface with international law and justice is that there are differing cultural perspectives on human rights. This topic is covered in detail in chapter 14.

Standards of Law for States and Individuals

Yet another issue related to the application of international law is whether states and individuals should be judged by the same standards (Erskine, 2003). Countries have generally not been held accountable for assassination, massive attacks on noncombatant civilians, and other acts that would be reprehensible if committed by individuals. Of course, we recognize differences between justifiable and inexcusable actions, but where do you draw the line? Some have argued that the state cannot be held to individual moral standards. Realist philosopher and statesman Niccolò Machiavelli wrote in *The Prince* (1513) that a ruler "cannot observe all those things which are considered good in men, being often obliged, in order to maintain the state, to act against faith and charity, against humanity, and against religion." Taking the opposite view, then Secretary of State Thomas Jefferson argued in 1793 that since a society is but a collection of individuals, "the moral duties which exist between individual and individual" also form "the duties of that society toward any other; so that between society and society the same moral duties exist as between the individuals composing them."

FIGURE 9.5   Sovereignty and Intervention

If a country seriously violates human rights, should its sovereignty bar UN intervention?

A large majority of Americans reject the idea that a country that is seriously abusing human rights should be able to claim immunity from UN intervention on grounds of sovereignty.

Data source: National Opinion Research Center poll, January 2005; data provided by The Roper Center for Public Opinion Research, University of Connecticut.

Questions about what principles should guide the foreign policy of countries are not abstract because countries are increasingly being held accountable for their actions in the court of international opinion and sometimes even in courts of law. Sovereignty, while still a powerful concept, is no longer a legal absolute. It is being eroded by a growing number of law-making treaties that limit states' actions and by changing attitudes that no longer see sovereignty as a defense against being called to account for illegal acts. As Figure 9.5 indicates, there is considerable public opinion to support UN Secretary-General Kofi Annan's argument that sovereignty "was never meant as a license for governments to trample on human rights and human dignity. Sovereignty implies responsibility, not just power."[3] Views such as this led, for instance, to international action that ended apartheid in South Africa (1993) and forced the military junta in Haiti to flee (1994), and to the NATO bombardment of Yugoslavia until it ceased its ethnic cleansing policy in Kosovo (1999), and to the international pressure on Sudan to stop the ethnic cleansing in Darfur. Also, as we will discuss further below, international tribunals are increasingly holding individual leaders responsible for their actions and for those of their subordinates.

There are numerous policy areas where international law is applicable to the actions of states. Many of these are covered in other chapters. Chapter 14, for example, examines the international law of human rights, and Chapter 15 takes up international law regarding the biosphere. Of all the policy areas, though, the oldest and arguably still the most critical is the law of war.

States, War, and International Law

Most of the early writing in international law focused on the law of war. This issue continues to be a primary concern of legal scholarship, but what has changed is that in addition to issues of traditional state-versus-state warfare, international law now also attempts to regulate revolutionary and internal warfare and terrorism.

Illustrating these diverse concerns is the long debate on when and how war can be justifiably fought. "Just war" theory has two parts: the cause of war and the conduct of war. Western tradition has believed that *jus ad bellum* (just cause of war) exists in cases where the war is (1) a last resort, (2) declared by legitimate authority, (3) waged in self-defense or to establish/restore justice, and (4) fought to bring about peace. The same line of thought maintains that *jus in bello* (just conduct of war) includes the standards of proportionality and discrimination. Proportionality means that the amount of force used must be proportionate to the threat. Discrimination means that force must not make noncombatants intentional targets (Rengger, 2002).

As laudable as limitations on warfare are, they present problems. One difficulty is that the standards of when to go to war and how to fight it are rooted in Western-Christian tradition. The parameters of *jus in bello* and *jus ad bellum* extend back to Aristotle's *Politics* (ca. 340 B.C.) and are especially associated with the writings of Christian theological philosophers Saint Augustine (Aurelius Augustinus, A.D. 354–430) and Saint Thomas Aquinas (1225–1274). As a doctrine based on Western culture and religion, not all the restrictions on war are the same as those derived from some of the other great cultural-religious traditions, including Buddhism and Islam (Silverman, 2002). Another difficulty with the standards of just war, even if you try to abide by them, is that they are vague and controversial (Butler, 2003).

Just Cause of War

WEB POLL
Just War?

The concept of *jus ad bellum,* the just cause of war, no longer exists only in theory. After World War II, the Nuremberg and Tokyo war crimes tribunals held German and Japanese leaders accountable for, among other things, waging aggressive war. More recently, UN tribunals have punished those found guilty of war crimes in the Balkans and in Rwanda. Moreover, the treaty that established the International Criminal Court (ICC) gives it jurisdiction over "the crime of aggression," which it defines as acts of war that are not consistent with the UN Charter. It recognizes "the inherent right of individual or collective self-defense if an armed attack occurs," but apart from that contingency requires that members "refrain in their international relations from the threat or use of force," and directs that other concerns be taken to the Security Council, which "shall determine the existence of any threat to the peace . . . or act of aggression and . . . decide what measures shall be taken." The Charter also stresses that every effort at a peaceful settlement should be made before resorting to force. These clauses closely parallel the traditional standards—that to be just, war must be the last resort, declared by legitimate authority, waged in self-defense or to establish/restore justice, and fought to bring about peace.

Because judging right from wrong is usually harder in an applied situation than in theory, it is worthwhile to examine a specific case, the U.S.-led invasion of Iraq in 2003, to explore the intricacies of *jus ad bellum* (Rodin, 2005). To find that Washington and London conducted a just war, the answer must be "yes" to all of the following questions:

Was the war the last resort? President George W. Bush argued it was. He told Americans, "For more than a decade, the United States and other nations have pursued patient and honorable efforts to disarm the Iraqi regime without war. . . . Every measure has been taken to avoid war."[4] President Jacques Chirac of France disagreed. He told reporters that he believed the "disarmament" of Iraq could "be done in a peaceful way," and that "War is always the worst of solutions. It's always a failure. . . . Everything should be done to avoid it."[5]

Was the U.S. action taken under legitimate authority? The United States made a legal argument that the authority to act did exist from the UN under earlier Security Council resolutions. As President Bush put it, "the Security Council did act in the early 1990s. Under Resolutions 678 and 687—both still in effect— the United States and our allies are authorized to use force in ridding Iraq of weapons of mass destruction." Taking an opposing view, Secretary-General Annan declared just before the war that if "action is taken without the authority of the Security Council, the legitimacy and support for any such action will be seriously impaired."[6]

Was the war waged in self-defense or to promote justice? Bush argued that the United States was threatened by the possibility that Iraq might give weapons of mass destruction (WMDs) to terrorists or someday use them itself. "The danger is clear," the president proclaimed, that the "United States has the sovereign authority to use force in assuring its own national security," and that "before it is too late to act, this danger will be removed." A statement issued by the heads of 60 Christian organizations disagreed. Explaining the group's position, Episcopal Bishop John B. Shane argued that just war theory differentiates between "anticipatory self-defense, which is morally justi- fied, and preventive war, which is morally prohibited." In the case of Iraq, he continued, "I don't see the threat from Iraq to the United States as an imminent threat, so . . . military action against Iraq is inappropriate."[7]

Was the war fought to bring about peace? Here again, President Bush argued "yes." He told Americans, "The cause of peace requires all free nations . . . to work to advance liberty and peace" in the Persian Gulf region. Taking a very different view of U.S. motives, one Middle East analyst contended that the U.S. invasion of Iraq "has to do with oil and to do with empire—getting control of Iraq's enormous oil resources." The analyst then explained her belief that the motive was "not just about importing oil to the United States." Instead, "The issue is control, undermining OPEC [Organization of Petroleum- Exporting Countries], and controlling access to oil for Germany, Japan, and the rest of Europe. This would give the United States tremendous political and economic clout in the rest of the world."[8]

When thinking about *jus ad bellum* and Iraq, fairness requires that you not apply 20-20 hindsight. If, in domestic law, a police officer shoots someone, the issue is not whether the person presented an immediate risk of injury or death to the officer, but whether the officer had reasonable cause to feel threatened. In the same way, the fact that WMDs were never found is not applicable to determining whether President Bush reasonably believed that a significant and imminent threat existed. Rather it is his intentions at the onset of the war, not the suc- cess or failure of the postwar occupation of Iraq in bringing about justice and peace that is the standard to apply.

After thinking about the just cause of war and about the circumstances of the U.S. invasion of Iraq in 2003, would you agree or disagree with the view of these people in Toulouse, France, that President George W. Bush should be considered a war criminal?

Web Link

The U.S. legal case for the Iraq war is in a State Department paper, "Decade of Defiance" (6/12/02), at **www.state.gov/p/ nea/rls/13456.htm.** An Australian government agency takes the opposite view, in "'Disarming' Iraq under International Law" (2/26/03) at **www.aph.gov.au/library/ pubs/cib/2002-03/03cib16.htm.**

Just Conduct of War

In the realm of *jus in bello,* there are some clear guidelines about what is unacceptable. The Hague Conferences (1899, 1907) and the Geneva Conventions (1949) set down some rules regarding impermissible weapons, the treatment of prisoners, and other matters. Other treaties have banned the possession and use of biological and chemical weapons, and the ICJ has ruled that in most circumstances the use of nuclear weapons would be illegal. Most recently, the treaty establishing the International Criminal Court includes an extensive list of war crimes.

Still, many uncertainties exist about *jus in bello.* The treatment of prisoners provides one example. American military personnel and CIA operatives violated just war standards in their egregious abuse of Iraqi prisoners of war at Abu Ghraib Prison and elsewhere in Iraq. But there is less clarity about whether the provision of the Geneva Conventions relating to the treatment of prisoners of war is applicable to the status of Iraqi insurgents or to Taliban and al Qaeda fighters captured by the United States in Afghanistan and held at the U.S. naval base at Guantánamo Bay, Cuba. The U.S. administration eventually took the position that Taliban prisoners were subject to the Geneva Conventions' provisions, but that al Qaeda members were "enemy combatants," not prisoners of war attached to a national military organization. As such, the White House reasoned, enemy combatants were not subject to protections of the Geneva Conventions and, furthermore, could not only be tried, but could be tried by special military courts (commissions) rather than civilian ones (de Nevers, 2006; Forsythe, 2006).

The Supreme Court ruled in *Hamdan v. Rumsfeld* (2006) that the president had no authority to create special military courts and that without such legislative authority, the legal process for prisoners like Salim Ahmed Hamdan, who had been Osama bin Laden's bodyguard, had to conform to existing U.S. law and to the Geneva Conventions. The controversy then moved to Congress, where there was a sharp struggle over how to treat enemy combatants. The resulting Military Commission Act of 2006 was largely a victory for the White House. The statute broadly defines an "unlawful enemy combatant" as anyone who has "purposefully and materially supported hostilities against the United States" and allows their criminal prosecution by military commissions. These courts can make use of hearsay evidence and even self-incrimination obtained by coercion falling short of "cruel, inhuman, or degrading treatment," and can bar the defendants from seeing evidence obtained from sensitive intelligence sources. The act does prohibit "grave breaches" of the Geneva Conventions, but it also gives the president authority to interpret the meaning of the Geneva Conventions and to bar prisoners from legally challenging these interpretations.

Another uncertainty about *jus in bello* involves how to gauge proportionality. Almost everyone would agree, for instance, that France, Great Britain, and the United States would not have been justified in using their nuclear weapons against Yugoslavia in 1999 to force it to withdraw from Kosovo or against Afghanistan in 2001 for refusing to surrender the al Qaeda terrorists. But what if Iraq had used chemical weapons against the forces of those three countries during the Persian Gulf War in 1991 or against U.S. and British forces in 2003? Would they have been justified if they had retaliated with nuclear weapons? Some people even argue that using nuclear weapons under any conditions would violate the rule of discrimination and would thus be unjust.

The *jus in bello* standard of discrimination also involves matters of degree rather than clear lines. There was heavy bombing, some of it in urban areas, during the

Web Link

The text of the Military Commissions Act of 2006 is available at **www.loc.gov/rr/frd/Military_Law/ pdf/PL-109-366.pdf.**

invasion of Iraq. American officials went to great lengths to give assurances that all efforts were being made to avoid unnecessary civilian casualties. For example, Secretary of Defense Donald H. Rumsfeld told reporters, "The targeting capabilities and the care that goes into targeting, to see that the precise targets are struck and other targets are not struck is as impressive as anything anyone could see—the care that goes into it, the humanity that goes into it."[9] Most Americans agree that the U.S. effort to avoid killing civilians was laudable, but some did not, as detailed in Figure 9.6. As this discussion illustrates, the law and justice of war remain highly controversial. Most observers would support neither of the two polar views: (1) that the United States could not be held responsible no matter what the level of civilian casualties; (2) that knowingly taking actions that would kill any civilians violates the standards of *jus in bello*. It is easier, however, to question two extreme views than to clearly demarcate the dividing line between what is just and unjust.

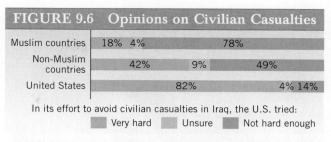

FIGURE 9.6   Opinions on Civilian Casualties

	Very hard	Unsure	Not hard enough
Muslim countries	18%	4%	78%
Non-Muslim countries	42%	9%	49%
United States	82%	4%	14%

In its effort to avoid civilian casualties in Iraq, the U.S. tried:

The Bush administration said, and 82% of Americans agreed, that the United States had tried very hard to avoid casualties to Iraqi civilians during the invasion in 2003. By contrast, 78% of respondents in mostly Muslim countries thought the United States had not tried hard enough. Opinions were much more mixed in predominantly non-Muslim countries, although a plurality agreed that the U.S. effort had been insufficient.

Note: The mostly Muslim countries were Indonesia, Jordan, Kuwait, Lebanon, Morocco, Pakistan, and Turkey. The mostly non-Muslim countries were Australia, Brazil, Canada, France, Germany, Great Britain, Israel, Italy, Russia, South Korea, and Spain.
Data source: Pew Research Center, "Views of a Changing World," 2003.

Applying International Law and Justice to Individuals

International law has begun to deal with the actions of individuals. It is possible to divide these developments into three topics: post–World War II tribunals, current international tribunals, and the International Criminal Court.

Post–World War II Tribunals

The first modern instances of individuals being charged with crimes under international law came in the aftermath of the horrors of World War II. In the Nuremberg and Tokyo war crimes trials, German and Japanese military and civilian leaders were tried for waging aggressive war, for war crimes, and for crimes against humanity. Twelve Germans and seven Japanese were sentenced to death. Many Germans and Japanese also went to prison. Three important precedents were established:

- Leaders are criminally responsible for war crimes they ordered.
- Leaders are responsible for war crimes committed by their subordinates unless the leaders tried to prevent the crimes or punished perpetrators.
- Obeying orders is not a valid defense for having committed atrocities.

Current International Tribunals

After an absence of nearly 50 years, international tribunals reemerged in the 1990s. The driving force was the atrocities that occurred in Bosnia and in Rwanda during the 1990s. In both places, people on all sides were abused, injured, and killed; in Bosnia it was the Muslims who were the principal victims and the Serbs who inflicted greater atrocities including death and degradation between 1990 and 1995. In Rwanda the Hutus were the murderous aggressors in 1994 and the Tutsis the victims of genocide in a ghastly slaughter that was revisited in the 2004 film *Hotel Rwanda* and the 2005 HBO special *Sometimes in April*.

Web Link

Links to documents of the Nuremburg trials and to such related sites as the U.S. Holocaust Memorial Museum are available on Yale University's Web site at **www.yale.edu/lawweb/avalon/imt/imt.htm.**

ANALYZE THE ISSUE
Nuremberg Trials

An advance in international law is that at least some of those accused of committing war crimes and crimes against humanity are now being brought before the international bar of justice. One of those is former Bosnian Serb senior officer Vidoje Blagojevic, here being guarded during his trial by an international tribunal in The Hague, the Netherlands. He was found guilty of committing genocide for his role in the massacre of more than 7,000 Muslims at Srebrenica in 1995 and was sentenced to 18 years in prison.

The atrocities in Bosnia and Rwanda shocked the conscience of the world and made it obvious, as a former UN official put it, that "a person stands a better chance of being tried and judged for killing one human being than for killing 100,000."[10] This jarring reality led to the establishment in 1994 of a tribunal for Bosnia and another for Rwanda to prosecute those who committed atrocities. The tribunal for the Balkans sits in The Hague, the Netherlands. The Rwanda tribunal is located in Arusha, Tanzania. In 1999, the authority of the Balkans tribunal was expanded to include war crimes in Kosovo.

The Hague tribunal has indicted over 160 individuals as war criminals, and 95% of them have been arrested. Charges have been dropped for about 10% of the accused. Of those whose trials were completed by mid-2005, 90% have been convicted, have received sentences of up to 40 years in prison, and have been transferred to other countries in Europe to serve their time (Kerr, 2004). The most important of the trials was that of Slobodan Milosevic, because of his prominence and stature as the former president of Yugoslavia. But he died in 2006 of heart failure before his trial was complete. The tribunal expects to complete all its initial trials by 2008 and the appeals process by 2010.

The Rwanda tribunal has made headway more slowly than its counterpart in The Hague, but it became the first international tribunal since the Tokyo War Crimes trials after World War II to punish a head of government when in 1998 former Rwandan Prime Minister Jean Kambanda pleaded guilty to genocide and was sentenced to life in prison. Through early 2007, the tribunal has completed the trials of 36 individuals, all but 5 of whom were convicted, and it was trying another 26 people. An additional 18 people who have been indicted are at large. Hutu civilian and military leaders have made up most, but not all, of the convicted and accused. For instance, a Belgian-born Italian citizen, Georges Henry Joseph Ruggiu, who was a radio journalist in Rwanda, was sentenced to 12 years in prison for inciting genocide. Among the many other chilling calls to mayhem he broadcast in 1994: "You [Tutsi] cockroaches must know you are made of flesh. . . . We will kill you."[11]

Web Link

Video presentations from the Special Court for Sierra Leone showing the prosecutors' cases against most of the defendants are available at **www.sc-sl.org/ video.html**.

Following a somewhat different pattern, a joint UN-Sierra Leone tribunal was established in 2002. It sits in Freetown, the capital of Liberia, and is guarded by UN peacekeepers. This court's mission is to deal with war crimes that occurred during the civil war in Sierra Leone (1996–2002). There three rebel groups killed and mutilated many thousands of noncombatants in an attempt to terrorize the population. Some of the tragedy that befell the country was captured in the 2006 film, *Blood Diamond*, with Leonardo DiCaprio. By early 2007, 11 individuals had been indicted, and 10 of them were in custody. These include former Liberian President Charles Taylor, who is charged with aiding the RUF (Romano, Nollkaemper, & Kleffner, 2005). Taylor's trial, which is slated to begin in late 2007, is considered so explosive that he has been moved to The Hague where a special session of the court will try him.

Yet another joint tribunal, this time linking the UN and Cambodia, is scheduled to begin proceedings in mid-2007. It is intended to prosecute members of Cambodia's former Khmer Rouge regime for the deaths of approximately 1.7 million people (about 25% of the population) during its reign of terror (1975–1979). It is uncertain, however, whether the tribunal will ever get under way, much less achieve any success amid the complexities of Cambodian politics. Among other issues, Cambodian Prime Minister Hun Sen was once a low-ranking Khmer Rouge official. Most recently, a joint tribunal was formed between the UN and Lebanon in May 2007. It is investigating specific crimes, such as the assassination of Prime Minister Rafik Hariri, and other examples of the alleged outside interference that has long destabilized the country and will prosecute those responsible if they can be identified.

The International Criminal Court

The advent of ad hoc international tribunals put war criminals at peril, and moving to the next step, the UN convened a global conference in 1998 to create a permanent International Criminal Court (ICC). During the conference, most countries favored establishing a court with broad and independent jurisdiction. A smaller number of countries, including the United States, wanted a much weaker ICC. The crux of U.S. opposition to a strong ICC was the fear that U.S. leaders and military personnel might become targets of politically motivated prosecutions. "The reality is that the United States is a global military power and presence. . . . We have to be careful that it does not open up opportunities for endless frivolous complaints to be lodged against the United States as a global military power," explained the U.S. delegate to the talks.[12] The U.S. stand drew strong criticism. For one, an Italian diplomat expressed disbelief "that a major democracy . . . would want to have an image of insisting that its soldiers be given license never to be investigated."[13]

While some of the U.S. reservations were met, over 80% of the 148 countries attending ultimately voted to create a relatively strong court. The treaty gives the ICC jurisdiction over wars of aggression, genocide, and numerous "widespread and systematic" crimes committed as part of "state, organization, or group policy" during international and internal wars. National courts remain the first point of justice, and the ICC is authorized to try cases only when countries fail to do so. The UN Security Council can delay a prosecution for a year, but the vote to delay or proceed is not subject to veto (Broomhall, 2004). The ICC treaty became operational in 2002 after 60 countries became party to it, and by July 2007 the number of ratifications stood at 105. They are shown in the map on page 298.

The countries party to the ICC treaty met in 2003 and elected the court's 18 judges and its other top officials, including its chief prosecutor. The court began to operate the following year. Several African countries soon filed complaints with the ICC in 2005 alleging atrocities by various forces in the long and gruesome fighting in the central African area that encompasses parts of the Democratic Republic of Congo, Uganda, Sudan, and the Central African Republic, and the ICC prosecutor has launched an investigation. ICC prosecutors began a second investigation in 2005 after the Security Council asked the ICC to address alleged criminal acts committed in the civil war afflicting the Darfur region of Sudan. That investigation led to an important first for the ICC. In 2007, its prosecutor issued the court's first arrest warrants, charging a Sudanese official who ironically is serving as minister for humanitarian affairs and a Janjaweed militia commander with 51 counts of crimes against humanity and war crimes. The Sudanese government immediately rejected the authority of the ICC, but other governments have derided other international tribunals only to later see the accused individuals turned over to the courts and tried.

There is little doubt that the creation of the ICC represents an important step in the advance of international law. However, French President Jacques Chirac was

MAP
Countries That Are Party
to the ICC Treaty

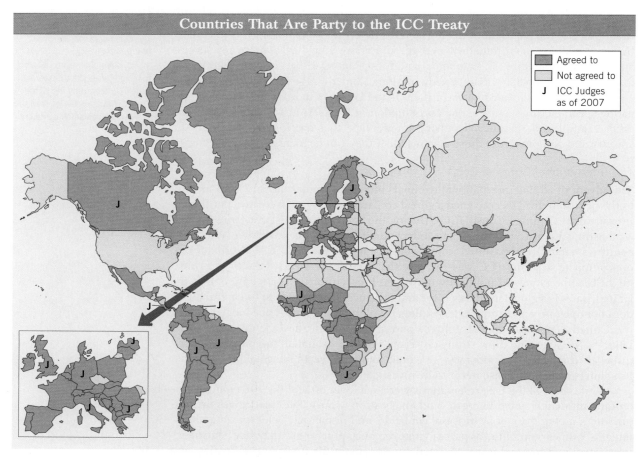

Countries That Are Party to the ICC Treaty

More than half the world's countries, including most of Europe and Latin America, have now ratified the International Criminal Court treaty. The widely dispersed home countries of the court's judges (16, with two vacancies) in 2007 is also evident. However, the absence among treaty adherents of such key countries as China, India, Russia, and the United States is a weak spot for the effectiveness of the ICC.

guilty of overstatement when he proclaimed, "Starting now, all those who might be inclined to engage in the madness of genocide or crimes against humanity will know that nothing will be able to prevent justice."[14] One issue is that the ICC treaty has not been ratified by 46% of the world states, including such notable countries as the United States, China, Russia, India, and Japan.

U.S. opposition remains adamant. President Clinton signed the treaty for technical reasons, but declined to submit it to the Senate for ratification unless revisions were made. Strengthening the U.S. stand, Congress passed the American Servicemembers' Protection Act (2002) barring U.S. cooperation with the ICC and authorizing the president to use force to free any American held by the ICC. President Bush agreed, and in 2002 the State Department informed the UN that the United States did not intend to ratify the ICC Treaty and did not believe there were any U.S. legal obligations arising from the earlier U.S. signing of the treaty. Bush also threatened to veto all UN peacekeeping operations unless the Security Council exempted U.S. troops from possible prosecution by the ICC. This issue has been resolved for now by a series

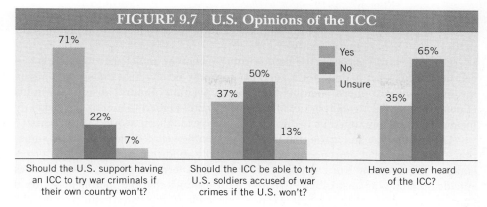

FIGURE 9.7   U.S. Opinions of the ICC

Legend: Yes / No / Unsure

Should the U.S. support having an ICC to try war criminals if their own country won't?
- 71%
- 22%
- 7%

Should the ICC be able to try U.S. soldiers accused of war crimes if the U.S. won't?
- 37%
- 50%
- 13%

Have you ever heard of the ICC?
- 65%
- 35%

If you ask Americans a general question about having the International Criminal Court try war criminals, as the left question does, you elicit a high level of support for the ICC. However, if you ask about the ICC possibly trying Americans accused of war crimes, as the middle question does, then only a minority of Americans supports the court. One reason for the varying opinions is, as the right question shows, that almost two-thirds of Americans admit that they have never even heard of the ICC.

Data sources: Left question: Chicago Council on Foreign Relations/German Marshall Fund poll, June 2002. Middle question: Pew Research Center poll, January 2003. Right question: Gallup International poll, 2005. All data provided by The Roper Center for Public Opinion Research, University of Connecticut.

of one-year exemptions given by the Security Council to U.S. peacekeepers. The Bush administration has also negotiated bilateral "Article 98 agreements" (for a clause in the ICC treaty) with 100 countries agreeing that neither country will surrender the other's citizens to the ICC for prosecution. Sometimes these agreements have been possible because another government agreed with Washington about the ICC; at other times U.S. threats of foreign aid cutoffs or other pressures have promoted agreement. What most Americans think about the ICC is unclear. As Figure 9.7 indicates, American views on the court depend on the question in part because most Americans know little or nothing about the ICC.

Given its hegemonic role in the international system, the U.S. position on the court is sure to be important—perhaps critical to its success (Johansen, 2006; Ralph, 2005). Little change is likely while President Bush is in office. But some observers are optimistic about the U.S. stance in the long run. For one, the ICC's chief judge, Philippe Kirsch of Canada, predicts, "In the end, this court is going to become universal. It will not happen overnight. I think it may take a few decades to reach universality, but I believe it is only a question of time."[15] Perhaps Judge Kirsch is correct and American attitudes will eventually change. Most movie viewers probably supported the idea of sending the odious dictator of the fictional country Matoba to the ICC for prosecution in the 2005 film *The Interpreter*, starring Nicole Kidman and Sean Penn, and perhaps in time the ICC will seem less threatening. Even the Bush administration relented just a bit when in 2005 it abstained rather than vetoed the Security Council resolution that referred the situation in Darfur to the ICC for investigation and possible prosecution.

The Pragmatic Application of Law and Justice

In a perfect world, all laws would be just, everyone would follow them and also act morally and ethically and insist that others conduct themselves in the same way. Moreover, everyone would agree on what is and is not legal, just, and moral. Finally, our choices would always be between good and evil, not between relative degrees of

JOIN THE DEBATE
The International Criminal Court: To Ratify or Not to Ratify–That Is the Question

good or of evil. Alas, our world is imperfect, and its standards and choices are often murky, which leads to several questions regarding the prudence of applying standards of law, justice, and morality.

Can ends justify means? One conundrum is whether an act that by itself is evil can be justified if it is done for a good cause. Some believe that ends never justify means. The philosopher Immanuel Kant took a position of **moral absolutism** in his *Groundwork on the Metaphysics of Morals* (1785) and argued that ends never justify means. He therefore urged us to "do what is right though the world should perish."

Others disagree and argue that faced with complex choices, lofty goals do sometimes justify acts that most people consider morally abhorrent in the abstract. Terrorism is a case in point. For example, the Middle East terrorist group Hamas justifies suicide bombings against Israeli civilians on the grounds that the "heroic martyrdom operations . . . represent the sole weapon" available to the Palestinian people. The statement goes on to argue that "denying the Palestinian people the right of self-defense and describing this as terrorism, which should have been linked with the occupation [of Palestinian lands by Israel], violates all laws and norms which granted the people the right of self-defense" and that "considering the Palestinian resistance as a terrorist act and an outlaw legitimizes occupation because it delegitimizes its resistance."[16]

On the other side are potential victims of terrorism who debate whether torturing terrorists to learn about and abort planned attacks is justified. The 1998 film *The Siege* took the moral position that FBI agent "Hub" Hubbard (Denzel Washington) was the hero when he arrested General William Deveraux (Bruce Willis) for torturing a suspected terrorist to death in an effort to gain information about other terrorist cells in a besieged New York City. But Americans are not so sure who was right. When asked the type of general question about torture posed in Figure 9.1 on p. 283, most Americans oppose torture. But a question in another poll that increased the incentive to torture by asking, "Would you support the use of torture by [the] U.S. if it might lead to the prevention of a major terrorist attack?" recorded 58% of Americans saying they would support torture compared to only 35% saying they would not.[17]

In practice, the primitive international political system can make the strict application of strong moral principles, adherence to international law, and other such altruistic acts unwise and even dangerous. Clearly, most of us do not take such an absolute position. Nor do we practice **amorality**. Instead, most people adhere to **moral relativism**. They believe that actions must be placed in context. For example, most Americans explicitly or implicitly accept capital punishment and the atomic bombings of Hiroshima and Nagasaki as somehow justifiable as retaliation or even as an unfortunate necessity to a better end. The problem, again, is where to draw the line, as presented to you in the box, "Would You Kill This Baby?"

Should we judge others by our own standards? The issue about whether to judge others rests on two controversies. The first, which we have already addressed, is whether one should apply standards of international law and justice given the divergent values of a multicultural world. Some claim that doing so is cultural imperialism; others believe that at least some universal standards exist.

A second objection to any country or even the UN imposing sanctions or taking other action against a country for committing supposedly illegal, unjust, or immoral acts is that it violates the sovereignty of the target country. Americans overwhelmingly supported sanctions and even war against Iraq for its invasion of Kuwait in 1990. Most Americans would have been outraged over the violation of U.S. sovereignty, however, had the UN imposed sanctions on the United States for what many, perhaps most people around the world considered the illegal U.S. invasion of Iraq in 2003.

Did You Know That:

A 2002 U.S. Justice Department memo relating to the treatment of terrorist suspects argued, "For an act to constitute torture as defined [in U.S. law] it must inflict pain . . . equivalent in intensity to the pain accompanying serious physical injury, such as organ failure, impairment of bodily function, or even death."

DEBATE THE POLICY SCRIPT

Would You Kill This Baby?

Here is a chance for you to rewrite the script and change the future. The setting is Braunau, Austria. The address is 219 Salzberger Vorstadt in a building known as the Gasthof zum Pommer. There, on Easter Sunday, April 20, 1889, a child was born. It is a year later, and you have been transported back to that time and are standing in the room with the baby boy. You are contemplating whether to kill him. If you do, you will be immediately transported back to the 21st century and will be beyond the reach of the Austrian police.

The infant is Adolf Hitler, the fourth child of Alois Schickel-gruber and Klara Hitler. He is a normal, cute baby, as you can see in the accompanying picture. His parents love him, and their neighbors think he is adorable. Unlike anyone in Braunau or indeed the world in 1890, however, you know what the future holds. Baby Adolf will grow up to be the führer of Nazi Germany. His Third Reich will be responsible for the horrors of World War II and the genocidal acts against Europe's Jews, Gypsies, and others. You know that he will die by his own hand on April 29, 1945, in a bunker in Berlin. But by then it will be too late. Tens of millions of people will have died in the war in Europe, and 6 million Jews and other people deemed undesirable will have perished in death camps. Should you kill the baby now?

All this may seem macabre, but the point is to struggle with whether the laudable ends sometimes justify distressing means. A moral absolutist would not kill young Hitler. Someone who is amoral would have no qualms about doing it. However, most people, probably including you, are moral relativists who make moral decisions in a context. Complicating the decision even further, the world drama is partly an improvisational play. So in a caution much like *Star Trek*'s "prime directive," interfering with the future is risky because you cannot be absolutely sure of what will occur in the 1930s and the first half of the 1940s if there is a simple marker reading "Adolf Hitler, 1889–1890" at the resting place in Braunau. Perhaps the Holocaust and World War II will never occur. Or perhaps a different German führer will come to power, one who is smart enough to defeat Great Britain before attacking Russia, to not declare war on the United States in 1941,

Would you kill this baby? Imagine you have been transported back to early 1890 and you are standing just out of this picture. No one but you and the child are present. The baby in this picture is Adolf Hitler, about a year after his birth on April 20, 1889, in Braunau, Austria. Given your knowledge of the horrors of World War II and the Holocaust, would you kill baby Adolf? Would the end justify the means? This and other issues are raised if one attempts to apply moral standards to the formation and conduct of foreign policy.

to focus on developing an atomic bomb, and to ultimately win World War II.

What Do You Think?

Should you rewrite the script of history by taking a pillow and smothering baby Adolf?

A third concern stems from what one might call "selective interventions." The United States has intervened in Haiti and Iraq at least partly in the name of democracy, yet in 1990 it sent its forces to defend Saudi Arabia and liberate Kuwait, both of which are ruled by distinctly undemocratic monarchies. Strong U.S. sanctions exist against communist Cuba, but U.S. trade with communist China is booming. Such selective interventions lead to a fourth concern: the suspicion that the invocation of international law and justice is often a smokescreen to cover old-fashioned imperialist intentions (Welsh, 2004; Orford, 2003).

Is it pragmatic to apply standards of legality and justice? Another objection to trying to apply moral principles is based on self-interest. Realists maintain that national interest sometimes precludes the application of otherwise laudable moral principles. They further contend that trying to uphold abstract standards of justice casts a leader as a perpetual Don Quixote, a pseudo knight-errant whose wish "To dream the impossible dream; to fight the unbeatable foe; . . . [and] to right the unrightable wrong," while appealing romantically, is delusional and perhaps dangerous. One danger is that you waste your reputation, your wealth, and the lives of your soldiers trying to do the impossible. A second peril springs from the reality that since not all states act morally, those who do are at a disadvantage: "Nice guys finish last."

Those who disagree with this line of reasoning contend that it fails the test of courageously standing up for what is right. They might even recall the remonstration of President John F. Kennedy, who, evoking Dante Alighieri's *The Divine Comedy* (1321), commented, "Dante once said that the hottest places in hell are reserved for those who in a period of moral crisis maintain their neutrality."[18] More pragmatically, advocates of applying principles of law and justice contend that greater justice is necessary for world survival. This argument deals, for example, with resource distribution. It contends that it is unjust to support a system in which a large part of the world remains both impoverished and without self-development possibilities. The inevitable result, according to this view, will be a world crisis that will destroy order as countries fight for every declining resource.

One way out of the dilemma about when and to what degree law, justice, and other principles should apply to foreign policy may be to begin with the observation that it is not necessary to choose between moral absolutism and amorality. Instead, there is a middle ground of moral relativism that relies on **moral pragmatism** as a guiding principle. There is a secular prayer that asks for the courage to change the wrongs one can, the patience to accept the wrongs that one cannot change, and the wisdom to know the difference. From this perspective, a decision maker must ask, first, whether any tangible good is likely to result from a course of action and, second, whether the good will outweigh negative collateral consequences. By the first standard, taking high-flown principled stands when it is impossible or unlikely that you will affect the situation is quixotic. By the second standard, applying standards of justice when the overall consequences will be vastly more negative also fails the test of prudence. But not taking action when change is possible and when the good will outweigh the bad fails the test of just behavior.

THE FUTURE OF INTERNATIONAL LAW AND JUSTICE

The often anarchic and inequitable world makes it easy to dismiss idealistic talk of conducting international relations according to standards of international law and justice. This view, however, was probably never valid and certainly is not true now. An irreversible trend in world affairs is the rapid growth of transnational interaction among states and people. As these interactions have grown, so has the need for regularized behavior and for rules to prescribe that behavior. For very pragmatic reasons, then, many people have come to believe, as one analyst notes, that "most issues of transnational concern are best addressed through legal frameworks that render the behavior of global actors more predictable and induce compliance from potential or actual violators" (Ratner, 1998:78). The growth of these rules in functional international interactions has been on the leading edge of the development of international law. Advances in political and military areas have been slower, but here too there has been progress. Thus, as with the United Nations, the pessimist may decry the glass as less than half full, whereas, in reality, it is encouraging that there is more and more water in the previously almost empty glass.

All the signs point to increasing respect for international law and a greater emphasis on adhering to at least rudimentary standards of justice. Violations of international standards are now more likely to draw criticism from the world community. It is probable, therefore, that international law will continue to develop and to expand its areas of application. So too will moral discourse have an increasing impact on the actions of international actors. There will certainly be areas where growth is painfully slow. A particular barrier is the change in the U.S. attitude from being a champion of international law and legal institutions after World War II to being a skeptic today (Murphy, 2004). There will also be those who violate the principles of law and justice and who sometimes get away with their unlawful and unjust acts. But, just as surely, there will be progress.

CHAPTER SUMMARY

FUNDAMENTALS OF INTERNATIONAL LAW AND JUSTICE

1. International law can be best understood as a primitive system of law in comparison with more developed domestic law. There are only the most rudimentary procedures and institutions for making, adjudicating, and enforcing international law. This does not mean, however, that international law is impotent, only that it is in an earlier stage of development than domestic law.

2. As a developing phenomenon, international law is dynamic and has been growing since the earliest periods of civilization. This growth accelerated in the 20th century because increasing levels of international interaction and interdependence required many new rules to govern and regularize contacts in trade, finance, travel, communication, and other areas. The possible consequences of war have also spurred the development of international law.

3. Thus far, international law is most effective when it governs functional international relations. International law works least well in areas of "high politics," where the vital interests of the sovereign states are at stake. Even in those areas, though, international law is gradually becoming more effective.

4. Justice is another factor in establishing the rules of the international system. It acts as a guide to action and as the basis for some international law.

THE INTERNATIONAL LEGAL SYSTEM

5. The international legal system has four essential elements: its philosophical roots, lawmaking, adherence, and adjudication.

6. The roots of law for any legal system may come from external sources, such as natural law, or from within the society, such as custom.

7. Regarding lawmaking, international law springs from a number of sources, including international treaties, international custom, general principles of law, and international representative assemblies. Some scholars argue that resolutions and other pronouncements of the UN General Assembly should be included as a significant influence.

8. Regarding adherence, international law, again like primitive law, relies mainly on voluntary compliance and self-help. Here again, though, there are early and still uncertain examples of enforcement by third parties, a feature that characterizes more advanced systems.

9. The fourth essential element of a legal system, adjudication, is also in the primitive stage in international law. Although there are a number of international courts in the world today, their jurisdiction and their use and effectiveness are limited. The International Court of Justice and other such international judicial bodies represent an increasing sophistication of international law.

APPLYING INTERNATIONAL LAW AND JUSTICE

10. In a culturally diverse world, standards of international law and justice have encountered problems of fit with different cultures. Most current international law and many concepts of justice, such as the stress on individualism, are based on Western ideas and practices, and many non-Western states object to certain aspects of international law as it exists.

11. The changes in the world system in this century have created a number of important issues related to international law. Among these are the status of sovereignty, the legality of war and the conduct of war, rules for governing the biosphere, and observing and protecting human rights.

12. International law has been interpreted as applying to states. Now it is also concerned with individuals.

Primarily, it applies to the treatment of individuals by states, but it also has some application to the actions of individuals. Thus people, as well as countries, are coming to have obligations, as well as rights, under international law.

13. It is not always possible to insist on strict adherence to international law and to high moral standards, yet they cannot be ignored. One middle way is to apply principles pragmatically.

THE FUTURE OF INTERNATIONAL LAW AND JUSTICE

14. With the growth of international interaction in the last century, international law has developed, and rudimentary standards of justice are being established. Although this growth has sometimes been slow, there will definitely be continued progress in the future.

For simulations, debates, and other interactive activities, a chapter quiz, Web links, and much more, visit **www.mhhe.com/rourke12/** and go to chapter 9. Or, while accessing the site, click on Course-Related Headlines and view recent international relations articles in the *New York Times*.

KEY TERMS

adjudication
amorality
codify
functional relations

ideological/theological school of law
International Court of Justice (ICJ)

jus ad bellum
jus in bello
moral absolutism
moral pragmatism

moral relativism
naturalist school of law
pacta sunt servanda
positivist school of law

National Security: The Traditional Road

Be wary then; best safety lies in fear.
—William Shakespeare, *Hamlet*

Cry "Havoc," and let slip the dogs of war.
—William Shakespeare, *Julius Caesar*

This image of this U.S. soldier grieving for a comrade recently killed in action in Iraq bears vivid testimony to the truth of U.S. Civil War General William Tecumseh Sherman's declaration, "War is hell!"

WAR IS AN ENIGMA. On the one hand, we have condemned it throughout history, and that refrain has become particularly persistent in recent centuries (Mueller, 2004). "O war, thou son of hell," Shakespeare has a character cry out in *King Henry VI, Part 2.* "War is hell," General William Tecumseh Sherman lamented, remembering the U.S. Civil War and "the shrieks and groans of the wounded." And General of the Army Dwight D. Eisenhower confessed, "I hate war . . . its brutality, its futility, its stupidity." War may be hell, but it is also a regular part of our political world. Perhaps that is because insecurity has also always been part of the human condition. "We make war that we may live in peace," Aristotle suggested in his *Nicomachean Ethics* (325 B.C.).

In this and the following chapter we will explore the human search for safety. National security, the traditional approach, is the focus of this chapter. It takes up the history and causes of warfare between states. Then chapter 11 contemplates international security, an alternative path to safety. As you will see, some people believe that security can be best achieved by disarming, not arming, and that creating collective security forces is a better approach than traditional self-reliance. As in this text's other juxtapositions of traditional and alternative approaches, the choice is not really A or B. There are no conceivable circumstances under which traditional politics would soon disappear. However, it is almost as unlikely that the status quo will remain unchanged and that alternative approaches to world politics, which are already under way, will not gain even further prominence. Thus the task for you while reading these two chapters is to decide what mix of the traditional and alternative approaches offer the best path to security.

WEB POLL
Your Knowledge of History

WAR AND WORLD POLITICS

Whatever the ultimate cost or morality of war, there is an element of truth to the classic observation of scholar Max Weber in "Politics as a Vocation" (1918): "The decisive means for politics is violence." Given the regrettable but regular role that force plays in the conduct of international relations, it behooves us to examine war and other forms of transnational political violence. Before beginning, it is important to note that chapter 8 on national power contains several elements that relate to our discussion here. One is a review of the elements of military power. A central focus of that commentary is the difficulty of measuring a country's military strength and comparing it to other countries or estimating its usefulness in a particular situation. For instance, having the world's most powerful air force has meant almost nothing to the power equation in Iraq. Chapter 8 also discusses the application of military power as an instrument of national diplomacy. The core of that discussion is that the military instrument is applied in a wide variety of ways ranging from serving as an unmentioned but still present backdrop to negotiations, through threats, to an escalating array of uses beginning with mobilizations and other ominous moves and ending with full-scale war.

War: The Human Record

War is as ancient as humanity. One reasonable number, as shown in Figure 10.1, is that there were almost 1,000 wars during the millennium that just ended. Looking even farther back, it is possible to see that the world has been totally free of significant interstate, colonial, or civil war in only about 1 out of every 12 years in all of

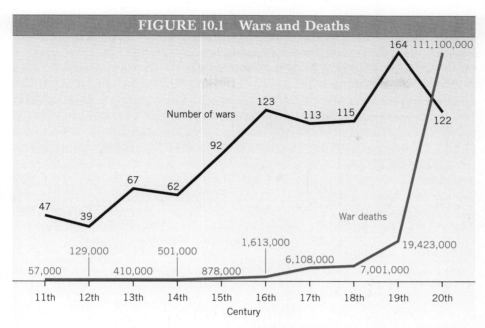

FIGURE 10.1 Wars and Deaths

This figure shows the long-term trend in the rise of both the frequency and severity of war. Beginning in the year 1000, the number of wars in each century has usually increased. The soaring death toll of the 20th century's wars, which accounted for 75 percent of the millennium's total, is a truly alarming figure.

Data sources: Eckhardt (1991); author. Eckhardt defines a war as a conflict that (1) involves a government on at least one side and (2) accounts for at least 1,000 deaths per year of the conflict.

recorded human history. The data also shows that war is not a tragic anachronism waged by our less civilized ancestors. To the contrary, political violence continues. Two ways to gauge this are by frequency and severity.

Frequency provides bad news. Since the year 1000, as Figure 10.1 shows, wars between countries have become more frequent, with some 30% occurring since 1800. Although the frequency of war in the 1900s declined somewhat from the horrific rate in the 1800s, and that ebbing has continued into the early 21st century, the number of civil wars increased (Eriksson & Wallensteen, 2004). This means that the overall incidence of interstate and intrastate warfare remains relatively steady.

Severity is worse news. Again as evident in Figure 10.1, about 150 million people have died during wars since the year 1000. Of the dead, an astounding 75% perished in the 20th century and 89% since 1800. Not only do we kill more soldiers, we also now kill larger numbers of civilians (Lacina, Gleditsch, & Russett, 2006). During World War I, six soldiers died for every civilian killed (8.4 million soldiers and 1.4 million civilians). World War II killed two civilians for every soldier (16.9 million troops and 34.3 million civilians). The worst news may lie ahead. A nuclear war could literally fulfill President John F. Kennedy's warning in 1961 that "mankind must put an end to war, or war will put an end to mankind."

The Causes of War: Three Levels of Analysis

Why war? This question has challenged investigators over the centuries (Caplow & Hicks, 2002). Philosophers, world leaders, and social scientists have advanced many different theories about the single root cause of war, but it is more likely that there is

MAP
International Conflicts in the
Post–World War II World

International Conflicts in the Post–World War II World

War is a continuing reality in the international system. As you can see, however, international wars do not occur equally around the world. Instead, the Middle East has seen the most conflicts, and the Balkans, Africa, and south-central Asia are also troubled regions.

	Conflict[1]	Start Date	Major Belligerent Countries[2] (in alphabetical order)	
1	Palestine	1948	Egypt Iraq Israel	Jordan Lebanon Syria
2	Korean	1950	China North Korea South Korea	UN, U.S., and 11 other countries
3	Soviet-Hungarian	1956	Hungary	Soviet Union
4	Sinai	1956	Egypt France	Israel United Kingdom
5	Sino-Indian	1962	China	India
6	Kashmir	1965	India	Pakistan
7	Vietnam	1965	North Vietnam South Vietnam	United States
8	Six-Day	1967	Egypt Israel	Jordan Syria
9	Soviet-Czech	1968	Czechoslovakia	Soviet Union
10	Football	1969	El Salvador	Honduras
11	Indo-Pakistani	1971	India	Pakistan
12	Yom Kippur	1973	Egypt Israel	Syria
13	Cyprus	1974	Cyprus	Turkey
14	Ogaden	1977	Ethiopia	Somalia
15	Cambodian-Vietnamese	1978	Cambodia	Vietnam
16	Ugandan-Tanzanian	1978	Tanzania	Uganda
17	Afghanistan	1979	Afghanistan	Soviet Union
18	Persian Gulf	1980	Iran	Iraq
19	Angola	1981	Angola Cuba	South Africa
20	Falklands	1982	Argentina	United Kingdom
21	Saharan	1983	Chad	Libya
22	Lebanon	1987	France Israel Lebanon	Syria United States
23	Panama	1989	Panama	United States
24	Persian Gulf	1990	Iraq UN	U.S. and 7 other countries
25	Yugoslavia	1990	Bosnia-Herzegovina	Croatia Serbia
26	Peruvian-Ecuadorian	1995	Ecuador	Peru
27	Albania	1995	Albania	Serbia Montenegro
28	Rwanda	1995	Burundi	Rwanda
29	East Timor	1995	Indonesia	Timorese insurgency
30	Cameroon	1996	Cameroon	Nigeria
31	Iraq	1998	Great Britain Iraq	United States
32	Democratic Republic of the Congo	1998	Angola Chad Congo	Namibia Sudan Zimbabwe
33	Eritrean-Ethiopian	1998	Eritrea	Ethiopia
34	Kosovo	1999	NATO	Yugoslavia
35	Chechnya	1999	Chechnya	Russia
36	"War on Terrorism"	2001	Afghanistan (Taliban) al-Qaeda organization Great Britain	United States
37	Iraq	2003	Great Britain Iraq	United States
38	Sudan-Darfur Rebels	2004	AU Darfur Rebels	Sudan UN

[1] "Conflict" implies at least 1,000 battle deaths.
[2] "Belligerent" implies country supplied at least 5% of the combat troops in the conflict.

International Conflicts in the Post-World War II World

✷ Area of conflict

no one reason why people fight. Given this, it is reasonable to discuss the causes of war by classifying them according to system-level analysis, state-level analysis, and individual-level analysis, as detailed in chapter 3.

System-Level Causes of War

Wars may be caused by a number of factors related to the general nature of the world's political system (Cashman, 1999). To illustrate that here, we can touch on four system-level variables.

The distribution of power. As noted in chapters 3 and 8, some analysts believe that the stability of the international system is influenced by factors such as the system's number of poles (big powers), their relative power, and whether the poles and their power are stable or in flux (Powell, 2006). Conflict is likely to occur, for example, when a system is experiencing a significant power transition because some powers are rising and others are declining. To a degree, for instance, the onset of World War I was about the attempt of the once powerful, but then moribund Austro-Hungarian Empire to defend its fading status as a big power. Postwar alliances that concentrate power by bringing victorious major countries together have also been found to be prone to conflict with other countries and alliances.

The anarchical nature of the system. In a sense, wars occur because there is no central authority to restrain them and to protect countries. Unlike domestic societies, the international system has no regularized and effective process of law creation, enforcement, or adjudication. When the gap between U.S. demands on Iraq and what Iraq was willing to do proved unbridgeable, there was no court that could either subpoena Iraqi records or enjoin an American attack. War ensued. This self-help system causes insecurity. Therefore, countries acquire arms in part because other countries do, creating a tension-filled cycle of escalating arms —→ tensions —→ arms —→ tensions.

System-level economic factors. The global pattern of production and use of natural resources is one of the system-level economic factors that can cause conflict. For example, when Iraq endangered the main sources of petroleum production by attacking Kuwait and threatening Saudi Arabia in 1990, a U.S-led coalition of countries dependent on petroleum rushed to defend the Saudis and to liberate the Kuwaitis (and their oil). The gap between wealthy and poor countries is another system-level factor. Some analysts believe that this wealth gap is one reason that a great deal of terrorism is rooted in the South.

System-level biosphere stress. Overconsumption of biosphere resources is yet another possible system-level cause of conflict. Water provides one example. This basic resource is becoming so precious in many areas, as related in chapter 15, that countries might soon go to war with one another over disputes about water supplies.

State-Level Causes of War

War may result from the nature of states. There are several ways that the internal processes and conditions of countries may lead to war (Finnenmore, 2004).

Militarism. One theory is that states inherently tend toward militarism. The argument is that as warfare required more soldiers as well as more and increasingly expensive weapons, it created a need for political units with larger populations and economies. This gave rise to the state.

Externalization of internal conflict. A theme found in movies such as *Wag the Dog* (1997, with Robert De Niro and Dustin Hoffman) and *Canadian Bacon* (1995, with Alan Alda and John Candy) is that of a faltering government trying to stay in power by fomenting a foreign crisis in order to rally the populace and divert its attention (Foster & Palmer, 2006). Scholars call this ploy diversionary war or the externalization of internal conflict (Kellett, 2006; Meernik & Ault, 2005; Pickering & Kisangani, 2005). Evidence indicates, for instance, that revolutionary regimes will attempt to consolidate their power by fomenting tension with other countries (Mitchell & Prins, 2004; Andrade, 2003). It is also the case that countries are more likely to go to war while they are experiencing times of economic distress. It is widely believed, for example, that Argentina's decision to try to seize the nearby Falkland Islands in 1982 was an attempt by Argentina's faltering military regime to divert the attention of its people away from the sagging economy.

Individual-Level Causes of War

It may be that the causes of war are linked to the character of individual leaders or to the nature of the human species.

Human characteristics. Those who have this perspective believe that although it is clear that human behavior is predominantly learned, there are also behavioral links to the primal origins of humans (Rosen, 2004). Territoriality, which we examined in chapter 3, is one such possible instinct, and the fact that territorial disputes are so frequently the cause of war may point to some instinctual territoriality in humans. Another possibility, some social psychologists argue, is that human aggression, individually or collectively, can stem from stress, anxiety, or frustration (Senese, 2005). The backlash of German society during the 1930s to its defeat and humiliation after World War I in the 1920s is an example.

Individual leaders' characteristics. The personal traits of leaders may also play a role in war (Bennett & Stam, 2004). A leader may have a personality that favors taking risks, when caution might be the better choice, or might have a psychological need for power. While discounting some of the more strident characterizations of Saddam Hussein as a madman, most personality analyses characterized him as driven to seek power and to dominate, traits that made it hard for him to cooperate completely with UN arms inspectors. Individual experiences and emotions also play a role, and it is not fatuous to ask what the impact of Iraq's attempt to assassinate former President George H. W. Bush in 1993 was on his son's view of that country once he became president.

Before leaving our discussion of the causes of war, it is important to note that whatever its root cause(s), war continues as a political instrument at least in part because it works. Countries that threaten or attack another country sometimes get their way, and, in particular, big powers win more often than not whether they begin a war or are attacked. Thus to some degree the decision for war is a rational process, one in which countries decide that the ever-present risks of war are worth the potential gains that victory will bring (Langlois & Langlois, 2006.)

The Changing Nature of War

Whatever its causes, warfare has changed greatly over the centuries. Technology, nationalism, participation, cost, and strategy are five dimensions of change.

Technology has rapidly escalated the ability to kill. Successive "advances" in the ability to deliver weapons at increasing distances and in the ability to kill ever more people with a single weapon have resulted in mounting casualties, both absolutely and as percentages of soldiers and civilians to total populations of the countries at war.

Nationalism has also changed the nature of war. Before the 19th century, wars were generally fought between the houses of nobles with limited armies. The French Revolution (1789) changed that. Wars were now fought between nations, with increases in intensity and in numbers involved. France proclaimed that military service was a patriotic duty and instituted the first comprehensive military draft in 1793. The idea of patriotic military service coupled with the draft allowed France's army to be the first to number more than a million men.

The scope of war has expanded as a result of technology and nationalism. Entire nations have become increasingly involved in wars. Before 1800, no more than 3 of 1,000 people of a country participated in a war. By World War I, the European powers called 1 of 7 people to arms. Technology increased the need to mobilize the population for industrial production and also increased the capacity for, and the rationality of, striking at civilians. Nationalism made war a movement of the masses, increasing their stake and also providing justification for attacking the enemy nation. Thus, the lines between military and civilian targets have blurred. Modern technology has, at other times, also reversed the connection between war effort and the nation (Coker, 2002). The high-tech forces deployed by the United States and its allies against Iraq (1991, 2003) and Yugoslavia (1995, 1999) and the quick victories over the opposing regular military forces that ensued largely separated the war effort from the day-to-day lives of Americans.

Participation by diverse individuals in war is a fourth area of change. Some of the changes in who is swept up in war relate to the discussion above regarding nationalism, the justification for both military drafts and attacks on factories and other facilities and areas heavily populated by civilians. Changing social attitudes are also impacting who serves in the military. Homosexuals were once universally banned from military service. Now some 24 countries such as Canada, Germany, and Thailand permit gays to openly serve. Since 1993 the United States under its "don't ask, don't tell" policy has tolerated gay members in its military as long as they do not disclose their sexual orientation. That policy is weakening. A 2006 poll found 60% of Americans in favor of allowing gays to serve openly in the military, with 32% opposed and 8% unsure.[1] Moreover, the argument that gays will disrupt military discipline has been contradicted by the uneventful integration of homosexuals into the ranks of other countries' armed services and by the changing views of some top-ranking U.S. officers. For example, retired General John Shalikashvili, who served as chairman of the Joint Chiefs of Staff (1993–1997) and opposed gays in the military, wrote in a 2007 op-ed piece, that "I now believe that if gay men and lesbians served openly in the United States military, they would not undermine the efficacy of the armed forces."[2]

Unlike gays, women have long served in the military, but what is changing is their increased presence on the field of battle. There are a few countries, such as Finland, in which women serve in all military units, including the three ground combat units: armor, artillery, and infantry. Here too, however, restrictions on women's roles have gradually declined because of changing social attitudes. A majority of Americans (67%) are now willing to have women serve in unspecific "combat jobs," although some ambivalence is evident in the fact that 54% oppose having women serve among "ground troops who are doing most of the fighting."[3]

Also, most Americans (55%) remain opposed to having women subject to the draft. How do you view the issues taken up in the box, Debate the Policy Script, "Should Women Serve in Combat?"

Costs of war have also escalated. Preparations, waging war, and repairing the damage have always been expensive, but the cost and destructive power of modern war technology have increased the price considerably. Precisely measuring the cost of a war is impossible, but one estimate of major U.S. wars and their costs calculated in 1990 dollars to adjust for inflation are the Revolutionary War ($1 billion), the Civil War ($44 billion), World War I ($197 billion), and World War II ($2.1 trillion).[4] Similarly the costs of the other U.S. wars have also generally gone up: War of 1812

DEBATE THE POLICY SCRIPT

Should Women Serve in Combat?

Throughout history, most of the women killed, wounded, or otherwise traumatized in war have been civilian noncombatants. Now women soldiers are increasingly becoming casualties. Lori Piestewa was the first of many U.S. servicewomen to fall in the Iraq War.

Private first class Piestewa was a member of the U.S. Army's 507th Maintenance Company who was serving her country as her father had in Vietnam and her grandfather had in World War II. Pfc Piestewa was 23, a Hopi from Tuba City, Arizona, and the mother of a son (age 4) and a daughter (age 3).

On March 23, soon after the war began, she was part of a convoy providing support for the U.S.-British offensive. Iraqi forces attacked the U.S. unit near Nasiriyah, Iraq, killing Piestewa and several other American soldiers. Her fate highlights the reality that the chances of women being killed, captured, or wounded as combatants have grown as the United States and many other countries have increasingly gender-integrated their armed forces. Some applaud this change. Others want to take it even further by abolishing the rules in the U.S. and most other armed forces that bar women from infantry, artillery, and armored units. Still others find women in combat abhorrent and would eliminate the possibility.

How would you decide policy regarding women serving in the armed forces? During the first three years of the U.S. operation in Iraq, women constituted 2% of the Americans killed, and your policy choice will almost certainly impact that percentage in future wars. One option is to maintain current U.S. policy, with women serving in most military positions, but barred from being in the most perilous ground forces (armored, artillery, and infantry units). A second possibility is to eliminate all barriers to women in the military by opening all positions to them. Your third choice is to remove women from all military jobs that might take them near the front lines.

What Do You Think?

How would you write the policy script regarding women in combat?

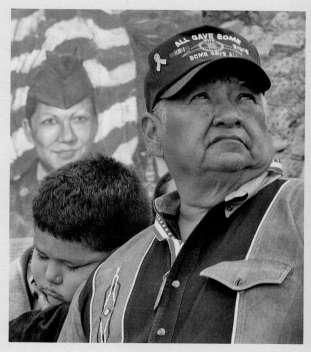

American women increasingly serve in military positions that have exposed them to enemy fire. Private first class Lori Piestewa, a Hopi, was killed when her combat maintenance unit was attacked by Iraqi forces in March 2003. She is shown here behind her father and her son, Brandon, at a 2005 memorial service. She also had a daughter, Carla. In 2005 Congress debated and rejected a proposal to end the prohibition on women serving in infantry, armor, and artillery units. Should women, including mothers of small children, serve in all military units?

($0.7 billion), Mexican-American War ($1 billion), Spanish-American War ($6 billion), Korean War ($264 billion), Vietnam War ($347 billion), Persian Gulf War ($61 billion), and Iraq War ($500 billion and rising). Yet another way to look at cost is by considering global military spending as presented in Figure 10.2.

Strategy is yet another aspect of war that has changed. Two concepts, the power to defeat and the power to hurt, are key here. The **power to defeat** is the ability to seize territory or overcome enemy military forces and is the classic goal of war. The **power to hurt**, or coercive violence, is the ability to inflict pain outside the immediate military sphere (Slantchev, 2003). It means hurting some so that the resistance of others

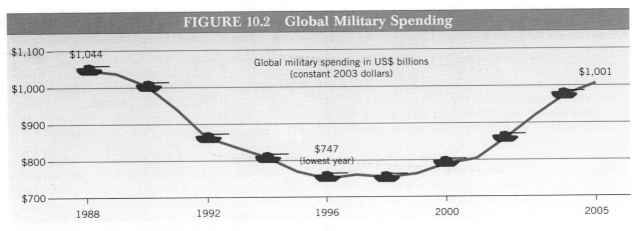

FIGURE 10.2   Global Military Spending

Global military spending in US\$ billions
(constant 2003 dollars)

Global military spending peaked in the late 1980s at the end of the cold war, then declined into the mid-1990s, reaching a low point in 1996 and being fairly steady for the rest of the decade. Beginning in 2000, arms spending began to accelerate more rapidly, increasing about 22% in constant 2003 dollars (adjusted for inflation) to just over \$1 trillion in 2005.

Data source: Stockholm International Peace Research Institute (SIPRI), 2004.

will crumble. The power to hurt has become increasingly important to all aspects of warfare because the success of the war effort depends on a country's economic effort and, often, the morale of its citizens. Perhaps the first military leader to understand the importance of the power to hurt in modern warfare was General William Tecumseh Sherman during the U.S. Civil War. "My aim was to whip the rebels, to humble their pride, to follow them to their inmost recesses, and [to] make them fear and dread us," the general wrote in his memoirs.

Traditionally wars were fought with little reference to hurting. Even when hurting was used, it depended on the ability to attack civilians by first defeating the enemy's military forces. During the American Revolution, for example, the British could have utilized their power to hurt—to kill civilians in the major cities they controlled—and they might have won the war. Instead they concentrated on defeating the American army (which they could not catch, and then it grew too strong to overpower), and they lost.

In the modern era, the power to defeat has declined in importance relative to the power to hurt. Terrorism, guerrilla warfare, and nuclear warfare all rely extensively on the power to hurt to accomplish their ends. Even conventional warfare sometimes uses terror tactics to sap an opponent's morale. The use of strategic bombing to blast German cities during World War II is an example.

Classifying Warfare

There are numerous ways to classify warfare. One has to do with causality and intent, and distinguishes among offensive, defensive, and other types of conflict. *Wars of aggression* are those that do not meet the standards of *jus ad bellum* (just cause of war) analyzed in chapter 9. *Defensive warfare* can include immediate self-defense, such as Kuwait's futile and short-lived resistance to Iraq's invasion in 1990, or coming to the defense of a country suffering aggression. Defense can also include responding collectively to aggression against others. For example, the countries in NATO and other alliances are pledged to protect one another, and a coalition of countries waged the

Persian Gulf War against Iraq in 1991 when the UN authorized action to liberate Kuwait. Often, of course, who is the aggressor and who is the victim is unclear, with each side claiming to be acting in self-defense or to be justifiably righting some other wrong.

Preemptive warfare is one such scenario that defies the simple dichotomy between offensive and defensive war. Whether preventive war is justified has been hotly debated in the aftermath of President Bush's declaration in 2002, known as the Bush Doctrine, as discussed in chapter 2, that, "To forestall or prevent hostile acts by our adversaries, the United States will, if necessary, act preemptively." The president soon put theory into practice by ordering U.S. forces into Iraq in March 2003. Countries have long struck first to forestall what they believed to be an impending attack, and the line between preemption as aggression (which violates international law) and preemption as self-defense (which does not) is not precise. Even in much more constrained domestic situations, a potential victim confronted by someone with a loaded gun does not have to wait to be shot at before exercising his or her right of self-defense. What the law generally says is that you must be reasonably afraid that you or someone with you faces immediate death or injury and your response must be proportionate to the threat. Thus the justifiability of a preemptive war must be evaluated within its context. The general public also holds this view, as evident in Figure 10.3.

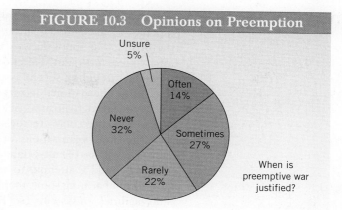

FIGURE 10.3 Opinions on Preemption

When is preemptive war justified?

For most people, the use of preemptive war is not a matter of absolute right or wrong. From one perspective, a majority (54%) of the respondents in 20 countries think that preemptive war is rarely or never justified. Another way to look at the data, though, is that 63% think preemption is at least conceivably justified. Americans were more aggressive than average, with responses of 22% often, 44% sometimes, 17% rarely, 13% never, and 4% unsure.

Data source: The Pew Research Center, "Views of a Changing World," June 2003.

Another approach to classifying war focuses on the weapons and tactics employed. Adopting this strategy, the remainder of this chapter discusses four categories of tactics and weapons: terrorism, unconventional military force, conventional force, and weapons of mass destruction.

SIMULATION
Classifying Wars

TERRORISM

When a quadrennial survey taken in 1999 asked Americans to name two or three top foreign policy concerns, only 12% mentioned terrorism. Four years later, with 9/11 on their minds, 75% of Americans identified terrorism as a critical threat, more than chose any other foreign policy issue.[5] Like the unknown in a horror movie, the shadow of terrorism may be greater than its actual presence, yet it is an important component of international violence.

The Nature and Limits of Terrorism

One of the challenges of examining terrorism is that there is no widely accepted definition. This is not just a problem of semantics. It has affected initiatives to establish treaties and other international efforts to combat terrorism. Most specifically, the UN has struggled intermittently for years to draft a comprehensive treaty on terrorism. Several treaties have been concluded, including one in 2005 to thwart nuclear terrorism. But a general agreement has failed in part because of definitional disagreements.

For instance, many LDCs want wording to indicate that armed struggles for national liberation, against occupation, or against a racist regime should not be considered terrorism. "The simple fact is that terrorism means different things to different people," one diplomat explained after one frustrating negotiation. "We couldn't find common political ground on several issues—despite the fact that the entire world is preoccupied with international terrorism."[6]

While recognizing this lack of consensus, it is, however, important to establish how the word is used here. **Terrorism** is (1) violence; (2) carried out by individuals, nongovernmental organizations, or covert government agents or units; that (3) specifically targets civilians; (4) uses clandestine attack methods, such as car bombs and hijacked airliners; and (5) attempts to influence politics. This definition stresses that terrorism focuses on harming some people in order to create fear in others by targeting civilians and facilities or systems (such as transportation) on which civilians rely (Kydd & Walter, 2006). The objective of terrorists is not just killing and wounding people and destroying physical material. Instead the true target is the emotions of those who see or read about the act of violence and become afraid or dispirited. Although the tactics are similar, it is useful to distinguish between **domestic terrorism**, which includes attacks by local nationals within their country against a purely domestic target for domestic reasons, and **international terrorism**, which involves terrorists attacking a foreign target, either within their own country or abroad. The attack by Timothy McVeigh and Terry Nichols on the Oklahoma City federal building in 1995 that killed 168 people and injured 800 more was clearly domestic terrorism. The 9/11 attack was international terrorism.

By inference, our definition of terrorism rejects the argument that noble ends can justify terrorist means. An example of this claim was made by Abu Musab al-Zarqawi, al Qaeda's chief of operations in Iraq, who was later killed by a U.S. air strike. He asserted that it was acceptable to kill "all infidels with all the kinds of arms that we have. . . . even if armed infidels and unintended victims—women and children—are killed together."[7] The definition of terrorism here also rejects the argument that actions taken by military forces against military targets that also result in civilian casualties should be classified as terrorism. Some would question why a civilian dissident who detonates a car bomb in a market, killing numerous noncombatants, is a terrorist, but a military pilot who drops a bomb that kills numerous noncombatants near the target is not a terrorist. There are two replies to this objection. The first is that intent is important. Terrorists intend to kill noncombatants. With rare exceptions, uniformed personnel attack military or hostile targets. Noncombatants may be inadvertently killed or wounded, but they are not the object of the attack.

Terrorism is attacking children and other noncombatants solely to inflict fear in an effort to advance a political cause. Whatever the justice of their desire to be independent of Russia, the 32 Chechen gunmen who in 2004 seized a Russian school in Beslan, Russia, were terrorists, not freedom fighters. This child being carried away by her traumatized father after Russian forces stormed the school was luckier than the 186 children, 191 teachers and other adult civilians, and 21 Russian soldiers and rescue workers who were killed.

This perspective does not mean all military actions are acceptable. When they are not, however, they are properly classified as war crimes under the principles of *jus in bello* (just conduct of war) discussed in chapter 9, and the perpetrators should be brought to justice in national or international courts. An additional note is that not all attacks categorized as terrorism by the United States fall within the definition used here. For example, Washington condemned as terrorism the October 2000, attack on the destroyer USS *Cole* while it was refueling in Aden. Yet despite the fact that it was suicide bombers operating a small boat laden with explosives that mangled the ship and killed 17 crew members, the fact that the target was a military vessel puts the act beyond the definition of terrorism used here. A final point is that like all definitions of terrorism, there are gray areas. For example, the attacks on American and other forces in Iraq during the postwar occupation fulfill the definition of guerrilla warfare rather than terrorism because they target military forces. Yet the use of car bombs that may kill dozens of civilians in order to also kill one or a few soldiers are at least war crimes and probably terrorism because they violate the standards of discrimination in *jus ad bellum* (just conduct of war). This is especially the case when the perpetrators are outside fighters, such as al-Zarqawi (a Jordanian) was, rather than Iraqis.

Sources of Terrorism

Two sources of political terrorism concern us here. One is state terrorism; the second is made up of transnational terrorist groups. As we shall see, they are closely linked.

State Terrorism

To argue that most acts, even if horrific, committed by uniformed military personnel are not properly regarded as terrorism does not mean that countries cannot engage in terrorism. They can, through **state terrorism**. This is terrorism carried out directly by an established government's clandestine operatives or by others who have been specifically encouraged and funded by a country.

From the U.S. perspective, the State Department repeatedly listed Cuba, Iran, Iraq, Libya, North Korea, Sudan, and Syria as countries guilty of state terrorism. Iraq has been deleted from the list, and reforms in Libya could also lead to its deletion. Each of these countries vehemently denies being involved in terrorism, and some of the U.S. allegations would fall outside the definition of terrorism used here. Not all would, though. For example, state terrorism would include Syria's involvement in the 2005 assassination of former Lebanese Prime Minister Rafiq Hariri, a strong opponent of Syria's long-time occupation of much of Lebanon. There have also been accusations of state terrorism against the United States. "We consider the United States and its current administration as a first-class sponsor of international terrorism, and it along with Israel form an axis of terrorism and evil in the world," a group of 126 Saudi scholars wrote in a joint statement.[8]

Here again, most, but not all, such charges fall outside our definition of terrorism. An example involves Washington's alleged complicity in assassinations and other forms of state terrorism practiced internally by some countries in Latin America and elsewhere during the anticommunist fervor of the cold war. A declassified secret document records the anguished views of an American diplomat in Guatemala regarding U.S. support of the Guatemalan army against Marxist guerrillas and their civilian supporters. After detailing a long list of atrocities committed by the army, the American diplomat told his superiors in Washington, "We have condoned counter-terror . . . even . . . encouraged and blessed it. . . . Murder, torture, and mutilation are all right if our side is doing it and the victims are Communists."[9]

Transnational Terrorist Groups

The global changes that have given rise to a rapid increase in the number of international nongovernmental organizations have also expanded the number of **transnational terrorist groups** that are organized and operate internationally and that commit **transnational terrorism**. One source, the U.S. State Department, identifies

Web Link

The Terrorism Research Center at **www.terrorism.com/** is a good source of information on all aspects of the topic.

Web Link

Pictures and profiles of the international terrorists "most wanted" by the FBI can be found at **http://www.fbi.gov/ wanted/terrorists/fugitives.htm.**

Web Link

A list and description of organizations classified as terrorist by the U.S. State Department is available at **http://www.state.gov/documents/organization/45323.pdf.**

40 such groups, including al Qaeda, and there are dozens of other such organizations that one source or another labels as terrorist.

Al Qaeda is surely the most famous of these, and its origins and operations provide a glimpse into transnational terrorism. According to U.S. sources, al Qaeda (the Base) was founded by Osama bin Laden, the son of a wealthy Saudi family, in the late 1980s to support Arabs fighting in Afghanistan against the Soviet Union. Once the Soviets were driven from Afghanistan in 1989, bin Laden's focus shifted to the United States. He was outraged by the presence of U.S. forces in Saudi Arabia near Mecca and Medina, the two holiest cities of Islam, and by American support of what he saw as Israel's oppression of Palestinian Muslims. Reflecting this view, he issued a *fatwa,* a religious call, in 1998 entitled "Jihad Against Jews and Crusaders," which proclaimed that "to kill the Americans and their allies—civilians and military—is an individual duty for every Muslim who can do it in any country in which it is possible to do it."[10] Subsequently, according to U.S. officials, bin Laden and his followers masterminded a number of other terrorist attacks of which the most devastating was the 9/11 assault. The group has also been linked to other terrorist activities ranging from the 2005 rush-hour attack on the London bus and subway system, in which four bombs killed 56 commuters, to the Arab *mujahedin* foreign fighters' campaign against Iraq's new government and the outside military forces there.

The Record of Terrorism

International terrorism is a regular occurrence, as evident in Figure 10.4. That figure details the more than 10,000 international terror attacks and over 14,000 deaths between 1968 and the end of 2006. It is also worth noting that while domestic terrorism as such is not our focus here, that form of terrorism is usually more common and claims more lives than does international terrorism. During the decade 1991–2000, for instance, there were 3,338 domestic terrorist attacks that killed 3,521 victims compared to 2,340 international terrorist attacks that killed 2,841. Since 2004,

FIGURE 10.4   International Terrorism Data

1081

Average annual deaths

502

Average annual attacks

424

159   246   299   312   310   256   262

78   195   275   380   273   192

| 1968–1974 | 1975–1979 | 1980–1984 | 1985–1989 | 1990–1994 | 1995–1999 | 2000–2004 | 2005–2006 |

Terrorism has long been a danger. There is an acute awareness of terrorism today, but the data shows that the average number of international terrorists attacks since 2000 does not differ dramatically from the overall record before that year. There has been an increase in the average number of deaths each year, but the more than 3,000 people who died in the 9/11 attacks influences that count. Apart from those victims, the yearly average number of deaths for 2000–2004 was 480.

Data source: Memorial Institute for the Prevention of Terrorism, MIPT Terrorism Knowledge Base, online.

domestic terrorist attacks have far exceeded international attacks in number and lethality, largely because of the sectarian violence in Iraq.

Geographically, international terrorism has touched all the regions of the world, but between 2000 and 2006 it has been by far the most common in the Middle East (60% of all attacks), followed by Asia (17%), Europe (13%), Latin America and the Caribbean (6%), and Africa (4%). North America was the safest region by a wide margin. It suffered the 9/11 attack, but that was one of only five such international attacks, or less than 0.03% of all incidents globally.

Terrorist Weapons and Tactics

The explosions that tore apart the World Trade Center and Pentagon and buried their victims under tons of rubble, the mangled remains of Israeli civilians in a bomb-shattered bus, the hollow stares of hostages held as pawns in the macabre game that terrorists play—these are the images of terrorism that have too often gripped us. For all the ghastly history of terrorism using conventional weapons, future possibilities are even more disturbing. Now there are new, more terrible threats—radiological terrorism, and nuclear, biological, and chemical (NBC) terrorism (Enders & Sandler, 2005). As a U.S. National Intelligence Estimate has described the situation, for the first time "U.S. territory is more likely to be attacked" with radiological, biological, or chemical weapons using "ships, trucks, airplanes, or other means" than by weapons of mass destruction from another country using its military missiles or bombers.[11]

Conventional Weapons Terrorism

With relatively few exceptions, most terrorist attacks have used bombs, guns, and other conventional weapons. During 2006, for example, bombs were used in 59% of the terrorist attacks, and firearms were used in another 19%. Kidnappings (17%) were also common, with a few cases of arson, hijackings, and assassinations. Even the attacks on the World Trade Center and Pentagon in 2001, as horrific as they were, would fall under the category of conventional weapons terrorist attacks.

Radiological Terrorism

The extraordinary difficulty of obtaining enough nuclear material to make a nuclear bomb, of mastering the complex process to cause a nuclear chain reaction, and of circumventing the security surrounding existing nuclear weapons all make it very unlikely that in the foreseeable future terrorists could get and use a mini version of a military nuclear weapon. There is a much greater possibility of terrorists being able to construct a radiological weapon, a so-called dirty bomb that would use conventional explosives to disperse radioactive material over a large area. A related approach would be to destroy a nuclear power plant, spewing radioactivity into the surrounding air and water. Such scenarios would result in very few immediate or near-term deaths. Rather, the danger would be from increased levels of radiation causing future cancers, pregnancy complications, and other medical risks. There is also potential for significant economic damage, since a radiological attack could render parts of a city or an important facility (such as a port) unsafe, perhaps for years. Thus, as one expert characterized the impact of a dirty bomb to Congress, "The effects are not instantaneous. You have long-term potential health hazards, and you also have longer-term psychological, social, and political impacts that can go on weeks, months, maybe years."[12]

The concern over the possibility of terrorists acquiring the material to fashion a radiological weapon has grown in recent years. According to the International Atomic Energy Agency (IAEA), there are hundreds of thousands of known industrial,

Did You Know That:

It takes about 17.5 pounds of plutonium to make a bomb with the explosive yield (about 15 kilotons of TNT) of the atomic bomb dropped on Hiroshima.

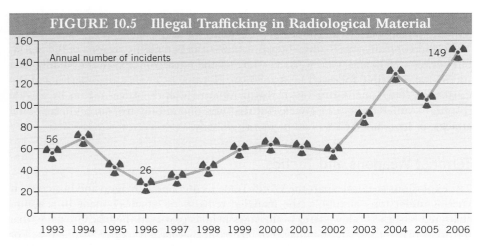

FIGURE 10.5   Illegal Trafficking in Radiological Material

Between 1993 and 2006 there were over 1,000 confirmed incidents of criminal trafficking in stolen radioactive material and almost certainly many more undetected illegal cases. Most incidents involved low-grade material, but about 8% involved weapons-grade enriched uranium or plutonium. It is unclear whether the sharp increase in recent years reflects more trafficking or better crime detection and reporting.

Data source: International Atomic Energy Agency Illegal Trafficking Database.

Web Link

For more on U.S. medical plans to deal with biological, chemical, and radiological attacks, go to the site of the Centers for Disease Control at **http://www.bt.cdc.gov/**.

medical, and other sites and thousands more "orphaned" (unregulated) sites that possess dangerous radioactive material. IAEA data also reveals over 1,000 confirmed cases of trafficking in stolen radiological material since 1993, and that thefts continue at an accelerating pace, as shown in Figure 10.5. Most of the known incidents have involved low-grade radiological material, but about 8% have involved extremely dangerous enriched uranium or plutonium. In just one such incident, officials in the former Soviet republic of Georgia arrested criminals attempting to sell almost three ounces of highly enriched uranium.

Of all possible sources, Russia is the most likely. That country is dismantling many of its nuclear weapons, and it needs to store tons of plutonium and uranium. Russia's desperate economic condition adds to the problem. There is concern that impoverished Russian military and scientific officials might be willing to sell radioactive material to terrorist groups or states. Additionally, the partial breakdown of governmental functions throughout the former Soviet republics (FSRs) creates the possibility that the material to make a radiological bomb could be stolen.

Chemical and Biological Terrorism

Public awareness of the possibility of chemical or biological attack grew after the 9/11 attacks. It was alarming to find out that one of the suicide hijackers had made repeated trips to rural airports to learn about crop dusters. Anxiety was further heightened by the spread of anthrax through the U.S. mail to postal facilities, news organizations, and congressional offices. The resulting atmosphere spawned a spate of doomsday images of chemical and biological attacks that would leave millions dead. Most experts consider such scenarios overdrawn, and it is important to have a balanced understanding of the possibilities and impact of such attacks.

Causes for concern. There surely are worrisome realities. The tons of chemical weapons and agents seized from Iraq in 1991 after the Persian Gulf War bear testimony to the amounts of such weapons in the world and the proliferation of the ability to produce them. Biological weapons are also a threat. For example, the U.S. Office of Technology Assessment has estimated that a light plane flying over Washington, D.C., and its surrounding area and releasing just 220 pounds of anthrax spores using a common crop sprayer could deliver a fatal dose to 3 million people. It would be comforting to think that no one would use such weapons, but that is not the case. Iraq used chemical weapons against Iran and rebellious Kurds in the 1980s, and in 1995 a Japanese terrorist group, Aum Shinrikyo (Supreme Truth), used nerve gas in an attack that killed 12 people and injured 5,000 on a Tokyo subway station. What is worse, a panel of UN experts has warned that the risk of terrorists groups "acquiring and using weapons of mass destruction . . . continues to grow."[13]

Calls for calm. While it is impossible to rule out a biological or chemical attack that may claim tens of thousands of lives, it is probably more realistic to see the likelihood of such an attack as remote because of the significant difficulties of amassing and delivering enough of a chemical or biological agent to cause widespread death and injury. According to one scientist, "When one retreats from the hyperbole and examines the intricacies involved in executing a mass casualty attack with [biological or chemical] agents, one is confronted with technical obstacles so high that even terrorists that have had a wealth of time, money, and technical skill, as well as a determination to acquire and use these weapons [would have difficulty doing so]."[14] This implies that the impact of a chemical or biological terrorist attack is most likely to be similar to that of a radiological attack. The psychological impact will far outweigh the actual casualties. This is what occurred during the anthrax incidents in the United States in late 2001. They caused only five deaths and about a dozen other infections, but that was enough to virtually close down Congress for a time and to frighten millions.

The Causes of Terrorism

Although the attacks of September 11, 2001, brought it to the front of the international agenda, terrorism has long existed. Understanding the causes of terrorism and its recent record are important parts of combating it (Laqueur, 2004; Sinclair, 2004).

Untangling the causes of terrorism is much like trying to understand why war occurs. At the *system level of analysis,* it is possible to argue that such political violence is in part a product of unequal global distribution of wealth. This has long existed, but globalization has brought the wealth gap into sharper focus and has also created a sense of cultural dislocation with its Westernizing impact. When the world's leaders met in Monterrey, Mexico, in 2002 to discuss globalization and economic development, many speakers made a connection between poverty and violence. The president of the UN General Assembly depicted poverty as "the breeding ground for violence and despair," and the president of Peru told the

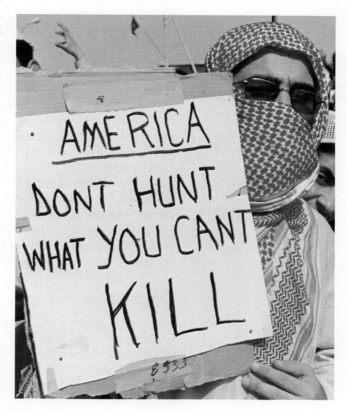

Although few Americans would agree with the view of this Pakistani man that it is a waste of time to try to hunt down Osama bin Laden and other terrorists, the placard does allude to the question about whether the military emphasis of the U.S. "war on terrorism" is the best approach for reducing terrorism. Some say that in the long run, alleviating poverty and other causes of desperation in many parts of the Muslim world and elsewhere would be a more effective way of combating terrorism than trying to kill the terrorists themselves.

conference that "to speak of development is to speak also of a strong and determined fight against terrorism."[15]

State-level analysis of the 9/11 attacks might argue that terrorism is partly caused by the continuing bloodshed between Israelis and Palestinians and the overwhelming view among Muslims that the United States favors Israel. Other possible state-level factors are the presence of U.S. forces in the Middle East, especially in Iraq, and U.S. support of authoritarian regimes in Saudi Arabia and elsewhere. On the *individual level of analysis,* one looks into the psychological drives of terrorists ranging from Osama bin Laden to the numerous suicide bombers who have blown themselves to pieces attacking Israelis in cafés, shops, and meeting rooms (Post, 2004). Like general war, analysts do not agree about the causes of terrorism along these dimensions.

On a pragmatic level, terrorism occurs because, like war, it can be effective, although, also like war, it is risky and often fails (Abrahms, 2006). As one expert puts it, "Terrorism has proved a low-cost, low-risk, cost-effective and potentially high-yield means of winning useful tactical objectives for its perpetrators."[16] From this perspective, terrorism usually is not the irrational acts of crazed fanatics (Bueno de Mesquita, 2005). Instead, it is usually carried out by those who consider it a necessary, legitimate, and effective tool to rid themselves of what they consider oppression. It is necessary, its proponents say, because it may be the only way for an oppressed group to prevail against a heavily armed government.

Moreover, modern conditions are ripe for terrorist operations. First, technology has increased the power of weapons available to terrorists. Explosives have become more deadly, huge airliners can be made into piloted missiles, and there is an increasing danger of terrorists obtaining the material and means to launch a biological, chemical, or radiological attack. Second, increased urbanization has brought people together so that they are easier targets, especially when gathered in such high-profile places as skyscrapers and sports stadiums. With eerie premonition, a U.S. senator warned in 1999, that Americans were vulnerable to attack on targets that might be "selected for their symbolic value, like the World Trade Center in the heart of Manhattan."[17] Third, modern communications have also made terrorism more efficacious because the goal of the terrorist is not to kill or injure, as such. Instead, the aim of terrorism is to gain attention for a cause or to create widespread anxiety that will, in turn, create pressure on governments to negotiate with terrorists and accede to their every demand. Without the media to transmit the news of their acts, terrorist attacks would affect only their immediate victims, which would not accomplish terrorists' goals.

Combating Terrorism

JOIN THE DEBATE
Understanding the National Security Threats of the 21st Century: Are Military Means the Best Way to Combat Terrorism?

The most immediate concern about terrorism is how to combat it. That is made difficult by the clandestine methods used by terrorists and also by the fact that, like other forms of political violence, there is no agreement on what causes terrorism. The U.S.-led "war on terrorism" in recent years has emphasized military and economic strategies to disrupt and destroy terrorist organizations and their ability to operate. Epitomizing this approach, a U.S. State Department report argues, "The world is fighting terrorism on five fronts: diplomatic, intelligence, law enforcement, financial, and military."[18] The report then explains how diplomacy had created cooperation to fight terrorism, how intelligence agencies had worked to identify terrorists and uncover their plans, how law enforcement agencies around the world have detained thousands of suspected terrorists since 9/11, and frozen hundreds of millions of dollars in assets of suspected terrorist groups and sympathizers, and how military operations have dealt heavy blows to terrorists in Afghanistan and elsewhere.

What the report does not mention are any efforts to address many of the causes of terrorism discussed earlier. Critics say it is a major error not to realize that the current wave of terrorism is prompted in significant part by turmoil in the Middle East, especially between Israelis and Palestinians, and the pattern of economic and cultural threat that globalization poses to many in less developed countries. As one such critic put it, "We need to understand the root causes behind terrorism" because "military action will not prevent future terrorism, but only delay it."[19] In a debate that in some ways resembles the one on the war on drugs, some people say that too much is being spent on countering the problem and not enough on trying to cure it.

UNCONVENTIONAL FORCE

As used here, **unconventional force** means outside intervention in local conflict through unconventional means including supplying arms and conducting special operations. This approach allows countries to use their military assets to support their policies while, at the same time, limiting their involvement.

Arms Transfers

The global flow of arms can be properly considered a form of intervention because it usually strengthens either government or antigovernment rebels favored by the supplying country. Thus to a substantial degree, the international flow of weapons is an indirect way to intervene abroad.

Arms Transfers: Where and Why

The export and import of arms has long been important economically and politically. It reached new heights during the cold war, as the two hostile superpowers struggled for influence. About two-thirds of the arms that flowed in the world during the cold war were exported by the United States and the Soviet Union, while LDCs were the destination of about two-thirds of the flow of weaponry. Annual global arms transfers peaked late in the cold war, then declined considerably into the late 1990s measured in constant dollars and have generally been steady since then. Between 2000 and 2005, arms transfers totaled about $246 billion and have been rising steadily. The United States was the largest arms merchant, with Russia close behind, as Figure 10.6 indicates. A number of Western European countries were also major exporters. About two-thirds of all weapons still flow to LDCs, and during 2000–2005, the rising Asian powers, China and India, were the two leading buyers of weaponry.

Several motives prompt countries to sell and give weapons to other countries or to insurgent groups. One of these, as noted, is political support of the recipient government or rebel group. A second and related factor is supplying arms as a way of furthering desired cooperation with another government. Although critics chastised the Bush administration's sale of F-16 fighters to Pakistan in 2005, contending that it fueled an arms race with India, the White House believed that it needed Pakistan's continued cooperation for the U.S. antiterrorist effort and operations in Afghanistan. Secretary of State Rice explained that view, "If you look at it, there is an entire arc there that is very important to American interests in the future, and we're going to pursue all of those relationships on their own terms, and in this context the F-16 issue with Pakistan makes sense."[20] Conversely, the withholding of weapons and their repair parts can serve as a sanction once another country is using your armaments.

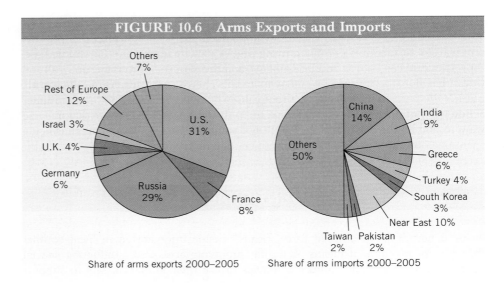

FIGURE 10.6   Arms Exports and Imports

Share of arms exports 2000–2005   Share of arms imports 2000–2005

World arms sales during the years 2000–2005 came to about $246 billion. A few countries dominated sales, as the pie chart on the left shows. The right pie chart indicates that purchases were a bit more spread out, but notice that tensions (China v. India, India v. Pakistan, China v. Taiwan, Turkey v. Greece, and the Middle East) go a long way to explaining the pattern of purchases.

Note: Data is for the delivery of conventional arms. Near East includes the Middle East and Iran.
Data source: SIPRI online.

President Hugo Chávez of Venezuela has become a growing irritant for the Bush administration, which in 2006 cut off supply parts for Venezuela's F-16s.

National economic benefit is yet another, and now perhaps the predominant, motive behind arms exports. As a 2006 congressional report commented, "Where before the principal motivation for arms sales [abroad] might have been to support a foreign policy objective, today that motivation may be based as much on economic considerations as those of foreign policy or national security policy."[21] To cite one example, selling F-16 fighters is crucial to the economic well-being of Lockheed Martin Company and the approximately 12,000 workers at its Fort Worth, Texas, plant. A majority of the more than 4,200 F-16s produced since 1976 have gone to other countries, and in recent years virtually the entire production of F-16s is for export. Thus, the economic welfare of Texas is not just linked to U.S. military needs; it also depends in part on the thousands of F-16s that have been sold to over 20 countries around the world. To ensure that economic health, the administration also provides incentives. Most U.S. military aid requires recipient countries to buy specific U.S. military weapons and supplies, which Washington then pays for. In 2003 and 2004, the Bush administration extended to Pakistan a $4.3 billion, multiyear military aid package. Much of it will be spent helping Pakistan to finance its $5 billion purchase of 36 new model F-16s and to modernize its existing 60 F-16s.

Arms Transfers: Drawbacks

There can be little doubt that arms transfers may help recipient countries meet legitimate defense needs, may be a valuable diplomatic tool, and may support the economy of the supplying country. It is also true, however, that the global flow of arms entails drawbacks to both the importing and the exporting countries. *Cost* is one concern, especially for LDCs. At least some of the billions of dollars that LDCs spend annually on arms might be better spent on funding economic development or social programs. *Increased violence* is a second problem because, at least sometimes, the arms flow increases the level and perhaps the frequency and intensity of violence between countries and within countries. One study concludes that the consequences of the flow of weapons, especially to the LDCs, are "likely to be severe" because they "now possess the capacity to conduct wars of greater intensity, duration, and reach" and because "there is a high correlation between the growing diffusion of war-making material and the increased tempo of global violence" (Klare & Lumpe, 2000:173).

Facing one's own weapons is a third problem that may occur. Countries that you supply today can wind up an opponent tomorrow. Also, weapons may later be sold by recipients to yet other governments or dissident groups, be stolen, or otherwise wind up in the vast arms black market. For example, Venezuela reacted to the U.S. cutoff of supply parts for its F-16s by threatening to sell them to Iran. *Hypocrisy* is a fourth problem. It is hard to persuade others not to do what you are doing. The United States regularly calls on other countries to embargo weapons sales to countries that abuse human rights, yet is a major supplier of weapons to such authoritarian countries as Saudi Arabia (Yanik, 2006).

Special Operations

Not all military action involves the use of large numbers of uniformed troops against other organized military forces in classic battle scenarios. Some approaches to violence fall under the heading of special operations.

Special operations include overtly or covertly sending one's own special operations forces (SOFs), intelligence operatives, or paramilitary agents into another country to conduct such small-unit activities as commando operations and intelligence gathering. When these actions are aimed at an opponent's armed forces or other military targets, then the activity falls under the general heading of special operations warfare. The use of SOFs as a form of military intervention has increased in recent decades for several reasons. First, there has been an increase in civil strife within countries. Second, attempts to topple governments or to create separatist states are now usually waged using guerrilla tactics, rather than the conventional tactics normally used in the past. More than any single reason, this change in tactics has occurred because the preponderance of high-tech weapons available to government forces makes it nearly suicidal for opposition forces to fight conventionally. Third, covert intervention avoids the avalanche of international and, often, domestic criticism that overt interventions set off. Fourth, clandestine operations allow the initiating country to disengage more easily, if it wishes, than would be possible if it overtly committed regular military forces.

Covert operations also have drawbacks. Escalating involvement can be a major problem. Interventions can begin with supplying weapons. If the arms flow does not bring victory, then the next step may be to send in advisers and special operations forces. Even if the supplier country has its doubts about wanting to commit its own armed forces, the process of intervention often causes that country's prestige to become associated with the fate of the recipient country or rebel group that is being supported. Therefore, if things continue to go badly for the recipient, then the supplier may be tempted to engage in limited combat support, and, finally, to commit to a full-scale military intervention with its own troops. This is how the United States waded ever deeper into the quagmire in Vietnam and how the Soviet Union fell into the abyss in Afghanistan.

Since the events of 9/11, SOFs have received renewed attention in the United States. President George W. Bush has dramatically increased the size of and funding for U.S. SOFs. In addition to their use in Afghanistan and Iraq, the president has deployed SOF units to Colombia to assist in the war against leftist guerrilla armies there and to the Philippines to help that country's army in the war against Abu Sayyaf, a Muslim rebel group. Whatever the justification of any specific use of SOFs, they can also lead to intervention where prudence might otherwise recommend restraint, as discussed in the section on the dangers of overemphasizing military power in chapter 8.

CONVENTIONAL FORCE

The most overt form of coercive intervention is for a country to dispatch its own forces to another country. That intervention can range from such limited demonstrations of power as the numerous U.S. aerial and cruise missile attacks on Iraq between 1991 and 2003 to the global warfare seen during World War I and World War II. With the exceptions of the U.S. atomic attacks on Hiroshima and Nagasaki in 1945 and some use of chemical weapons, wars have been waged using conventional weapons.

The **conventional warfare** that has been the norm throughout most of history is distinguished from other types of warfare by the tactics and weapons used. The overt use of uniformed military personnel, usually in large numbers, is what separates conventional tactics from special operations and terrorism. As for weapons, it is easier to indicate what conventional weapons are not than what they are. Generally, conventional weapons are those that rely on explosives for impact but are not nuclear/radiological, biological, or chemical weapons.

Goals and Conduct of War

Masterful generals and diplomats from ancient to modern time have recognized the intimate connection between force and diplomacy. The great Chinese strategist Sun Tzu in *The Art of War* (about 500 B.C.) counseled, "A government should not mobilize its army out of anger . . . Act when it is beneficial; desist when it is not." Extending that view, the Prussian strategist Carl von Clausewitz's *On War* (1833) described war as a "political instrument . . . carrying out [diplomacy] by other means." And somewhat reversing Clausewitz's view, China's Premier Zhou Enlai in 1954 depicted diplomacy as "a continuation of war by other means."

Whatever their particular emphasis, the thrust of these observations implies three principles that civilian and military decision makers should keep in mind. (1) *War is a part of diplomacy, not a substitute for it.* Therefore, channels of communication to the opponent should be kept open in an attempt to limit the conflict and to reestablish peace. (2) *Wars should be governed by political, not military, considerations.* Often commanders chafe under restrictions, as General Douglas MacArthur did during the Korean War (1950–1953) over his lack of authority to attack China. When generals become insubordinate, as MacArthur did, they ought to be removed from command, as he was. (3) *War should be fought with clear political goals.* When goals are not established or are later ignored, disaster looms. After the Persian Gulf War, some criticized President George H. W. Bush for not driving on to Baghdad and unseating Saddam Hussein. Others strongly defended him for halting hostilities once U.S.-led forces had achieved the stated UN goal in 1991 of liberating Kuwait. By doing so, he ended the killing and stayed within the legal confines of the UN resolution that authorized

ANALYZE THE ISSUE
NATO

the action. Moreover, in retrospect, invading Iraq in 1991 and unseating Saddam might have led to the same morass for U.S. forces that bogged them down after the 2003 war.

The fact that most wars are fought within limits does not mean that those boundaries are never violated. **Escalation** occurs when the rules change and the level of combat increases. Stepping up the scope and intensity of a war, however, has always been dangerous, and it is particularly so in an era of horrifically destructive weapons. Not long after their entry into the war in Vietnam in the mid-1960s, Americans began to realize that continuing it within the limits it was being fought offered little chance of victory and carried a heavy cost in lives and economics. Escalating the war by invading North Vietnam might have brought about China's involvement and increased the cost monumentally. Also, many Americans were sickened by the human cost to both sides; if the war had continued or escalated, there surely would have been an increase of deep divisions within the United States. Ultimately, the United States could have achieved a military victory by "nuking" North Vietnam and killing everyone there. Americans finally accepted, though, that victory was not the only thing (Tannenwald, 2006). American troops began to withdraw from Vietnam in 1969; all U.S. troops were gone by 1973; Vietnam was reunited under Hanoi's control in 1975.

Avoiding Unchecked Escalation

The dangers of escalation and the prudence of keeping limited wars limited make it important to understand how to avoid unchecked escalation. As with most things political, there is no set formula. There are, however, a few useful standards.

- *Keep lines of communication open.* The basic principle is that escalation (or de-escalation) should be a deliberate strategy used to signal a political message to the enemy. Accordingly, it is also important to send signals through diplomatic or public channels so that the opponent will not mistake the escalation as an angry spasm of violence or misconstrue the de-escalation as a weakening of resolve.

- *Limit goals.* Unlimited goals by one side may evoke unlimited resistance by the other, so limiting goals is another way to avoid unchecked escalation. It is usually appropriate, for instance, that a goal should fall short of eliminating the opponent as a sovereign state! Even where unconditional victory is the aim, obliteration of the enemy population is not an appropriate goal.

- *Restrict geographical scope.* It is often wise to limit conflict to as narrow a geographical area as possible. American forces refrained from invading China during the Korean War. Similarly, the Soviets passed up the temptation to blockade Berlin in 1962 in response to the U.S. blockade of Cuba.

- *Observe target restrictions.* Wars can be controlled by limiting targets. Despite their close proximity, the Arabs and Israelis have never tried to bomb each other's capitals. Iraq's launch of Scud missiles against Tel Aviv and other Israeli cities in 1991 was, by contrast, a serious escalation, but it was not repeated in 2003.

- *Limit weapons.* Yet another way to keep war limited is to adhere to the principle that the level of force used should be no greater than the minimum necessary to accomplish war aims. The stricture on weapons has become even more important in an era when there is such a great potential for the use of limited, on-the-battlefield NBC weapons. In addition to moral issues, even the limited use of NBC weapons might well set off a serious escalation that could lead to strategic nuclear war or massive biological and chemical attacks. This stricture has been followed in all international wars in recent decades, with the exception of the Iran-Iraq war in the 1980s during which Iran used mustard gas (which causes chemical burns to the lungs) and Iraq used mustard gas and tabun (a nerve agent).

WEAPONS OF MASS DESTRUCTION

Web Link

The horror of German bombing in Spain is presented in Pablo Picasso's iconic painting, *Guernica,* depicting people in that city under air attack. View it at **www.pbs.org/treasuresoftheworld/ guernica/gmain.html.**

The world's history of waging war primarily with conventional weapons does not guarantee that this restraint will continue. Science and technology have rapidly increased the ability of countries to build, deploy, and potentially employ devastating **weapons of mass destruction (WMDs)**. The term was first used by the British press in 1937 to describe German bombers deployed to Spain in support of the eventually successful effort of fascist forces to overthrow the government during that country's civil war (1936–1939). Now, however, the term weapons of mass destruction is used to denote nuclear, biological, and chemical weapons in the amounts and potencies that are available to national militaries and can cause horrific levels of death and injury to enemy forces or civilian targets. In the pages that follow, we will deal briefly with biological and chemical weapons, then turn to a more extensive examination of nuclear weapons and strategy.

Biological Weapons

Biological warfare is not new. As early as the 6th century B.C., the Assyrians poisoned enemy wells with a parasitic fungus called rye ergot that caused gangrene and convulsions. More catastrophically, the Tartar army besieging Kaffa, a Genoese trading outpost in the Crimea in 1346, catapulted plague-infected corpses and heads over the walls to spread the disease among the defenders. Many of those who fled back to Italy carried the disease with them and, according to some historians, set off the Black Death that killed millions of Europeans. North America first experienced biological warfare in 1763 when, during an Indian uprising, the British commander in North America, Sir Jeffrey Amherst, wrote to subordinates at Fort Pitt, "Could it not be contrived to send the smallpox among those disaffected tribes of Indians?"[22] As it turns out, Sir Jeffrey's prompting was unnecessary. Soldiers at the fort had already given disease-infected blankets to members of the Shawnee and Delaware tribes.

The specter of biological warfare still looms large. Although the 1972 Biological Weapons Convention (BWC) bans the production, possession, and use of germ-based *biological weapons,* there are persistent rumors that some countries maintain bioweapons stocks or are seeking them. North Korea, Iran, Russia, and Syria are most often mentioned. Such possibilities are given credence by relatively recent evidence of bioweapons activity. For example, a top Russian official admitted in 1992 that the Soviet Union had been violating the BWC by conducting biological weapons research and, among other things, had amassed 20 tons of smallpox solution. The UN-led inspections of Iraq after the 1991 Persian Gulf War indicated that the country also had a germ warfare program that had, at minimum, produced 132,000 gallons of anthrax and botulism toxins.

Chemical Weapons

Of the three components of NBC warfare, chemical weapons are the most prevalent because they are relatively easy and inexpensive to produce. Indeed, they have earned the sobriquet of "the poor man's atomic bomb." As one CIA director told Congress, "Chemicals used to make nerve agents are also used to make plastics and [to] process foodstuff. Any modern pharmaceutical facility can produce biological warfare agents as easily as vaccines or antibiotics."[23]

Most ominously of all, chemical weapons have been used recently. Both Iran and Iraq used them during their grueling war (1980–1988), and Iraq used them internally to attack rebellious Kurds. Recordings of meetings later captured by U.S. forces chillingly verify the personal involvement of Saddam Hussein in the use of the weapons against Kurds. In one meeting he reminds other participants, "chemical weapons are not used unless I personally give the orders." When Iraq's vice president asks if chemical weapons are effective, Saddam replies, "Yes, they're very effective if people don't wear masks."

"You mean they will kill thousands?" the vice president wonders.

"Yes, they will kill thousands," the president assures him.[24] And so they did, killing perhaps 5,000 people in a 1988 attack on the Kurdish city of Halabja and many thousands of other Kurds in other attacks elsewhere in the region, apart from leaving yet thousands of others with long-term illnesses.

UN inspections in Iraq after the Persian Gulf War (1991) also uncovered huge stores of chemical weapons, including over 105,000 gallons of mustard gas; 21,936 gallons of tabun, sarin, and other nerve gases; and over 453,000 gallons of other chemicals associated with weapons. Some of this supply was contained in munitions, such as 12,786 artillery shells filled with mustard gas and 18 warheads or bombs filled with nerve agents. There is no evidence that any chemical weapons were used during the war, but traces of mustard gas and sarin were detected on the battlefield. These may have been released inadvertently when the allied attacks destroyed Iraqi weapons depots, and some analysts suspect that exposure to these chemicals may be the cause of Gulf War syndrome, which has afflicted many veterans of the war.

Chemical weapons remain a threat because humans have used them against one another, and some countries continue to possess them. This photograph, a grim reminder of the horror of chemical weapons, shows a child and its mother who were killed in 1988 in Halabja, Iraq. Saddam Hussein's government launched a chemical weapons attack on Halabja and other Kurdish communities in northern Iraq to punish the Kurds for their political restiveness.

Nuclear Weapons

Web Link

For a look at the impact of a nuclear attack, go to the PBS site **http://www.pbs.org/wgbh/amex/bomb/sfeature/index.html.**

The Bible's Book of Revelation speaks of much of humankind suffering a fiery death during an apocalyptic end to the world: A "hail of fire mixed with blood fell upon the earth; and . . . the earth was burnt up. . . . The sea became blood . . . and from the shaft rose smoke like the smoke of a great furnace and the sun and the air were darkened." Whatever your religious beliefs, such a prophecy is sobering because we now have the capability to sound "the blast of the trumpets" as Revelations put it, by loosing the awesome array of nuclear weapons that we possess.

Nuclear Weapons States and Their Arsenals

The world joined in a collective sigh of relief when the cold war ended. Almost overnight, worry about the threat of nuclear war virtually disappeared from the media and from general political discussion. Unfortunately, the perception of significantly greater safety is illusory. It is true that the number of strategic nuclear weapons has declined. Nevertheless, many extremely powerful nuclear weapons remain in the arsenals of several states, and yet other countries aim to acquire such WMDs.

The United States and Russia The United States and Russia remain the nuclear Goliaths, as evident in Figure 10.7. In 2006, the U.S. deployed strategic-range (5,550 kilometers/3,416.8 miles) arsenal included 5,021 nuclear warheads and bombs and 951 **strategic-range delivery vehicles** (missiles and bombers). Russia's deployed strategic inventory was 3,500 weapons and 639 delivery vehicles. Additionally, the United States has about 500 deployed tactical (shorter-range, battlefield) nuclear weapons, and Russia has some 2,330. Both countries also keep a substantial number

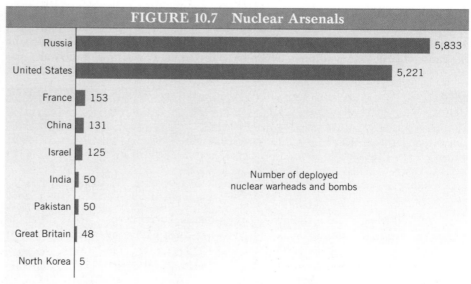

FIGURE 10.7 Nuclear Arsenals

Country	Number of deployed nuclear warheads and bombs
Russia	5,833
United States	5,221
France	153
China	131
Israel	125
India	50
Pakistan	50
Great Britain	48
North Korea	5

Although the cold war is history and there has not been much in the news about nuclear weapons proliferation, the United States and Russia are still by far the dominant nuclear powers. The United States has 46% and Russia 49% of all the deployed nuclear warheads and bombs. These two countries also have a large number of nuclear weapons stored "in reserve," while the other countries do not.

Notes: Data is for 2006 except for North Korea, which is a 2007 estimate. The weapons counts of North Korea, Israel, Pakistan, and India are all speculative to some degree and should be read as estimates or averages of various estimates.
Data sources: SIPRI online; *Bulletin of the Atomic Scientists*, various 2006 and 2007 editions.

of nuclear warheads and bombs in reserve. The U.S. stockpile in 2006 was 4,226 such weapons, Russia's came to about 10,200.

Washington and Moscow have both long relied on a triad of strategic weapons systems that includes (1) submarine-launched ballistic missiles (SLBMs) carried aboard ballistic missile nuclear submarines (SSBNs), (2) land-based intercontinental ballistic missiles (ICBMs), and (3) bombers. Most ICBMs are located in silos, although Russia has some that are railroad-mobile. ICBMs and SLBMs carry up to ten warheads, with multiple warhead missiles having multiple independent reentry vehicle (MIRV) capability. This allows each warhead to attack a different target. The most powerful of these explosive devices is currently deployed on Russia's SS-18 ICBMs, each of which carries 10 MIRV warheads, each with the explosive power of 750 kilotons of TNT. The largest U.S. weapons are D-5 SLBMs that carry six 475-kiloton warheads.

Nuclear weapons designed for tactical use also come in a relatively miniaturized form. Among currently deployed tactical nuclear weapons, the explosive power of U.S. B-61 bombs can be as low as 0.3 kilotons (30 tons of TNT), a yield that is approximately nine times as powerful as the ammonium nitrate bomb that destroyed the Federal Building in Oklahoma City on April 19, 1995.

> **Did You Know That:**
>
> The array of 750-kiloton warheads on Soviet ICBMs each has an explosive yield 50 times larger than that of the atomic bomb dropped on Hiroshima in 1945.

Other Nuclear Weapons States China, France, Great Britain, India, and Pakistan all openly have nuclear weapons, and Israel and (perhaps) North Korea have undeclared nuclear weapons, adding another 1,300 or so nuclear devices to the volatile mix of over 13,000 deployed tactical and strategic nuclear devices. China, for example, has about 130 nuclear warheads and bombs, of which 40 are deployed on bombers, 12 on single warhead SLBMs, 78 on single warhead missiles with ICBM or near-ICBM ranges. Additionally, several countries, most notably Iran, have or are suspected of having nuclear weapons development programs, and another 30 countries have the technology base needed to build nuclear weapons.

The Role of Nuclear Weapons

Given the reality of the huge number of nuclear weapons that still exist and the increase in the number of countries that have them, it would be unwise to discount the continuing impact of nuclear weapons on world politics. One role that nuclear weapons play is to be a part of the "backdrop" of power and influence. There can be little doubt that the continuing importance of Russia, despite its tremendous travails, rests in part on its still-immense nuclear arsenal. Deterrence is a second role played by nuclear weapons. Whether or not nuclear weapons will always deter conventional or nuclear attack is uncertain, but at least sometimes they have been and remain a restraining factor that deters an opponent from attacking in the first place or that limits an opponent's weapons or tactics. It is not unreasonable to conjecture, for instance, that the nuclear option that the United States, France, and Great Britain all had in the Persian Gulf War may have helped deter Saddam Hussein from using his chemical weapons in 1991. The United States again used its nuclear weapons in 2003 to threaten Iraq. Among other warnings, Secretary of Defense Donald Rumsfeld publicly declared that the administration would "not foreclose the possible use of nuclear weapons if attacked" by WMDs.[25] Similarly,

Concern with nuclear weapons has declined in the press and among the public since the end of the cold war. Nevertheless, as represented by this fiery cloud from a long-ago test of a nuclear weapons in Nevada, the world's countries still have huge nuclear arsenals. Moreover, since more countries now have nuclear weapons, the chances of nuclear war have arguably increased rather than decreased, and nuclear weapons play an ongoing role in world diplomacy.

Secretary of State Condoleezza Rice's pointed remark in 2005 that, "the U.S. maintains significant—I want to underline significant—deterrent capability of all kinds in the Asia-Pacific region," served notice on North Korea that any use of WMDs might evoke a U.S. nuclear response.[26]

Actual use is a third role for nuclear weapons. Strategic analysts envision several scenarios that could lead to nuclear war. These include:

- *An irrational leader,* one who is fanatical, deranged, drunk, or otherwise out of control is one possible cause of nuclear war. For instance, Russian generals were reportedly worried about what hard-drinking President Boris Yeltsin (1990–1999) might do during a crisis.

- *A calculated attack* could also occur if one country felt that it could deliver a first strike that would disable all or most of its opponent's strategic forces and force it into submission. Similarly, a leader might launch a preemptive strike to try to destroy an enemy's nuclear forces if convinced that country was itself about to launch a nuclear strike. An unprovoked nuclear attack could also come as a result of a nuclear country attacking a nonnuclear country, especially if that country used chemical or biological weapons against the nuclear country.

- *Last gasp nuclear war* could come as a final attempt to fend off conventional defeat. This scenario is called the Samson option after the biblical character who pulled a building down on himself in order to slay his captors. Some analysts believe that a key reason behind Israel's nuclear arsenal is to have the Samson option if its vaunted conventional forces are ever overwhelmed by numerically superior Arab invaders (Beres, 2004; Moaz, 2004).

- *Inadvertent nuclear war* based on bad information or misperceptions is one of the most likely scenarios. False intelligence that a nuclear attack is imminent or even under way, for example, might cause a leader to inadvertently strike first. Such an event nearly occurred when Russian radar detected what appeared to be an incoming missile over the Norwegian Sea. Moscow moved to launch a retaliatory strike on the United States, halting its missile launch only after it was discovered at the last minute that the radar blip was an outgoing Norwegian scientific rocket, not an incoming U.S. missile. "For a while," said a Russian defense official, "the world was on the brink of nuclear war."[27] This was neither the first nor last such close call. The time for American and Russian leaders to make decisions in a nuclear crisis is short—at most 30 minutes—given the flight time of a nuclear missile between the two countries. Leaders of countries close to one another, like Pakistan and India, would have much, much less time to respond. This will decrease the time to confirm reports that a nuclear attack has been launched or is about to be launched. It will also vastly increase the chances of erroneously launching what a leader sees as a counterstrike, but what, in fact, is a first strike.

- *Escalation* in a deadly spiral is a final, not unlikely, path to nuclear war. History has demonstrated that leaders are willing to risk nuclear war even when there is no immediate and critical threat to national security. Perhaps the closest the world has ever come to nuclear war was during the 1962 Cuban missile crisis, when the Soviets risked nuclear war by placing missiles with nuclear warheads in Cuba, and the United States risked nuclear war by threatening to invade Cuba and attack the Russian forces guarding the missiles unless Moscow withdrew them.

Did You Know That:

Eighteen Japanese survived the atomic attack on Hiroshima and also (three days later) the atomic blast in Nagasaki, where they and others had fled seeking safety after the first mushroom cloud.

Nuclear Deterrence and Strategy

There are issues about a country's nuclear arsenal and doctrines that seldom enter the public debate, but that are crucial to an effective and stable arsenal. The two main issues are (1) how to minimize the chance of nuclear war and (2) how to maximize the chance of survival if a nuclear exchange does occur. It is not possible here to review all the factors that impinge on these issues, but we can illustrate the various concerns by examining deterrence and then two strategy issues, first-strike use and national missile defense.

Deterrence

The concept of deterrence remains at the center of the strategy of all the nuclear powers. **Deterrence** is persuading an enemy that attacking you will not be worth the cost. Deterrence relies on two factors. *Capability* is the first. Effective deterrence requires that even if you are attacked you must be able to preserve enough strength to retaliate powerfully. Of all current strategic weapons systems, SLBMs are least vulnerable to attack and therefore the most important element of deterrence. Fixed-silo ICBMs are the most vulnerable to being destroyed in an attack. *Credibility* is the second foundation of deterrence. An opponent must also believe that you can and will use your weapons if attacked. You might be thinking at this point, Why would a country not respond to an attack? In the sometimes perverse logic of nuclear war, as we shall see, there are times when doing so might not be an option. This leads some analysts to believe that relying exclusively on retaliation is not a credible deterrent stance and that, therefore, countries should be able and willing to initiate a nuclear war in an extreme circumstance.

Mutual assured destruction (MAD) advocates would base deterrence exclusively on having the ability and will to deliver a devastating counterstrike. They believe that deterrence is best achieved if each nuclear power's capabilities include (1) a sufficient number of weapons that are (2) capable of surviving a nuclear attack by an opponent and then (3) delivering a second-strike retaliatory attack that will destroy that opponent. In essence, this approach is *deterrence through punishment*. If each nuclear power has these three capabilities, then a mutual checkmate is achieved. The result, MAD theory holds, is that no power will start a nuclear war because doing so will lead to its own destruction (even if it destroys its enemy).

An alternative approach to deterrence is **nuclear utilization theory (NUT)**. Its advocates contend that the MAD strategy is a crazy gamble because it relies on rationality and clear-sightedness when, in reality, there are other scenarios (discussed earlier) that could lead to nuclear war. Therefore, NUT supporters prefer to base deterrence partly on *deterrence through damage denial* (or limitation). This requires the ability and willingness to destroy enemy weapons before the weapons explode on one's own territory and forces. The ways to do this are to prevent weapons from being launched by either destroying an enemy's command and communications structure or the weapons themselves before the weapons are launched and/or destroying the weapons during flight.

Both U.S. and Russian nuclear doctrine are a mixture of MAD and NUT strategies. The approaches of most of the lesser nuclear powers, such as China, Great Britain, and France, are almost pure MAD doctrine. As you will see, though, in the following two discussion of strategy, U.S. doctrine under the Bush administration has taken on a decidedly NUT orientation (Glaser & Fetter, 2006).

Strategy: First-Use

One long-standing strategy debate is when, if ever, to employ the **first-use option**, to launch a nuclear attack rather than respond to one. *Last-gasp use* is one possibility.

This involves using nuclear weapons to stave off defeat by a conventional attack. The NATO alliance long held that it might launch a nuclear strike to destroy oncoming, overwhelming Soviet ground forces (Quackenbush, 2006). *Employing mini-nukes* is a second first-use possibility. The idea is to use very low-yield nuclear weapons (under 5 kilotons of TNT explosive power) against very select targets that are impervious to conventional bombardment. For example, the Bush administration advocates developing a "robust nuclear earth penetrator" (RNEP) nuclear weapon, informally dubbed a "bunker buster," arguing that 70 countries that are potential enemies have 10,000 hardened sites that could withstand U.S. weapons. Critics reply that building a RNEP would promote first-use and also contend that even low-yield weapons would kill a huge number of civilians. In 2006, legislators rejected funding for mini-nukes after a congressional study estimated that one might kill as many as a million people if used in an urban area. It is likely that the White House will persist in its effort to add bunker busters to the U.S. arsenal, but the chances of doing so dimmed even more when the Democrats took control of Congress in 2007.

Preemption, launching a nuclear attack against an opponent you are convinced is about to attack you with nuclear weapons, is a third possibility and one that is permissible under current U.S. doctrine.

Responding to a chemical or biological weapons attack is a fourth first-use scenario. This is also possible under U.S. doctrine. Presidents Bush, the father and the son, each indirectly warned Saddam Hussein that if Iraq used biological or chemical weapons in the impending wars (1991 and 2003), Iraq faced U.S. nuclear retaliation. Similarly, President Clinton issued a presidential direction indicating he might respond with nuclear weapons to a biological or chemical attack on the United States. As for the American public, it is closely divided on whether to resort to nuclear weapons for either preemption or to respond to a chemical or biological weapons attack, as detailed in Figure 10.8.

MAD advocates are very leery of first-use. They warn that using nuclear weapons against another nuclear power could lead to uncontrolled escalation. As for using nuclear weapons against a nonnuclear country, MAD supporters worry that doing so could undermine the norm against nuclear warfare and make it easier in the future for other nuclear powers to use their weapons against nonnuclear foes. NUT advocates argue that there are scenarios when first-use would be good policy. One is when faced with a major attack by biological or chemical weapons. NUT advocates reason that these are WMDs and therefore deterring their use or responding to them with another type of WMD, nuclear weapons, is valid. A second scenario in which NUT supporters would use nuclear weapons first is one in which their country faced a nuclear attack and decided to use nuclear weapons to kill off the enemy's leadership, destroy its communications and control system, and disarm it before it could attack by obliterating as many of its nuclear weapons as possible. This approach is roughly akin to the Bush Doctrine's advocacy of preemptive war in the realm of conventional warfare. MAD supporters believe the preemptive nuclear first-strikes could be launched in error, much as the Iraq War was launched on the false premise of Iraqi WMDs in 2003, and that the result might well be an apocalyptic nuclear counterstrike.

Strategy: National Missile Defense

Another long-standing controversy in the area of nuclear planning is whether or not to build a national missile defense (NMD) system, also called a ballistic missile defense (BMD) system or an anti-ballistic missile (ABM) system. After early U.S. and Soviet attempts to build a NMD system both failed, the two countries agreed in the

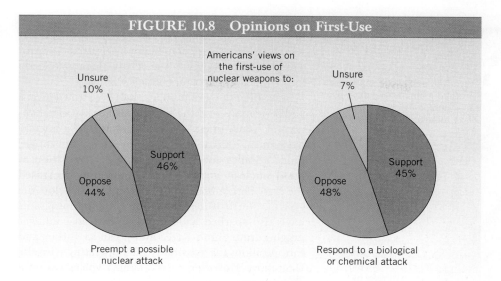

FIGURE 10.8   Opinions on First-Use

Americans' views on the first-use of nuclear weapons to:

Unsure 10%

Support 46%

Oppose 44%

Preempt a possible nuclear attack

Unsure 7%

Support 45%

Oppose 48%

Respond to a biological or chemical attack

Nuclear doctrine under the Bush administration allows the United States to be the first to use nuclear weapons in several circumstances. Two of these scenarios are illustrated in this figure. Americans are evenly split on whether first-use would be appropriate to preempt a possible nuclear attack on the United States or to respond to a biological or chemical weapons attack on U.S. forces. The normal margin of error in reputable national polls is ±3%, meaning that both responses shown above are best considered a tie.

Data sources: The data on preemption is the average of the responses to identical questions asked of a subset of the entire sample in a Pew Research Center/Council on Foreign Relations poll, October 2005. The question on biological or chemical weapons attack is from an ABC News/*Washington Post* poll, March 2003. All data provided by The Roper Center for Public Opinion Research, University of Connecticut.

Anti-Ballistic Missile (ABM) Treaty (1972) to abandon such efforts. A decade later, President Ronald Reagan renewed the controversy by proposing the Strategic Defense Initiative (SDI, labeled "Star Wars" by its critics) to develop BMD capability. Reagan's vision of a comprehensive shield from missile attack was abandoned as too expensive and technically infeasible.

The Current U.S. NMD Program   More recently, advances in technology and concern about future possible nuclear attacks by "rogue states" such as North Korea, Iran, and, it was thought, Iraq combined to resurrect the goal of building an NMD system. Soon after entering office in 2001, President Bush gave Moscow the required one-year notice that the United States would withdraw from the ABM Treaty. He also directed the Pentagon to develop an NMD capability. It is a challenging task that needs to overcome the immense technical difficulties of reliably attacking missiles early in their flight or shooting down warheads traveling through space at 18,000 miles per hour among numerous decoy warheads. The NMD system will also be expensive. Annual funding during the Bush administration has averaged about $9 billion, and the first NMD missile site has been built at Fort Greeley, Alaska, with some 20 ground-based interceptors that are meant to physically hit and destroy an incoming warhead. These interceptors are a rudimentary beginning, and trial tests to intercept missiles have had very mixed results. Even the Pentagon describes the current U.S. capability as "very basic" and admits there is a need for additional tests "under stressing conditions . . . to increase confidence in the models, simulations, and assessment of

Web Link

The U.S. National Missile Defense Agency Web site is at **www.mda.mil/.**

Ballistic missile defense system

1. **Defense satellites** use infrared sensors to detect heat from a missile launch.

2. **Land- and sea-based** sensors are directed to search for the missile along predicted trajectories.

3. A ground-based interceptor missile is launched with an intercept course calculated from tracking data.

4. The Upgraded Early Warning Radar – UEWR – tracks the warhead after it separates from the missile; data is sent to the interceptor missile.

5. Once in position, the interceptor missile releases its "kill vehicle" outfitted with onboard sensors to locate the warhead. The kill vehicle destroys the warhead by colliding with it.

As attractive as the idea of building a defense system against incoming ballistic missiles might seem, doing so has several drawbacks. Among these are the high costs of the system, doubts about whether it can ever reach an acceptable level of reliability, and concerns that trying to build a defensive system could launch a new nuclear arms race, reversing the downward trend in the U.S. and Russian nuclear arsenals.

system capability."[28] There are also numerous efforts under way to develop even more sophisticated NMD weapons, including a high-energy laser situated aboard a modified Boeing 747 to attack ballistic missiles early in flight before they launch their warheads.

Despite the preliminary status of the current NMD weapons and the highly speculative effectiveness of future ones, North Korea's test of a nuclear weapon in 2006 accompanied by its tests of longer range missiles and Iran's seeming determination to build nuclear weapons has significantly increased the U.S. determination to continue to develop the system. North Korea's and Iran's nuclear programs have also sparked widespread interest in countries ranging from South Korea and Japan to Turkey and Europe about the possibility of cooperating with the U.S. effort. However, there are also voices warning against moving ahead.

Arguments For and Against Building an NMD Capability. Some argue that an NMD system will be too expensive (at least $150 billion), that it is unlikely to ever be very effective, and that it can be easily overcome by an opponent by either building more missiles or developing capabilities (such as radar jamming devices) to neutralize the NMD system. Whatever the merits of the financial and technical arguments, they are not as important as the question of whether an NMD system should be built even if it is technically and financially feasible (Cimballa, 2003). NUT supporters favor the project because it follows the damage-denial strategy by, hopefully, allowing you to destroy all or some of your opponent's weapons in flight. They also argue that if an enemy believes that its weapons may not get through, it will be less likely to attack and risk retaliation. Advocates of an NMD system also point out that even if it never got to the point where it could provide safety from a large nuclear attack from Russia, the system would provide a degree of protection from North Korea, Iran, and other "rogue states."

MAD proponents claim that an NMD system would make the world more, not less, dangerous, by reigniting the nuclear arms race and destabilizing deterrence. They contend the arms race would resume as other nuclear powers deployed a massive number of delivery devices capable of overwhelming any defensive system even after they had suffered a first-strike. For one, French President Jacques Chirac believed that building an NMD system "cannot fail but to re-launch the arms race in the world" (Bradley, 2006:97). MADs also contend that developing an NMD capability will be destabilizing for two reasons. First, an NMD capability might tempt its possessor to strike first in a crisis, since an anti-missile system would be most effective against a reduced retaliatory strike rather than a full-scale first-strike by an opponent (Lieber & Press, 2006). Second, China, Russia, and perhaps other countries will see a U.S. NDM system as a threat. They worry about the possibility that having one might tempt the United States to attack them, a concern that could tempt them to launch their own first-strike if they believed that a U.S. first-strike was coming. The other country would reason that since many of its weapons would be destroyed by a U.S. first-strike and that the U.S. NMD system would deflect the remaining weapons in the retaliatory strike, the only chance for survival might be to go first. In such a scenario, the chance of inadvertent nuclear war would soar.

A hint of such a reality has come in the reaction of Russia to the news in 2007 that U.S. NMD batteries might be deployed in Poland and the Czech Republic, ostensibly to defend against a potential threat from Iran. Moscow suspects a different purpose, and the commander of Russia's nuclear missiles warned, "If the government of Poland, the Czech Republic and other countries make this decision . . . [Russia's] strategic missile troops will be able to have those [NMD] facilities as targets. Consequences in case of hostilities will be very grave for both sides."[29] China conducted its first successful test of an anti-satellite (ASAT) system by shooting down one of its own orbiting satellites with a missile in early 2007. Many analysts saw this as a step toward countering U.S. NMD developments by being capable of attacking not only spy satellites but also other potentially space-based devices, such as tracking radars and NMD lasers and missiles.

Thus, the issue about whether to proceed with developing a NMD system is momentous. Even a limited capability defense against a nuclear attack is immensely appealing. Yet in the strange logic of nuclear deterrence, an NMD system would diminish the "assured" part of mutual assured destruction, thereby arguably detracting from nuclear stability and making nuclear war more likely. What would you do?

Web Link

The Claremont Institute maintains a pro-NMD system site at **www.missilethreat.com,** and an anti-NMD system link is on the main page of the organization Nuclearfiles at **www.nuclearfiles.org/.**

CHAPTER SUMMARY

WAR AND WORLD POLITICS

1. War is organized killing of other human beings. Virtually everyone is against that. Yet war continues to be a part of the human condition, and its incidence has not significantly abated. Modern warfare affects more civilians than it traditionally did; the number of civilians killed during war now far exceeds that of soldiers.

2. The study of force involves several major questions: When and why does war occur? When it does happen, how effective is it? What conditions govern success or failure? What options exist in structuring the use of force?

3. Although much valuable research has been done about the causes of war, about the best we can do is to say that war is a complex phenomenon that seems to have many causes. Some of these stem from the nature of our species, some from the existence of nation-states, and some from the nature and dynamics of the world political system.

4. The nature of war is changing. Technology has enhanced killing power; nationalism has made war a patriotic cause. As a result, the scope of war has expanded, which has also changed the strategy of war. The power to defeat is a traditional strategy of war, while the power to hurt has increased in significance and incidence.

TERRORISM

5. The definition of terrorism—what acts are terrorist— has been an ongoing controversial issue. The sources of terrorism can be state-sponsored or transnational, and terrorist acts have taken place in all regions of the world, with some fluctuations in their numbers over the years.

6. Terrorist weapons and tactics have become important issues that states and policy makers must combat, as modern conditions have facilitated the growth of terrorist activities. Apart from using conventional weapons, terrorist threats include the potential use of radiological, chemical, and biological weapons.

7. Governments around the globe have devoted increasing resources and cooperative efforts to find new strategies to combat terrorism as well as to address its root causes.

UNCONVENTIONAL FORCE

8. Warfare can be classified into three categories: unconventional warfare (including arms transfers, special operations), conventional warfare, and weapons of mass destruction warfare (including nuclear, biological, and chemical weapons).

9. Arms transfers and special operations are unconventional methods of warfare. These have assumed more importance in recent times.

CONVENTIONAL FORCE

10. Conventional warfare has been the norm throughout most of history. The goals and conduct of war include avoiding unchecked escalation.

WEAPONS OF MASS DESTRUCTION

11. Biological, chemical, and nuclear weapons are now developed to the point where they can cause horrific levels of death and destruction. The debate (MAD versus NUT) involving how to structure nuclear weapons systems and doctrines is an example of the issues that arise as the ability to conduct war continues to change and new technology develops new weapons.

For simulations, debates, and other interactive activities, a chapter quiz, Web links, and much more, visit **www.mhhe.com/rourke12/** and go to chapter 10. Or, while accessing the site, click on Course-Wide Content and view recent international relations articles in the *New York Times*.

KEY TERMS

conventional warfare
deterrence
domestic terrorism
escalation
first-use option
international terrorism

mutual assured
    destruction (MAD)
nuclear utilization theory
    (NUT)
power to defeat
power to hurt

special operations
state terrorism
strategic-range delivery
    vehicles
terrorism
transnational terrorism

transnational terrorist
    groups
unconventional force
weapons of mass
    destruction (WMDs)

International Security:
The Alternative Road

Weapons! arms! What's the matter here?
—William Shakespeare, *King Lear*

Out of this nettle, danger, we pluck this flower, safety.
—William Shakespeare, *King Henry IV, Part 1*

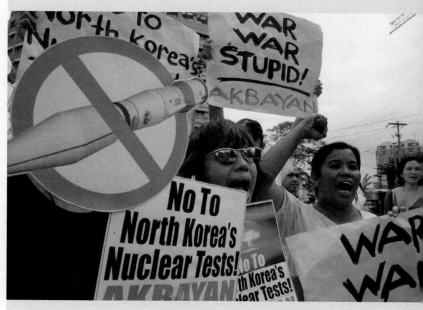

This chapter presents alternatives to seeking security through national defense. Alternative approaches include international security forces, arms control and disarmament, and, as these Filipino women protesting North Korea's recent nuclear weapons test suggest, total rejection of war as a stupid form of human interaction.

ECURITY IS THE ENDURING YET elusive quest. "I would give all my fame for a pot of ale, and safety," a frightened boy cries out before a battle in Shakespeare's *King Henry V*. Alas, Melpomene, the muse of tragedy, did not favor the boy's plea. The English and French armies met on the battlefield at Agincourt. Peace—and perhaps the boy—perished. Today most of us similarly seek security. Yet our quest is tempered by the reality that while humans have sought safety throughout history, they have usually failed to achieve that goal for long.

THINKING ABOUT SECURITY

Web Link

The Bulletin of the Atomic Scientists has calculated a "Doomsday Clock" since 1947 to estimate how close humankind is to midnight (nuclear annihilation). The clock's history and "current time" are at **www.thebulletin.org/ minutes-to-midnight/**.

Perhaps one reason that security has been elusive is that we humans have sought it in the wrong way. The traditional path has emphasized national self-defense by amassing arms to deter aggression. Alternative paths have been given little attention and fewer resources. From 1948 through 2007, for example, the world states spent about $43 trillion on their national military budgets, and the UN spent approximately $49 billion on peacekeeping operations. That is about $878 spent on national security for each $1 spent on peacekeeping. Perhaps the first secretary-general of the United Nations, Trygve Lie, was onto something when he suggested that "wars occur because people prepare for conflict, rather than for peace."[1]

The aim of this chapter is to think anew about security from armed aggression in light of humankind's failed effort to find it. Because the traditional path has not brought us to a consistently secure place, it is only prudent to consider whether to supplement or even replace the traditional approach with alternative, less-traveled-by, paths to security. These possible approaches include limiting or abandoning our weapons altogether, creating international security forces, and even adopting the standards of pacifism.

A Tale of Insecurity

One way to think about how to increase security is to ponder the origins of insecurity. To do that, let us go back in time to the hypothetical origins of insecurity. Our vehicle is a mini-drama. Insecurity may not have started exactly like this, but it might have.

A Drama about Insecurity

It was a chilly autumn day many millennia ago. Og, a caveman of the South Tribe, was searching for food. After unsuccessful hunting in his tribe's territory, the urge to provide for his family carried Og onto the lands of the North Tribe. There one of its members, Ug, was also hunting. He had been luckier than Og. Having just killed a large antelope, Ug was using his long knife to clean his kill. At that moment, Og, with hunting spear in hand, came upon Ug. Both hunters felt fear. Ug was troubled by the lean and hungry look of the spear-carrying stranger, and he unconsciously grasped his knife more tightly. The tensing of his muscles alarmed Og, who instinctively dropped his spear point to a defensive position. Fear increased. Neither Og nor Ug wanted to fight, but violence loomed. Their alarmed exchange went something like this (translated):

Ug: You are eyeing my antelope and pointing your spear at me.

Og: And your knife is menacing. Believe me, I mean you no harm. Your antelope is yours. Still, my family is hungry and it would be good if you shared your kill.

Ug: I am sympathetic and want to be friends. But this is my antelope and my tribe's valley. If there is any meat left over, I may give you a little. But first, put down your spear so we can talk more easily?

Og: A fine idea, Ug, and I'll be glad to put down my spear, but why don't you lay down that fearful knife first? Then we can be friends.

Ug: Spears can fly through the air farther. . . . You should be first.

Og: Knives can strike more accurately. . . . You should be first.

And so the confrontation continued, with Og and Ug equally unsure of the other's intentions, each sincerely proclaiming his peaceful purpose but unable to convince the other to lay his weapon aside first.

Critiquing the Drama

Think about the web of insecurity that entangled Og and Ug. Each was insecure about providing for himself and his family in the harsh winter that was approaching. Security extends farther than just being safe from armed attacks. Ug was a "have" and Og was a "have-not." Ug had a legitimate claim to his antelope; Og had a legitimate need to find food. Territoriality and tribal differences added to the tension. Ug was in "his" valley; Og could not accept the fact that the lack of game in the South Tribe's lands meant that his family would starve while Ug's family would prosper. Their weapons also played a role. But did the weapons cause tension or was it Ug and Og's clashing interests?

We should also ask what could have been done to ease or even avoid the confrontation. If the South Tribe's territory had been full of game, Og would not have been driven to the lands of the North Tribe. Or if the region's food had been shared by all, Og would not have needed Ug's antelope. Knowing this, Ug might have been less defensive. Assuming, for a moment, that Og was dangerous—as hunger sometimes drives people to be—then Ug might have been more secure if somehow he could have signaled the equivalent of today's 911 distress call and summoned the region's peacekeeping force, dispatched by the area's intertribal council. The council might even have been able to aid Og with some food and skins to ease his distress and to quell the anger he felt when he compared his ill fortune with the prosperity of Ug.

The analysis of our allegorical mini-drama could go on and be made more complex. Og and Ug might have spoken different languages, worshipped different deities, or had differently colored faces. That, however, would not change the fundamental questions regarding security. Why were Og and Ug insecure? More important, once insecurity existed, what could have been done to restore harmony?

Seeking Security

Now bring your minds from the past to the present, from primordial cave dwellers to yourself. Think about contemporary international security. It is easy to determine our goal: to be safe. How to achieve it is, of course, much more challenging. To begin our exploration, we will take up various approaches to security, then turn to standards of evaluation.

Approaches to Security

There are, in essence, four possible approaches to securing peace. The basic parameters of each are shown in Table 11.1. As with many, even most matters in this book, which approach is best is part of the realist-liberal debate.

				Primary	
Security Approach	Sources of Insecurity	World Political System	Armaments Strategy	Peacekeeping Mechanism	Strategy
Unlimited self-defense	Many; probably inherent in humans	State-based national interests and rivalries; fear	Have many and all types to guard against threats	Armed states, deterrence, alliances, balance of power	Peace through strength
Limited self-defense	Many; perhaps inherent, but weapons intensify	State-based; limited cooperation based on mutual interests	Limit amount and types to reduce capabilities, damage, tension	Armed states; defensive capabilities, lack of offensive capabilities	Peace through limited offensive ability
International security	Anarchical world system; lack of law or common security mechanisms	International political integration; regional or world government	Transfer weapons and authority to international force	International peacekeeping/ peace enforcement	Peace through law and universal collective defense
Abolition of war	Weapons; personal and national greed and insecurity	Options from pacifist states to global village model	Eliminate weapons	Lack of ability; lack of fear; individual and collective pacifism	Peace through being peaceful

TABLE 11.1 Four Approaches to Security

Concept source: Rapoport (1992).

The path to peace has long been debated. The four approaches outlined here provide some basic alternatives that help structure this chapter on security.

ANALYZE THE ISSUE
Choosing an Alternative Path

Unlimited self-defense, the first of the four approaches, is the traditional approach of each country being responsible for its own defense and amassing weapons it wishes for that defense. The thinking behind this approach rests on the classic realist assumption that humans have an inherent element of greed and aggressiveness that promotes individual and collective violence. This makes the international system, from the realists' perspective, a place of danger where each state must fend for itself or face the perils of domination or destruction by other states.

Beyond the traditional approach to security, there are three alternative approaches: *limited self-defense* (arms limitations), *international security* (regional and world security forces), and *abolition of war* (complete disarmament and pacifism). Each of these will be examined in the pages that follow. Realists do not oppose arms control or even international peacekeeping under the right circumstances. Realists, for instance, recognize that the huge arsenals of weapons that countries possess are dangerous and, therefore, there can be merit in carefully negotiated, truly verifiable arms accords. But because the three alternative approaches all involve some level of trust and depend on the triumph of the spirit of human cooperation over human avarice and power-seeking, they are all more attractive to liberals than to realists.

Standards of Evaluation

Our central question is to determine which or what mix of the various approaches to security offers us the greatest chance of safety. To begin to evaluate various possibilities, consider the college community in which you live. The next time you are in class, look around you. Is anyone carrying a gun? Are you? Probably not. Think about why you are not armed. The answer is that you feel relatively secure. Are you?

The answer is yes and no. Yes, you are relatively secure. For example, the odds you will be murdered are quite long: only 56 in 1 million in 2005. But, no, you are not absolutely safe because dangerous people who might steal your property, attack you, and even kill you are lurking in your community. There were 16,692 murders, 93,934 reported rapes, and 1,280,069 other violent crimes in the United States during 2005. Criminals committed another 10,166,159 burglaries, car thefts, and other property crimes, which cost the victims about $18 billion. Yet most of us feel secure enough to forgo carrying firearms.

The important thing to consider is why you feel secure enough not to carry a gun despite the fact that you could be murdered, raped, beaten up, or have your property stolen. There are many reasons. *Domestic norms* against violence and stealing are one reason. Most people around you are peaceful and honest and are unlikely, even if angry or covetous, to attack you or steal your property. Established *domestic collective security forces* are a second part of feeling secure. The police are on patrol to deter criminals; you can call 911 if you are attacked or robbed; courts and prisons exist to deal with perpetrators. *Domestic disarmament* is a third contributor to your sense of security. Most domestic societies have disarmed substantially, have rejected the routine of carrying weapons, and have turned the legitimate use of domestic force beyond immediate self-defense over to their police. *Domestic conflict-resolution mechanisms* are a fourth contributor to security. There are ways to settle disputes without violence. Lawsuits are filed, and judges make decisions. Indeed, some crimes against persons and property are avoided because most domestic political systems provide some level of social services to meet human needs.

What is important to see here is that for all the protections and dispute-resolution procedures provided by your domestic system, and for all the sense of security that you usually feel, you are not fully secure. Nor are countries and their citizens secure in the global system. For that matter, it is unlikely that anything near absolute global security can be achieved through any of the methods offered in this chapter or anywhere else. But it is also unlikely that absolute domestic security is possible.

Security is relative and a state of mind. Like this student at Virginia Tech University who is being carried away after being shot by a gunman during the campus massacre in April 2007, individuals can suddenly fall victim to violent crime. Yet most people do not carry guns because they feel safe in their domestic system. By contrast, there is no overreaching security force that will necessarily come to the aid of a country if it finds itself an international victim of aggression. Therefore, countries in the anarchical international system rely on self-protection and create armies to defend themselves.

Therefore, the best standard by which to evaluate approaches to security—domestic or international—is to compare them and to ask which one or combination of them makes you the most secure.

LIMITED SELF-DEFENSE THROUGH ARMS CONTROL

The first alternative approach to achieving security involves limiting the numbers and types of weapons that countries possess. This approach, called **arms control**, aims at reducing military (especially offensive) capabilities and lessening the damage even if war begins. Additionally, arms control advocates believe that the decline in the number and power of weapons systems will ease political tensions, thereby making further arms agreements possible. Several of the arms control agreements that will be used to illustrate our discussion are detailed in the following section on the history of arms control, but to familiarize yourself with them quickly, peruse the agreements listed in Table 11.2.

Methods of Achieving Arms Control

There are many methods to control arms in order to limit or even reduce their number and to prevent their spread. These methods include:

- *Numerical restrictions.* Placing numerical limits above, at, or below the current level of existing weapons is the most common approach to arms control. This approach specifies the number or capacity of weapons and/or troops that each side may possess. In some cases the numerical limits may be at or higher than current levels. For example, the two Strategic Arms Reduction Treaties (START I and II) were structured to significantly reduce the number of American and Russian nuclear weapons. Although START II never went into effect because Russia's Duma refused to ratify it, both countries later agreed to cuts in their nuclear arsenals that in many cases will exceed the reductions outlined in the treaty.

- *Categorical restrictions.* This approach to arms control involves limiting or eliminating certain types of weapons. The Intermediate-Range Nuclear Forces Treaty (INF) eliminated an entire class of weapons—intermediate-range nuclear missiles. The new Anti-Personnel Mine Treaty will make it safer to walk the earth.

- *Development, testing, and deployment restrictions.* This method of limiting arms involves a sort of military birth control, ensuring that weapons systems never begin their gestation period of development and testing or, if they do, they are never deployed. The advantage of this approach is that it stops a specific area of arms building before it starts. For instance, the countries that have ratified the Nuclear Non-Proliferation Treaty (NPT) and that do not have such weapons agree not to develop them. The U.S. Congress has barred the development of new types of low-yield tactical nuclear weapons (mini-nukes), and refuses to lift that ban despite the Bush administration's repeated requests to do so.

- *Geographic restriction.* An approach that prohibits the deployment of any weapons of war in certain geographic areas. The deployment of military weapons in Antarctica, the seabed, space, and elsewhere is, for example, banned. There can be geographic restrictions on specific types of weapons,

TABLE 11.2 Selected Arms Control Treaties

Treaty	Provisions	Date Signed	Number of Parties
Treaties in Force			
Geneva Protocol	Bans using gas or bacteriological weapons	1925	133
Limited Test Ban	Bans nuclear tests in the atmosphere, space, or underwater	1963	124
Non-Proliferation Treaty (NPT)	Prohibits selling, giving, or receiving nuclear weapons, materials, or technology for weapons. Made permanent in 1995	1968	189
Biological Weapons	Bans the production and possession of biological weapons	1972	162
Strategic Arms Limitation Talks Treaty (SALT I)	Limits U.S. and USSR strategic weapons	1972	2
Threshold Test Ban	Limits U.S. and USSR underground tests to 150 kt	1974	2
SALT II	Limits U.S. and USSR strategic weapons	1979	2
Intermediate-Range Nuclear Forces (INF)	Eliminates U.S. and USSR missiles with ranges between 500 km and 5,500 km	1987	2
Missile Technology Control Regime (MTCR)	Limits transfer of missiles and missile technology	1987	33
Conventional Forces in Europe Treaty (CFE)	Reduces conventional forces in Europe	1990	30
Strategic Arms Reduction Treaty (START I)	Reduces U.S. and USSR/Russian strategic nuclear forces	1991	2
Chemical Weapons Convention (CWC)	Bans the possession of chemical weapons after 2005	1993	182
Anti-Personnel Mine Treaty (APM)	Bans the production, use, possession, and transfer of land mines	1997	155
Strategic Offensive Reduction Treaty (SORT)	Reduces U.S. and Russian strategic nuclear forces	2002	2
Treaties Not in Force			
Anti-Ballistic Missile (ABM) Treaty	U.S.-USSR pact limits anti-ballistic missile testing and deployment. U.S. withdrew in 2002	1972	1
START II	Reduces U.S. and Russian strategic nuclear forces. Not ratified by Russia	1993	1
Comprehensive Test Ban Treaty (CTBT)	Bans all nuclear weapons tests. Not ratified by U.S., China, Russia, India, and Pakistan	1996	138

Notes: The date signed indicates the first date when countries whose leadership approves of a treaty can sign it. Being a *signatory* is not legally binding; becoming a *party* to a treaty then requires fulfilling a country's ratification procedure or other legal process to legally adhere to the treaty. Treaties to which the Soviet Union was a party bind its successor state, Russia.

Data sources: Numerous news and Web sources, including the United Nations Treaty Collection at http://untreaty.un.org/.

Progress toward controlling arms has been slow and often unsteady, but each agreement listed here represents at least an attempted step down the path of restraining the world's weapons.

such as the Treaty for the Prohibition of Nuclear Weapons in Latin America (1989).

■ *Transfer restrictions.* This method of arms control prohibits or limits the flow of weapons and weapons technology across international borders. Under the NPT, for example, countries that have nuclear weapons or nuclear weapons technology pledge not to supply nonnuclear states with weapons or the technology to build them.

This review of the strategies and methods of arms control leads naturally to the question of whether they have been successful. And if they have not been successful, why not? To address these questions, in the next two sections we will look at the history of arms control, then at the continuing debate over arms control.

The History of Arms Control

Attempts to control arms and other military systems extend almost to the beginning of written history. The earliest recorded example occurred in 431 B.C. when Sparta and Athens negotiated over the length of the latter's defensive walls. Prior to the beginning of the 20th century, however, arms control hardly existed. Since then there has been a buildup of arms control activity. Technology, more than any single factor, spurred rising interest in arms control. Beginning about 1900, the escalating lethality of weapons left many increasingly appalled by the carnage they were causing on the battlefield and among noncombatants. Then in midcentury, as evident in Figure 11.1, the development of nuclear, biological, and chemical (NBC) weapons of mass destruction (WMDs) sparked a growing sense that an apocalyptic end of human life had literally become possible.

Arms Control through the 1980s

Beginning in the second half of the 1800s there were several multilateral efforts to limit arms. The most notable of these were the Hague Conferences (1899, 1907). Although limited in scope, they did place some restrictions on poison gas and the use

FIGURE 11.1 Arms Control Treaties

Arms control treaties
■ During period
— Total treaties

The development and use of increasingly devastating weapons has spurred greater efforts to limit them. This graph shows the number of treaties negotiated during various periods and the cumulative total of those treaties. The real acceleration of arms control began in the 1960s in an effort to restrain nuclear weapons. Of the 37 treaties covered here from 1675 to 2007, 26 (70%) were concluded between 1960 and 1999.

Note: Treaties limited to those that went into force and that dealt with specific weapons and verification rather than peace in general, material that could be used to make weapons, and other such matters.
Data sources: Web sites of the Federation of American Scientists, the UN Department for Disarmament Affairs, and the U.S. Department of State, and various historical sources.

of other weapons. The horror of World War I further increased world interest in arms control. The Geneva Protocol (1925) banned the use of gas or bacteriological warfare, and there were naval conferences in London and Washington that set some limits on the size of the fleets of the major powers. Such efforts did not stave off World War II, but at least the widespread use of gas that had occurred in World War I was avoided. Arms control efforts were spurred even more by the unparalleled destruction wrought by conventional arms during World War II and by the atomic flashes that leveled Hiroshima and Nagasaki in 1945. One early reaction was the creation in 1946 of what is now called the International Atomic Energy Agency (IAEA) to limit the use of nuclear technology to peaceful purposes.

The bitter cold war blocked arms control during the 1950s, but by the early 1960s worries about nuclear weapons began to overcome even that barrier. The first major step occurred in 1963 with the Limited Test Ban Treaty prohibiting nuclear weapons tests in the atmosphere, in outer space, or under water. Between 1945 and 1963, there were on average 25 above-ground nuclear tests each year. After the treaty was signed, such tests (all by nonsignatories) declined to about three a year, then ended in the 1980s. Thus, the alarming threat of radioactive fallout that had increasingly contaminated the atmosphere was largely eliminated.

Later in the decade, the multilateral nuclear **Non-Proliferation Treaty (NPT)** of 1968 pledged its parties (adherents, countries that have completed their legal process to adhere to a treaty) to neither transfer nuclear weapons to a nonnuclear state nor to help one build or otherwise acquire nuclear weapons. Nonnuclear adherents also agree not to build or accept nuclear weapons and to allow the IAEA to establish safeguards to ensure that nuclear facilities are used exclusively for peaceful purposes. Overall, the NPT has been successful in that many countries with the potential to build weapons have not. Yet the NPT is not an unreserved success, as discussed below in the section on its renewal in 1995 and subsequent five-year reviews.

During the 1970s, with cold war tensions beginning to relax, and with the U.S. and Soviet nuclear weapon inventories each passing the 20,000 mark, the pace of arms control negotiations picked up. The **Anti-Ballistic Missile Treaty (ABM)** of 1972 put stringent limits on U.S. and Soviet efforts to deploy national missile defense (NMD) systems, which many analysts believed could destabilize nuclear deterrence by undermining its cornerstone, mutual assured destruction (MAD). As discussed in chapter 10, President Bush withdrew the United States from the ABM Treaty in 2002 to pursue the development of an NMD system.

The 1970s also included important negotiations to limit the number, deployment, or other aspects of WMDs. The most significant of these with regard to nuclear weapons were the **Strategic Arms Limitation Talks Treaty I (SALT I)** of 1972 and the **Strategic Arms Limitation Talks Treaty II (SALT II)** of 1979. Each put important caps on the number of Soviet and American nuclear weapons and delivery vehicles. Moscow and Washington, already confined to

Two soldiers at a base near Little Rock, Arkansas, are attaching explosives to the nose cone of a U.S. Titan II ICBM in order to destroy it under the provisions of the SALT II Treaty. The nose cone once housed a nuclear warhead with a 9-megaton explosive yield, a force about 60 times more powerful than the atomic bombs dropped on Japan in 1945.

underground nuclear tests by the 1963 treaty, moved to limit the size of even those tests to 150 kilotons in the Threshold Test Ban Treaty (1974). In another realm of WMDs, the **Biological Weapons Convention** (1972), which virtually all countries have ratified, pledges its adherents that possess biological weapons to destroy them, and obligates all parties not to manufacture new ones.

Arms control momentum picked up even more speed during the 1980s as the cold war began to wind down. The **Missile Technology Control Regime (MTCR)** was established in 1987 to restrain the proliferation of missiles. The designation "regime" comes from the pact's status as an informal political agreement rather than a formal treaty. Under it, signatory countries pledge not to transfer missile technology or missiles with a range greater than 300 kilometers. The MTCR has slowed, although not stopped, the spread of missiles. The countries with the most sophisticated missile technology all adhere to the MTCR, and they have brought considerable pressure to bear on China and other noncompliant missile-capable countries.

A second important agreement was the U.S.-Soviet **Intermediate-Range Nuclear Forces Treaty (INF)** of 1987. By eliminating an entire class of nuclear delivery vehicles (missiles with ranges between 500 and 5,500 kilometers), it became the first treaty to actually reduce the global nuclear arsenal. The deployment of such U.S. missiles to Europe and counter-targeting by the Soviet Union had put Europe at particular risk of nuclear war.

Arms Control since 1990: WMDs

The years since 1990 have been by far the most important in the history of the control of WMDs. The most significant arms control during the 1990s involved efforts to control nuclear arms, although progress was also made on chemical weapons.

Web Link

The lead U.S. office for arms control is the State Department's Bureau of Arms Control at **http://www.state.gov/t/ac/**.

Strategic Arms Reduction Treaty I   After a decade of negotiations, Presidents George H. W. Bush and Mikhail Gorbachev signed the first **Strategic Arms Reduction Treaty I (START I)** in 1991. The treaty mandated significant cuts in U.S. and Soviet strategic-range (over 5,500 kilometers) nuclear forces. Each country was limited to 1,600 delivery vehicles (missiles and bombers) and 6,000 strategic explosive nuclear devices (warheads and bombs). Thus, START I began the process of reducing the U.S. and Soviet strategic arsenals, each of which contained more than 10,000 warheads and bombs.

Strategic Arms Reduction Treaty II   Presidents Boris Yeltsin and George Bush took a further step toward reducing the mountain of nuclear weapons when they signed the **Strategic Arms Reduction Treaty II (START II)** in 1993. Under START II, Russia and the United States agreed that by 2007 they would reduce their nuclear warheads and bombs to 3,500 for the United States and 2,997 for Russia. The treaty also has a number of clauses relating to specific weapons, the most important of which was the elimination of all ICBMs with multiple warheads (multiple independent reentry vehicles, MIRVs). The U.S. Senate ratified START II in 1996, but Russia's Duma delayed taking up the treaty until 2000. Then it voted for a conditional ratification, making final agreement contingent on a U.S. pledge to abide by the ABM Treaty. When President George W. Bush did the opposite and withdrew from the ABM Treaty, Moscow announced its final rejection of START II. As a result, the reduction of U.S. and Russian strategic nuclear weapons slowed, but it continued as both countries sought to economize. Cuts have continued under the Strategic Offensive Reductions Treaty (SORT) discussed next, but the provision requiring elimination of all MIRV-capable ICBMs died, and both countries maintain a significant number of these missiles (U.S.–350; Russia–214).

Strategic Offensive Reductions Treaty   Even while START II awaited Russia's ratification, Presidents Bill Clinton and Boris Yeltsin agreed in 1997 to a third round of START aimed at further cutting the number of nuclear devices mounted on strategic-range delivery systems to between 2,000 and 2,500. That goal took on greater substance in May 2002 when President George W. Bush met with President Vladimir Putin in Moscow and the two leaders signed the **Strategic Offensive Reductions Treaty (SORT)**, also called the Treaty of Moscow. Under its provisions, the two countries agree to cut their arsenals of nuclear warheads and bombs to no more than 2,200 by 2012. However, SORT contains no provisions relating to MIRVs.

Most observers hailed the new agreement, and both countries' legislatures soon ratified it. There were critics, however, who charged that it was vague to the point of being "for all practical purposes meaningless." For one, there is no schedule of reductions from existing levels as long as they are completed by 2012. Second, the treaty expires that year if the two sides do not renew it. Thus the two parties could do nothing, let the treaty lapse in 2012, and still not have violated it. Third, either country can withdraw with just 90 days notice. And fourth, both countries will be able to place previously deployed warheads in reserve, which would allow them to be rapidly reinstalled on missiles and redeployed.

Such concerns, although important, are somewhat offset by the fact that between 2002 and 2006, the U.S. stockpile of deployed nuclear warheads and bombs declined 23% and Russia's arsenal dropped 30%. Moreover, these reductions are part of an overall trend that has lowered the mountain of global nuclear weapons by 80% between 1986 and 2002, as Figure 11.2 illustrates. If the reductions outlined in the SORT are put into place, and if the nuclear arsenals of China and the other smaller nuclear powers remain relatively stable, the world total of nuclear weapons in 2012 will be further reduced by about 25%. Even now the silos at several former U.S. ICBM sites are completely empty, some of the bases have even been sold, and part of the land has reverted to farming, bringing to fruition the words from the Book of Isaiah (2:4), "They shall beat their swords into plowshares, and their spears into pruning hooks."

The Comprehensive Test Ban Treaty   Banning all tests of nuclear weapons has been another important arms control effort. Following the first atomic test on July 16, 1945, the number of tests mushroomed to 171 blasts in 1962. Then testing began to ebb in response to a number of treaties (see Table 11.2, p. 345), a declining need to test, and increasing international condemnation of those tests that did occur. For example, Australia's prime minister in one of the milder comments labeled France's series of underground tests in 1995 on uninhabited atolls in the South Pacific "an act of stupidity."[2] Those tests, China's two in 1996, and the series that India and Pakistan each conducted in 1998 brought the total number of tests since 1945 to 2,051. Then in 2006, North Korea tested a weapon, taking the total to 2,052, as shown in Figure 11.3.

Those who share the goal of having nuclear tests totally banned forever have pinned their hopes on

> **Did You Know That:**
> START I is about 700 pages long. SORT is 3 pages long.

FIGURE 11.2   Global Nuclear Arsenal, 1945–2006

The mountain of strategic and tactical nuclear warheads and bombs grew rapidly from 1945 to the mid-1980s when it peaked at just over 70,000. Then it began a steep decline and in 2006 stood at about 27,000. Furthering the reduction even more, the number of deployed weapons, which is indicated by the dotted line, is less than half the 2006 total, with the balance of U.S. and Russian weapons in reserve (not deployed).

Data source: Bulletin of the Atomic Scientists, July/August 2006 for the United States, Russia, China, France, and Great Britain. Calculations by author for other nuclear weapons countries.

FIGURE 11.3   Nuclear Tests, 1945–2006

There have been 2,052 known nuclear weapons tests since the first by the United States in August 1945. Perhaps the 2,052nd conducted by North Korea in 2006 will be the last. The goal of the Comprehensive Nuclear Test Ban Treaty is to turn that hope into a universal international commitment, but the unwillingness of several of the existing nuclear-weapons countries to ratify the treaty leaves further tests possible.

Data source: Bulletin of the Atomic Scientists, 45/6 (November/December 1998); author's calculations.

the **Comprehensive Test Ban Treaty (CTBT)**. The treaty was concluded in 1996 and 138 countries have become parties to it. Nevertheless, it has not gone into force. The reason is that it does not become operational until all 44 countries that had nuclear reactors in 1996 ratify it, and several of them, including the United States, have not. President Bill Clinton signed the treaty, but the Republican-controlled Senate rejected it in 1999. His successor, President Bush, is unwilling to try to resurrect the treaty, in part because his administration favors developing and possibly testing mini-nukes, as discussed earlier, and a new generation of "reliable replacement warheads" (RRWs) for the current inventory. Thus testing remains a possibility, and any new tests could set off a chain of other tests. As the Russian newspaper *Pravda* editorialized, "The Moscow hawks are waiting impatiently for the USA to violate its nuclear test moratorium. . . . If the USA carries out tests . . . , the Kremlin will not keep its defense industries from following the bad U.S. example. They have been waiting too long since the end of the cold war."[3]

Chemical Weapons Convention   Nuclear weapons were not the only WMDs to receive attention during the 1990s. Additionally, the growing threat and recent use of chemical weapons led to the **Chemical Weapons Convention (CWC)** in 1993. The signatories pledge to eliminate all chemical weapons by the year 2005; to "never under any circumstance" develop, produce, stockpile, or use chemical weapons; to not provide chemical weapons, or the means to make them, to another country; and to submit to rigorous inspection.

As with all arms control treaties, the CWC represents a step toward, not the end of, dealing with a menace. One issue is that the United States and many other countries that are parties to the treaty have not met the 2005 deadline. Second, about a dozen countries have not agreed to the treaty. Some, such as North Korea and Syria, have or are suspected of having chemical weapons programs, and they, along with others, view chemical weapons as a way to balance the nuclear weapons of other countries. Some Arab nations, for instance, are reluctant to give up chemical weapons unless Israel gives up its nuclear weapons. Third, monitoring the CWC is especially difficult because many common chemicals are dual-use (they have both commercial and weapons applications). For example, polytetrafluoroethene, a chemical used to make nonstick frying pans, can also be used to manufacture perfluoroisobutene, a gas that causes pulmonary edema (the lungs fill with fluid).

Arms Control since 1990: Nuclear Non-Proliferation

Stemming the spread of nuclear weapons to additional countries has arguably been the greatest arms control challenge since the end of the cold war. A recent poll of Americans found that 76% of them believed that "preventing the spread of nuclear weapons" should be "a very important" U.S. foreign policy goal, a support level 2% higher even than combating international terrorism.[4]

The centerpiece of the nuclear containment campaign, as noted earlier, is the Non-Proliferation Treaty (NPT) of 1968. It obligates countries that have nuclear weapons not to transfer either any of them or the technology to make them to a non-nuclear weapons country. In turn, states are obliged not to try to produce or otherwise acquire nuclear weapons and to also submit to inspections by the IAEA to ensure no nuclear weapons program is under way. Under the terms of the NPT, its members met in 1995 to review it and, among other things, to determine how long, if at all, to continue it. They decided to not only extend it, but to make it permanent (Braun & Chyba, 2004). As of mid-2007, 189 countries had ratified the NPT, and one had withdrawn (North Korea in 2003), leaving 188 parties to the treaty.

The Record of the NPT   Clearly the record of the NPT is not one of complete success. In contrast to the decline in the number of nuclear weapons that has occurred since the end of the U.S.-Soviet confrontation in the early 1990s, the number of countries with nuclear weapons has increased. India, Israel, and Pakistan never agreed to the NPT, and, as noted, North Korea has withdrawn its ratification. All have developed nuclear weapons. This doubles the number of countries with nuclear weapons from the time the NPT was first signed. As the accompanying map indicates, there are now eight countries that openly possess nuclear weapons and one (Israel) whose nuclear arsenal is an open secret. Several other countries have or had active programs to develop nuclear weapons, and unless the diplomats from the European Union can persuade Iran to change course, it too will arm itself with nuclear weapons. Still further proliferation is not hard to imagine. For example, North Korea's acquisition of nuclear weapons may eventually push neighboring South Korea and Japan to develop a nuclear deterrent. The list could go on.

Yet despite the proliferation that has occurred, it would be an error to depict the NPT as a failure. Now all but four countries are party to the NPT. Furthermore, somewhat offsetting the march of India, Pakistan, North Korea, and perhaps Iran to become nuclear weapons countries, other pretenders to that title have given up their nuclear ambitions. Libya ratified the NPT in 2004 and agreed to dismantle its nuclear weapons and missile programs and allow IAEA inspections. Why Libya abandoned its 30-year effort to develop nuclear weapons and the missiles to deliver them is uncertain, but among the reasons cited by various analysts were the negative impact of the long-term sanctions on the Libyan economy, the cost of continuing the faltering program, and fear that it would become a target of U.S. military action, as Iraq had.

MAP
The Spread of Nuclear
Weapons

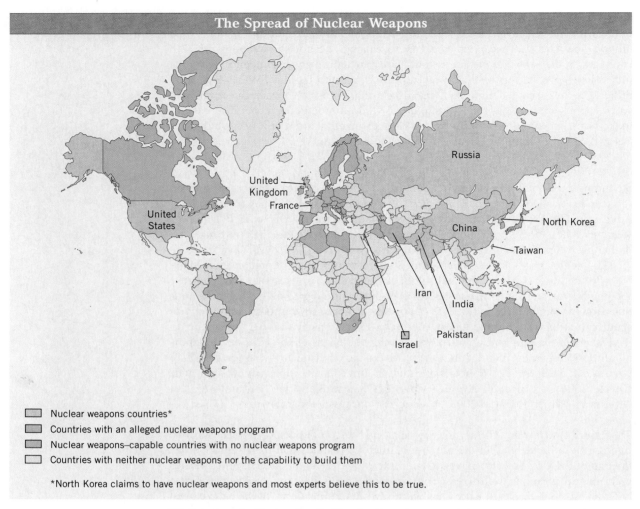

The Spread of Nuclear Weapons

Nuclear weapons countries*
Countries with an alleged nuclear weapons program
Nuclear weapons–capable countries with no nuclear weapons program
Countries with neither nuclear weapons nor the capability to build them

*North Korea claims to have nuclear weapons and most experts believe this to be true.

Efforts such as the Nuclear Non-Proliferation Treaty have slowed, but not stopped, the proliferation of nuclear weapons. There are now nine declared and undeclared nuclear weapons countries. Numerous other countries have the ability and, in some cases, the desire to acquire nuclear weapons.

*Israel has never acknowledged that it has nuclear weapons.

Similarly, Argentina and Brazil halted their nuclear programs in the early 1990s and adhered to the NPT in 1995 and 1997 respectively. Algeria and South Africa both also had nuclear weapons programs, and South Africa may have even tested a weapon, before they both changed course and also became party to the NPT (1995 and 1991 respectively). The agreement concluded by the Six Party Talks in 2006 may be a first step in getting North Korea to someday dismantle its nuclear weapons. Beyond these countries that once pursued nuclear weapons, there are many countries such as Canada, Germany, and Japan that long ago could have developed nuclear weapons and have not.

Challenges to Halting Proliferation   Although the parties to the NPT made it permanent in 1995, the difficult negotiations illustrate some of the reasons that proliferation is hard to stop (Singh & Way, 2004). One stumbling block was that many nonnuclear countries resisted renewal unless the existing nuclear-weapons countries set a timetable for dismantling their arsenals. Malaysia's delegate to the conference charged, for instance, that renewing the treaty without such a pledge would be "justifying nuclear states for eternity" to maintain their monopoly.[5] One important factor in overcoming this objection was a pledge by the United States and other nuclear-weapons states to conclude a treaty banning all nuclear tests.

A second reason that nuclear proliferation is difficult to stem is that some countries still want such weapons. Israel developed its nuclear weapons soon after the NPT was first signed, India and Pakistan joined the nuclear club when each tested nuclear weapons in 1998, and North Korea became the newest member in 2006.

Iran is yet another country that appears determined to acquire nuclear weapons. Even though it is a party to the NPT and claims that it is developing only a peaceful nuclear energy program, most outsiders believe that Tehran is nearing the ability to produce nuclear weapons. This has led to ongoing efforts since 2003 to pressure Iran to comply with the NPT. Whether by design or happenstance, the United States has acted as the "bad cop" by pressing for at least economic sanctions against Iran. The "good cop" role has been played by the European Union represented by the foreign ministers of France, Germany, and Great Britain. They have offered Iran various diplomatic carrots, including admission to the World Trade Organization and economic aid, in exchange for it permanently ending its nuclear enrichment program. Iran's continued refusal to cooperate finally led to the issue being taken up by the UN Security Council. The Europeans came to favor significant sanctions, but China and Russia opposed them, and each possesses a veto on the Council. The Council did call on Iran to halt all activities related to the production of nuclear weapons, and in late 2006 imposed mild sanctions on Iran. These were increased in March 2007 in response to Iran's continued refusal to comply. Sanctions included a ban on Iranian weapons exports, and seizure of a very limited range of the country's foreign assets. Iran's President Mahmoud Ahmadinejad immediately rejected the UN action, calling the Security Council resolution "a torn piece of paper" and vowing it would have no impact on either Iran's actions or its will.[6]

The continuing challenges to the NPT were also highlighted in the stalemated quinquennial (five yearly) review meeting in 2005. Washington's complaints about the nuclear programs of North Korea and Iran were met by the countercharge by many other countries that the United States was seeking to keep its nuclear weapons advantage by reneging on its pledge in Article 6 of the NPT to seek "cessation of the nuclear arms race at an early date and . . . general and complete disarmament under strict and effective international control." A similar charge is that when the United States rejected the CTBT, Washington ignored its 1995 agreement to join a treaty barring all nuclear weapons testing in return for an agreement by nonnuclear-weapons countries to support moves to make the NPT permanent. Muslim countries also accused the United States of hypocrisy for condemning their acquisition of such weapons while accepting Israel's nuclear weapons. When the meeting adjourned with no progress, a frustrated Mohamed El Baradei, head of the IAEA, lamented, "The conference after a full month ended up where we started, which is a system full of loopholes, ailing, and not a road map to fix it."[7]

Arms Control since 1990: Conventional Weapons

Arms control efforts since the advent of nuclear weapons in 1945 have emphasized restraining these awesome weapons and, to a lesser degree, the other WMDs and their delivery systems. In the 1990s, the world also began to pay more attention to conventional weapons inventories and to the transfer of conventional weapons.

Conventional Weapons Inventories The virtual omnipresence of conventional weapons and their multitudinous forms makes them more difficult to limit than nuclear weapons. Still, progress has been made. One major step is the **Conventional Forces in Europe Treaty (CFE)**. After 17 years of negotiation, the countries of the North Atlantic Treaty Organization (NATO) and the Soviet-led Warsaw Treaty Organization (WTO) concluded the CFE Treaty in 1990 to cut conventional military forces in Europe from the Atlantic to the Urals (the ATTU region). In the aftermath of the cold war, adjustments have been made to reflect the independence of various European former Soviet republics (FSRs) and the fact that some of them have even joined NATO. Such details aside, the key point is that the CFE Treaty as amended reduced the units (such as tanks and warplanes) in the ATTU region by about 63,000 and also decreased the number of troops in the area.

An additional step in conventional weapons arms control came in 1997 with the **Anti-Personnel Mine Treaty (APM)**, which prohibits making, using, possessing, or transferring land mines. Details of the creation of the APM Treaty and directions for what you can do to support or oppose it can be found in the Get Involved box, "Adopt a Minefield." By early 2007, 153 countries had ratified the APM Treaty, and it has had an important impact. Since the treaty was signed, countries that had stockpiles of mines have destroyed about 40 million of them. Additionally, the associated effort to clear land mines has removed some 6 million of the deadly devices and millions of other pieces of unexploded ordinance from former battle zones. The APM Treaty has not been universally supported, however. Several key countries (China, India, Pakistan, Russia, and the United States) are among those that have not adhered to it, arguing that they still need to use mines. For example, U.S. military planners consider land mines to be a key defense element against a possible North Korean invasion of South Korea.

Conventional Weapons Transfers Another thrust of conventional arms control in the 1990s and beyond has been and will be the effort to limit the transfer of conventional weapons. To that end, 31 countries in 1995 agreed to the Wassenaar Arrangement on Export Controls for Conventional Arms and Dual-Use Goods and Technologies. Named after the Dutch town where it was negotiated, the "pact" directs its signatories to limit the export of some types of weapons technology and to create an organization to monitor the spread of conventional weapons and **dual-use technology**, which has both peaceful and military applications.

A more recent attempt to control conventional weapons is the work of the UN Conference on the Illicit Trade in Small Arms and Light Weapons (2001). It is a huge task considering the estimated 639 million small arms and light weapons (revolvers and rifles, machine guns and mortars, hand grenades, antitank guns and portable missile launchers) that exist in the world, mostly (60%) in civilian hands. To address this menacing mass of weaponry, the conference called on states to curb the illicit trafficking in light weapons through such steps as ensuring that manufacturers mark weapons so that they can be traced, and tightening measures to monitor the flow of arms across borders. Most of these arms, initially supplied by the United States, Russia, and the European countries to rebel groups and to governments in less developed countries, eventually found their way into the multibillion-dollar global arms black market. Now there are some 92 countries making small arms and

GET INVOLVED

Adopt a Minefield

A common sight throughout the United States are roadside adopt-a-highway signs naming one or another group that has pledged to keep a section of the road clear of litter. Fortunately for Americans, a discarded beer can or fast-food wrapper is about the worst thing they might step on while working along the country's roadways or in its fields and forests.

People in many other countries are not so lucky. In the fields of Cambodia, along the paths of Angola, and dotting the countryside in dozens of other countries, land mines wait with menacing silence and near invisibility to claim a victim. Mines are patient, often waiting many years to make a strike, and they are also nondiscriminatory. They care not whether their deadly yield of shrapnel shreds the body of a soldier or a child. Cambodian farmer Sam Soa was trying to find his cow in a field near his village when he stepped on a mine. "I didn't realize what had happened, and I tried to run away," he remembers.[1] Sam Soa could not run away, though; his left lower leg was gone. Millions of land mines from past conflicts remain in the ground in over 50 countries. In 2005 alone these explosive devices killed or maimed 7,328 civilians, one-third of them children, and unreported incidents almost surely put the toll of dead and injured over 10,000.

The effort over the past three decades to ban land mines and clear existing ones has been a testament to the power of individuals at the grass roots. For example, Jody Williams of Vermont, a former "temp agency" worker in Washington, converted into action her horror at the toll land mines were taking. In 1991, she and two others used the Internet to launch an effort that became the International Campaign to Ban Landmines (ICBL). "When we began, we were just three people sitting in a room. It was utopia. None of us thought we would ever ban land mines," she later told a reporter.[2] Williams had underestimated herself. The ICBL has grown to be a transnational network of 1,400 nongovernmental organizations (NGOs) based in 90 countries. More importantly, 79% of world countries have now ratified the Anti-Personnel Mine Treaty. Williams's work in fostering the 1997 pact won her that year's Nobel Peace Prize.

Reflecting the tragedy of many children, as well as adults, who are killed or maimed by old land mines each year, this sign, erected with the help of UNICEF, warns of a minefield in Sri Lanka. One of the many ways you can get involved in world politics is by supporting an NGO or IGO involved in the international effort to rid the world of land mines.

Be Active!

If you share Williams's view, much remains to be done to get the United States and other countries that have not agreed to the APM Treaty to do so and to clear existing minefields. Certainly the efforts of individual countries and the UN and other IGOs will be important. But individuals can also get involved through such organizations as the ICBL, a network of NGOs (**http://www.icbl.org**), or Adopt-A-Minefield (**www.landmines.org**). No pro–land mine NGOs exist, but you can find President Clinton's rationale for not signing the treaty at the Department of Defense site, **www.defenselink.mil/speeches/speech.aspx?speechid=785**. The Bush administration has followed Clinton's lead. Whatever your opinion, let your members of Congress and even the president know what you think.

light weapons for export. Often these manufacturers are an important part of the economy. For example, the plant in Eldoret, Kenya, that makes 20 million rounds of small arms ammunition each year is an important employer. Yet such production often exacts a toll elsewhere. A 2006 look at the black market in Baghdad found weapons for sale from Bulgaria, China, the Czech Republic, Hungary, Romania, Russia, and Serbia.

The UN program is nonbinding, but it does represent a first step toward regulating and stemming the huge volume of weapons moving through the international system. Speaking at a UN conference to review progress in curbing the illicit arms trade, Chairperson Kuniko Inoguchi of Japan commented, "I would not claim we have achieved some heroic and ambitious outcome," but she did point to heightened awareness of the problem and to the greater willingness of countries to cooperate on the issue as evidence that the world's countries had "started to implement actions against small arms and explore what the United Nations can do."[8]

The Barriers to Arms Control

Limiting or reducing arms is an idea that most people favor. Yet arms control has proceeded slowly and sometimes not at all. The devil is in the details, as the old maxim goes, and it is important to review the continuing debate over arms control to understand its history and current status. None of the factors that we are about to discuss is the main culprit impeding arms control. Nor is any one of them insurmountable. Indeed, important advances are being made on a number of fronts. But together, these factors form a tenacious resistance to arms control.

International Barriers

A variety of security concerns make up one formidable barrier to arms control. Some analysts do not believe that countries can maintain adequate security if they disarm totally or substantially. Those who take this view are cautious about the current political scene and about the claimed contributions of arms control.

Worries about the possibility of future conflict are probably the greatest security concern about arms control. For example, the cold war and its accompanying huge arms buildup had no sooner begun to fade than fears about the threat of terrorists and "rogue" states with WMDs escalated in the aftermath of 9/11. This concern has, for instance, accelerated the U.S. effort to build a national missile defense system, as discussed in chapter 10.

At least to some degree, nuclear proliferation is also a product of insecurity. India's drive to acquire nuclear weapons was in part a reaction to the nuclear arms of China to the north, which the Indian defense minister described as his country's "potential number one enemy."[9] India's program to defend itself against China raised anxieties in Pakistan, which had fought several wars with India. So the Pakistanis began their program. "Today we have evened the score with India," Pakistan's prime minister exulted after his country's first test.[10] Similarly, North Korea has repeatedly maintained that it needs nuclear weapons to protect itself against the United States. Many Americans discount that rationale, but it is not all that far-fetched given the U.S. invasion of Iraq and other uses of force.

Much the same argument about a dangerous world helps drive other military spending and works against arms reductions. The U.S. military is the most powerful in the world, with a bigger budget than the next five or six countries combined. Yet security worries drive U.S. spending even higher. Presenting Congress in 2007 with an approximately $700 billion annual and supplementary (for Iraq and Afghanistan)

FIGURE 11.4   Arms, Tension, and War

Theory A approximates the realist view, and Theory B fits the liberal view of the causal relationship between arms, tension, and use. Theory C suggests that there is a complex causal interrelationship between arms, tension, and war in which each of the three factors affects the other two.

budget request, Secretary of Defense Robert M. Gates conceded that the request would cause "sticker shock" and that "the costs of defending our nation are high." But he also warned, "The only thing costlier, ultimately, would be to fail to commit the resources necessary to defend our interests around the world, and to fail to prepare for the inevitable threats of the future."[11]

Doubts about the value of arms control are a second security concern that restrains arms control. Those who are skeptical about arms control and its supposed benefits begin with the belief that humans arm themselves and fight because the world is dangerous, as represented by Theory A in Figure 11.4. Given this view, skeptics believe that political settlements should be achieved before arms reductions are negotiated. Such analysts therefore reject the idea that arms control agreements necessarily represent progress. In fact, it is even possible from this perspective to argue that more, not fewer weapons, will sometimes increase security.

By contrast, other analysts agree with Homer's observation in the *Odyssey* (ca. 700 B.C.) that "the blade itself incites to violence." This is represented by Theory B in Figure 11.4, and it demonstrates the belief that insecurity leads countries to have arms races, which leads to more insecurity and conflict in a hard-to-break cycle (Gibler, Rider, & Hutchison, 2005). From this perspective the way to increase security is by reducing arms, not increasing them.

While the logic of arms races seems obvious, empirical research has not confirmed that arms races always occur. Similarly, it is not clear whether decreases in arms cause or are caused by periods of improved international relations. Instead, a host of domestic and international factors influence a country's level of armaments. What this means is that the most probable answer to the chicken-and-egg debate about which should come first, political agreements or arms control, lies in a combination of these theories. That is, arms, tension, and wars all promote one another, as represented in Theory C of Figure 11.4.

Concerns about verification and cheating constitute a third international barrier to arms control stemming from security concerns. The problem is simple: Countries suspect that others will cheat. This worry was a significant factor in the rejection of the CTBT by the U.S. Senate. A chief opponent characterized the treaty as "not effectively verifiable" and therefore "ineffectual because it would not stop other nations from testing or developing nuclear weapons. . . . The CTBT simply has no teeth."[12]

There have been great advances in verification procedures and technologies. Many arms control treaties provide for **on-site inspections (OSI)** by an agency such as the IAEA, but in some cases weapons and facilities can be hidden from OSI. **National technical means (NTM)** of verification using satellites, seismic measuring devices, and other equipment have also advanced rapidly. These have been substantially offset, however, by other technologies that make NTM verification more difficult. Nuclear warheads, for example, have been miniaturized to the point where one could literally be hidden in a good-sized closet. Dual-use chemicals make it difficult to monitor the CWC, and the minute amounts of biological warfare agents needed to inflict massive casualties make the BWC daunting to monitor. Therefore, in the last analysis, virtually no amount of OSI and NTM can ensure absolute verification.

Because absolute verification is impossible, the real issue is which course is more dangerous: (1) coming to an agreement when there is at least some chance that the other side might be able to cheat, or (2) failing to agree and living in a world of un-restrained and increasing nuclear weapons growth? Sometimes, the answer may be number 2. Taking this view while testifying before the U.S. Senate about the Chemical Weapons Convention, former Secretary of State James A. Baker III counseled, "The [George H. W.] Bush administration never expected the treaty to be completely verifi-able and had always expected there would be rogue states that would not participate." Nevertheless, Baker supported the treaty on the grounds that "the more countries we can get behind responsible behavior around the world . . ., the better it is for us."[13]

Ultimately, the decision with the most momentous international security impli-cations would be to opt for a world with zero nuclear weapons. Whether you favor overcoming the many barriers to that goal or would consider such an effort a fool's errand is asked in the debate box, "Is 'Zero Nukes' a Good Goal?"

Domestic Barriers

All countries are complex decision-making organizations, as chapter 3 discusses. Not all leaders favor arms control, and even those who do often face strong opposition from powerful opponents of arms control who, as noted above, are skeptical of arms control in general or of a particular proposal. Additionally, opposition to arms control often stems from such domestic barriers as national pride and the interrelationship among military spending, the economy, and politics.

National pride is one domestic barrier to arms control. The adage in the Book of Proverbs that "pride goeth before destruction" is sometimes applicable to arms acqui-sitions. Whether we are dealing with conventional or nuclear arms, national pride is a primary drive behind their acquisition. For many countries, arms represent a tangible symbol of strength and sovereign equality. EXPLOSION OF SELF-ESTEEM read one newspaper headline in India after that country's nuclear tests in 1998.[14] LONG LIVE NUCLEAR PAKISTAN read a Pakistani newspaper headline soon thereafter. "Five nuclear blasts have instantly transformed an extremely demoralized nation into a self-respecting proud nation," the accompanying article explained.[15] Such emotions have also seemingly played a role in Iran's alleged nuclear weapons program. "I hope we get our atomic weapons," Shirzad Bozorgmehr, editor of *Iran News,* has com-mented. "If Israel has it, we should have it. If India and Pakistan do, we should, too," he explained.[16]

Military spending, the economy, and politics interact to form a second domestic barrier to arms control. Supplying the military is big business, and economic interest groups pressure their governments to build and to sell weapons and associated tech-nology. Furthermore, cities that are near major military installations benefit from jobs provided on the bases and from the consumer spending of military personnel stationed on the bases. For this reason, defense-related corporations, defense plant workers, civilian employees of the military, and the cities and towns in which they reside and shop are supporters of military spending and foreign sales. Additionally, there are often bureaucratic elements, such as ministries of defense, in alliance with the defense industry and its workers. Finally, both interest groups and bureaucratic

DEBATE THE POLICY SCRIPT

Is "Zero Nukes" a Good Goal?

Most of the commentary on nuclear weapons takes the view that they are dangerous and that reducing their number will create a safer world. By extension, a "zero-nuke" world, one with no nuclear weapons, would be even safer yet and, therefore, is a worthwhile goal. The logic is straightforward. Nuclear weapons have horrific destructive power. Even a relative handful could cause devastating casualties and damage to large countries and virtually wipe out many smaller ones. Because weapons that do not exist cannot hurt you, it would seem that if nuclear arms cuts are considered progress, then having no such weapons would be the ultimate success. Most people, even Americans with their powerful nuclear arsenal, agree with this line of thought, as Figure 11.5 shows.

It is possible, though, that the majority is wrong on this issue. Nuclear weapons may actually provide safety by making war between nuclear-armed countries too terrible to fight. Taking this view, British Prime Minister Winston Churchill observed early in the atomic age, "It may be that we shall by a process of sublime irony" come to a point "where safety will be the sturdy child of terror and survival the twin brother of annihilation."[1] Arguably Sir Winston's point was well taken; during the cold war, despite its intense hostility, the United States and the Soviet Union avoided war and its risk of nuclear counterstrikes and mutual destruction. That was the view of British Prime Minister Margaret Thatcher, who told Soviet President Mikhail Gorbachev in 1987 that, "A world without nuclear weapons would be less stable and more dangerous for all of us."[2]

Some analysts make much the same point in the post–cold war world. For example, one top U.S. government nuclear weapons expert argues that "the world, in fact, would become more dangerous, not less dangerous, were U.S. nuclear weapons to be absent. The most important role for our nuclear weapons is to serve as a 'sobering force,' one that can cap the level of destruction of military conflicts and thus force all sides to come to their senses."[3]

Not all top U.S. officials agree with this view. For instance, a number of former high-ranking U.S. military officers were among the 57 retired generals and admirals from countries with nuclear weapons who published a 1996 manifesto declaring that nuclear weapons are "of sharply reduced utility" in the post–cold war world, calling for "substantially reducing their numbers," and proclaiming that "the ultimate objective . . . should be the complete elimination of nuclear weapons from all nations" (Schultz & Isenberg, 1997:87).

What Do You Think?

Do you favor a zero-nuke world? Assume this could be achieved by a treaty in which all the countries with nuclear weapons agreed to turn them over to the International Atomic Energy Agency for immediate destruction, in which all nonnuclear countries agreed not to develop nuclear weapons, and in which all countries agreed to unlimited and unscheduled IAEA inspections to verify treaty compliance. Do not debate the possibility of cheating. For our scenario here, the treaty is foolproof, and the issue is whether the world would be safer with zero nuclear weapons or if Churchill was right when he warned, "Be careful above all things not to let go of the atomic weapon until you are sure, and more sure than sure, that other means of preserving the peace are in your hands."[4]

FIGURE 11.5   The Zero-Nukes Option

Those with them now 11%
Any 5%
Unsure 4%
U.S. only 1%
U.S. and its allies only 13%
None 66%
Which countries should be allowed to have nuclear weapons?

About two-thirds of all Americans favor a nuclear weapons–free world.

Data source: AP Poll, March 2006. Data provided by The Roper Center for Public Opinion Research, University of Connecticut.

actors receive support from legislators who represent the districts and states that benefit from military spending. This alliance between interest groups, bureaucracies, and legislators forms a military-industrial-congressional complex that has been termed the **iron triangle**.

INTERNATIONAL SECURITY FORCES

The idea of forming international security forces to supplement or replace national military forces is a second approach to seeking security on the road less traveled by. This approach would enhance, not compete with, the first approach, arms control. Indeed, the creation of international security forces and the advance of arms control are mutually supportive.

International Security Forces: Theory and Practice

The idea of seeking security through an international organization is not new. Immanuel Kant foresaw the possibility over two centuries ago in *Idea for a Universal History from a Cosmopolitan Point of View* (1784). "Through war, through the taxing and never-ending accumulation of armament . . . after devastations, revolutions, and even complete exhaustion," Kant predicted, human nature would bring people "to that which reason could have told them in the beginning": that humankind must "step from the lawless condition of savages into a league of nations" to secure the peace. These ideas have evolved into attempts to secure the peace through such international structures as the Concert of Europe, the League of Nations, and the United Nations (Price & Zacher, 2004). An increased UN peacekeeping role has been especially evident, and other international governmental organizations (IGOs) also have occasionally been involved in international security missions.

An important point is that while our discussion here will focus on the UN as a global organization, much of what is said is also applicable to regional IGOs and their security forces. The **North Atlantic Treaty Organization (NATO)** is providing international security forces in Afghanistan, Bosnia-Herzegovina, and Kosovo province. Also in Europe, the European Union took on its first peacekeeping mission in 2003 when it assumed that role in Macedonia from NATO, and a second EU initiative sent its peacekeepers to the Congo later that year. Additionally on the continent, the **Organization for Security and Cooperation in Europe (OSCE)** has taken on some functions of a regional security structure. Established in 1973, the OSCE now has 56 members, including almost all the countries of Europe, Kazakhstan and several other states in Central Asia, and Canada and the United States. Operationally, it has begun limited field activities to prevent or settle conflicts. These efforts primarily involve sending monitors and other personnel to try to resolve differences, and in 2007, OSCE missions were operating along the border between Georgia and Russia, in Kosovo, and in more than a dozen other countries or hot spots. The largest OSCE peacekeeping effort involved the dispatch of 6,000 troops from eight countries to Albania in 1997 when that country's political system collapsed into anarchy amid factional fighting.

Beyond Europe, the **African Union** has begun to take on peacekeeping duties. The AU was formed in 2001, succeeding the Organization of African Unity (founded in 1963). The AU's membership includes 52 of Africa's 53 generally recognized states and also the so-called Sahrawi Arab Democratic Republic. This territory is also called

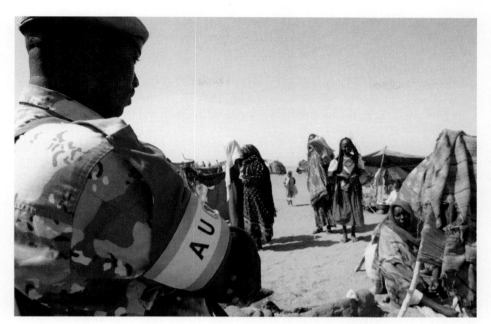

Although peacekeeping is generally associated with the UN, other international organizations such as the African Union also field international security forces. Here an AU soldier from Nigeria stands guard at a refugee camp in the Darfur region of Sudan. Unfortunately, the undermanned and lightly equipped AU force was not enough to halt the killing.

the Western Sahara, an area that Morocco claims to have incorporated in the 1970s after Spain gave up its colonial presence, and that the UN considers a non-self-governing territory. Because of this dispute and the AU's acceptance of SADR, Morocco is not an AU member. To return to the AU peacekeeping activities, it sent a force to the Darfur region of Sudan in 2004. The force was supposed to grow to 7,000, but reached only about half that size because of various reasons including the AU's limited financial resources. The UN has authorized an even larger force to supplement the AU mission, bringing the combined strength up to about 20,000 peacekeepers, but as of early 2007 the resistance of the Sudanese government has blocked the deployment of UN troops. Beginning in March 2007, the AU also deployed a limited force in Somalia to help stabilize that chronically beleaguered and fragmented country. At the subregional level in Africa, the **Economic Community of West African States (ECOWAS)** has dispatched troops over the past decade or so to Guinea-Bissau, Ivory Coast, Liberia, and Sierra Leone.

The idea of regional forces has been drawing increased support for two reasons. One is the belief that being aware of regional sensitivities, local troops are often a better option than a more international force. Second, regional organizations may sometimes be able to act more easily than the UN, which is encumbered by the veto-restricted ability of the Security Council to authorize missions. To promote African peacekeeping, the leading industrialized countries, the Group of 8 (G-8, see chapter 12) have agreed to help the AU establish a stand-by force of 15,000 peacekeeping troops by 2010. To that end, there were initial pledges in 2006 of $80 million from the United States and about $400 million from the European Union. Additionally, several European countries and Canada have agreed to fund a training center in Ghana, to prepare ECOWAS soldiers for UN, AU, and local duties.

On the other side of the South Atlantic Ocean, the Organization of American States (OAS) has advanced peace on a number of fronts, including helping to settle the long and seemingly intractable border dispute between Ecuador and Peru. The potential cause of war was eliminated in 1998 when the presidents of the two countries met in

Brazil to sign the Acta de Brasilia demarcating their border and establishing Argentina, Brazil, Chile, Spain, and the United States as the guarantors of the pact.

Collective Security

One theory behind the use of international security forces through the UN and other IGOs is the concept of **collective security**. This idea was first embodied in the Covenant of the League of Nations and is also reflected in the UN Charter.

The Theory of Collective Security   Collective security is based on three basic tenets:

- All countries forswear the use of force except in self-defense.
- All agree that the peace is indivisible. An attack on one is an attack on all.
- All pledge to unite to halt aggression and restore the peace by supplying to the UN or other IGOs whatever material or personnel resources are necessary to deter or defeat aggressors and restore the peace.

This three-part theory is something like the idea that governs domestic law enforcement. First, self-defense and the defense of someone in the case of an attack or dire threat that could lead to death or serious injury are the only times an individual can use force legally. Second, acts of violence are considered transgressions against the collective. If one person assaults another, the case is not titled the victim versus the aggressor (such as *Jones v. Smith*); it is titled the society versus the aggressor *(Ohio v. Smith);* the prosecutor takes legal action and presents the case on behalf of the people. Third, domestic societies provide a collective security force, the police, and jointly support this force through taxes.

Collective security, then, is not only an appealing idea but one that works—domestically, that is. It has not, however, been a general success on the international scene. In part, applying collective security is limited by problems such as how, in some cases, to tell the aggressor from the victim. But these uncertainties also exist domestically and are resolved. The more important reason that collective security fails is the unwillingness of countries to subordinate their sovereign interests to collective action. Thus far, governments have generally maintained their right to view conflict in terms of their national interests and to support or oppose UN action based on their nationalistic points of view. Collective security, therefore, exists mostly as a goal, not as a general practice. Only the UN-authorized interventions in Korea (1950–1953) and in the Persian Gulf (1990–1991) came close to fulfilling the idea of collective security. The United States and Great Britain tried to convince the Security Council in 2003 that the situation in Iraq warranted a third such collective security action, but that effort failed.

Collective Security, Preemption, and Iraq   The refusal of the Security Council to authorize action against Iraq and the subsequent American- and British-led invasion raised a storm of controversy over whether that action had violated the UN Charter. President George Bush and Prime Minister Tony Blair argued that they were justified in ordering action as a matter of self-defense. Secretary-General Annan disagreed, as detailed in the chapter 2 box, "Is Preemptive War Good Policy?" At the center of the dispute is the meaning and interface between Article 51 of the Charter, recognizing that every country retains "the inherent right of individual or collective self-defense if an armed attack occurs," and Article 39, which states that except in cases of self-defense, the UN Security Council has the sole authority to "determine the existence of any threat to the peace, breach of the peace, or act of aggression and . . . decide what measures shall be taken."

Not unexpectedly, an international panel subsequently appointed by Annan supported his view. In its late-2004 report, the High-Level Panel on Threats, Challenges, and Change said that while nations could act in self-defense if under attack or facing an incontrovertible and imminent attack, preemption was another matter. The report concluded that on the question of the legality of a preemptive attack,

> The short answer is that if there are good arguments for preventive military action, with good evidence to support them, they should be put to the Security Council, which can authorize such action if it chooses to. If it does not so choose, there will be, by definition, time to pursue other strategies, including persuasion, negotiation, deterrence and containment—and to visit again the military option. For those impatient with such a response, the answer must be that, in a world full of perceived potential threats, the risk to the global order and the norm of nonintervention on which it continues to be based is simply too great for the legality of unilateral preventive action, as distinct from collectively endorsed action, to be accepted. Allowing one to so act is to allow all.[17]

This reasoning cheered critics of Washington and London, but it did not address some of the political realities of Security Council politics. France, for example, may well have truly believed that more time to conduct inspections for WMDs was needed. It is also the case, though, that Paris saw the issue as a chance to frustrate American power and to reduce its hegemonic sway, at least marginally. Thus the views of the secretary-general and the panel he appointed may have been technically correct but they were also politically naïve. What the views did not adequately address is the possibility of members blocking action by the Security Council for reasons not connected to the crisis even if action is warranted.

Peacekeeping

What the United Nations has been able to do more often is to implement a process commonly called **peacekeeping**. Peacekeeping is quite different from collective security. The latter identifies an aggressor and employs military force to defeat the attacker. Peacekeeping takes another approach and deploys an international military force under the aegis of an international organization such as the UN to prevent fighting, usually by acting as a buffer between combatants. The international force is neutral between the combatants and must have been invited to be present by at least one of the combatants.

Some of the data regarding the use of UN peacekeeping forces and observer groups to help restore and maintain the peace is given in chapter 7, but it bears repeating briefly here. From 1945 to 2007, the United Nations sent over 9 million soldiers, police officers, and unarmed observers drawn from two-thirds of the world's countries to conduct 61 peacekeeping or truce observation missions. Almost 2,300 of these individuals have died in UN service. The frequency of such UN missions has risen sharply, as can be seen in Figure 7.9 on page 218. At the beginning of 2007 there were 16 UN peacekeeping forces of varying size, totaling nearly 81,000 troops, police, and military observers drawn from 114 countries in the field in Africa, Asia, Europe, and the Middle East, as shown in the map on page 364. The cost of these operations was about $4.8 billion in 2006.

Several characteristics of UN peacekeeping actions can be noted. First, most have taken place in LDC locations, as evident on the map. Second, UN forces have generally utilized military contingents from other LDCs (Lebovic, 2004). In 2006, Bangladesh, India, and Pakistan alone combined for 36% of all UN peacekeepers, and those countries plus Jordan, Ghana, Nepal, Uruguay, and Nigeria accounted for about half of all troops wearing the renowned UN blue helmets. Troops from larger

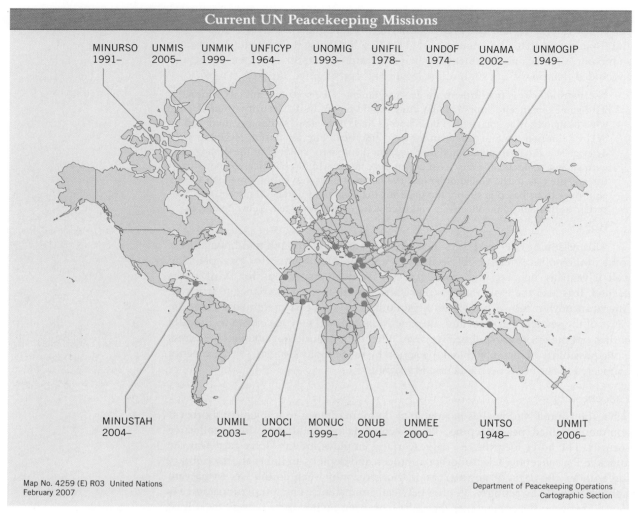

Current UN Peacekeeping Missions

MINURSO 1991– UNMIS 2005– UNMIK 1999– UNFICYP 1964– UNOMIG 1993– UNIFIL 1978– UNDOF 1974– UNAMA 2002– UNMOGIP 1949–

MINUSTAH 2004–   UNMIL 2003– UNOCI 2004– MONUC 1999– ONUB 2004– UNMEE 2000–   UNTSO 1948–   UNMIT 2006–

Map No. 4259 (E) R03 United Nations
February 2007

Department of Peacekeeping Operations
Cartographic Section

The United Nations has played a valuable peacekeeping role. This map shows the 16 peacekeeping operations active at the end of 2006. It is a testament to the ever-growing record of UN peacekeeping that the map would have become too confusing if it had included the other 43 peacekeeping missions that the UN had undertaken and concluded in its history. The Nobel Peace Prize for 1988 was awarded to the soldiers who have served in peacekeeping missions, thousands of whom have been killed or wounded in UN service.

Notes: UNTSO—UN Truce Supervision Organization
UNMOGIP—UN Military Observer Group in India and Pakistan
UNFICYP—UN Peacekeeping Force in Cyprus
UNDOF—UN Disengagement Observer Force
UNIFIL—UN Interim Force in Lebanon
MINURSO—UN Mission for the Referendum in Western Sahara
UNOMIG—UN Observer Mission in Georgia
UNMIK—UN Interim Administration Mission in Kosovo
MONUC—UN Mission in the Democratic Republic of the Congo
UNMEE—UN Mission in Ethiopia and Eritrea
UNMIT—UN Integrated Mission Timor-Leste
UNMIL—UN Mission in Liberia
UNOCI—UN Operation in Côte d'Ivoire
MINUSTAH—UN Stabilization Mission in Haiti
ONUB—UN Operation in Burundi
UNMIS—UN Mission in the Sudan
UNAMA—United Nations Assistance Mission in Afghanistan
Source: http://www.un.org/Depts/dpko/dpko/home.shtml.

powers have taken a greater part in international security missions since the end of the cold war, but those number are still small, including in 2006 the United States (324 troops and police), China (1,666), and Russia (291).

Peacekeeping Issues

There are a number of important issues related to UN peacekeeping. Some of those are discussed elsewhere. For example, chapter 7 outlines the budget restraints and the unwillingness of numerous countries to pay their dues for peacekeeping to the United Nations. Yet another issue covered in chapter 7 is the use of veto power held by the five permanent members of the UN Security Council and the growing number of countries that are voicing their discontent with a system they claim is neither fair nor any longer resembles world power realities. A third issue, addressed in chapter 9 on international law, is the demand made by the United States that its troops serving with UN peacekeeping forces be exempted by the Security Council from the jurisdiction of the International Criminal Court, and the threat of Washington to withhold its dues or veto new and continuing missions if the American stipulations are not met. Two other issues involved with peacekeeping are whether UN forces should play a relatively passive peacemaking role or a more assertive peace enforcement function and how to ensure that humanitarian interventions by UN and other IGO military police forces are not neocolonialism by another name.

Peacekeeping and Peace Enforcement For all the contributions that UN peacekeeping efforts have made, they have sometimes been unable to halt fighting quickly (or even at all) or to keep the peace permanently. The numerous reasons for the limited effectiveness of UN forces can be boiled down to two fundamental and related problems: First, countries frequently do not support UN forces politically or financially. Second, it is often difficult to get the self-interested UN Security Council members, especially the five veto-wielding permanent members, to agree to authorize a UN mission. Even when the mission is authorized, it is often given a very narrow scope of authority to act and few troops. When, for example, the UN initially sent forces to the Balkans in 1992, the secretary-general asked for 35,000 peacekeepers. However, the Security Council authorized only 7,000 troops restricted to light arms and not authorized to take strong action. These limits prevented the peacekeepers from being effective and even led, at one point, to UN troops being taken hostage and chained to potential targets to deter threatened action by NATO forces.

The mounting frustrations with the reactive, passive peacekeeping approach of UN forces led to an upsurge of support for the idea of proactive **peace enforcement**. This new role would involve heavily armed UN forces with the authority to restore and maintain the peace. Such UN units would not only intervene where fighting had already broken out. They could also be deployed to imperiled countries before trouble starts, thereby putting an aggressor in the uncomfortable position of attacking UN forces as well as national defense forces.

In an effort to implement change, successive secretaries-general have called on UN members to better fund and equip UN forces and to give them sufficient personnel and a broad enough mandate (rules of engagement) that will allow them to be effective. A report issued in 2000 by a special panel appointed by the secretary-general to study peacekeeping operations made several key points.[18] The report noted that when major forces are needed to respond to aggression, "the United Nations does not wage war." Instead, to respond, it relies on "coalitions of willing states, with the authorization of the Security Council." Nevertheless, the panel urged that when peacekeepers are deployed, "The United Nations must be prepared to deal effectively with spoilers

MAP
Current UN Peacekeeping Operations

Did You Know That:

In late 2006, the five countries with the most UN peacekeepers were Pakistan (9,867), Bangladesh (9,6818), India (9,483), Jordan (3,820), and Ghana (2,694).

Web Link

The site of the UN's Department of Peacekeeping Operations is at **http://www.un.org/Depts/dpko/dpko/**.

JOIN THE DEBATE
The United Nations and the Establishment of International Peace: Debating the Scope of UN Peacekeeping Mandates

[of the peace] if it expects to achieve a consistent record of success in peace-keeping." One step toward that goal, according to the report, is closing "the gap between verbal postures and financial and political support for prevention" by the UN's member-states. The panel also recommended a change in posture for UN troops. For example, instead of maintaining impartiality toward all combatants, the report said that when one side was clearly at fault, the UN should take a more assertive stand. To implement this, it recommended bigger and better equipped forces with enough freedom of action to be "a credible deterrent," to "mount an effective defense against violent challengers," and when faced with flagrant violence "to stop it." Additionally, the panel called for the UN to have a "rapid and effective deployment capacity" so that it could deploy peacekeepers more rapidly. This could involve options ranging from national troops predesignated and trained for UN missions to a standing UN military force.

Reflective of the gap between the member-states' rhetoric and reality, such calls for a more effective UN peace-enforcing ability have often drawn accolades from national leaders and sometimes even pledges of support. However, change has been slow and limited. As one analyst explains the resistance of countries to further empowering the UN, "Robust peace enforcement is beyond the capacity of the United Nations. The Security Council does not have the stomach for it, contributing countries don't want to put their troops under other commanders and then have to answer questions at home when their troops get killed."[19]

WEB POLL
The United Nations and
International Security

Peace Enforcement: Humanitarian Intervention or Neocolonialism?   Doubts about a more aggressive UN military role are not just based on nationalism and other such factors. There is also a concern that creating a more powerful, proactive UN will undermine the sovereignty of the smaller LDCs and that the UN will become a neocolonial tool of the big powers. In the words of one UN report, "there is the understandable and legitimate concern of member-states, especially the small and weak among them, about sovereignty."[20] The chaos and abuses that engulf weak countries sometimes render them mere legal fictions that have no coherent government, and they are considered so-called failed states. In such a situation, other states may have powerful emotional and political incentives to intervene, either to alleviate the suffering or to take political advantage of the turmoil. One observer notes, for example, that "the new rule whereby human rights outrank sovereignty must still prevail, because the old rule is simply dead." The problem, the analyst continues, is the "places where this new rule could be applied all too easily: weak states" (Luttwak, 2000:61). That, arguably, allows powerful states like China to continue to abuse human rights while small countries may be "invaded" by international security forces and have their sovereignty abridged. To make matters worse, the concern about neocolonialism sometimes helps countries fend off intervention even when it seems clearly justified. Despite the atrocities it has committed in Darfur, the Sudanese government rejects UN peacekeepers on the grounds, President Omar al-Bashir argues, that they are "part of a comprehensive conspiracy for confiscating the country's sovereignty."[21] This complaint has enough resonance with enough countries in the UN to have so far helped frustrate the UN's efforts to deploy peacekeepers to Darfur.

Other commentators worry that once the barrier of sovereignty is breached, the powerful countries will have license through the UN to impose their will on weaker countries. That suspicion is not voiced only from within LDCs; it also receives some scholarly support. A study of the record from 1945 to 1990 concluded that the political consideration the countries applied to supporting peacekeeping led to a record during the cold war "bordering on imperialism" by the Western countries and that a post–cold war "expansion of UN peacekeeping activities . . . [might] signal an era in which sovereignty is eroded, but only for non-Western states" (Neack, 1995:194).

International Security and the Future

What does the future hold for international security? Certainly many impediments, but it would be foolish to dismiss the idea as impossible. First, it is in almost everyone's interest to prevent or contain crises, and there is a growing recognition that using an international security force cooperatively may often be a more effective way to maintain or restore peace than is continued reliance on unlimited national self-defense in a world capable of producing and using WMDs. As such, the peacekeeping is largely a functional response to an international problem, and the increased number of missions by the UN and regional IGOs is evidence that the international security efforts are necessary, have achieved some successes, and almost certainly have become a permanent part of world politics (Fortna, 2004).

Second, it is important to see that many of the shortcomings of previous international security missions have not been due to an inherent failure of the UN. Certainly the UN has problems, as any large political and bureaucratized organization does. But the central problem, according to one secretary-general, is that the UN has "been asked to do too much with too little."[22]

Events in the first years of the new millennium somewhat revived interest in strengthening UN forces and giving them more proactive authority. As has occurred too often before, UN forces in Sierra Leone in 2000 were outnumbered, outgunned, and hamstrung by a very limited authority to initiate action. Then after a humiliating incident in which rebels took several dozen UN peacekeepers hostage, the Security Council more than tripled UN forces in the country and gave them a broader mandate. The improved UN position played an important role in creating enough stability to allow elections in 2002. Stability has continued in Sierra Leone. Reflecting that, the Security Council ended the UN peacekeeping mission there in December 2005, replacing it with a much smaller monitoring group to report on any future threats to peace.

Does peacekeeping work? Sometimes it does. Haiti is one of the recent success stories. Here a Brazilian peacekeeper, who is part of the UN force that has been in Haiti since 2004, stands on guard in front of graffiti in the slum area Cite-Soleil in Port-au-Prince in 2007. The desperately poor area is now relatively peaceful, a calm advanced in part when UN forces arrested 400 suspected members of violent gangs that were terrorizing the residents.

Unfortunately, such success stories are offset by others demonstrating the barriers to effective peacekeeping. Darfur provides a tragic example. The effort to get a UN force into Darfur has been extraordinarily frustrating despite continued attacks on civilians. Part of the problem has been the resistance of Russia and China on the Security Council to strong measures. Some of that reflects their general positions against interventions and sanctions, but their stand also stems from self-interests. China, for example, buys about two-thirds of Sudan's petroleum exports. Russia also has commercial interests in Sudan and, among other things, has sold the Sudanese government over $500 million in weapons since 2000. Even after the UN finally authorized a UN force to go to Sudan to supplement the African Union force there, the Sudanese government refused to let it enter, and the politics of the UN prevented a forced entry or even strong sanctions on Sudan.

Darfur also demonstrates the limitations to the idea of instituting a stronger peace enforcement element to UN troop deployment. Sudan has responded to pressure to allow UN troops in by declaring that it would consider any attempt to send in peacekeepers without the permission of the Sudanese government a "hostile act" and "an invasion." This implied threat to use the Sudanese military to attack the peacekeepers was made to dissuade countries from contributing troops, and it had its effect. In late 2006, Jean-Marie Guehenno, head of the UN peacekeeping department, told reporters that UN members had not been "forthcoming" with pledges of peacekeepers for the new force authorized by the Security Council and that the UN was neither well-enough equipped to fight a war nor powerful enough to force its way into Darfur. As he summed up the situation, "When you try to apply peacekeeping to any kind of situation and confuse peacekeeping with peace enforcement, you run very quickly into great difficulties."[23] At least for Americans, the accuracy of Guehenno's analysis is evident in Figure 11.6.

Another approach for the immediate future may be to distinguish between types of international security efforts, including peacekeeping and peace enforcement missions, and to handle them differently. The UN's undersecretary-general for peacekeeping has contended, "Peace enforcement and serious peace restoration campaigns will . . . be the responsibility of a coalition of interested countries using their own forces but with a green light from the Council."[24] This model is much like the NATO-led interventions in Bosnia in 1995 and in Kosovo in 1999 and the International Force in East Timor in 1999. This Australian-led multinational force restored stability in East Timor before handing over responsibility for the territory to the UN in 2000. According to this model, peace enforcement would be up to heavily armed regional forces, with peacekeeping assigned to more lightly armed UN contingents. As one U.S. diplomat explains it, "There has to be a peace to keep before the blue helmets are put on the ground."[25] In the case of East Timor, at least, the model worked well. Peace was restored and protected, and the UN established a transitional administration that prepared East Timor for full independence in May 2002.

This model also resembles the intervention in Afghanistan beginning in 2001. The initial action was taken under UN authority by a U.S.-led coalition of forces that routed al Qaeda and toppled the Taliban government. Then in 2002 the UN Security Council turned over authority to the NATO-led International Security Assistance Force to provide security in Kabul in support of the efforts of the interim government to begin the reconstruction of the country's physical and political structures.

In sum, the exact configuration of international security forces in the future is not clear. They face many problems, and there is no consensus on how to fix them. The UN process, especially the veto in the Security Council, makes it difficult to take action or institute change. Additionally, countries are not willing to pay enough money,

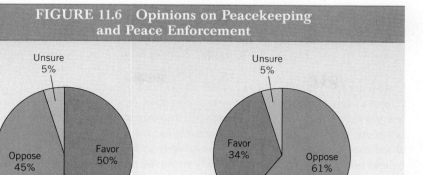

FIGURE 11.6   Opinions on Peacekeeping and Peace Enforcement

Unsure
5%

Oppose
45%

Favor
50%

Do you favor or oppose sending U.S.
troops to Darfur as a small part of a
UN peacekeeping force?

Unsure
5%

Favor
34%

Oppose
61%

Do you favor or oppose sending 10,000 U.S.
troops to Darfur as part of a UN peacekeeping
mission that may cost 100 U.S. lives?

One restraint on UN peacekeeping is that while most people support the concept and are even willing to contribute a limited number of their country's troops, support declines substantially when faced with the possibility of sending larger numbers of troops and sustaining casualties. This attitudinal pattern among Americans is evident here in their responses to two questions asked in the same poll. Half were willing to send a few U.S. troops to Darfur, but when asked about sending more troops and perhaps having 100 killed, opinion shifted, with a majority opposed. This result also relates to the discussion in Chapter 8 about whether U.S. power has been eroded by an alleged unwillingness of Americans to tolerate casualties to U.S. troops.

Data source: Genocide Intervention Network poll, December 2006; data provided by The Roper Center for Public Opinion Research, University of Connecticut.

send enough troops, or give the UN enough authority to not just keep peace, but to enforce it if necessary. There is fear, legitimate to some degree, that despite its appealing name, peacekeeping is a form of intervention that is never applied to the mighty, only to the weak by the mighty. Yet for all the failures, half-successes, and ongoing problems, it is also the case that international security forces have become an integral part of world politics in the little more than half a century since they were first deployed; they are here to stay, and we are even likely to see their use increase.

ABOLITION OF WAR

The last of the four approaches to security that we will examine in this chapter looks toward the abolition of war. For our purposes, we will divide the discussion into two parts: complete disarmament and pacifism.

Complete Disarmament

The most sweeping approach to arms control is simply to disarm. The principal argument in favor of disarmament is, as noted, the idea that without weapons people will not fight. This rests in part on sheer inability. **General and complete disarmament (GCD)** might be accomplished either through unilateral disarmament or through multilateral negotiated disarmament.

In the case of *unilateral disarmament,* a country would act on its own to dismantle its arms. Its safety, in theory, would be secured by its nonthreatening posture, which would prevent aggression, and its example would lead other countries to also disarm. Unilateral disarmament draws heavily on the idea of pacifism, or a moral and resolute refusal to fight. The unilateral approach also relies on the belief that it is arms that cause tension rather than vice versa. *Negotiated disarmament* between two or more countries is a more limited approach. Advocates of this path share the unilateralists' conviction about the danger of war. They are less likely to be true pacifists, however, and they believe one-sided disarmament would expose the peace pioneer to unacceptable risk.

The GCD approach has few strong advocates among today's political leaders. Even those who do subscribe to the ideal also search for intermediate arms limitation steps. Still, the quest goes on. The UN Disarmament Committee has called for GCD, and the ideal is a valuable standard by which to judge progress as "real."

Pacifism

The second war-avoidance approach, pacifism, relies on individuals. As such, it very much fits in with the idea that people count and that you can affect world politics if you try. Unlike other approaches to security, **pacifism** is a bottom-up approach that focuses on what people do rather than a top-down approach that stresses government action.

Pacifism begins with the belief that it is wrong to kill. Leo Tolstoy, the Russian novelist and pacifist, told the Swedish Peace Conference in 1909, "The truth is so simple, so clear, so evident . . . that it is only necessary to speak it out completely for its full significance to be irresistible." That truth, Tolstoy went on, "lies in what was said thousands of years ago in four words: *Thou Shalt Not Kill.*"

Beyond this starting point, pacifists have varying approaches. There are *universal pacifists,* who oppose all violence; *private pacifists,* who oppose personal violence but who would support as a last resort the use of police or military force to counter criminals or aggressors; and *antiwar pacifists,* who oppose political violence but would use violence as a last resort for personal self-defense.

The obvious argument against pacifism is that it leads to getting killed or conquered. Those who support pacifism make several counterarguments. One is that pacifism has proven effective. As one scholar points out, "Nonviolence is as old as the history of religious leaders and movements." The analyst goes on to explain that "traditions embodied by Buddha and Christ have inspired successful modern political movements and leaders [such as] . . . the Indian struggle for independence under the leadership of [Mohandas K.] Gandhi and the struggle of the American blacks for greater equality under the leadership of Martin Luther King, Jr." (Beer, 1990:16).

Gandhi was the great Indian spiritual leader. He began his career as a London-trained attorney earning what was then an immense sum of £5,000 annually practicing in Bombay. Soon, however, he went to South Africa, where, earning £50 a year, he defended Indian expatriates against legal white oppression. Gandhi returned to India in 1915 to work for its independence. He gave up Western ways for a life of abstinence and spirituality. Gandhi believed that the force of the soul focused on (to use the Hindi terms) *satyagraha* (truth seeking) and *ahimsa* (nonviolence) could accomplish what resorting to arms could not. He developed techniques such as unarmed marches, sit-downs by masses of people, work stoppages, boycotts, and what might today be called "pray-ins," whereby *satyagrahi* (truth seekers) could confront the British nonviolently.

SIMULATION
Make Love Not War

"The sword of the *satyagrahi* is love," he counseled the Indian people (Lackey, 1989:14). Gandhi became known as Mahatma (great soul) and was the single most powerful force behind Great Britain's granting of independence to India in 1947. The Mahatma then turned his soul toward ending the hatred and violence between Hindus and Muslims in independent India. For this, a Hindu fanatic, who objected to Gandhi's tolerance, assassinated him in 1948. Earlier, after the United States had dropped atomic bombs on Japan, Gandhi was moved to write that "mankind has to get out of violence only through nonviolence. Hatred can be overcome only by love. Counter-hatred only increases the surface as well as the depth of hatred." One has to suspect that had he been able to, Gandhi would have repeated this to the man who shot him.

Pacifists, especially antiwar pacifists, would also make a moral case against the massive, collective violence that is war. They would say that no gain is worth the loss. This view, they would argue, has become infinitely more compelling in the nuclear age. Consider the description of Nagasaki filed by the first reporter who flew over the city after a U.S. bomber dropped an atomic bomb, killing at least 60,000 people. "Burned, blasted, and scarred," he wrote, "Nagasaki looked like a city of death." It was a scene, he continued, of "destruction of a sort never before imagined by a man and therefore is almost indescribable. The area where the bomb hit is absolutely flat and only the markings of the building foundations provide a clue as to what may have been in the area before the energy of the universe was turned loose" (Lackey, 1989:112). Pacifists contend that even by the standards of just war conduct (*jus in bello*) adopted by nonpacifists, any nuclear attack would be unconscionable.

A final point about pacifism is that it is not an irrelevant exercise in idealist philosophy. There are some countries, such as Japan, where at least limited pacifism represents a reasonably strong political force. Moreover, in a changing world, public opinion, economic measures, and other nonviolent instruments may create what is sometimes called a "civilian-based defense." Indeed, there are efforts, such as the Program on Nonviolent Sanctions in Conflict and Defense at Harvard University's Center for International Affairs, that are working to show that those who favor nonviolence should not be considered "token pacifists" who are "tolerated as necessary to fill out the full spectrum of alternatives, with nonviolent means given serious considerations only for use in noncritical situations" (Bond, 1992:2). Instead, advocates of this approach believe that the successes of Gandhi, King, and others demonstrate that proactive techniques, including nonviolent protest and persuasion, noncooperation, and nonviolent intervention (such as sit-ins), can be successful (Schell, 2003).

It is true that pacifists are unlikely to be able to reverse world conflict by themselves. They are a tiny minority everywhere. Instead, pacifism may be part of a series of so-called peace creation actions. It is an idea worth contemplating.

Pacifism's simple message that killing and war are absolutely unacceptable is considered naïve by most people, but perhaps those who dismiss pacifism are cynics standing in the way of permanent peace.

Web Link

"Shakespeare's Pacifism," an article by Steven Marx in *Renaissance Quarterly* (1992) arguing that the Bard's plays shifted from being militaristic to favoring pacifism, is available at **http://cla.calpoly.edu/~smarx/ Publications/pacifism.html.**

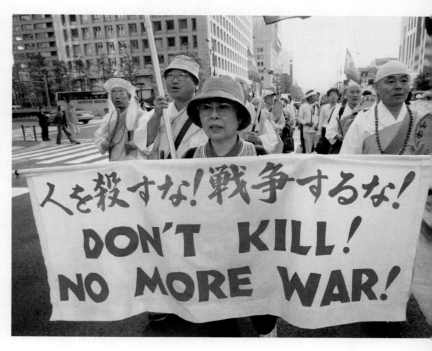

CHAPTER SUMMARY

THINKING ABOUT SECURITY

1. The goal of the chapter is to discuss alternative paths to security. Security is not necessarily synonymous with either massive armaments or with disarmament. There are four approaches to security: unlimited self-defense, limited self-defense, international security, and abolition of war. The first was the subject of the last chapter. This chapter investigates the other three.

2. There are four possible approaches to ensuring security. They involve restrictions on the number of arms; their development, testing, and deployment; restrictions on certain types of weapons; and the transfer of weapons. Additionally, the standards of evaluation are determined by domestic norms, domestic collective security forces, domestic disarmament, and the established domestic conflict-resolution mechanism. Despite all of the protections and dispute-resolution procedures provided by a domestic system, security is a relative term, thus making full security impossible.

LIMITED SELF-DEFENSE THROUGH ARMS CONTROL

3. Some people believe that, because of the nature of humans and the nature of the international system, unlimited self-defense is the prudent policy. Advocates of this approach are suspicious of arms control.

4. Limited self-defense is one means of alternative security. People who favor limited self-defense would accomplish their goals through various methods of arms control.

5. From the standpoint of pure rationality, arms control, or the lack of it, is one of the hardest aspects of international politics to understand. Virtually everyone is against arms; virtually everyone is for arms control; yet there are virtually no restraints on the explosive arms escalation in which we are all trapped. It is a story that dates back far into our history, but unless progress is made, we may not have a limitless future ahead.

6. There are many powerful arguments against continuation of the arms race. Arms are very costly, in direct dollars and in indirect impact on the economy. Arms are also very dangerous and add to the tensions that sometimes erupt in violence.

7. During the 1990s, efforts increased to regulate arms. Several START treaties, renewal of the Nuclear Non-Proliferation Treaty (NPT), the Comprehensive Test Ban Treaty (CTBT), conventional weapons inventories, conventional weapons transfer regulation, and biological and chemical arms control are among the efforts made. There are heavy domestic pressures from the military-industrial-congressional complex and sometimes from the public against arms control.

8. There are a number of ways to implement approaches to arms control, including arms reductions, limits on the expansion of arms inventories, and prohibitions against conventional arms transfers and nuclear proliferation.

INTERNATIONAL SECURITY FORCES

9. Some people favor trying to achieve security through various international security schemes. Collective security, peacekeeping, and peace enforcement are among the most significant attempts of an international security effort. The most likely focus of this approach would be the United Nations with a greatly strengthened security mandate and with security forces sufficient to engage in peace enforcement, rather than just peacekeeping.

ABOLITION OF WAR

10. Abolition of war is a fourth approach to security. One way to avoid war is through general and complete disarmament. This makes violence difficult and may also ease tensions that lead to violence. Individual and collective pacifism is another way to avoid violence. Pacifists believe that the way to start the world toward peace is to practice nonviolence individually and in ever-larger groups.

For simulations, debates, and other interactive activities, a chapter quiz, Web links, and much more, visit **www.mhhe.com/rourke12/** and go to chapter 11. Or, while accessing the site, click on Course-Wide Content and view recent international relations articles in the *New York Times*.

KEY TERMS

African Union

Anti-Ballistic Missile Treaty (ABM)

Anti-Personnel Mine Treaty (APM)

arms control

Biological Weapons Convention

Chemical Weapons Convention (CWC)

collective security

Comprehensive Test Ban Treaty (CTBT)

Conventional Forces in Europe Treaty (CFE)

dual-use technology

Economic Community of West African States (ECOWAS)

general and complete disarmament (GCD)

Intermediate-Range Nuclear Forces Treaty (INF)

iron triangle

Missile Technology Control Regime (MTCR)

national technical means (NTM)

Non-Proliferation Treaty (NPT)

North Atlantic Treaty Organization (NATO)

on-site inspections (OSI)

Organization for Security and Cooperation in Europe (OSCE)

pacifism

peace enforcement

peacekeeping

Strategic Arms Limitation Talks Treaty I (SALT I)

Strategic Arms Limitation Talks Treaty II (SALT II)

Strategic Arms Reduction Treaty I (START I)

Strategic Arms Reduction Treaty II (START II)

Strategic Offensive Reductions Treaty (SORT)

National Economic Competition: The Traditional Road

Our wealth increased
By prosperous voyages I often made.
> —William Shakespeare, *The Comedy of Errors*

I greatly fear my money is not safe.
> —William Shakespeare, *The Comedy of Errors*

In this chapter and the next one, you will be asked to evaluate different approaches to the global economy. One, economic nationalism, argues that tariffs and other protectionist measures are valid ways to protect a country's industries and workers. Representing this view is the group of Australians protesting what they see as the negative impact of free trade on their country.

GIVEN THE DEGREE TO WHICH this text has already discussed the interplay of politics and economics, you have probably concluded correctly that, to a significant extent, economics is politics and vice versa. Chapter 8, for example, discusses the elements of national economic power and also how economic power is applied by states to achieve their diplomatic goals. This chapter and the next explore the **international political economy (IPE)**, that is, how economics and politics intertwine. The subject of this chapter is economic competition among countries, the traditional IPE approach (Goddard, Cronin, & Dash, 2003). We begin by explaining IPE theories and also the general state of the world economy before turning to national economic competition. Then chapter 13 discusses international economic cooperation, the alternative IPE path.

It is important before delving into the subject to familiarize yourself with the distinctions between some economics terms that you will encounter frequently in this and the next chapter. **Gross national product (GNP)**, also called gross national income (GNI), is the value of all domestic and international economic activity by a country's citizens and business. **Gross domestic product (GDP)** is the value of all economic activity within a country by its own and foreign individuals and companies. Some sources use raw numbers to report GNP and GDP, while others adjust these two measures for **purchasing power parity** (**PPP**, as in GNP/PPP, GDP/PPP). This process adjusts the GNP and GDP to a relative value against the U.S. dollar based on differentiations in the cost of food, housing, and other "local" purchases. For example, the unadjusted 2005 per capita GNPs of the United States and Mexico are $43,740 and $7,310 respectively. Because it is the standard against which other currencies are measured, the U.S. GNP/PPP remains the same ($43,740), while Mexico's GNP/PPP ($10,030) is 37% more than its unadjusted GNP because of the lower cost of living in Mexico. By contrast, Japan's per capita GNP/PPP ($31,410) is 19% lower than its unadjusted GNP ($38,980) because of its relatively high cost of living compared to the United States.

Both measures have advantages and disadvantages. GNP does not take prices of locally produced and consumed items into account. But GNP-PPP misses the fact that many items we all consume come through international trade, and prices of a barrel of imported petroleum or an imported computer are pretty much the same, whether you are paying for them in U.S. dollars, Mexican pesos, or Japanese yen. Finally, it is important to understand the difference between **current dollars** and **real dollars**. Current (inflated) dollars report values in terms of the worth of the currency in the year being reported. Real (constant, uninflated) dollars express value in terms of a base year adjusted for inflation. For example, if your current dollar earnings were $50,000 a year in 2006 and you got a raise to $60,000 in 2008, but there was 10% annual inflation, then using 2006 as the base year, your real dollar earnings in 2008 would be just $55,000 with the other half of your $10,000 raise being offset by inflation.

A final technical note is about sources and statistics. You may find that the data used here for any given indicator may vary somewhat from another source. The reason is that for most of the data the methodology used to calculate it varies among reporting organizations, such as the World Bank, IMF, WTO, UN, and U.S. government. Second, the data itself is imperfect. For example, if you have ever been paid for an odd job such as cutting grass or babysitting and not reported the income, then you have detracted from the precise calculation of your country's GNP. Economic data for poorer countries is especially imperfect, given the limited resources those countries' governments have to collect statistics. None of this means that you can ignore the data. Instead, it means that it is best to concentrate on trends, such as the rapid growth of international trade, and on major differences, such as the per capita income gap between the wealthy and poor countries. For instance, whatever the precise amount,

Web Link

The United Bank of Switzerland analyzes the PPP factor among major world currencies by comparing the prices of a Big Mac hamburger at McDonald's restaurants around the world. To learn more, go to the UBS site **www.ubs.com** and type "Big Mac" into the search window.

MAP
Gross National Income
Per Capita

trade has risen vastly during the last half-century. Also, whether the difference in per capita wealth between Americans and Mexicans is $36,430 measured in unadjusted GNP or is $33,710 measured in GNP-PPP, the key point is that it is huge.

THEORIES OF INTERNATIONAL POLITICAL ECONOMY

As chapter 1 discusses, many political scientists believe that economic forces and conditions are the key determinants of the course of world politics. The various theories that these scholars have advanced to explain the interaction between politics and economics can be roughly divided into economic nationalist, economic internationalist, and economic structuralist approaches. Each of these three approaches purports to describe how and why conditions occur and also offers prescriptions about how policy should be conducted. These descriptions and prescriptions are summarized in Table 12.1. You should further note that economic nationalism is a realpolitik school of IPE, while economic internationalism and, especially, economic structuralism are liberal schools.

Economic Nationalism

The core of **economic nationalism** is the realpolitik belief that the state should use its economic strength to further national interests. By extension, economic nationalists also advocate using a state's power to build its economic strength. Early economic nationalism writings include those of the first Secretary of the U.S. Treasury Alexander Hamilton in his *Report on Manufactures* (1790) and German economist George List's influential study *National System of Political Economy* (1841). In the latter, List argued that the prosperity of individuals was inextricably linked to that of their nation and its political expression, the nation-state. Therefore, List advocated strong government action to promote and protect domestic industries. He rejected the idea of free trade and instead believed in protectionism and other trade policies designed to gain an economic advantage. List also argued for government subsidies for industry, government investment in transportation, education, and other infrastructure improvements that would benefit the economy. Economic nationalists also believe that conflict characterizes international economic relations and that the international economy is a zero-sum game in which one side can gain only if another loses. From the economic nationalist perspective, political goals should govern economic policy because the aim is to maximize state power in order to secure state interests.

To accomplish their ends, economic nationalists rely on a number of political-economic strategies such as exploiting weaker countries. *Colonialism* (imperialism) seeks national economic gain by directly controlling another land and its people. It was this motive that propelled Europeans outward to conquer and build the great colonial empires. Classic colonialism has largely died out, but many observers charge that **neocolonialism** (neoimperialism, indirect control) continues to exist, with the powerful **economically developed countries (EDCs)** of the North dominating and exploiting the **less developed countries (LDCs)** of the South. Economic nationalists also advocate furthering their country's policy goals by using *economic incentives*, such as foreign aid and favorable trade terms, and *economic disincentives*, such as sanctions. For example, a U.S. State Department official justified putting "pressure on the Cuban government through the embargo and [other sanctions]" on the grounds

TABLE 12.1	Approaches to International Political Economy		
	Economic Nationalism	**Economic Internationalism**	**Economic Structuralism**
Associated terms	Mercantilism, economic statecraft	Liberalism, free trade, free economic interchange, capitalism, laissez-faire	Marxism, dependency, neo-Marxism, neoimperialism, neocolonialism
Primary economic actors	States, alliances	Individuals, multinational corporations, IGOs	Economic classes (domestic and state)
Current economic relations	Competition and conflict based on narrow national interest; zero-sum game	National competition but cooperation increasing; non-zero-sum game	Conflict based on classes of countries; wealthy states exploit poor ones; zero-sum game
Goal for future	Preserve/expand state power; secure national interests	Increase global prosperity	Eliminate internal and international classes
Prescription for future	Follow economic policies that build national power; use power to build national economy	Eliminate/minimize role of politics in economics; use politics	Radically reform system to end divisions in wealth and power between classes of countries
Desired relationship of politics and economics	Politics controls economic policy	Politics used only to promote domestic free markets and international free economic interchange	Politics should be eliminated by destruction of class system
View of states	Favorable; augment state power	Mixed; eliminate states as primary economic policy makers	Negative; radically reform states; perhaps eliminate states
Estimation of possibility of cooperation	Impossible; humans and states inherently seek advantage and dominance	Possible through reforms within a modified state-based system	Only possible through radical reform; revolution may be necessary
Views on development of LDCs	No responsibility to help. Also could lose national advantages by creating more competition, higher resource prices	Can be achieved through aid, loans, investment, trade, and other assistance within current system; will ultimately benefit all countries	Exploitation of countries must be ended by fundamentally restructuring the distribution of political and economic power

Conceptual sources: Isaak (2000). Balaam & Veseth (1996), Gilpin (1996), author.

Analysts take very different approaches in describing how the international political economy works and in prescribing how it should work.

that they "can be and are a valuable tool for . . . protecting our national interests."[1] *Protectionism,* such as tariffs, and *domestic economic support,* such as tax breaks for companies that manufacture exports, are a third set of tools that economic nationalists favor. Because they favor using economic measures as a policy tool, economic nationalists are suspicious of free trade and many other aspects of economic globalization on the grounds that these take away important economic levers and thus reduce their state's sovereignty and its power.

Economic Internationalism

A second theoretical and policy approach to IPE is **economic internationalism**, which is also commonly called economic liberalism. Other associated terms include capitalism, laissez-faire, and free trade. Economic internationalists are liberals. They believe that international economic relations should and can be conducted cooperatively because, in their view, the international economy is a non-zero-sum game in which prosperity is available to all. To spread prosperity, economic internationalists favor freeing trade and other forms of economic interchange from political restrictions. Therefore, economic internationalists (in contrast to economic nationalists) oppose tariff barriers, domestic subsidies, sanctions, and any other economic tools that distort the free flow of trade, investments, and currencies.

The origins of economic liberalism lie in the roots of **capitalism**. One early proponent of capitalist theory, Adam Smith, wrote in *The Wealth of Nations* (1776) that people seek prosperity "from their regard to their own interest" and that this self-interest constituted an "invisible hand" of competition that created the most efficient economies. Therefore, he opposed any political interference in trade. Smith argued that "if a foreign country can supply us with a commodity cheaper than we ourselves can make it, better buy it of them with some part of the produce of our own industry, employed in a way in which we have some advantage."

The pure capitalism advocated by Smith has few adherents today. Instead, most modern economic liberals favor a "mixed economy" using the state to modify the worst abuses of capitalism by preventing the formation of monopolies and by taking other steps to ease the brutal competition and unequal distribution of wealth inherent in capitalism. At the international level, the liberal approach of modified capitalism makes its adherents moderate reformers who would alter, but not radically change either capitalism or the state-based international system. Instead they would use intergovernmental organizations (IGOs), such as the International Monetary Fund (IMF), to promote and, when necessary, to regulate international economic interchange. Modern liberals also favor such government interference as foreign aid and a degree of concessionary trade agreements or loan terms to assist LDCs to develop.

In sum, modern economic liberals generally believe in the capitalist approach of eliminating political interference in the international economy. They are modified capitalists, though, because they also favor using IGO and national government programs for two ends: (1) to ensure that countries adopt capitalism and free trade, and (2) to ease the worst inequities in the system so that future competition can be fairer and current LDCs can have a chance to achieve prosperity. Thus economic liberals do not want to overturn the current political and economic international system.

Economic Structuralism

Advocates of the third major approach to IPE, **economic structuralism**, believe that economic structure determines politics; they argue that the way the world is organized economically determines how world politics is conducted. Economic structuralists contend that the world is divided between have and have-not countries and that the "haves" (the EDCs) work to keep the "have nots" (the LDCs) weak and poor in order to exploit them. To change this, economic structuralists favor a radical restructuring of the economic system to end the uneven distribution of wealth and power. There are several subsets of economic structuralist thought.

Marxist theory is the first of these subsets. It is based on the ideas of Karl Marx, who with Friedrich Engels in *The Communist Manifesto* (1848) depicted the struggle between the propertied and powerful *bourgeoisie* and the poor and oppressed *proletariat* over the distribution of wealth as the essence of politics. The first Soviet Communist Party chief, V. I. Lenin, applied Marxism to international politics. He argued in

Imperialism: The Highest Stage of Capitalism (1916) that capitalist, bourgeois leaders had duped their proletariat workers into supporting the exploitation of other proletariat peoples through imperialism. Thus, the class struggle also included an international class struggle between bourgeois and proletariat countries and peoples.

Dependency theory, like Marxism, holds that underdevelopment and poverty in the LDCs is the result of exploitation by the EDCs. However, dependency theorists focus on nationalist effort and, unlike Marxists, do not believe that the workers of the world would unite if freed of their respective bourgeoisie masters. Dependency theorists contend that the EDCs' exploitation of the LDCs is driven by the EDCs' need for cheap **primary products** (such as oil), large external markets for the EDCs' expensive **manufactured goods**, profitable investment opportunities, and low-wage labor. Because this economic structure enriches the EDCs and impoverishes the LDCs, dependency theories argue that the EDCs follow policies designed to keep LDCs dependent. For this reason, economic structuralists call the system that has been created *neocolonialism* because it operates without colonies but is nevertheless imperialistic. The dependency of LDCs is maintained in a number of ways. Some are subtle, such as giving rich countries much greater voting power in the IMF and some other IGOs, thereby allowing the EDCs to manipulate the world economy to their advantage. Other techniques are less subtle. These include corrupting and co-opting the local elite in LDCs by allowing them personal wealth in return for governing their countries to benefit the North or, if the local elite is defiant, using military force to overthrow it and replace it with a friendlier regime.

World systems theory traces the current global economic inequality to the rise of the Western political and economic domination, especially following the Western-centered industrial revolution in the mid-1700s. Theorists who take this perspective contend that the evolution of the Western-dominated capitalist system has distorted development, leaving vast economic, social, and political disparities between the core of the international system (the EDCs) and the periphery (the LDCs). As for countries such as South Korea, which have achieved considerable prosperity, world system theorists are apt to argue that these semiperiphery states have achieved success only by dutifully serving the interests of the EDCs. Like all economic structuralists, world systems theorists favor dramatic changes to the prevailing economic model of Western-dominated capitalism. Sharing the view of dependency theorists, and unlike their Marxist counterparts, world system theorists do not believe that capitalism and the state system should be wiped away. Yet even those not totally opposed to capitalism are skeptical of it. They contend that it can be supported only if it is radically reformed from exploitive capitalism to cooperative capitalism, which recognizes the moral and practical advantages of ensuring at least minimally acceptable economic and social conditions for all.

Whatever their exact theoretical perspective, economic radicals would argue, for example, that the U.S. role in the Persian Gulf region dating back to World War II epitomizes neoimperialism. The devil's bargain, in the view of structuralists, is this: The United States protects or tries to protect the power of obscenely rich, profoundly undemocratic rulers of oil-rich states, such as Saudi Arabia and Kuwait, as it did in 1991. In return, the king and emir keep the price of oil down, which benefits the

GOMAA
AL AHRAM WEEKLY
Cairo
EGYPT

Cartoonists & Writers Syndicate

Poverty Line

This Egyptian editorial drawing captures the belief of economic structuralists that the world's wealthier countries exploit the world's poorer countries and want to keep them weak and poor in order to dominate and further take advantage of them.

Web Link

For a site lauding the virtues of capitalism, go to **www.capitalism.org/**. For an opposing view, visit the Web site of the World Socialist Movement at **www.worldsocialism.org/**.

economies of the United States and other oil-importing EDCs. Crude oil sold for an average of about $20 a barrel (equal to 42 gallons) in 1990. After the Persian Gulf War through 1999, oil prices dropped to an average of about $17 a barrel, a significant economic advantage to the United States and other imported-oil-dependent countries. Then, beginning in 2000, oil prices began to rise, and when the U.S. invaded Iraq in 2003, economic radical theorists were suspicious that Washington was motivated, at least in part, by the prospects of driving down prices by dominating and increasing Iraqi oil production. From this perspective, it is possible to argue that, in light of the continued oil price increases, the postwar pressure on the Arab oil states to democratize is not the result of a sincere U.S. concern with democracy but a threat to undermine the autocratic "oil sheiks" if they do not reduce petroleum prices.

Before turning to the main theme of this chapter, national economic competition, it is important to set the stage by surveying the state of the world economy. This analysis contains two parts. First, we will see that the world economy is globalizing and becoming increasingly interdependent. Second, we will take up the often-dramatic differences in economic circumstances that exist among the world's countries.

THE WORLD ECONOMY: GLOBALIZATION AND INTERDEPENDENCE

Economic interchange across political borders predates written history. Trading records extend back to almost 3000 B.C., and archaeologists have uncovered evidence of trade in the New Stone Age, or Neolithic period (9000–8000 B.C.). Since then, economics has become an ever more important aspect of international relations. This is evident in expanding world trade and the resulting increased interrelationship between international economic activity and domestic economic circumstances. It has reached the point that we can speak of true economic **globalization** and its accompanying **interdependence** among countries. We can see this by examining trade, investment, and monetary exchanges and by looking at both the general expansion of these factors and the uneven pattern of each.

Trade

In the quest for prosperity, the international flow of goods and services is a vital concern to all world states. **Merchandise trade** is most frequently associated with imports and exports. These goods are tangible items and are subdivided into two main categories: primary goods (raw materials) and manufactured goods. **Services trade** is less well known but also important. Services include things that you do for others. When U.S. insurance companies earn premiums for insuring foreign assets or people, when American movies earn royalties abroad, when U.S. trucks carry goods in Mexico or Canada, the revenue they generate constitutes the export of services. Note that exported services do not have to be performed overseas. American colleges and universities, for example, are one of the country's largest exporters of services. During 2006, the 591,050 foreign students studying in U.S. colleges spent over $14 billion for tuition, room, board, and the other aspects of college life ranging from textbooks to pizzas. Whatever their nature, services are a major source of income for countries, amounting to 19% of the entire flow of goods and services across international borders.

Expanding Trade

Whether merchandise or services, trade is booming. In 1913 it totaled only $20 billion. In 2005 world trade stood at $12.4 trillion. Even considering inflation, this represents a tremendous jump in world commerce, as indicated in Figure 12.1. Trade growth has been especially rapid during the post–World War II era of significant tariff reductions. During the 1913–1948 period of world wars, depression, and trade protectionism, trade increased at an average annual rate of only 0.8%. The postwar period has seen average annual increases at a rate of about 6% overall. The rapid growth of trade has been caused by a number of supply and demand factors and the implementation of a free trade philosophy.

Factors Promoting Expanded Trade

A number of supply and demand factors have spurred increased trade. First, *improved production technology* has increased the supply of goods. The industrial revolution, which began in 18th-century Europe, led to mass manufacturing. As production rates sped up, manufacturers increasingly had to seek markets for their burgeoning supply of goods farther away and even across national borders. This, in turn, created an *increased demand for resources* to supply the factories. Trade in raw materials imported by the industrialized European countries peaked during the 19th century and through World War II, as increased demand outstripped domestic resource availability. This demand has decreased for several reasons, such as the use of synthetic materials in the manufacturing process. Today, primary products account for only about one-fifth of all goods in international trade. *Materialism* is a third factor that accounts for increased trade. The rise in the world's standard of living, especially in the industrialized countries, has also contributed to "demand" pressure on international trade as people have sought more material goods and improved services. A fourth factor, *improved transportation,* has increased our ability to carry the growing supply of materials and manufactured goods and to meet the demand for them. Modern developments in transportation technology have also greatly decreased per-unit transportation costs.

Wide acceptance of a *free trade philosophy* is a fifth factor that has promoted trade. The early advocacy of free trade by Adam Smith and others came into vogue in the wake of the global trauma of the great economic depression of the 1930s and World War II in the early 1940s. One cause for these miseries, it was believed, was the high tariffs that had restricted trade and divided nations. To avoid a recurrence, the United States took the lead in reducing barriers to international trade. As a result, countries accounting for 80% of world commerce began in 1947 to cooperate to reduce international trade barriers through the General Agreement on Tariffs and Trade (GATT). This and a series of related efforts have dramatically decreased world tariff barriers. American import duties, for example, dropped from an average of 60% in 1934 to a current level of less than 4%. The tariffs of other EDCs have similarly dropped, and while the duties charged by LDCs tend to be higher, the average global tariff rate is only about 15%. Tariffs, as we will soon see, are not the only trade barrier, but their sharp reductions have greatly reduced the cost of imported goods and have strongly stimulated trade.

FIGURE 12.1 Increasing World Trade

World exports (U.S.$ billions)

$12,418

$6,912

$3,492

$1,524

$20 $33 $12 $53 $94 $304

1913 1928 1933 1948 1958 1968 1978 1988 1998 2005

Trade, measured here in the export of goods and services calculated in current dollars, has grown meteorically in recent decades. This growth is one sign of the vastly increased importance of international economic relations to all countries and their citizens.

Data source: World Bank.

Web Link

You can find more information on the less familiar type of trade—services—at the World Trade Organization's Web site, **www.wto.org/english/tratop_e/serv_e/serv_e.htm.**

SIMULATION
Free Trade or Domestic Industry? You Make the Decision

International Investment

Trade has not been the only form of international economic activity that has grown rapidly. A parallel globalization of international investment has created increased financial interdependence among countries. For example, Americans had $7.2 trillion in investments, bank deposits, property, stocks, and other assets abroad in 2004, making not only individual investors but also the health of the entire U.S. economy dependent to a degree on the state of the world economy. Conversely, foreigners had a $12.7 trillion stake in the United States, and the ebb and flow of those funds into the country are also a central factor in Americans' prosperity, or lack of it. Of the variety of assets that countries have in one another, the two most important types are foreign direct investments and foreign portfolio investments.

Foreign Direct and Portfolio Investment

When Americans invest in British or Nigerian companies, or when Canadians invest in U.S. corporations, a web of financial interdependency is created. There are two types of foreign investments, **foreign direct investment (FDI)**, which involves buying a major stake in foreign companies or real estate, and **foreign portfolio investment (FPI)** in stocks and bonds on a smaller scale that does not involve controlling companies or owning real estate. Such investments have long existed, but they have accelerated greatly in recent decades as Figure 12.2 shows for FDI. American individuals and corporations are the leading investors, with $2.1 trillion in FDI and another $4 trillion in FPI abroad in 2005.

The flow of investment capital into and out of countries is an important factor in their economic well-being. FDI and, to a degree, FPI help support and expand local businesses, thus supplying jobs. Foreign investors can also help finance a country's budget deficit. The U.S. Treasury would be in dire straits if it were not for the $2.1 trillion in bonds (44% of the total public debt) it has sold to foreigners to fund the chronic U.S. federal budget deficits (see Figure 8.8, p. 254). Foreign investments also create earnings for investors. American investors earned $463 billion in 2005 alone from their overseas investments.

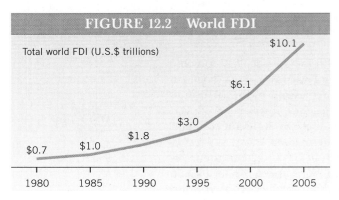

FIGURE 12.2   World FDI

Total world FDI (U.S.$ trillions)

$10.1

$6.1

$3.0

$1.8

$1.0

$0.7

1980   1985   1990   1995   2000   2005

One indication of economic globalization is the rapid increase in recent decades of foreign direct investment (FDI) capital that people and corporations have invested in other countries. As you can see, total global FDI rocketed from $700 billion in 1980 to $10.1 trillion in 2005.

Data source: United Nations Conference on Trade and Development.

International Investment and Multinational Corporations

The world's **multinational corporations (MNCs)**, also called transnational corporations (TNCs), account for the lion's share of the global FDI. MNCs are businesses that operate in more than one country. These operations can involve sales outlets, mines and other natural resource–extraction processes, farms and ranches, manufacturing plants, or offices that supply banking and other services. MNCs date back at least to the Dutch East India Company in 1602, but it was not until after World War II that they began to expand in number and size at a rapid pace. Now over 60,000 MNCs exist, and they pack enormous economic muscle. Their annual revenues (gross corporate product, GCP) provide one good measure. The top 500 MNCs alone had a collective GCP of

$18.9 trillion in 2005. That is equal to an astounding 42% of the world's collective GNP ($45 trillion) that year. Figure 12.3 presents a second perspective on GCP by comparing the revenues of the largest MNC with the GNPs of a number of countries. ExxonMobil was the world's largest MNC in 2005, with revenues of $377 billion. It had $208 billion in assets and 84,000 employees. These numbers give ExxonMobil an "economy" the size of Sweden's. Indeed, Exxon-Mobil's GCP is larger than the GNPs of all but 16 of the world's countries.

The immense wealth of the largest MNCs gives them considerable influence (Navaretti & Venables, 2004). As a key player in the world's energy supply, ExxonMobil wields considerable influence on policy in that area. For example, critics charge that it has been a leader in the campaign to block or limit restrictions on the use of fossil fuels as part of the effort to slow or reverse global warming. Two such critics, U.S. senators Olympia Snowe (R-ME) and Jay Rockefeller (D-WV) wrote to the head of ExxonMobil accusing the corporation of supporting supposedly scientific groups who "are producing very questionable data" that denies the reality of global warming. Snowe and Rockefeller went on to urge ExxonMobil to accept what they said was its "responsibility to the global community to refrain from lending their support, financial and otherwise, to bogus, nonsubstantiated articles and publications on climate change that serve only to cloud the important global debate of rigorous peer-reviewed research and writings."[2] Exxon-Mobil did not reply, but a *Wall Street Journal* editorial characterized the letter as part of a "campaign of intimidation against any global warming dissent." The editorial went on to wonder how the senators could "say that everyone agrees on the facts and consequences of climate change," yet "at the same time [be] so afraid of debate that they want Exxon to stop financing a doughty band of dissenters who can barely get their name in the paper."[3]

FIGURE 12.3 An MNC and National Economies

GCP/GNP (U.S.$ billions)

Comparing the gross corporate product (GCP, revenues) of the world's largest multinational corporation in 2005, ExxonMobil, with the gross national product (GNP) of countries highlights the economic power of MNCs. As evident, ExxonMobil's 2005 GCP ($377 billion) was about equal to Sweden's GNP, a third larger than that of Indonesia, the world's fourth most populous country (pop.: 221 million); twice as big as Iran's; and about four times Chile's GNP. Indeed, Exxon's GCP equaled 68% of the combined GNPs of all the countries of sub-Saharan Africa, with its 741 million people.

Data sources: Fortune, July 24, 2006; World Bank.

Did You Know That:

ExxonMobil's 2005 profit of $39.5 billion was alone larger than the GNPs of about half of the world's countries.

Monetary Relations

The globalization of trade and investments means that **monetary relations** have become an increasingly significant factor in both international and domestic economic health. *The globalization of money* is one aspect. A torrent of money amounting to about $700 trillion a year is circulating around the world. Much of this flow involves exchanging one country's currency for another's, greatly increasing the importance of **exchange rates**. These are the values of currencies in relation to each other—for example, how many U.S. dollars per Japanese yen or EU euro and vice versa. Exchange rates are important because they strongly influence the flow of trade and investment. Consider, for example, the changes in the exchange rate of the U.S. dollar against the yen and the euro in Figure 12.4. It shows that the U.S. dollar increased in strength between 1997 and 1998; dropped dramatically in the next two years; then rose, dropped, and rose yet again in more

FIGURE 12.4   Dollar versus Yen/Euro Exchange Rates

Currencies vary in their value against one another. As you can see, the exchange rate of Japan's yen (¥) and the U.S. dollar between 1997 and 2007 varied from a low of $1 = ¥106 in 2000 to a high of $1 = ¥140 in 1998 before settling into a narrower exchange range of $1 = ¥118 through mid-2007. The exchange rate of the European Union euro (€), which was launched on January 1, 1999, at first went to $1 = 1.11€ in 2001, then began to decline steadily to a low in mid-2007 of $1 = 0.76€. Changes in exchange rates have an important impact on the flow of trade, investment, and other international financial transactions.

Note: Yen and euro values average per year.
Data source: U.S. Federal Reserve Board.

recent years. By contrast, the number of euros a dollar could buy rose at first after the EU's currency was introduced in 1999, before starting a continuing downward trend.

Weak and strong currency should not be equated with good and bad, though, because exchange rates are a two-edged sword. For example, there are advantages and disadvantages for Americans both when the dollar is strengthening (can buy more units of a foreign currency) and weakening (can buy fewer units of a foreign currency). According to the U.S. Federal Reserve Board, these advantages and disadvantages are:[4]

Strong Dollar

Advantages for Americans	Disadvantages for Americans
>Lower prices for foreign goods/services.	>U.S. exports more costly in foreign markets.
>Lower prices on foreign goods/services restrain inflation.	>U.S. firms must compete with lower priced imports.
>Less costly to travel to foreign countries.	>More costly for foreigners to visit/ study in U.S.
>Foreign stocks/bonds cost less.	>U.S. stocks/bonds cost more abroad, restricting flow of capital to the U.S.

Weak Dollar

Advantages for Americans	**Disadvantages for Americans**
>Easier for U.S. firms to sell goods and services abroad.	>Higher prices for foreign goods/services.
>Less pressure on U.S. firms to keep wages/benefits low.	>Higher prices on imports add to higher cost-of-living.
>More foreign tourists can afford to visit the U.S.	>More costly to travel to foreign countries.
>U.S. investments more attractive to foreign investors.	>Foreign investments more costly.

As this comparison of a "strong" and a "weak" U.S. dollar reveals, the phrase "it depends" captures whether, overall, Americans should be cheered or dismayed by whichever way the dollar is trending versus any or all currencies. A stronger dollar tends to increase low-cost imports, keeping down the cost of living. But at the same time, the inflow in imports can cause the shutdown of competing U.S. firms, putting Americans out of work. A weaker dollar may restrain imports and even save U.S. jobs, but the cost of the foreign goods that Americans want or need will go up. Some economic factors are even affected both ways. Low-cost goods help keep down inflation because of a strong dollar, but at the same time the strong dollar makes it harder for foreigners to buy U.S. stocks and bonds. This may lead to increased inflation if the U.S. Treasury offers higher interest rates on the U.S. bonds it sells to finance the federal government's chronic budget deficits. The interest rate on these bonds affects interest rates across the U.S. economy, increasing the cost of loans for mortgages, vehicles, college study, and many other usages.

To accommodate the globalization of money, there has been a parallel *globalization of financial services,* such as banking. In recent decades, banks have grown from hometown to national to multinational enterprises that operate in many countries and whose power to lend money—or not—gives them immense financial clout. Just the top 10 multinational banks controlled assets of over $15 trillion in 2006, giving them immense financial power in the global economy because of the influence they have over the flow of loans, investment capital, and other financial transactions across borders. For example, multinational banks in 2006 had about $25.6 trillion in foreign loans, foreign currency holdings, and other foreign assets. American banks alone have $5.8 trillion in such assets. Moreover, many of these multinational banks are involved in international financial services beyond traditional banking. For example, the world's largest bank in 2007, Citigroup (assets: $1.9 trillion), owns, among other companies, Diners Club International and the Smith Barney brokerage house.

A third aspect of monetary relations is the *international regulation of money.* As trade, transnational investing, and other forms of international economic interchange increased during the 20th century, it became clear that some mechanisms needed to be created to help regulate the rapidly expanding flow of currencies across borders. The most pressing problem was, and still is, how to stabilize the values of currencies against one another. To that end, there have been a number of regional and global efforts to keep exchange rates stable and to otherwise ensure that currency issues do not impede economic activity. Globally, the International Monetary Fund (IMF), which is detailed in chapter 13, has the primary responsibility for attempting to maintain monetary stability. Regionally, the most advanced efforts have been in the European Union, which has the European Central Bank and now a common currency, the euro.

Web Link

The historical exchange rate between the U.S. dollar and a range of other currencies can be found at **www.eh.net/hmit/ exchangerates/.**

ANALYZE THE ISSUE
The IMF and the International Political Economy

THE WORLD ECONOMY: DIVERSE CIRCUMSTANCES

Every country, whatever its domestic economic system, has citizens whose circumstances range from wealthy to poor. Similarly, the countries of the world range from rich to destitute.

Traditionally, analysts have divided the world's countries into two spheres. One, the **North**, consists of the generally prosperous EDCs. The other sphere, the **South**, is composed of the relatively, and in some cases absolutely, poor LDCs. The poorest of these LDCs are low-income countries also referred to as **least developed countries (LLDCs)**. The North-South designations result from the fact that most EDCs lie to the north in North America and Europe and most LDCs are farther to the south in Africa, Asia, and Central and South America.

From a closely parallel categorization, Table 12.2 looks at world countries using four income categories (high, upper middle, lower middle, and low) established by the World Bank. It is important to note that the North and South categories are somewhat fluid and do not exactly match the dichotomy between the high-income countries and the low- and middle-income countries. One variance is that five oil-producing countries (Brunei, Kuwait, Qatar, Saudi Arabia, and the United Arab Emirates), which are usually classified as part of the South, fall into the high-income group. Second, two of the **newly industrializing countries (NICs)** in the South, Singapore and South Korea, have achieved high-income status. If Taiwan were considered a country, it too would fall into this group. Third, a few high-income countries such as Israel, Malta, and Cyprus (with a well-off Greek Cypriot majority and a much poorer Turkish Cypriot minority) do not fall easily into either the North or South category. Also worth noting is the status of Russia, other former Soviet republics (FSRs), and the former communist countries of Eastern Europe. Some of these have a reasonable industrial base, but only one, Slovenia, falls in the high-income group. Russia and most of the other European FSRs are middle-income countries, and Tajikistan and most of the other Asian FSRs are low-income countries.

Did You Know That:

The world had 946 billionaires with collective assets of $3.52 trillion in 2007. The richest was Bill Gates with a net worth of $56 billion, an amount about equal to the GNP of Vietnam and its 83 million people.

TABLE 12.2 Country Economic Classification

Category	Income Range Per Capita GNP	Number of Countries	% of World Population	Average Per Capita GNP	Average Per Capita GNP/PPP
High Income	≥$10,066	42	16%	$32,112	$31,009
Upper Middle Income	$10,065–$3,256	38	9%	$4,769	$10,186
Lower Middle Income	$3,255–$826	53	38%	$1,686	$5,829
Low Income	≤$825	59	37%	$587	$2,258

Note: The Holy See is not included.
Data source: World Bank.

Whether you measure economic circumstances in per capita GNP or per capita GNP/PPP, the world is generally divided into two spheres, the "economic haves" in the high-income group and the "have nots" made up of the low- and middle-income countries. The high-income countries include a small minority of the world's countries and an even smaller minority of its population, yet generate an average per capita income that is 21 (GNP) or 7 (GNP/PPP) times the average for the rest of the world.

North-South Patterns

Despite some imprecision, the North-South dichotomy is used in this analysis because it captures the reality that there is a great divide in the world pattern of economic and social circumstances. In addition to their economic circumstances, most of the countries of the South share a history of having been colonially or neo-colonially dominated by one or another EDC, often within living memory. According to economic structuralists, this dependency relationship continues to a great degree today.

North-South Economic Patterns

"Significantly poorer" is an apt phrase to begin any analysis of the economies of the South compared to those of the North. The most common measure of any country or group of countries' economic prosperity is per capita GNP or GDP. By this measure, as detailed in Figure 12.5, there is a huge wealth gap between the high-income countries and the middle- and low-income countries. Furthermore, while the wealth gap has narrowed a bit in recent decades, the improvement is so slight that it would

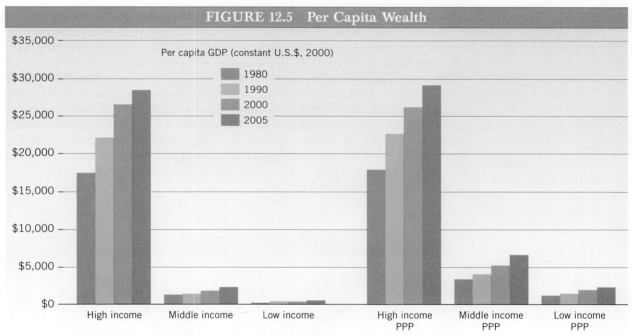

FIGURE 12.5   Per Capita Wealth

This figure shows the per capita GDPs between 1980 and 2005 of the high-, middle-, and low-income countries calculated in constant (real, controlled for inflation) dollars. The group to the left shows GDP unadjusted for cost of living, and the group on the right shows GDP adjusted for cost of living (PPP: purchasing power parity). Note the huge gap on both measures between the high-income countries and the middle- and low-income countries. The gap is narrower on the PPP basis, but only marginally so. Also notice that while the per capita income of all three groups has increased on both measures, the income gap has remained relatively stable. As one example, for every dollar of per capita GNP generated by the low-income countries in 1980, the high-income countries generated $68; in 2005 that ratio had improved only slightly to $1:$59. The PPP measure tells the same general story, with the wealth ratio between high-income countries and low-income countries narrowing only a bit, $1:$16 to $1:$13.

Data source: World Bank.

take centuries at the current rate to approach anywhere near equal prosperity for all countries.

There are many reasons why the South fares so poorly compared to the North, and these are taken up later in this chapter and in chapter 13. One reason, though, is that the LDCs take in considerably less capital through such methods as exports and the inflow of investment money, both of which are major sources of income for the EDCs. *Trade differences* leave the North advantaged. Overall, the EDCs, which form 22% of the world's countries and have 16% of the world population, exported 77% of all the goods and services in 2005. That left less than a quarter of all exports for the vast majority of countries and people that make up the South. Moreover, China accounted for 33% of all LDC exports, while many other LDCs had few. For example, sub-Saharan Africa, with 11% of the world population, managed to ship only 1.5% of world exports. Trade differences are depicted in Figure 12.6. What products a country exports also makes a difference. A diverse range of manufactured goods and services exports account for more than 90% of what EDCs sell abroad. By contrast, manufactured goods and services make up only 69% of middle-income country exports and only 50% of low-income country exports. These LDCs rely more than do EDCs on the export of primary products, such as food, fibers, fuels, and minerals. This disadvantages the LDCs because the price of primary products is often unstable and also generally has not risen as fast as the price of manufactured goods.

Similarly, *investment differences* also favor the North. First, the North has the flow of most investment capital. Of the 500 largest MNCs, 89% are based in an EDC, with U.S. firms alone making up 34% of the Global 500. Only 13 of the 150 LDCs are the site of the headquarters of one of the Global 500, and of 56 such firms based in an LDC, 20 are in China and another 12 are in South Korea. Therefore the flow of the profits that the 500 largest MNCs generate ($535 billion in 2005) mostly benefits the North. Second, about two-thirds of all FDI, and an even greater percentage of FPI, flows from one EDC to another, rather than to the South where the need is greatest. Furthermore, the newly industrialized countries and a few others receive most of the investment capital, and most LDCs receive little or none. China alone is the recipient of over 40% of the FDI going to LDCs.

FIGURE 12.6   North/South Share of Exports

South 24%

North 76%

Total exports

South $889

North $8,281

Exports per capita

The pattern of world trade is very uneven. The North exports over three times more goods and services than does the South. Trade is even more unbalanced on a per capita basis, with the North's exports exceeding the South by more than 9 to 1.

Data source: World Bank.

North-South Societal Patterns

Economic data can seem dry until you realize the social implications of differences in per capita GNP and similar statistics. Consider what it means for their comparative quality of life that on a per capita basis, the people who live in the EDCs produce $61 for every $1 produced by those living in the LLDCs. In these countries, about 1 billion people live in **extreme poverty**, which the World Bank defines as less than $1 a day. Another 1.5 billion people struggle to sustain themselves on between $1 and $2 a day, with the two impoverished groups combining to make up almost 40% of the world's population. In societal terms, these numbers translate into poor health care, limited education, lack of safe drinking water, inadequate nutrition, and other grim realities. For example, 38% of all adults in LLDCs are illiterate; less than 1% of EDC adults are. Medical facilities in the South are overwhelmed. Each physician in an LLDC is responsible for about 2,500 people, 10 times as many people as a physician in the North. Moreover, hundreds of millions of people in the South have no access to any kind of health care. These conditions lead to disease and death on a wide scale. A child born in an LLDC is 17 times more likely to die before age 5 than a child in an EDC. Having children is also risky, with the maternal mortality rate in LLDCs 48 times higher than in EDCs. Overall, just 58% of the people in LLDCs (compared to 91% in EDCs) live to age 65, and the average person in a low-income country dies 20 years earlier than a resident in a high-income country.

Evaluating the North-South Gap

Although annual data about economic and societal factors are important in evaluating the indisputable gap between North and South, such statistics do not tell the whole story. Trends are of at least equal importance. Are things getting better or worse? On this question, the data is mixed and somewhat subject to interpretation. There is also a highly uneven pattern of development.

Mixed Data on Development

Statistics about development in the South do not tell a consistent story. Analyses of conditions in the South tend to be gloomy, but it is important to see that significant advances are being made. Table 12.3 shows that, by many health, education, and economic measures, circumstances in the LDCs are improving. A greater percentage of the LDC population has access to safe water and adequate sanitation facilities. There has been a marked decrease in child mortality and substantial increase in overall longevity in the LDCs. Literacy has improved. As a whole, the LDCs have at least a little greater share of the world's collective GNP, its trade, and its inflow of FDI capital. These are not the only signs of progress. For example, a distressing 19% of the LDCs' population still lives in extreme poverty, but that is a distinct improvement over the 28% in that condition in 1990.

It is also important to see, though, that while such statistics are a cause to celebrate the progress that has occurred, they are not an indication that conditions are good or that many of the LDCs do not continue to need substantial help. One factor is that the stark contrast between conditions in LDCs and EDCs still endures. Yes, for example, it is good that the child mortality rate in the LDCs has plummeted, but even in the middle-income countries it remains six times what it is in the high-income countries. Second, as evident in Figure 12.5 and to a degree in Table 12.3, the progress that is being made is often painfully slow. Third, statistics can sometimes tell almost contradictory stories. Extreme poverty provides an illustration. As noted,

Category	Measure	Income group	1960	1980	1990	2005*
Health	Population with clean water	Low income			21%	38%
		Middle income			48%	62%
	Population with improved sanitation	Low income			64%	75%
		Middle income			78%	84%
	Children dying before age 5	Low income	25%	18%	15%	12%
		Middle income	19%	8%	6%	4%
	Life expectancy (years)	Low income	43	52	56	59
		Middle income	46	65	68	70
Education	Literacy rate (%)	Low income			48%	62%
		Middle income			81%	90%
Economy	Share of world GDP	Low income			3%	3%
		Middle income			14%	17%
	Share of world exports	Low income			2%	2%
		Middle income			15%	22%
	Share of inflow of FDI	Low income			1%	3%
		Middle income			10%	31%
Population	Share of world population	Low income	28%	31%	33%	37%
		Middle income	50%	50%	49%	47%

TABLE 12.3 Indicators for LDCs

*2005 or most recent year available

Note: In some categories, reliable data prior to 1990 is not available for these income classifications. For 1960 and 1980 the data is omitted in the economic categories because the large number of former colonies becoming independent and entering the low-income categories skews the data.

Data source: World Bank.

This table indicates that by many health, education, and economic measures, the situation of the LDCs is getting better. Notice that the middle-income countries have often progressed faster than the low-income countries. Indeed, for share of world exports and for share of world GDP, the low-income countries have not progressed. It is also important to note that some of the signs of progress here are partially offset for the low-income countries by their increasing share of the world population and, conversely, enhanced for the middle-income countries by their decreasing share of the global population.

the percentage of people in the LDCs who live in extreme poverty has decreased, but because populations continue to rise rapidly, especially in the LLDCs, there are still more than 1 billion people in these countries trying to survive on the equivalent of less than a dollar a day.

Uneven Patterns of Development

The good news about the growth in the economies of the LDCs and the improvements in their societal conditions is also tempered by uneven patterns of development. *Disparity between countries* is one warp in the overall picture of economic growth in the South. As noted, the middle-income countries have advanced more quickly than the low-income countries. There are also regional differences. Some regions such as East Asia have made major economic and societal strides. At the other end of the regional spectrum, sub-Saharan Africa has struggled and in some cases lost ground. Its per capita GNP is less than half that of the other LDCs. The region's merchandise exports are only 31% manufactured goods and services, compared to 64% for all LDCs. Of the FDI going to LDCs, only 5% goes to sub-Saharan countries. Life expectancy in

MAP
Central Government
Expenditures Per Capita

the region has actually declined from 49 years in 1990 to 46 years now, and two-thirds of the population will die before reaching age 65. About a third of sub-Saharan Africans were malnourished in 1990, and no improvement has been made. The child mortality rate has fallen from a horrific 19% in 1990, but is still a disturbing 17%. The litany of woes need not continue to make the point that the overall data for the LDCs does not always reflect the wide array of circumstances among them.

Disparity within countries is a second characteristic of LDC economic development that can make the overall data deceiving. All countries have disparities in income and other measures of wealth within their population, but unequal distribution is particularly strong within most LDCs. More than in EDCs, the LDCs tend to have a very small, very wealthy upper class and a vast, very poor lower class. Figure 12.7 shows the percentage of income earned by the wealthiest and poorest 20% each of the populations of an LDC (Brazil), an EDC (Japan), and the world's largest economy (the United States).

Negative by-products of development are a third aspect of the uneven pattern because some of the South's advances have been partially offset by several negative side effects. *Explosive population growth* has occurred as a result of medical advances, which have decreased infant mortality and increased longevity. The population of sub-Saharan Africa, for instance, rose 253% from 210 million in 1960 to 741 million in 2003, and the region is expected to reach 866 million people by 2015. *Rapid urbanization* has also beset the South, as the hope of finding jobs and better health, sanitation, and other social services has set off a mass migration from rural areas to cities in the South. Between 1965 and 2005 the share of the South's population living in urban areas grew from 22% to 43%, and it is projected to reach 53% in the year 2020. There are now approximately 175 cities in LDCs with populations over 1 million, and of the world's 20 most populous cities, all but 3 (Tokyo, New York, and London) are in the LDCs. This rapid urbanization process has created a host of problems. One is the weakening of the social order. Older tribal, village, and extended-family loyalties are being destroyed, with few new offsetting values and other social support systems to take their place. Second, the hope of employment is often unfulfilled, and unemployment and poverty in many cities is staggering. Third, struggling LDC governments are often unable to meet the sanitary, housing, and other needs of the flood of people moving to or being born in the cities. About a quarter of the South's urban population is living in conditions below the minimum standards for health. In Nigeria, for example, less than half the urban households are connected to a sewer; only about half the urban population in Haiti has access to safe drinking water; and 58% of Bangladesh's urban population lives in dwellings without a "durable structure," that is, in makeshift shacks.

Industrial and environmental dangers have also been undesirable by-products of development. The impact of development on the environment is detailed in chapter 15,

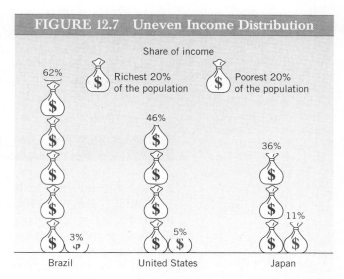

FIGURE 12.7   Uneven Income Distribution

Share of income

Richest 20% of the population

Poorest 20% of the population

Brazil: 62%, 3%
United States: 46%, 5%
Japan: 36%, 11%

The unequal distribution of income within countries is shown for each of three countries by a pair of moneybags. One represents the share of the country's income that goes to the richest 20% of its citizens and the other, the share of the country's income that goes to the poorest 20% of its citizens. All countries have unequal distributions, but LDCs generally have the greatest inequality. Notice that in Japan, the wealthiest 20% make only about 3 times as much as the country's poorest citizens. In Brazil the top 20% make about 31 times what the poorest 20% receive. The "wealth gap" in the United States is greater than in most EDCs.

Data source: World Bank (2005).

Web Link

The Population Reference Bureau has good commentary, maps, and data on urbanization in the South and the rest of the world at **www.prb.org/**. Type "urbanization" into the search window.

but a brief note of the dangers is appropriate here. One problem is rapid deforestation due to demands for wood, expanding farm and ranch acreage, and general urban growth. Loss of these forests increases soil erosion and has numerous other deleterious effects. LDC industrial development also adds to air, water, and soil pollution, and most major cities in the LDCs are now far more polluted than are major metropolitan areas in the EDCs.

NATIONAL ECONOMIC RELATIONS

A key economic change within countries since the end of the 1800s has been the expansion of government regulation of their national economies. Even countries like the United States that see themselves as bastions of capitalism have myriad laws that significantly restrain economic competition by barring monopolistic practices and other unwanted manifestations of capitalism. Furthermore, most countries have accepted the notion that the self-interest of individual citizens must be balanced to some degree with the collective welfare of the national society.

In contrast to domestic systems, the international system is still a largely unregulated arena in which countries pursue their economic self-interests in competition with other countries and in which there is little sense of shared responsibility for the welfare of the global society. Two factors have eased the maneuvering for economic advantage among states. One is globalization and its attendant economic theory, economic internationalism, which has made countries much less likely now than earlier to use tariffs and other forms of barriers to manipulate the free exchange of trade, investment capital, and currencies. Second, as chapter 13 discusses, the last half century or so has seen the emergence of a greater global sense that the EDCs should help the LDCs. An illustration is foreign aid. It did not exist before World War II; now over $100 billion in aid flows annually from North to South. Thus, the dog-eat-dog image of the international political economy is not quite as stark as it once was. Nevertheless, competition and self-reliance, not cooperation and mutual assistance, remain the prevailing IPE realities. This struggle for advantage and prosperity exists both between and within the North and South.

North-North Economic Relations

Although the North is extraordinarily advantaged compared to the South, the EDCs face many economic challenges. In addition to the normal competitive tensions of the system, economic and political changes are creating strong competitive pressures on the EDCs.

Changes in the North's Economic Climate

One factor accounting for increasing economic tensions within the North is that its economic growth rate has slowed. The average annual real GDP growth rate of the EDCs during the 1980s was 3.4%; during the 1990s that declined to 2.3%; and between 2000 and 2006 it rebounded only marginally to 2.6%. Europe and Japan in particular have been in the doldrums since the early 1990s, as detailed in Figure 12.8. During 2000–2006, Japan's economy had a lackadaisical 1.5% annual growth rate, and the EU's was barely better at 1.8%. Although the reasonably healthy U.S. growth rate of 3% for the period was much better than its main economic rivals, U.S. GDP growth

Web Link

The best source for data on the economic position of the North is the Web site of the Organization for Economic Cooperation and Development at **www.oecd.org.** The most recent data overview can be found by entering "Economic Outlook" and the current year in the search window of the OECD's home page to find the latest issues of its monthly publication of that name.

was below its even more robust levels of the 1980s and 1990s.

The EDCs' slowing economies have sharpened the competition among them to export their products to one another and to the LDCs and to protect their domestic economies against imports. Adding to this pressure, there is increasing competition from China and a few other LDCs in the manufacturing and service sectors. To make matters worse, companies in the North have tried to deal with the competition in some cases by reducing their workforces and using robotics and other high-tech manufacturing processes to replace workers. In other cases, companies have eliminated entire plants, laid off their employees, and moved operations overseas to take advantage of cheaper labor. Many of the workers displaced by the shift of manufacturing jobs abroad are either unemployed or find jobs in the usually lower-paying service sector. Now even service sector jobs are increasingly subject to foreign competition. In what is called "outsourcing," companies in the United States and other EDCs are hiring workers abroad to do data entry work, to respond to service telephone calls and e-mail inquiries, to write software, and do many other service jobs. The economic impact of outsourcing has created mounting domestic pressures on EDC governments to protect jobs. For example, a survey of Americans that asked them to name their high-priority foreign policy goals found that more Americans listed protecting jobs from foreign competition as a high priority (78%) than those who chose stopping the spread of nuclear weapons (73%) or combating international terrorism (71%).[5]

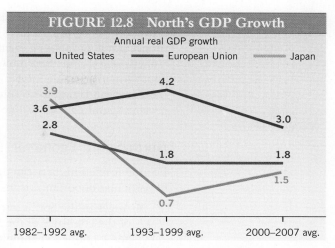

FIGURE 12.8 North's GDP Growth

Annual real GDP growth

—— United States —— European Union —— Japan

4.2
3.9
3.6
2.8
1.8
1.8
3.0
1.5
0.7

1982–1992 avg.   1993–1999 avg.   2000–2007 avg.

Economic competition among the countries of the North has been sharpened by the falloff in economic growth since the booming 1980s. The real (controlled for inflation) growth rates of the European Union and, even more so, of Japan dropped sharply in the 1990s. Japan's recovered partially after 2000, but the EU countries did not. By contrast, the U.S. growth rate improved during the 1990s, but then in recent years declined somewhat.

Note: The EU data includes only those countries using the euro.
Data source: OECD.

Changes in the North's Political Climate

Declining political accord is also increasing the sense of rivalry among the EDCs. The end of the cold war and with it the looming threat of the Soviet Union lessened the need for strategic cooperation among the industrialized Western allies. As a result, the long-standing economic disputes among the so-called trilateral countries (Japan, the United States/Canada, Western Europe) that had once been suppressed in the name of allied unity have become more acrimonious. The strains between the United States, on one hand, and France, Germany, and other European countries, on the other, over the U.S. determination to topple the Iraqi regime of Saddam Hussein in 2003 is but one of the latest examples of the discord.

The United States and most of Europe have also parted ways on a range of political issues. There is broad resentment of President George W. Bush's unilateralist approach to foreign policy and many of his specific policies. Europeans were distressed by his refusal to support the Kyoto Protocol on the environment, by his rejection of the International Criminal Court, by his abrogation of the Anti-Ballistic Missile Treaty, and, perhaps most of all, by his military action against Iraq. These political strains have intensified the U.S.-European rivalry and entwined it with European concerns about U.S. hegemony. Most European leaders believe that increasing the size and unity of the European Union is one way to maintain their region's global power and, especially, to counterbalance the United States. As President Jacques Chirac of France put it, developing "genuine European power" is necessary to stand up to "the United States, and other emerging economic blocs, like China, India, Brazil and South America, [and] Russia." He warned, "Only our political power at the heart of the European Union today allows us to defend our interests," and that if Europeans became disunited, "we will no longer have any power."[6]

North-South Economic Relations

Economic relations between the North and South are often strained, with four factors of particular importance:

- Anger in the South over its past and present treatment by the North. Most of the countries of the South were once colonies of or otherwise dominated and exploited economically by one or another country in the North. Moreover, remnants of the exploitive relationship often continue to exist. Typically during the colonial period, the dominant country imported fuels, agricultural produce, ores, and other raw material from the colony and exported manufactured goods to it. Although formal colonialism has almost entirely disappeared, the same flow of goods continues to a degree. Most of Africa was once a colonial dependent of a country now in the EU, and still today, 63% of EU imports from Africa are raw materials, and another 17% are low-tech goods such as textiles and clothing. By contrast, manufactured goods make up 81% of EU exports to Africa.

- New assertiveness by the LDCs of their claim that they have a right to a much greater share in the world's economic wealth.

- The North's general rejection of the South's demands for unilateral and compensatory economic reforms by the North. Instead, as we shall see, the North is apt to demand reciprocal concessions from the South. These the South often rejects on the grounds that its plight is partly the fault of the North to begin with and, furthermore, that it is unfair to ask relatively poor countries of the South to swap concessions with the richer countries of the North.

- Increase in the number of LDCs that have become major exporters of manu-factured goods and, to a lesser degree, services that directly compete with the EDCs' products and services, thus undermining EDC dominance in those economic areas.

The South's Reform Agenda

To understand the South's perspective, a basic point to realize is that many people there share parts of the structuralist argument that by design or happenstance the in-ternational system works to the advantage of the EDCs and serves to keep the LDCs relatively poor and dependent. As a result, the LDCs have joined together to insist on a more equitable distribution of global financial resources. To promote that, a coalition of LDCs cooperated to convene the first United Nations Conference on Trade and Development (UNCTAD) and to create an LDC organization, the Group of 77, both in 1964. Now the Group of 77 has grown to 130 members, and the ongoing UNCTAD organization includes all countries with UN membership and serves as a vehicle for the LDCs to discuss their needs and to press demands on the North.

The new LDC coalition soon led to an assertive South pressing the North to reform its policies and the international economic system. Proposals were first put forward in the Declaration on the Establishment of a **New International Economic Order (NIEO)**, which was drafted by UNCTAD and approved by the UN General Assembly in 1974. These largely unmet demands have regularly been reiterated, refined, and expanded by UNCTAD and the Group of 77. A recent reassertion occurred at the 2005 summit meeting of the South's leaders in Doha, Qatar (the first was in Havana, Cuba, in 2000). The leaders adopted the "Doha Program of Action" that reiterated a number of earlier declarations and pledged its signatories to "continue strengthening the unity and solidarity among countries of the South, as an indispensable element in the defense of our right to development and for the creation of a more just and equitable international order."[7] The document asserted the need for policy change in these areas:

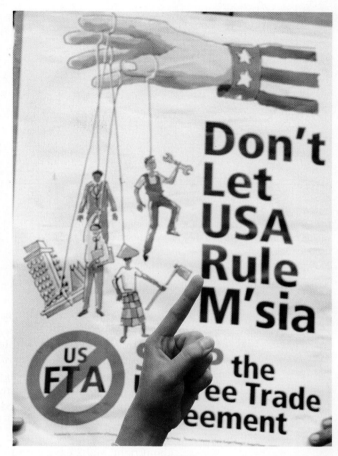

Many in the South are demanding reforms called the New International Economic Order on the grounds that trade and other aspects of international economic exchange favor the countries in the North. This placard in Malaysia protesting the newly negotiated free trade agreement with the United States portrays Malaysia in the position of being an economic puppet.

- *Trade reforms,* such as lowering EDC barriers to agricultural imports, that will expand and stabilize markets for LDC exports.

- *Monetary reforms* that will create greater stability in the exchange rates of LDC currencies and will also moderate the sometimes sudden and significant ebb and flow of FDI and FPI into and out of the LDCs.

- *Institutional reforms* that will increase the South's influence over policies of the International Monetary Fund, the World Bank, and other such international financial agencies. Currently, as chapter 13 details, wealthy countries dominate decision making in these institutions.

- *Economic modernization* of LDCs with significant assistance by EDCs through such methods as relaxing patent rights to permit easier technology transfers to LDCs.

- *Greater labor migration* for LDC workers seeking employment in more prosperous EDCs.

- *Elimination of economic coercion,* including the use of sanctions, which the South tends to see as a tool by which EDCs punish and control LDCs.

- *Economic aid* to the South by the North that steadily increases to meet the UN's target of 0.7% of each EDC's GNP, to be spent on promoting the development of LDCs. The current aid level is a bit over 0.2%.

- *Debt relief* granted by EDCs, the World Bank, and the IMF, based on reducing the money owed to them by many LDCs and eliminating the debt for the poorest LLDCs. Currently, LDCs owe about $2.4 trillion and have annual debt service payments over $400 billion.

Web Link

A good source for the South's view on the international political economy is the Web site of the Group of 77 at **www.g77.org.**

FIGURE 12.9 EDC Foreign Aid Effort

Aid as a percent of EDCs' GNP

The foreign aid effort of the EDCs, measured as the share of their annual combined GNPs that they give in foreign aid, has declined since the 1960s. As you can see, the effort dropped sharply until 2000, before recovering somewhat in recent years.

Data source: Organization of Economic Cooperation and Development.

The North's Response to the South's Reform Agenda

To say that the North has ignored the South's plight would be inaccurate. But it would also be misleading to assert that the North has gone very far to meet the South's demands. One reason for the North's limited response is the view of many that the main barriers to the South's development are internal issues, including political instability, inefficient market controls, and corruption. Taking that view, President George W. Bush told one international development conference that LDCs had not done enough to reform themselves and that, "The lesson of our time is clear: When nations close their markets and opportunity is hoarded by a privileged few, no amount—no amount—of development aid is ever enough." Instead of more aid, the president continued, the LDCs needed to accept "a higher, more difficult, more promising call . . . to encourage sources that produce wealth: economic freedom, political liberty, the rule of law and human rights."[8]

Domestic resistance within the EDCs is a second factor that has limited their response to the LDCs. Many of the changes that the LDCs want are very unpopular in the EDCs. Greater labor migration is an example. One survey of the United States, Canada, Japan, and four Western European EDCs found that an average of 71% of their people opposed increased immigration.[9] Foreign aid also faces stiff opposition in most EDCs. A recent poll of Americans found 64% saying that U.S. foreign aid was too high and only 9% thinking it was too low. Another 24% thought the aid level was about right, and 2% were unsure.[10] The result of this attitude in the United States and elsewhere is, as Figure 12.9 shows, that foreign aid as a percentage of the EDC's GNP has gone down, instead of up toward the 0.7% standard that the LDCs and the UN advocate. Yet other steps that would help LDCs are opposed by one or another powerful interest group in the EDCs. For instance, numerous LDCs have large sugar crops, yet their exports to the United States are limited by an array of strict quotas and high tariffs that the U.S. sugar lobby has persuaded the U.S. government to impose. These are a sweet deal for American sugar producers, leaving the price of U.S. sugar more than three times the world market price. However, the protection is a bitter pill for both American consumers, annually costing them an extra $2 billion for sugar, soda, and other products containing sugar, and for poor LDCs that cannot export their crop freely to the United States.

New Developments in North-South Competition

A relatively recent and growing development in North-South relations is that a few LDCs are beginning to compete with the EDCs for markets, resources, and other economic assets, creating global repercussions. China is the prime example. With a 2006 per capita GNP of only $1,740, China is distinctly an LDC. Yet its overall annual GNP of $2.3 trillion is the world's third largest, just behind Germany and just ahead of Great Britain. Moreover, on a PPP basis, China's GNP ($8.6 trillion) is second only to that of the United States ($12.4 trillion) and more than twice that of third-place Japan ($4.0 trillion). Thus, China is an economic giant on an overall basis.

Among myriad impacts, China's large economy has increased its needs for energy imports, which the EDCs also need. Between 2000 and 2006, China's annual petroleum consumption increased 63% from 70 billion gallons to 114 billion gallons. Indeed, China now consumes 9% of the world's annual oil supply, second only to—but still far behind—the United States (24%). Because China produces increasingly less petroleum than it needs, its oil imports have risen steadily and now supply half its needs. Soaring oil prices are one outcome of the sharply increased demand for petroleum. There have also been diplomatic ramifications. China has resisted strong UN intervention in Sudan to ease the situation in Darfur in part because China imports oil from Sudan. China has also lent support to the anti-American government of Venezuela's President Hugo Chávez by agreeing to invest billions of dollars to modernize the country's production facilities, and in return Chávez has guaranteed substantial deliveries of his country's petroleum to China in the coming years. "The United States as a power is on the way down, China is on the way up. China is the market of the future," Chavez predicted to explain his redirection of Venezuela's oil exports toward China.[11]

Trade is another source of tension between China and the North. A major factor has been the mounting U.S. trade deficit with China, as shown in Figure 12.10, p. 398 located in the box "Sanctions on China?" The U.S. deficit in 2006 at (−)$233 billion set a record for any one country. The European Union also has an escalating trade deficit with China that stood at (−)$92 billion in 2006. Some of the trade imbalance is explainable by such economic factors as China's vastly lower labor costs. Some of the deficit also reflects Americans' near insatiable appetite for consumer goods.

However, U.S. officials and others blame part of the problem on what they term illegal or unfair practices by China. One U.S. charge is that China does far too little to suppress the rampant *"piracy" of intellectual property*. This means reproducing and selling patented goods and copyrighted music, software, and other material. Washington also alleges that China gives economic subsidies to its industries, enabling them to compete unfairly with foreign companies. A third charge by U.S. officials is that China has manipulated the exchange rate of its currency, the yuan, to keep it artificially high relative to the dollar in order to promote Chinese exports and to discourage foreign imports. Each of these charges, with China's responses and subsequent U.S. reaction, are further explained in the policy-making box, Debate the Policy Script, "Sanctions on China?" It also asks you to help chart future U.S. economic policy vis-à-vis China.

South-South Economic Relations

Although the South generally shows a united front in calling on the North for economic reform, the LDCs also compete with one another. One contentious example is the price of oil. Increased prices benefit those few LDCs that export oil, but higher prices restrict the economies of oil-importing LDCs, which are much less able to afford them than are the EDCs.

Additionally, LDCs compete among themselves for investment capital from the North and for its markets. For example, Chinese goods are flooding the United States, the EU, and other countries of the North, but only a minority of the factories exporting goods are owned by the Chinese. The rest are owned by MNCs of the EDCs. At one time these factories may have been in the United States and other countries of the North and employed those countries' workers. But in most cases, the

DEBATE THE POLICY SCRIPT

Sanctions on China?

China and the United States may be on a collision course. The path to conflict begins with the U.S. trade deficit with China, as detailed in Figure 12.10. It has been steadily mounting and reached $233 billion in 2006, accounting for 30% of the entire U.S. trade deficit that year.

U.S. officials put part of the blame for the deficit on China's halfhearted effort to deal with the illegal production of everything from music through movies and software, to machinery. The U.S. entertainment and software industries alone estimated that they lost $2.6 billion to the piracy of their products in China, for use there and for export to other countries. U.S. officials also claimed that Beijing is maintaining an artificially high yuan-to-dollar exchange value at a time when the dollar has weakened against most other currencies. Repeated de-

mands by U.S. officials that China mend its ways have been backed by Congress, which, among other things, threatened in 2005 to enact a 27.5% increase in the U.S. tariff on Chinese goods unless Beijing gave way. A third U.S. allegation is that China provides economic subsidies to many of its industries, which gives them an unfair advantage in the international marketplace.

Beijing routinely rejects such charges as unfounded, but it has relented somewhat in response to increasingly urgent U.S. demands. There was some evidence that China was trying to increase its imports of American goods. Beijing also let the yuan drift lower against the dollar, but only by a little. The 7% decline from 8.3 to 7.7 yuan to the dollar fell far short of the 40% drop to about 5 yuan to the dollar that some thought

FIGURE 12.10   U.S.–China Trade

- U.S exports to China
- Imports from China
- Deficit with China
(in U.S.$ billions)

This figure shows two clear trends about U.S. trade with China. First, after growing only moderately in the 1980s, it began to rise more quickly in the 1990s, then really shot up after 2000. Second, the U.S. trade deficit with China (exports minus imports) followed a similar course, changing from a relative balance in 1985 to a (−)$4 billion deficit in 2000, to a (−)$233 billion deficit in 2006, a year in which China sent over $5 in goods to the United States for every $1 in American exports it took in. These lopsided numbers have created increasing tension between the two countries.

Data source: U.S. Bureau of Economic Analysis.

plants had long ago left the North and had gone to such LDCs as Mexico. In the past few years, however, Mexico's role as a provider of low-cost exports to the United States has been substantially undercut by China, where an average factory worker's wages are less than half those of the average Mexican worker. As a result, production dropped 30% between 2000 and 2002 in Mexico's *maquiladora* manufacturing zone would be the exchange level if the yuan were trading freely. These and other measures led to a 32% increase in 2006 of U.S. exports to China compared to a more modest 18% increase in China's exports to the United States. Still, the size of the U.S. trade deficit with China grew 16% from $201 billion in 2005 to $233 billion in 2006.

The issue facing Washington in 2007 was whether to continue negotiating with China to increase the limited concessions that it had made or to take strong measures to retaliate and otherwise try to force China to change its policies. The key argument for confronting China is that trade deficits cost Americans workers their jobs. "Until [the Chinese] start playing by the rules, our manufacturing industry will continue to bleed jobs," charged one U.S. senator.[1] Another argument for retaliating against China might be termed the "enough's enough" argument. It does not focus on one thing, but on the pattern of China allegedly not playing fairly by keeping the value of the yuan high, by continuing to allow the massive pirating of U.S. movies and software, and by a range of other practices that distort trade and investment.

Those who opposed sanctions on China make several counterarguments. One is that a major revaluing of the yuan or imposing sanctions on China will not save jobs. Former Federal Reserve Board Chairman Alan Greenspan told Congress that few if any American jobs would be protected because if the price of Chinese goods increased, the affected items would be imported from other low-cost countries rather than supplied by U.S. manufacturers. Opponents of retaliation against China also warn that substantially revaluing the yuan or increasing the tariff would harm most Americans. For instance, China produces about 90% of the world's toys, and the price of the nearly $18 billion in toys that the U.S. imports annually from China would increase, making birthdays and other gift-giving occasions more expensive.

It is also the case that China has used part of the inflow of U.S. currency to amass $230 billion in U.S. Treasury bonds (second only to Japan), thereby helping the U.S. government finance its budget deficit. A falling yuan would reduce bond purchases, the reduced demand would push up the interest rate the U.S. Treasury has to pay to sell its supply of bonds, and an increase in the Treasury rate would push up U.S. consumer interest rates on credit cards, mortgages, student loans,

and other debt. On the political front, opponents of strong actions against China cautioned that it could react by lowering or ending its cooperation with such U.S. goals as ending North Korea's nuclear weapons program and having an effective UN force intervene in the Darfur region of Sudan.

The Bush administration acted in 2007 to ramp up the pressure on Beijing, but U.S. moves fell far short of determined retaliation. In March, the United States, alleging illegal subsidies by China's government to support its industries, imposed increased tariffs on glossy paper and intimated that other Chinese goods might soon also face increased barriers. The following month, Washington filed two complaints with the World Trade Organization (WTO), one alleging that China was failing to enforce antipiracy rules as required under international trade law and the other protesting against policies restricting access to U.S. products and services in China. Supporters of the administration's actions said that they represented a limited but important step to demonstrate U.S. resolve to challenge China. The tariff move, for example, was the first time in 20 years a U.S. president had ordered a tariff hike against Chinese goods. Critics offered two opposite opinions. Some argued that China was already making concessions, and applying more pressure would be counterproductive because the Chinese were unlikely to risk damaging their economy by making major changes quickly. From the opposite perspective, others charge that the Bush administration was making minimoves designed more to diffuse efforts in Congress to enact strong retaliatory moves against China than to persuade it to reform its trade policies.

What Do You Think?

Imagine you are the U.S. senator deciding on whether to vote on three competing measures. One is a resolution urging the White House to follow quiet diplomacy and persuade China to continue its economic reforms rather than imposing tariffs and filing legal actions. The second measure, also a resolution, supports the limited moves taken by the Bush administration. The third is a bill to impose a 25% tariff on all U.S. imports from China until the president certifies that it is fulfilling all its trade obligations under WTO rules. Help make U.S. foreign economic policy. Would you vote for or against a major tariff increase on Chinese goods?

near the U.S. border. Some 850 maquiladora factories shut down and employment in the zone declined by 20%. Since then the economic fortunes of the maquiladoras and their Mexican workers have improved somewhat, but that has come in part at the cost of wage restraints for low-paid workers and tax breaks to lure MNCs back to the border.

APPLIED ECONOMIC NATIONALISM

Economic nationalism is more than a theory. It also has been and remains a powerful force in determining the economic and political policies of the world's sovereign states. Economic nationalists believe that a state's political, military, and economic powers are inextricably linked, leading them to advocate interference in the international political economy in three ways. One is the use of a country's economic power to accomplish its political goals. This usage is detailed in chapter 8's discussion of economic sanctions and economic incentives. The second approach advocated by economic nationalists is manipulation of a country's international economic policy to preserve or, even better, to enhance the national economy. The third is use of a country's military and other noneconomic power resources to achieve its economic goals. These second and third uses for economic goals are our focus in the following section.

Using Economic Means to Achieve Economic Ends

Globalization is increasingly linking the economies of all countries, and chapter 13 takes up the argument that in the long run the chances of prosperity of every country are improved if all other countries have sound economies. Be that as it may, all countries still follow the traditional approach of shaping their economic policy primarily to promote their own prosperity; the welfare of the world is a secondary issue. To accomplish their self-interested goals, all states practice **protectionism** to some degree by using a variety of tools to manipulate the flow of trade, investments, and other forms of economic interchange into and out of the country. Each of these protectionist measures has benefits and drawbacks, a cost-benefit analysis that is taken up in the chapter 13 section on debating the future of globalization, cooperation, and interdependence.

Trade and Investment Barriers

Countries can erect a range of barriers to limit import or foreign investment. These include tariffs, nontariff barriers, monetary manipulation, and investment restrictions.

Tariff Barriers   Restrictions on trade and investments are the most familiar form of protectionism. Of the tools available, **tariffs**, taxes imposed on foreign goods imported into a country, are the most widespread. Tariff rates are quite low relative to what they once were, but two qualifications are important. One is that tariff rates for EDCs are generally much lower than those for LDCs, which believe they need higher rates to protect their smaller industries from being overpowered by foreign competition. For example, the average U.S. tariff is 4% compared to 10% for China, 31% for Brazil, and 50% for India. Second, globally and for almost every country individually, the average tariff on agricultural products is much higher than it is on manufactured products. U.S. tariffs on agriculture average 10% in contrast to 3% on manufactured goods.

Beyond the normal tariff levels, countries sometimes impose economic sanctions by increasing import duties in response to an alleged abuse of international trade rules by other countries. As noted earlier, for example, President Bush fired a warning shot related to China's exports by using his power as president to find that China was violating trade rules and by imposing special tariffs of an extra 11% to 20% on Chinese exports of various types of glossy paper for high-end printing and other uses.

Nontariff Barriers   A less-known but more common way that countries restrict trade is by using **nontariff barriers (NTBs)**. *Health and safety standards* are one form of NTB. These are sometimes reasonable regulations to protect the well-being of the importing country's citizens. At other times, they are simply an excuse for protectionism, and trade disputes are common over whether the restriction is reasonable or protectionist. One current example has been the EU's resistance to the importation of genetically modified (GM) crops, a barrier that hurts farmers in the United States and many other countries that grow and seek to export GM crops. Under pressure by the WTO, the EU relented in 2004, but many member-countries have maintained or enacted national legislation that bars the importation or sales of GM crops. These countries claim that GM crops pose a health threat, while the United States, Canada, and other GM crop exporters condemn the bans as an ill-disguised effort to protect Europe's inefficient farms, claiming they are "driven much more by politics than by science."[12]

Quotas limiting the number of units that can be shipped are another form of NTB. The European Union has quotas on textile imports from China that will limit the annual growth rate on imports to 10% through 2008. Quotas are sometimes tied into tariffs. The United States sets quotas on imported raw and refined sugar by estimating U.S. sugar production, subtracting that from estimated U.S. needs, and permitting an amount of sugar imports equal to the difference at a low tariff rate of $33 a ton. Any imports beyond that quota face a tariff of $353 a ton. This added to the world price of sugar ($179 a ton) drives the price of nonquota sugar to over $532 a ton, and it effectively protects the U.S. sugar industry, which sells its product domestically for $520 a ton.

Administrative requirements are a third type of NTB. These are particularly important in limiting service imports. For example, many countries license architects, engineers, insurance agents, stock and bond traders, and other professionals, and these licensing requirements can be used to make it difficult for foreign professionals and companies to provide services in another country. One study that compared licensing and similar restrictions that 34 countries place on domestic (citizens, companies) and foreign service providers found that countries almost uniformly put more difficult requirements on foreign providers of accounting, banking, engineering, legal, telecommunications, transportation, and other services.[13]

ANALYZE THE ISSUE
E-Commerce and the WTO

Monetary Barriers   Another way that a country protects its domestic producers by limiting imports and promoting exports is by manipulating the exchange rate so that its currency is weaker against other currencies than it would be if it were allowed to float, that is, trade freely. As discussed earlier, Washington alleges (and Beijing denies) that China is keeping the value of the yuan artificially low versus the U.S. dollar. Through mid-2005, as shown in Figure 12.11, China managed to keep the value of its currency at a steady 8.3 yuan = $1 even though during the same period the dollar varied significantly against a "market basket" of currencies monitored by the IMF. This monetary manipulation is one reason that U.S. exports from China and the trade deficit with it rose so quickly.

Investment Barriers   Most countries want to attract international investment because it brings outside capital into their national economy. Yet countries are also wary of outside control of their companies and real estate. The most common form of investment restriction limits foreign ownership of companies. All countries have some limits. For example, foreigners are barred from controlling airlines in the European Union, Canada, and the United States. Japan does not allow foreign ownership of its telecommunications companies. Only citizens may own fishing and energy enterprises

FIGURE 12.11 Dollar-SDR-Yuan Exchange Rates

Countries sometimes try to manipulate their currencies to achieve certain economic goals. In order to stimulate its exports and to attract foreign investment capital, China kept the yuan at a weak rate of 8.3 yuan to the dollar until 2005. The artificiality of that rate is evident when compared with the exchange rate of the dollar with SDRs (special drawing rights), a market basket of currencies designated by the International Monetary Fund. Since 2005, China has allowed the yuan to trade with somewhat more freedom, and it has strengthened against the dollar, just as SDRs have. However, while SDRs strengthened against the dollar by 18% between 2001 and August 2007, the yuan strengthened only 7%. This indicates China's continued unwillingness to let its currency fluctuate freely.

Note: All exchange rates are yearly averages except *2007, which is August 2007.
Data source: IMF.

in Iceland. Some countries directly control companies, such as Mexico's state-owned oil monopoly Petróleos Mexicanos.

Trade and Investment Supports

In addition to erecting protectionist barriers to foreign trade and investment, countries also try to increase the economic prospects of their domestic products and producers through a variety of support techniques. Subsidies, dumping, and cartels are three of note.

Subsidies   Countries give tax breaks, provide low-cost services (such as energy and transportation), and offer various other forms of financial support to subsidize domestic producers, who can then lower the price they charge for their product. Less direct supports include such techniques as funding research for product development and undertaking government trade promotion campaigns (advertising). Agriculture is the most heavily subsidized economic sector. The EDCs provide an estimated $280 billion annually in support of agricultural business ("agribusiness") in those countries. On average 30% of all agricultural income in the EDCs comes from subsidies. The United States is on the low end of the subsidization scale, providing 18% of all agricultural receipts. The EU at 33% of receipts is about average, and Japan at 56% on the high end. Many LDCs also give subsidies, with Mexico (17%) an example. Like other forms of economic intervention, agricultural subsidies benefit one segment of a country's economy at the expense in taxes and prices of the country's citizenry and also at the expense of foreign competitors.

Subsidies can also play an important part in the competitive position of manufactured goods. For example, a major trade dispute broke out in 2005 between the

United States and the European Union, with each charging the other was violating international trade rules by providing billions of dollars in tax breaks, loan waivers, and other economic subsidies to promote the development of competing new commercial airliners. At the center of the dispute are Boeing's 787 jetliner, which is scheduled to enter service in 2008, and the Airbus 380, which is being developed by Airbus, a subsidiary of the European Aeronautic Defense and Space Company (EADS) and is scheduled for deliveries beginning in 2010. At stake are tens of billions of dollars in orders plus the prestige of being the leading commercial aircraft producer. Each has filed various complaints with the World Trade Organization (WTO), and in one the trade organization's judicial body ruled against U.S. policy. Both contestants have also levied retaliatory tariffs on selected goods against one another in the ongoing battle.

The United States and the European Union are engaged in a dogfight over their competing commercial airliner producers Boeing and Airbus. The stakes run into billions of dollars. Each combatant accuses the other of illegally subsidizing their aircraft industry, and each has filed charges against the other in the World Trade Organization.

Dumping   Yet another trade tactic is dumping. This occurs when a company, often with the support of its national government, violates trade laws by selling its products abroad at a price lower than what it sells them for at home. When in 2005, for instance, Vietnamese Prime Minister Phan Van Khai became the first of his united country's leaders ever to visit the United States, one item on his and President Bush's agenda was the 27% tariff on shrimp imports from Vietnam imposed by the U.S. International Trade Commission after it found that Vietnam was dumping the seafood on the U.S. market. Similar punitive tariffs were also put on other countries' shrimp, ranging up to 112% on Chinese shrimp. Such matters may seem small, but they are not for the U.S Southern Shrimp Alliance, which faces competition from imported shrimp worth $5 billion annually.

Cartels   Countries, especially EDCs, also have occasionally tried to control trade by establishing cartels. A **cartel** is an international trading agreement among producers who hope to control the supply and price of a primary product. The first cartel was established in 1933 to regulate tea, but the decade of the 1960s, when 18 came into existence, was the apex of cartel formation. They ranged in importance from the Organization of Petroleum Exporting Countries (OPEC) to the Asian and Pacific Coconut Community. Cartels, however, have not always proven to be successful. Even OPEC has had to struggle to maintain prices in the face of internal economic and political disputes (such as the Iraq-Iran war in the 1980s), the production of about 60% of the world's petroleum by non-OPEC countries, and other factors. Over the years, price increases, including sharp rises beginning in 2004, have had less to do with the efforts of OPEC to increase prices by manipulating supply than with uncertainty in the oil markets caused by the Iraq War, tension with Iran, and other events and with the increasing demand for oil by an energy-addicted world, as evident in Figure 12.12.

> *Did You Know That:*
>
> Cotton growers in poor countries are harmed by a U.S. cotton subsidy program that in 2003 gave American farmers $3.2 billion in cotton acreage subsidies and $1.6 billion in export credits. The total ($4.8 billion) in subsidies was greater than the market value ($3.9 billion) of the U.S. crop that year.

Using Economic Means to Achieve Political Ends

Tariffs, quotas, and other tools of economic nationalist policy are primarily used to achieve economic ends such as the protection of domestic producers. However, it is not uncommon for countries to also use a range of economic techniques to support noneconomic political goals. This type of policy was considered in detail in chapter 8's discussion of economic power, but it is worth recapping that discussion here.

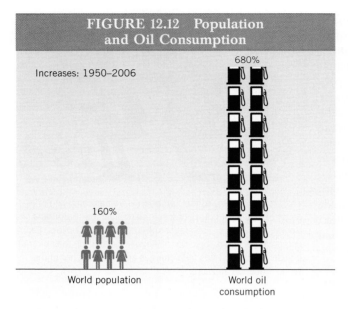

FIGURE 12.12   Population and Oil Consumption

Increases: 1950–2006

680%

160%

World population   World oil consumption

Rising energy costs are sometimes attributed to price manipulation by the OPEC cartel. The steep increase, however, has been more significantly influenced by the fact that consumption is growing much faster than the population. From 1950 to 2006, world oil consumption increased from 10.9 to 85.0 million barrels a day, a 680% rise, even though the population grew only 160% from 2.5 billion to 6.5 billion. Thus we are consuming more than three times as much oil per person globally as we did in 1950.

Data sources: UN Population Fund; U.S. Department of Energy.

National security restrictions are one aspect of such policy. All countries that produce major military weaponry require government approval of foreign sales. In many cases there are blanket prohibitions of sales to other countries that are considered current or potential enemies. As circumstances change, such bans can prove controversial. For example, the EU is considering dropping the West's long-time embargo on selling high-tech weapons to China. The United States, among others, strongly opposes this move for various reasons, including the possibility that U.S. forces could face European-supplied weaponry if China were to invade Taiwan. Another often-controversial area involves "dual-use" goods, anything from supercomputers to nuclear plant machinery to chemicals that can be used for both civilian and military purposes. As one example, the United States restricts the sale of the most advanced semiconductors, computers, avionics equipment, and other high-tech items to China.

As chapter 8 details, countries also sometimes use economic incentives or economic sanctions to try to convince one or more other countries to commence, continue, or cease acting in a certain way. For example, incentives have played a prominent role in recent efforts to stem nuclear proliferation. Both the diplomatic effort by the EU to persuade Iran to halt its alleged nuclear weapons development program and the effort by the United States and other countries to get North Korea to build no more nuclear weapons and dismantle its ability to do so include offers of energy aid and important additional economic incentives.

Countries apply their economic power in a negative way by imposing sanctions. Sanctions applied for political reasons most often occur when there has been a major event, such as Iraq's invasion of Kuwait in 1990, or amid a long-term hostile relationship, with U.S. sanctions on Cuba serving as an example. A last point is that incentives and sanctions can be used simultaneously. In May 2006 the UN Security Council endorsed a series of incentives offered by the EU and others if Iran stopped developing its capacity to create plutonium and weapons-grade uranium. When Iran failed to do so, the Security Council voted two rounds of escalating sanctions, the first in December 2006, the second in March 2007, while leaving the earlier incentives in place if Iran complied.

THE FUTURE OF ECONOMIC NATIONALIST POLICY

There can be no doubt that global economics during the last half-century has been marked by three main stories. The first has been the almost complete triumph of capitalism over competing economic models, especially Marxism and socialism. Even two (China and Vietnam) of the four remaining officially communist countries have largely adopted capitalism, with Cuba and North Korea the last holdouts still following the Marxist model.

The second important development has been a steady movement toward ever-greater economic interdependence based on an increasingly free exchange of trade, investment, and other financial activity. An array of statistics presented in this and the following chapter show conclusively that the movement of goods, services, investment capital, and currencies across borders has expanded exponentially. Furthermore, as chapter 13 discusses, the international system has created the EU, IMF, World Bank, WTO, and numerous global and regional organizations and arrangements to facilitate and promote free international economic interchange. A third important change, also a topic addressed in chapter 13, has been the growth of a sense of global responsibility for the plight of the poorer countries. Whether the EDCs are doing enough for the LDCs is a question chapter 13 addresses, but at least the EDCs are now doing something.

For all this evidence, it would be erroneous to conclude that the world is on a path to inevitable economic integration and cooperation and that the eclipse of economic nationalism is inescapable. Certainly it has weakened somewhat, but it remains the dominant approach to the international political economy (Helleiner & Pickel, 2005). The most important reason for the persistence of economic nationalism is the continuing status of sovereign states as the dominant actors in the international system and the enduring strength of nationalism as the primary focus of political identity. As integrationists once again learned when French, then Dutch voters rejected the new EU constitution in 2005, nationalist opposition to integration and cooperation remains potent. Furthermore, resistance to liberal changes in the international political economy is not just confined to Europe. Protectionist sentiment is also strong in the United States. As Great Britain's minister of trade warned in 2007, "Around the world we are seeing an increasing trend towards protectionism, putting up barriers to trade that will make us all poorer. We are seeing the growth of economic nationalism. It won't work. Protectionism dressed up as patriotism is still protectionism."[14]

Indirectly, economic nationalism is also being reinforced by doubts about globalization. Many in the North perceive their prosperity to be threatened by the flight of jobs to countries with low-cost labor and by the immigration of low-wage laborers from other countries to take many of the jobs that are left. Ironically, many in the South perceive globalization as a process that has enriched the North even further and harmed the poorer countries. President Hosni Mubarak of Egypt has portrayed the "emerging world" as a place where "there is a bitter sentiment of injustice, a sense that there must be something wrong with a system that wipes out years of hard-won development because of changes in market sentiment."[15] Such views prompted UN Secretary-General Kofi Annan to characterize globalization as "fragile" and to warn, "The unequal distribution of benefits and the imbalances in global rule-making, which characterize globalization today, inevitably will produce backlash and protectionism."[16] All this lends credence to one analyst's observation that, "We have gotten used to the idea that globalization will inevitably succeed, but I am not so sure anymore."[17]

WEB POLL
National and Global
Economic Demands:
Where Do Your
Loyalties Lie?

CHAPTER SUMMARY

THEORIES OF INTERNATIONAL POLITICAL ECONOMY

1. Economics and politics are closely intertwined aspects of international relations. This interrelationship has become even more important in recent history. Economics has become more important internationally because of dramatically increased trade levels, ever-tightening economic interdependence between countries, and the growing impact

of international economics on domestic economics. The study of international political economy (IPE) examines the interaction between politics and economics.

2. There are many technical aspects to explaining and understanding the international political economy, and it is important to understand such concepts as gross domestic product, gross national product (and purchasing power parity for each of these), and current and real dollars.

3. The approaches to IPE can be roughly divided into three groups: economic nationalism (mercantilism), economic internationalism (liberalism), and economic structuralism.

4. The core of the economic nationalist doctrine is the realist idea that the state should harness and use national economic strength to further national interest. Therefore, the state should shape the country's economy and its foreign economic policy to enhance state power.

5. Economic internationalists are liberals who believe that international economic relations should and can be harmonious because prosperity is available to all and is most likely to be achieved and preserved through cooperation. The main thrust of economic internationalism is to separate politics from economics, to create prosperity by freeing economic interchange from political restrictions.

6. Economic structuralists hold that world politics is based on the division of the world into have and have-not countries, with the EDCs keeping the LDCs weak and poor in order to exploit them. There are two types of economic structuralists. Marxists believe that the entire capitalist-based system must be replaced with domestic and international socialist systems before economic equity can be achieved. Less radical economic structuralist theories include dependency and world systems theory, which stress reform of the current market system by ending the system of dependency.

THE WORLD ECONOMY: GLOBALIZATION AND INTERDEPENDENCE

7. Globalization and interdependence have increased at an exponential rate since the beginning of the second half of the 20th century, with a rapid rise in the level of economic interchange (trade, investments and other capital flows, and monetary exchange) in the international political economy.

THE WORLD ECONOMY: DIVERSE CIRCUMSTANCES

8. The world is generally divided into two economic spheres: a wealthy North and a much less wealthy South. There are some overlaps between the two spheres, but in general the vast majority of the people and countries of the South are much less wealthy and industrially developed than the countries of the North and their people. The South also has a history of direct and indirect colonial control by countries of the North.

9. While a wealth gap persists between North and South, and in some ways has grown, the data must be carefully analyzed. By many measures, economic and social conditions in the South have improved greatly during recent decades. Also, data about overall improvements in the South is skewed downward by the worsening conditions in sub-Saharan Africa.

NATIONAL ECONOMIC RELATIONS

10. There is economic competition across the analytical categories of countries, including North-North competition, North-South competition, and South-South competition.

APPLIED ECONOMIC NATIONALISM

11. Countries attempt to advance their economic policy and prosperity by using their economic power through a mixture of protectionist barriers and incentives in the areas of trade and investment. While each approach is sometimes successful, both incentives and, particularly, sanctions are difficult to apply successfully and have numerous drawbacks.

THE FUTURE OF ECONOMIC NATIONALIST POLICY

12. Although globalization and interdependence are undermining economic nationalism, it remains the driving force behind states' international economic policy. Moreover, persistent state sovereignty, nationalism, and problems with globalization are all helping to maintain the central role of economic nationalism in world politics.

For simulations, debates, and other interactive activities, a chapter quiz, Web links, and much more, visit **www.mhhe.com/rourke12/** and go to chapter 12. Or, while accessing the site, click on Course-Wide Content and view recent international relations articles in the *New York Times*.

KEY TERMS

capitalism

cartel

current dollars

dependency theory

economic internationalism

economic nationalism

economic structuralism

economically developed countries (EDCs)

exchange rates

extreme poverty

foreign direct investment (FDI)

foreign portfolio investment (FPI)

globalization

gross domestic product (GDP)

gross national product (GNP)

interdependence

international political economy (IPE)

least developed countries (LLDCs)

less developed countries (LDCs)

manufactured goods

Marxist theory

merchandise trade

monetary relations

multinational corporations (MNCs)

neocolonialism

New International Economic Order (NIEO)

newly industrializing countries (NICs)

nontariff barriers (NTBs)

North

primary products

protectionism

purchasing power parity (PPP)

real dollars

services trade

South

tariffs

world systems theory

CHAPTER

13

International Economic Cooperation:
The Alternative Road

Join we together, for the public good.
—William Shakespeare, *King Henry VI, Part II*

For my part, I had rather bear with you than bear you;
yet I should bear no cross if I did bear you,
for I think you have no money in your purse.
—William Shakespeare, *As You Like It*

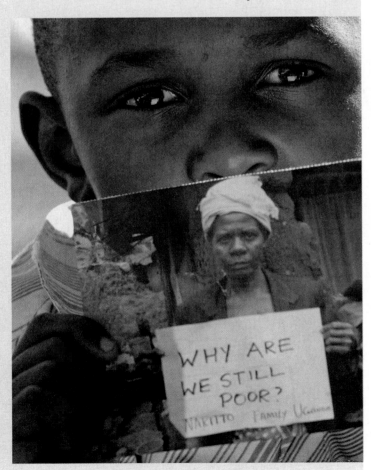

This South African boy is holding a photograph that poses a poignant question: Why do so many countries, particularly those in sub-Saharan Africa and South Asia, remain so poor? This chapter addresses that question and the international efforts to remedy the plight of these countries.

THIS CHAPTER IS THE SECOND of two that examine the international political economy (IPE). Chapter 12, the first of the pair, takes up economic nationalism, the traditional approach to the international political economy. That path is characterized by self-interested economic competition among countries. Economic nationalism persists as the dominant set of values behind the international economic policy of states. But it is not unchallenged. Instead, economic internationalists and structuralists believe that the global economic future would be better if countries cooperate economically, or even integrate their economies. This chapter assesses the alternative route of greater international cooperation. Our assessment will first examine global cooperation, then turn its attention to regional efforts. As you will see, one aspect of cooperation among the economically developed countries (EDCs) of the North is an effort to ensure that their relative prosperity continues. An even more important goal of economic cooperation, arguably, is to improve the circumstances of the less developed countries (LDCs) of the South. Therefore we will pay particular attention to what is needed for economic development and the programs that are addressing that need.

ECONOMIC COOPERATION AND DEVELOPMENT: BACKGROUND AND REQUIREMENTS

The thought of moving toward a very different way of dealing with the international economy is more than theory. It is a process that has made substantial progress and one that many think can and should become the dominant paradigm in the future. At the global level, it is appropriate to first look at basic IPE theory and the origins of economic cooperation. Then we will turn to detailing the development needs of the South, the most important focus of international economic cooperation today.

IPE Theory and Cooperation

Chapter 12 details the three main IPE theories, economic nationalism, economic internationalism, and economic structuralism. Still, it is appropriate to also briefly consider them here, with an emphasis on what each says about cooperation and development.

Economic nationalists operate from a realpolitik orientation and believe that each country, be it North or South, should look out for itself first and foremost by promoting its own national interest when formulating policy related to trade, investment, and aid. They also view the political economy as a zero-sum game in which gains made by some players inevitably mean losses for other players. As for development, economic nationalists are apt to be wary of giving extensive aid or other forms of economic assistance to the LDCs. One reason is that today's LDC could become tomorrow's competitor, just as China has become. Economic nationalists are particularly averse to taking steps such as ending agricultural subsidies, which would help the LDCs that export such products but would hurt farmers in the EDCs. Furthermore, economic nationalists suspect that the South's calls for greater equity are, in essence, attempts to change the rules so that LDCs can acquire political power for themselves.

Economic internationalists believe that international economic policy should emphasize cooperation. In their view, the global economy is a non-zero-sum game in which prosperity is available to all because the economic advancement of countries does not have to come at the expense of other countries. From this perspective, economic internationalists favor generally unfettered economic interchange. They therefore oppose tariff and nontariff barriers (NTBs) and incentives, the very tools that economic nationalists heartily endorse. As for LDC development, economic internationalists contend that the major impediments are the South's weakness in acquiring capital, its shortage of skilled labor, and some of its domestic economic policies, such as centralized planning and protectionism. These difficulties can be overcome, according to economic internationalists, through free trade, foreign investment supplemented by loans, foreign aid, and reduced government interference in the economy. Such policies will allow unimpeded international economic exchange among states, benefiting all of them. This view that the global economy is not a zero-sum game leads economic internationalists to believe that it is possible to integrate LDCs into the world economic system by eliminating system imperfections while maintaining the basic structure and stability.

Economic structuralists argue that how the world economy is structured determines the conduct of world politics. They portray a world split between rich countries (EDCs, the North) and poor countries (LDCs, the South), and they contend that the EDCs consciously strive to keep the LDCs poor and dependent so that EDCs can exploit them. From this perspective, economic structuralists maintain that the political-economic organization of the world's patterns of production and trade must be radically altered for the LDCs to develop. To accomplish this, economic structuralists believe that not only should LDCs be given substantial economic assistance and concessions, but that they should also be politically empowered and given a greater say over the operation of IGOs such as the IMF and World Bank.

The Origins of Economic Cooperation

Did You Know That:

Within two years after Congress enacted the highly protectionist Smoot-Hawley Tariff in 1930 and the European countries retaliated with their own protectionist tariffs, U.S. imports from Europe declined 71% and U.S. exports to Europe dropped 67%.

The liberal idea of creating global **interdependence** based on free economic interchange and cooperation for the economic good of all dates back several hundred years. It was slow to take hold, though, and did not begin to shape international economic relations to any great extent until the 1930s and 1940s. The violence of two world wars and the economic dislocation during the Great Depression in the 1930s led an increasing number of leaders to rethink current policies, and they agreed with the view that unrestrained economic nationalism had played a role in causing these disasters. To avoid such catastrophes in the future, the United States led the EDCs of the anti-Axis alliance and then the anticommunist West to create the foundation of a new international economic order. During the years 1943–1948, the EDCs created a number of global and regional intergovernmental organizations (IGOs) to promote economic stability and the free flow of trade and capital across national boundaries. Most notable among these IGOs are the World Bank, the International Monetary Fund (IMF), and the General Agreement on Tariffs and Trade (GATT, both a treaty and an organization; the organization was renamed the World Trade Organization, WTO). The United Nations also came into existence, and it has grown to have numerous economic agencies and responsibilities.

The immediate post–World War II era also saw the first major foreign aid program. The United States launched the European Recovery Program (the Marshall Plan), which gave over $13 billion (or about $100 billion in current dollars) to the countries of Western Europe between 1948 and 1951. Certainly there was some degree of humanitarian concern with Europe's plight, but the main U.S. motives were political self-interest (to strengthen Western Europe against communism) and an economic self-interest (to revive major trading partners so that they could buy U.S. exports).

DEVELOPMENT OF THE SOUTH

Although the economic cooperation that began after World War II focused initially on the rebuilding of the devastated EDCs, the emphasis gradually shifted to the economic development of the South (Seligson & Passé-Smith, 2003). The reorientation occurred for several reasons. Among these are the general return to prosperity of the North, the independence movements that changed dozens of colonies into countries, and a growing awareness of the economic plight of the South. Reflecting this shift, the commentary in this chapter will mostly deal with LDC development. A first step toward developing this topic is to briefly outline the criteria that characterize a developed economy. Then we will turn to what the countries of the South need in order to develop their economies more fully.

Criteria for Economic Development

Per capita income is the standard way to distinguish the LDCs from the EDCs, but the question here is what factors are necessary to promote development and to establish a prosperous economy. Some of the following criteria that characterize most EDCs and are partly or entirely missing from many LDCs, especially LLDCs (lower-income, least developed countries), are economic, others are political.

Economic diversification: A broadly based economy is a key component of prosperity. Any country's prosperity is enhanced if it produces and exports a wide variety of manufactured goods, is agriculturally self-sufficient, and produces at least some of the minerals and other raw materials that a modern economy consumes or can sell. It is true that there are some LDCs, like Kuwait with its oil, that are prosperous despite a very narrow economic base. It is also true that some EDCs, like Japan, have limited agricultural capacity and few natural resources. But such countries are highly vulnerable.

Limited economic reliance on primary products: A related trait that distinguishes most EDCs from most LDCs is that a greater proportion of the economic activity of the latter group is devoted to the production of primary products, including fibers (such as cotton), food, fuels, wood, and other minerals and raw materials. By contrast, the manufacturing and services sectors dominate EDC economic activity. With the exception of energy-exporting countries, a rule of thumb is that the more dependent a country's economy is on primary products, the poorer that country is likely to be. One indication is found in Figure 13.1.

International market and investment access: In order to develop, LDCs need to sell their goods and services abroad. Trade is an important source of income for the LDCs, like all countries, and tariffs, quotas, and other barriers to LDC exports restrict their ability to bring in foreign capital. Barriers to the provision of services such as banking, insurance, and transportation are usually higher than for merchandise, but as a country's economy develops, so does its ability to provide services abroad. Similarly, as an LDC's economy develops, some of its companies may well seek investment opportunities abroad that offer the potential of creating an inflow of capital to the

FIGURE 13.1   GDP and Primary Products

Share of GDP from primary products

Low-income countries: 36%
Middle-income countries: 27%
High-income countries: 10%

A shift away from the production of fuels, food, minerals, and other primary products to manufacturing and providing services is one mark of the shift from LDC to EDC status.

Data source: World Bank.

investing LDC. One indication of the slow economic progress of the LDCs is that their share of the world's FDI rose from 8% in 1990 to 12% in 2005. The more rapidly developing LDCs saw the greatest jumps in their FDI holdings, with, for example, China's growing 10 times between 1990 and 2005 and South Korea's expanding sixteenfold.

A stable currency: A country's currency is the lifeblood of its economy because it allows buying, selling, payments for services, and other key economic functions to proceed smoothly. Most EDCs have fairly stable currencies that, among other things, permit commerce to flow freely and promote investment by keeping interest rates low. Inflation is one important factor that affects a currency's stability. Between 1987 and 2007, average annual inflation in the EDCs was 2.7%; in LDCs it was 30.1%. Among other impacts, low inflation promotes both foreign investing and domestic borrowing for investment. In 2005, the U.S. lowest annual lending rate was about 4%, in Japan it was 2%. By contrast, the LDCs tend to have higher inflation and experience other destabilizing factors. These left, for example, the 2005 annual lending rates at about 82% in Angola and 67% in Colombia. In some cases, inflation can get truly out of hand and devastate an economy. The inept monetary policies of Zimbabwe's dictatorial President Robert G. Mugabe created hyperinflation that reached an annualized rate of 2,200% by mid-2007. In one especially bad week alone, the prices of food and other basics rose 256%. With the Zimbabwean dollar almost worthless, most businesses could no longer function, and workers could no longer go to their jobs because the weekly cost of taking the bus was more than their weekly wage. As a result, unemployment reportedly reached 80%.

A strong human infrastructure: Chapter 8's discussion of measures of a country's power, economic and otherwise, highlights the importance of having a population with a good age distribution (neither too many children nor senior citizens), one that is healthy, well educated, and capable of maximizing the use of everyone's talents, rather than marginalizing some based on gender, race, ethnicity, or some other trait. Currently less than half of all high school–age youth in low-income countries are in school; almost everyone in this age group in high-income countries is in school.

A strong physical and technological infrastructure: Chapter 8 also discusses the importance of advanced communications systems and of efficient transportation systems, as well as the widespread availability and use of computers, robotics, and many other forms of modern technology. As one example, for every 1,000 people, high-income countries on average have 574 computers; low-income countries have only about 11.

Domestic order: Civil war and other forms of internal violence destroy prosperity where it exists and prevent prosperity where it does not. Liberia provides a tragic, if all too common, example. From 1980 until 2003, the country was torn by almost constant fighting that killed perhaps 200,000 people, displaced about a million others, and demolished the country's infrastructure and economy. During the nearly quarter century of turmoil, the country's real (controlled for inflation) per capita GDP declined 82%, transforming Liberia from one of the most prosperous in sub-Saharan Africa to one of the poorest.

Effective government: Most EDCs have, and many LDCs do not have, a reasonably stable political system and a government that tries to promote prosperity rather than enrich its members and supporters. Among other government characteristics that the World Bank considers important to development are the level of corruption, the willingness of the courts to uphold property rights, the crime rate, and efficiency in issuing permits and addressing other regulations. A World Bank survey of business leaders found, for example, that in Guatemala, 81% said corruption was a major constraint to doing business, 71% lacked confidence in the courts, and 81% worried about the crime rate. In Germany, by contrast, these were minor factors: corruption (2%), courts (2%), and crime (4%). A regional look at one indication of corruption is found in Figure 13.2. Wherever it is located, corruption tends to hinder both domestic and international investment in an economy.

Is a supportive government a democratic one? Not necessarily. The discussion in chapter 6 and Figure 6.3, p. 180, indicate that there is a correlation between poor countries and authoritarian governments on the one hand and wealthier countries and democratic governance on the other. It is not clear, though, whether there is a causal relationship or, if so, whether democratic countries become more prosperous or prosperous countries become more democratic. Certainly, the case of China, the fastest growing economy in the world over the last decade or so, indicates that development can occur within authoritarian states.

FIGURE 13.2   Corruption by Region

Percentage of households reporting they paid a bribe in the last year

Region	
Western Europe	2%
U.S./Canada	2%
Asia	7%
Eastern Europe	9%
Latin America	17%
Africa	36%

Bribery and other forms of corruption inhibit economic development and, on average, are more prevalent in LDCs than in EDCs.

Data source: Transparency International, *Report on the Transparency International Global Corruption Barometer* 2006 (Berlin, Germany: December 7, 2006).

Achieving Economic Development

Laying out in print some of the criteria for being an EDC is far easier than it is for an LDC to achieve those criteria. To examine how LDCs can advance toward EDC status, we will first look at economic factors. Perhaps the greatest need for the LDCs is to attract capital (money) to improve their human and technological infrastructures, to increase the size of their manufacturing and service sectors, and to diversify their economies so that no single product or service alone determines whether they are prosperous or not. Much akin to the old saying that "it takes money to make money," the problem for LDCs is that they are poor and find it difficult to raise capital internally. Therefore, they need massive inflows of **development capital** from the EDCs to expand and diversify their economies. "Uganda needs just two things," according to its president. "We need infrastructure and we need foreign investment. That is what we need. The rest we shall do ourselves."[1]

Obtaining capital from any source is important, but inflows from the EDCs are particularly important because they bring in relatively stable **hard currencies**, such as American dollars, Japanese yen, and European Union euros, that are widely accepted in international transactions. Most LDC currencies are not readily convertible because they are unstable. So if Guatemala wants to bring in foreign expertise, equipment, and material to improve its port facilities at San José, it will usually need dollars or some other hard currency because its suppliers are unlikely to accept quetzals.

Five important external sources of capital are loans, investment, trade, aid, and remittances. Unfortunately, there are limitations and drawbacks to each. Unless significant changes are made to increase the flow of development capital to the LDCs and to distribute it more broadly among all LDCs, many of them are destined to remain relatively poor for the foreseeable future. It is also the case that the LDCs

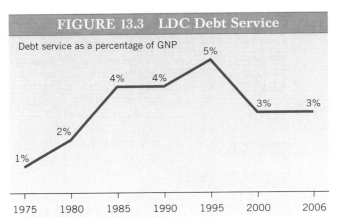

FIGURE 13.3   LDC Debt Service

Debt service as a percentage of GNP

1975   1980   1985   1990   1995   2000   2006

Many LDCs began to borrow heavily in the early 1980s to speed their development. Excessive borrowing proved counterproductive, however, because of the cost of servicing the debt (paying principal and interest). One way to measure debt service is to compare it to the LDCs' combined GNPs. As you can see, the burden grew rapidly and persisted at a high level before declining after 1995. Still, the debt-to-GNP percentage remains higher than in the past and continues to hinder economic development in many LDCs.

Data source: World Bank.

need to institute some internal reforms so that they can better utilize their own capital resources and those that flow in from EDCs.

Loans

One source of hard currency is loans extended by private or government sources. Based on a number of economic factors, the LDCs moved in the 1970s to finance their development needs by borrowing heavily from external sources. By 1982 LDC international debt had skyrocketed to $849 billion, and while the rate of increase has eased, the total debt owed by LDCs has continued to grow and stood at $3.1 trillion in 2004. Banks and other private institutional and individual bondholders hold about half the debt, with banks and official sources (EDC governments and IGOs such as the IMF) each holding about 25%.

Borrowing abroad to meet current domestic needs is common. The United States, for example, owes foreigners over $2 trillion on the bonds the U.S. Treasury has sold them to finance the U.S. national debt. Both borrowers and lenders must manage money carefully, however. Many LDCs have struggled to meet their **debt service** (principal plus interest payments) on their loans. A standard measurement of any country's ability to meet its debt payments is the amount of its annual debt service compared to its annual export earnings. As Figure 13.3 shows, in 1975, LDC debt stood at only 1% of the economic productivity (GNP), but soon quintupled. That set off a broad crisis, which pushed Argentina, Brazil, Mexico, Nigeria, and several other LDCs to the edge of bankruptcy and also threatened the financial well-being of the lenders, who stood to lose billions of dollars. The debt crisis was finally solved. Several programs were instituted by the EDCs and the IMF to refinance the debt of those LDCs with a long-term ability to pay and to forgive all or most of the debt for the poorest, most debt-burdened countries. The IMF designates this latter group of 38 countries, 32 of them in Africa, as Heavily Indebted Poor Countries (HIPCs). Among other debt relief initiatives, the EDCs agreed in 2005 to provide the HIPCs with $55 billion in debt relief, wiping out the debt of 27 of the HIPCs and substantially lowering the debt of others.

The immediate LDC debt crisis abated, but the issue of LDC debt remains troubling for several reasons. One concern is that the LDCs still have a towering debt of more than $3 trillion. Second, as also evident in Figure 13.3, the debt burden remains much higher than it once was, and in 2006, the LDCs had to pay out $629 billion in much-needed capital to service the debt. Third, the overall data about the declining debt burden disguises the crushing continuing debt of some countries. Argentina, for one, is $244 billion in debt, a figure that amounts to 159% of its annual GNP and requires service payments that equal almost 9% of its GNP. In 2001 and 2002, a combination of Argentina's monetary policies, its faltering economy, and its immense debt set off a political and financial crisis that weakened the value of the peso by 71%, sent inflation up to 65%, caused the economy to shrink, tripled unemployment, and caused

Many poorer countries are being hindered from developing economically by their need to pay off their mountains of foreign debt. Their funds could instead be spent to improve themselves. The debt crisis has eased somewhat in the past few years, but the debt burden remains a major problem for many LDCs.

several governments to fall. Internal reforms and IMF assistance eased the crisis, and Argentina has begun to recover, but it will take years to repair. Argentina's example shows that as a way to finance development and to meet short-term needs, loans can play a positive role in moderation, but they present a perilous path to long-term development.

Private Investment

A second source of capital for LDCs is private investment through foreign direct investment (FDI) and foreign portfolio investment (FPI), as discussed in chapter 12. The flows of investment capital are growing in importance for LDCs. For example, the annual net inflow of FDI into the LDCs grew twelvefold between 1990 and 2006 from $20 billion to $241 billion. FPI is also important, and it stood at a net $53 billion in 2004. However, FPI is volatile. The funds tend to be short-term investments, and the flow can turn sharply negative when investors lose confidence. As Figure 13.4 indicates, the ten years 1997–2006 saw an initial net inflow of FPI, followed by a strong outflow, then a return of net inflow, although it was tapering off in 2006. Sudden outflows can disrupt a country's economy and helped cause financial crises in Mexico in 1995, much of Asia in the late 1990s, and Argentina in 2001–2002. For Argentina the economic woes, already noted related to its debt and other factors, caused investors both within the country and internationally to lose confidence, and their efforts to divest themselves of their holdings of Argentinean bonds and other assets added to the general destabilization of the country's currency and its economy.

As with other overall data, the seemingly huge flow of FDI and, sometimes, FPI into the LDCs is only part of the story. One less positive aspect of the details is that most investment capital flowing to the LDCs goes to only a handful of them. China alone receives 40%, and that combined with FPI flows into Brazil, Mexico, Singapore, and South Korea account for about two-thirds of all the FDI going to the South. The LLDCs are particularly disadvantaged, receiving only 8% of the LDCs' net inflow, and less than 3% of the world total.

Trade

Export earnings are a third source of development capital. In theory, the vast size of the world market makes trade the optimal source of hard currency for LDCs. Yet, in reality, the LDCs are disadvantaged by the pattern and terms of international trade.

There are several sources of LDC trade weakness. First, as detailed in chapter 12 and Figure 12.6, p. 388, LDC exports are only 24% of the world total overall, and only 10% on a per capita basis. With exports equal to only $889 per person, they provide nowhere near the economic stimulus generated by the North's exports, which are $8,281 per capita.

Second, just a few LDCs account for the lion's share of all goods exported by the South. China alone accounts for 32% of all the South's exports, another five LDCs combine for 35%, and the handful of petroleum and natural gas exporters share another 14%. This leaves a scant 19% of the South's exports for the rest of the LDCs.

MAP
Global Flows of
Investment Capital

FIGURE 13.4   FPI Flow to LDCs

Net flow of FPI to LDCs (US$ billions)

$14.0

$47.5 $42.4

$11.0

$14.3

Net inflow

–$0.6   Net outflow

–$17.2

–$44.5   –$39.8

1998 1999 2000 2001 2002 2003 2004 2005 2006

The purchase of stocks in private companies and of bonds of both companies and governments, which together make up foreign portfolio investment (FPI), bring important capital into LDCs. However, the net flow (money invested minus money withdrawn) can be volatile. After a positive inflow in 1998, new FPI for the LDCs was in the red (negative) the next four years, causing a drain of $102.1 billion, before turning to the black (positive) in 2004. Sharp outflows, especially the sale of government bonds, can cause inflation in an LDC and otherwise destabilize its currency.

Data source: OECD.

Third, many LDCs have a negative trade balance. That is, they import more than they can export. This is a particular problem for the LLDCs, which need many goods they cannot produce for themselves and have relatively few products to sell on the world market. For these countries, imports exceeded exports by 10% in 2004. The net result is that almost all the export earnings for most LDCs go toward buying imports, leaving little to invest in new development, and LLDCs with a trade deficit have a net loss of capital.

Fourth, the overdependence of many LDCs on primary products for exports is disadvantageous. With the exception of energy-exporting countries, a rule of thumb is that the more dependent a country is on the export of primary products, the poorer that country is likely to be. Between 1990 and 2004, the LDCs' manufactured goods as a share of all exported goods rose from 51% to 64%, but this still compares unfavorably with the North's 81%. Furthermore, manufactured goods are only 50% of LLDC exports, and some individual countries export hardly any manufactured goods. For example, primary products make up 85% of Uganda's exports and 90% of Ecuador's exports. The accompanying map shows the extent to which world countries are dependent on the export of primary products.

Dependence on one or a few primary products for export earnings leaves LDCs disadvantaged because of several factors. *Product instability* is one factor. When, for example, the disease pod rot attacks the cocoa crop in Ghana, it loses a substantial portion of one of its leading exports. *Price weakness* also afflicts most primary products. During the past decades, world demand for products such as cotton and other natural

MAP
Exports of Primary Products

The less developed countries of the South are disadvantaged compared to the economically developed countries of the North. One reason is that the LDCs are much more reliant on primary products for export earnings. The dependency is a disadvantage because the demand for and price of primary products is unstable. Also, over the long term the value of primary products rises more slowly than manufactured products. Therefore most LDCs have increasing difficulty earning the foreign capital needed for economic development. This map shows the distribution of countries according to the percentage of their exports accounted for by primary products.

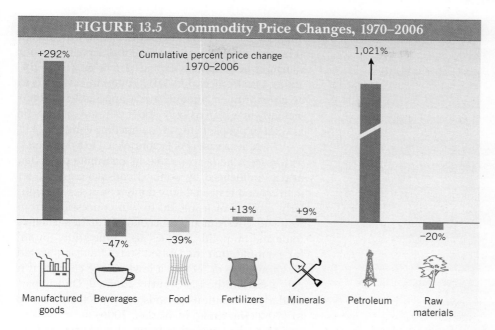

FIGURE 13.5 Commodity Price Changes, 1970–2006

Cumulative percent price change 1970–2006

+292% 1,021%

+13% +9%

−47% −39% −20%

Manufactured goods Beverages Food Fertilizers Minerals Petroleum Raw materials

LDCs that rely on primary products other than oil for export earnings have had an increasingly difficult time earning enough foreign capital through their exports to modernize their economies. Measured in real dollars, the price of manufactured goods increased 292% between 1970 and 2006. Even worse, most LDCs import petroleum, against which their primary product exports have lost even more value than against manufactured goods, while primary product prices rose little or even declined.

*Measured in real dollars
Data source: World Bank (2006).

fibers has declined due to the development of synthetics, and sugar sales have been undercut by artificial substitutes and by dietary changes. Lower demand has led to level or even reduced prices in keeping with the classic economic relationship of greater supply and less demand. Between 1970 and 2004, the price of cotton fell 42% and the price of sugar dropped 48% in real dollars. Making matters worse, the price of manufactured goods has risen steeply, which means that most of the primary products the LDCs export have lost value against the manufactured goods the LDCs need to import. This "double trouble" relationship is shown in Figure 13.5.

The use of trade, then, to acquire capital and to improve economic conditions has not been highly effective for most LDCs. Their pattern of merchandise trade deficits, overreliance on primary product exports, and price weaknesses are all disadvantages for LDCs in their trade relations with the EDCs.

Foreign Aid

A fourth possible external source of capital for LDCs is foreign aid. In some ways the flow of official development assistance (ODA) to LDCs has been impressive, amounting to over $4 trillion (measured in 2005 real dollars) since World War II. For 2006, ODA was $103 billion. Currently, 95% of all foreign aid that is given comes from the 22 EDCs that are members of the **Development Assistance Committee (DAC)** of the Organization for Economic Cooperation and Development (OECD). In 2006, 73% of the assistance was extended through **bilateral aid** (country to country), with 27% channeled through **multilateral aid** (via the United Nations, the World

Did You Know That:

For the first time since the Mexican-American War of 1848, Mexican military forces entered the United States in 2005. This time Mexican troops were delivering foreign aid in the form of disaster relief supplies to American victims of Hurricane Katrina along the Gulf Coast.

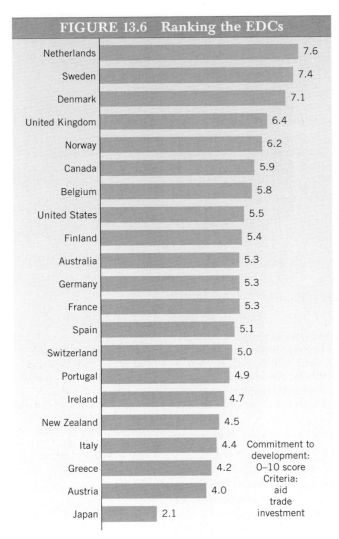

FIGURE 13.6 Ranking the EDCs

Country	Score
Netherlands	7.6
Sweden	7.4
Denmark	7.1
United Kingdom	6.4
Norway	6.2
Canada	5.9
Belgium	5.8
United States	5.5
Finland	5.4
Australia	5.3
Germany	5.3
France	5.3
Spain	5.1
Switzerland	5.0
Portugal	4.9
Ireland	4.7
New Zealand	4.5
Italy	4.4
Greece	4.2
Austria	4.0
Japan	2.1

Commitment to development: 0–10 score
Criteria:
aid
trade
investment

An advocacy NGO, the Center for Global Development (CGD), calculates an annual index called "Ranking the Rich." The CGD assigns EDCs a score from 0 (poor) to10 (excellent) depending on the CGD's evaluation of how well the policies of each promote development according to six measures: aid, trade, investment, migration, environment, and security/technology transfer supports. This figure shows the average score of the EDCs using only those three criteria (aid, trade, and investment) emphasized in this chapter. It is worth noting that the rankings using all six criteria were not dramatically different from those shown here, with the Netherlands ranking first and Japan last on both.

Note: For a full explanation of the three criteria used here and the others, go to the Web site of the Center for Global Development at www.cgdev.org.
Data source: Center for Global Development.

Bank, and other IGOs). Without disparaging the value or intent of foreign aid, the primary issue with foreign aid is that there is not enough of it to serve as a major source of development capital (Travis & Zahariadis, 2002). On the face of it, $103 billion in aid seems to be an enormous amount, but it appears less monumental when seen as only about $43 for each of the 2.4 billion people living in low-income countries.

There are a variety of factors related to aid that limit its impact. One factor is that its distribution is often heavily influenced by political considerations rather than economic need. Many donor countries are regularly accused of using aid to win concessions from recipient governments on economic matters such as trade and on political issues also. One study found, for example, that the United States increases its aid by an average of 59% to a low-income country if it gets a seat on the UN Security Council. During particularly contentious periods, U.S. aid soared by up to 170% (Kuziemko & Werker, 2006).

More than any other factor, though, the amount of foreign aid, both in total dollars and in effort—as a percentage of the donor country GNP—is controversial. These two standards—total giving and giving as a share of wealth—yield very different results in the debate over whether individual EDCs are generous or penurious in their aid. From the perspective of the amount of aid, the United States in 2006 stood a laudable first among donors, giving $22.7 billion in aid, or 21% of all the aid. Great Britain ranked second ($12.6 billion), with Japan ($11.6), and France and Germany ($10.4 billion each) not far behind.

Does this make the United States a model of generosity? Not according to its critics, who argue from the share-of-wealth perspective. As chapter 12 noted, the UN has adopted a standard of 0.7% of GNP as a goal for foreign aid giving. In 2006, only 5 of the DAC countries met that mark. Sweden was the most generous at 1.03% of GNP; Norway, Luxembourg, the Netherlands, and Denmark also exceeded 0.7%. But with smaller economies, their aid amounts were relatively small. Luxembourg gave only $291 million, less than U.S. donations about every 5 days. Yet in terms of the share of its wealth that it was willing to give, the United States at 0.17% ranked next to last, barely edging out Greece (0.16%). Two other marks of comparison are that the average country gave 4.5% of its GNP in aid (foreign and domestic), and overall the DAC members donated 3% of their collective GNPs to aid. What is your view? Should the United States be lauded or lambasted for its foreign aid program? As part of that consideration, the record of the United States or any other EDC should be considered within the overall effort to assist LDCs, as in Figure 13.6, which ranks the comparative contributions of the EDCs to the development of the LDCs along a number of dimensions.

Remittances

Temporary or permanent emigrants are another important source of foreign capital to those LDCs that have substantial number of their nationals living and working abroad and sending money home (remittances) to their families and other contacts. Remittances are growing quickly, as Figure 13.7 indicates, and in 2005, according to the World Bank, totaled $203 billion and probably much more. This figure is easily double that year's foreign aid. About 90% of remittances go from EDCs to LDCs. Latin America is probably the region that benefits the most from remittances. A study by the Inter-American Development Bank concludes that Latinos in the United States sent about $45 billion in remittances to Latin America in 2006. About half of that went to Mexico.[2] India, however, at nearly $25 billion was the single country that got the most in remittances in 2006. Measuring remittances as a percentage of the recipient country's GNP is probably the best standard to see their impact. For most countries the amounts were small, with remittances equaling perhaps 3% of India's and Mexico's GNPs. However, some countries benefit greatly, with remittances equaling over 30% of Moldova's GNP and between 20% and 25% of the respective GNPs of such countries as Haiti, Lesotho, Lebanon, and Tajikistan. For all the benefits that remittances can bring, they are something of a double-edged sword. The World Bank warns that the outflow of workers seeking higher pay in other countries can drain the home country of some of its most motivated and talented workers, the very people it needs at home to progress.

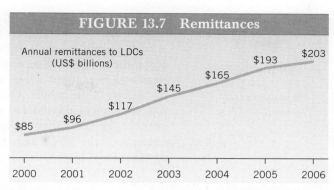

FIGURE 13.7   Remittances

Annual remittances to LDCs (US$ billions)

$85 — $96 — $117 — $145 — $165 — $193 — $203

2000   2001   2002   2003   2004   2005   2006

Remittances, money that immigrants send to their home country, have become an important source of foreign capital for some LDCs. Remittances in 2006 were about twice the amount of foreign aid that year.

Data source: Ratha (2007).

Did You Know That:

A 2002 survey found that on average Americans thought that foreign aid consumed 31% of the federal budget and should be cut back to 17%. That year foreign aid was actually less than 1% of the federal budget.

Internal Reforms

Although not a capital need as such, internal reforms are a closely associated and controversial topic. One criticism of the LDCs is that development funds and other assistance programs have had effects ranging from suboptimal to failure because of protectionism, corruption, and problems within the countries. President Bush, Prime Minister Tony Blair of Great Britain, other EDC leaders, and the IMF and World Bank have all pressed countries to open their economies further to trade and investment, to privatize state-run enterprises, and to assure greater "transparency," something of a code word for reducing corruption. Symbolic of this thrust, the World Bank's *World Development Report 2005* is subtitled *A Better Investment Climate for Everyone*. The report argues (p. xii) that "improving the climate for investment in developing countries is essential to provide jobs and opportunities." It states that some countries have taken steps to improve their investment climate. Nevertheless, it continues, "Progress remains slow" because many "governments still saddle firms and entrepreneurs with unnecessary costs, create substantial uncertainty and risks, and even erect unjustified barriers to competition." In its table rating countries by their investment climate, the report takes up such standards as the unpredictability of how officials interpret regulations, bribes, confidence in the court system, crime, tax rates, and the amount of bureaucratic red tape.

Certainly, some of these factors, such as being safe from crime, would elicit no dispute. Others are more controversial. For example, leaders in LDCs wonder

JOIN THE DEBATE
Is Debt Relief Good for
the Global Economy?

how the United States would do on the regulatory predictability scale, given that Washington is populated by hordes of lobbyists trying to influence government, as well as armies of attorneys trying to interpret, and to a degree manipulate, government regulations. Another criticism is that the demand for reductions in taxes and regulations serves to improve the profits of capitalist corporations, not the welfare of the people. There are yet other objections, but as you will see in several subsequent discussions of North-South relations, there is suspicion among many in the LDCs that the calls for "reform" are in truth an effort to advance the interests of the EDCs and their corporations and to continue their neocolonial domination of the South.

ECONOMIC COOPERATION AND DEVELOPMENT: THE INSTITUTIONS

Our next step toward understanding economic cooperation and its emphasis on the development of the South is to examine the array of global and regional IGOs, treaties, and other efforts to try to regulate and enhance the world economy in general and conditions in the South in particular. Of the global IGOs, the most important are the UN, the WTO, the IMF, and the World Bank. A number of EDC institutions and regional institutions also play a role.

The United Nations and Economic Cooperation

Among its many functions, the UN serves as a global umbrella organization for numerous agencies and programs that deal with economic issues through the United Nations Economic and Social Council (UNESCO), and other UN divisions and associated agencies. The economic focus of the UN can be roughly divided into two categories: global economic regulation and the economic development of the South.

The UN and Global Economic Regulation

The UN is involved in a number of areas related to global economic cooperation such as the regulation of transnational (or multinational) corporations (TNCs/MNCs). Many observers argue the MNCs need to be regulated by IGOs because globalization has allowed businesses to escape a great deal of domestic regulation. "Are we really going to let the world become a global market without any laws except those of the jungle?" France's president asked at a UN-sponsored economic conference.[3] In response to such concerns, the UN's Center for Transnational Corporations was established as part of the effort to create global standards and regulations to limit the inherently self-serving practices of capitalist corporations.

The UN and Development

The second focus of UN economic activity has been development of the LDCs. One role that the UN has played since 1981 is sponsor of North-South economic summit conferences that have helped increase international awareness among the policy makers of the North about the need for development, have elicited expressions of concern, and have even brought some financial support. For example, the Millennium Summit held at the UN in 2000 brought together 150 national leaders who established eight goals to be reached by 2015 in such areas as reducing extreme poverty, increasing education, and improving health. It is unlikely that most, perhaps any of the goals will be met completely, but setting a standard by which progress can be measured is an important step.

The Millennium Summit also agreed that in 2002 the leaders of North and South should meet again at the UN-sponsored **International Conference on Financing for Development (ICFD)** held in Monterrey, Mexico. Fifty national leaders, including President George Bush, the heads of the top financial IGOs, and other world leaders, attended the conference. The UN secretary-general called on the EDCs to increase annual economic foreign aid from the current .025% of their GNPs to .07%. Meeting that standard in 2006 would have required an increase in aid that year from $104 billion to $240 billion. Some leaders supported that goal, but President Bush and most other EDC officials were more cautious. Still, the pressure to respond to the South's needs had an effect, with Bush, for example, pledging to ask Congress to increase U.S. economic aid by 50% within three years. Congressional appropriations fell short of that mark, but U.S. international assistance did increase by about 30%.

The UN also has numerous development programs. For example, the **UN Development Programme (UNDP)** was established in 1965 to provide technical assistance (such as planning) and development funds to LDCs. It spends about $3 billion annually, has offices in 134 LDCs, and focuses on grassroots economic development, such as promoting entrepreneurship, supporting the Development Fund for Women, and transferring technology and management skills from EDCs to LDCs.

Another important UN organization, the **UN Conference on Trade and Development (UNCTAD)**, was founded in 1964 to promote the positive integration of the LDCs into the world economy. Virtually all countries are members of UNCTAD. UNCTAD primarily gives voice to the South, especially at the summit conferences it holds every four years. The most recent of these, held in São Paulo, Brazil, in 2004, emphasized "ways to make trade work for development," and called on the North to increase its support for achieving the goals set by the Millennium Summit.

A related organization is the **Group of 77 (G-77)**, a name derived from the Joint Declaration of the Seventy-Seven Countries that the LDCs issued at the end of the first UNCTAD conference. Since then the G-77 has expanded to include 130 members. It has recently tried to increase its profile by holding its first summit meeting since it was founded in the mid-1960s. That meeting, in Havana, Cuba, in 2000, as well as the second summit in Doha, Qatar, in 2005, have played an important role in having the leaders of the LDCs gather, establish their development agenda, and press the EDCs to support it, as discussed in chapter 12.

Trade Cooperation and Development: The WTO

While the UN addresses the broad range of global economic issues, there are a number of IGOs that focus on one or another specific area of economic interchange. One of the most prominent of these is the **World Trade Organization (WTO)**. It was founded in 1947, and until 1995 the organization had the same name as its underlying treaty, the **General Agreement on Tariffs and Trade (GATT)**. Whatever its name, the organization's initial membership of 23 countries has expanded to 148 members, and most of the nonmembers are seeking to join. In keeping with the GATT's original mission, the reduction of trade barriers, the WTO has sponsored a series of trade negotiations called "rounds" that have greatly enhanced the free flow of trade and capital. Although the WTO was established and remains a general

Web Link

You can get the details of the goals set by the Millennium Summit at **www.un.org/millenniumgoals/**.

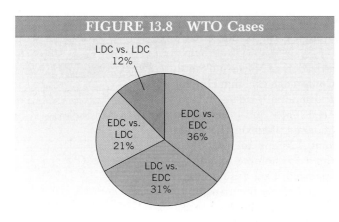

FIGURE 13.8   WTO Cases

This figure analyzes WTO cases: who filed charges (complainants) against whom (respondents, defendants) in the 363 WTO cases filed between 1995 and April 10, 2007. An EDC was either the respondent or the defendant in 88% of the cases. This is not surprising, though, given the high levels of EDC trade and the resulting sensitivity of other EDCs and LDCs to perceived violations of GATT rules.

Note: Each segment shows complainants vs. defendants.
Data source: WTO; author's calculations.

SIMULATION
IGOs and Economic
Cooperation

trade organization, its latest series of negotiations, the Doha Round, heavily focuses on North and South perspectives on the intersection of economic globalization and development. Before turning to that, however, it is important to take a look at the WTO itself.

The Structure and Role of the WTO

The function of the WTO is to deal with the complexities of the GATT and to handle the disputes that will inevitably arise under the GATT. WTO headquarters are in Geneva, Switzerland, and it is currently headed by Director-General Pascal Lamy of France, a former trade commissioner of the European Union (EU), who took office in 2005. Countries can file complaints against one another for alleged violations of the GATT. The WTO uses three-judge panels to hear the complaints, and if a panel finds a violation, the WTO may authorize injured countries to levy sanctions on the offending country. Each country has one vote in the WTO, and sanctions require a two-thirds vote. While any country can withdraw from the WTO by giving six months' notice, that country would suffer significant economic perils because its products would no longer be subject to the reciprocal low tariffs and other advantages WTO members accord one another.

Despite grumbling by critics about countries losing their sovereignty, the WTO judicial process has been busy, with an average of about 30 cases filed annually in recent years (Leitner & Lester, 2006). The pattern since this process began in 1995, as illustrated in Figure 13.8, shows that EDCs are both the most common complainants (57%) and respondents (67%). The United States was involved in 51% of those cases, 88 times as a complainant and 97 times as a respondent. It is reasonable to conclude that the frequency of the U.S. status of respondent is almost surely a function of the size of the U.S. economy, rather than any tendency to target the United States, given the fact that the European Union was involved in 36% of all cases, filing 76 complaints and responding to 56 others.

The significance of the WTO hearing process was evident in the dispute that flared up in 2005 between the United States and the EU, each charging that the other was violating GATT rules by subsidizing their commercial airliner manufacturing industry. As detailed in chapter 12, both took their cases to the WTO, but they also began negotiations with one another to seek the equivalent of an out-of-court settlement. Such resolutions are not uncommon. The most difficult times arise when a WTO ruling runs counter to the desires of a powerful interest group in a respondent country and requires a change in domestic law. When in 2005 the WTO decided in favor of Brazil's complaint that U.S. subsidies to its cotton farmers violated GATT rules, powerful members of Congress from cotton-growing states decried the WTO's intervention in supposedly domestic American matters. But the following year the White House proposed and Congress enacted reductions in U.S. cotton subsidies. Brazil argued the reductions did not go far enough, and the dispute continues, but it is important to see that the United States did respond positively, if perhaps not fully, despite powerful political pressure not to do so. Typical of many cases, an effort was made to limit the impact on the U.S. cotton industry. But simply rejecting the WTO finding would expose the United States to sanctions that would hurt other areas of American commerce, would encourage other countries to reject WTO rulings that favored the United States, and, indeed, would imperil the WTO and the entire structure of economic globalization that Washington has so steadily promoted for over a half-century.

Revising the GATT: The Doha Round

As noted earlier, the GATT has been revised in a series of negotiations. The eighth and most recently completed of these, the **Uruguay Round**, was convened in 1986 in Punta del Este, Uruguay, and was not concluded until 1994. The resulting GATT revisions further reducing economic barriers are complex beyond our telling here, addressing about 10,000 products and myriad businesses and other commercial interchanges. There were, for example, four paragraphs on the importation of "soft-ripened cow's milk cheese" and how to distinguish that kind of cheese from other kinds of cheese.

What is important, though, is that, overall, the countries that signed the Uruguay Round document agreed to reduce their tariffs $744 billion over a 10-year period by cutting them one-third on average. Agricultural tariffs were included in the GATT for the first time, and the agreement also further reduced or barred many NTBs. The signatories also agreed to institute within five years effective protection of intellectual property, such as patents, copyrights, trade secrets, and trademarks. These changes did not end the process of economic globalization, however. Instead, they set the stage for the next round of negotiations to further enhance the free flow of global trade and finance.

This newest round of negotiations began when the WTO decided during one of its periodic ministerial meetings, which had gathered in Doha, Qatar, in 2001, to reach agreements in just three years, less than half the time it took to complete the Uruguay Round. The **Doha Round** failed to meet that deadline, and the story of the stalled negotiations is in considerable part about conflict between North and South priorities on further development and globalization.

North-South disagreements came to a head in 2003 during the second ministerial meeting of the Doha Round negotiations, which were held in Cancún, Mexico. The EDCs wanted to focus on matters that mostly require reform in the South such as lowering LDCs tariffs, permitting competition (the EDCs want barriers against cartels and price fixing), promoting transparency (ensuring corruption does not hinder trade), enforcing intellectual property rights (protecting the patents of EDC companies), limiting government procurement (ensuring foreign companies can compete), and curtailing investment restrictions (such as limits of foreign ownership of business and real estate). By contrast, LDCs wanted to focus on reducing EDC barriers to agricultural imports. A particular target is the approximately $300 billion in annual subsidies that the EDCs give to their farmers and agribusinesses. These subsidies allow EDC agricultural products to be sold at artificially low prices, thereby often pricing LDC exports of those products out of the global market (Cline, 2004). The LDCs have strengthened their leverage by presenting a generally united front in the negotiations, with leading LDCs forming a coalition informally headed by Brazil, China, India, and South Africa.

Unable to reach a compromise, the talks in Cancún collapsed. LDC delegates blamed the EDCs. "They were not generous enough; there was just not enough on the table for developing countries," argued the delegate from Jamaica.[4] Reflecting the EDC view, the EU commissioner of agriculture rejoined, "If I look at the recent extreme proposal co-sponsored by Brazil, China, India and others [in Cancún], I cannot help

International trade negotiations are more intense than ever since 2003. That year the less developed countries formed a loose alliance, called the Group of 20 (G-20), including Brazil, China, India, and South Africa, to strengthen their negotiating position vis-à-vis the North. In this photo, World Trade Organization Director-General Pascal Lamy, center, consults with Brazil's Foreign Minister Celso Amorim, left, and India's Commerce Minister Kamal Nath during a G-20 meeting in Rio de Janeiro, Brazil.

[having] the impression that they are circling in a different orbit. If they want to do business, they should come back to Mother Earth. If they choose to continue their space odyssey they will not get the stars, they will not get the moon, they will end up with empty hands."[5]

Despite the impasse, there was also wide recognition that failure to reach an agreement might mean more than just no new progress; it might lead to an unraveling of more than 50 years of progress toward ever freer international economic exchange. As UN Secretary-General Ban Ki-moon put it, "Should this round of trade talks fail, serious damage will be done . . . to the multilateral trading system and to multilateralism itself."[6] Therefore negotiations have continued, but yet another ministerial meeting (Hong Kong, 2005) and a number of other somewhat lower-level negotiations yielded only scant results. Somewhat renewed hope arose in 2007 after a White House meeting between President Bush and the EU's top officials, the president of the Council, German Chancellor Angela Merkel, and the president of the Commission, José Manuel Barroso. The three agreed to try to reenergize negotiations. "We told our trade ministers: Work hard, work often, work constructively," Bush said.[7] Whether hard work will be enough remains to be seen. The problem, according to WTO Director-General Pascal Lamy, is that even though all sides want the Doha Round to succeed, they also "are somewhat paralyzed by fear that any move in the negotiation by any one of them will be pocketed by the others and will not lead to reciprocal moves."[8]

Monetary Cooperation in Support of Development: The IMF

As trade and the level of other international financial transactions have increased, the need to cooperate internationally to facilitate and stabilize the flow of dollars, euros, yen, pounds, and other currencies has become vital. To meet this need, a number of organizations, of which the **International Monetary Fund (IMF)** is the most important, have been established. As with many other aspects of international economic cooperation, the focus of the IMF has shifted substantially toward concerns with LDC development.

The genesis of the IMF in the early 1940s was rooted in the importance the United States placed on monetary stability and the easy convertibility from one currency to another, as discussed in chapter 12. To this end, Washington organized a conference of World War II Allies in 1944 at Bretton Woods, New Hampshire. There the delegates established the IMF. Thus, like the WTO, it was created by the West, with the United States in the lead, as part of the liberalization of international economic interchange. When the IMF began operations 1947, it had 44 member-countries. That number stood at 185 in 2007. Its headquarters are in Washington, D.C, and its managing director since 2004 is Rodrigo de Rato y Figaredo, formerly Spain's economic minister. At first the IMF followed a system under which currencies were exchanged against the U.S. dollar on a "fixed-rate" tied to the price of gold. This worked for a time, but by the early 1970s a new system was put in place that relied on "free-floating" currency relations. Under this system, supply and demand is the principal determinant of the exchange rate of currencies.

To fund its operations, the IMF utililizes hard currency reserves ($327 billion in 2007) placed at its disposal by EDCs and from interest on loans it has made to countries that draw on those reserves. On rare occasions, the IMF also sells part of its gold reserve, currently at over 3,200 tons and worth over $68 billion, to support its operations. The agency can also borrow up to about $25 billion to meet emergency needs. Whatever their source, the value of IMF resources are expressed in terms of **special drawing rights (SDRs)**, a virtual currency whose value is based on an average, or market basket, value of the EU euro, Japanese yen, British pound, and U.S. dollar. In mid-2007, the exchange rate was 1 SDR = $1.53.

The Role of the IMF

The IMF's primary function is to help maintain exchange-rate stability by making short-term loans to countries with international balance-of-payments problems because of trade deficits, heavy loan payments, or other factors. In such times, a country can use the IMF's loan to help meet debt payments, to buy back its own currency (thus maintaining exchange-rate stability by balancing supply and demand), or take other financial steps.

Over time, the focus of the IMF has turned almost entirely to LDCs. Reflecting their increased number and their frequent monetary difficulties, the total loans that the IMF has outstanding at any one time have grown significantly. As recently as 1980, IMF loans were under $15 billion. The challenges of dealing with the crunch brought on by the LDCs' loan repayment crisis and by financial crises in Mexico (1995), Asia (late 1990s), and Argentina (2001–2002) increased IMF's outstanding loans to a peak of $103 billion in 2003. After that through 2006, as detailed in Figure 13.9, an easing of international monetary pressures allowed IMF lending to drop sharply. Whether this change is a trend or an anomaly is unclear. To that end, IMF in 2006 had over $35 billion in loans outstanding to 74 countries, all of them LDCs. As part of its program, the IMF has the Poverty Reduction and Growth Facility (PRGF) program that provides loans at "concessional" (very low) interest rates to low-income countries, and another program to provide loans at concessional rates to very poor countries under the Heavily Indebted Poor Countries (HIPC) Initiative. Of the overall 78 loans in mid-2007, 56 worth $9 billion were concessionals.

In addition to responding to monetary difficulties, the IMF tries to head them off by encouraging member-countries to follow sound fiscal policies and providing them technical support to achieve that goal. Under its "surveillance program," the

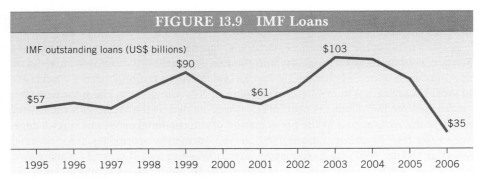

FIGURE 13.9   IMF Loans

IMF outstanding loans (US$ billions)

$57 $90 $61 $103 $35

1995 1996 1997 1998 1999 2000 2001 2002 2003 2004 2005 2006

The IMF now extends all its loans to LDCs in an effort to increase their financial stability and advance their development. As evident, the amount of loans that the IMF has outstanding in any given year varies significantly and is based on the problems that it is addressing. Whether the recent easing of needs for IMF loans is a trend or a short-term anomaly remains to be seen.

Note: Source expresses loans in SDRs; conversion to U.S. dollars by author using average SDR rate for year.
Data source: IMF.

IMF regularly conducts detailed analyses of each country's economic situation and discusses the findings of the appraisal with the country's financial officials. The IMF also offers countries technical assistance in such areas as developing monetary and exchange rate policy, regulating banks and other financial institutions, and gathering and interpreting statistics.

Criticisms of the IMF

Although the IMF has played a valuable role and has many supporters, it is often criticized. The controversies regarding the IMF may be divided into two categories: voting and conditionality.

Voting   One criticism centers on the formula that determines voting on the IMF board of directors. Voting is based on how much each member-country contributes to the IMF's resources. On this basis, the United States has over 17% of the votes, 242 times the voting strength of Palau's 0.07%. By another calculation, the United States and just seven other large EDCs control a majority of the IMF vote under the wealth-weighted system. The weight of the EDC vote is a key reason why the director-general of the IMF has always been a Western European. This record and the voting apportionment leads critics of the IMF to charge that it is undemocratically controlled by the North and is being used as a tool to dominate the LDCs.

One of the criticisms of the International Monetary Fund and the World Bank is that their voting formulas allow a few wealthy countries to dominate decisions. This photograph shows members of an NGO, Global Call to Action Against Poverty, protesting what they charge is an unfair lack of voice by poorer countries in the operations of the leading economic IGOs.

Conditionality   Critics also accuse the IMF of imposing unfair and unwise conditions on countries that borrow from it. Most IMF loans are subject to **conditionality**. This refers to requirements that the borrowing country take steps to remedy the practices and conditions that, according to the IMF, either caused the recipient's financial problems or will retard its recovery. The IMF also often requires borrowing governments to make significant changes in domestic policy such as reducing their budget deficits by cutting domestic programs and/or raising taxes. While such requirements may seem reasonable, critics take exception. One objection is that IMF conditions *violate sovereignty* by interfering in the recipients' policy-making processes. When the IMF and Argentina were negotiating the provisions of an IMF loan to that country in 2002 amid its financial crisis, many Argentine political leaders denounced the IMF's demand that they slash their budget deficit and make other changes in their domestic policy. Reflecting a common view, one Argentine official growled, "The only thing lacking is for us to pull down the Argentine flag and replace it with the IMF's."[9]

A second and closely related charge is that as part of its conditions, the IMF generally *promotes the capitalist model* by pressing LDCs to move toward easing restrictions on their economies and adopting free international economic exchange. It advocates such steps as privatizing state-run enterprises, reducing barriers to trade and investment, and devaluing currencies to increase exports and decrease imports. According to one of the IMF's detractors, such policies as the "liberalization and deregulation of trade and finance" only serve to "bring about crises, widen inequalities within and across countries, and increase global poverty."[10]

Third, some critics have contended that given the North's control of IMF policy, conditionality *promotes a neocolonial relationship*. Argentina's president decried this status as the "domination" of the LDCs by the EDCs.[11]

Fourth, critics charge that *IMF conditions often harm economies in LDCs* by requiring fiscal austerity and other stringent conditions that are counterproductive. During the IMF-Argentina negotiations, economist Jeffrey Sachs compared the IMF's approach to "the 18th-century medical practice in which doctors 'treated' feverish patients by drawing blood from them, weakening the patients further and frequently hastening their deaths."[12] A fifth and related charge is that *IMF conditions often destabilize governments* by forcing them to institute policies that cause a domestic backlash. Reflecting on riots that occurred in Argentina, one observer commented, "The IMF has the wrong idea if they think . . . any president can immediately make the kinds of reforms they are demanding and still be left standing in the morning."[13] A sixth line of criticism contends that *the IMF conditions undermine social welfare* by pushing countries to cut their budget, thereby reducing social services, laying off government workers, and taking other steps that harm the quality of life of their citizens. Taking that view, Argentina's president portrayed the IMF's conditions as "delaying education and the good health of Argentina's children."[14]

Defense of the IMF

Those who defend the IMF reject these charges. With respect to the *voting formula*, defenders argue that since it is the EDCs that provide the funds, they should have a proportionate share of the say in how they are invested. As for *conditionality*, the IMF acknowledges that its demands often cause hardship. But it argues that the required reforms are necessary to correct the problems that led the borrower-country into financial difficulty in the first place in order to avoid a continuing cycle of crisis and loans. Taking this view during Argentina's economic meltdown, the head of the IMF, argued that, "without pain, [Argentina] won't get out of this crisis, and the crisis—at its root—is homemade."[15]

It is also the case that the IMF has responded to the criticism of its conditionality standards and eased them during Argentina's monetary crisis and after formal reviews that took place in 2002 and 2005. As is often true of compromises, those in Argentina left many on both sides dissatisfied. Some talked of an IMF "cave in," while others protested that "if the national government . . . with the IMF . . . [causes] utility rate increases, there will be more hunger and there will be more unemployment."[16]

To the charge of promoting *capitalism and economic internationalism*, those who defend the IMF argue that it is doing just what it should do to promote global prosperity. From this perspective, "Free markets and free trade and free choices transfer power to individuals at the expense of political institutions," and, "People who have acquired a taste of economic liberty and expanded horizons will not consent to be shut in again by walls or fences. They will work to create a better existence for themselves. The aim of our politics should be to give them that freedom."[17] Those who agree with the IMF approach also point to statistics such as those found in Figure 13.10 to support their position. Not everyone would agree with the "pro-capitalist" conclusions that Figure 13.10 would seem to suggest. For example, closer inspection of the data raises many questions. China, for one, is making rapid economic progress, yet its economic freedom score puts it in the next to lowest 20% of all countries. There are some countries, including El Salvador, that are in the top 20% but remain poor. France has a lower score than Botswana and Italy's ranking is below that of Namibia, yet both the European countries are much better off economically than either of the two southern African states. The point is to do both macro and micro analysis, and the Web link in the margin directs you to the source to begin that.

Web Link

The Heritage Foundation and the *Wall Street Journal* compile an annual Index of Economic Freedom, rating countries on how closely they adhere to capitalism. The index is available at **www.heritage.org/research/features/index/.**

FIGURE 13.10   Capitalism and Prosperity

There is considerable pressure on countries from the IMF, WTO, and elsewhere to institute economic reforms that reduce the presence of government in both the domestic and foreign economic systems. The argument is that systems adhering to capitalism (free enterprise) and open international economic exchange according to the economic internationalist model are the most likely to achieve prosperity. One analysis annually ranks countries according to 10 criteria of their degree of "economic freedom." The resulting data, some of which is shown here, indicates a generally positive relationship between how free a country's economy is domestically and internationally and having a higher per capita GDP, a lower unemployment rate, and a lower annual inflation rate. As the text notes, however, not everyone agrees with such analyses.

Note: The 10 criteria were business, trade, fiscal, monetary, investment, financial, and labor freedom; freedom from government and from corruption; and property rights.
Data source: Heritage Foundation and *Wall Street Journal, Index of Economic Freedom 2007.*

Development Cooperation: The World Bank Group

A third type of multilateral economic cooperation involves granting economic development loans and aid to LDCs. The most significant development agency today is the **World Bank Group**, commonly referred to as just the World Bank. The designator "group" stems from the fact that the World Bank consists of several distinct agencies.

World Bank Operations

Like the IMF, the World Bank was established in the World War II era to promote the postwar economic prosperity of the United States and its allies. However, like the IMF, the World Bank's priorities have shifted to assisting the development of the South.

Almost every country is a member of each agency of the World Bank Group. One agency, the *International Bank for Reconstruction and Development* (IBRD, established 1946) has lending policies that resemble those of a commercial bank in that the IBRD analyzes the financial worth of projects it funds and charges some interest. In 2006, the IBRD made new loans totaling $14 billion to fund 87 projects in 33 countries and had total outstanding loans of $103 billion. By 2006, cumulatively during its history the bank had loaned $367 billion to 130 countries; it additionally had $35 billion in reserves. Its funding is based on $110 billion that member-countries have given or pledged to it, from the interest it earns on its loans, and from the returns it gets from investment activities. The country with the greatest amount of loans was China ($16 billion), followed by Brazil, Mexico, India, and Turkey (all $10 billion or more).

A second agency, the *International Development Association* (IDA, created 1960) focuses on making loans at no interest to the very poorest countries to help them provide better basic human services (such as education, health care, safe water, and sanitation), to improve economic productivity, and to create employment. All of the IDA's loans are on a concessional basis, with no interest, no repayments for 10 years, then a 15- to 30-year repayment schedule. During 2006, the IDA extended $9.5 billion in loans to fund 167 projects in 61 countries, most of them in sub-Saharan Africa. As the numbers indicate, most loans are for small amounts. During its history, IDA credits and grants have totaled $161 billion, about half of which has gone to Africa. Some of the IDA's funding comes from the income of the IRBD, but most comes from member-country contributions. Of these, the United States has been the largest donor, giving $29 billion, about 23% of the funds the association has received from national governments.

The third agency, the *International Finance Corporation* (IFC, founded 1956) makes loans to companies in LDCs and also guarantees private investment for projects supporting development. This contrasts with the IBRD and the IDA, which mostly make loans to governments for public projects. The IFC's loans for 2006 came to $6.7 billion to 284 private enterprises in 66 countries. IFC also guaranteed $2.8 billion in private investment in various LDCs. Because of the unstable business climates in many countries, many of the IFC's loans are risky. Nevertheless, it is now largely self-sustaining and had a net income of $1.2 billion in 2006 based on the interest from its loans and earnings from other investments. The fourth of the World Bank Group agencies, the *Multilateral Investment Guarantee Agency* (MIGA, created 1988) promotes the flow of private development capital to LDCs by providing guarantees to investors for about 20% of any losses they might suffer due to noncommercial risks (such as political instability). In 2004, MIGA issued $1.3 billion in 41 guarantees.

Controversy about the World Bank Group

Like the IMF, the World Bank has done a great deal of good, but it has also come under criticism. Many object to the fact that, like the IMF, the World Bank is dominated by the EDCs. It also uses a wealth-based voting formula. This gives the United States 16% of the votes and, along with Western Europe, majority control of the bank's board of directors. One result is that the president of the World Bank is and always has been an American. The informal rule that an American will head the bank was reconfirmed in 2007 when the tenth president, former U.S. Deputy Secretary of Defense Paul Wolfowitz, was forced to resign after only two years in office, amid a scandal that involved his ongoing romantic relationship with a bank staff member. He had arranged to have her placed temporarily at the U.S. State Department to avoid a conflict of interest, but had also agreed to not only have the bank continue to pay her salary but also to have it increased from $130,000 annually to $190,000. Yet despite this clouded end, President Bush soon nominated yet another member of his administration, former U.S. Trade Representative Robert Zoellick, to be the bank's eleventh president and, despite some grumbling globally, he appeared virtually assured of the support of the bank's board of directors.

Beyond its immediate cause, the Wolfowitz imbroglio also illustrated some of the other issues with the bank. One, the view expressed by the *Financial Times* of Great Britain when Wolfowitz first became president, is that the bank is too much of "an instrument of U.S. power and U.S. priorities."[18] Indeed, there were some suspicions that Europeans and others seized upon Wolfowitz's personal indiscretion as an opening to unseat him in part because of his close association with the Iraq War and in part to try to embarrass the Bush administration for its alleged unilateral highhandedness. For one, the *Wall Street Journal* editorialized that Wolfowitz was being "Euro-railroaded."[19] Wolfowitz was also vulnerable because his policies angered many of the staff at the bank. They especially opposed his stress on corruption on the grounds that it tended to stereotype LDCs and also, by laying part of the blame for the lack of development on the LDCs themselves, it might strengthen the forces that opposed greater aid to the South. Reflecting Wolfowitz's rocky relationship with the bank staff, Zoellick was quick to say assuringly, "The most important thing, to start off, is to try to reach out to the staff."[20]

For now, then, the leadership of the World Bank will remain in the hands of the North. From the South's perspective, the North's ongoing domination of the World Bank limits its ability to understand the views and problems of the LDCs. A harsher interpretation in line with economic structuralism is that the EDCs use the World Bank and other IGOs to maintain neoimperialist control of the South. For example, Malaysian economist and activist Martin

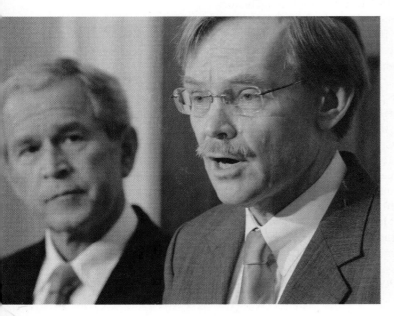

The domination of the World Bank by the North in general and the United States in particular was demonstrated anew when its president, former U.S. Deputy Secretary of Defense Paul Wolfowitz, was forced to resign in 2007 amid scandal. To replace him, U.S. President George Bush, left, nominated and the bank's board accepted former U.S. Deputy Secretary of State Robert Zoellick, right. There were no other candidates, although any country could have nominated one.

Kohr charges, "Economically speaking, we are more dependent on the ex-colonial powers than we ever were. The World Bank and the IMF are playing the role that our ex-colonial masters used to play."[21]

Critics also grumble that the World Bank provides too little funding. Figures such as the approximately $600 billion the World Bank has distributed in its history and the $30 billion it loaned LDCs in 2004 sound less impressive in light of the fact that in real dollars, World Bank funding is no greater than it was in 1995 despite the North's rhetoric about being committed to increasing development funds for the South. A third criticism charges that the World Bank is too conservative in the distribution of its loans. Almost a third of World Bank loans in 2006 went to just five countries (Brazil, China, India, Mexico, and Turkey), none of which was in dire economic straits. In fact there is a growing question of whether the bank should be loaning money to countries like China that can get loans on the world's commercial credit markets, have large foreign reserves (China: $1 trillion), or that spend huge sums on their nuclear weapons and other military programs (China and India). Regarding this concern, conservative critics suggest that the bank is no longer needed at all, while liberal critics urge the bank to devote most or all of its resources to giving grants, not loans, to the poorest countries. Finally, liberal critics also charge that the World Bank's conservatism causes it, like the IMF, to use its financial power to impose the capitalist economic model on recipient countries.

Web Link

For a critique of the IMF and World Bank, go to the Bretton Woods Project site at **www.brettonwoodsproject.org/.** The institutions defend themselves at **www.worldbank.org** and **www.imf.org.**

Economic Cooperation and Development: EDC Institutions

As globalization progressed in the latter half of the 20th century, the EDCs created several organizations to help ensure their own post–World War II economic health. While these IGOs still do that to some degree, they, like the IMF and other economic IGOs, have expanded their focus to include development.

Organization for Economic Cooperation and Development

Of the two major EDC organizations, the first to be created was the **Organization for Economic Cooperation and Development (OECD)**. It was established in 1961 by the United States, Canada, 15 Western European countries, and Turkey. It has subsequently admitted several LDCs that have close economic ties to an EDC, such as Mexico, or that are relatively prosperous, such as South Korea. Still, the bulk of the OECD's 30 member-states are EDCs, making the organization something of a "rich man's club." The OECD serves as a forum for member-countries to discuss economic issues; it generates copious statistics and numerous studies and offers economic advice and technical assistance. It has also become increasingly involved with the LDCs and such issues as globalization and sustainable development, and it has established links with some 70 LDCs, ranging from Brazil, China, and Russia to the low-income, or least developed countries (LLDCs), in sub-Saharan Africa and elsewhere.

The Group of Eight (G-8)

If the OECD is a reasonably exclusive club of prosperous member-countries, the **Group of Eight (G-8)** is equivalent to the executive board. The G-8 does not have a formal connection to the OECD, but it does represent the pinnacle of economic power, with its members combining to generate 62% of the world's GDP. The G-8 began in 1975 as the Group of Seven (G-7) to coordinate economic policy among the seven most economically powerful noncommunist countries (Canada, France, Germany, Great Britain, Italy, Japan, and the United States). In 1997 the G-7 became the G-8 when it added Russia in recognition of its economic potential and geostrategic importance. The president of the Commission of the EU also regularly attends meetings.

The apex of G-8 activity comes at its annual summit meeting. These have increasingly concentrated on development and other matters related to LDCs. One indication of this focus on LDCs is that a number of them have been invited as participating nonmembers to each G-8 summit since 2000. The leaders of Brazil, China, India, Mexico, and South Africa now regularly attend. Additionally, the 2007 summit in Heiligendamm, Germany, included UN Secretary-General Ban Ki-moon, the head of the African Union, and leaders of Algeria, Ethiopia, Nigeria, Senegal, and South Africa. The agenda of individual meetings is somewhat driven by events, with global warming and global health threats the central items of the 2007 meeting. With respect to climate change, most G-8 leaders had hoped to persuade President Bush to support the Kyoto agreements, but he countered with a proposal calling for countries that produce the most emissions leading to global warming to set targets to reduce them. Critics denounced the proposal as meaningless, but it was the first public commitment by the United States to reduce emissions, and its timing did reflect Bush's desire to avoid appearing completely obstructionist by arriving at the summit without any proposal. On the second main agenda item, the G-8 leaders pledged their countries would spend $60 billion to fight AIDS, tuberculosis, and other diseases in Africa. However, some critics condemned the announcement as misleading in that it did not indicate when the money would be given and also in that the amount mostly represented earlier commitments, with at most $3 billion in new money pledged. For one, veteran AIDS activist Bono, of the group U2, described the seemingly large pledge as "bureau-babble" based on the assumption that "rock stars might not be able to add

The Group of Eight (G-8) consists of the seven leading economic powers plus Russia. During its annual summit, the G-8 leaders set goals, and those have increasingly included assistance for the world's poorest countries. This picture shows the G-8 leaders plus the president of the European Union Commission seated under their respective flags during the 2007 summit in Heiligendamm, Germany. From left to right are Prime Minister Shinzo Abe (Japan), Prime Minister Stephen Harper (Canada), President Nicolas Sarkozy (France), President Vladimir Putin (Russia), Chancellor Angela Merkel (Germany), President George Bush (United States), Prime Minister Tony Blair (United Kingdom), Prime Minister Romano Prodi (Italy) and President of the EU Commission José Manuel Barroso.

and subtract or spell or read," and he promised to move on to the "obscure village in Japan" (Toyako), where the 2008 G-8 summit will convene.[22]

Opinions on the importance of the G-8 vary widely. One factor is that the high-profile summits become an important part of the public diplomacy regarding development. Prior to the 2005 meeting, for example, music promoter Bob Geldof organized Live 8 popular music concerts in ten cities. They were broadcast around the world and starred such groups and performers as U2, Coldplay, Sting, Elton John, the Who, Pink Floyd, and Green Day. Adding to the public pressure, HBO aired a movie, *The Girl in the Café,* about a young woman who travels to the G-8 summit with a British financial expert and confronts the gathered leaders, charging them with not doing enough to meet the UN Millennium Development Goals to alleviate poverty and its related social ills. Like most major meetings of the leading economic institutions, the summit also drew thousands of antiglobalization protesters, although there were far fewer than previous summits held in less tightly controlled host countries.

As for the importance of the G-8 and its resolutions, one analyst depicts it as an emergent "shadow world government."[23] A less expansive view, according to another scholar, is that G-8 members "do comply modestly with the decisions and consensus generated [at their summit meetings]."[24] There are also opinion differences over whether the G-8 is a positive or negative force. Representing the range of opinions, some observers applauded the decisions of the 2005 summit. U2 lead singer Bono, a cofounder of DATA (Debt AIDS Trade Africa), exulted, "We've pulled this off. The world spoke, and the politicians listened." More cautiously, Bob Geldof advised, "It is only time that will decide whether this summit is historic or not. The check has been written and signed, now we need to cash it."[25] Yet other views were neutral or negative. Sue Mbaya, director of the Southern Africa Regional Poverty Network, was even more hesitant. "As optimistic as we would like to be," she said, "we should be wary based on [the G-8] track record, which has often been far short compared to the pledges." Mbaya expressed suspicion of the G-8's sincerity in light of the fact that its pledge of added aid had been made on the condition that African countries reduce corruption and institute other reforms. She called demand for reform "the latest trick on the conditionalities front," and warned that it could be used "as a loophole" by the G-8 to renege on its pledge.[26]

Web Link

The University of Toronto includes the G8 Information Centre at **www.g7.utoronto.ca/.**

REGIONAL AND BILATERAL ECONOMIC COOPERATION AND DEVELOPMENT

In addition to activity promoting economic cooperation and development from a global perspective, there are important efforts under way at the regional and bilateral level to reduce the barriers to economic interchange. This activity does not exclusively involve LDCs. Still, similar to global cooperation, regional and bilateral ties have become extensively intermeshed with and important to the development of the South.

Regionally, one area of cooperation is finance through nine regional development banks. In terms of loan commitments, the largest of these (and their loans in 2006) were the Asian Development Bank ($7.4 billion), the Inter-American Development Bank ($6 billion), the African Development Bank ($1.8 billion), and the European Bank for Reconstruction and Development ($5.6 billion), which focuses on projects in the LDCs in Eastern Europe, and in Russia and the former Soviet republics. There are other regional banks, but they are not as well funded, as exemplified by the Caribbean

Development Bank which, despite its region's pressing needs, only had the assets to make $162 million in loans in 2006. In addition to the development banks, numerous IGOs are dedicated to promoting economic cooperation and development among groups of countries based on their geographical region (such as the 12-member Black Sea Economic Cooperation Zone), culture, or some other link (for example, the 21-member Arab Monetary Fund).

An even more common type of international effort involves one or another Free Trade Agreement (FTA). These are treaties among two or more countries to reduce or eliminate tariffs and other trade barriers and to otherwise promote freer economic exchange. Before discussing FTAs in depth, it is important to note that different IGOs, governments, and studies designate them with different names and accompanying acronyms. Here we will use **regional trade agreement (RTA)** to designate an FTA among three or more countries within a region, and **bilateral trade agreement (BTA)**, an FTA between two countries or between an RTA and any other non-member-country. There is no precise count of FTAs, but the WTO estimates that there are about 30 RTAs and perhaps another 270 BTAs. We will begin with and emphasize multilateral regional economic cooperation, but we will also take up bilateral activity at the end of the section.

RTAs range from the tiny Melanesian Spearhead Group (Fiji, Papua New Guinea, Solomon Islands, and Vanuatu) to the huge European Union. Indeed, there are very few countries that are not members of an RTA, and numerous countries are in two or more. Some are little more than shell organizations that keep their goals barely alive, yet each represents the conviction of its members that, compared to standing alone, they can achieve greater economic prosperity by working together through economic cooperation or even economic integration. RTAs are particularly important to the development plans of the South. One indication is that about 75% of them have memberships that are exclusively made up of or include LDCs, and several others mix EDCs and LDCs as members. This pattern is evident in our following discussion of the major RTAs.

The Western Hemisphere

Proposals for regional economic cooperation date back to a U.S. effort in 1889 to create a hemispherical customs union that would reduce trade barriers among the hemisphere's countries and adopt common external tariff and nontariff barriers. The notion of RTAs in the Western Hemisphere then lay dormant for almost a century until globalization began to convert the idea into reality.

The North American Free Trade Agreement

The largest RTA in the Western Hemisphere, measured in trade volume, is the **North American Free Trade Agreement (NAFTA)** among Canada, Mexico, and the United States. The 2,000-page agreement, which took effect in 1994, established schedules for reducing tariff and nontariff barriers to trade by 2004 in all but a few hundred of some 20,000 product categories and by 2009 for all products. NAFTA also reduced or eliminated many restrictions on foreign investments and other financial transactions and facilitated transportation by allowing trucking largely unimpeded access across borders. There is a standing commission with representatives from all three countries to deal with disputes that arise under the NAFTA agreement.

NAFTA has had an important impact on the three trading partners. For example, intra-NAFTA trade is a key component of the exports of all three partners, as can be

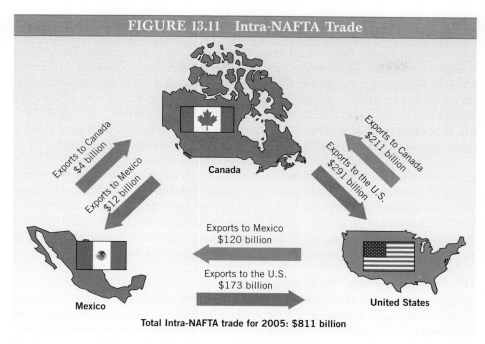

FIGURE 13.11   Intra-NAFTA Trade

Exports to Canada
$4 billion

Exports to Mexico
$12 billion

Canada

Exports to Canada
$211 billion

Exports to the U.S.
$291 billion

Exports to Mexico
$120 billion

Exports to the U.S.
$173 billion

Mexico

United States

Total Intra-NAFTA trade for 2005: $811 billion

The North American Free Trade Agreement has accounted for a rapid rise in trade among Canada, Mexico, and the United States since the treaty went into effect in 1994. There are now plans for a Western Hemisphere free trade zone, the Free Trade Area of the Americas.

Data source: OECD.

seen in the data on merchandise trade in Figure 13.11. Mexico and Canada are especially dependent on intra-NAFTA trade, with each sending between 80% and 90% of their exports to the United States and to one another. The United States is least dependent, albeit still heavily so, with NAFTA trade accounting for 26% of U.S. exports.

A vigorous debate continues in each of the three countries about the pros and cons of NAFTA. Canada is the least affected because it has relatively little interchange with Mexico and because preexisting U.S.-Canada trade was already quite high. For Americans, there certainly have been losses. Many American businesses have relocated their facilities to Mexico, establishing *maquiladoras,* manufacturing plants just south of the border. These produce goods for export to the United States. According to a U.S. Department of Labor study, U.S. job losses from this shift of production and from Mexican imports totaled 507,000 between late 1993 and late 2002. Yet economists point out that those jobs would have probably gone to other LDCs if they had not been shifted to Mexico. Furthermore, American consumers benefited from lower prices for goods imported from Mexico. Such gains often are less noticed, however, than are losses. As one economist explains, "The gains are so thinly spread across the country that people don't thank NAFTA when they buy a mango or inexpensive auto parts."[27]

NAFTA has had the greatest effect on Mexico, in large part because both the size and strength of its economy are so much less than those of the United States and Canada. Some aspects have been clearly positive. For example, NAFTA has diversified Mexico's economic base by increasing the percentage of its exports that are manufactured goods. The country's maquiladora program, dating back long before NAFTA, was set up to promote industrialization by giving special tax and other advantages to

ANALYZE THE ISSUE
Is NAFTA a Success
or Failure?

industries in a zone near the U.S. border. But after NAFTA went into effect, the maquiladora zone boomed, doubling its production and tripling its workers by 2000. Then fortunes turned down in the zone, in part because of competition from China for the U.S. market. More recent data, however, shows a new upswing. Moreover, Mexico's GDP growth rate nearly tripled in the decade after NAFTA, compared to the decade before it. And the country's 2005 per capita GNP of $7,310 was 25% higher than that of Chile, the next wealthiest country in Central and South America. Reflecting on such data, Mexican President Vincente Fox contended, "NAFTA gave us a big push. It gave us jobs. It gave us knowledge, experience, technological transfer."[28]

It is also true that for Mexicans, as well as for Americans and Canadians, NAFTA has had some very negative effects on some, such as displaced workers. Some segments of Mexico's economy have been particularly hard hit. For example, corn farmers in central and southern Mexico have suffered greatly from the incoming tidal wave of subsidized U.S. corn, which increased about 1,400% between 1993 and 2004. Many Mexicans also worry about the loss of their culture amid the influx of Pizza Huts, KFC outlets, and other elements of American culture.

The Free Trade Area of the Americas

At the same time that NAFTA went into effect in 1994, efforts were under way to create a much broader hemispheric RTA tentatively named the **Free Trade Area of the Americas (FTAA)** that would include all or most of the countries in North, Central, and South America, and in the Caribbean. To that end, the heads of every country in the Western Hemisphere except Cuba, which was barred at U.S. insistence, met in 1994 at the Summit of the Americas in Miami, Florida, and agreed to create a free trade zone in the hemisphere by 2005. Soon, the optimistic predictions of the summit meeting gave way to difficult and slow negotiations. Subsequent summits in Santiago, Chile (1999), Quebec City, Canada (2001), Monterrey, Mexico (2004) and Mardel Plata, Argentina (2005) failed to reach any breakthroughs, and 2005, the original target date for an FTAA agreement, passed into history without one.

The disagreements that have ensnared the FTAA negotiations are very similar to the North-South issues that have beset the WTO's Doha Round, as discussed earlier. As much as the hemisphere's LDCs are anxious to improve their access to U.S. markets, they are equally nervous about dropping their protections and being drowned in a tidal wave of American imports and services, and about having American investors snap up local businesses and other property. The increasingly anti-American tone of Venezuela's Hugo Chávez and funds flowing into the country's treasury from surging oil prices have increased the opposition to the FTAA even more. In fact, Chávez is trying to expand an existing limited trade agreement among his country, Cuba, Bolivia, and Nicaragua into a much larger Bolivarian Alternative of the Americas encompassing much of Latin America and the Caribbean. "The idea here is to promote cooperation between countries of the South—seeking out complementary exchanges in terms of trade and technological transfer—rather than, as has traditionally been the case, further extending North-South dependencies,'" a Venezuelan official explained.[29]

There is also resistance to the FTAA in the United States, especially among some interest groups. Unions fear that American jobs will wind up in the hands of underpaid Central and South Americans; agricultural organizations are determined to protect their subsidies. Other groups fear that an FTAA will eventually increase labor migration, as the EU has done among its member-countries, leading to a greater inflow of Latin Americans into the United States than already exists. For now, then, the fate of the FTAA remains cloudy at best.

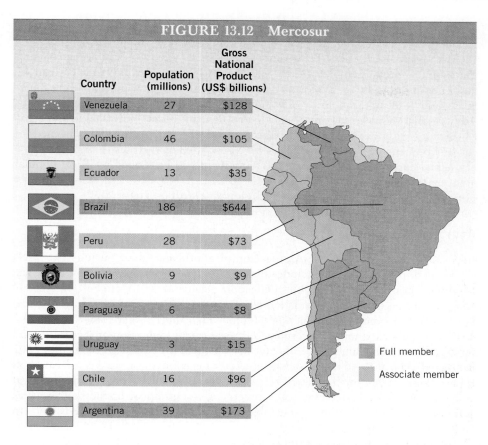

FIGURE 13.12   Mercosur

Country	Population (millions)	Gross National Product (US$ billions)
Venezuela	27	$128
Colombia	46	$105
Ecuador	13	$35
Brazil	186	$644
Peru	28	$73
Bolivia	9	$9
Paraguay	6	$8
Uruguay	3	$15
Chile	16	$96
Argentina	39	$173

Full member

Associate member

Mercosur is an important RTA. A key issue for the Western Hemisphere is whether it, NAFTA, and other RTAs will merge into a single FTAA or remain divided, overlapping, and to a degree competitive.

Data source: World Bank.

Mercosur

Whatever the future of the FTAA, a number of countries have undertaken or continued efforts to establish or expand their own trade treaties. The **Southern Common Market (Mercosur)** is of particular note. Mercosur was established in 1995 by Argentina, Brazil, Paraguay, and Uruguay. Venezuela has joined since then as a full member, and Bolivia, Chile, Colombia, Ecuador, and Peru have become associate members. Including just its five full and five associate members, Mercosur is a market of 372 million people with a combined GDP of over $1.2 trillion, as shown in Figure 13.12.

A number of issues, including Argentina's economic crisis and some countries' concerns about the powerful role that Brazil plays in Mercosur, have slowed the negotiations to expand and strengthen it, but other factors exist that are pushing for its enlargement and invigoration. One is the desire to provide a counterweight to the United States in the hemisphere. "We have to unite," Brazil's President Lula da Silva told an audience. "We need to create a South American nation. The more policies we have in common, the better we will be able to succeed in big negotiations, above all in trying to break down WTO's protectionist barriers and prevent the FTAA becoming an instrument that suffocates our chances of growth."[30]

Taking a step in that direction, the South American leaders agreed at summits in 2004 and again in 2007 to seek to merge Mercosur and the Andean Community (Bolivia, Colombia, Ecuador, Peru, Venezuela) into a Union of South American Nations that would eventually emulate the EU with its own currency, a continental parliament, and a common passport. Mercosur itself also continues to develop, and all the countries of the Andean Community of Nations are now either full or associate members. Additionally, Mercosur may reach north, and there are at least informal membership discussions with Mexico. Mercosur also established a parliament that convened for the first time in 2007. It first members were appointed by their respective home governments, but like the EU, Mercosur's parliament will be elected by direct popular vote beginning in 2010. The RTA has also expanded its scope by negotiating a number of BFTAs with individual countries, including one with India in 2007.

Asia and the Pacific

In Asia, the first RTA was the **Association of Southeast Asian Nations (ASEAN)** established in 1967. It now includes Brunei, Cambodia, Indonesia, Laos, Malaysia, Myanmar (Burma), the Philippines, Singapore, Thailand, and Vietnam. The ASEAN countries have a combined population of over 568 million, a GNP of just over $1 trillion, and total exports of about $767 billion. Like the EU and some other RTAs, ASEAN is also expanding its responsibilities to include development, health, and other matters. For example, the disaster management program it developed in 2002 facilitated a coordinated response when in 2004 a tsunami devastated coastal areas in Indonesia and other member-countries. ASEAN is working to forge greater political cooperation among its members and to bargain as a group with external countries and other trade organizations. Some observers view the RTA as a counterbalance to China in the region.

More recently, the **Asia-Pacific Economic Cooperation (APEC)**, an oddly named structure, was founded in 1989. Its Web site declares that it is the "only intergovernmental grouping in the world operating on the basis of non-binding commitments . . . [with] no treaty obligations required of its participants . . . decisions made by consensus, and commitments . . . undertaken on a voluntary basis." Despite its amorphous nature, APEC is important because among its 21 members are most of the countries of the greater Pacific Ocean region, including China, Japan, Russia, and the United States. Additionally, APEC members account for 41% of the world population, about half the global GDP, and over 40% of world trade. There is a small APEC secretariat based in Singapore, but it is symbolic of APEC's still-tentative status that it has not added a word such as "organization" or "community" to the end of its name.

Somewhat like the G-8, APEC facilitates numerous routine economic consultations among members. Its focus, however, is the annual APEC summit meeting, which serves as a forum for discussions among the United States, Japan, China, and other leading members. Although APEC does not claim to be moving toward RTA status, there have been agreements in principle, for example, to achieve "free and open trade and investment" in the Asia-Pacific region. Japan and the United States are to remove all their barriers by the year 2010, with the rest of the APEC members achieving a zero-barrier level by 2020. It remains unclear whether this will occur, given such factors as China's huge trade surplus with the United States and Japan's uncertain economy. Beyond this, few specific agreements have resulted from these summits, but they are part of a process of dialogue that helps keep lines of communication open. Among other Asia/Pacific RTAs are the 14 island-states of the South

In addition to having an annual summit meeting, the organization Asia-Pacific Economic Cooperation (APEC) works through many lower level meetings to address common problems. This less-visible interchange is represented in this photograph of an APEC ministerial meeting in Da Nang, Vietnam, to address the potential avian influenza crisis. Here Vietnam's Deputy Prime Minister Vu Khoan addresses the meeting.

Pacific Regional Trade and Economic Cooperation Agreement, and the South Asian Preferential Trade Agreement among India and six other countries.

Other Regions

The impulse for regional ties has not been confined to the Americas and the Asia-Pacific region. In Europe, the 25-member European Union is by far the most extensive regional effort. Other European or partly European RTAs are the four-member European Free Trade Association and the Commonwealth of Independent States, which includes the former Soviet republics. Given the expanded coverage of the EU in chapter 7, further commentary here is unnecessary other than to point out that with a population about 50% larger than the U.S. population and with a collective GNP that rivals that of the United States, the EU is a powerful economic force. The setback to EU political integration when French and Dutch voters rejected its constitution in 2005 does not detract from its importance as an RTA. To some degree, competing with it is one factor that has driven the creation of other RTAs, including NAFTA.

Among the most important RTAs in Africa are the 19-member Common Market for Eastern and Southern Africa, northern Africa's 24-member Community of Sahel-Saharan States, the 15-member Economic Community of West Africa States, the 11-member Economic Community of Central African States, and the 14-member South Africa Development Community. Another range of RTAs are based in the Middle East. These include the Gulf Cooperation Council and its six oil-wealthy members. All these share a common purpose of increasing the members' economic strength. Yet because most RTAs are made up of countries with weak economies, their goal is something akin to trying to build a solid structure on quicksand.

Bilateral Trade Agreements

Countries have long concluded bilateral trade agreements with one another, but, as with RTAs, recent years have seen a rapid expansion of BTAs between countries and between RTAs and individual countries. As noted, the WTO estimates that at least 270 and probably many more RTAs are currently in effect. The United States, for example, has concluded BTAs with 21 individual countries such as Australia, Chile, Israel, Morocco, and South Korea, and with one RTA, the five-member Southern Africa Customs Union (Botswana, Lesotho, Namibia, South Africa, and Swaziland). Among the U.S. BTAs is the confusingly named Central American Free Trade Association—Dominican Republic (CAFTA-DR). In addition to the United States and the Dominican Republic, it includes Costa Rica, El Salvador, Guatemala, Honduras, and Nicaragua. Despite its RTA-like name, CAFTA-DR is a series of similar bilateral trade agreements between the United States and the other countries, and those countries with each other.

Before leaving our discussion of RTA and BTAs, it is important to inquire into their impact. They have the advantages of opening trade, investment, and other forms of economic interchange among countries. That is good insofar as it generally improves the economic circumstances of most people in all the countries party to any FTA. Such agreements can also potentially create commonalities and ease tensions among nations and lead to greater regional cooperation on many fronts. The current EU serves as an example of what can evolve from a very limited RTA.

Yet there are also downsides to RTAs and BTAs. One is that their proliferation has created a patchwork of agreements that undermine global trade liberalization (Haftel, 2004). This may harm, rather than advance the South's economic development. According to the WTO's director-general, RTAs are an unsatisfactory substitute for global trade liberalization because "they are by their very nature discriminatory. None has really succeeded in opening markets in sensitive areas like agriculture. They add to the complexities of doing business by creating a multiplicity of rules. And the poorest countries tend to get left out in the cold."[31]

COOPERATION AND DEVELOPMENT: DEBATING THE FUTURE

There is no doubt that the expansion of world trade, investment, and currency exchange has profoundly affected countries and their citizens. Economic interdependence has inexorably intertwined personal, national, and international prosperity. Domestic economics, employment, inflation, and overall growth are heavily dependent on foreign markets, imports of resources, currency exchange rates, capital flows, and other international economic factors. Economic globalization is a reality.

The process of globalization has also brought the issue of development much more to center stage than it was in the past. Globalization has had advantages and disadvantages for all countries, but there is widespread agreement that both within countries and among countries those with the greatest wealth have benefited the most and those with the least wealth have gained the least and, in some cases, have been harmed. That has brought increasing resistance to globalization in the South and from those sympathetic to its stand (Drainville, 2004).

Globalization and the cooperation it entails are also beginning to have a significant impact on the way we organize our world politically. Globalization and sovereignty are not mutually exclusive, but cooperation requires that countries surrender some of their sovereign rights to make unilateral policy and accept international rules. The authority of the WTO to find a country's trade practices legal or illegal serves as an example. Some see this diminution of sovereignty as acceptable, even a positive development. Others are appalled by it.

There are yet other arguments for and against globalization and its accompanying commitment to cooperate and support development, and it is to this debate that we can now turn. Consider the arguments below, and then decide where you stand. Even better, take action to support globalization, modify its course, or reverse it. This much is sure: the script for the future remains unwritten. Because there is little likelihood that the major upheavals favored by economic structuralists will take place, we will shape the argument as a choice between economic internationalism and economic nationalism.

The Case for Economic Internationalism

Economic internationalists make a number of arguments in favor of furthering free economic interchange and increasing support for development. They advance both economic and noneconomic reasons to support their case (Bhagwati, 2004).

Economic Advantages

According to economic internationalists, there are several economic advantages to globalization and to assisting the LDCs as part of that process. These positive results include general prosperity, the benefits of specialization, the cost of protectionism, the advantages of competition, and the advancement of the LDCs through the provision of development capital.

General Prosperity   Economic internationalists argue that unhindered trade and other forms of free economic exchange promote prosperity. Especially since the mid-20th century, trade has accounted for a rapidly growing share of the world's economic activity. As Figure 5.4 on p. 138 shows, exports have grown from 11% of the world's collective GDP in 1955 to 29% in 2005. This means that more and more of what countries and their workers produce goes abroad. Without trade, then, or with a marked decline in trade, national economies would slow, perhaps stall, or might even decline. Figure 13.13 further demonstrates that trade growth helps drive economic expansion by comparing the annual growth of exports and the world's collective GDP. More specifically, for example, the U.S. government calculates that because of trade liberalization since the founding of GATT in 1947, the income of the average American household is $9,000 higher than it would otherwise have been.[32]

A corollary of this argument, according to economic internationalists, is that EDC prosperity will be increased by the development of the South. Although assisting the LDCs will require a substantial short-term cost to the North in aid, debt reductions, and other assistance, many analysts argue that in the long run this investment would create a world in which many more of the 1.3 billion Chinese, 1.1 billion Indians, and the other 3 billion people living in LDCs could buy products labeled "Made in America," visit the United States as tourists, and otherwise benefit the U.S. economy.

Benefits of Specialization   A second advantage of globalization according to economic internationalists is based on the long-standing theory that all countries will

FIGURE 13.13 World Trade and GDP

World trade measured in exports, which generate GDP, has grown faster in each period between 1960 and 2005 than did the collective GDPs of the world's countries. This means that exports have played an important role in driving overall economic growth. Globalization supporters point to such data to show that freer trade is having an overall positive impact on world economic circumstances.

Data source: IMF.

benefit if each sells what it can produce most efficiently. Among those who have propounded this idea are English economists David Ricardo in *On the Principles of Political Economy and Taxation* (1817) and John Stuart Mill in *Principles of Political Economy* (1848). Ricardo developed the theory of "comparative advantage," which held that everyone would benefit if each country produced and exported its most cost-efficient products. Based on this view, Mill argued that trade's "advantage consists in a more efficient employment of the productive forces of the world."

The Cost of Protectionism   Protecting jobs from foreign imports has a tremendous emotional appeal, but most economists argue that trade barriers result in higher prices because tariff costs are passed on to consumers or because consumers are forced to buy more expensive domestically produced goods. The U.S. Federal Reserve Bank argues that "protectionism is pure poison for an economy" and estimates that each American job that is saved by protectionism costs an average of $231,289, with an overall cost of nearly $100 billion annually to U.S. consumers.[33] How does a protected job cost over $200,000? The cost includes not just the higher price of the protected items but downstream products as well. For example, protecting sugar not only raises its price to consumers, it also raises prices of candy, soft drinks, and many other products. The higher price of candy also exposes that industry and its jobs to foreign competition. LifeSavers, Jaw Breakers, and Red Hots used to be made in the Chicago area. Now they are produced in Canada using cheaper sugar, and Chicago has lost half its candy manufacturing jobs since 1970. These wages are lost, unemployment compensation is paid, and the rippling costs add up higher and higher.

Promotion of Competition   A fourth contention by economic internationalists is that free economic interchange promotes beneficial competition. Without foreign competition, the argument goes, domestic manufacturers have a captive market, which can have a variety of ill effects, such as price fixing and lack of innovation. For example, American automakers did not begin to offer U.S. consumers well-built, inexpensive, fuel-efficient small cars until pressure from foreign competition forced them to reshape their product and modernize their production techniques.

Providing Development Capital   Fifth, economic internationalists maintain that free economic interchange increases the flow of investment capital to the LDCs. The IMF calculates that between 1997 and 2005 alone, a net $1.3 trillion (investments minus withdrawals) foreign direct investment (FDI) flowed into LDCs to bolster their economic development, and FDI also benefits EDCs. It is also the case that MNC-directed investments provide EDCs with a wide variety of economic benefits. Jobs are one example. Foreign-owned MNCs employ 6.3 million people in the United States, pay them $350 billion a year, and contribute tens of billions of dollars in U.S. federal, state, and local taxes.

Noneconomic Advantages

Arguably, there are also several noneconomic advantages to economic internationalism. These include advancing world cooperation, inhibiting conflict, and promoting democracy.

World Cooperation   A sixth, and this time political, argument made by economic internationalists is that free economic interchange promotes world cooperation. The logic is that if countries can trade together in peace, their interactions will bring greater contact and understanding. Cooperation will then become the rule rather than the exception, and this, it is thought, will lead to political cooperation and interaction. The move toward the political integration of Europe, which began with economic cooperation, is the most frequently cited example.

Decreased Violence   A seventh, and again political, argument for free economic interchange is that it restrains conflict by promoting interdependence, which makes fighting more difficult and more unlikely (McDonald, 2004; Pevehouse, 2004). In the words of one study, "Higher levels of economically important trade . . . are associated with lower incidences of militarized interstate disputes and war" (Oneal & Russett, 1997:288). One link between peace and trade is the contention that a high degree of interdependence among countries may dissuade or even prevent them from fighting. If oil and iron are necessary to fight, and if Country A supplies Country B's oil, and B supplies A's iron, then they are too enmeshed to go to war.

A related argument is that the North will be more secure as the South achieves prosperity. This view contends that the poor are becoming increasingly hostile toward the wealthy. Modern communications have heightened the South's sense of relative deprivation—the awareness of a deprived person (group, country) of the gap between his or her circumstances and the relatively better position of others. Research shows that seeing another's prosperity and knowing that there are alternatives to your own impoverished condition causes frustration and a sense of being cheated, often leading to resentment and sometimes to violence. Perhaps it was the 9/11 attacks that provided the wake-up call, but when world leaders met in Monterrey, Mexico, in

2002 to discuss LDC development, a constant theme was the connection between poverty and violence (Li & Schaub, 2004). "Poverty in all its forms is the greatest single threat to peace [and] security," the head of the WTO told delegates.[34] Similarly, the UN secretary-general warned, "Left alone in their poverty, [very poor] countries are all too likely to collapse or relapse into conflict and anarchy, a menace to their neighbors and potentially, as the events of the 11th of September so brutally reminded us, a threat to global security."[35]

ANALYZE THE ISSUE
International Economic
Cooperation

Promoting Democracy   An eighth, and once more political, argument advanced by some economic internationalists is that the openness required for free economic exchange promotes democracy. The idea is that it is difficult to simultaneously have a free enterprise system and an authoritarian political system. Gradually the habits of independent decision making inherent in a capitalist system, the flow of ideas within the country and between it and the outside world, and the growth of powerful financial interests all work to undercut the authoritarian political regimes. For example, during the past few years, such newly industrializing countries as Mexico, South Korea, and Taiwan have had their first truly democratic elections either ever, or in many decades. Particularly appealing is the thought that globalization will eventually moderate China's authoritarian government. According to one analyst, "Global markets and information technology are multiplying the channels through which outside actors can influence Chinese society and, simultaneously, undermining the regime's strict control" (Moore, 2001:63; Li & Reuveny, 2003).

The Case for Economic Nationalism

There are also several political and economic arguments for economic nationalism. Some of these involve trade or some other single aspect of international economic exchange; other arguments are more general.

Economic Advantages

Economic nationalists advance a number of economic arguments to support their position. These include the benefits of protecting the domestic economy, diversification, and compensating for existing distortions.

Protecting the Domestic Economy   The need for economic barriers to protect threatened domestic industries and workers from foreign competition is a favorite theme of economic nationalists. "I'm not a free trader," one U.S. secretary of commerce confessed. "The goal," he said, "is to nurture American workers and industry. It is not to adhere to some kind of strict ideology."[36] An associated argument seeks protection for new or still small, so-called infant industries. This is an especially common contention in LDCs trying to industrialize, but it is heard worldwide. Many economists give the idea of such protection some credibility, at least in the short term.

Economic nationalists also argue that the positive impact of creation or preservation of jobs by the inflow of investment is offset by the loss of jobs when MNCs move operations to another country or when MNCs create new jobs in another country rather than in their own home country. American MNCs, for example, employ about 1.9 million more workers in other countries than foreign MNCs employ American workers in the United States. Furthermore, these opponents say, forcing well-paid

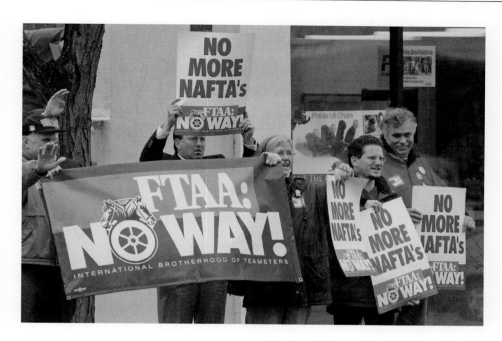

A key debate about the world's future centers on the pros and cons of economic globalization. Critics charge that globalization harms many people who lose their jobs when the companies they work for shift their production or other operations overseas. Among the antiglobalization forces are these members of the Teamsters Union in New Hampshire, seen here during an appearance of candidates in the state's approaching presidential primary. The union members are protesting the existing North American Free Trade Association and the proposed Free Trade Area of the Americas.

workers in the United States and elsewhere to compete with poorly paid workers in LDCs depresses the wages and living conditions in EDCs in what they call "a race to the bottom." The U.S. clothing industry, for example, has been devastated, with its workforce dropping 47% between 1990 and 2005 from 929,000 to 260,000. Some of this loss is due to robotics and other forms of mechanization, but most is the result of foreign competition.

Lost jobs and wages must also be measured in terms of the ripple effect that multiplies each dollar several times. A worker without a job cannot buy from the local merchant, who in turn cannot buy from the building contractor, who in turn cannot buy from the department store, and so on, rippling out through the economy. Displaced workers also collect unemployment benefits and may even wind up on public assistance programs. These costs are substantial and diminish the gains derived from free trade. Finally, there is the psychological damage from being laid off and from other forms of economic dislocation that cannot be measured in dollars and cents.

Diversification   Another economic nationalist argument holds that economic diversification should be encouraged. Specialization, it is said, will make a country too dependent on a few resources or products; if demand for those products falls, then economic catastrophe will result. In reality, no modern, complex economy will become that specialized, but the argument does have simplistic appeal.

Compensating for Existing Distortions   Yet another economic nationalist argument is that protectionism and other trade distortions continue, and that nice-guy free traders will finish last when faced with such realities as cartels that set petroleum prices and governments that use tariffs, subsidies, currency manipulation, and other techniques to benefit themselves at our expense. As an example, take the issue raised in chapter 12 of China's refusal to substantially revalue its artificially low currency, the yuan, against the dollar. The economic nationalist argument is that the United States should retaliate against China by raising tariffs and setting quotas or even embargos on Chinese goods (Shambaugh, 2004).

Putting Domestic Needs First   According to economic nationalists, citizens forge a government and support it to look after their welfare and safety, not to lead idealistic quests to solve other people's problems. From this perspective, the amounts of funding recommended by the UN and other development advocates are prohibitive. It would cost the EDCs nearly $147 billion extra a year to increase foreign aid to the recommended level of 0.7% of their GNPs. Debt forgiveness, trade concessions, and other financial measures would add to the annual expenses. With most EDCs already running annual budget deficits, the added funds would mean higher taxes for their people, fewer social programs for them, or larger deficits.

Noneconomic Advantages

Economic nationalists also argue that their perspective protects national sovereignty, enhances national security, and permits the beneficial use of their country's economic power as a policy tool. There is an additional argument that globalization is harming the welfare of many individuals and also increasing damage to the environment.

National Sovereignty   One of the fastest-growing sources of sentiment against globalization is the belief of many people that the process is eroding their country's national sovereignty. Many people are shocked to find that sometimes their country's laws and regulations must give way when they clash with rules of the WTO or some other international organization or agreement.

A closely related phenomenon involves the fear that foreign investors will gain control of your country's economy and will be able to influence your political processes and your culture. In the late 1980s the value of the dollar plunged and set off a feeding frenzy of acquisition as foreign investors snapped up such quintessential American brand names as Capitol Records (Great Britain), Roy Rogers (Canada), Alka-Seltzer (Germany), and 7–Eleven (Japan). Cries rang out that the British, among others, were coming. One member of Congress fretted that "for the first time since the Revolution, Americans are being subjected to decisions and dictates from abroad."[37] In time, the flow of FDI reversed itself, and American acquisitions abroad once again outpaced foreign buying of U.S. companies and other assets. But American sensitivities are now rising anew, this time in response to the bids by Chinese investors to take control of such brand names as Maytag, RCA, and IBM's personal computer line.

National Security   A related economic nationalist argument involves national defense. The contention is somewhat the reverse of the "conflict inhibition," pro–free trade argument made earlier. Protectionists stress that the country must not become so dependent on foreign sources that it will be unable to defend itself. In recent years, the U.S. government has acted to protect industries ranging from specialty steels to basic textiles, partly in response to warnings that the country was losing its ability to produce weapons systems and uniforms. Economic nationalists also warn of the dangers of unchecked FDI acquisitions by foreign investors. A Chinese company's bid to take control of the major U.S. oil company Unocal in 2005 sparked the warning from one analyst that, "Clearly, in today's China, we are up against a country that has a strategy to acquire U.S. critical technology companies. If we continue to ignore it—let alone enable it by acquiescing to the sale of companies like Unocal—we will do so at our peril."[38] Many Americans agreed, and the ensuing uproar in the United States ultimately persuaded the Chinese company to withdraw its bid.

Also under the rubric of national security, there is the issue of what can be called strategic trade. The question is how far a country should go in restricting trade and other economic interchanges with countries that are or may become hostile. Currently, the primary focus of the strategic trade debate is on dual-use technology that has peaceful uses but also has military applications. Here too, China is the cause of the greatest current concern. The export of U.S. computers and other high-tech items to China has led one staff member in Congress to worry that there has been a serious undermining of U.S. national security due to relaxed restrictions on export of "dual-use technologies," and that "The Chinese threat of a 'high-tech Pearl Harbor' is well within their reach."[39]

Policy Tool   Yet another economic nationalist argument maintains that trade "follows the flag" (Keshk, Pollins, & Reuveny, 2004). This means that politics determines economic relations, more than the other way around, and that trade is a powerful political tool that can be used to further a country's interests. The extension or withdrawal of trade and other economic benefits also have an important—albeit hard-to-measure—symbolic value. Clearly, economic tools can be used to promote a country's political goals, and free economic interchange necessarily limits the availability of economic tools to pursue policy. A current example is the U.S. embargo on most trade with and travel to Cuba, which has existed since 1960. It is justified, President Bush has argued, because "Well-intentioned ideas about trade will merely prop up this dictator, enrich his cronies, and enhance the totalitarian regime."[40]

Social and Environmental Protection   The chairman of Dow Chemical Company once confessed, "I have long dreamed of buying an island owned by no nation and establishing the world headquarters of the Dow company on . . . such an island, beholden to no nation or society" (Gruenberg, 1996:339). Critics of MNCs claim that such statements confirm their suspicions that these global enterprises use their ability to move operations around the world to undercut protections relating to child labor, minimum wages, and many other socioeconomic standards and also to escape environmental regulations. In the estimate of one analyst, "National governments have lost much of their power to direct their own economies because of the power of capital to pick up and leave." The result of the "quantum leap in the ability of transnational corporations to relocate their facilities around the world," he continues, is to make "all workers, communities and countries competitors for these corporations' favor." This competition, he worries, has set off "a 'race to the bottom' in which wages and social and environment conditions tend to fall to the level of the most desperate" (Brecher, 1993:685).

Critics of globalization also charge that, among other evils, the race to the bottom will mean gutting desirable social programs. Europe has built an extensive social welfare support system through government programs and mandates on industries (such as health insurance for workers, paid vacations, and other benefits). Such programs and benefits are costly, however, and European economies struggle to meet them while also keeping the price of their products low enough to be competitive in world markets or even at home compared to imported goods and services. Similarly, critics worry that countries attempting to maintain high standards of environmental

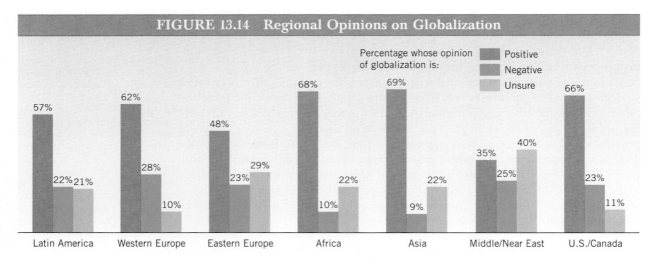

FIGURE 13.14 Regional Opinions on Globalization

Percentage whose opinion of globalization is: Positive / Negative / Unsure

A majority or plurality of people globally in every region but the Middle/Near East supports globalization.

Note: Countries in the Middle/Near East stretch from Egypt to Pakistan. The question was: Do you think that globalization is a very good thing, somewhat good, somewhat bad or a very bad thing? The data averages country results within a region, not overall results.

Data source: Pew Research Center for the People and the Press (2003).

protection or institute new safeguards will be penalized by companies moving their production facilities and jobs elsewhere.

The Globalization Debate in Perspective

To return to the point with which we began this section, the clash between the forces of economic internationalism and those of economic nationalism will be one of the most pivotal struggles in the years ahead (Helleiner & Pickel, 2005). The rapid globalization process that began after World War II has brought the world much closer to a truly global economy than seemed possible not long ago. The EDCs have generally prospered, and even most of the LDCs have improved their health, education, and many other social conditions. Moreover, globalization enjoys substantial public support worldwide, as Figure 13.14 shows.

The advances that globalization has made and the general support for it do not mean, however, that it is an unmitigated success. The changes associated with globalization have occurred in a largely unregulated international system, and, as a result, the benefits and costs that accompany most change have been unequally distributed. Other countries, their citizens, and even many people in prosperous countries have either not benefited or have been harmed. This has left the global public somewhat cautious about globalization, as Figure 13.14 can also be interpreted (Kaltenthaler, Gelleny, & Ceccoli, 2004).

For us here, the key question is not the world's opinion, but yours. Should globalization proceed or be halted? You can also take the position that globalization is good in theory, but the practice so far has been unsatisfactory and needs to be reformed. If that is your view, what would you do to make globalization a positive process? Of course, answering such questions in the abstract and responding to them in a specific situation are not quite the same, so the decision box, "Economic Nationalism or Economic Internationalism?" asks you to make some policy choices.

DEBATE THE POLICY SCRIPT

Economic Nationalism or Economic Internationalism?

Economic internationalists favor few restrictions on free trade and investment. They believe that a mostly unfettered flow of goods, services, and capital will, in the long term, advance the prosperity of all countries. Economic nationalists disagree. They see the international economy as a generally zero-sum game in which prosperity of some often comes at the expense of others. Therefore, economic nationalists believe that restrictions are often warranted to protect their country's economy and to advance its political interests.

You can test where you stand by deciding on several policy issues. Some have been put in generic terms, but each is related to a current or recent U.S. policy decision. The first involves the continuation of the long-standing economic embargo on Cuba. The second is whether you think the United States should make sufficient concessions on its agricultural subsidies to satisfy the LDCs and move the Doha Round forward. The third involves whether you would approve of a Chinese company acquiring a controlling interest in a major U.S. energy company, such as the move by Chinese investors to buy Unocal. Fourth, would you renew the president's "fast track" authority to negotiate trade agreements? This limits congressional authority to only approving or disapproving the agreements. Congress cannot amend them, which would require their renegotiation. Fifth, what are your views about limiting the importation of foreign footwear to protect jobs of U.S. workers? Sixth, would you abide by a ruling by the WTO that U.S. subsidies of Boeing were a violation of trade law?

What Do You Think?

Assume that you are a member of Congress facing votes today on six issues. For each issue, a yea vote casts you as an economic internationalist; a nay vote aligns you with the economic nationalists. Cast your vote!

	Yea	Nay
Repeal the embargo on Cuba	___	___
Make concessions to reenergize the Doha Round	___	___
Permit Chinese acquisition of a U.S. energy company	___	___
Renew the president's fast-track authority	___	___
Reject limits on footwear imports	___	___
Abide by WTO ruling	___	___

CHAPTER SUMMARY

ECONOMIC COOPERATION AND DEVELOPMENT: BACKGROUND AND REQUIREMENTS

1. This chapter assesses the alternative route of economic nationalism and focuses on the approach advocated by economic internationalists and structuralists, which stresses global economic cooperation with a particular emphasis on the economic development of the South.

2. The idea of creating global interdependence based on free economic interchange and cooperation for the economic good of all dates back several hundred years, but it did not begin to significantly shape international economic relations until about 60 years ago.

3. There has been considerable improvement in the socioeconomic development of the South, but those positive indications should not obscure other, more distressing realities in many LDCs.

4. To modernize their economies, the LDCs need to get more development capital, the four main sources of which are loans, investment, trade, and aid. Unfortunately, there are limitations and drawbacks to each. The South also needs to undertake internal reforms.

ECONOMIC COOPERATION AND DEVELOPMENT: THE INSTITUTIONS

5. Numerous IGOs and international programs focus on economic cooperation, and most give the development of the South top priority. The largest general IGO, the UN, maintains a number of efforts aimed at general economic development, with an emphasis on the less developed countries (LDCs).

6. The IMF is the primary IGO dedicated to stabilizing the world's monetary system. The IMF's primary

role in recent years has been to assist LDCs by stabilizing their currencies and reducing their foreign debt. There is, however, considerable controversy over how the IMF is run and the conditions it attaches to its loans.

7. The World Bank Group is the best known of the IGOs that provide developmental loans and grants to LDC. Like the IMF, there is controversy about the governance of the World Bank and its policies.

8. There are two main economic organizations associated with the North, the OECD and the G-8, but they also devote considerable attention to LDC development.

REGIONAL ECONOMIC COOPERATION AND DEVELOPMENT

9. In addition to the activity promoting economic cooperation and development at the global level, there are important efforts under way at the regional level. The most important of these is the expansion in the number and size of regional trade organizations.

10. Receiving particular attention here are NAFTA, the FTAA, and Mercosur in the Western Hemisphere; ASEAN and APEC in the Asia-Pacific Region. The EU in Europe is detailed in chapter 7, and other RTAs are of less significance.

11. There is disagreement whether the growth in the number and membership of regional trade organizations and the establishment of other forms of preferential trade agreements is a positive or negative development for global economic cooperation, and, by extension, cooperation in other areas.

COOPERATION AND DEVELOPMENT: DEBATING THE FUTURE

12. There are significant arguments on both sides of the question of whether or not to continue to expand economic globalization, including advancing both free international economic interchange and LDC development. Economic internationalists advance a series of economic and noneconomic arguments in support of their view. Economic nationalists counter with their own set of economic and noneconomic contentions.

For simulations, debates, and other interactive activities, a chapter quiz, Web Links, and much more, visit **www.mhhe.com/rourke12/** and go to chapter 13. Or, while accessing the site, click on Course-Wide Content and view recent international relations articles in the *New York Times*.

KEY TERMS

Asia-Pacific Economic Cooperation (APEC)
Association of Southeast Asian Nations (ASEAN)
bilateral aid
bilateral trade agreement (BTA)
conditionality
debt service
Development Assistance Committee (DAC)
development capital

Doha Round
Free Trade Area of the Americas (FTAA)
General Agreement on Tariffs and Trade (GATT)
Group of Eight (G-8)
Group of 77 (G-77)
hard currency
interdependence
International Conference on Financing for Development (ICFD)

International Monetary Fund (IMF)
multilateral aid
North American Free Trade Agreement (NAFTA)
Organization for Economic Cooperation and Development (OECD)
regional trade agreement (RTA)
Southern Common Market (Mercosur)

special drawing rights (SDRs)
UN Conference on Trade and Development (UNCTAD)
UN Development Programme (UNDP)
Uruguay Round
World Bank Group
World Trade Organization (WTO)

Preserving and Enhancing Human Rights and Dignity

The sun with one eye vieweth all the world.
—William Shakespeare, *Henry VI, Part I*

And your true rights be term'd a poet's rage.
—William Shakespeare, "Sonnet XVII"

HIGH COMMISSIONER FOR HUMAN RIGHTS

An important change in world affairs in the last half century is that the topic of this chapter, human rights, has gone from being largely ignored to becoming a significant concern. The change in focus is represented by this photograph of UN High Commissioner for Human Rights Louise Arbour, a former justice of Canada's Supreme Court, addressing the UN Human Rights Council in Geneva, Switzerland.

A BUSES OF THE HUMAN RIGHTS of individuals, groups, and indeed, whole segments of humanity have existed throughout history and continue today. What is new is a rising global consciousness and condemnation of such travesties and a resolve to help the oppressed. That is what this chapter is about. We will begin by looking at the nature of human rights, then turn to areas of concern and what is being done at the international level to improve conditions.

Unlike chapters 4 through 13, which contrast the traditional and alternative approaches to global affairs in successive chapters, this chapter includes both the traditional approach and the alternative approach to human rights. Addressing the traditional approach is relatively simple: It has been to largely ignore human rights abuses in other countries or at best to denounce them without doing anything to alleviate the situation. A separate chapter on the traditional approach to human rights would have mostly blank pages. Sovereignty and nationalism are the two main reasons for a history of hands-off policy. *Sovereignty,* the legal concept that countries have absolute control over what happens within their borders, has kept human rights out of the interplay of world politics because most violations occur within state borders and, therefore, have been seen as domestic matters. Intervening to address them would constitute a violation of sovereignty. What is worse, violating another country's sovereignty might set a precedent for the future violation of your own sovereignty by others. *Nationalism* has created a we–they complex, as discussed in chapter 4. To a significant degree, our sense of responsibility and even of human caring is much greater for members of our we-group, our nation, than for people of other nations, the they-groups. Thus, traditionally, if members of a they-group were suffering, well, that was a shame, but not really something we were obligated to address.

While this traditional approach to human rights continues as the dominant modality of international politics, things are beginning to change slowly to provide an alternative approach. Technology is one factor. There is a much more extensive and graphic detailing of human rights through television and the Internet. Hearing and reading about human rights abuses do not have anywhere near the emotional impact of seeing images of violence, torture, and other abuses in vivid color on the television screens and computer monitors in the intimate surroundings of our family rooms and bedrooms. Such images are harder to ignore than reporting in other media and have added to slowly changing attitudes about abuses. The World War II era was an important turning point. Shocked by the Holocaust, the horrendous treatment of the Chinese, Koreans, and others by the Japanese, and other horrific abuses of human rights, the victorious nations of the world proclaimed in the Preamble to the United Nations Charter that they were establishing the UN in part, "To reaffirm faith in fundamental human rights, in the dignity and worth of the human person, [and] in equal rights of men and women." It is easy to dismiss such words as mere lofty rhetoric, and, in truth, the "talk" has been far greater than the "action."

Yet it is also the case, as we shall see, that real changes have begun to take hold. Human rights are now "on the table" in diplomatic discussions within international governmental organizations (IGOs) and among countries, and there are hundreds, perhaps thousands, of international nongovernmental organizations (NGOs) whose focus is the promotion of human rights. More importantly, the international community is sometimes taking action. To preview the many instances of action that are discussed below, the former presidents of Serbia and Liberia and dozens of other alleged criminals have been brought to trial before an international tribunal for abusing human rights and other crimes. Additionally, UN peacekeepers are in the Darfur region of Sudan trying to protect the population from marauding militia backed by the government in Khartoum. Such steps remain the exception to the rule of the still dominant traditional approach of remaining uninvolved, but ignoring abuses is no longer the only alternative.

MAP
Human Rights: Political
Rights and Civil Liberties

Web Link

For links to a wide variety of human rights–oriented organizations and material go to the "Human Rights, Globalization and Disaster Relief " page of the Human Rights Interactive Network at **www.webcom.com/hrin/.**

THE NATURE OF HUMAN RIGHTS

Before moving to a detailed discussion of human rights, it is important to explain the broad concept of human rights used here and also some of the controversies in defining human rights. This will entail discussions of proscriptive and prescriptive rights, universal and culture-based rights, and individual and community rights.

Proscriptive and Prescriptive Human Rights

We generally think about human rights as freedom from specific abuses or restrictions that are proscribed (forbidden). Most commonly, certain actions by governments are proscribed. The U.S. Bill of Rights, for example, prohibits (except in extreme cases) the government from abridging individual Americans' rights to exercise their religion or free speech. **Proscriptive rights** also include those things that the government cannot do to groups, such as discriminate based on race, ethnicity, or gender. The obligation to respect many of these proscriptive rights also extends to private individuals and organizations. For instance, employers in the United States may not decide to hire only white males. Such rights are also called negative rights, because they involve what *cannot* be done legally.

Many people believe that humans also possess a range of **prescriptive rights**. They include the basic necessities that a society and its government are arguably prescribed (obligated) to try to provide in order to assure certain qualitative standards of life for everyone in the community. These include receiving adequate education, nutrition, housing, sanitation, health care, and the other basics necessary to live with dignity and security and to be a productive individual. Whether society is defined in narrow national terms or broader global terms is a matter of controversy. Such rights are also called positive rights because they place a positive obligation on societies and their governments to ensure they are met.

Whatever the focus, though, one scholar suggests that the most fruitful way to think about human rights is to begin with the idea that "ultimately they are supposed to serve basic human needs." These basic human needs, which generate corresponding rights, include, among others (Galtung, 1994:3, 72):

- "Survival needs—to avoid violence": The right of individuals and groups to be free from violence.
- "Well-being needs—to avoid misery": The right to adequate nutrition and water; to movement, sleep, sex, and other biological wants; to protection from diseases and from adverse climatological and environmental impacts.
- "Identity needs—to avoid alienation": The right to establish and maintain emotional bonds with others; to preserve cultural heritage and association; to contribute through work and other activity; and to receive information about and maintain contact with nature, global humanity, and other aspects of the biosphere.
- "Freedom needs—to avoid repression": The right to receive and express opinions, to assemble with others, to have a say in common policy; and to choose in such wide-ranging matters as jobs, spouses, where to live, and lifestyle.

The degree to which proscriptive and prescriptive rights should be used as a standard to judge countries is increasingly being debated internationally. For example, the United States, which emphasizes proscriptive rights, regularly criticizes China for a

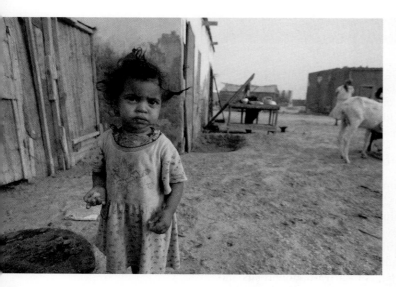

Most people accept the idea of negative, or proscriptive, human rights, those that forbid certain actions like suppressing free speech. More controversial are positive, or prescriptive, human rights, those that arguably require a society to do certain things. Ask yourself, Does this child standing in front of the hovel where she lives in Nouakchott, Mauritania, have a right to adequate health, education, and housing? If she does, and her own government is too poor to honor her rights, then is the global society obligated?

wide range of rights abuses. Typically, a U.S. State Department annual review of global human rights characterized China as an "authoritarian state" whose "human rights record throughout the year remained poor" on such matters as freedom of speech and religion.[1] China countered by accusing the United States of violating prescriptive human rights. "Human rights protection provided by the U.S. Constitution is very limited," a Chinese government report asserted. It noted, for instance, that in the United States there is no right to "food, clothing, shelter, education, work, rest, and reasonable payment."[2]

One source of differing views about prescriptive and proscriptive rights is linked to a society's conceptions of individual success or failure: Is it based on each person's effort or on outside forces such as that person's place in society? Most Americans and Canadians believe that individuals are responsible for their personal success and other conditions, but throughout much of the rest of the world a majority disagree. They believe that outside forces, not personal actions are the most important factor in determining an individual's success or failure in life. These contrasting views are detailed for different regions in Figure 14.1. Given the differences, it is hardly surprising that there are different views of prescriptive and proscriptive liberty. This is apparent in a survey that asked Americans, Western Europeans, and Eastern Europeans which they thought more important for a government to do: (1) follow the proscriptive liberty standard of not interfering in people's freedom to pursue their goals, or (2) adhere to the prescriptive liberty standard by acting to ensure that no one in the society is in need. Among Americans, 58% favored the proscriptive liberty approach; only 33% of Western Europeans and 29% of Eastern Europeans did. By contrast, 59% of Western Europeans and 60% of Eastern Europeans favored the prescriptive approach; only 33% of Americans agreed.

As you read the balance of this chapter, think about how you feel about proscriptive rights and prescriptive rights. What proscriptive rights, "freedoms from" specific abuses do you possess? Also ponder prescriptive rights. Doing so is more challenging because they are probably less familiar to you and whether they even exist is debatable. The ultimate question, which is posed in a decision box at the end of the chapter, is what rights you would include and exclude in a global bill of rights.

Universal and Culture-Based Rights

Scholars generally agree that a right is a justified claim to something. To say, for instance, that you have a right to freedom of religion means you have a legitimate claim to believe whatever you wish. However, a key question is what justifies claiming a

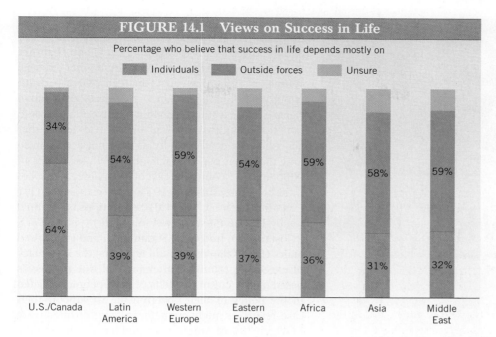

FIGURE 14.1   Views on Success in Life

Percentage who believe that success in life depends mostly on

■ Individuals   ■ Outside forces   ■ Unsure

U.S./Canada	Latin America	Western Europe	Eastern Europe	Africa	Asia	Middle East
34%	54%	59%	54%	59%	58%	59%
64%	39%	39%	37%	36%	31%	32%

How a society perceives proscriptive and prescriptive rights is based in part on how it feels about the importance of individual traits and effort in achieving success compared to the role of outside forces. Examples of such outside forces may be what country a person is born in, or whether, within a country, a person is a member of a privileged or disadvantaged demographic group. Most Americans and Canadians believe that an individual's personal qualities are more important than circumstances in determining success or failure. By contrast, a majority of people in every other region believe that circumstances play the dominant role. These different views are related to why Americans and Canadians are more likely to see rights in proscriptive terms and others are more likely to also support prescriptive rights.

Note: The question was, "Is success in life pretty much determined by forces outside our control?" For clarity, the "agree" answer is labeled "outside forces," and the "disagree" answer is labeled "individual traits." Data points for "unsure" are omitted and can be equated by subtracting the sum of the other two answers from 100%.
Data source: The Pew Research Center, "Views of a Changing World," June 2003.

right. Where does it come from? As noted in chapter 9, there are two schools of thought about where rights originate.

The Source of Rights

Universalists believe that all humans possess the same rights and that they are immutable. This perspective begins with the idea that rights originate from outside a society. Among the possible external sources, theology leads many universalists to believe that rights are granted by a deity and therefore may not be transgressed by humans. A second external source is the very nature of human existence. Universalists who believe in natural rights contend that people inherently possess such rights as the right to life, which may not be legitimately abridged. Whatever the specific source, those who contend that rights originate outside a society and transcend it are called universalists.

Relativists contend that rights are relative to culture. That is, rights are the product of a society's contemporary values. Relativists therefore assert that in a world of diverse cultures, no single standard of human rights exists or is likely to exist short of the world becoming homogenized culturally. This point of view also means that rights are not timeless; they can change with changing social norms.

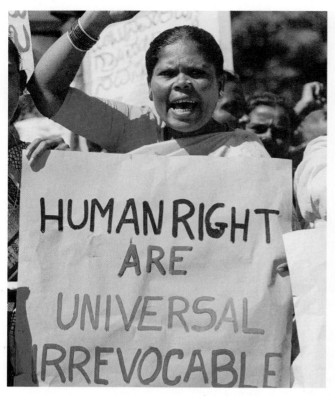

This woman in India is one of many people globally who argue that human rights are universal: the same for everyone, everywhere. Others contend that human rights are based in culture and can vary across the world. Which view do you support?

MAP
Capital Punishment

To see the difference between the two views of rights, consider capital punishment. Whether they cite the theological commandment, "Thou shalt not kill," the natural right to life, or some other external source, many universalists believe that the death penalty is an abomination that violates the human rights of the executed individual. Universalists would note that about two-thirds of all countries have either abolished the death penalty or have not used it in so long that it has been de facto abolished. Moreover, in 2006, only 25 countries executed anyone, and six of these countries carried out 91% of the estimated 1,591 executions. China, with 1,010 executions, accounted for by far the most. It was followed by Iran (177), Pakistan (82), Iraq (65), Sudan (65), and the United States (53). Relativists would reply that the legitimacy of executing criminals after judicial due process is based on the cultural beliefs of their people reflected in the policy of their government. To support their case, relativists might point, for instance, to one survey in which 70% of American respondents expressed the belief that capital punishment is "morally acceptable," compared to 25% who held it be "morally unacceptable," and 5% who were uncertain.[3] Such disagreements over whether a right is universal or culturally relative are not simply abstract arguments. One political repercussion is that numerous countries refuse to extradite accused individuals to a country if they might be sentenced to death. At some point, also, the global consensus against capital punishment might be strong enough to make it a violation of international law under international custom and the general principles of law, as explained in chapter 9. Unlike in the United States, as Figure 14.2 shows, opposition to the death penalty is strong enough in many countries that majorities in them did not even support the execution of a figure as diabolical as Saddam Hussein.

Applying Universalism and Relativism

Given the differences in perspective between cultures, the question arises as to whether it is reasonable to try to apply human rights standards to international relations (Arat, 2006). Relativists contend that trying to impose human rights standards on the world stage constitutes **cultural imperialism**. Advocates of this view are apt to note that the prevailing definitions of human rights substantially reflect the values of the dominant Western powers and are much less attuned to some of the beliefs of Asian, African, and other societies. One American scholar writes, for instance, "We must understand and learn from other traditions while seeing them as historically conditioned—and this includes our own tradition. What we must not do . . . is elevate our own tradition to the status of 'universalism.' This is just rehashed cultural imperialism and has its roots in the dogmatic religious outlooks of the past and present." In sum, he argues, "We should realize that we create our own values, reacting to the times and climes, and rational people can disagree on what these values are."[4]

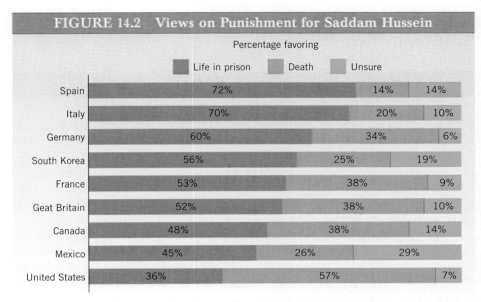

FIGURE 14.2   Views on Punishment for Saddam Hussein

Percentage favoring

■ Life in prison   ■ Death   ■ Unsure

Country	Life in prison	Death	Unsure
Spain	72%	14%	14%
Italy	70%	20%	10%
Germany	60%	34%	6%
South Korea	56%	25%	19%
France	53%	38%	9%
Geat Britain	52%	38%	10%
Canada	48%	38%	14%
Mexico	45%	26%	29%
United States	36%	57%	7%

Even for an individual like Saddam Hussein, who directed horrific crimes, a majority or plurality of people in every country but the United States favored life in prison rather than execution. At what point is the weight of world opinion heavy enough to make capital punishment a violation of international law no matter what the citizens of any individual country may think?

Data source: AP/Ipsos Poll, February 2006; data courtesy of World Public Opinion.org.

Others reject such claims of cultural imperialism as poor attempts to justify the unjustifiable. They argue that the nature of humankind is not based on culture, and, therefore, human rights are universal (Donnelly, 2003). For one, UN Secretary-General Kofi Annan told an audience, there is "talk of human rights being a Western concept, . . . [but] don't we all suffer from the lack of the rule of law and from arbitrariness? What is foreign about that? What is Western about that? And when we talk of the right [of people] . . . to live their lives to the fullest and to be able to live their dreams, it is universal."[5]

Individual and Community Rights

An issue closely related to the debate over cultural relativism is the controversy over the respective rights of individuals and society. Imagine a scale that ranges, on one end, from **individualism**, a value system in which the rights of an individual are more important than those of the society to, at the other end, **communitarianism**, a value system in which the good of the community takes precedence over the good of the individual. Western states would generally fall toward the individualistic end of the scale; non-Western states would generally fall farther toward the communitarian end of the scale. Singapore, for example, does not extend all the "Miranda rights" and other legal protections given to suspects in the United States. Singapore also imposes punishment that Americans might think is "cruel and unusual," including the extremely painful caning of a convict's bared buttocks with a rattan cane for about 30 crimes ranging from attempted murder through vandalism. To defend their position, Singapore officials point to the fact that people there are threatened by a vastly lower crime rate than found in most major U.S. cities. "We believe that the

WEB POLL
The Sources of Human Rights: Are You a Universalist or a Cultural Relativist?

legal system must give maximum protection to the majority of our people. We make no apology for clearly tilting our laws and policy in favor of the majority."[6]

PROSCRIPTIVE HUMAN RIGHTS

Most rights that societies and their states extend (the relativist view) or recognize as inherent (the universalist view) are proscriptive rights that prohibit the government and often others (such as organizations and companies) from doing certain things. Although they overlap, these rights can be subdivided into individual rights, such as freedom of speech and assembly, and group rights, which involve prohibitions against discriminating against categories of people based on ethnicity, gender, race, and other such "inborn" factors. These are often thought of as civil rights.

Rights are abused for many reasons. For example, oppression of individual rights often comes at the hands of dictators, who violate them by arbitrarily arresting and punishing people; by depriving them of their property without the due process of law; and by abridging their freedom to freely speak, organize, travel, and associate with other individuals and groups.

As for group rights, whether the focus is race, ethnicity, gender, sexual orientation, religious choice, or some other trait, there are few human characteristics or beliefs that have not been the target of discrimination and abuse somewhere in the world. One important cause, as discussed in chapter 4, is the "we–they" sense of group identification often associated with nationalism. This leads people to value the group they identify with and to see those in other ("they") groups as different. Too frequently, different does not mean "I'm OK, you're OK," but instead means that you are inferior and someone to be feared or oppressed. Evidence of such attitudes extends as far back into history as we can see. Genocide is a modern term, but the practice is ancient. The Roman philosopher and statesman Seneca (ca. 8 B.C.–A.D. 65) wrote in *Epistles* that Romans were "mad, not only individually, but nationally" because they punished "manslaughter and isolated murders" while accepting "the much vaunted crime of slaughtering whole peoples."

Other sources of discrimination and abuse of groups within a society or across borders come from any one or a combination of feelings of superiority, lack of tolerance, or lack of concern. For example, the status of women has always been determined in significant part by the traditional assumption of most men and even many women that male dominance is natural. The reasoning, Plato explained in *The Republic,* is that men are the "watchdogs of the flock" and should bear the burden of conducting war and "the other duties of guardianship," whereas "in these duties the light part must fall to the women because of the weakness of their sex." The work of Charles Darwin also lent a patina of scientific theory to the practice of male dominance, based on his argument in *The Descent of Man* (1871) that "man is more courageous, pugnacious and energetic than woman, and has a more inventive genius." Darwin went on to assert that "the chief distinction in the intellectual powers of the two sexes is [shown] by man's attaining to a higher eminence, in whatever he takes up, than can woman— whether requiring deep thought, reason, or imagination, or merely the use of the senses and hands." Such attitudes are less pervasive than they once were, but they continue to exist widely, and are especially strong in some societies. This was documented in a survey's finding that approval of gender equality ranged from a high of 82% in Western countries, through 60%–65% in Asia and sub-Saharan Africa, to 55% in Muslim countries (Inglehart & Norris, 2002, 2003).

Human Rights: Problems and Progress

With some exceptions, the abuses of individual and group rights occur within countries. As such, they have traditionally been treated as domestic matters and beyond the scope of world politics. This attitude is changing, and that in turn has brought international pressure on governments to respect the basic rights of their citizens.

Human Rights Problems

It is likely that you, like most of the people who read this book, live in the United States, Canada, or some other country where individual and group rights, while far from ideal, have progressed over time. Indeed, it is hard for those of us fortunate enough to live in such countries to imagine how widespread and how harsh oppression can be. Whether or not you agreed with the U.S.-led invasion of Iraq in 2003, there can be no doubt that President George Bush was correct in his 2004 State of the Union message when he asserted, "Had we failed to act . . . Iraq's torture chambers would still be filled with victims—terrified and innocent. The killing fields of Iraq— where hundreds of thousands of men and women and children vanished into the sands—would still be known only to the killers." The victims were not just individuals who opposed Saddam Hussein's regime. Whole groups were attacked with near genocidal intensity. The Sunni-dominated regime ruthlessly oppressed Shiite Muslim political activity and dealt even more harshly with the Kurds, many of whose villages were attacked with chemical weapons during the 1980s and then razed after survivors had been herded into trenches and executed by bullets to the brain. Detailing lurid tales of repression would be easy, for there are many, but perhaps it is best to turn to the data about the continuing widespread abuse of individual rights. Among other sources of evidence is one survey that ranked countries' respect for civil liberties such as freedom of religion and expression on a scale of 1 (free) to 7 (oppressive). Figure 14.3 illustrates that individual rights are still moderately to severely restricted in most of the world's countries. Indeed, 30% of all countries fall at or below the seriously oppressive score of 5. It is a sad note on the travails of the Iraqi people that their country had managed to progress from a 7 before the war to only a 6 in 2006.

Human Rights Progress

It would be naïve to argue that the world has even begun to come close to resolving its numerous human rights issues; it would be equally wrong to deny that a start has been made and that one aspect of globalization is the increased concern for and application of human rights principles (Cardenas, 2004; Tomuschat, 2004). The way to evaluate the worth of the efforts that we are about to discuss is to judge their goals and to see them as the beginnings of a process that only a few decades ago did not exist at all. Whatever country you live in, the protection of human rights has evolved over an extended period and is still far from complete. The global community has now embarked on an effort similar to your country's effort (Hawkins, 2004). It will take time, however, and it will be controversial (Monshipouri, et al., 2003).

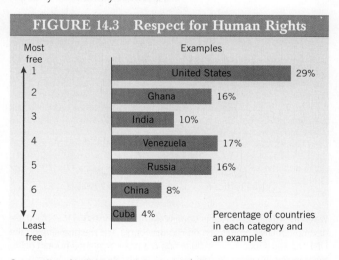

FIGURE 14.3 Respect for Human Rights

Most free

1 United States — 29%
2 Ghana — 16%
3 India — 10%
4 Venezuela — 17%
5 Russia — 16%
6 China — 8%
7 Cuba — 4%

Least free

Percentage of countries in each category and an example

Oppression of individual and group rights remains common. Although 45% of all countries fall into the laudable 1 and 2 categories, 28% fall into categories 5–7, which includes those countries where rights are tenuous at best and brutally abused at worst.

Note: Scores are based on a rating system of 1 to 7 used by Freedom House to evaluate civil liberties.
Data source: Freedom House, *Freedom House Survey 2006* at www.freedomhouse.org/. Calculations by author.

ANALYZE THE ISSUE
Human Rights

The UN is at the center of the international human rights effort. It has sponsored numerous human rights treaties that, along with human rights in general, are monitored by the Office of the United Nations High Commissioner on Human Rights (OHCHR).

From 1946 through early 2006, the UN Commission on Human Rights (UNCHR) was also a leading UN organization on human rights. It consisted of 53 member-countries elected for three-year terms by the United Nations Economic and Social Council (ECOSOC), and during its annual meetings it was often the site of clashes over human rights. However, it was plagued by numerous problems. One was a penchant for regularly condemning Israel for violating the rights of Arabs while just as regularly ignoring the human rights violations of many other countries. Adding to the dismay in many quarters about the commission, ECOSOC regularly named countries with poor human rights records as members. Making matters even worse, in 2003 the commission elected authoritarian Libya, which has a deplorable human rights record, to its chairmanship. Then in 2004, ECOSOC elected Sudan to the Commission virtually at the same time the Security Council was calling on Khartoum to cease its genocidal policies in Darfur.

Responding to such absurdities, the UN General Assembly in 2006 replaced the UNCHR with a new organization, the UN Human Rights Council (UNHRC). It is a 47-member body elected by the General Assembly, and its members are supposed to uphold the highest human rights standards. Nevertheless, the United States was one of the few countries that voted against creating the UNHRC, arguing that there was little to keep it from repeating the flaws of the UNCHR. Only time will tell, but the initial election of members was not especially auspicious. The scores of the 47 members using Freedom House's 2006 rating of countries' civil liberties record, from 1 (best) to 7 (awful), averaged a not-too-bad 2.6. However, 43% of the members fell into the dubious 4 and below categories, including Cuba with a bottom-dwelling score of 7. The details of the distribution of the council are in Figure 14.4. In another discouraging turn, the council soon followed the defunct UNCHR's practice of paying inordinate attention to alleged human rights abuses by Israel. This issue of objective balance soon led the UN secretary-general to write an open letter in which he said that to advance human rights, "We must realize the promise of the Human Rights Council, which so far has clearly not justified all the hopes that so many of us placed in it." The secretary-general went on to say that he was "worried by its disproportionate focus on violations by Israel," and he urged, "Instead, the Council's agenda should be broadened to reflect the actual abuses that occur in every part of the world."[7]

Concerns with the council led Washington to decline to seek a council seat in 2006 and again in 2007. A State Department official explained, "We believe that the [council] has thus far not proved itself to be a credible body in the mission that it has been charged with. There has been a nearly singular focus on issues related to Israel, for example, to the

FIGURE 14.4   UNHCR Member Rankings

7
2%

6
9%

1
21%

5
15%

2
21%

4
17%

3
15%

Percentage of council members with
civil liberties records from 1 (best) to 7 (worst)

When the UN Human Rights Council was created in 2006 to replace the discredited UN Commission on Human Rights, the membership on the UNHRC was supposed to include only countries with good human rights records. Yet the initial 47 members elected by the General Assembly fell short of that. This figure uses the Freedom House civil liberties score from 1 (best) to 7 (worst) that each council member earned in 2006. Laudably, 57% of the members earned scores of 3 and above, but 43% had dubious records of 4 and below. Indeed, 5 members (11%) were in the woeful 6 or 7 categories.

Data source: Civil liberties scores from Freedom House, *Freedom House Survey 2006* at www.freedomhouse.org/. Calculations by author.

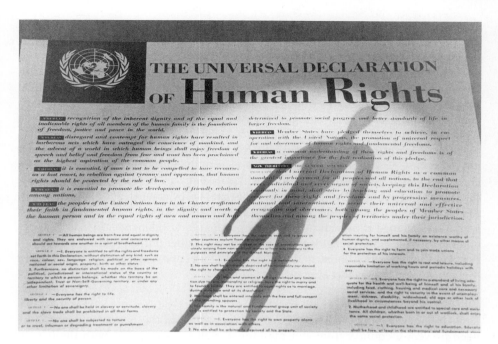

The UN's Universal Declaration of Human Rights was drafted in 1948. It is the most fundamental statement of global human rights, and most countries have agreed to it. The decision box at the end of this chapter asks your view of the various clauses of the declaration and whether you would call for any changes in these clauses or make additions.

exclusion of examining issues of real concern to the international system, whether that's in Cuba or Burma or in North Korea. . . . We hope that over time, that this body will expand its focus and become a more credible institution representative of the important mission with which it is charged."[8]

On a more positive note, there are a number of UN-sponsored human rights treaties that serve as standards for conduct (Neumayer, 2005). The most far-reaching is the **Universal Declaration of Human Rights**, which was overwhelmingly adopted by the UN General Assembly in 1948. The Universal Declaration clearly supports the universalist approach, rather than the relativist approach to human rights by declaring in Article 1, "All human beings are born free and equal in dignity and rights," and by further proclaiming in Article 2, "Everyone is entitled to all the rights and freedoms set forth in this Declaration, without distinction of any kind."

Because it is not a treaty, the declaration does not directly bind countries, but its overwhelming passage makes it arguably part of the global norms. Many of the rights enunciated in the Universal Declaration are also included in two multilateral treaties: the International Covenant on Civil and Political Rights (ICCPR, 1966) and the International Covenant on Economic, Social and Cultural Rights (ICESCR, 1966). Each pact has been ratified by more than 80% of all countries, but there are some major exceptions. For example, China has not become a party of the ICCPR, and the United States has not ratified the ICESCR. In addition to these two basic treaties and the Universal Declaration, there are numerous other UN-sponsored covenants that address the rights of specific groups, as will be detailed below.

There are also several multilateral treaties that address specific types of abuse. Of these, the Convention against Torture and Other Cruel, Inhuman or Degrading Treatment or Punishment (1984) has drawn considerable recent attention because of confirmed and alleged abuses of prisoners by U.S. personnel in Iraq, Afghanistan, and elsewhere. The treaty, to which the United States became a party in 1994, defines torture as "any act by which severe pain or suffering, whether physical or mental, is

ANALYZE THE ISSUE
The Rights of Our Enemies

intentionally inflicted on a person for such purposes as obtaining . . . information [or a confession]. Additionally, the treaty specifies, "No exceptional circumstances whatsoever, whether a state of war or a threat of war, internal political instability or any other public emergency, may be invoked as a justification of torture." Some low-ranking military personnel that committed indisputable abuses have been punished. However, the larger issue is whether the tactics authorized by the Bush administration for use during questioning of suspected terrorists (see chapter 9) violate the UN treaty.

A number of regional conventions and IGOs supplement the principles and efforts of the UN. The best developed of these are in the European Union (EU) and include two human rights covenants and the European Court of Human Rights. Domestic courts also increasingly apply human rights law (Jayawickrama, 2003). Additionally, many NGOs, such as Amnesty International and Human Rights Watch, are concerned with a broad range of human rights. These groups work independently and in cooperation with the UN and regional organizations to further human rights. They add to the swell of information about, and criticisms of, abuses and help promote the adoption of international norms that support human rights.

Barriers to Progress on Human Rights

Unfortunately, being a party to one, some, or even all of these treaties does not by itself prevent a country from abusing human rights. Iraq ratified both the ICCPR and the ICESCR in 1971, yet throughout its 33 years, Saddam Hussein's regime egregiously abused many, even most, of the rights set forth in both covenants. Indeed, the impact of such treaties, the efforts of IGOs and NGOs, and the general progress of human rights have, as noted, been mixed. One problem is sovereignty. Countries jealously guard it and reject outside criticism of their internal practices. When in 2007 a reporter asked a Chinese Foreign Ministry spokesperson about a resolution in Germany's Bundestag criticizing China's labor camps for political dissidents, he replied testily, "The question you mentioned involves China's internal affairs. We are opposed to irresponsible remarks on China's internal affairs by other countries including the German parliament."[9] Although the sovereignty argument as a defense has weakened, it still remains powerful. Smaller countries and those of the South are particularly sensitive to what they see as a pattern of powerful countries in the North criticizing weaker countries in the South while refusing to accept criticism themselves and generally being unwilling to criticize one another. Especially alarming for countries of the South is the assertion that such human rights violations give other countries the right to intervene, a course of action that is never contemplated with regard to a powerful EDC. Thus for many in the South, the human rights campaign seems tinged with neocolonialism and perhaps even racism.

A second and closely related impediment is the claim that cultural standards are different, and, therefore, what is a human rights violation in one country is culturally acceptable in another (De Bary, 2004). This is part of the argument discussed above about the source of law and whether cultural relativism is an acceptable standard. Like the matter of sovereignty, the issue of law based in cultural standards is particularly sensitive for the South since the Universal Declaration of Human Rights and, to a lesser degree, the ICCPR, the ICESCR, and some of the other major human rights treaties were written at a time when the UN was dominated by the West much more than it is today.

A third barrier is political selectivity, which disposes all countries to be shocked when opponents transgress human rights and to ignore abuses by themselves, by their allies, and by countries that they hope to influence. The United States regularly proclaims its commitment to the global spread of democracy, yet continues to support the governments of Saudi Arabia and several other unabashedly authoritarian regimes. Making matters worse, the self-proclaimed U.S. role of championing democracy and human rights was badly undercut by disclosures including secret prisons abroad under CIA auspices where prisoners could be questioned using tactics illegal in the United States; turning over prisoners for questioning by other governments that operate without the limits on prisoner treatment that bind American officials; and abuses inflicted on prisoners in Iraq at Abu Ghraib prison and elsewhere and on Muslim detainees at Guantánamo Bay. When the U.S. State Department issued its 2005 report on human rights and criticized numerous other countries, many of them retorted that, in essence, Americans should address their own abuses before pointing a finger at anyone else. The Russian Foreign Ministry charged that the report once again showed a "double standard" and that, "Characteristically off-screen is the ambiguous record of the United States itself." Venezuela's vice president portrayed the United States as "not qualified from any point of view" to lecture others on human rights, and a Mexican official said that Washington criticizing other countries' human rights records was like "the donkey talking about long ears"—the Spanish-language equivalent of "the pot calling the kettle black."[10]

Fourth, concern with human rights remains a fairly low priority for most countries. In the abstract, most people support advancing human rights, but in more applied situations it becomes clear that support is shallow. For example, a recent survey that asked people in the United States and India about important foreign policy goals for their country found that promoting human rights ranked 11th of 14 possible goals among Americans and 11th of 11 goals presented to Indians.[11] It can also be said, however, that while still not at the forefront of concern of most people, the importance given to human rights has increased in recent years, as Figure 14.5 indicates, and that increased sensitivity is strengthening international pressure on those abusing the rights of others.

Thus, while it would be wrong to overestimate the advance of human rights, it would equally be an error not to recognize that progress has been achieved in the advancement of human rights by declarations of principle, by numerous treaties, and by the work of the UN, Amnesty International, and other IGOs and NGOs. The frequency and horror of the abuses that they highlight are increasingly penetrating the international consciousness, disconcerting the global conscience, and having a positive effect on the world stage. To see that more clearly and to also see how much remains to be done, it is appropriate to turn to the status of human rights for women, children, and several other groups.

Women's Rights

In our discussion of the status of the rights of a diversity of demographic groups, it is appropriate that we begin with the largest of all minority groups, women. The status of women has improved in recent decades, but only somewhat and slowly.

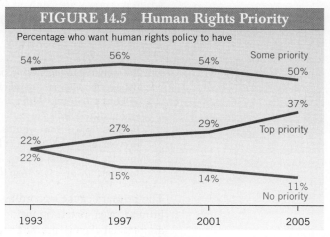

FIGURE 14.5 Human Rights Priority

Percentage who want human rights policy to have

54%   56%   54%   Some priority
  50%

  37%
22%   27%   29%   Top priority
22%

15%   14%   11%
No priority

1993   1997   2001   2005

Most people, including Americans, give less foreign policy priority to defending and promoting the human rights of others than to such matters as protecting jobs from foreign competition and combating terrorism. Still, it is clear here that the percentage of Americans who rank human rights as their top priority has increased steadily and those who see human rights as unimportant has declined steadily.

Note: Data for those who were unsure, 2–3% each year, is omitted.
Data source: Pew Research Center and Chicago Council on Foreign Relations, *America's Place in the World, 2005.*

Women's Rights Problems

Economic and educational deprivations seem to pale when compared to the violence inflicted on women. They are subject to abuse during international and internal armed conflicts and to domestic abuse in their homes.

Political, Economic, and Social Discrimination   Females constitute about half the world's population, but they are a distinct political-economic-social minority because of the wide gap in their societal power and resources compared to men. Chapter 6 detailed this gap with respect to political power, noting among other things that only about 5% of countries are headed by women; they make up only about 8% of all national cabinet ministers, 17% of the membership of national legislatures, and about 9% of the world's judges. In a few countries women are still not allowed to vote, much less hold national office. Women are also disadvantaged economically. Compared to men, women are much less likely to have a salaried job or to hold a professional position. There is no country in the world where women wage earners make as much as men, and in a majority of countries women earn salaries that are less than half of what men make. An even more compelling statistic is that women globally constitute 70% of all those living below the poverty line. Women also suffer from a range of types of social discrimination. In many countries they are less likely than men to be literate or, if educated, go on to secondary school, let alone college or technical training. The degree of gender discrimination differs significantly among countries, with the gap between men and women generally narrower in economically developed countries (EDCs) than in less developed countries (LDCs). Nevertheless, female disadvantages are universal, as the Gender Gap map in chapter 5, page 160 shows.

Women, Armed Conflict, and Abuse   The image of men fighting and dying in wars while women wait safely at home is substantially a myth. In many armed conflicts, women noncombatants suffer as much or more than male soldiers and civilians. A recent UN Development Fund for Women (UNIFEM) report, *War, Women, and Peace* (2002), begins with the observation of the study panel members that,

> We were completely unprepared for the searing magnitude of what we saw and heard in the conflict and post-conflict areas we visited . . . [and] for the horrors women described. Wombs punctured with guns. Women raped and tortured in front of their husbands and children. Rifles forced into vaginas. Pregnant women beaten to induce miscarriages. Fetuses ripped from wombs. Women kidnapped, blindfolded, and beaten on their way to work or school. We heard accounts of gang rapes, rape camps, and mutilation. Of murder and sexual slavery. We saw scars of brutality so extreme that survival seemed for some a worse fate than death.

The primary cause, according to the report, is that women's "bodies become a battleground over which opposing forces struggle." Rape, forced impregnation and birth, and sexual slavery are not uncommon, and women are also kidnapped and used as servants to soldiers. To escape such fates, many women flee and become refugees. In fact, up to 80% of all refugees from violence are women and their children. Such women find themselves in dire conditions. Many die of disease; others "are forced . . . to become sex workers . . . their bodies . . . a form of exchange that buys the necessities of life" (p. 11). Desperation often continues after women return home to face razed dwellings, dead husbands and other family members, and no means of economic support. Much of this goes unnoticed. As the UNIFEM report puts it, "Violence against women in conflict is one of history's great silences."

Women, Society, and Abuse   All the abuses noncombatant women suffer are but a small proportion of physical abuse that women endure globally. According to the UN, at least one-third of all women have been beaten, coerced into sex, or otherwise abused at least once in their life, and, depending on the country, 40% to 70% of all female murder victims are killed during domestic violence.

Another form of assault on women comes through sex-selective abortions or female infanticide. Globally, there are about 60 million fewer girls (age 0 to 15) than normal population figures would expect. The reason is that female fetuses are aborted more often than male fetuses after ultrasound technology is used to determine sex or, more grimly, infant girls are killed outright or allowed to die through neglect more often than boys. The UN estimates that in India 7,000 fewer baby girls are born each day than normally expected. The problem is even more severe in China, as evident in Figure 14.6, where among the 85 million children through age 4, there are 6.4 million more boys than girls. "Society needs to recognize this discrimination," a recent UN Population Fund (UNFPA) study counsels. "Girls have a right to live just as boys do. Moreover, a missing number of either sex, and the resulting imbalance can destroy the social and human fabric as we know it."[12]

Other girls are subjected to female genital mutilation (FGM), sometimes euphemistically called female circumcision. This procedure ranges in severity from, at minimum, a clitoridectomy (the excision of the clitoris), which deprives a female of all sexual sensation, to infibulation, the cutting away of all of a female's external genitalia and labial tissue. It is widely performed on adolescent and preadolescent girls in central and North Africa, and the UN estimates that as many as 130 million women and girls alive currently have undergone the procedure and that each year another 2 million are subjected to it. Beyond the psychological trauma, FGM, which is usually performed by individuals without medical training operating in unsanitary settings, is extraordinarily painful and dangerous, carrying a significant rate of infection.

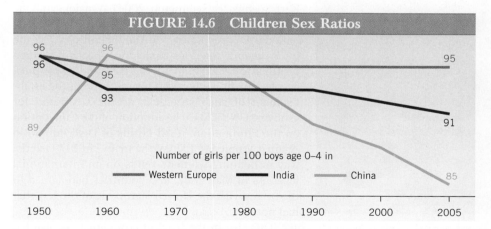

FIGURE 14.6   Children Sex Ratios

Number of girls per 100 boys age 0–4 in

—— Western Europe   —— India   —— China

Arguably a genocidal attack on females is occurring in some parts of the world through the abortion of female fetuses and the killing of female infants. This figure shows how many girls there were for every 100 boys ages 0 to 4 in the populations of Western Europe, China, and India between 1950 and 2005. Without outside intervention, it is normal for about 4% fewer girls than boys to be born. Therefore the ratio of about 96 girls per 100 boys is "normal" in the natural sense. As you can see here, Western Europe has maintained close to that ratio, but in India and even more in China, the ratio of girls has declined considerably. The low ratio for China in 1950 probably reflects female infanticide during the very difficult times surrounding World War II and the Communist Revolution.

Data source: UN Population Data Base.

Another unhappy fate awaits the impoverished women in many countries who annually are sold or forced to go into de facto slavery in their own countries or abroad. According to the UN, "human trafficking" is the world's third largest commercial enterprise, earning at least $39 billion annually. The International Labour Organization (ILO) estimates that 1.2 million people a year are trafficked. About 80% of them are women and girls.[13] Some become domestic servants, who are often mistreated. The sale of young women and even girls (and young men and boys) into heterosexual or homosexual slavery is also relatively common in some places. Most of the women in sexual servitude are located in the LDCs, but many are also in the EDCs. All countries have laws against sexual slavery and child prostitution, but some governments do little to enforce them. Economic incentives are one reason that governments ignore the problem. Prostitution is a huge business in Southeast Asia, as elsewhere, and the UN has estimated that the revenue generated by sex tourism and other aspects of the illicit sexual trade ranges between 2% and 14% of the GNPs of Indonesia, Malaysia, Thailand, and the Philippines.[14] According to the UN report, the "revenues [the sex trade] generated are crucial to the livelihoods and earning potential of millions of workers beyond the prostitutes themselves."

Women's Rights Progress

Numerous international human rights efforts in recent years have focused on women, and progress has been made in defining the maltreatment of women as a global problem, identifying some of the causes and worst abuses, and enumerating women's rights (Johnstone, 2006). This has placed the issue of women solidly on the international agenda (Antrobus, 2004; Kerr, Spenger, & Symington, 2004). A major symbolic step occurred when the UN declared 1975 as International Women's Year and the kickoff of a Decade for Women. Numerous conferences brought women together to document their status. Funding for projects to benefit women was begun through the establishment of such structures as the UN Fund for Women (UNIFEM). The adoption of the **Convention on the Elimination of All Forms of Discrimination Against Women (CEDAW, the treaty)** in 1979 led the way in defining women's rights on an international level. As of May 2007, 185 countries had agreed to the treaty, with the United States one of the few that had not.

This rise in the level of consciousness also led the UN to create the Division for the Advancement of Women, which is responsible for addressing women's issues and promoting their rights. In this role, the division administratively supports both the Commission on the Status of Women (CSW), which is the main UN policy-making body for women, and the Committee on the Elimination of Discrimination Against Women (CEDAW, the committee), which monitors

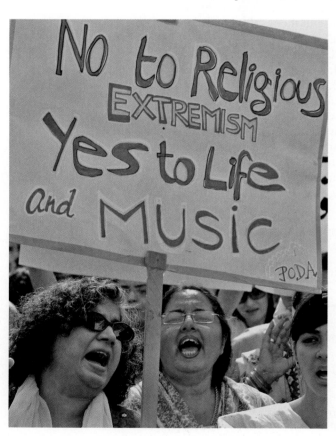

Women's rights have advanced almost everywhere in the world in recent decades, but much remains to be done. First, there is no country where men and women are equal. Second, the advances that women have made are threatened in some places. These members of the Potohar Organization for Development Advocacy (PODA) are chanting "Down with Talibanization" during a 2007 rally in Islamabad, Pakistan. The chant refers to the ousted Taliban regime in Afghanistan, which had denied almost all rights to women. Also reflected is the worry of the women shown here that the growing strength of Islamic fundamentalism in Pakistan will result in its Talibanization.

the implementation of the 1979 convention on women's rights. The division has also organized four UN world conferences on women.

Of these, the most important was the fourth **World Conference on Women (WCW)**. It convened in Beijing in 1995, and 180 countries sent some 3,000 delegates. Additionally, about 30,000 delegates representing some 2,000 NGOs gathered nearby at the parallel NGO convention. The combined meetings constituted the largest conclave of women in history. Not only were their already formidable network of women's groups strengthened, but their message was carried outward by the 2,500 reporters who covered the conferences. The WCW demanded an end to discrimination against and the abuse of women, called for their economic empowerment, and urged public and private organizations to lend their moral and economic support to the cause of advancing the status of women worldwide. These stands were not binding on states, but they set a standard that has had an impact. The following year, for example, the Hague tribunal for war crimes in the Balkans for the first time held that sexual abuse was a war crime and indicted eight Bosnian Serb soldiers for the rape of Bosnian Muslim women.

Five years later a special UN General Assembly session and a parallel NGO conference, collectively called the Beijing +5 Conference, brought 10,000 delegates together in New York City to review the progress of the goals adopted by the WCW. In addition to continuing with important networking and exerting pressure on governments to address women's issues, Beijing +5 adopted goals such as increasing the availability and affordability of treatment for women and girls with HIV and AIDS.

Finally, there have been advances in other contexts to further the rights of women. One notable stride, which is discussed in chapter 9, was the recent founding of various international tribunals that are trying individuals for rape, among other crimes against humanity. To cite just one example, in 2007 the tribunal for war crimes in the Balkans that sits in The Hague, the Netherlands, sentenced Bosnian Serb Radovan Stankovic to 20 years in prison for the mass rapes, torture, and enslavement of Bosnian Muslim women in 1992. The recent creation of the **International Criminal Court (ICC)** offers further hope for the protection of women. Its charter defines war crimes to include violence "committed as part of a widespread or systematic attack directed against any civilian population," including such offenses as "rape, sexual slavery, enforced prostitution, forced pregnancy, enforced sterilization, or any other form of sexual violence of comparable gravity." The ICC, now investigating alleged war crimes, including sexual abuse, in Sudan and other countries, is described by MADRE, a U.S.-based women's rights NGO, as "a critical new tool in the defense of human rights for women and their families around the world."[15]

There is also evidence that the rising international condemnation of the abuse of women is having some impact on norms and practices within countries. Data for a number of societal opportunity measures indicates that the gap between men and women is narrowing. For example, the difference in the literacy rate of men and women worldwide narrowed from 13% in 1990 to 10% in 2005. During that time, there has been a 7% increase in percentage of national legislative seats held by women. Women's share of paying jobs in the manufacturing and service sectors has increased 3.5% to 35%. The percentage of countries with laws against domestic violence has nearly doubled to 47%. Regarding a more specific concern, several countries where FGM has been practiced have passed laws against it, and there are indications that the procedure is on the decline. Women in Kuwait won the right to vote and to hold office in 2005, and nearby Yemen ratified CEDAW, created a Ministry of Human Rights, and appointed a woman as its first head. All these advances and many more are also

Web Link

One of the many NGOs promoting the rights of women is the International Women's Rights Action Watch at **http://iwraw.igc.org/**.

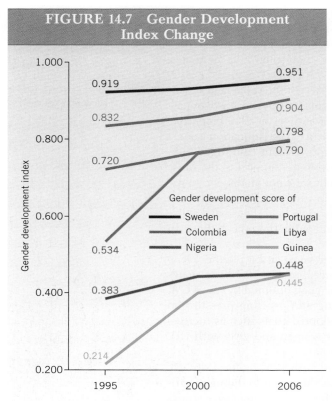

FIGURE 14.7 Gender Development Index Change

The UN Development Programme's Gender Development Index evaluates the status of women compared to men by country using several health, education, and economic criteria. A score of 1.000 would mean statistical equality. In general terms, a 0.900 means women measure 90% compared to men's 100%, a 0.600 means 60% as equal, and so on. This figure shows the scores since 1995 for that year's top-ranked country (Sweden) and the countries ranked 25 (Portugal), 50 (Colombia), 75 (Libya), 100 (Nigeria), and 125 (Guinea) of the 130 ranked countries. Notice the upward trend of all countries.

Data source: UNDP, *Human Development Report* (1995, 2000, 2006). Calculations by author.

evident in the upward trend shown in Figure 14.7 of the Gender Development Index (GDI), a measure of women's conditions relative to men using a variety of health, education, and economic measures. Surely, reforms have come slowly, and there continues to be significant global disparity in the conditions of men and women across the political-social-economic spectrum. Yet there has been progress.

Children's Rights

Children are not commonly considered a political group, but they are perhaps the most vulnerable of all humans. Also, children have rights like all humans, and those rights are all too often violated (Ensalaco & Majka, 2005).

Children's Rights Problems

If anything, the abuses that children suffer globally have received even less notice than those of women. In addition to the lack of adequate nutrition, medical care, and education that prevent a vast number of children in many countries from achieving a fulfilling life or even surviving at all, they endure a variety of abuses. Being forced to work is one of them. According the International Labour Organization (ILO), there are 246 million children aged 5 to 14 who are performing more than light or casual economic work. About 75% of these children do hazardous work. Among children ages 5 to 9, 12% work, and nearly 25% between ages 10 and 14 do so. Adding further to the problem, about half these children age 10 and under work full-time and do not go to school. Child labor ranges from about 2% of all children in the EDCs to as high as 29% in sub-Saharan Africa.

The most disturbing statistics of all relate to the 8.4 million children involved in what the ILO terms "unconditional worst forms of child labor." This includes children in five categories (and the number of children in each): internationally trafficked children (1.2 million), forced and bonded labor (5.7 million), armed conflict (so-called boy soldiers, 0.3 million), prostitution and pornography (1.8 million), and illicit activities (such as drug sales, 0.6 million). Child prostitution is especially prevalent in southern Asia and Latin America. There are many reasons—ranging from abuse at home to economic desperation—why children turn to prostitution; it is also the case that many children are sold by their families. A recent UN report related the example of Lam, a 15-year-old Vietnamese girl who was sold by her grandmother to purveyors for a brothel in Cambodia. According to the report, the price for girls like Lam ranges between $50 and $200. Other individuals are kidnapped by sex-slavers to supply the multibillion-dollar sex trade. An astronomical rate of AIDS and other sexually transmitted diseases are among the myriad dangers these children face.

The treatment of children is certainly the proper concern of national governments, but it is also an international issue. It is estimated that each year 10 to 12 million men travel internationally as "sex tourists" to exploit children. An unknown but substantial number of children are transported across international borders for sexual purposes, and technology has brought child pornography to the Internet. Clothes, shoes, and other products manufactured by children are sold in international trade; you may be wearing one of these products even as you read these words. The wars and civil strife that ruin the lives of boy soldiers and other children are often rooted in world affairs.

Children's Rights Progress

Serious international efforts to protect children's rights were symbolically kicked off in 1979, which the UN designated as the International Year of the Child. The United Nations Children's Fund (UNICEF) is the most important agency promoting the rights of children, but it is supported by numerous other IGOs and NGOs. Their common goal, in the words of UNICEF's executive director, is to "ensure that exploitive and hazardous child labor becomes as unacceptable in the next century as slavery has become in this. Children should be students in school, not slaves in factories, fields, or brothels."[16]

One advance is the **Convention on the Rights of the Child** (1989). It defines a wide range of collective and individual rights in such areas as the sexual exploitation of children, the use of boy soldiers, and the diversion of children from their education to work. The convention garnered enough ratifications to go into force in less than a year and also quickly became the most widely ratified human rights treaty in history. Indeed, as of mid-2007, every country in the world save the United States and the failed state of Somalia was party to the treaty. Among other U.S. concerns was whether the convention would abridge the possibility in some U.S. states that minors convicted of capital crimes can be executed once they reach age 18. However as noted in chapter 9, the U.S. Supreme Court declared such executions unconstitutional in the 2005 case *Roper v. Simmons,* and that could open the way for U.S. ratification of the treaty. Whatever the U.S. concerns, the treaty has begun to protect children. Under it and other global prohibitions against the use of boy soldiers, the UN's tribunal prosecuting war crimes in Sierra Leone convicted three former rebel commanders in June 2007 of a range of offenses including, for the first time in any international court, forcing children to be combatants.

Children's rights have also been advanced through a series of global conferences. In 1990, top officials from 156 countries met at the World Summit for Children at UN headquarters, adopted the Declaration on the Survival, Protection and Development of Children, and put forth a 10-point Plan of Action. The world's countries also joined together during the first (1996) and second (2001) World Congresses Against Commercial Sexual Exploitation of Children. Such international meetings serve a valuable function by focusing attention on issues and defining international norms.

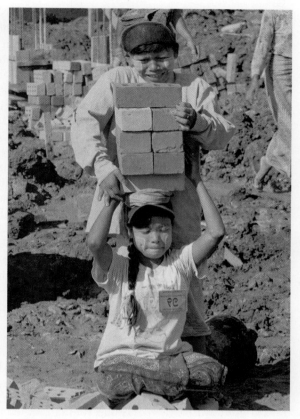

Ending child labor is a major goal of the International Labor Organization, a leader in the effort to create a world where scenes such as the one pictured here cease to exist. This young girl is carrying bricks at a construction site in Myanmar rather than going to school and playing as she should be. Bricks such as the eight she is carrying weigh between 3 and 4 kilos each, meaning that the total weight pressing down on her neck and spine is between 53 and 71 pounds.

As one official of the first congress noted, "There can be no more delusions—no one can deny that the problem of children being sold for sex exists, here and now, in almost every country in the world."[17]

The increasing awareness of child labor and determination to end it is also evident in many other ways. For example, an ILO-sponsored international conference led to an agreement known as the Worst Forms of Child Labour Convention (1999). The convention bars the use of children for any form of compulsory labor similar to slavery (including being forced to become a child soldier), for illicit activities (prostitution, pornography, drug trafficking), and for work that is inherently dangerous. As of mid-2007, the treaty had been ratified by 163 countries and become part of international law, although the continuing absence of India as a party is a particular concern. A report by the head of the ILO also cites evidence of progress in such factors as the number of countries passing new or tougher child labor laws and the adoption of codes of conduct by multinational corporations barring the use of child laborers. "The global challenge remains daunting," the ILO director-general concedes in the report, but he also advised, "We can take heart that already there has been a great deal of progress achieved in knowledge and experience, as well as an impressive worldwide movement to combat child labor."[18]

Ethnic, Racial, and Religious Group Rights

Among humans, the "we–they" complex is most destructive when it engenders hostility toward "others" and often violent oppression of "others" based on their ethnicity, race, and religion. There is hope, though. Tolerance can be taught to many, and it can be enforced for those who do not want to learn.

Group Rights Problems

Strife and oppression based on ethnicity, race, and religion remain common. There are racial and religious overtones in the gruesome violence in Sudan between the government dominated by Arab-heritage Muslims and the black Muslims in the western region of Darfur. Fighting between the mostly Buddhist Sinhalese who control the government and the mostly Hindu Tamil minority has beset Sri Lanka for many years. People in Northern Ireland have traditionally divided themselves between warring Protestant and Catholic factions, and in Cyprus fences and troops separate Greek-heritage citizens from Turkish-heritage citizens. Religious fundamentalism has strengthened in recent decades and has sparked numerous efforts in India, Israel, several Muslim countries, and elsewhere to align the legal codes and religious laws of their respective countries and to force everyone, regardless of their personal beliefs, to follow those theocratic laws. It hangs in the balance whether Iraq will become a tolerant democracy, an oppressive quasi-theocracy, or will dissolve into civil war among Shiite Muslims, Sunni Muslims, and Kurdish Muslims. Even in countries where there is no move to supplant civil with theocratic law, religious intimidation is not uncommon.

Most of the worst instances of oppression are in the LDCs, but the EDCs do not escape the stain. The persecution of Jews and Gypsies, properly called Roma, did not perish with Adolf Hitler's Nazi Third Reich. Instead, they persist in Europe and elsewhere. In 2005, the European Court of Human Rights found racist motivations in an incident in Romania in which an altercation between Romas and ethnic Romanians ended when Romanians, encouraged by police, surrounded a house where several Roma men were hiding and set it on fire. One man burned to death; those who fled the flames were beaten to death. Charges brought against the town police were

Web Link

One way to learn more about child labor is to see the documentary *Stolen Childhoods* released in 2005. More on the film and about how to get involved in halting child labor can be found at **www.stolenchildhoods.org/mt/index.php.**

Web Link

Learn more about the Roma and their human rights concerns at **http://www.romani.org/index.html.**

dismissed by a Romanian court, which commented, "The Roma community has marginalized itself, shown aggressive behavior and deliberately denied and violated the legal norms acknowledged by society. Most of the Roma have no occupation and earn their living by doing odd jobs, stealing, and engaging in all kinds of illicit activities."[19]

Anti-Semitism also troubles Europe and other EDCs. Between 1989 and 2006, Tel Aviv University's annual review on global anti-Semitism recorded a twelvefold increase in major anti-Semitic incidents to 572. Russia is one country with a worrisome record. There a poll found 59% of Russians agreeing with the statement, "Jews have too much power in the world of business." Such attitudes are evident even in the government. In a 2005 incident, 20 members of the Duma, Russia's parliament, called for a ban of all Jewish groups. The legislators claimed, "The whole democratic world today is under the financial and political control of the Jews. We would not want our Russia, which is subject to a permanent illegal war seeking to prevent its rebirth, to find itself among unfree countries."[20] President Vladimir Putin and the Duma both condemned the idea, but they imposed no sanctions on the offending legislators. The list of ethnic, racial, and religious divisions, oppression, and violence could go on at length, but that is not necessary here. Chapter 4 details the world's ethnonational divisions and chapter 5 does the same for religion. The question is what is being done to address the problem.

Group Rights Progress

The international effort to increase ethnic, racial, and religious tolerance and to eliminate their worst forms quickly is only a few decades old. It has made progress, but negative attitudes are so widespread and deep-seeded that change has been limited.

One early notable advance came in South Africa. Years of international pressure through economic sanctions and other penalties finally compelled South African whites to surrender political power in 1994, ending official racism through the apartheid system that permitted 6.5 million whites to dominate the other 29 million black, Asian, and "colored" (mixed-race) people.

The global effort to combat intolerance has also been furthered by three international conferences. The first two met in Geneva, Switzerland, in 1978 and 1983. The third, the World Conference against Racism, Racial Discrimination, Xenophobia and Related Intolerance (WCAR) convened in Durban, South Africa, in 2001 and brought together official delegations from 160 countries. Like most UN conferences, there was also an unofficial parallel conference that included representatives of hundreds of NGOs ranging alphabetically from ABC Ulwazi (South Africa) to the Zoroastrian Women's Organization (Iran).

Unfortunately the Durban conference fell into acrimonious debate over two issues. One was the demand by African delegates that the United States and the countries of Western Europe that had once been involved in the slave trade apologize and pay reparations. The other sore point was the effort by Muslim countries to label Israel a "racist apartheid state" and to demand an end to the "ongoing Israeli systematic perpetration of racist crimes, including war crimes, genocide, and ethnic cleansing."[21] When some countries insisted on bringing a resolution with this language to a vote, Canada and several European countries downgraded their delegations, and the U.S. delegation walked out of the conference. Secretary of State Colin Powell said he regretted doing so, but added, "I know that you do not combat racism by conferences that produce declarations containing hateful language," he concluded.[22]

More positively, efforts to define the rights of ethnic, racial, and religious groups have been part of the major human rights documents such as the International Covenant on Economic, Social, and Cultural Rights and the Convention on the Prevention and Punishment of the Crime of Genocide. There have also been some specific agreements, such as the **International Convention on the Elimination of All Forms of Racial Discrimination** (1969). It is a step forward that 170 countries, including the United States, have been willing to agree to this document, which, among other things, proclaims that its signatories are "convinced that . . . there is no justification for racial discrimination, in theory or in practice, anywhere."

There are also regional efforts. At a 2005 conference in Sofia, Bulgaria, eight countries (Bulgaria, Croatia, the Czech Republic, Hungary, Macedonia, Romania, Serbia and Montenegro, and Slovakia) pledged to begin a 10-year program to improve the social and economic status of Eastern Europe's Roma people. One observer optimistically noted, "There has been a huge lack of political will on behalf of the countries that are now participating in this effort," and called it "a huge leap forward in this respect." More cautiously, a Roma activist commented, "It is now at the level of good will and speeches. How it will work we will have to wait and see."[23] Both were right.

Enforcement of the standards of tolerance and equality have been limited, but they have not been absent. The earlier international pressure on South Africa to end legal racism was an important step. The international tribunals investigating and trying war crimes committed in the Balkans and in Rwanda are further evidence that persecution based on ethnicity, race, or religion are increasingly considered an affront to the global conscience, as are the investigations that the ICC has begun into atrocities in Sudan and elsewhere.

The Rights of Indigenous Peoples

World history is a story of mass migrations and conquests that have often left indigenous people as minority groups in national political systems imposed on them. All together, there are approximately 5,000 indigenous groups with more than 300 million people residing in more than 70 countries on five continents.

Indigenous Peoples' Rights Problems

Most of the world's indigenous peoples live in socioeconomic circumstances below those of the non-native population of their country. For example, the socioeconomic status of Mexico's indigenous peoples, such as the Mayas, is 21% below that of the country's general population according to the UNDP. There is also a long history in many countries of trying to force indigenous groups to adopt mainstream culture by giving up their language, customs, and other aspects of their culture.

One of the particular efforts of indigenous peoples in recent years has been their attempt to protect their traditional home areas from the incursion of the surrounding cultures. For example, the influx of people and commercial activities such as logging and mining into the vast interior areas of the Amazon River system has increasingly degraded the health, environment, and other aspects of the life of the indigenous peoples of that region such as the Yanomami of Brazil and Venezuela. The Yanomami (which means "human being") had little contact with outsiders before the mid-1980s when the lure of gold brought prospectors and miners far up Brazil's rivers and into the Yanomami's forest retreats. The invasion has left the Yanomami devastated by diseases, by mercury and other toxins brought by the miners, and, on occasion, by violence aimed at forcing the tribe off its lands. Their numbers have shrunk since the mid-1980s by about 10%, to 19,000.

Indigenous Peoples' Rights Progress

The UN proclaimed 1993 to be the International Year of the Indigenous Peoples. The following year, representatives of some of the more than 5,000 indigenous peoples agreed to an International Covenant on the Rights of Indigenous Nations that pre-scribed relations among the groups and between each of them and the country in which it is located. The increased focus on the plight of many groups led the UN to further designate 1995 to 2004 as the International Decade of the Indigenous Peoples and to subsequently extend that to a second decade (2005–2014). Additionally, in 2000 the UN Economic and Social Council established the UN Permanent Forum on Indigenous Issues (UNPFII) as an advisory body. Its purpose, declared Mary Robinson, UN High Commissioner for Human Rights, is "to give indigenous peoples a unique voice within the United Nations system."[24] The UNPFII has a permanent staff, meets annually, and serves to study problems faced by indigenous populations and to bring those issues to the attention of the UN and other IGOs. The efforts of indigenous people have also been furthered by numerous NGOs, including the International Indian Treaty Council, the World Council of Indigenous Peoples, the Inuit Circumpolar Conference, and the Unrepresented Nations and Peoples' Organization. The causes of indigenous peoples were also furthered when the Nobel Peace Prize Committee made its 1992 award to Rigoberta Menchú of Guatemala in recognition of her efforts to advance the rights of her Mayan people in her country and to further the welfare of indigenous people globally.

Refugee and Migrant Workers' Rights

Driven by war, economic desperation, and other factors, the movement of humans ranging from individuals to entire nations has occurred throughout history. "Migration is the visible face of social change," a report by UNFPA explains.[25] This face is evident in the early 21st century. In 2006 according to the United Nations High Commissioner for Refugees (UNHCR) there were 8.4 million people in the UNHCR's "core con-stituency," those who have fled their country to a neighboring country because of violence, famine, or some other disaster. The largest single group is Afghanis, 1.9 mil-lion of whom no longer live in their country. While still distressingly high, the core constituency is below its peak in the 1990s, as indicated in Figure 14.8. In addition to these international refugees, there were 12.4 million people who the UNHCR calls "internally displaced persons," those who have been displaced within their own countries, or who otherwise fell into one of the agency's refugee categories. Beyond those classes of people and beyond the UNHCR data, many millions of others have legally or illegally entered other countries to find work.

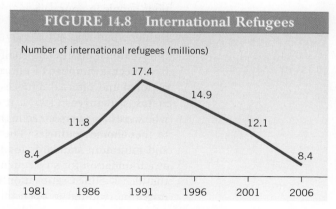

FIGURE 14.8   International Refugees

Number of international refugees (millions)

Although the number of refugees living outside their home country has declined since its peak in the early 1990s because of reduced ethnonational violence (see chapter 4), there is still a huge number of displaced people in the world who have been forced from their homelands by violence, hunger, and other causes.

Data source: UNHCR.

Refugee and Migrant Workers' Rights Problems

Human history is a story of populations either mi-grating in their entirety or expanding to new territo-ries. When those on the move or expanding have come to dominate their new homes, they have often reduced the indigenous population to second-class citizenship, as discussed in the section above. Where the newcomers have not dominated, it is they who have often been relegated to second-class status or even worse through discrimination and nativist violence against them. This latter pattern is a tale of current times, and the tide of refugees and immigrants, legal and illegal, has been met with increasing resistance. When asked whether immigrants have a good or bad effect on their country, a plurality of people in almost two-thirds of the 41 countries surveyed replied bad. Moreover, almost three-fourth of all respondents favored stricter controls on immigration, with at least 61% of people in each geographic region taking that position.[26]

To a degree, the feelings against immigrants, refugees, and others entering a country may result from racial, ethnic, religious, and other biases. But there are other causes. As discussed in chapter 5, people in most countries see their national cultures being diluted by the cross-acculturation associated with globalization. Coping with refugees and economically driven illegal immigrants is costly, whether you are trying to keep people out or trying to assist those who have been admitted or who have slipped in. Such costs can be a severe strain for LDCs that suffer a large influx of refugees, and the funds available through the UN and other IGOs and private NGOs are almost never adequate to fully house, feed, and otherwise care for the refugees.

Whatever attitudes may be about refugees and immigrants, it is certain that the tide will persist as long as people in some countries are subject to endemic violence and poverty. Immigration reform has become a major issue in the United States, for example, and a major component of the suggested response to the millions of illegal aliens coming into the country from Mexico and elsewhere in Latin America is to increase the number of border guards, build a long fence, and otherwise create physical barriers. These can lower the stream, but in the long run it might be better to address the cause by helping the South develop quickly and achieve political stability so that it can provide its people reasonable sustenance and safety. It is conceivable that if Mexico's standard of living were to increase substantially, for example, many of its citizens would no longer undergo the dislocation and risk the physical danger entailed in leaving home and slipping into the United States. "We have a good argument now, a very concrete one," for helping the LDCs, the prime minister of Denmark told a UN conference, "which is, if you don't help the Third World . . . , then you will have these poor people in your society."

Refugee and Migrant Workers' Rights Progress

International efforts on behalf of refugees have provided very mixed results. There have been a number of efforts to define the status and the rights of both international and internal refugees. An early effort was the Convention Relating to the Status of Refugees (1951). It charged the UN with providing assistance to people who were being persecuted in their countries or who feared persecution if they returned to their home countries. The convention also defined the basic rights of refugees and minimum standards for their treatment and has served, among other things, as a foundation for subsequent efforts on behalf of refugees. It is also true, though, that it has gained ratifications only slowly because some countries worry that they might be required to open their borders to refugees or extend rights to those who managed to arrive unbidden. As of mid-2007, only 144 countries had ratified the convention, with the United States and India prominent among the countries that had not.

Aid to refugees, while scant compared to their actual need, presents a somewhat brighter picture. The effort on behalf of displaced persons in the early 1950s led to the creation of the UNHCR in 1951 with wide responsibility for refugee rights and needs. Among other things, it oversees the feeding and sheltering of refugees and works toward restoring them to their homes. The agency has a staff of about 6,700, who are located in 116 countries, and a budget of $1.5 billion (2005), or about $77 for each of the 19.5 million people it was trying to help that year. Most of the UNHCR's funding comes from voluntary contributions by countries, with the United States accounting for about one-third. A related IGO, also formed in 1951, is the International Organization for Migration (IOM). It has 120 member-countries and an annual budget over $700 million, and it is concerned with the movement of refugees either to new homes or back to their former homes, as appropriate. Additionally, there are a number of NGOs, such as the International Red Cross (and its Muslim counterpart, the International Red Crescent), Oxfam, and others, that are involved in providing food, clothes, shelter, and other necessities.

Although migrant workers are not refugees as such, their transnational status makes them an international issue. However, most countries have not been willing to recognize any international role in protecting the rights of migrant workers and their families. Indicative of that attitude is the history of the Convention on the Protection of the Rights of All Migrant Workers and Members of Their Families. It extends the rights noted in several other UN human rights to all migrants, both legal and illegal, and obligates states to protect their rights equally with citizens. The UN submitted the treaty to states for ratification in 1990, but few have responded positively. As of 2007, only 36 countries were party to the treaties, and none of these included the United States or any other EDC.

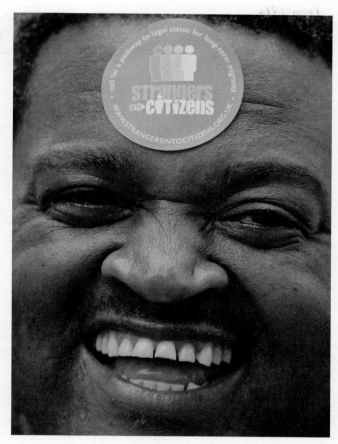

Whether it is Latin Americans in the United States, North Africans in France, Turks in Germany, or other people in another country, the presence and the rights of documented and undocumented immigrants from poor countries is an increasing point of contention globally. This man represents the side of the debate that such immigrants should be given greater support. He is a participant in a 2007 march in London and is displaying a sticker with the logo of the British NGO, Strangers into Citizens.

PRESCRIPTIVE HUMAN RIGHTS

Compared to the proscriptive rights that we have been discussing, prescriptive human rights are much less often recognized or enumerated by countries or in international law. Yet they exist. South Africa's post-apartheid constitution (1996), for one, obligates the government to ensure that everyone has access to adequate food. The U.S. Constitution mostly includes proscriptive rights, but it does prescriptively specify in Article IV, "The United States shall guarantee to every state in the union a republican form of government, and shall protect each of them against invasion and . . . domestic violence." In other words, the U.S. federal government is obligated to ensure that all states maintain a democratic form of government, to repel invaders, and to preserve domestic order. Many U.S. state constitutions are more expansive in extending prescriptive rights. For one, Connecticut's constitution requires the state legislature to "implement . . . free public elementary and secondary schools in the state." Less clearly, there has been an effort at both the U.S. federal and state levels to establish the notion that providing many basic services (such as housing, food, and health care for the needy) are obligations on the government, not merely options. This move is evident in the vast array of federal programs, such as food stamps and Medicare, which provide funding according to a formula (rather than by specific legislative appropriation) and which are commonly referred to as "entitlement programs." Those who favor this phrase meant it to imply a prescriptive obligation.

At the international level, the Universal Declaration of Human Rights mostly contains proscriptive rights, but it does also enumerate prescriptive rights. Article 22 specifies that:

> Everyone, as a member of society, has the right to social security and is entitled to realization, through national effort and international co-operation and in accordance with the organization and resources of each State, of the economic, social and cultural rights indispensable for his dignity and the free development of his personality.

Being more specific about some of these prescriptive rights, Article 25 states in part:

> Everyone has the right to a standard of living adequate for the health and well-being of himself and of his family, including food, clothing, housing and medical care and necessary social services, and the right to security in the event of unemployment, sickness, disability, widowhood, old age or other lack of livelihood in circumstances beyond his control.

Certainly one set of pressing problems involves preserving and enhancing human dignity by protecting and improving the physical condition of humans. These issues are partly economic in nature and are being addressed by the international economic cooperation efforts discussed in chapter 13. It is also the case, in the view of many, that food, health, and the other quality of life matters that we will take up in this section fall under the rubric of human rights. For example, the UN-sponsored World Food Summit that met in 1996 reasserted the principle found in the Universal Declaration by declaring that there is a "right to adequate food and the fundamental right of everyone to be free from hunger."[27] If, indeed, there is such a right, then an obligation also exists. As one scholar explains it, "Since adequate food is a human right, the obligations apply internationally. The rights and the corresponding obligations do not end at national borders. Under human rights law, the international community is obligated to create conditions that will end hunger in the world" (Kent, 2002). A right to adequate nutrition, to a reasonable standard of health, and to a basic education are not the only ones that some people lay claim to as prescriptive rights, but they will serve to illustrate the need and the response.

A final important point about prescriptive rights is that those who are without adequate health care, education, and the other necessities that support survival and a decent level of dignity are not spread evenly across the globe. This is evident in the accompanying map showing the pattern of the Human Development Index. This is a measure established by the UNDP that includes various measures of health, education, and per capita income. As you can see, the countries the UNDP rates as having "high human development" (levels 8 and 9) are mostly in Europe and North America. The low human development countries (levels 4 and below) are in Africa and southern Asia, with the remaining medium human development countries (levels 5 through 7) concentrated in South America, northern Asia, and the Middle East.

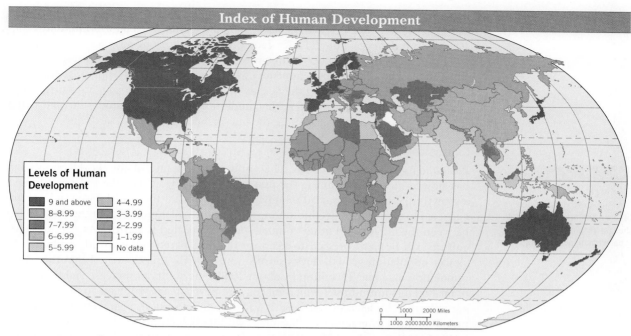

Index of Human Development

Levels of Human Development

- 9 and above
- 8–8.99
- 7–7.99
- 6–6.99
- 5–5.99
- 4–4.99
- 3–3.99
- 2–2.99
- 1–1.99
- No data

0 1000 2000 Miles
0 1000 2000 3000 Kilometers

The level of human rights and dignity around the world is measured in part by the Index of Human Development. The index, which was developed by the United Nations Development Programme, includes such gauges as health, literacy, income, and education. As you can see, the level of development that people enjoy or endure, as the case may be, varies greatly.

Adequate Nutrition

Long ago, Thomas Malthus predicted in his *Essay on the Principle of Population* (1798) that the population of the world would eventually outpace its agricultural capacity. To date, human ingenuity has defied his predictions. The question is whether it can continue to do so, given the increasing global population.

There are two basic food problems. One is the *short-term food supply*. The UN's Food and Agriculture Organization (FAO) estimates that 891 million people, about 14% of the world population, are undernourished. Sub-Saharan Africa, where 33% of the people are undernourished, is the most severely affected region. In addition to the death of 15 million people annually from starvation or diseases stemming from malnutrition, food shortages rob individuals and their societies of part of their future. Poor nutrition among pregnant women leads to 20 million "low birthweight" (less than 5.5 pounds) babies being born each year in the LDCs. In some countries, including India, more than 30 percent of all children are born underweight. Infant mortality for such infants is four times the normal rate. Moreover the malnourishment that they have already suffered and continue to experience, not just in calories but also in protein, vitamins, minerals, and other nutritional necessities, stunts their growth both physically and cognitively in ways that often limit them for the rest of their lives and deprive their societies of talents and vigor they might have developed.

The *long-term adequacy* of the food supply is also a significant issue. There have been important strides in the LDCs over the past few decades toward agricultural self-sufficiency. The food supply and crop yields (amount produced per acre) have grown over 50% since 1970 due to the "green revolution" (the development and widespread introduction of high-yielding rice, wheat, and other grains), the increased use of fertilizers and pesticides, better irrigation, more mechanization, and other agricultural advances. For all LDCs, food production grew by 35% between 1994 and 2004, far outpacing their population growth (16%). But among the poorest countries (the LLDCs, the low-income countries) where the problem has been most acute, the food production index during the decade increased only at the same rate as the population, 30% each. One result is that undernourishment in middle-income LDCs stood at 10% in 2004 and at 25% in the low-income LDCs.

Causes of the Food Problem

Web Link

The World Food Programme has an interactive world hunger map at **www.wfp.org/country_brief/ hunger_map/map/hungermap _popup/map_popup.html.**

Population growth is one cause. The annual growth rate of the world population has slowed measurably during the past two decades. However, the LLDCs still have a growth rate that is about 50% higher than the rest of the world. Growth rates are expected to continue to decline among all categories of countries, but the relative gap between the LLDCs and other countries is not expected to narrow. As a result, agriculture will be hard pressed to keep up in some parts of the world. Additionally, slower population growth does not mean no growth; it is estimated that the world population may reach 9 billion by about 2050. The ability to increase yields per unit of farmland is not infinite, which means that new acreage will have to be devoted to agriculture. This clearing of land is causing deforestation, aggravating a range of problems such as greenhouse warming, wildlife habitat destruction, and water pollution from pesticide and fertilizer runoff. Accelerating the problem is the fact that a great deal of current agricultural land is being lost to urbanization, degradation due to ill-use, and other causes. The FAO calculates that 38% of the world's original cropland (some 2.1 million square miles, almost two-thirds the area of the United States) has been lost to agriculture, and that a combination of increasing population and loss of arable land has cut the world's cultivated land to six-tenths of an acre per mouth to feed.

It is also important to note that some countries are already not keeping up. Whether the problem is inability to afford modern methods and technology, lack of adequate water and arable land, or political strife, many countries are in serious trouble. There are 34 LDCs whose per capita food production declined between 1996 and 2005. More than half of these were in sub-Saharan Africa. As a region, its annual per capita food production declined 0.2% annually between 1996 and 2005 after declining 0.4% annually the decade prior to that.

Maldistribution of food is a second problem. In 2000 the world produced enough food to allow for 2,790 calories per person in the world. Thus, for now at least, the world has the agricultural capacity to feed everyone adequately. Resources and consumption, however, are concentrated in relatively few countries. In the EDCs, daily food consumption averages a waist-expanding 3,490 calories a day. In significant segments of the South calorie intakes were at belt-tightening low levels. The sub-Saharan countries of Africa, for example, averaged only 2,260 calories per capita daily. Some countries in that region are in especially desperate shape. The people of Burundi average only 1,640 calories a day, 67% of them are undernourished, one of every six babies has a low birthweight, and 57% of the children are stunted.

Nutritional content represents a third, and even greater dietary problem. Protein deficiency is particularly common in the LLDCs. Most people in Africa, for instance, consume less than 60 grams of protein per day per capita and in some countries they average as little as 30 grams. The recommended daily intake is about 55 grams for sedentary individuals, which means that in the LLDCs, where manual labor is the norm, protein deficiency is also the norm. The lack of protein is especially detrimental to children because of the role it plays in developing both healthy bodies and brain tissue, and there are over 300 million children who suffer from stunted growth, poor cognitive development, and other ills due to protein malnutrition. Vitamin A deficiency, also common in LLDCs, is the cause of visual impairment in over 100 million children a year. Adding to the nutritional woes of the South, over 800 million people suffer from iodine deficiency, which inhibits motor skill development and also, according to the FAO, causes losses of 10 to 15 points on IQ tests.

Political strife is a fourth problem. In many countries with severe food shortages, farms have been destroyed, farmers displaced, and food transportation disrupted by internal warfare. Sierra Leone, one of the recent tragic examples, now produces 23% less food per capita than the already meager supply it managed to provide in 1991 before it was overtaken by strife.

The International Response to the Food Problem

A number of international efforts are under way. Some deal with food aid to meet immediate needs, while others are dedicated to increasing future agricultural productivity.

Emergency Food Aid   Supplying food aid to areas with food shortages is a short-term necessity to alleviate malnutrition and even starvation. Cereal grains, mostly rice and wheat, constitute about 85% of food aid. Some of the aid is given bilaterally, but most of the assistance goes through a number of multilateral food aid efforts. The UN's World Food Programme (WFP) is the largest. It distributes food in crisis situations, delivering over 4 million tons of food in 2006 to feed 97 million people in 82 countries. About 90% of WFP aid goes to countries that have experienced food emergencies because of natural causes or political strife; the other 20% goes to development projects. In 2006, the WFP received $2.7 billion in grains and other foodstuffs. Of this, 41% came from the United States. While these contributions are laudable, they do not meet all the emergency food needs identified by the WFP and amounted in 2006 to

The efforts of the World Food Program (WFP) have saved millions from starvation. Here a WFP truck convoy brings food to refugee camps in Chad that house about 200,000 Sudanese who have fled the killing in the Darfur region.

only about $28 per WFP individual recipient. There are also a variety of NGOs, such as Food for the Hungry International, that are active in food aid.

Specific Nutritional Needs Numerous programs also exist to address the lack of adequate dietary vitamins and minerals and other nutritional problems. Iodine deficiency provides an example. The 1990 World Summit for Children set the goal of eliminating iodine deficiencies by 2000. That did not occur, but substantial progress has been made. With WHO and UNICEF in the lead among IGOs and such NGOs as Kiwanis International also playing a leading role, the proportion of LDC households using iodized salt has risen from less than 20% in 1990 to over 70% today. As a result, 50 million more children who are born each year are now protected against learning impairment and other problems related to iodine deficiency than would have been the case without the international programs.

Agricultural Development The development of agricultural techniques and capabilities is crucial to remediate conditions in countries that already cannot adequately feed their people and to meet the needs of the 9 billion people that will constitute the world's population less than five decades from now. On a bilateral basis, many countries' programs include agricultural development aid. There is also a multilateral effort. The oldest agricultural IGO is the FAO. Founded in 1945, it has 189 members and an annual budget of approximately $770 million. The FAO sponsors agricultural research and provides technical assistance to LDCs through field offices in 74 countries. In the past, the agency had been criticized for a variety of its policies, including putting too much emphasis on short-term food aid and not enough effort into long-range agricultural growth. This, in addition to the growing recognition of the food problem, has led to the establishment of several other global food efforts.

One of these is the International Fund for Agricultural Development (IFAD), a specialized UN agency. IFAD began operations in 1977 and is specifically dedicated to environmentally sustainable agricultural development projects in rural areas of the LLDCs. The agency raises its funds through the voluntary contributions of its 165 member-countries, and disburses about $400 million annually in loans and grants to support projects in agriculturally struggling countries. These efforts are supplemented by several UN-associated organizations involved in various donor, investment, and research efforts in agriculture. Finally, there are a variety of regional and specialized organizations that address agricultural issues.

World Food Conferences A key event in both the effort to increase both short- and long-term food was the 1974 World Food Conference held in Rome. Among its other actions, the conference sponsored the creation of IFAD and various structures associated with the UN Economic and Social Council to monitor the global food supply and its delivery to needy countries and people.

A second global conference, the 1996 **World Food Summit**, met in Rome and was attended by representatives of 180 countries. It established the goal of reducing the number of undernourished people from 800 million to 400 million by 2015, but tensions between the EDCs and LDCs limited its accomplishments. The EDCs were dismayed when the LDCs pushed to reaffirm the UN's traditional standard that the EDCs should devote 0.7% of their respective GDPs to development aid, including food and agricultural assistance. Additionally, in a move that rankled Washington and some other capitals, the conference resolved that "food should not be used as an instrument for political and economic pressure."[28] This swipe at economic sanctions came just days after the UN General Assembly voted overwhelmingly to urge the United States to end its embargo against Cuba. The delegates also declared their belief in "the right of everyone to have access to safe and nutritious food [and] . . . the fundamental right of everyone to be free from hunger." The recognition of a prescriptive right to adequate nutrition had little immediate meaning, but such rhetorical flourishes are often one of the building blocks that change attitudes and eventually lead to action.

The continuing problems with supplying adequate calories and nutrition to a large number of LDCs occasioned a review of the efforts since the 1996 conference. The World Food Summit—Five Years Later conference, organized by the FAO, was held in Rome during June 2002. The fifth year review was necessary, in the estimation of Jacques Diouf, the FAO's director-general, because little progress was being made toward achieving the goal to cut the number of malnourished people in half, set by the 1996 conference. "There is very little evidence," according to Diouf, "of the large-scale purposive action needed to get to grips with the underlying causes of hunger."[29]

Adequate Health Standards

Those who believe that humans have prescriptive rights would put living in reasonably healthy conditions and having access to adequate health care on the list of those rights. Reality is far from this ideal.

Health Needs

The state of medical care, sanitation, and other conditions related to health in some areas of the world is below a level imaginable by most readers of this book. While health care is well below EDC standards in most LDCs, it is in the LLDCs that the greatest need exists. As one measure, the EDCs annually spend $115 per capita on health care for every $1 spent by the LLDCs (Ghobara, Huth, & Russett, 2004). By another measure, there are 10 times as many physicians per person and 5 times as many hospital beds per capita in the EDCs as there are in the LLDCs. The health of people within these countries is an international concern for reasons beyond altruism. A healthy population is vital to economic growth because healthy people are economically productive and because unhealthy people often consume more of a society's resources than they produce.

The fate of children is one way to think about health care. In LLDCs, children under age five die at a rate that is 16 times higher than for children in the North. Compared to children in EDCs, those in LLDCs are more frequently exposed to disease because of poor sanitation and other factors, they are more vulnerable to disease because of malnutrition, and they more often succumb to disease because basic medical care is not available. Overall, an estimated 70% of the children under age five in LDCs who die each year perish from infectious and parasitic diseases that are easily preventable and claim only 1% of the children in EDCs. "No famine, no flood, no earthquake, no war has ever claimed the lives of this many children a year," the director of UNICEF once lamented.[30]

Adults also suffer from poor health conditions and lack of adequate health care. Nearly all births in EDCs are attended by skilled health professionals; only 40% of the births in LLDCs are. That is one reason for the maternal mortality rate in the LLDCs being 49 times the rate in the EDCs. Also, diseases once thought to be on the decline can reassert themselves catastrophically. Tuberculosis is one such disease. It has resurged in recent decades. Now each year over 9 million new cases occur and about 1.7 million people die of the disease. TB is found everywhere, but the rate in LLDCs is 13 times the rate in EDCs. Plague is another old disease that refuses to die.

Did You Know That:

LLDCs are home to 37% of the world population, yet they have 89% of children age 0–4 who die of diarrheal diseases.

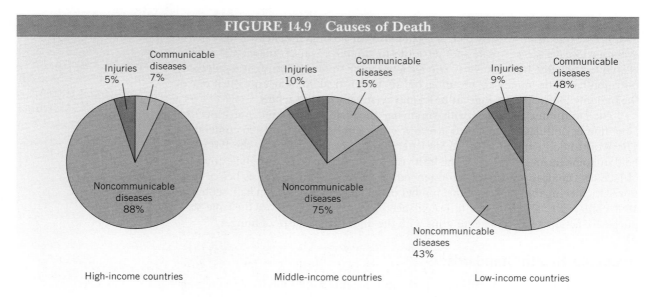

FIGURE 14.9 Causes of Death

People in poor countries die from readily preventable and curable diseases much more frequently than do people in high-income and even middle-income countries. Communicable diseases such as tuberculosis, malaria, and measles are responsible for 48% of the deaths in low-income countries, but only 15% of the deaths in middle-income countries and 7% of the deaths in high-income countries. By contrast, people in these two wealthier groups are much more likely to succumb to cancer and other noncommunicable diseases. Injuries from accidents and violence claim the rest of the lives. Compared to the noncommunicable diseases, many of the communicable ones are more likely to be contracted earlier in life, and they are easier to prevent and to cure.

Data source: World Health Organization.

The plague, or "Black Death," that killed one-third of Europe's population in the mid-1300s, still afflicts over 2,000 people a year, 99% of them in Africa. If strains resistant to antibiotics develop, as has happened with TB, plague could once again travel widely, as the Black Death did from Asia to Europe in 1347.

Figure 14.9 captures some of the impact of health conditions by comparing the percentage of people who die of communicable diseases in the LLDCs, the low-income countries, with people in middle-income LDCs and high-income EDCs. These are diseases caused by "germs" such as viruses, bacteria, fungi, or protozoa. As you can see, people in low-income countries are almost seven times as likely to perish from a communicable disease. Since these tend to occur more often earlier in life than noncommunicable diseases, such as cancer and cardiovascular afflictions, the high rate of communicable disease in the LLDCs means that tens of millions of people die each year much earlier than they would have if they live in an EDC. In some regions of the world the numbers are even more dramatic than those in the figure. Fully 70% of Africans die of communicable diseases.

New problems add to these old worries. The worldwide AIDS epidemic, for one, is a global killer. At the beginning of 2007, one of every 162 humans, almost 40 million people, worldwide were HIV-positive. That was a net annual increase of 1.4 million cases, a grim statistic derived from subtracting the 2.9 million people who died from AIDS-related causes from the 4.3 million new HIV-positive people. Sub-Saharan Africa has been especially devastated. The region has 63% of the world's HIV-positive people, and 6% of the region's adults are HIV-positive. The incidence in some countries is horrific, ranging up to 33% of all adults in Swaziland. AIDS is a key factor in the economic struggles of sub-Saharan Africa. It attacks the workforce, overwhelms the meager budgets of countries, creates millions of orphans, and diverts outside funding that could be used for development. During 2005 in Zambia, for example, 40% of the teachers who left that country's already-too-small corps of educators did so because they had AIDS and could no longer work. Overall, as the World Bank puts it, "The epidemic continues to reverse life expectancy gains, erode productivity, decimate the workforce, consume savings, and dilute poverty reduction efforts."[31]

Yet other horrific emerging diseases lurk in the shadows and threaten to spread, as AIDS has, to a world with few or no natural or manufactured immunological defenses. SARS (severe acute respiratory syndrome) and West Nile virus (see chapter 1) have broken out in recent years, but neither is as scary as the threat of avian influenza (avian flu, bird flu). An outbreak in Southeast Asia that began in 2003 was traced to a strain of avian flu that, unusually, had spread from domestic fowl to humans. Only 200 cases were confirmed through early 2007, and those have been confined to just six countries: Cambodia, China, Indonesia, Thailand, Turkey, and Vietnam. However, half of all those stricken have died, and migrating birds with the H5N1 virus have been found throughout Asia and as far away as Western Europe and Africa. WHO officials warn that if the disease spreads globally it might kill 50 million people within a year or two. Such numbers are not scare tactics: The great influenza pandemic of 1918–1919 caused an estimated 40 to 50 million deaths worldwide. In the United States, 28% of the population came down with the "Spanish flu," and 675,000 died from it. Possibly a strain of avian influenza, the disease spawned its own morbid child's verse used to skip rope:

> I had a little bird,
> Its name was Enza.
> I opened the window,
> And in-flu-enza.

So far, preventive measures that include the slaughter of more than 140 million chickens and other domestic fowl in Southeast Asia have kept bird flu in check. There is also a scramble to create vaccines, both for domestic fowl and for humans. But viruses mutate and with so few cases so far, clinical trials for vaccines fall far short of ideal. That means, according to one scientist in the field, "We can't get the answer to [how effective any given vaccine will be] until the pandemic comes. There's just no way."[32]

At least to a minor degree, combating a potential avian flu outbreak has been hampered by North-South tension. Some LDCs took heed of the observation of World Health Organization (WHO) Director General Margaret Chan that "Faced with a universal threat, each country will look after itself, at least in the immediate pandemic period. This is a natural behavior of governments." The LDCs worry that the EDCs, which contain most of the major pharmaceutical companies, will horde their vaccines or try to charge exorbitant prices for them. This led Indonesia, which has seen the most cases of avian flu, to withhold samples taken from victims that researchers need to monitor any changes in the virus and develop effective vaccines, while demanding the creation of an international stockpile of vaccine available to all. This move sparked outrage in some quarters, but an Indonesian editorial replied, "Self-defense is no crime. Withholding H5N1 samples is the only way Indonesia can protect its people." Whatever the right or wrong of the policy, it was effective, and

Did You Know That:

The impact of the Black Death on Europe is evident in a children's rhyme that reputedly originated in 14th-century England among wagon drivers collecting plague victims for burial:

> Ring-around the rosy,
> A pocket full of posies,
> Ashes, ashes!
> We all fall down!

"Ring-around the rosy" refers to a plague symptom, a ring-shaped skin lesion caused by internal bleeding that initially was rosy red, but then turned black, hence the name Black Death. Europeans often carried a "pocket full of posies," hoping the flowers' scent would mask the stench of rotting bodies. "Ashes, ashes" is an interpretation of "atishoos," the violent sneezing sound plague victims made. As for "We all fall down," the unspoken final word is "dead."

SIMULATION
Threats to World Health

the WHO has taken steps toward establishing a global stockpile. "This is a perfect example of a small developing country standing up against a world body and developed countries," an editorial in an Indian newspaper noted approvingly.[33]

What makes these diseases even more of a world problem than they once were is the flow of humans and their products around the globe, which means that diseases can be spread very quickly from continent to continent. A person who contracts an exotic disease in one place can board an airplane and, 12 hours later, be stifling a sneeze while sitting next to you in a restaurant. Such diseases are more than just a threat to individual health; they are also a national security risk. For example, a U.S. Central Intelligence Agency report concludes that, "New and reemerging infectious diseases . . . pose a rising global health threat and . . . complicate U.S. and global security over the next 20 years" because they "endanger U.S. citizens at home and abroad, threaten U.S. armed forces deployed overseas, and exacerbate social and political instability in key countries and regions in which the United States has significant interests."[34]

International Response to Health Issues

Although avian influenza lurks alarmingly on the horizon, the greatest current threat to global health is HIV/AIDS. Reflecting that, the most intense single international health initiative is coordinated by the Joint United Nations Programme on HIV/AIDS (UNAIDS), an alliance of ten UN agencies and other IGOs such as the World Bank. Founded in 1995 and with a budget of about $320 million, UNAIDS gathers information, works with national governments, and coordinates the international effort to slow and someday halt new HIV infections, to care for those already infected, and to ease the impact of the epidemic on the countries and families of the afflicted. The organization also works with other IGOs and NGOs, private donors, and governments, which combined spend another $1.8 billion annually on the campaign against HIV/AIDS. When national treatment efforts and other related spending is added in, global spending on the disease came to about $8.5 billion in 2006. While the number of people infected each year is still climbing, the various international efforts have reached many millions of people with AIDS prevention information and assistance and have provided some who are already infected with medical help. For example, the number of people in sub-Saharan Africa receiving antiretroviral treatment increased tenfold to 1 million by 2007, a hopeful advance even if it represents only 25% of the need in that region.

Combating AIDS is proving frustrating, but much better progress is being made on other health fronts. Overall, health conditions and health care in the LLDCs has improved. A few decades ago only 5% of the children in LLDCs received any vaccinations; now 67% receive protection against diphtheria, whooping cough, tetanus, and polio. For this and other reasons, child mortality in the LLDCs is down from one in four children in 1960 to one in eight children now. Adults are also healthier in the LLDCs. As discussed in chapter 13, their health prospects remain far below those in EDCs, but also like the children in the LLDCs, the adults are in better health and live longer than in previous decades.

Much of the credit for these advances goes to the **World Health Organization (WHO)**, headquartered in Geneva, Switzerland. The UN-affiliated WHO was created in 1946. It has 193 members and an annual budget of about $2 billion from member-countries and from other sources. The crusade against smallpox provides a heartening example of WHO's contributions. Smallpox was a scourge throughout human history. There were over 131,000 cases worldwide in 1967 when WHO began a 10-year campaign to eradicate the disease. It succeeded. The last case of smallpox, perhaps forever, occurred in Somalia in 1977.

Taking on another disease, WHO began a campaign against polio in 1988, and in 2004 organized an all-out effort to finally eradicate polio. During 2005 alone, 400 million children in 49 countries were immunized. As Figure 14.10 shows, the annual global incidence has been cut by 99% since the campaign began in 1988. From about 350,000 cases globally that year, the incidence of polio dropped to 315 cases in 2006, of which 285 were in just four countries: Nigeria, India, Afghanistan and Pakistan. Perhaps when the next edition of this text is written, polio will have joined smallpox in the garbage can of history.

Basic Education

Education, like health, affects more than just the quality of life. Education is also a key to increased national and international productivity, population control, and other positive social goals.

Educational Needs

As with most other socioeconomic indicators, there is a vast gulf in the educational experience of children and young adults in the North and in the South. The LLDCs, the lowest-income countries, manage to annually spend only about $50 per student. The EDCs spend 110 times as much per student. Even factoring in purchasing power parity (see chapter 12) to account for the lower cost of living in LLDCs, the gap narrows to 23:1. The overall teacher-pupil ratio in EDC primary schools is 1:14; it is 1:43 in the LLDCs. About two-thirds of all students in EDCs go on to college or technical postsecondary training; only about 10% of students in the LLDCs do so. In our technological age, the lack of advanced training is a major impediment to development. In the North there are nearly 80 times as many scientists and technicians per capita as there are in the LLDCs.

FIGURE 14.10   Annual Polio Cases

Number of new polio cases

350,000 (1988), 100,000 (1993), 7,000 (1999), 1,255 (2004), 325 (2006)

Global cooperation to provide better health wiped out smallpox and is on the verge of doing the same for polio. There were about 350,000 new cases of polio in 1988, the year that the World Health Organization resolved to eliminate the disease. With tens of millions of children being immunized each year, polio has become a rare disease. Overall, the number of countries where it occurred dropped from 125 in 1988 to 17 in 2006, with only 325 new cases.

Note: Cases for 1988, 1993, and 1999 are approximate.
Data source: Global Polio Education Initiative and UNICEF.

The International Response to Education Issues

Promotion of education remains primarily a national function, but there are a number of international efforts. For one, the United Nations Educational, Scientific, and Cultural Organization (UNESCO) sponsors several programs. These national and international efforts are slowly paying off. In the 1950s less than 30% of all children in LLDCs ever attended any school; now almost all children begin the first grade and more than two-thirds complete primary school. This means that while the adult literacy rate in the LLDCs is still only 61%, the literacy rate for those ages 15 to 24 is now 73%. Data on secondary education is incomplete, but the indications are that there is progress at these levels also. Fairly typical of sub-Saharan Africa, only 8% of Malawi's high-school-age children were attending secondary school in 1990, now 33% are. Progress is also being made to narrow and eventually eliminate the gender gap in education. Among adults in LLDCs age 25 or older, men are 23% more likely to be literate than women.

DEBATE THE POLICY SCRIPT

Support a Global Bill of Rights?

It is easy to favor rights when ours are being violated. It is much harder to agree on what rights everyone, everywhere should have and which, therefore, we and our governments are obligated to respect and protect. There is also considerable controversy over whether rights are universal or culturally based and, even more, over whether prescriptive rights should be accorded the same support as the more familiar proscriptive rights.

The rights in the following list are paraphrased from most of those contained in the Universal Declaration of Human Rights (1948). That document arguably rejects culturally defined rights and favors universal rights in its preamble, which asserts the existence of "inalienable rights of all members of the human family." Many of them are very close to the proscriptive rights that most Americans and others are familiar with. For example, the language in the Universal Declaration and in clause 3 below is very much like the prohibition in the Eighth Amendment to the U.S. Constitution barring "cruel and unusual punishments." Other rights listed here are prescriptive. These

obligate governments to assist people to achieve something, not to just protect people from being denied something. Clauses 23, 24, and 25 fall into that category; others may if you believe that they carry with them a positive obligation for societies and their governments to fulfill them.

What Do You Think?

In your class or with your friends, constitute yourselves as the World Constitutional Convention, debate the various clauses of the UNDHR, and decide whether to ratify or reject each one of them. You might also decide to open them up for amendment. For example, would you add "sexual orientation" to clause 11? You could even add a new clause, such as one that said, "The pronouns everyone and no one in this enumeration of rights include men and women without distinction." Also, note clause 27 and ponder whether it provides too much of an escape clause that potentially allows governments to violate rights. How say you to the propositions that:

1. Everyone has the right to life, liberty, and security of person.   Ratify _____   Reject _____

2. No one shall be held in slavery or servitude.   Ratify _____   Reject _____

3. No one shall be subjected to torture or to cruel, inhuman, or degrading treatment or punishment.   Ratify _____   Reject _____

4. Everyone is equal before the law and entitled to equal protection of the law.   Ratify _____   Reject _____

5. No one shall be subjected to arbitrary arrest, detention, or exile.   Ratify _____   Reject _____

6. Everyone charged with a crime shall be presumed innocent until proved guilty according to law in a public trial and shall be guaranteed the necessities for an adequate defense.   Ratify _____   Reject _____

7. Everyone has the right to freedom of movement and residence in their country.   Ratify _____   Reject _____

8. Everyone has the right to leave their country or any other and to return to their country whenever they wish.   Ratify _____   Reject _____

9. Everyone has the right to seek asylum in other countries to escape persecution.   Ratify _____   Reject _____

10. No one shall be arbitrarily deprived of their citizenship or the right to change it.   Ratify _____   Reject _____

11. Adults have the right to marry and have a family, without restrictions based on ethnicity, race, or religion. Both adults are entitled to equal rights both during marriage and at its dissolution.   Ratify _____   Reject _____

That gap is only 14% among young people age 15 to 24, and indicating a further narrowing in the future, the male-female gap primary school completion rate is only 8%.

At the end of this section on prescriptive rights and the lengthier discussion of proscriptive rights, it is worthwhile to ask yourself how you feel about them. If a

12. Everyone has the right to own property alone. No one shall be deprived of his property.   Ratify _____   Reject _____

13. Everyone has the right to freedom of thought, conscience, and religion and to express their beliefs in public and in private through teaching, practice, worship, and observance.   Ratify _____   Reject _____

14. Everyone has the right to freedom of opinion and expression to seek, receive, and impart information and ideas through any media and regardless of frontiers.   Ratify _____   Reject _____

15. Everyone has the right to freedom of peaceful assembly and association.   Ratify _____   Reject _____

16. No one may be compelled to belong to an association.   Ratify _____   Reject _____

17. Everyone has the right to take part in their country's government, either directly or through freely chosen representatives.   Ratify _____   Reject _____

18. Everyone has the right to equal access to public services in his country.   Ratify _____   Reject _____

19. The will of the people shall be the basis of the authority of government; this will shall be expressed in periodic and genuine elections which shall be by universal and equal suffrage and shall be held by secret vote or by equivalent free voting procedures.   Ratify _____   Reject _____

20. Everyone has the right to work, to choose their work, to reasonable work conditions, and to protection against unemployment.   Ratify _____   Reject _____

21. Everyone has the right to equal pay for equal work.   Ratify _____   Reject _____

22. Everyone has the right to form and to join trade unions.   Ratify _____   Reject _____

23. Everyone has the right to an adequate standard of living, including food, clothing, housing, medical care, and other necessary social services regardless of age, health, or any other circumstance beyond their control.   Ratify _____   Reject _____

24. Mothers and children are entitled to special assistance and to equal help, regardless of marital or any other circumstance.   Ratify _____   Reject _____

25. Everyone has the right to education. It shall be compulsory and free, at least at the elementary level. Enrollment in more advanced levels shall be based on merit.   Ratify _____   Reject _____

26. Parents have a right to choose the kind of education given to their children.   Ratify _____   Reject _____

27. Everyone must uphold these rights, except as determined by law to be necessary to meet the just requirements of morality, public order, and the general welfare in a democratic society.   Ratify _____   Reject _____

right is a justifiable claim, are these claims justified by whatever standard you believe should apply? Also, to the extent that you believe various rights exist, do the restraints of proscriptive rights and the obligations of prescriptive rights apply only in your own country or are they universal? To begin to answer these questions, consider the rights contained in the decision box, "Support a Global Bill of Rights?"

Educational opportunities in much of the South are still far below those of the North, but important progress has been made in recent decades. These advances are symbolized here by this geography lesson using an inflatable globe in a school in Rwanda.

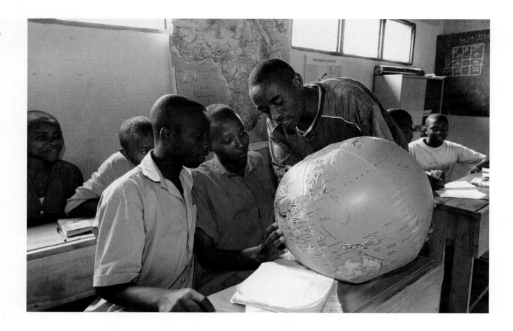

Think about and debate them, as the box suggests. While doing that, particularly note which rights you believe are or should be prescriptive rights. If you believe that an obligation exists, does it end at national borders, or does it extend to humankind?

CHAPTER SUMMARY

THE NATURE OF HUMAN RIGHTS

1. Rights may be designated as proscriptive rights, those that others cannot violate, and prescriptive rights, those that others are obligated to ensure everyone attains.
2. The universalist and relativist schools of thought have different approaches to the origin of rights.
3. Universalists argue that human rights apply to all people; relativists contend that human rights are culturally oriented, and imposing rights based on Western cultural traditions on non-Western people is cultural imperialism.
4. Another clashing view is the slant of rights. In Western countries, individualism is stressed. An individual's rights are accorded more weight than in non-Western societies that stress communitarianism. The collective rights of the community take precedence over an individual.

PROSCRIPTIVE HUMAN RIGHTS

5. The discussion of proscriptive human rights, the abuses of them, and the efforts to ease them focuses on women, children, ethnic and racial groups, religious groups, indigenous peoples, and refugees and immigrants.
6. The area of human rights is one of the most difficult to work in because violations are usually politically based. Therefore, efforts to redress them are often resented and rejected by target countries. The greatest progress has been made in adopting a number of UN declarations, such as the Universal Declaration of Human Rights, and multilateral treaties that define basic human rights. The enforcement of human rights is much less well developed, but the rising level of awareness and of disapproval of violations on a global scale are having a positive impact. There are also many IGOs,

such as the UN Human Rights Commission, and NGOs, such as Amnesty International, that work to improve human rights.

PRESCRIPTIVE HUMAN RIGHTS

7. The discussion of prescriptive human rights focuses on what some people claim are the rights to adequate nutrition, health prevention and care, and education.

8. Population growth, the underproduction of food, and the maldistribution of the food that is produced are factors contributing to food shortages and inadequate nutrition for many people in LDCs and LLDCs. International organizations, such as the Food and Agriculture Organization, attempt to provide short-term food relief and long-term agricultural assistance to countries facing nutritional shortages.

9. Many people in LDCs face disease and lack of medical care to degrees that boggle the minds of most people in EDCs. Some of the diseases, such as AIDS, can become a world health threat. The World Health Organization, other IGOs, and many NGOs are attempting to bring better health care to people globally.

10. The ability of individuals to achieve a higher quality of life and the ability of countries to develop economically depend in substantial part on education. More than 1 billion adults are still illiterate, many more have only the most rudimentary education, and the personal and societal productivity of these people is limited. The United Nations Educational, Scientific, and Cultural Organization is one of many international organizations working to improve education in the LDCs and LLDCs.

For simulations, debates, and other interactive activities, a chapter quiz, Web links, and much more, visit **www.mhhe.com/rourke12/** and go to chapter 14. Or, while accessing the site, click on Course-Wide Content and view recent international relations articles in the *New York Times*.

KEY TERMS

communitarianism
Convention on the
    Elimination of All Forms
    of Discrimination Against
    Women (CEDAW)
Convention on the
    Rights of the Child

cultural imperialism
individualism
International
    Convention on the
    Elimination of All
    Forms of Racial
    Discrimination

International Criminal
    Court (ICC)
prescriptive rights
proscriptive rights
relativists
Universal Declaration
    of Human Rights

universalists
World Conference on
    Women (WCW)
World Food Summit
World Health
    Organization (WHO)

Preserving and Enhancing the Biosphere

Comfort's in heaven, and we are on the earth.
—William Shakespeare, *Richard II*

Dear earth, I do salute thee with my hand.
—William Shakespeare, *Richard II*

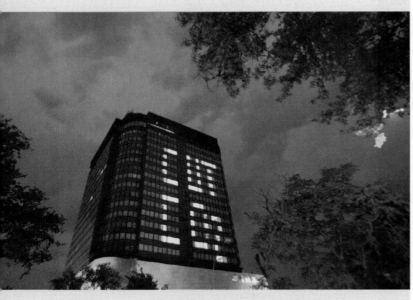

Of all the concerns about the biosphere that this chapter covers, the one many people consider the most critical is the increasing discharge of carbon dioxide (CO_2) and other "greenhouse gases" into the atmosphere. Most scientists believe that this trend is accelerating global warming. The campaign to cut CO_2 emissions is depicted in this photograph of a light display orchestrated by the NGO Greenpeace on a darkened building in New Delhi, India.

THIS CHAPTER DEALS with the **biosphere**: Earth's ecological system (ecosystem) that supports life—its land, water, air, and upper atmosphere—and the living organisms, including humans, that inhabit it. One certainty and two issues related to it are at the center of our discussion here. What is certain is that the well-being of each of us is connected to the ecological state of the world. As one scientist warns, "Common sense . . . tells us that if we ruin the Earth, we will suffer grievously."[1]

We will begin our examination of the biosphere by asking two questions: Are there major problems and, if so, how threatening are they? If there are significant concerns—and there are—then the next step is to consider such topics as what is being done to address problems, what the politics of environmental protection are, and what more should be done. A final note before turning to our topic is that this chapter, like chapter 14 on human rights, combines both the traditional and alternative approaches. The reason is that, like human rights, environmental issues have only very recently become part of the international dialogue. Thus the traditional approach was to consider the environment a domestic issue with little or no relevance to world politics. Some people continue to favor that approach, arguing that each country should set its own standards and not compromise its sovereignty by submitting to international regulation. By contrast, others see their country's interests as inextricably tied to those of the world and, therefore, favor protecting the biosphere through a cooperative approach that includes international standards and regulations.

THE ECOLOGICAL STATE OF THE WORLD

Just as the U.S. president delivers an annual State of the Union address each year, a regular evaluation of Earth is a worthwhile exercise. A good place to start our survey of the state of the world is **green accounting**. This measures a country's strength by beginning with overall and per capita gross national product (GNP) and other traditional measures of national wealth and then adding two other factors. One is "human capital," the productive capacity of a country's population as determined by its education, health, and other factors (see chapter 8). "Natural capital" including land, air, water, and natural resources is the second factor. Some of these factors, such as the importance of petroleum and other natural resources and agricultural capacity, are also included in chapter 8's discussion of national power. Other aspects of green accounting, such as clean air and water, are less standard, but they too impact present and future power and prosperity. Therefore, as one scholar advises, green accounting "is a valuable thing to do even if it can only be done relatively crudely."[2]

"How are we doing?" is the question that the bottom line of any accounting system seeks to answer. On this issue, there is agreement on the immense financial value of the biosphere and our dependence on it. Consensus ends, however, when we turn to the question of the current and future ecological state of the world. Here the range of opinions can be roughly divided into two camps: the environmental pessimists and the environmental optimists.

Environmental pessimists are those analysts who assess the state of the world and believe that humans are causing serious, even irreversible, damage to the environment. They further worry that the environmental damage will increasingly cause human suffering: severe and devastating storms due to global warming, skin cancer due to ozone layer depletion, warfare over scarce natural resources, and other problems. Representing this camp, a WorldWatch Institute study warns that, "depending on the

SIMULATION
Worldwatch Issue Alerts

Web Link

For an interactive green accounting site, go to
http://web.nmsu.edu/~dboje/
TDgreenaccounting.html.

As does the annual publication, *The State of the World*, environmental pessimists give the biosphere a checkup, find it seriously ailing, and advocate strong measures to restore its health. Environmental optimists come to a different diagnosis. They argue that any problems that do exist are not severe and that they can be addressed without taking dramatic measures.

degree of misery and biological impoverishment that we [humans] are prepared to accept, we have only one or perhaps two generations [20 to 40 years] in which to reinvent ourselves." It is imperative to do so, the study continues, because, "by virtually every broad measure, our world is in a state of pervasive ecological decline."[3] Some pessimistic analysts even foresee environmental issues or resource scarcities as the cause of future warfare among states desperate to sustain their economies and quality of life. Oil is one obvious example, but we shall also see that countries may increasingly clash over water or even over such matters as "invasions" of acid rain and similar pollutants from other countries.

Environmental optimists are those who reject this gloomy view of the world environment and its future. Some optimists believe that the pessimists resemble Chicken Little, the protagonist in a children's story who was hit on the head by a shingle that had fallen off the barn roof. Convinced that he had been struck by a piece of the sky, Chicken Little panicked and raced around the barnyard crying, "The sky is falling, the sky is falling," thereby creating unfounded pandemonium. Optimists tend to chastise the ecology movement for promoting "green guilt" by alarming people. "On average we over-worry about the environmental areas," one such critic notes. That is not necessary, he continues, because "things are actually getting better and better, and they're likely to do so in the future." He concedes that "problems exist," but reassuringly argues they "are getting smaller" (Lomborg, 2003:312). This school of thought is especially optimistic that most biosphere problems can be solved through technological innovation. They believe that new technology can find and develop additional oil fields. Synthetics can replace natural resources. Fertilizers, hybrid seeds, and mechanization can increase crop yields. Desalinization and weather control can meet water demands. Energy can be drawn from nuclear, solar, thermal, wind, and hydroelectric sources.

SUSTAINABLE DEVELOPMENT

Throughout most of history, Earth has provided humans with the necessities of life, has absorbed their waste, and has replenished itself. Now, the mounting human population and technology have changed this, and environmental pessimists warn that we are straining Earth's **carrying capacity**: the largest number of humans that the planet can sustain indefinitely at current per capita rates of consumption of natural resources and discharges of pollution and other waste. Not only are there more than six times as many people as there were just a little over 200 years ago, but our technological progress has multiplied our per capita resource consumption and our per capita waste and pollutant production. Whether or not technological wizardry will eventually provide solutions remains uncertain, but if that does not happen soon, then the world is approaching, or may have even reached a crisis of carrying capacity—the potential of no longer being able to sustain its population in an adequate manner or being able to absorb its waste. To put this as an equation:

$$\text{Exploding population} \times \text{Spiraling per capita resource consumption} \times \text{Mounting waste and pollutant discharges} = \text{Biosphere catastrophe}$$

If the environmental pessimists are correct in their equation, then a primary goal should be to ensure we do not reach or, for safety's sake, even approach full carrying capacity. That will not be easy, however, because another fundamental goal of humans has been and remains to increase their economic well-being and to reap the other benefits, such as better health, that come with prosperity. The world's economically developed countries (EDCs) have largely achieved that goal; the world's less developed countries (LDCs) are intent on also doing so. Industrialization and science are key elements of development, yet they are two-edged swords in their relationship to the environment and the quality of human life. On the positive side, industrialization has vastly expanded global wealth, especially for the EDCs. Science has created synthetic substances that enhance our lives; medicine has dramatically increased our chances of surviving infancy and has extended adult longevity. Yet, on the negative side, industry consumes natural resources and discharges pollutants into the air, ground, and water. Synthetic substances enter the food chain as carcinogens, refuse to degrade, and have other baleful effects. Similarly, decreased infant mortality rates and increased longevity have been major factors promoting the world's rapid population growth.

Given that all these factors are part of modernization and unlikely to be reversed, the dilemma is how to achieve **sustainable development**, the process of protecting the biosphere while simultaneously advancing human socioeconomic development. Can the biosphere survive if we bring the 5.4 billion people who live in the LDCs up to the standard of living—with all its cars, air conditioners, throwaway plastic containers, and other biosphere attacking amenities—enjoyed by the 1 billion people in the EDCs? If so, how?

Web Link

More information on sustainable development is available on the Web site of the Canada-based IGO, International Institute for Sustainable Development at **www.iisd.org/.**

The Conundrum of Sustainable Development

Central to what you should ponder as you read the rest of this chapter is if and how we can meet the legitimate but resource-consuming and waste-creating modernization goals of LDCs without severely damaging the environment. For example, think about what consumption would be like if India with its 1.1 billion people was as economically developed as the United States and had the same resource use and waste patterns. There are now 6.6 million cars in India; there would be 535 million if automobiles were as commonplace there as in the United States. One impact would be astronomically increased pressure on petroleum supplies. The additional cars and other accoutrements of a developed economy would put India on the road to consuming as much petroleum per capita as Americans. Since the United States uses 31 times more petroleum per capita than does India, annual oil consumption in India would skyrocket from 36 billion gallons to 1.1 trillion gallons. In addition to the drain on the world's oil supply, this would increase pollution enormously. For one, carbon dioxide (CO_2) emissions would rise ominously. Americans discharge 20 times more CO_2 per capita than do Indians, and India already emits 1.2 billion metric tons of CO_2 annually. That figure would rise to 24 billion metric tons, escalating the threat to the environment. It is not necessary to continue this example to make the point that if Indians, as they have a right to do, achieve the same level of prosperity as Americans and also have the same resource consumption and waste pattern as prevails today in the United States, that would be very bad for the ecological future of the planet. Furthermore, if you were to bring the rest of the LDCs up to the U.S. level of resource use and emissions discharge, then you would hyperaccelerate the depletion of natural resources and the creation of pollution. Figure 2.5 on p. 61 indicates that at existing current rates of increase, LDC emissions of CO_2 will surpass those of

FIGURE 15.1 Current and Projected CO_2 Emissions

Annual CO_2 emissions
(billions of metric tons)

■ Economically developed countries
■ Less developed countries
■ World

One challenge of sustainable development is restraining pollution. If LDCs were as economically developed as the EDCs and had per capita carbon dioxide (CO_2) discharges equal to those of the EDCs, then LDC discharges would be 277% greater than they are now and overall world discharges would be 133% greater than now. Global warming would speed up disastrously.

Data source: World Bank.

Did You Know That:

Texas, population 22 million, discharges 50% more CO_2 than sub-Saharan Africa, population 511 million.

EDCs in about 10 years, and if LDCs discharged CO_2 at the same per capita rate as the EDCs, then current world emissions would be 133% greater than the already-too-high level, as Figure 15.1 details. Clearly, this is not acceptable. Less clear is what to do. Other than doing nothing, the options fall into two broad categories: restricting development and paying the price for environmentally sustainable development.

Option 1: Restrict/Rollback Development

Preserving the environment by consuming less is one possibility. Those who advocate stringent programs believe that even if they seem unpalatable to many people now, eventually we will be better off if we make the sacrifices necessary to restrain development and preserve the environment.

Objections to such solutions leap to mind. Are we, for instance, to suppress LDC development? If people in India do not acquire more cars, if Chinese are kept in the fields instead of in factories, and if Africans continue to swelter in the summer's heat without air conditioners, then accelerated resource use and pollution discharges can be partly avoided. As we saw in chapter 12, however, the LDCs are asserting their right to industrialize and to acquire the conveniences of life, such as cars and air conditioning, on an equal basis with the EDCs. As such, the LDCs reject any suggestion that they restrain their development. No one can "try to tell the people of Beijing that they can't buy a car or an air-conditioner" because they pollute, cautions one Chinese energy official. "It is just as hot in Beijing as it is in Washington."[4]

Another possible answer is for the people of the North to use dramatically fewer resources and to take the steps needed to reduce pollution by drastically curtailing some of the luxuries they currently enjoy. This could include forfeiting SUVs and other large passenger vehicles, commuting by public transportation instead of by car, or keeping the heat down in winter and using air conditioners only sparingly in the summer. Polls show that most people favor the theory of conservation and environmental protection. Yet practice indicates that, so far, most people are also unwilling to suffer a major reduction in their own conveniences or standards of living. Efforts to get more Americans to use mass transit, for example, have had very little success. There are other possibilities that would apply greater pressure on the public to conserve. A steep "gas guzzler" tax could be levied on any private passenger vehicle that gets, say, less than 25 miles per gallon (mpg). How would you react to such a tax of $1,000 at the time of sale for each mpg under 25 mpg that the vehicle got? That would raise the price of a 17-mpg SUV an extra $8,000. Yet another approach would be to dramatically raise gasoline taxes, an option presented to you in the decision box, "Pay More at the Pump?"

Option 2: Pay for Environmentally Sustainable Development

A second possibility is to pay the price to create and distribute technologies that will allow the LDCs to maximize the balance between economic development and environmental protection. Without modern technology and the money to pay for it, China, for example, poses a serious environmental threat. China now stands second behind the United States in terms of national CO_2 emissions. China's increased

DEBATE THE POLICY SCRIPT

Pay More at the Pump?

Americans make up less than 5% of the world population, yet they consume about 25% of its petroleum. With a private passenger vehicle for every two Americans, the largest single item (45%) in U.S. petroleum consumption is gasoline. Private vehicles use about two-thirds of all gasoline in the United States; Americans drive their private vehicles about 9,800 miles a year per capita or about 26,500 miles a year per household.

This freedom of movement comes at a price. U.S. dependence on foreign petroleum imports is high (75%) and expensive ($325 billion in 2006 for oil imports). Pollution is another cost. Carbon dioxide (CO_2) is one of several pollutants produced by motor vehicles. Given Americans' free-wheeling driving habits and preference for large vehicles, it is not surprising that the United States emits about 24% of all the world's CO_2. Private (noncommercial) driving by Americans generates one-fifth of that, or about 5% of world CO_2 emissions.

American motorists could thus make a major contribution to reducing CO_2 emissions and easing global warming by driving less or using more fuel-efficient cars. So far, most Americans seem little inclined to do either. One way to try to impact the driving habits of Americans would be to drastically hike gasoline taxes. Figure 15.2 shows that per capita use of the fuel is much lower in the three countries with high gasoline taxes than in the three countries with lower gasoline taxes. The United States was the least taxed of these three, with an 18 cents a gallon federal tax and an average 21 cents a gallon gas tax. If increasing the U.S. tax to the level of the Netherlands resulted in American motorists adopting the driving habits of the Dutch, U.S. gasoline consumption would drop 77%, resulting in billions of dollars in saving on imports and about 938 million metric tons less of annual CO_2 emissions. This would roll U.S. CO_2 emissions almost all the way back to the U.S. level in 1990.

What Do You Think?

Would you support an increase in federal and state taxes on gasoline from the current average of 39 cents a gallon to $4.11 a gallon? In mid-2007, that would increase the price per gallon at the pump from $3.25 ($2.86 for the product, $0.39 in taxes) to $6.97 a gallon ($2.86 for the product, $4.11 in taxes). What is the reasoning behind your position?

FIGURE 15.2   Gasoline Taxes and Consumption

Gasoline tax per gallon (US$)
Weekly per capita gasoline use (gallons)

Netherlands $4.18 — 1.3
Italy $3.59 — 1.4
United Kingdom $4.11 — 1.7

Countries with high gasoline taxes and low per capita gasoline consumption

Australia $1.38 — 3.5
Canada $0.96 — 4.8
United States $0.39 — 5.7

Countries with low gasoline taxes and high per capita gasoline consumption

The pre-tax cost of gasoline in these six countries was about the same, ranging from $1.83 in Canada and the United Kingdom to $2.15 in the Netherlands. Taxes were the biggest difference in gasoline costs at the pump. The group of three countries to the left had high gasoline taxes and an average total price per gallon of $5.93. The group of three to the right had much lower gasoline taxes and an average total price per gallon of $2.85. At least partly because of these price differences, the three high-tax, high-total-cost countries used a per capita average of 1.5 gallons of gasoline weekly, while the three low-tax, low-total-cost countries used a per capita average of 4.7 gallons of gasoline weekly.

Data source: "Ranking the Rich," *Foreign Policy,* September/October, 2006, p. 73.

The economic leaps that China and some other less developed countries are making highlight the problem of sustainable development. China's development is captured in these high-voltage transmissions lines and towers. The problem is that the electricity is almost certainly produced either by coal-burning power plants that put massive amounts of greenhouse gases into the atmosphere or by oil-burning power plants, which discharge less, but still substantial amounts of greenhouse gases and additionally increase the strain on the world's finite petroleum reserves.

WEB POLL
Opportunity and Costs

industrialization is one reason. But a second important factor is that China generates most of its commercial power by burning coal. The problem is that coal produces 45% more CO_2 per unit of energy generated than gasoline, 41% more than heating oil, and 97% more than natural gas. China annually consumes over 2 billion tons of coal, about 38% of the world total. This combined with the country's economic development, is a major reason why China's CO_2 emissions rose 57% between 1990 and 2004, while the rest of the world's emissions went up 19%. Even on a per capita basis, China's emissions increased more than four times the global per capita increase.

There are choices, but each has trade-offs. One option is to install pollution control equipment such as "stack scrubbers" to clean the emissions from burning coal. That would aid the environment, but it would be hugely expensive. For example, a recent proposal to retrofit a huge coal-fired generating plant in Bulgaria with stack scrubbers and other equipment, which would clean up its sulfur dioxide emissions by 95%, came with an estimated price tag of $650 million. Bulgaria had EU backing for the project, and China and other LDCs would need similar support to meet the costs of reducing the discharge of pollutants. Another approach China could take is to consume more oil to decrease the use of coal. Oil imports are vastly expensive, however, and act as a drag on the country's socioeconomic development. Increased oil consumption at the level China would need would also rapidly accelerate the depletion of the world's finite petroleum reserves. Moreover, the new oil fields that are being found often lie offshore, and drilling endangers the oceans.

A third possibility is using hydroelectricity to provide relatively nonpolluting energy. This requires the construction of dams that flood the surrounding countryside, displace its residents, and spoil the pristine beauty of the river valley downstream. China, for example, is trying to ease its energy crunch and simultaneously develop clean hydroelectric power by building the massive $25 billion Three Gorges Dam and hydroelectric project on the Yangtze River. The project, which rivals the Great Wall of China in scope, will vastly increase the availability of clean power to rural provinces by generating 18,200 megawatts of electricity without burning highly polluting coal. The dam will also help stem floods that have often caused catastrophic damage and death downstream. To accomplish these benefits, however, the dam will create a 370-mile-long reservoir, inundating over 200 cities, towns, and villages, forcing 1.3 million people from their homes. The rising water will submerge numerous archeological sites and what many consider one of the most scenic natural areas in the world. Moreover, a collapse of the dam from structural failure, earthquake or other natural disaster, or military attack could cause a flood of unimaginable proportions. Critics also charge that as the reservoir covers some 1,500 factories, hospitals, dumps, and other sites containing human and industrial waste, the water will become contaminated as the pollutants seep into it. Thus, the Three Gorges project is an almost perfect illustration of the difficulty of sustainable development.

Although the project will ease some environmental problems (in this case, coal burning) it will also have an adverse impact on people and create or worsen other environmental problems. Even if you can cut such Gordian knots, you will encounter other problems: the short-term costs of environmental protection in terms of taxes to pay for government programs; the high costs of products that are manufactured in an environmentally acceptable way and that are themselves environmentally safe; and the expense of disposing of waste in an ecologically responsible manner.

Moreover, since the LDCs are determined to develop economically, yet must struggle to pay the costs of environmentally sound progress, the North will have to extend significant aid to the South to help it develop in a relatively safe way. Money is needed to create nonpolluting energy resources, to install pollution control devices in factories, and to provide many other technologies. The costs will be huge, with some estimates exceeding $120 billion a year. Billions more are needed each year to help the LDCs stem their—and the world's—spiraling population.

Is the North willing to pay this price? Polls show that people in many countries are concerned about global warming, ozone layer destruction, deforestation, wildlife destruction, and acid rain. Cross-national polls also regularly find that a majority of respondents say that their governments should do more to protect their country's environment and also to be involved in the global environmental effort. Yet surveys additionally find that a majority of citizens think that their tax burdens are already too heavy and are reluctant to support large expenditures on environmental programs. In an indication about how Americans might respond to the question posed in the earlier box "Pay More at the Pump?" a 2007 survey recorded 58% of Americans rejecting and only 38% approving (with 4% unsure) the idea of increased gasoline taxes as a way to cut consumption and ease global warming.[5] Given Americans' historic antipathy to foreign aid, it is hard to imagine much support for higher taxes to pay other countries to protect the environment.

Web Link

An excellent informational and visual site, including film clips, on the Three Gorges Dam is associated with the PBS Great Wall across the Yangtze program at **www.pbs.org/itvs/greatwall/ yangtze.html.**

The Politics of Sustainable Development

There is not a great deal of debate over the fact that future development has to occur in a way that does not lay further waste to the biosphere. But what to do and who is responsible for doing it is a much more difficult question, and the lack of resolution of that issue has hampered efforts to fashion an overall global approach to achieving the goal of sustainable development. There are sections later in this chapter that address problems and programs associated with the atmosphere, water, land, and other elements of the biosphere, but before taking those up, it is appropriate to review the global approach to sustainable development and its politics at its broadest level.

The first step to dealing with any problem is recognizing that it exists. This has occurred with regard to sustainable development, as indicated by the two UN-sponsored "Earth Summits" in 1992 and 2002. However, both illustrate the limits to progress and the political disagreements that stand in the way.

Earth Summit I

The 1992 **United Nations Conference on Environment and Development (UNCED)** in Rio de Janeiro symbolized the growing concern with the environment and how to achieve sustainable development. Popularly dubbed Earth Summit I, most of the 178 countries in attendance were represented by their head of state. Additionally, 15,000 representatives of NGOs attended a nearby parallel conference. The official conference produced Agenda 21 (a 112-topic, nonbinding blueprint for sustainable development in the 21st century) and two treaties (the Biodiversity Convention and the Global Warming Convention).

Earth Summit I also featured the often-divisive politics of environmental protection. In particular, the North and the South were at odds on many issues. First, the LDCs argued that the burden of sustainable development should fall substantially on the EDCs because they were responsible for most of the pollution and depletion of resources. Second, LDCs also contended that they should be exempt wholly or in part from environmental restrictions because the EDCs had already developed and it was unfair to ask LDCs not to achieve the same national standards as the EDCs. Indeed, some in the LDCs suspect that EDC efforts to restrict their development may be part of a neocolonial effort to keep the LDCs poor, weak, and dependent. Third, LDCs maintained that they were too poor to develop their considerable resources in an environmentally sustainable way and, therefore, EDCs should significantly increase aid to help LDCs do so. For their part, most of the EDCs, especially the United States, disagreed with each of these LDC positions.

A stand-off occurred. The EDCs averted LDC efforts to set binding timetables for the EDCs to reduce their emissions of CO_2 and other gases that contribute to global warming. The North also resisted making major financial commitments. "We do not have an open pocketbook," President George H. W. Bush observed.[6] Similarly, the South avoided restrictions on such activities as deforestation. "Forests are clearly a sovereign resource. . . . We cannot allow forests to be taken up in global forums," Malaysia's chief negotiator asserted.[7] Given the various divisions, it was not surprising that neither the Biodiversity nor Global Warming Convention created legally binding mandates. It would be an overstatement to call the conference a failure, however, because important global initiatives normally gestate for an extended period, and the two treaties, Agenda 21, and the attention the conference generated all helped firmly plant the environment on the world political agenda.

Earth Summit II

A decade later, delegates from almost all of the world's countries and representatives from some 8,000 NGOs gathered in Johannesburg, South Africa, at Earth Summit II, the **World Summit on Sustainable Development (WSSD)** to address what the UN secretary-general called the "gap between the goals and the promises set out in Rio and the daily reality [of what has been accomplished]."[8] However, the political disputes that had bedeviled Earth Summit I also afflicted the WSSD, creating what an Indonesian diplomat portrayed as "a battle, a conflict of interest between developed and developing countries."[9] The United States and some other EDCs were unwilling to provide LDCs with substantially increased aid for sustainable development or to accept environmental restrictions that did not also apply at least partly to LDCs. The EDCs also opposed the creation of international agencies to monitor conditions and enforce mandatory standards. Articulating this view, one U.S. official insisted that the only path to progress was for "both developing and developed nations" to agree to mutual restrictions.[10] Taking the opposite view, the secretary-general asserted, "The richest countries must lead the way. They have the wealth. They have the technology. And they contribute disproportionately to global environmental problems."[11]

In the end, the EDCs did announce some new funding commitments, and the conference also adopted some important new, albeit voluntary, targets for reducing pollution and resource depletion, and for easing other biosphere problems. Although it is impossible to be satisfied with these modest steps, it would be wrong to judge the WSSD a dismal failure. Providing a good perspective, the UN secretary-general advised, "I think we have to be careful not to expect conferences like this to produce miracles. It is not one isolated conference that is going to do this whole thing." Instead, he suggested, "What happens is the energy that we create here, the commitments that have been made, and what we do on the ground as individuals, as civil society, as community groups and as governments and private sector."[12]

We can gain further perspective on the problems facing Earth Summits I and II by examining some of the key issues regarding the biosphere and the possibility of achieving international cooperation toward sustainable development. We will first consider population. Then we will turn to concerns over such resources as minerals, forests, wildlife, and water. Last, the chapter will take up environmental issues, including pollution of the ground, water, air, and upper atmosphere.

SUSTAINABLE DEVELOPMENT: POPULATION PROBLEMS AND PROGRESS

On Tuesday, October 12, 1999, the world population passed the 6 billion mark. That is a stunning number. Humans in their modern form date back about 40,000 years, and their number did not reach 1 billion until 1804. It took only another 195 years, to 1999, to get to the 6 billion mark. The jump from 5 billion to 6 billion had only taken 12 years. The world is awash in humanity, with China alone having more people than had been on Earth in 1804. The upward spiral has begun to slow, but only slightly. Current UN projections, as depicted in Figure 15.3, show the world population continuing to grow to 9 billion by midcentury. Given a reasonably finite amount of resources and ability to absorb waste, this growing population presents a challenge to Earth's carrying capacity. That will be an especially acute problem in some regions because their populations will continue to grow at a relatively rapid rate. Sub-Saharan

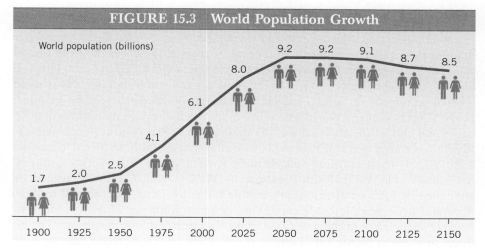

FIGURE 15.3   World Population Growth

The UN expects the world population to peak at 9.2 billion by midcentury, to stabilize briefly at that level, and then to gradually decline. Adding another 2.7 billion more people between 2005 and 2050 will strain Earth's resources, especially given the increased use of resources and the generation of waste due to economic development.

Data source: UN Population Division.

MAP
Population Growth Rate

Africa will be the most troubled. Its population is projected to grow annually by 2.43% between 2005 and 2115, while the world population is projected to grow at an annual rate of just 1.14%. The percentages may seem small, but they mean that Sub-Saharan Africa will have about 9 million more people a year than it would have at the 1.14% rate.

The acceleration of population growth beginning about 1950 that is evident in Figure 15.3 occurred for several reasons. *High fertility rates* is one. Between 1950 and 1970 the average woman had five children, with an average between 6 and 7 children per family in the LDCs. That overall rate has fallen, but the world population continues to grow too fast. *Fewer deaths* is a second and increasingly important factor. Better health means that more infants survive to grow up and adults live longer. In 1950, 20 of every 1,000 people worldwide died each year; now only 9 of every 1,000 do. A third factor causing population growth is the *population base multiplier effect*. This problem is one of mathematics. During the next decade, some 3 billion women will enter their childbearing years. At the current fertility rate, these women will have 7.5 billion children, who in turn will have yet more children. Thus the population will continue to grow until the world fertility falls to 2.1, the approximate "replacement rate" at which each set of parents has two surviving children.

Global Recognition of the Population Problem

The United Nations has led the effort to control global population growth. Among the UN divisions and associated agencies involved, the United Nations Population Fund (UNFPA) is the largest. It began operations in 1969 and focuses on promoting family planning services and improving reproductive health in LDCs. During its history, UNFPA has provided over $6 billion to support population programs in the vast majority of the world's countries. In addition to its own programs, the agency helps coordinate programs of other related IGOs and national governments. UNFPA's efforts are further supplemented by and often coordinated with NGOs such as the International Planned Parenthood Federation (IPPF). This British-based organization, which was founded in 1952, operates its own international family planning programs and also links the individual planned parenthood organizations of about 150 countries.

Additionally, the need to control global population growth led the UN to sponsor three world population conferences. The most recent of these was the 1994 **United Nations Conference on Population and Development (UNCPD)** in Cairo, Egypt. It brought together delegates from over 170 countries and a large number of NGOs and focused on population control and on reproductive health. Each year, for example, about 529,000 women (99% of whom live in LDCs) die from complications of pregnancy and childbirth. Abortion was the most controversial issue at the conference. Abortion is widely available in about 60% of all countries, fairly restricted in another 15%, and very restricted or unavailable in the remaining 25% of the world's countries. According to the World Health Organization (WHO), about 22% of all pregnancies are ended by induced abortions (those that occur for other than natural causes). Abortions performed in unsafe conditions, either in countries where it is illegal or severely restricted or in countries with an inadequate health care system, are a major threat to women's health. WHO estimates that about 68,000 women a year die from unsafe abortions. There are estimates that in some countries, which both restrict abortions and are exceptionally poor, over half of all maternal mortality is the result of illegal abortion.

Controversy at the conference centered on how far it should go toward supporting abortion as a health measure or even as a population control approach. Predominantly

Muslim countries were particularly opposed to the conference's support of abortion, with the Sudanese government charging that this would result in "the spread of immoral and irreligious ideas."[13] The Roman Catholic Church was also critical, with the pope warning the conference not to "ignore the rights of the unborn."[14] Among those with the opposite view was Norway's Prime Minister Gro Harlem Brundtland, who charged, "Morality becomes hypocrisy if it means accepting mothers' suffering or dying in connection with unwanted pregnancies and illegal abortions and unwanted children."[15]

The result of this conflict was a compromise, with the language in the conference report promoting safe abortion qualified by the phrase, "in circumstances in which abortion is legal," and the caveat, "In no case should abortion be promoted as a method of family planning." The 1994 Cairo conference unanimously approved a "Program of Action" calling for spending $5.7 billion annually by the year 2000 on international programs to foster family planning. Funding never reached that goal, but the heightened awareness of the population problem and the closely associated issue of women's reproductive health and the postconference activity of the delegates and others did help to increase funding from $1.3 billion in 1993 to $2.2 billion in 2000. Most importantly, maternal mortality has declined by about one-third since the conference.

Approaches to Reducing the Birthrate

There are two basic approaches to reducing the birthrate. *Social approaches* provide information about birth control and encouragement to practice it by making birth control devices and pills, sterilization, and, in some cases, abortion programs available. The combined efforts of national governments, UNFPA and other IGOs, and NGOs, have had an impact. During the early 1960s, the contraceptive prevalence rate (the percentage of couples practicing contraception) in the LDCs was only 9%. Now it is 60%. This contraceptive prevalence rate falls off drastically in the least developed countries (LLDCs), where it is only 40%.

Economic approaches to population growth also work. There is a clear relationship between poverty and the number of children a woman bears. The fertility rate (average number of children a woman will have) is 1.7 in high-income countries, 2.1 in middle-income countries, and 3.7 in low-income countries. How does one explain the link between population and wealth? One view is that overpopulation causes poverty. This view reasons that with too many people, especially in already poor countries, there are too few resources, jobs, and other forms of wealth to go around. Perhaps, but that is only part of the problem, because it is also true that poverty *causes* overpopulation. The low-income countries tend to have the most labor-intensive economies, those in which children are economically valuable because they help their parents with farming or, when they are somewhat older, provide cheap labor in mining and manufacturing processes. As a result, cultural attitudes in many countries have come to reflect economic utility. Having a large family is also an asset in terms of social standing in many societies with limited economic opportunities.

Furthermore, women in low-income countries have fewer opportunities to limit the number of children they bear. Artificial birth control methods and counseling services are less readily available in these countries. Another fact is that women in LDCs are less educated than are women in EDCs. It is therefore harder to convey birth control information, especially written information, to women in LDCs. Additionally, they have fewer opportunities than do women in EDCs to gain paid employment and to develop status roles beyond that of motherhood. The lack of educational and economic opportunities are related to both the use of contraception and the fertility

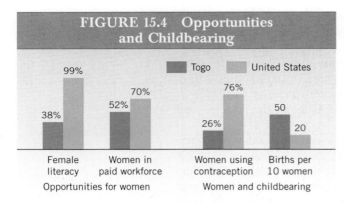

FIGURE 15.4 Opportunities and Childbearing

The greater the educational and economic opportunities that women have, the more likely they are to use contraception and to have fewer babies. The two measures on the left show educational opportunities (the percentage of adult women who are literate) and economic opportunities (the percentage of working-age women who have a paid job). The two measures on the right show the likelihood that women (ages 15–49) are using contraception and how many children they have on average. Notice that American women have better educational and economic opportunities compared to women in Togo and are also more likely to use contraception and less likely to have numerous children.

Data source: World Bank.

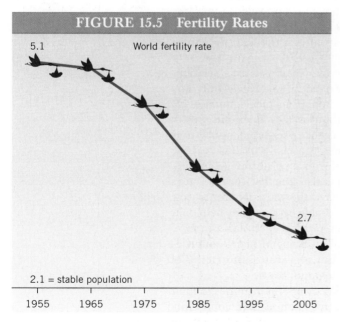

FIGURE 15.5 Fertility Rates

The number of children the average woman bears has dropped by almost 50% since the 1950s. This welcome change is the result of numerous factors, including the work of international agencies to improve educational and economic opportunities for females and to provide information and other forms of assistance to women who wish to practice planned parenthood.

Data source: UN Population Division, *World Population to 2003* (UN: New York, 2004).

rate, as evident in Figure 15.4, which compares Togo and the United States.

The evidence that poverty causes population increases has spurred efforts to advance the economic and educational opportunities available to women as an integral part of population control. This realization was one of the factors that led the UN to designate 1975 as International Women's Year and to kick off the Decade for Women. That year the UN also convened the first World Conference on Women (WCW). These initiatives were followed in 1976 by the establishment of the UN Development Fund for Women (UNIFEM, after its French acronym). The Fund works through 10 regional offices to improve the living standards of women in LDCs by providing technical and financial support to advance the entry of women into business, scientific and technical careers, and other key areas. UNIFEM also strives to incorporate women into the international and national planning and administration of development programs and to ensure that issues of particular concern to women such as food, security, human rights, and reproductive health are kept on the global agenda. The UN also established the International Research and Training Institute for the Advancement of Women with the task of carrying out research, training, and information activities related to women and the development process. Headquartered in the Dominican Republic, the institute conducts research on the barriers that impede the progress of women in social, economic, and political development.

The Impact of International Population Control Efforts

The effort to reduce global population growth is a success story. Part of the credit goes to the work of IGOs, NGOs, and national governments. Improved economic conditions in many LDCs and the slowly improving economic and educational status of women in many countries have also played a role. As a result, the average global fertility rate has declined dramatically, as evident in Figure 15.5. The goal is 2.1, which is about the stable replacement rate. The UN expects that standard to be reached by mid-century. Indeed, after that the UN expects the fertility rate to drop below the replacement rate, which will for a time at least decrease the world population late in this century. As recently as 1994, the population was expanding at 94 million a year, and the UN was estimating that it would reach 11.6 billion by 2150. Now the population is projected to peak at more than 2 billion people short of that. That is stellar news, but it merits two cautions. One is that population is hard to predict; a UN "worse-case scenario" projects the population at 14 billion at the end of this century and peaking at 36 billion in 2300. Second, despite the slowdown, the substantial population increase that is looming will challenge Earth's carrying capacity.

SUSTAINABLE DEVELOPMENT: RESOURCE PROBLEMS AND PROGRESS

Recent decades have witnessed increased warnings that we are using our resources too quickly. Most studies of the rates at which we are depleting energy, mineral, forest, land, wildlife, fishery, and water resources have expressed a level of concern ranging from caution to serious alarm.

Petroleum, Natural Gas, and Minerals

The supply of oil, gas, and mineral resources is one area of concern. At the forefront of these worries are the cost and supply of energy resources. World energy needs are skyrocketing. Global energy production increased 80% between 1960 and 2005. Seventy-five percent of the output is generated by burning fossil fuels (coal, oil, and gas); following in declining order are burning wood, crop residue, and other forms of biomass; then, nuclear energy. Only about 3% of energy is produced by such environmentally friendly sources as hydroelectric, solar, geothermal, and wind power. At one time the world had an estimated 2.3 trillion barrels of oil beneath its surface. Current known reserves are a bit more than half of that. At the rate that oil is being consumed—34 billion barrels in 2007—simple math would suggest that the world's oil wells will go dry in 2046. Natural gas supplies are a bit better, but at current reserves and use they will be depleted in 2072. But projections are tricky because demand changes, because new sources of oil and gas are sometimes discovered, and because new techniques such as deep sea drilling are developed to tap previously unusable deposits. For example, known reserves of petroleum actually increased from 1.01 trillion barrels in 1996 to 1.32 trillion barrels in 2007. Nevertheless, petroleum and natural gas reserves are a concern because the supply is indisputably exhaustible and because new finds are smaller and less attractive to utilize (deeper, under the ocean, in environmentally sensitive land areas).

The story for natural gas is nearly the same. New discoveries, enhanced extraction methods, and other factors may have an impact on the timing, but the bottom line is that the supply is finite and at some point, perhaps within the lifetime of those being born today, it will be exhausted. Coal will last almost 500 years at current consumption rates, but it is a major pollutant if not controlled by expensive technology. The development of hydroelectric power is attractive in some ways, but it is expensive to develop, and damming rivers creates environmental and social problems. Nuclear power is yet another alternative, and some countries rely heavily on it. For one, France generates 80% of its electricity by nuclear power. However, only 30 countries generate nuclear power, and on average it amounts to only about 20% of their total commercial energy production. Additionally, there are high costs and obvious hazards to nuclear power. Some people advocate developing wind, solar, geothermal, and other such sources of power. So far, though, cost, production capacity, and other factors have limited the application of these energy sources and will continue to do so unless there are major technological breakthroughs.

Did You Know That:

The world's first oil well was drilled in 1859 in Titusville, Pennsylvania. Sold as a lubricant, oil initially averaged $25 a barrel, compared to over $75 a barrel in August 2007. Adjusted for inflation, the 1859 price is equal to about $624 a barrel today.

JOIN THE DEBATE
Is a Government-Sponsored
Clean Energy Program the
Answer to Rising Oil Prices
and Overall Economic and
Environmental Security?

Another factor in the supply and demand for energy is usage patterns. With 10% of the world population, the EDCs consumed 50% of the energy. But in terms of increasing use, LDC energy consumption increased 105% between 1975 and 2005, while the increase in energy consumption by EDCs was lower at 76%. This pattern indicates that while the North may bear much of the responsibility to date for the resources used to create the energy and the waste products discharged, no solution is possible unless the South is a full participant. In addition to oil and natural gas, many other minerals are also being rapidly depleted. Based on world reserves and world use, some minerals that are in particularly short supply (and estimates of the year that Earth's supply will be exhausted given known reserves) include copper (2056), lead (2041), mercury (2077), tin (2053), and zinc (2042). Certainly, discoveries of new sources or the decline of consumption based on conservation or the use of substitutes could extend those dates. But it is also possible that the time interval to depletion could narrow if, for instance, extraction rates accelerate as LDCs develop.

The resource puzzle, as mentioned, is how to simultaneously (1) maintain the industrialized countries' economies and standards of living, (2) promote economic development in the South (which will consume increased energy and minerals), and (3) manage the problems of resource depletion and environmental damage involved in energy and mineral production and use. If, for instance, the South were to develop to the same economic level as the North, if the LDCs' energy-use patterns were the same as the North's currently are, and if the same energy resource patterns that now exist persisted, then petroleum reserves would almost certainly soon be dry. Natural gas and many other minerals probably would also quickly follow oil into the museum of geological history.

Forests and Land

For many who will read this book, the trees that surround them and the very land on which they stand will hardly seem like natural resources and will certainly not seem to be endangered. That is not the case. There are serious concerns about the depletion of the world's forests and the degradation of its land.

Forest Depletion

The depletion of forests and their resources concerns many analysts. Data compiled by the UN Food and Agriculture Organization (FAO) and other sources indicates that the increase in world population and, to a lesser degree, economic development have been destroying the world's forests. Some 1 billion people depend on wood as an energy source, and many forests have been depleted for fuel to cook food and heat homes. Forests are also being cleared to make room for farms and grazing lands. Forests and woodland still cover about 30% of Earth's land area. Once, however, they occupied 48% of the land area, and tree cover has been declining by about 1% every ten years. Logging is a major factor, but forests are also being drowned by hydroelectric projects and being strip-mined for minerals. Acid rain and other environmental attacks increase the toll on trees. The result is that in recent years an average 35,000 square miles of forest, an area about the size of Portugal, have been lost annually. Forest loss is greatest in the LLDCs, whose forests are disappearing at the rate of 1% every two years. Tropical forests, which account for over 80% of all forest losses, are in particular peril. Fifty years ago, 12% of Earth's land surface was covered by tropical forest; now just 6% is. The Amazon River basin's tropical forest in Brazil and the surrounding countries is an especially critical issue. This ecosystem is by far the largest of its kind in the world, covering 2.7 million square miles, about the size of

The charred remains shown here of what was once lush rain forest in Brazil are just a minute fraction of the forest lands that have been destroyed around the world. The environmental costs of deforestation are enormous. They include loss of trees to convert CO_2 into oxygen, runoff that fills rivers with silt, destruction of endangered flora and fauna, loss of human life from mudslides, and exhaustion of the land's fertility.

the 48 contiguous U.S. states. The expanding populations and economic needs of the region's countries have exerted great pressure on the forest. For example, the Amazon basin has recently been losing 9,000 square miles (an area about the size of Massachusetts) of forest every year.

LDCs recognize the problem, but economic need drives them to continue to clear forestland for farming, building material, roads and other facilities, and many other domestic uses. Wood and wood products (such as paper, pulp, and resins) are also valuable exports, annually bringing in about $100 billion in needed earnings to the LDCs. It is easy to blame the LDCs for allowing their forests to be overcut, but many in those countries ask what alternative they have. "Anyone . . . who comes in and tells us not to cut the forest has to give us another way to live," says an official of Suriname. "And so far they haven't done that." Instead, what occurs, charges the country's president, is "eco-colonialism" by international environmental organizations trying to prevent Suriname from using its resources.[16]

Deforestation has numerous negative consequences. One is global warming, which we will discuss in a later section. Another ill effect of forest depletion is that wood in many areas has become so scarce and so expensive that poor urban dwellers have to spend up to a third of their meager incomes to heat their homes and cook. Poor people in rural areas have to devote the entire time of a family member to gather wood for home use. The devastation of the forests is also driving many forms of life into extinction. A typical 4-square-mile section of the Amazon basin rain forest contains some 750 species of trees, 125 kinds of mammals, 400 types of birds, 160 different kinds of reptiles and amphibians, and perhaps 300,000 insect species. The loss of bio-diversity has an obvious aesthetic impact, and there are also pragmatic implications. Some 25% of all modern pharmaceutical products are "green medicines" that contain ingredients originally found in plants. Extracts from Madagascar's rosy periwinkle, for example, are used in drugs to treat children's leukemia and Hodgkin's disease. Taxol is a drug derived from the Pacific yew for use in cancer chemotherapy, and a soil fungus is the source of the anticholesterol drug Mevacor. Many plants also

MAP
Hot Spots of Diversity

contain natural pesticides that could provide the basis for the development of eco-logically safe commercial pesticides to replace the environmental horrors (such as DDT) of the past.

Fortunately, the story of the world's forests is not all bleak. Recent research indicates that overall forest depletion may have stopped. One study found that about half of the countries with the largest forests are having positive forest growth. "This is the first time we have documented that many countries have turned the corner, that gradually forests are coming back," commented a scholar involved in the study. The head of the FAO's forest division cautioned that while he was glad about the study's "positive indications of an important change," he also felt that the lack of good data on forests in many parts of the world meant it would be wise not to be overly optimistic.[17]

Land Degradation

Not only are the forests beleaguered, so too is the land. Deforestation is one of the many causes of soil erosion and other forms of damage to the land. Tropical forests rest on thin topsoil. This land is especially unsuited for agriculture, and it becomes exhausted quickly once the forest is cut down and crops are planted or grazing takes place. With no trees to hold soil in place, runoff occurs, and silt clogs rivers and bedevils hydro-electric projects. Unchecked runoff can also significantly increase the chances of down-river floods, resulting in loss of life and economic damage, and deadly mudslides down barren slopes with no trees to hold the dirt in place.

According to the United Nations Environmental Programme (UNEP), 3.5 million square miles (about the size of China or the United States) of land are moderately degraded, 1.4 million square miles (about equal to Argentina) are strongly degraded, and 347,000 square miles (about the same as Egypt) are extremely degraded (beyond repair). At its worst, *desertification* occurs. More of the world's surface is becoming desertlike because of water scarcity, timber cutting, overgrazing, and overplant-ing. The desertification of land is increasing at an estimated rate of 30,600 square miles a year, turning an area the size of Austria into barren desert. Moreover, that rate of degradation could worsen, based on UNEP's estimate that 8 billion acres are in jeopardy.

Forest and Land Protection

Because almost all of the world's land lies within the boundaries of a sovereign state, international programs have been few. Desertification is one area in which there has been international action. Almost all countries are party to the Convention on Desertification (1994), which set up a structure to monitor the problem and to assist countries in devising remedial programs to reclaim barren land. There have also been some advances at the regional level. Most European countries abide by a 1979 treaty to reduce acid rain, and addressing that issue was the main goal of the Canada-U.S. Air Quality Agreement (1991). More recently, and addressing another problem, leaders of seven central African countries agreed in 2005 to a treaty to protect their region's rain forest, which is second in size to the one in the Amazon basin.

Progress is also being made at the national level in the preservation of forest and land resources, as well as on other resource and environmental concerns. Member-ship in environmental groups has grown dramatically. In several European countries and in the European Union, "green parties" have become viable political forces. For example, they have 42 (5%) of the seats in the European Parliament and Germany's Green Party has 51 seats (8%) in the Bundestag. The growing interest in flora and fauna is also increasing the so-called ecotourism trade, which some sources estimate makes up as much as a third of the nearly $500 billion annual tourism industry. For this reason, many countries are beginning to realize that they can derive more economic benefit from tourists than from loggers wielding chain saws.

Wildlife

World wildlife is amazingly diverse. These life forms (and the approximate number of known species for each) include mammals (4,300), reptiles (6,800), birds (9,700), fish (28,000), mollusks (80,000), insects (+1,000,000), and arachnids (44,000).

Global Pressure on Wildlife

The march of humankind has driven almost all the other creatures into retreat and, in some cases, into extinction. Deforestation, land clearing for settlement and farming, water diversion and depletion, and pollution are but a few of modernization's by-products that destroy wildlife habitat. There are pragmatic, as well as aesthetic, costs. The blood-pressure drug Capoten is derived from the venom of the Brazilian pit viper, and vampire bat saliva is the basis of an anti–blood-clotting drug being tested to prevent heart attacks and stroke.

While some species are the unintended victims of development, others are threatened because they have economic value. The estimated $10 billion annual illegal trade in feathers, pelts, ivory, and other wildlife products is leading to the capture and sale or slaughter of numerous species, including many that are endangered. Tigers are dying because their bodies are so valuable. A pelt fetches up to $15,000; powdered tiger humerus bone, said to cure typhoid fever and other ailments, sells for $1,450 a pound; and men in some parts of the world pay $1,200 for a tiger's penis in the hope that eating it will improve their virility. Other endangered animals wind up on someone's dinner plate. Rising prosperity in China has increased the number of *ye wei* (wild taste) restaurants, where for $100 or so a buffet of elephant, tiger, and other exotic fare can be eaten (Marshall, 2006). Much of the slaughter occurs in LDCs, but the EDCs are not guiltless. For example, poachers illegally kill more than 40,000 bears each year in the United States in part to harvest their gall bladders. These supposedly relieve a range of ailments (including hemorrhoids) and sell for up to $3,000 when smuggled abroad.

It should be noted that on the issue of wildlife, like many other matters discussed in this chapter, there are optimists who believe that the problem is being grossly overstated. According to one, "a fair reading of the available data suggests a rate of extinction not even one–one-thousandth as great as the one the doomsayers scare us with." He cautioned against ignoring "possible dangers to species," but stressed, "We should strive for a clear and unbiased view of species' assets so as to make sound judgments about how much time and money to spend on guarding them."[18] Other analysts have agreed with that assessment (Lomborg, 2001).

Protecting Wildlife

Although the world's list of endangered species is still growing, these threatened species are also now gaining some relief through the Convention on the International Trade in Endangered Species (CITES, 1975) and the 167 countries that are party to it. Elephants were added in 1989 to the CITES list of endangered species, and the legal ivory trade has dropped from 473 tons in 1985 to zero. About 500 elephants a year are still being killed for their ivory by poachers, but that is far better than the annual toll of 70,000 elephants during the last decade before they were protected under CITES. Wild cats, reptiles, and other types of wildlife have also found greater refuge,

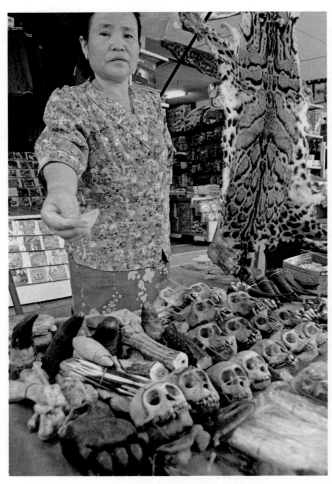

The Convention on the International Trade in Endangered Species (CITES) has provided some relief to many endangered species by banning the international sale of live wildlife or wildlife products, such as skins. However, the limits of CITES are evident in this recent photograph of a woman in the street market in Tachileik, Myanmar (Burma), openly selling wildlife parts including monkey skulls and the pelt of a clouded leopard, an endangered species.

and the international sale of their skins has declined drastically. The global trade in live primates, birds, and reptiles has seen similar decreases. Individual countries have also acted to suppress poaching and punish those engaged in the illegal sales of wildlife. In 2003, for example, Chinese officials impounded 1,276 illegal pelts from 32 tigers, 579 leopards, and 665 otters that had been smuggled into the country. It was the largest seizure in China's history, and a particularly helpful sign from a region that is the destination of a great deal of the illegal trade in wildlife, especially in parts used in traditional medicine. Penalties, it should be noted, are especially stringent for such activity in China, which has executed at least 28 wildlife smugglers since 1990.

Freshwater

"Water, water everywhere, Nor any drop to drink," cries out an adrift seaman in Samuel Taylor Coleridge's *Rime of the Ancient Mariner* (1798). That cannot quite be said of the world's freshwater, but there is less of it than you might think. Yes, 71% of Earth's surface is covered by water, but 97% of it is salt water and another 2% is frozen in the polar ice caps. This leaves only 1% readily available for drinking, watering livestock, and irrigating crops. Moreover, some of the freshwater supply that exists is being depleted or being tainted by pollution. Freshwater use, after tripling between 1940 and 1975, has slowed its growth rate to about 2% to 3% a year. Much of this is due to population stabilization and conservation measures in the EDCs. Still, because the world population is growing and rainfall is a constant, the world needs to use an additional 7.1 trillion gallons each year just to grow the extra grain needed to feed the expanding population.

Complicating matters even more, many countries, especially LDCs, have low per capita supplies of water, as you can see in the map on page 509. The world per capita availability is 8,549 cubic meters (1 m^3 = 264.2 gallons), but it is unevenly distributed. Indeed, about 20% of all countries have an annual availability of less than 1,000 cubic meters of water per person. Given the fact that Americans annually use 1,682 cubic meters of water per capita, the inadequacy of less than 1,000 cubic meters is readily apparent.

To make matters worse, the water usage in LDCs will increase as they develop their economies. These increases will either create greater pressure on the water supply or will limit a country's growth possibilities. Globally, most freshwater is used for either agriculture (70%) or industry (20%), with only 10% for domestic (personal) use. Industrialized countries, however, use greater percentages for industry and more water per capita overall than LDCs. It follows then, that as LDCs industrialize, their

Per Capita Water Availability

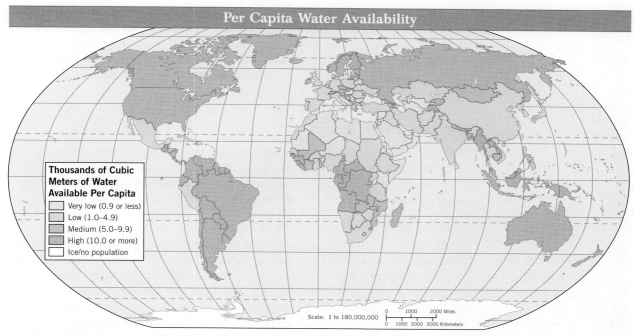

Thousands of Cubic Meters of Water Available Per Capita
- Very low (0.9 or less)
- Low (1.0–4.9)
- Medium (5.0–9.9)
- High (10.0 or more)
- Ice/no population

Scale: 1 to 180,000,000

0   1000   2000 Miles
0 1000 2000 3000 Kilometers

A report by the United Nations Commission on Sustainable Development warns that 1.2 billion people live in countries facing "medium-high to high water stress."

Data source: World Resources Institute, 2006.

water needs will rise rapidly. China provides an example: Water use for industry, which was 46 billion cubic meters in 1980, has increased 107% to 95 billion cubic meters. Adding to the problem in many countries, a great deal of the water needed for drinking is being contaminated by fertilizer leaching, industrial pollution, human and animal wastes, and other discharges.

Compounding demands on the water supply even further, global population growth means that the water supply worldwide will decline by one-third by 2050, leaving 7 billion people in 60 countries facing a water shortage. "Of all the social and natural crises we humans face, the water crisis is the one that lies at the heart of our survival and that of our planet Earth," the director-general of the United Nations Educational, Scientific, and Cultural Organization (UNESCO) has commented.[19]

If this projection proves accurate, it could lead to competition for water and to international tensions. There are, for example, 36 countries with a water "dependency ratio" above 50, that is they get more than 50% of their freshwater from rivers that originate outside their borders. The security of these countries would be threatened if upstream countries diverted that water for their own purposes or threatened to limit it as a political sanction. For example, Israel, which only has 2.041 cubic meters of water per capita to begin with, also has a dependency ratio of 55, with a majority of its water sources originating in the surrounding, often hostile Arab states. Such possibilities have led some analysts to suggest that in the not-too-distant future the access to water supplies could send "thirsty" countries over the brink of war.

Such concerns are not new. The first known water treaty was negotiated 4,500 years ago by two Sumerian city-states to end their dispute over water in the Tigris River.

Just since 1820, according to the UN, more than 400 treaties have been concluded relating to water as a limited and consumable resource. Nevertheless, old disputes reemerge and new ones break out. Such disputes recently moved the head of UNEP to contend that there is an "urgent need" for IGOs to "act as the water equivalent of marriage counselors, amicably resolving differences between countries . . . [that] may be straying apart."[20]

The Seas and Fisheries

The saltwater oceans and seas cover about two-thirds of Earth's surface. The water may not be useful for drinking or irrigation, but the seas are immensely valuable resources. Their fish and the food they provide are covered in this section; marine pollution is taken up later in this chapter under environmental concerns.

Pressures on the Seas and Fisheries

Human food requirements put increasing pressure on the ocean's fish, mollusks, and crustaceans. The importance of marine life as a source of food plus the demands of a growing world population increased the marine (saltwater) catch from 17 million tons in 1950, to 62 million tons in 1980, to 84 million tons recently. Saltwater accounts for 63% of the world's fisheries production, with aquaculture providing 30%, and freshwater wild fisheries supplying the remaining 7%. Given an estimate by the Food and Agriculture Organization (FAO) that the sustainable annual yield of Earth's oceans is no more than 96 million tons, it is clear that a critical point is approaching rapidly. One recent study concluded that 29% of species that provide seafood had either been fished so heavily or so damaged by pollution or loss of habitat, such as reef destruction, that they had been reduced to 10% of peak levels. Most other species were also depleted to a greater or lesser degree. "I don't have a crystal ball and I don't know what the future will bring, but this is a clear trend," one researcher commented. "There is an end [to the marine fisheries] in sight, and it is within our lifetimes."[21] Given that the world's fisheries supply 15% of the animal protein humans consume, the danger to the fisheries poses a health threat to countries that rely on fish for vital protein supplies. Especially imperiled would be Asia and Africa, where fish contribute 20% or more to the often inadequate animal protein in the diet of the regions' inhabitants (Williams, 2005).

Protecting Fisheries

One major step at the international level came in 1994 when the UN's convention on the Law of the Sea went into effect. Agreed to by 148 countries, not including the United States, the treaty gives countries full sovereignty over the seas within 12 miles of their shores and control over fishing rights and oil and gas exploration rights within 200 miles of their shores. That should improve conservation in these coastal zones. Additionally, an International Seabed Authority, headquartered in Jamaica, has been established. It will help regulate mining of the seabed in international waters and will receive royalties from those mining operations to help finance ocean-protection programs.

National and international efforts are also being made in other areas. A huge decline in demersal fish (such as cod, flounder, and haddock) in the northwest Atlantic prompted Canada and the United States to severely limit catches in rich fishing grounds such as the Grand Banks and the Georges Bank off their North Atlantic coasts. On an even broader scale, 99 countries, including all the major fishing countries, agreed in 1995 to an international treaty that will regulate the catch of all the species of fish (such as cod, pollock, tuna, and swordfish) that migrate between national and international waters. As evident in Figure 15.6, the treaty was part of the rapidly growing number of international pacts to regulate the marine catch that have made fishing, as one diplomat put it, "no longer a free-for-all situation."[22]

Despite its relatively minor economic impact, there is no issue of marine regulation that sparks more emotion than the control of whaling. At the center of the controversy is the International Whaling Commission (IWC), which was established in 1946. With whale populations plummeting and some species nearing extinction, the IWC banned commercial whaling in 1986. That did not end whaling, however. Norway, although an IWC member, objects to the ban and under a loophole in the IWC treaty takes about 1,000 whales a year; Japan takes another 700 whales under the pretext of scientific study, which is permitted under IWC rules; and Iceland takes 60 for science. A number of other counties or indigenous peoples add to the annual whale harvest, which totals about 1,900. About 80% of all whales taken each year are minke whales, but more than a half dozen other types, including sperm and humpback whales, are also harpooned.

The controversy over whaling has occasioned strong clashes at each year's IWC meeting. Japan leads the move to abolish the moratorium, and in 2006 managed to get a one-vote majority in the IWC saying that the number of many species of whales makes the ban no longer necessary. However, abolishing the prohibition requires a three-fourths vote of the IWC's 73 members, and Japanese diplomacy has not mustered nearly that many votes. Critics accuse Japan of using its foreign aid to win votes on the IWC and point, for example, to the decision of landlocked Laos to join the IWC in 2007 soon after the Laotian prime minister visited Tokyo and reconfirmed its aid package to his country. However, Great Britain and other countries that oppose Japan have also been active in encouraging other landlocked, but antiwhaling countries like Slovakia to join the IWC. Those who advocate whaling claim that the minke population, which is between 300,000 and 1,000,000, will support limited commercial whaling. They also argue that whaling can provide an important source of food and income. As an official from Dominica put it, "This is a creature like all others that people depend upon for food, and therefore because of its abundance we think that we can take a limited amount and make some money out of it."[23] The whaling issue has also become enmeshed with issues of national pride. "There is a consensus in Japan that as part of the natural right for a sovereign nation it is perfectly right to continue whaling," explained a Japanese Ministry of Foreign Affairs official.[24] Advocates for the moratorium argue that too little is known about whale numbers and reproduction to allow commercial whaling. As for whaling for supposedly scientific study, the antiwhaling view is typified by a U.S. government statement, "The United States believes that lethal research on whales is not necessary, and that the needed scientific data can be obtained by well-established nonlethal means."[25]

FIGURE 15.6   Fisheries Treaties

Number of multilateral treaties in force

53

1

1930 1940 1950 1960 1970 1980 1990 2000 2006

The world's marine fisheries are in danger of being exhausted. International recognition of this fact is evident in the rapid growth in the number of treaties regulating fishing, whaling, crabbing, and other forms of wildlife harvests in international waters. In addition to the 53 multilateral treaties, there are over 700 bilateral treaties regulating shared freshwater and marine fisheries.

Data source: Internet Guide to Fisheries Law, at http://www.oceanlaw.net/texts/index.htm.

Web Link

For a prowhaling point of view, visit the Web site of the Japan Whaling Association at **www.whaling.jp/english/.** Whale-Watch has one of the numerous antiwhaling sites at **www.whalewatch.org.**

Did You Know That:

In 2006, whale meat was selling for about $10 a pound in Japan.

SUSTAINABLE DEVELOPMENT: THE ENVIRONMENT

In the environmental equation on p. 492, the growing world population and its increasing consumption of resources are only part of the problem. The third part of that equation is the increasing waste and pollution from the excretions of over 6 billion people and the untold billions of domestic animals they keep for food or companionship and from the discharges of polluting gases, chemicals, and other types of waste into the water, air, and ground by industry, governments, and individuals.

The state of the biosphere is related to many of the economic and resource issues we have been examining. Like the concerns over those issues, international awareness and activity are relatively recent and are still in their early stages. Several concerns that have an environmental impact, such as desertification, deforestation, and biodiversity loss, have already been discussed. The next sections will look at threats to the quality of the ground we walk on, the water we drink, the air we breathe, and to the dangers posed by global warming and ozone layer depletion.

Ground Quality

It seems almost comical to observe that there are serious concerns about the dirt getting dirty. Ground quality is no joke, however. Industrial waste and other discharges have polluted large tracts of land, some of the largest construction projects engineered by mankind are garbage dumps (euphemistically called landfills), and destructive farming techniques have depleted the soil of its nutrients in many areas.

International Ground Quality Issues

Did You Know That:

A dumped computer monitor contains up to 8 pounds of toxic lead.

The pollution of the land is a significant problem, but the territorial dominance of states usually leaves this issue outside the realm of international action. Exporting solid waste for disposal does, however, have an international impact. With their disposal sites brimming and frequently dangerous, EDCs annually ship millions of tons of hazardous wastes to LDCs. Financial considerations have persuaded some LDCs to accept these toxic deliveries. Along with sending old tires, batteries, and other refuse to LDCs, the EDCs also practice so-called e-dumping, shipping millions of discarded computers and other electronic devices overseas for disposal. Some 63 million computers become obsolete in the United States each year, and many of those are shipped overseas, supposedly for recycling. According to one report, "The Digital Dump: Exporting Reuse and Abuse to Africa," Nigeria alone receives 400,000 such computers each month.[26] What occurs, though, is that small amounts of valuable minerals (gold, platinum, silver, copper, and palladium) found on some motherboards are sometimes extracted, and the rest of the unit is dumped, where it adds to ground and water pollution. In the view of one NGO report, "The export of e-waste remains a dirty little secret of the high-tech revolution."[27]

Although this practice—in essence, using LDCs as disposal sites—is widely condemned and illegal in some shipping and receiving countries, the UN reports that "the volume of transboundary movements of toxic wastes has not diminished." Even more alarmingly, the report warns, "The wastes are sent to poor countries lacking the infrastructure for appropriate treatment. They are usually dumped in overpopulated areas in poor regions or near towns, posing great risks to the environment and to the life and health of the poorest populations and those least able to protect themselves."[28] A closely associated international aspect of ground pollution

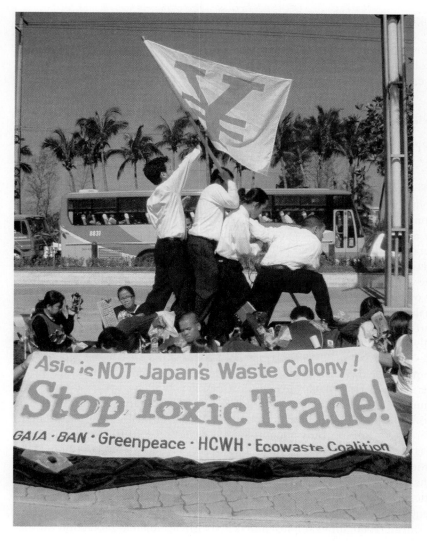

Although exporting toxic wastes is banned by treaty, wealthier countries regularly send millions of tons of castoffs such as obsolete computers that contain toxic material to poorer countries for "recycling." In this photograph, Filipino activists outside the Japanese Embassy in Manila are re-creating the iconic raising of the American flag over Mount Suribachi on Iwo Jima during World War II, to protest what the demonstrators said were Japan's efforts to export toxic wastes throughout Asia under various bilateral trade agreements. The symbol on the flag is for Japan's currency, the yen.

is that it is often caused by waste disposal by multinational corporations (MNCs), which may set up operations in LDCs because they have fewer environmental regulations.

International Efforts to Protect Ground Quality

There has been progress on international dumping. The 1992 Convention on the Control of Transboundary Movements of Hazardous Wastes and Their Disposal (the Basel Convention), which was signed by 105 countries in Switzerland, limits such activity. It has been ratified by 170 countries, with the United States among the missing. There have also been several regional agreements including the Bamako Convention (1998), which includes almost all African states and bans the transboundary trade in hazardous wastes on their continent, and the Waigani Convention (2001), which takes the same measures for its parties in the South Pacific. The limits in the Basel Convention were stiffened further in reaction to the continued export of hazardous wastes under the guise of declaring that the materials were meant for recycling or as foreign aid in the form of recoverable materials. At one time Great Britain alone annually exported up to 105,000 tons of such toxic foreign aid to LDCs, a practice that one British opposition leader called the "immoral . . . dumping of our environmental problems in someone else's backyard."[29] Now all such shipments for recycling and recovery purposes are banned.

Water Quality

There are two water environments: the marine (saltwater) environment and the freshwater environment. The quality of both is important.

International Water Quality Issues

Marine pollution has multiple sources. Spillage from shipping, ocean waste dumping, offshore mining, and oil and gas drilling combine for a significant part of the pollutants that are introduced into the oceans, seas, and other international waterways. Petroleum is a particular danger. Spills from tankers, pipelines, and other parts of the transportation system during the 1990s dumped an annual average of 110,000 tons of oil into the water, and discharges from offshore drilling account for another 20,000 tons. The flow of oil from seepage and dumpsites on land or oil discharge into inland waters making their way to the ocean is yet another large man-made source, with these sources annually adding about 41,000 tons of oil to the marine environment. Some spills are spectacular, such as the August 2003 grounding on Pakistan's coast of the Greek oil tanker *Tasman Spirit,* which spilled 28,000 tons (7.5 million gallons), but less noticed are the many smaller spills that add to the damage.

Other major carriers of marine pollution are rivers, which serve as sewers transporting human, industrial, and agricultural waste and pollutants into the seas. The runoff from fertilizers is a major pollutant, and their annual global use at about 153 million metric tons is nearly quadruple what it was in 1960. The exploding world population, which creates ever more intestinal waste, adds further to pollution. Many coastal cities are not served by sewage treatment facilities. Sewage is the major polluter of the Mediterranean and Caribbean seas and the ocean regions off East Africa and Southeast Asia. Industrial waste is also common. Because they often have neither modern equipment nor standards, discharges are especially common and dangerous in LDCs. During 2006, for example, China's State Environmental Protection Administration (SEPA) recorded 161 "serious" spills and many more minor ones off the coast of China, leading SEPA's deputy director to characterize 2006 as "the most grim year for China's environmental situation."[30]

Of these pollutants, the influx of excess nitrogen into the marine system is especially damaging. Human activities, such as using fertilizers and burning fossil fuels, add about 210 million metric tons to the 140 million metric tons of nitrogen generated by natural processes. Excess nitrogen stimulates eutrophication, the rapid growth of algae and other aquatic plants. When these plants die in their natural cycle, the decay process strips the water of its dissolved oxygen, thereby making it less and less inhabitable for aquatic plants, fish, and other marine life. To make matters worse, some algae blooms are toxic and take a heavy toll on fish, birds, and marine mammals. The Baltic Sea, Black Sea, the Caribbean, Mediterranean Sea, and other partly enclosed seas have been heavily afflicted with eutrophication, and even ocean areas such as the northeast and northwest coasts of the United States have seen a significant increase in the number of algae blooms in the last quarter century. Inasmuch as 99% of all commercial fishing is done within 200 miles of continental coasts, such pollution is especially damaging to fishing grounds.

Freshwater pollution of lakes and rivers is an international as well as a domestic issue. The discharge of pollutants into lakes and rivers that form international boundaries (the Great Lakes, the Rio Grande) or that flow between countries (the Rhine River) is a source of discord. Additionally, millions of tons of organic material and other pollutants that are dumped into the inland rivers around the world eventually find their way to the ocean. Freshwater pollution is also caused by acid rain and other contaminants that drift across borders.

International Efforts to Protect Water Quality

Marine pollution control has been on the international agenda for some time, and progress has been made. One of the first multilateral efforts was the International Maritime Organization, founded in 1958 in part to promote the control of pollution from ships. Increased flows of oil and spills led to the International Convention for the Prevention of Pollution from Ships (1973). More recently, 43 countries, including the world's largest industrial countries, agreed to a global ban effective in 1995 on dumping industrial wastes in the oceans. The countries also agreed not to dispose of nuclear waste in the oceans. These efforts have made a dramatic difference for marine oil spills as Figure 15.7 demonstrates. During the 1970s, the average year saw 314,000 tons of oil spew into the oceans and seas; that spillage was down to 29,000 tons a year during 2000–2004. National governments are also taking valuable enforcement steps, with, for instance, the U.S. Justice Department fining 10 cruise lines a total of $48.5 million between 1993 and 2002.

On another front, 146 countries (not including Russia or the United States) have ratified the Stockholm Convention on Persistent Organic Pollutants (2001), a treaty that bans 12 so-called dirty dozen pollutants, such as various insecticides, PCBs, and dioxins, which have been linked to birth defects and other genetic abnormalities. These pollutants contaminate water either directly, through seepage from the land, or from rainfall and eventually enter the food chain. Some also cause other forms of destruction. DDT, for example, has attacked eagle and other populations by significantly reducing the chances that eggs will hatch.

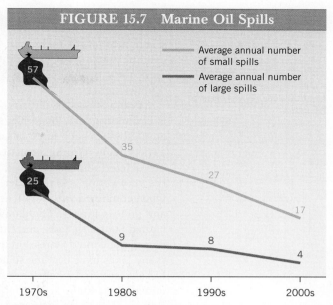

FIGURE 15.7 Marine Oil Spills

- Average annual number of small spills
- Average annual number of large spills

57
35
27
17
25
9
8
4

1970s   1980s   1990s   2000s

While improvements in some areas of environmental concern have been frustratingly slow or even absent, other areas such as preventing oil spills in the oceans have made impressive advances. As evident here, overall incidents in the 2000s are down 74% from the 1970s and large spills are down 84%.

Notes: Small spills are those from 7 tons to 699 tons. Large spills are those of 700 tons and over. 2000s is through 2006.
Data source: International Tanker Owners Pollution Federation, "Oil Tanker Spill Statistics," at www.itopf.com.

Air Quality

Air is the most fundamental necessity of the biosphere. It sustains life, but it can also contain pollutants that can befoul lungs as well as the land and water. Moreover, the world's air currents ignore national boundaries, making air quality a major international concern.

International Air Quality Issues

The quality of the air we breathe has deteriorated dramatically since the beginning of the industrial revolution. Now, air pollution from sulfur dioxide (SO_2),

Web Link

For information on the health and other impacts of SO_2, NO_x, PM, and other air pollutants, go to the site of the U.S. Environmental Protection Agency at **http://www.epa.gov/air/urbanair/6poll.html.**

nitrogen dioxide (NO_x), and particulate matter (PM, such as dust and soot) cause about 2 million deaths a year, according to WHO. The majority of those are in Asia, where most of the major cities exceed WHO guidelines for suspended particles. For example, Beijing's SO_2 concentration is 4.5 times higher than the WHO's health standard, the city's NO_x level is 3 times higher, and its suspended particulate matter is 5 times higher.

Using SO_2 as an illustration, we can dig a bit deeper in air quality issues. Sulfur is common in raw materials such as petroleum, coal, and many metal ores. SO_2 is emitted when such materials are burned for fuel or during such industrial processes as petroleum refining, cement manufacturing, and metal processing. SO_2 has numerous deleterious effects. It can cause or aggravate respiratory problems, especially in the very young and the elderly. The sulfurous gas in the atmosphere forms an acid when combined with water, and the resulting acid rain contaminates water resources and attacks forests. The damage done by acid rain has followed development. The United States, Canada, and Europe were the first to suffer. Especially in the northern part of the United States and in Canada there has been extensive damage to trees, and many lakes have become so acidified that most of the fish have been killed. Europe has also suffered extensive damage. About a quarter of the continent's trees have sustained moderate to severe defoliation. The annual value of the lost lumber harvest to Europe alone is an estimated $23 billion. The ecotourism industry in once-verdant forests around the world is also in danger, imperiling jobs. The death of trees and their stabilizing root systems increases soil erosion, resulting in the silting-up of lakes and rivers. The list of negative consequences could go on, but that is not necessary to make the point that acid rain is environmentally and economically devastating.

Protecting Air Quality

On the positive side, annual EDC emissions of air pollutants have declined dramatically. Since 1940, for instance, U.S. emissions have dropped 51% for SO_2, 30% for NO_x, and 80% for particulate matter. Unfortunately, the improvement in the EDCs is being more than offset by spiraling levels of air pollution in the LDCs. This is particularly true in Asia. There, rapid industrialization combined with the financial inability to spend the tens of billions of dollars needed to control SO_2 emissions is expected to more than triple annual SO_2 emissions from 34 million tons in 1990 to about 115 million tons in 2020. Even now, according to the World Bank, China has 16 of the 20 most polluted cities globally. Among the ill effects, China's Ministry of Science and Technology estimates that air pollution annually kills 50,000 newborn babies.

There have also been several international efforts to address air quality. Some regional agreements, such as the 1985 Helsinki Protocol for reducing SO_2 emissions in Europe, have been followed by improved air quality (Ringquist & Kostadinova, 2005). Various international agencies, such as UNEP and WHO work to warn against the danger of air pollution and help countries reduce it. Some funding is also available. For example, about 6% of the loans the World Bank made in 2004 were for environmental improvement programs. In the end, though, countries will have to be at the forefront of the effort to improve air quality. The costs are significant. In 2007, China's government pledged to spend $180 billion over five years on environmental protection. With 90% of the country's SO_2 emissions, 70% of its NO_x emissions, and a significant part of its PM discharges produced by burning coal, China plans to devote about 10% of its environmental funds to such efforts as flue gas desulfurization. China predicts that it can meet WHO SO_2 standards by 2020, but that is a significant technological and budgetary challenge.

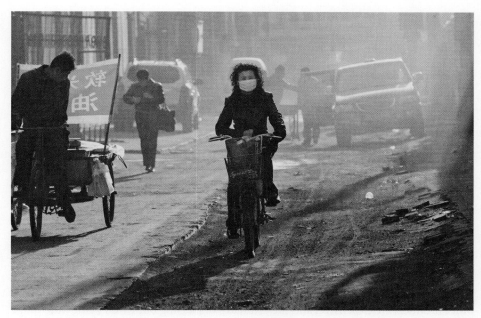

One of the by-products of economic development in the South has been rapidly declining air quality as a result of emissions from factories, cars, and other sources of pollution. The often dire conditions are captured in this 2007 photograph of a woman wearing a mask to try to shield her lungs from the murky air in Linfen, a city in China's Shangxi province. Linfen may be the world's most polluted city. Illustrating one dilemma of sustainable development, an official of the province's environment agency commented, "If we closed all Linfen's polluting factories, the environment would clear up. . . . But then a new problem would emerge—how would people afford to eat?"

The Ozone Layer

Atmospheric ozone (O_3) absorbs ultraviolet (UV) rays from the sun. About 90% of all O_3 is found within the ozone layer, which rings Earth 10 to 30 miles above the planet. Without it, human life could not exist.

Ozone Layer Depletion

There is little doubt that the ozone layer has been thinned or that the consequences are perilous. The ozone layer is being attacked by emissions of chlorofluorocarbons (CFCs), a chemical group used in refrigerators, air-conditioners, products such as Styrofoam, many spray can propellants, fire extinguishers, and industrial solvents. The chemical effect of the CFCs is to deplete the ozone by turning it into atmospheric oxygen (O_2), which does not block ultraviolet rays. This thinning of the ozone layer increases the penetration through the atmosphere of ultraviolet-B (UV-B) rays, which cause cancers and other mutations in life forms below. The impact of this on Americans was noted in chapter 1. Australia and New Zealand have measured temporary increases of as much as 20% in UV-B radiation, and light-skinned Australians have the world's highest skin cancer rate. Another possible deleterious effect of increased UV-B bombardment came to light during a study of the water surrounding Antarctica. Over the area, a hole 3.86 million square miles in size—about the size of Europe and with as much as a 70% depletion of atmospheric O_3—occurs annually. There scientists found evidence of a 6% to 12% decline in plankton organisms during the period of the annual ozone hole. Such losses at the bottom of the food chain could restrict the nutrition and health of fish and eventually of humans farther up the food chain. Ozone levels over the rest of the world have declined less than over the South Pole, but they are still down about 10% since the 1950s.

Protecting the Ozone Layer

Among its other accomplishments, the UNEP sponsored a 1987 conference in Montreal to discuss protection of the ozone layer. There, 46 countries agreed to reduce their CFC production and consumption by 50% before the end of the century. Subsequent amendments to the Montreal Convention were negotiated at quadrennial conferences, the last of which was held in Nairobi, Kenya, in 2003. The major issue was a U.S. move to increase its permitted use of methyl bromide, a pest control. The effort was rejected.

Overall, there is relatively good news on ozone depletion. The annual buildup of CFC concentrations reversed itself from 5% in the 1980s to a slight decline beginning in 1994, only seven years after the Montreal Convention. Somewhat modifying this good news is the fact that the CFC buildup had increased so rapidly in the years before 1987 that it will take many decades before the damage is substantially reversed. Moreover, even that is far from certain. The most important caveat has to do with the economic advancement of the LDCs. The substitutes for CFCs in refrigerants and other products are expensive, and the estimates of phasing out CFCs worldwide range up to $40 billion. Therefore LDCs will be hard-pressed to industrialize and provide their citizens with a better standard of living while simultaneously abandoning the production and use of CFCs. For example, refrigerators, which not long ago were rare in China, are becoming more and more commonplace. China has pledged to end CFC production by 2010, but it still has 27 CFC plants operating, and ending production with outside help now would be better than ending it (hopefully) alone later.

Global Warming

During the past few years, **global warming**, the increase in Earth's average annual temperature has become the leading environmental concern and point of controversy. Global warming's place at center stage was symbolized in 2007 by former Vice President Al Gore Jr., as he stepped up to center stage to claim his Oscar award for the documentary *An Inconvenient Truth*. Gore told the Hollywood audience and several hundred million television viewers that addressing global warming was not just a political issue, but a "moral issue." "We have everything we need to get started," he urged, "with the possible exception of the will to act." As if to second the call to action, singer Melissa Etheridge also received an Oscar for the movie's theme song, "I Need to Wake Up." There can be little doubt that Earth is warming, but what Gore and many others believe is that its cause is the accumulation in the upper atmosphere of carbon dioxide (CO_2) and other **greenhouse gases (GHGs)**, especially methane and chlorofluorocarbons (CFCs), generated mostly by human activity. These gases create a blanket effect, trapping heat and preventing the nightly cooling of Earth. Reduced cooling means warmer days, producing what is known as the **greenhouse effect** based on the way an agricultural greenhouse builds up heat by permitting incoming solar radiation but hindering the outward flow of heat.

Global Warming: What We Know

Three things are clear. Each is detailed in Figure 15.8. First, global emissions of greenhouse gases have risen significantly. The primary cause has been a huge increase in the emissions of GHGs from burning fossil fuels because of industrialization and the

To understand global warming, it is helpful to consider these three graphs together. Each covers the period 1880–2006. The top left graph shows that during that period carbon dioxide (CO_2) emissions increased nearly 34 times. These increased emissions caused a significant build-up of CO_2 in the atmosphere, which is evident in the upper-right graph. Most, but not all, scientists believe that the increase in atmospheric CO_2 has created a greenhouse effect that is substantially or wholly responsible for the steady increase in Earth's average temperature, as shown in the last of the three graphs.

Data sources: World Resources Institute, U.S. Energy Information Agency, and U.S. Carbon Dioxide Information Analysis Center.

need of the growing world population to warm itself and cook its food. The rate of increase has accelerated in recent decades. For example, CO_2 emissions more than tripled between 1960 and 2006 alone. Deforestation accelerates the build up of CO_2 in the atmosphere because it destroys trees needed to convert CO_2 into oxygen by the process of photosynthesis. One way to calculate this is to compare the CO_2 impacts of an SUV and a big tree. Based on the amount of CO_2 discharged by an SUV, which burns 800 gallons of gas to go 12,000 miles a year (at 15 miles per gallon), and the amount of CO_2 a large tree can absorb and convert to oxygen, it takes 333 trees to absorb the CO_2 emitted annually by each SUV.

A second certainty is that atmospheric CO_2 concentrations have risen, as also clear in Figure 15.8. That most of this added CO_2 comes from human intervention is evident in the fact that the start of the growing increases coincides with the beginning of the industrial revolution in the mid-1700s. Not only did factories and other commercial uses of fossil fuels put more CO_2 into the atmosphere, but it built up because the greenhouse gases emitted into the atmosphere linger there for up to 200 years before dissipating. As a result, CO_2 concentrations have increased 38% over the last 250 years or so. The increase was slow at first, then gradually grew steeper before accelerating even more beginning in the 1950s. Of the overall increase between 1750 and 2006, half occurred after 1975.

Third, there is no doubt that the global temperature is rising, that is, global warming is occurring. Between 1880 and 2006, as Figure 15.8 additionally shows, Earth's average temperature has risen 0.7°C/1.3°F. In fact, the 10 warmest years since records were first kept in 1856 occurred during the ten-year span 1997–2006. The warmest year on record was 2005, 2006 was fifth, and at this writing 2007 appears headed to being warmer than 2006. Almost certainly the first decade of the 21st century will replace the last decade of the 1900s as the hottest decade since the mid-1800s and probably much earlier. Because it can be shown experimentally that a CO_2 buildup traps heat, there is certainly a strong prima facie case that the causality chain is: greater CO_2 emissions $\longrightarrow$ a buildup of atmospheric CO_2 $\longrightarrow$ global warming. Most, but as we shall see, not all believe that this causal chain is valid.

Global Warming: What Is in Dispute

Four things about global warming are controversial. One is whether or what part of global warming is caused by humans. It is possible that some or all of it is a natural phenomenon. As one atmospheric scientist notes, no one is "arguing over whether there's any global warming. The question is, What is the cause of it?"[31] The second issue is whether global warming will have dire environmental consequences or an impact that will in some cases be beneficial and in other cases can be addressed using modern technology. Third, what will the economic consequences of global warming be? Fourth, what economic and lifestyle changes will be necessary to halt or at least significantly slow down the rate of global warming?

The Cause of Global Warming To restate the question: What are the relative contributions, if any, of human activity and natural phenomena to global warming? Representing the *environmental optimists'* point of view, a former U.S. secretary of energy rejects the "political alarmism over global warming" and argues that the "cold, hard facts take the heat out of global warming."[32] One counterargument that optimists make is to point out that Earth has natural warming and cooling trends, and they attribute a good part of the current global warming to this natural cycle, rather than human activity. They note, among other things, that many scientists believe that the world experienced a gradual temperature rise for at least a millennium that was interrupted beginning in about 1200 by the "Little Ice Age." This period of sharply cooler temperatures reached its frosty nadir in the 1600s and it was not until around 1850 that temperatures once again reached what they had been over 600 years earlier. There is no disputing that temperatures have continued to rise since that point. What optimists contend is that all or most of the increase is an extension of the natural warming cycle that brought Earth out of the Little Ice Age or, from an even longer perspective, has been going on for at least 2,000 years, interrupted only by the Little Ice Age. If all this is the case, as optimists claim, then human activity has only a limited role, at best, in global warming. Therefore, taking on large costs and making significant lifestyle sacrifices to curb GHG emissions will have little impact on global warming.

Did You Know That:

As of 2006, the ten hottest years since records have been kept were, in order: 2005, 1998, 2002, 2003, 2006, 2004, 2001, 1997, 1999, and 2000.

ANALYZE THE ISSUE
Global Warming

Did You Know That:

The first warning about global warming was issued in 1896 by Swedish chemist Svante Arrhenius, who wrote, "We are evaporating our coal mines into the air."

Environmental pessimists contend that humans are the cause of all or most of current global warming. The most recent report (2007) of the UN-sponsored Intergovernmental Panel on Climatic Change (IPCC) declares that there is "high agreement" among scientists based on "much evidence" that, "since pre-industrial times, increasing emissions of GHGs due to human activities have led to a marked increase in atmospheric GHG concentrations." Moreover, the report found that the "widespread warming of the atmosphere and ocean, together with ice mass loss, [make it] *extremely unlikely* that global climate change of the past 50 years can be explained without external forcing, and *very likely* that it is not due to known natural causes alone."[33] While the IPCC does not rule out some role for natural global warming, it notes several things. One is that GHGs are higher than they have ever been. Methane levels, for example, are three times what they ever were. Second, the rate of temperature increase in the past 50 years or so is much faster than earlier, whether that increase was driven by human activity or natural warming, and this sharp upturn coincides with the sharp upturn in the emissions of GHGs. Third, temperatures are now beyond what even accepting natural warming would predict. For example, the temperatures at the poles are higher today than in any time in the last 125,000 years.

The Environmental Impact of Global Warming *Environmental pessimists* predict dire consequences from global warming. The IPCC estimates that the world's average temperature could rise several more degrees by the year 2100, about doubling the temperature increase since the last ice age. Potential global temperature changes are shown in the map on page 522. The pessimists believe this change has already altered rainfall, wind currents, and other climatic patterns, and that the deleterious effects, such as the melting of the polar ice caps and the rise of sea levels, will escalate during the coming century as temperatures continue to rise. For example, a 2004 study, "Arctic Climate Impact Assessment" found that in the previous 30 years the area of the Arctic ice had shrunk by 8% (the equivalent of Norway, Sweden, and Denmark disappearing) and that the average thickness of the ice had declined 10% to 15%. According to IPCC, such melting could cause sea levels in different regions to rise up to 3 feet, with the floods displacing well over 100 million people during this century. Particularly at risk are island countries. Expressing their concerns during the UN Millennium Summit in 2000, the president of the Maldives, an Indian Ocean island country, asked rhetorically, "When the UN meets [in 2100] to usher in yet another century, will the Maldives and other low-lying nations be represented here?"[34]

Destructive weather changes are yet another possible peril because global warming affects ocean temperatures and currents and upper atmosphere wind patterns, which, in turn, control rainfall, temperature, and other climatic variables. Droughts could occur in some places; other areas could see much heavier precipitation including periods of torrential rainfall. "It's going to be a wild ride, especially for specific regions," one climatologist recently predicted.[35] An important factor in such weather changes are the El Niño/La Niña (unusual warming/cooling) conditions that are natural but have been occurring with increasing frequency and intensity in the equatorial Pacific Ocean. Just one impact, according to the head of the U.S. Bureau of Land Management's weather program, is "increasing fire problems because of global warming" because "drier conditions will exist over the next 10 to 20 years."[36]

The IPCC projects many other negative impacts of global warming, but detailing them is not as important as the panel's primary point: Global warming is disruptive. The panel concedes that there are and will be some benefits. For example, some

Web Link

The Arctic Climate Impact Assessment, which has great maps, photographs, and data presentations, is available at **http://amap.no/acia/**.

Web Link

Information and graphics on El Niño/La Niña are available from the National Oceanic and Atmospheric Administration at **www.elnino.noaa.gov/**.

Did You Know That:

La Niña is marked by unusually cold water in the mid-Pacific; El Niño is marked by unusually warm water in the same region. The term *El Niño* originated with South American fishermen who noticed that unexpectedly warm water would appear some years near Christmas. This led to the name, which means "little boy" and refers to the Christ child. Since La Niña is the opposite of El Niño, that name soon came into use.

Climate shifts from global warming will range from dramatic to modest if this map's projected changes in temperature and precipitation (measured by soil humidity) are correct. It would be an error to assume that you can necessarily feel relieved if you live in a low-change area or even one in which the climate will improve. Shifts in one part of the world can have impacts far away. For example, some scientists believe warmer ocean temperatures fuel more and stronger hurricanes. If that is correct, then hurricanes such as Katrina in 2005 may become the rule instead of the exception.

areas that were once very dry or extremely cold are becoming more agriculturally productive. Overall, though, the IPCC concludes that the positive results "are expected to diminish as the magnitude of climate change increases. In contrast many identified adverse effects are expected to increase in both extent and severity with the degree of climate change. When considered by region, adverse effects are projected to predominate for much of the world, particularly in the tropics and subtropics."

Environmental optimists downplay the damage from global warming. "It should be pretty clear," says one, "that warming to date didn't demonstrably dent health and welfare very much." There is no reason, he added, "to expect a sudden [greater danger] in the next 50 years."[37] Moreover, the optimists predict that some areas could benefit and most could adapt to the changes brought on by global warming. Drought in some regions would damage their present agricultural areas, but new arable areas would be created and would prosper in other regions. Farmers in colder regions might have their growing seasons and bounty increased. Moreover, optimists contend that the world can use its technological and financial resources to deal with whatever climate change does occur without causing major changes to our economies or

Web Link

A global warming site representing the environmental optimists' point of view is that of the Cooler Heads Coalition at **www.globalwarming.org/.** The environmental pessimists' perspective is presented by a coalition of environmentalist groups at **www.climatehotmap.org/.**

lifestyles. Optimists believe for example, that nuclear power plants can safely replace environmentally unfriendly coal- and oil-fueled power plants. France and Great Britain have similar economies, yet Great Britain, which generates only 25% of its electricity from nuclear power, emits 50% more CO_2 per capita than does France, where nuclear plants generate 75% of its electricity. In sum, according to one optimistic scientist, "The prospects for having a modest climate impact instead of a disastrous one are quite good."[38]

The Economic Impact of Global Warming   Projections of what it will cost to protect against the damage from global warming range very widely. One problem is that studies make different assumptions about how much danger there is from flooding, more violent weather, the loss of agricultural land to arid conditions, and many other factors that environmental pessimists stress and environmental optimists minimize. Another problem is the diverse cost estimates of preventing or repairing damage. At the pessimistic end of the spectrum, a recent study by the British government estimates that global warming costs could eventually rise to 5% to 20% of the world's annual GDP, a level associated with world wars and the Great Depression. The lead author of the report warned that "delaying action [to address global warming], even by a decade or two, will take us into dangerous territory."[39] At the other end of the spectrum, one economist predicts that global warming will cost the EDCs less than 1% of their collective GDPs through 2050. Similarly, a Danish scientist argued in 2002 that the damage from global warming of the next half century would come to between $5 trillion and $8 trillion. This can be put into context by taking that year's global GNP ($31.5 trillion), projecting it out over 50 years ($1.56 quadrillion), and calculating that $8 trillion would come to one-half of 1% of that total. Compounding the puzzle even more, the longer-term the economic projections are, the less reliable they inevitably become. Regarding such projections, one economist commented, "Going past 2050, the cleverness really has to kick in."[40]

The Costs of Halting or Substantially Slowing Global Warming   Projections of what it will cost economically and in terms of lifestyle to address global warming also range widely, with pessimists saying that the cost will be high and the optimists prone to diminishing them. It would take volumes to cover the different cost estimates, and resolving them is impossible because they rest on vastly different assumptions, just as do the estimates of the economic impact of global warming. What it is safe to say is that there will be significant costs that will impact people's wallets or their lifestyles or both. Consider, for example, one existing proposal for a U.S. tax on CO_2 emissions of $14 a ton to promote conservation and to raise money to combat global warming.[41] That would mean an added tax of about 12 cents a gallon on gasoline. Given that Americans drive 9,800 miles a year per capita (not per driver) and the U.S. government estimate that the average private vehicle gets 17.1 mpg, that comes to an added annual tax of $69 per person, or $276 for a family of four. The cost of electricity from coal- and oil-fuel plants would also go up, and people would pay more for a wide range of goods because of the added cost of producing and delivering them. Surely, such costs might be lower than the expense of dealing with the damage from global warming. The bottom line, as one economist puts it, is "There's no easy way around the fact that if global warming is a serious risk, there will be serious costs" from its damage, the costs to address it, or both.[42] There is also wisdom in the observation, "It's important for the people arguing for action to make the case that it's worth it, rather than the promise that it will be free."[43]

The International Response to Global Warming

The early movement toward addressing global warming came at the World Climate Conference (WCC, 1990), at which most EDCs other than the United States made nonbinding pledges to stabilize or reduce greenhouse gas emissions, and Earth Summit I's Global Warming Convention (1992, more formally the United Nations Framework Convention on Climate Change, UNFCCC), whereby virtually all countries, including the United States, agreed to ease pressure on the climate and to work toward a global solution through annual meetings to discuss policy.

The Kyoto Protocol   During the 1997 round of these discussions in Kyoto, Japan, conferees drafted a supplement to the treaty called the **Kyoto Protocol**. This agreement came after intense negotiations, often divided along familiar North-South lines. The South wanted the EDCs to cut GHG emissions by 12–15% by 2012 and to provide the LDCs with massive new aid to cut pollution. Most EDCs found neither of these proposals acceptable. The EDCs wanted the LDCs to commit to upper limits on future emissions, but the LDCs rejected this idea, arguing, "Very many of us are struggling to attain a decent standard of living for our people. And yet we are constantly told that we must share in the effort to reduce emissions so that industrialized countries can continue to enjoy the benefits of their wasteful lifestyle."[44] The compromise was to require the EDCs to reduce GHG emissions by about 7% below their 1990 levels by 2012 and to urge, but not require LDCs to do what they can to restrain GHG emissions. The protocol specified that it would go into effect when ratified by at least 55 countries representing at least 55% of the world's emissions of GHG at that point. Those standards were met in 2005, and by mid-2007, 173 countries had ratified the treaty (Fisher, 2004).

Of the handful of countries that have not ratified the treaty, the United States is the most prominent. Although Vice President Gore was the chief U.S. negotiator in Kyoto and signed the protocol on behalf of the United States, President Clinton did not send it to the Republican-controlled Congress for ratification because he knew it faced certain death there. Among other indications, the Republican leader in the Senate condemned the Kyoto Protocol as a "flawed treaty" that would cripple the U.S. economy.[45] The election of President Bush in 2000 ended any immediate chance of U.S. adherence to the treaty. One reason he cites for his opposition is the lack of requirements for LDCs. "It is ineffective, inadequate, and unfair to America," he told reporters, "because it exempts 80% of the world, including major population centers such as China and India, from compliance."[46] Bush also argues that complying with "the Kyoto treaty would severely damage the United States' economy." Placing himself squarely in the camp of environmental optimists, he argued, "We can grow our economy and, at the same time, through technologies, improve our environment."[47]

Recent Developments   More recently, the debate over what to do about global warming has heated up anew. The change has been driven by the increasingly certain IPCC declarations that global warming is manmade, amid more and more dramatic warnings about the impact of global warming; by the campaign of Al Gore and such other events as the Live Earth concerts held around the world in July 2007, featuring entertainers including Bon Jovi, Madonna, and Snoop Dogg; and by the recapture of Congress by the Democrats in 2007 and the impending end of Bush's presidency in 2009.

Among other initiatives, Great Britain in 2007 introduced global warming for the first time as a topic in the UN Security Council, arguing that it presented a threat

THE CHRISTIAN SCIENCE MONITOR Bennett

THE G-8 TEAM PHOTO

When the leaders of the Group of Eight gathered in Germany in 2007, all but President Bush of the United States were in agreement that countries should agree to strict limits of greenhouse gases (GHGs). President Bush's plan to call a new conference to negotiate voluntary targets for, not mandatory limits on GHGs is captured in this editorial drawing of seven of the G-8 leaders dressed for one form of football (soccer in American parlance), and a lone one for American-style football.

to world security. British Foreign Secretary Margaret Beckett contended, "Our responsibility in this Council is to maintain international peace and security, including the prevention of conflict. An unstable climate will exacerbate some of the core drivers of conflict, such as migratory pressures and competition for resources."[48] But the ongoing North-South divide stymied the British effort, with China's representative rejecting the initiative on the grounds that, "The developing countries believe that the Security Council has neither the professional competence in handling climate change, nor is it the right decision-making place for extensive participation leading up to widely acceptable proposals."[49] The European countries and Canada also pushed hard for a strong statement of the Group of Eight leaders (see chapter 13) at their 2007 meeting in Germany, but the United States insisted on moderating the language.

In part all such efforts were skirmishes leading up to the 2007 round of WCC talks scheduled for Bali, Indonesia, and its agenda for extending the Kyoto Protocol beyond 2012 (the year that it expires) and expanding its limitations on GHG emissions. Japan, for example, proposed a 50% mandatory cut in emissions by 2050. The diplomatic maneuvering that precedes the talks features familiar themes in environmental politics. First the EU countries, most other EDCs, and the LDCs were pressuring the United States to reengage with the Kyoto process and agree to roll back its emissions. The prospects of that were dim, though, with the U.S. delegate to the talks commenting, "I just think that it's not going to happen. It's certainly not something we think the time is right for."[50] Second, the EDCs were insisting that China, India, and other LDCs that have become major sources of GHG emissions accept limits. These are needed because of the rapid increase in LDC emissions, as detailed in Figure 2.5 on p. 61, which gives substance to one scholar's view that, "Unless China and India are brought in, it won't matter much what the developed world does."[51] Third, the LDCs will resist limits. "Any legally mandated measures [on the LDCs] for reducing emissions are likely to have significant adverse impacts on GDP growth and this will have serious implications for poverty alleviation efforts," India's minister of the environment complained.[52] The LDCs also restated their long-standing position, as China's chief environmental negotiator put it, that the "developing countries need assistance in technology and financial resources from developed countries."[53] Looking on the upside, one UN official noted the strong commitment of the EU, Japan, and other EDCs to GHG emissions controls and the willingness of Brazil, South Africa, and some other LDCs to contemplate limits on LDC emissions. He declared optimistically, "I think there are quite encouraging signals from both developed and developing countries that they are willing to go to the next level."[54] Perhaps, but the barriers to the United States and to China, India, and other LDCs agreeing to limits left Japan's delegate characterizing himself as "really, really pessimistic" about the negotiations at Bali.[55] Thus for all the debate over the scientific evidence, the future of global cooperation to address global warming "is not something that goes on inside a computer," according to one analyst, "but a grand political calculation."[56]

CHAPTER SUMMARY

THE ECOLOGICAL STATE OF THE WORLD

1. This chapter deals with international ecological concerns and cooperation. Self-interest—some people would say self-survival—compels us to attend to issues concerning the world's expanding population, the depletion of natural resources, the increase of chemical discharges into the environment, and the impact of these trends on the global biosphere.

SUSTAINABLE DEVELOPMENT

2. A key concept and goal is sustainable development. The key questions are how to ensure that LDCs develop industrially, how to maintain the standard of living in the EDCs, and how to also simultaneously protect the environment. Given the justifiable determination of the LDCs to develop economically, the potential for accelerated resource depletion and pollution production is very high.

3. There is a wide range of views about how great the threats to the biosphere are and what can and should be done to address them.

SUSTAINABLE DEVELOPMENT: POPULATION PROBLEMS AND PROGRESS

4. Population is a significant problem facing the world, with the global population surpassing the 6 billion mark. The 1994 UN Conference on Population and Development in Cairo marked the latest step in the effort to control population and the associated attempts to improve women's reproductive and other rights. There are also numerous international organizations, such as the United Nations Population Fund, working in the area. The most effective way to control population is to improve the educational and economic status of women and to make contraceptive services widely available.

SUSTAINABLE DEVELOPMENT: RESOURCE PROBLEMS AND PROGRESS

5. Increasing population and industrialization have rapidly accelerated the use of a wide range of natural resources. It is possible, using known resources and current use rates, to project that petroleum, natural gas, and a variety of minerals will be totally depleted within the present century. The world's forests, its supply of freshwater, and its wildlife are also under population and industrialization pressure. There are many international governmental and nongovernmental organizations and efforts, symbolized by the 1992 Earth Summit, to address these problems.

SUSTAINABLE DEVELOPMENT: THE ENVIRONMENT

6. Population growth and industrialization are also responsible for mounting ground pollution, water pollution, air pollution, global warming, and ozone

layer depletion due to atmospheric pollution. Work in other areas, such as reducing CO_2 emissions, has only just begun and is difficult because of the high costs.

7. The efforts at international cooperation in the areas discussed in this chapter return us to the question of standards of judgment. It is easy to view the vast extent of the problems facing the globe, to measure the limited effort being made to resolve them, and to dismiss the entire subject of international cooperation as superficial. It is true that not nearly enough is being done. But it is also true that only a very few decades ago nothing was being done. From that zero base, the progress made since World War II is encouraging. The only question is whether or not we will continue to expand our efforts and whether or not we will do enough, soon enough.

For simulations, debates, and other interactive activities, a chapter quiz, Web links, and much more, visit **www.mhhe.com/rourke12/** and go to chapter 15. Or, while accessing the site, click on Course-Wide Content and view recent international relations articles in the *New York Times*.

KEY TERMS

biosphere
carrying capacity
environmental optimists
environmental pessimists
global warming

green accounting
greenhouse effect
greenhouse gases (GHGs)
Kyoto Protocol

sustainable development
UN Conference on Environment and Development (UNCED)

UN Conference on Population and Development (UNCPD)
World Summit on Sustainable Development (WSSD)

An Epilogue to the Text/
A Prologue to the Future

Where I did begin, there shall I end.
—William Shakespeare, *Julius Caesar*

SO HERE IT is some months later, and we are at the end of this book and this course. Finals await, and then, praise be, vacation. That well-deserved break from your academic labors brings you to an implicit point of decision about what to do with this text, the other course readings, and the knowledge you have gained from your instructor. One option is to sell what books you can back to the bookstore and forget the rest. I can remember from my undergraduate days how attractive an idea that sometimes seemed.

But then, is that really the best option? Probably not. We began our semester's journey with the idea that we are all inescapably part of the world drama. There may be times when we want to shout, "Stop the world, I want to get off," but we cannot. We have also seen that we are both audience and actors in the global play's progress. At the very least, we are all touched by the action in ways that range from the foreign designer jeans that we wear to, potentially, our atomized end.

We can leave it at that, shrug our shoulders, and complain and mumble at the forces that buffet us. But we also can do more than that. We do not have to be just passive victims. We can, if we want and if we try, help write the script. The plot is ongoing and improvisational. The final scene is yet unwritten. We are not even sure when it will occur. It could be well into the far distant future—or it could be tomorrow. This, more than any particular point of information, is the most important message. You are not helpless, and you owe it to yourself and your fellow humans to take an active role in your life and in the world's tomorrows.

The world is beset by great problems. War continues to kill without cessation. The specter of terrorism increasingly haunts many people as they go about their daily lives. A billion-dollar diet industry prospers in many countries of the North because many of its citizens are overweight, while in the South, infants and the elderly starve to death in the dry dust. As if localized malnutrition were too slow and selective, we globally attack our environment with the waste products of our progress, and the human population tide threatens to overwhelm Earth's ability to sustain the people who live on it. Of even more immediate peril, an expanse of nuclear mushroom clouds could instantly terminate our biosphere's more evolutionary decay.

To face these problems, we have, at best, a primitive political system. Sovereignty strengthens nationalities but divides the world. Frontier justice is the rule. As in a grade-B western, most of the actors carry guns on their hips and sometimes shoot it out. The law is weak, and the marshals have more authority in theory than in practice.

There are few anymore who really try to defend the system of assertive sovereignty as adequate for the future. Clearly, it is not. What is less certain is what to do next and how to do it. Cooperation, humanitarianism, enlightenment, and other such words provide easy answers, but they are vague goals. Real answers are difficult to come by. They may involve tough choices; we may be asked to give up some things now so that they will not be taken later, to curb our lifestyle, to risk arms control in the hope of avoiding nuclear war, and to think of the world in terms of "we."

At every step there will be those who urge caution, who counsel self-preservation first, who see the world as a lifeboat. Maybe they will be right—but probably not. We *have* begun to move toward a more rational order. Many chapters clearly show this. But they also show how limited and fragile this progress has been. This is where you come in. Your job is to work to make the world the place you want it to be. It is your job to consider the problems, to ponder possible solutions, to reach informed opinions, and to act on your convictions. Think? Yes, of course. But also DO!! That is what is really important.

We began this study with the thought from Shakespeare's *Henry V* that "the world [is] familiar to us and [yet] unknown." My hope is that this text and the course you have just about completed have made the world more familiar, less unknown to you. What you do with what you have learned is now the issue. Will you treat this moment as an end? Or is it a beginning? Heed, if you will, the counsel of Shakespeare's King Lear:

Be governed by your knowledge and proceed.

Endnotes

CHAPTER 1

1. Pew Research Center report, July 30, 2006.
2. National Geographic Society, "National Geographic—Roper 2002 Global Geographic Literacy Survey," November 2002.
3. Former Assistant Secretary of Defense Lawrence J. Korb, quoted in the *New York Times,* January 22, 1996.
4. CNS News, October 26, 2004.
5. Paul Epstein, associate director of the Center for Health and Global Environment at Harvard University's medical school, quoted in the *Hartford Courant,* May 4, 2003.
6. Analyst William Schneider on Cnn.com, November 8, 2006.
7. Wilson's address to Congress asking for a declaration of war, April 2, 1917.
8. *Washington Post,* January 21, 2001.
9. *New York Times,* November 28, 1995.
10. *New York Times,* January 21, 2005.
11. *New York Times,* July 29, 1996.
12. *Washington Post,* February 3, 2005.
13. *Washington Post,* March 25, 2005.

Debate the Policy Script box, "Applying Theory to Policy" p. 26

1. James A. Baker, III and Lee H. Hamilton, co-chairs, *The Iraq Study Group Report,* Washington, D.C., December, 2006, p. 3.
2. *Washington Post,* December 7, 2006.
3. Walter Isaacson, "The Return of the Realists," *Time,* November 20, 2006.

CHAPTER 2

1. French Foreign Minister Hubert Védrine, quoted by Joseph Nye (2002) in *The Economist,* October 23, 1999.
2. *New York Times,* February 8, 2005.
3. Putin was quoted in the *Moscow Times,* May 28, 2003; Vajpayee was quoted in the *Hartford Courant,* May 29, 2003.
4. *Hartford Courant,* September 5, 1995.
5. Speech by President Hugo Chávez, at the opening of XII G-15 Summit, March 1, 2004, in Caracas, Venezuela.
6. U.S. Government, White House, "A National Security Strategy for the United States: A Report to the Nation," September 17, 2002.
7. *Hartford Courant,* September 5, 1995.
8. U.S. Government, White House, "A New Security Strategy for a New Century," January 5, 2000.
9. *Time,* June 1, 1992.

Debate the Policy Script box, "Is Preemptive War Good Policy?" p. 51

1. *Hartford Courant,* March 20, 2003.
2. *New York Times,* September 24, 2003.

CHAPTER 3

1. The interview was with Dan Rather and aired on CBS News, February 26, 2003.
2. *Washington Post,* February 12, 2002.
3. *Washington Post,* October 30, 2002.
4. *Washington Post,* January 10, 2007.
5. *Washington Post,* January 27, 2002.
6. *New York Times,* September 21, 2001.
7. Frank Newport, editor-in-chief of the Gallup Poll at http://www.gallup.com/poll/summits/islam.asp.
8. *New York Times,* June 1, 1998.
9. *Hartford Courant,* June 18, 1998.
10. The adviser was Arthur Goldberg, and the quote is from Robert B. Dallek, *Flawed Giant: Lyndon Johnson and His Times, 1961–1973* (New York: Oxford University Press, 1998), as quoted in Sean Wilentz, "Lone Star Setting," *New York Times Book Review,* April 12, 1998, p. 6.
11. *Washington Post,* March 4, 2003.
12. Pew Research Center, "Global Gender Gaps," May 2004.
13. This section relies on quotes drawn from Kenneally (2006) and the pages in Mansfield (2006) cited therein rather than from the original.
14. Pew Research Center, "Views of a Changing World: War with Iraq Further Divides Global Publics," June 3, 2003.
15. *New York Times,* October 12, 2001.
16. Pew Research Center, "Views of a Changing World: War with Iraq Further Divides Global Publics," June 3, 2003.
17. *Washington Post,* January 27, 2002.
18. Interview of retired Marine General Joseph P. Hoar, televised February 15, 2005 on *Frontline,* a PBS program.
19. All quotes from the *Washington Post,* January 11, 2007. The security official was Kori Schake, then director for defense strategy on the National Security Council staff; the senator was Lindsey Graham (R-SC).
20. Charles Duelfer, "Comprehensive Report of the Special Advisor to the DCI on Iraq's WMD," September 30, 2004.
21. *New York Times,* October 2, 1993.
22. *Washington Post,* February 3, 2002.
23. Charles Duelfer, "Comprehensive Report of the Special Advisor to the DCI on Iraq's WMD," September 30, 2004.
24. *New York Times,* June 17, 1991.
25. Interview of former U.S. Deputy Secretary of State Strobe Talbot, May 30, 2002, Salon.com at http://www.salon.com/books/.
26. Bush's remarks were made during an interview with Linda Douglas of KNBC, Jim Lampley of KCBS, and Paul Moyer of KABC in Los Angeles, California, June 15, 1991.

27. Doug Wead, "Bush Completes Father's Unfinished Business," op-ed piece, *USA Today,* June 15, 2003.Wead was an aide to George H. W. Bush.
28. *Albany Times-Union,* November 10, 2002.
29. Richard Brookhiser, "The Mind of George W. Bush," *Atlantic Monthly,* April 2003, pp. 55–69.
30. *Guardian Unlimited,* April 15, 2003.
31. *Investor's Business Daily, Christian Science Monitor* poll, 2002. Data provided by The Roper Center for Public Opinion Research, University of Connecticut.
32. "Letter from the President to the Speaker of the House of Representatives and the President Pro Tempore of the Senate," October 9, 2001, State Department Web site at http://usinfo.state.gov.
33. Transcript of joint press conference, October 21, 2001, White House Web site at http://www.whitehouse.gov.
34. *New York Times,* September 17, 1995.
35. Fox News, July 11, 2004.
36. *Washington Post,* July 23, 2003. The official was Stephen J. Hadley.
37. All quotes in this paragraph are from the *Washington Post,* July 25, 2003.
38. *New York Times,* October 12, 2003.
39. Representative James Leach, quoted in the *New York Times,* September 26, 2003.
40. *New York Times,* February 20, 2005.
41. From the *American Machinist,* December 22, 2006, at http://www.americanmachinist.com/304/Issue/Article/False/43786/Issue.
42. Fox News/Opinion Dynamics poll, August 2006, data provided by The Roper Center for Public Opinion Research, University of Connecticut.
43. *Washington Post,* February 1, 2002.
44. *New York Times,* December 15, 2005.
45. *Washington Post,* February 11, 2007.
46. BBC News, December 12, 1999.
47. *Washington Post,* April 30, 2003.
48. *New York Times,* May 5, 1994.
49. CBS News, November 15, 2002.
50. Robert Dreyfuss, "The Thirty-Year Itch," *Mother Jones,* March/April 2003, online.
51. Michael Klare, professor of peace and world security studies at Hampshire College, quoted in Dreyfuss, "The Thirty-Year Itch."
52. Michael Lynch, managing director, Strategic Energy and Economic Resources, quoted in Faye Bowers, "Driving Forces in War-Weary Nations," *The Nation,* February 25, 2003, online.
53. *Investor's Business Daily, Christian Science Monitor* poll, April 2003. Data provided by The Roper Center for Public Opinion Research, University of Connecticut.

Debate the Policy Script box, "Who Should Decide on War?" p. 83

1. "Letter from the President to the Speaker of the House of Representatives and the President Pro Tempore of the Senate," October 9, 2001, State Department Web site at http://usinfo.state.gov.
2. *Washington Post,* January 27, 2007.

CHAPTER 4

1. All quotes from the *Sydney Morning Herald,* November 26, 2006. Historian John English was the scholar.
2. BBC online, November 22, 2006.
3. Masoud Barzani, head of the Kurdistan Democratic Party, quoted in the *New York Times,* February 18, 2005.
4. Voice of America online, November 30, 2006.
5. Martha Brill Olcott of the Carnegie Endowment for International Peace, quoted in *The Kansas City Star,* November 26, 2001.
6. Quoted on the Web site of Consortiumnews.com, February 7, 2000.
7. *Washington Times,* March 14, 2005.
8. *New York Times,* October 6, 1995.
9. Program for International Policy Attitudes, September 2006.
10. *New York Times,* June 8, 1994.
11. Chicago Council on Foreign Relations, *Global Views 2004: American Public Opinion and Foreign Policy* (Chicago: Chicago Council on Foreign Relations, 2004).
12. Chicago Council on Foreign Relations, German Marshall Fund. Methodology survey, June 2002. Data provided by The Roper Center for Public Opinion Research, University of Connecticut.
13. From "Patrie" in *Dictionaire Philosophique,* 1764.
14. Comment by anthropologist Eugene Hammel in the *New York Times,* August 2, 1994.
15. *New York Times,* April 10, 1994.
16. Statement in "Report of the Secretary-General on the Work of the Organization," quoted in the *Hartford Courant,* September 9, 1999.
17. *Time,* March 12, 1990.
18. Irakli Gogava, chairman of the Georgian parliamentarian subcommittee on CIS issues, quoted in the *Hartford Courant,* July 17, 2001.
19. BBC News, December 9, 2006.
20. *Financial Times,* December 13, 2006.
21. Wilson's speech to Congress was on February 11, 1918.
22. Political scientist Rupert Emerson of Harvard University, quoted in Wiebe (2001), p. 2.
23. *Washington Post,* September 23, 1996.

CHAPTER 5

1. Pauline Maier, "No Sunshine Patriot," a review of *Tom Paine: A Political Life* (Boston: Little Brown, 1995) in the *New York Times* Book Review, March 12, 1995, 1–et. seq.
2. Thomas L. Friedman, "It's a Flat World, After All," *Sunday Magazine, New York Times,* April 3, 2005.
3. *Washington Post,* November 19, 2000. President Clinton's remark was during a speech at the Vietnam National University, Hanoi, Vietnam, November 17, 2000.
4. BBC News, January 30, 2004.
5. *Washington Post,* January 29, 2000.
6. *Time,* November 18, 1993.
7. State of the Union message transcript, *Washington Post,* January 28, 2000.
8. *Washington Post,* December 23, 2006.
9. Randall L. Tobias, Director of U.S. Foreign Assistance & USAID Administrator Address Before the U.S. Conference of Catholic Bishops, Washington, D.C., December 13, 2006.
10. The former diplomat was Jonathan Clarke, president of the American Journalism Foundation, quoted in *The Washington Diplomat,* June 2001.

11. All data on attitudes toward European and national political identification in this section are drawn from *Eurobarometer* 59, Spring 2003.
12. Richard M. Nixon, *Beyond Peace* (New York: Random House, 1994), excerpted in *Time,* May 2, 1994.
13. The Pew Research Center for People and the Press, "Views of a Changing World," June 2003.
14. The Reverend J. Bryan Hehir of Harvard University, quoted in the *New York Times,* August 24, 1994.
15. *Time,* April 11, 2005.
16. *New York Times,* June 9, 1996.
17. *New York Times,* January 25, 2004.
18. Pew Research Center poll, June 2004.
19. "Why Evangelical Christians Support Israel," a speech at the Herzliya Conference, Lauder School of Government, Diplomacy, and Strategy, December 17, 2003.
20. The Pew Research Center for People and the Press, "What the World Thinks in 2002."
21. *New York Times,* February 27, 1998.
22. Gallup Poll Web site at http://www.gallup.com/poll/ releases/pr020308.asp.
23. USA-CNN-Gallup poll, reported in the *Arizona Republic,* March 5, 2002.
24. All quotes from the *Washington Post,* February 12, 2007. The second quote is by Ghassan Charbel, editor of the Arabic-language daily al-Hayat. The Egyptian man in the third quote was Abdel-Hamid Ibrahim, a "man on the street."
25. UNDP, 2003.
26. UNDP, 1995, p. 1.
27. *Hartford Courant,* July 10, 1992.
28. Survey in the *New York Times,* June 7, 2000.
29. *New York Times,* September 16, 1995.
30. *New York Times,* April 10, 1995.
31. *New York Times,* April 10, 1995.
32. David Shenk of the Columbia University Freedom Forum Media Studies Center, quoted in the *New York Times,* April 14, 1996.

CHAPTER 6

1. *New York Times,* February 26, 1992.
2. *Washington Post,* January 15, 2007.
3. From Woodrow Wilson's *The State: Elements of Historical and Practical Politics* (1911), quoted on the Web site of the Woodrow Wilson International Center for Scholars at www.wilsoncenter.org.
4. Maurice Glele-Ahanhanzo, UN Special Rapporteur of the Commission on Human Rights. InterPress Service World News, September 20, 1998.
5. *Le Monde,* May 8, 1998.
6. National Public Radio transcript, November 21, 2006.
7. Spiegel Online, January 9, 2007.
8. *New York Times,* January 28, 1998.
9. *International Herald Tribune,* October 26, 2006.
10. The Pew Research Center for People and the Press, "Views of a Changing World," June 2003.
11. *New York Times,* September 24, 2006.
12. The Pew Research Center for People and the Press, "Views of a Changing World," June 2003.
13. Chicago Council on Foreign Relations, "Americans on Promoting Democracy," September 2005.

14. *Hartford Courant,* April 2, 2005.
15. *Hartford Courant,* April 4, 2005.
16. Shigeru Omi, director of WHO's Western Pacific regional office, quoted in a Reuters dispatch, November 30, 2004.
17. CNN.com, April 2000.
18. Opening statement by Han Seung-soo, president of the General Assembly of the UN, at the International Conference on Financing for Development, Monterrey, Mexico, March 21, 2002.
19. CNN.com, January 24, 2003.
20. *Hartford Courant,* February 25, 1994.

CHAPTER 7

1. "The History of the European Union and European Citizenship," on the Web site www.historiasiglo20.org.
2. Group of 77, Declaration of the Twenty-Seventh Annual Ministerial Conference, United Nations headquarters, New York City, September 25, 2003.
3. Senator Richard Lugar (R-IN), quoted on CNN.com, April 12, 2005.
4. BBC News, February 11, 2003.
5. Valery Fyodorov, director of the Center for Political Trends in Moscow, quoted in the *Christian Science Monitor,* February 11, 2003.
6. Churchill made the widely quoted statement on June 26, 1954, while visiting the United States.
7. Address to the General Assembly, July 16, 1997, UN Document SG/SM/6284/Rev.2.
8. The Web site of the World Federalist Movement is at www.wfm.org/.
9. President Frederick J. T. Chiluba of Zambia, quoted in the *New York Times,* October 23, 1995.
10. Permanent Mission of Germany to the United Nations at http://www.new-york-un.diplo.de/Vertretung/newyorkvn/ en/Startseite.html.
11. UN press release GA/9692, December 20, 1999.
12. *New York Times,* March 6, 1995.
13. Press conference, January 15, 2007, UN press release.
14. *Time,* October 8, 2006.
15. *New York Times,* March 6, 1995.
16. CNN.com, September 23, 2003.
17. BBC, March 29, 2005.
18. UN Secretary-General Ban Ki-moon's address to the Center for Strategic and International Studies in Washington, D.C., January 16, 2006. UN press release.
19. BBC online, October 16, 2006.
20. BBC online, December 12, 2006.
21. Address to the Council on Foreign Relations, New York, January 19, 1999, UN Document SG/SM/6865.
22. James Traub, "Kofi Annan's Next Test," *New York Times Magazine,* March 29, 1998.
23. *Asia Times,* January 10, 2007.
24. UN, Secretary-General, "Renewing the United Nations: A Programme for Reform," Report to the General Assembly, Document A/51/950, July 14, 1997.
25. *Washington Post,* April 29, 2006.
26. U.S. General Accounting Office, "United Nations Reforms Progressing, but Comprehensive Assessments Needed to Measure Impact," Report GAO-04-399, February 2004.
27. *New York Times,* September 12, 1995.

28. Address to "Empower America," Washington, D.C., October 16, 1998, UN Document SG/SM/6754.

29. *Time,* October 30, 1995.

30. 16 January 2007—Address at the Center for Strategic and International Studies, January 16, 2007. UN press release.

31. Press conference, December 16, 2006, UN press release.

32. Address at Princeton University, November 24, 1997, UN Document SG/SM/6404.

33. *New York Times,* July 17, 1997.

34. *Washington Post,* April 12, 2005.

35. *New York Times,* January 8, 1997.

36. *New York Times,* September 18, 1994.

37. Jacques Santer, president of the European Commission (1995–1999), quoted in the *Manchester Guardian Weekly,* July 27, 1997.

38. *Daily Mail,* February 2, 2007.

39. BBC, March 29, 2005.

40. Eurobarometer poll, June 2005.

41. Eurobarometer poll, June 2005.

42. *New York Times,* January 17, 2007.

43. CNN and BBC, April 15, 2005.

44. *Christian Science Monitor,* December 12, 2003.

Debate the Policy Script box, "Santa or Scrooge? The United States and the UN Budget" p. 217

1. Pew Research Center poll, December 2006; data provided by The Roper Center for Public Opinion Research, University of Connecticut.

2. Worldview 2002 survey, June 2002; data provided by The Roper Center for Public Opinion Research, University of Connecticut.

3. Gallup Poll, February 2003; data provided by The Roper Center for Public Opinion Research, University of Connecticut.

CHAPTER 8

1. From Henry A. Kissinger, *Diplomacy* (1994), quoted in *Newsweek,* April 11, 1994.

2. George W. Bush, "The National Security Strategy of the United States of America," a report to Congress, September 19, 2002.

3. Ambassador Howard H. Baker Jr. and Foreign Minister Nobutaka Machimura quoted in the *Washington Post,* November 7, 2004.

4. *Newsweek,* November 26, 1994.

5. *Washington Post,* January 11, 2002.

6. National Center for Education Statistics, *Comparative Indicators of Education in the United States and other G-8 Countries, 2002.* The study looked at eighth-grade students.

7. Andrei Memin, president of the Public Health Association, quoted in the *Hartford Courant,* November 24, 1995.

8. *New York Times,* June 8, 1997.

9. Commission on the Intelligence Capabilities of the United States Regarding Weapons of Mass Destruction. Report to the President of the United States, March 31, 2005.

10. "Scientific Balance of Power," *Nature,* 439 (February 9, 2006), pp. 646–647.

11. Retired General Andrei Nikolayev, who chairs the defense affairs committee in the lower house of parliament, the State Duma, quoted in the *Boston Globe,* May 9, 2003.

12. *Washington Post,* July 20, 2003.

13. Jacob Heillbrunn and Michael Lind, "The Third American Empire," an op-ed piece in the *New York Times,* January 2, 1996.

14. *New York Times,* February 24, 1998.

15. *Washington Post,* April 13, 2001.

16. Elements for success are from Alexander L. George, David K. Hall, and William R. Simons, *The Limits of Coercive Diplomacy* (Boston: Little Brown, 1971) and include (1) strong determination, (2) a less determined opponent, (3) clear goals, (4) a sense of urgency to accomplish these goals, (5) adequate domestic political support, (6) usable military options, (7) fear of escalation by the opponent, and (8) clarity concerning terms of the peaceful settlement. Other elements of success are from Barry Blechman and Stephen Kaplan, *Force without War: U.S. Armed Forces as a Political Instrument* (Washington, DC: Brookings, 1978) and include (1) opponent finds the threat credible, (2) opponent is not yet fully committed to a course of action, (3) goal is maintaining the authority of a particular regime abroad, (4) force is used to offset force by an opponent, (5) goal is to have an opponent continue current behavior, that is, to deter a change in behavior, (6) action is consistent with prior policy, (7) there has been previous U.S. action in the area, (8) involvement begins early in the crisis, (9) military action is taken rather than threatened, and (10) strategic forces become involved, thus signaling seriousness of purpose. Secretary of Defense Caspar Weinberger's six criteria included (1) vital interests at stake, (2) a clear intention of winning, (3) clear political and military objectives, (4) sufficient military force to succeed employed, (5) reasonable congressional and public support, and (6) combat as a last resort. General Colin Powell basically subscribed to the Weinberger Doctrine, as evident in the *New York Times,* September 29, 1992.

17. *New York Times,* February 10, 2007.

18. *New York Times,* October 23, 1995.

19. *Time,* April 9, 1990.

20. Hans-Ulrich Klose, head of the foreign affairs committee in the German parliament, quoted by the Associated Press, May 18, 2003.

21. Ambassador J. Stapleton Roy's recollection of what President Jiang Zemin said. *New York Times,* July 3, 1995.

22. *Los Angeles Times,* February 25, 2003.

23. Associated Press, March 17, 2003.

24. *Washington Post,* February 1, 2002.

25. MSNBC online, March 7, 2006.

26. *Washington Post,* February 2, 2002.

27. KnightRidder News Service, October 19, 2003.

28. *New York Times,* February 27, 2000.

29. Undersecretary of Defense for Policy Walter Slocombe quoted in the *New York Times,* March 6, 2000.

30. Acting Assistant Secretary of State Michael G. Kozak quoted in the *Washington Post,* March 29, 2005.

31. *Washington Post,* March 14, 2005.

32. *Washington Post,* March 22, 2005.

33. *New York Times,* April 30, 1988.

34. Assistant to the President for National Security Affairs Stephen Hadley, quoted in the *Hartford Courant,* May 9, 2005.
35. *Hartford Courant,* May 8, 2004.
36. *New York Times,* March 18, 1996.
37. *New York Times,* September 13, 2002.
38. Kurt Campbell of the Center for Strategic and International Studies, quoted in the *Washington Post,* December 29, 2002.
39. *New York Times,* March 3, 1998.
40. CBS News, January 16, 2003.
41. *Washington Post,* November 8, 2006.

Debate the Policy Script box, "Is Immigration a Solution to Demographic Graying?" p. 245

1. NBC News, *Wall Street Journal* poll, April 2005. Data provided by The Roper Center for Public Opinion Research, University of Connecticut.
2. Gallup Poll, June 2004. Data provided by The Roper Center for Public Opinion Research, University of Connecticut.

CHAPTER 9

1. *Washington Post,* October 23, 2006.
2. Reuters, February 8, 2007.
3. Address at Ditchley Park, United Kingdom, June 26, 1998, UN Document SG/SM/6313.
4. All quotes from President George W. Bush are from his address to the nation, March 17, 2003.
5. CNN.com, February 24, 2003.
6. *New York Times,* March 11, 2003.
7. Quoted on the Web at http://www.why-war.com/news/2002/10/12/iraqwarn.html.
8. Phyllis Bennis of the Institute for Policy Studies, quoted in Margot Patterson, "Beyond Baghdad: Iraq Seen as First Step to Extend U.S. Hegemony," *National Catholic Reporter,* December 12, 2002.
9. Radio Free Europe release, April 9, 2003.
10. Taken from the Web at http://worldnews.miningo.com/msub.12.htm. (URL no longer operative.)
11. CNN.com, June 1, 2000.
12. *New York Times,* August 13, 1997.
13. *New York Times,* June 15, 1998.
14. *Washington Post,* April 12, 2002.
15. Interview of April 29, 2002, in Judicial Diplomacy on the Web at http://www.diplomatiejudiciaire.com/UK/ICCUK7.htm. (URL no longer operative.)
16. Statement of the Islamic Resistance Movement, Hamas-Palestine, issued December 17, 2001, in reaction to the speech of President Arafat on the Web at http://www.jmcc.org/new/01/dec/hamasstate.htm.
17. *Newsweek* poll, November 2005; data provided by The Roper Center for Public Opinion Research, University of Connecticut.
18. Kennedy's remark on June 24, 1963, can be found in the *Public Papers of the President of the United States: John F. Kennedy, 1963.*

CHAPTER 10

1. Pew Research Center poll, March 2006.
2. John Shalikashvili, "Second Thoughts on Gays in the Military," op-ed piece, *New York Times,* January 2, 2007.
3. Gallup/CNN/*USA Today* polls of June 2005 and May 2005 respectively; data provided by The Roper Center for Public Opinion Research, University of Connecticut.
4. Al Nofi, "Statistical Summary: America's Major Wars," online at http://www.cwc.lsu.edu/other/stats/warcost.htm, February 12, 2003.
5. *Global Views 2004: American Public Opinion and Foreign Policy,* The Chicago Council on Foreign Relations.
6. Interpress Service World News, November 29, 2001.
7. *Hartford Courant,* May 19, 2005.
8. *Washington Post,* April 24, 2002.
9. *Hartford Courant,* March 12, 1999.
10. World Islamic Front Statement, "Jihad Against Jews and Crusaders," February 23, 1998, on the Web site of the Federation of American Scientists at http://www.fas.org/irp/world/para/docs/980223-fatwa.htm.
11. *Washington Post,* January 11, 2002.
12. John Pike, director of the Global Security Organization, testifying before the U.S. Senate Committee on Foreign Relations, quoted in an ABC News report, March 6, 2002.
13. Associated Press, November 15, 2003.
14. Amy Smithson testifying before the U.S. House Committee on Energy and Commerce, October 10, 2001.
15. BBC News, March 22, 2002.
16. Paul Wilkenson, "The Strategic Implications of Terrorism," on the Web site of the Center for the Study of Terrorism and Political Violence at www.ciaonet.org/wps/wip05/.
17. Senator Pat Robert of Kansas, quoted in the *Washington Post National Weekly Edition,* October 1–7, 2001.
18. U.S. Department of State, *Patterns of Global Terrorism 2002,* p. iii.
19. Bill Christison, a retired CIA official, "Why the War on Terror Won't Work," *Counterpunch,* March 4, 2002.
20. BBC, March 26, 2005.
21. *Boston Globe,* November 13, 2006.
22. Elizabeth A. Fenn, "Biological Warfare, Circa 1750," an op-ed piece in the *New York Times,* April 11, 1998.
23. John M. Deutch quoted in the *New York Times,* February 25, 1996.
24. *New York Times,* January 9, 2007.
25. *New York Times,* February 14, 2003.
26. Fox News, May 5, 2005.
27. *Time,* May 19, 1997.
28. Associated Press, February 3, 2007.
29. General Nikolai Y. Solovtsov quoted in the *New York Times,* February 21, 2007.

CHAPTER 11

1. *Labor,* September 6, 1947.
2. *Time,* September 18, 1995.
3. *Pravda,* December 16, 2003.
4. Chicago Council on Global Affairs, *Global Views 2006: The United States and the Rise of China and India. Results of a 2006 Multination Survey of Public Opinion.*
5. *New York Times,* May 12, 1996.
6. BBC News online, March 16, 2007.
7. *Los Angeles Times,* May 25, 2005.
8. United Nations Foundation, UN Wire, July 14, 2003.
9. *New York Times,* May 16, 1998.

10. *New York Times,* May 29, 1998.
11. Testimony before the Senate Armed Services Committee, February 6, 2007.
12. Majority Leader Trent Lott in the *Congressional Record,* October 13, 1999, p. S12549.
13. *New York Times,* September 12, 1996.
14. *Newsweek,* May 25, 1998.
15. *New York Times,* May 31, 1998.
16. *Washington Post,* March 11, 2003.
17. High-Level Panel on Threats, Challenges, and Change, 2004, "A More Secure World: Our Shared Responsibility," a report commissioned by the Secretary-General of the United Nations, Anand Panyarachun, former prime minister of Thailand, chair (December 2, 2004).
18. Report of the Panel on United Nations Peace Operations, 2000.
19. J. Stephen Morrison, the director of Africa programs at the Center for Strategic and International Studies in Washington, quoted in the *New York Times,* May 10, 2000.
20. Report of the Panel on United Nations Peace Operations, 2002.
21. *Guardian Unlimited,* September 5, 2006.
22. Kofi Annan, quoted in the *New York Times,* January 6, 1995.
23. All quotes in the paragraph from the *Washington Post,* October 6, 2006.
24. *New York Times,* May 4, 1997.
25. *New York Times,* October 3, 1999.

Get Involved box, "Adopt a Minefield" p. 355

1. *New York Times,* May 1, 1996.
2. CNN, June 18, 1997.

Debate the Policy Script box, "Is Zero Nukes a Good Goal?" p. 359

1. *Time,* March 14, 1955.
2. *Time,* April 27, 1987.
3. C. Paul Robinson, president and director, Sandia National Laboratories, "A White Paper: Pursuing a Nuclear Weapons Policy for the 21st Century," March 22, 2001.
4. Attributed to Churchill by Prime Minister Margaret Thatcher in an address to a joint session of the U.S. Congress, February 20, 1985.

CHAPTER 12

1. Michael Ranneberger, testifying at U.S. Congress, House of Representatives, Hearings Before the Subcommittee on Trade of the Committee on Ways and Means, May 7, 1998.
2. Press release, office of Senator Olympia J. Snowe, October 30, 2006.
3. *Wall Street Journal,* December 4, 2006.
4. Federal Reserve Bank of Chicago, *Strong Dollar, Weak Dollar: Foreign Exchange Rates and the U.S. Economy* at www.chicagofed.org.
5. Chicago Council on Foreign Relations, *Global Views 2004: American Public Opinion and Foreign Policy.*
6. *Hartford Courant,* April 14, 2005.
7. www.g77.org/southsummit2/en/intro.html.
8. President Bush's comments were made to the International Conference on Financing for Development in Monterrey, Mexico, as quoted in the *Hartford Courant,* March 23, 2002.
9. Pew Research Center, "Views of a Changing World," 2003.
10. Gallup Poll, February 2004; data provided by The Roper Center for Public Opinion Research, University of Connecticut.
11. BBC online, March 25, 2007.
12. An unnamed U.S. trade official quoted by the BBC, June 25, 2005.
13. Productivity Commission, Government of Australia, "Measures of Restrictions on Trade in Services Database," Canberra, March 8, 2005.
14. BBC.com, April 24, 2007.
15. *New York Times,* February 1, 1999.
16. Address to the World Economic Forum, January 28, 2001, at http://www.weforum.org/.
17. Klaus Schwab, director of the Davos Forum, quoted in Thomas L. Friedman, "The Revolt of the Wannabees," a column in the *New York Times,* February 7, 1996.

Debate the Policy Script box, "Sanctions on China?" p. 398

1. Senator Lindsey Graham (R-SC) quote by CNN, May 5, 2005.

CHAPTER 13

1. *New York Times,* March 2, 1997.
2. *New York Times,* October 26, 2006.
3. *Hartford Courant,* March 12, 1995.
4. *Washington Post,* September 15, 2003.
5. *Guardian Unlimited,* September 5, 2003.
6. BBC, April 24, 2007.
7. Reuters, April 30, 2007.
8. Speech to the U.S. Chamber of Commerce, Washington, April 23, 2007.
9. Inter Press Service News Agency, April 17, 2002.
10. Walden Bello, from "Justice, Equity and Peace Are the Thrust of Our Movement," acceptance speech at the Right Livelihood Award ceremonies, Swedish Parliament, Stockholm (December 8, 2003).
11. President Eduardo Duhalde of Argentina (2002–2003), quoted in the *Washington Post,* January 15, 2002.
12. Jeffrey D. Sachs, "IMF 'Cure' Is Adding to Crisis in Argentina," op-ed piece in the *Irish Times,* May 4, 2002.
13. Artemio Lopez, chief economist for Equis Research, quoted in the *Washington Post,* May 3, 2002.
14. President Nestor Kirchner, quoted by BBC News, May 26, 2003.
15. *Washington Post,* April 30, 2002.
16. BBC News, September 11, 2003.
17. Johan Norberg, "Three Cheers for Global Capitalism," American Enterprise Online (June 2004).
18. BBC, March 21, 2005.
19. *Wall Street Journal,* May 1, 2007.
20. *International Herald Tribune,* June 11, 2007.
21. Comments in a speech, January 22, 1999, on the Web at www.oneworld.net/guides/imf_wb/front.shtml.
22. BBC.com, June 9, 2007.
23. Professor John Kirton of the University of Toronto G-8 Information Centre, quoted by the BBC, July 12, 2005.

24. Nicholas Bayne, "Impressions of the Evian Summit, 1–3 June 2003," 2003 Evian Summit: Analytical Studies, G-8 Information Center, University of Toronto, http://www.g7.

25. *Rolling Stone,* July 11, 2005.

26. Reuters, July 13, 2005.

27. Gary Hufbauer of the Institute for International Economics, quoted in the *Virginian-Pilot,* January 14, 2004.

28. *BusinessWeek,* December 22, 2003.

29. *Miami Herald,* April 28, 2007.

30. *Miami Herald,* September 13, 2003.

31. *New Zealand Herald,* January 14, 2004.

32. John K. Veroneau, "Introduction," *eJournal USA,* an Electronic Journal of the U.S. Department of State, January 2007.

33. U.S. Federal Reserve Bank of Dallas, "2002 Annual Report, The Fruits of Free Trade," W. Michael Cox and Richard Alm.

34. BBC, March 22, 2002.

35. Associated Press, February 5, 2002.

36. *New York Times,* November 2, 1996.

37. Representative Joseph Gaydos in the *Congressional Record,* April 13, 1988.

38. Frank J. Gaffney Jr., "China's Charge," *National Review,* June 28, 2005.

39. Quoted in Charles R. Smith, "Rand Report Warns of Conflict with China," June 20, 2001, on the NewsMax Web site at http://www.newsmax.com/.

40. White House press release, May 20, 2002.

CHAPTER 14

1. U.S. State Department, Bureau of Democracy, Human Rights, and Labor, Country Reports on Human Rights Practices, 2002, released March 31, 2003.

2. *New York Times,* March 5, 1997.

3. Gallup Poll, May 2005. Data provided by The Roper Center for Public Opinion Research, University of Connecticut.

4. Thomas Riggins, "Why Humanists Should Reject the Social Contract," March 20, 2001, Corliss Lamont Chapter of the American Humanist Association Web site at http://www .corliss-lamont.org/hsmny/contract.htm. Professor Riggins teaches the history of philosophy at the New School for Social Research and at New York University.

5. Address at the University of Tehran on Human Rights Day, December 10, 1997, UN Document SG/SM/6419.

6. *New York Times,* May 5, 1994.

7. Secretary-General Kofi Annan, "Address to Mark International Human Rights Day," New York City, December 8, 2006, text in a UN press release, December 8, 2006.

8. U.S. State Department, Daily Press Briefing, Sean McCormack, spokesman, March 6, 2007.

9. China, Ministry of Foreign Affairs, Foreign Ministry spokesperson Jiang Yu's regular press conference, May 8, 2007.

10. *Washington Post,* March 4, 2005.

11. Chicago Council on Global Affairs, *The United States and the Rise of China and India: Results of a 2006 Multination Survey of Public Opinion* (Chicago: Chicago Council on Global Affairs, 2006).

12. UN Population Fund (UNFPA), *Missing: Mapping the Inverse Child Sex Ratio in India,* June 2003, p. 1.

13. United Nations Population Fund, *State of the World Population 2006,* chapter 3, "Selling Hope and Stealing Dreams: Trafficking in Women and the Exploitation of Domestic Workers."

14. International Labour Organization, *The Sex Sector: The Economic and Social Bases of Prostitution in Southeast Asia,* 1998.

15. MADRE press release, April 12, 2002, on the Web at http://www.madre.org.

16. *Hartford Courant,* December 12, 1996.

17. Report on the World Congress Against Commercial Sexual Exploitation of Children, taken in December 1996 from the UNICEF Web site at http://www.childhub.ch/webpub/.

18. International Labour Organization, Juan Somavia, director-general, *Eliminating Child Labor: A Moral Cause and a Development Challenge,* May 2005.

19. European Union, Council of Europe press release 397a, July 12, 2005.

20. *The Telegraph,* January 26, 2005.

21. Draft resolution presented to the conference, quoted in the *Guardian Unlimited,* September 3, 2001.

22. Secretary of State Powell on the State Department Web site at www.state.gov/p/io/uncnf/wcar/.

23. *Hartford Courant,* September 8, 2001.

24. UN High Commissioner for Human Rights press release, May 12, 2002.

25. *New York Times,* March 31, 1996.

26. The Pew Research Center, "Views of a Changing World," June 2003.

27. Final document of the World Food Summit, November 17, 1996.

28. Final document of the World Food Summit, November 17, 1996.

29. United Nations *Chronicle,* 2001, Issue 3.

30. *Hartford Courant,* December 17, 1992.

31. www.worldbank.org. Search for AIDS.

32. Dr. Robert Webster, a flu researcher from St. Jude Children's Hospital, Memphis, TN, quoted on the CBC, May 14, 2007.

33. All quotes from R. Prasad, "Bird Flu Vaccine: Benefit to Developing Countries," *Hindu,* May 10, 2007.

34. Central Intelligence Agency, "The Global Infectious Disease Threat and Its Implications for the United States" (2000).

CHAPTER 15

1. *New York Times,* May 20, 1997.

2. Robert Repetto of the World Resources Institute quoted in the *New York Times,* September 19, 1995.

3. Christopher Flavin, et al., *State of the World 2003* (World-Watch Institute: Washington, D.C. 2005), p. 5.

4. *New York Times,* November 29, 1995.

5. CBS News/New York Times poll, April, 2007; data provided by The Roper Center for Public Opinion Research, University of Connecticut.

6. *Hartford Courant,* June 8, 1992.

7. *Hartford Courant,* June 6, 1992.

8. September 2, 2003, on the WSSD site at http://www.un.org/ events/wssd/.

9. Reuters, June 7, 2002.

10. Under Secretary of State for Global Affairs Paula Dobriansky, on the Web site of the U.S. Embassy in Indonesia at http://www.usembassyjakarta.org.

11. September 2, 2003, on the WSSD site at http://www.un.org/events/wssd.

12. September 4, 2003, on the WSSD site at http://www.un.org/events/wssd.

13. *New York Times,* August 31, 1994.

14. *L'Observatore Romano,* n.d.

15. *New York Times,* September 6, 1994.

16. *New York Times,* September 4, 1995.

17. Quotes are from the *New York Times,* November 14, 2006, reporting on an article by Pekka Kauppi, Jesse Ausubel, and others in *The Proceedings of the National Academy of Sciences.*

18. Julian Simon, "Environmentalists May Cause the Truth to Become Extinct," an op-ed piece in the *Hartford Courant,* June 15, 1992.

19. *Washington Post,* March 5, 2003.

20. *Arizona Republic,* March 23, 2003.

21. Boris Worm of Dalhousie University in Nova Scotia, Canada, quoted in the *New York Times,* November 3, 2006.

22. Satya Nandan of Fiji, chairman of the conference that in 1995 concluded the Agreement for the Implementation of the Law of the Sea Convention Relating to the Conservation and Management of Straddling Fish Stocks and Highly Migratory Fish Stocks; quoted in the *Hartford Courant,* August 4, 1995.

23. BBC, June 22, 2005.

24. BBC, June 15, 2006.

25. U.S. Department of State press release, August 7, 2003.

26. Report by the NGO, Basel Action Group, quoted in the *New York Times,* October 24, 2005.

27. Quote is from the *Asia Times,* August 8, 2003. The NGOs that issued the report were the Basel Action Network and the Silicon Valley Toxics Coalition.

28. UN Human Rights Commission, UN Document E/CN.4/1998/10, "Adverse Effects of the Illicit Movement and Dumping of Toxic and Dangerous Products and Wastes on the Enjoyment of Human Rights," January 20, 1998.

29. *Manchester Guardian Weekly,* March 20, 1994.

30. *Guardian Unlimited,* January 6, 2007.

31. *New York Times,* February 29, 2000.

32. James Schlesinger, an op-ed piece in the *Hartford Courant,* January 27, 2004.

33. IPCC, Working Group III Report, "Mitigation of Climate Change," May 4, 2007, and Working Group I Report "The Physical Science Basis," February 2, 2007.

34. *New York Times,* September 6, 2000.

35. Claudia Tebaldi, a scientist at the National Center for Atmospheric Research quoted in the *Washington Post,* October 21, 2006.

36. CNN.com, May 31, 2003.

37. *New York Times,* February 29, 2000.

38. *New York Times,* August 19, 2000.

39. Nicholas Stern, head of the U.K. Government Economic Service, quoted in the *Washington Post,* October 31, 2006.

40. John M. Reilly, an economist at the M.I.T. Joint Program on the Science and Policy of Global Change, quoted in the *New York Times,* December 12, 2006.

41. The proposal was made by Harvard economist Richard Cooper.

42. W. David Montgomery, economist at Charles River Associates, quoted in the *New York Times,* December 12, 2006.

43. Yale environmental law and policy professor Dan Esty quoted in the *Washington Post,* October 31, 2006, A18.

44. Mark Mwandosya of Tanzania, head of the LDC caucus in Kyoto quoted in the *New York Times,* November 20, 1997.

45. *New York Times,* December 12, 1997.

46. *New York Times,* December 13, 1997. Bush's remark was made while still a presidential hopeful.

47. *Washington Post,* June 5, 2002.

48. *New York Times,* April 7, 2007.

49. *New York Times,* April 7, 2007.

50. BBC.com, May 18, 2007.

51. Scott Barrett, professor of environmental economics, School of Advanced International Studies, The Johns Hopkins University, quoted in the *New York Times,* December 12, 2006.

52. Reuters, May 28, 2007.

53. MSNBC.com, May 18, 2007.

54. Yvo de Boer, executive secretary of the United Nations Framework Convention on Climate Change quoted in ShanghaiDaily.com, May 19, 2007.

55. Reuters, May 18, 2007.

56. Stephen H. Schneider of Stanford University, quoted in the *New York Times,* December 12, 2006.

Glossary

Absolute power An element of power, such as nuclear weapons, that indisputably exists and can be potentially used irrespective of other considerations.   237

Adjudication   The legal process of deciding an issue through the courts.   284

African Union   The continent's leading intergovernmental organization; all of Africa's countries but Morocco are members. The successor to the Organization of African Unity.   360

Amorality   The philosophy that altruistic acts are unwise and even dangerous, or that morality should never be the absolute guide of human actions, particularly in regard to international law.   300

Anarchical international system   The traditional structure of world politics in which there is no central authority to set and enforce rules and resolve disputes.   3

Anarchical political system   An anarchical system is one in which there is no central authority to make rules, to enforce rules, or to resolve disputes about the actors in the political system. Many people believe that a system without central authority is inevitably one either of chaos or one in which the powerful prey on the weak. There is, however, an anarchist political philosophy that contends that the natural tendency of people to cooperate has been corrupted by artificial political, economic, or social institutions. Therefore, anarchists believe that the end of these institutions will lead to a cooperative society. Marxism, insofar as it foresees the collapse of the state once capitalism is destroyed and workers live in proletariat harmony, has elements of anarchism.   41

Anti-Ballistic Missile Treaty (ABM)   A treaty signed by the United States and the Soviet Union (now Russia) in 1972 that barred the two countries from developing and deploying a system to shoot down ballistic missiles. The United States withdrew from the treaty in 2001 in order to pursue the development and deployment of a national missile defense system.   347

Anti-Personnel Mine Treaty (APM)   A treaty signed in 1997 and effective in 1999 that commits its adherents not to produce, stockpile, or transfer antipersonnel land mines, to destroy any current inventory of mines, and to remove all mines they have planted. The United States is among the handful of countries that has not agreed to the treaty.   354

Appeasement policy   A policy advocated by the British and French toward the Germans following World War I. The hope was to maintain peace by allowing Hitler to annex the Sudentenland region of Czechoslovakia.   45

Arms control   A variety of approaches to the limitation of weapons. Arms control ranges from restricting the future growth in the number, types, or deployment of weapons; through the reduction of weapons; to the elimination of some types of (or even all) weapons on a global or regional basis.   344

Asia-Pacific Economic Cooperation (APEC)   A regional trade organization founded in 1989 that now includes 21 countries.   438

Association of Southeast Asian Nations (ASEAN)   A regional organization that emphasizes trade relations, established in 1967; now includes Brunei, Cambodia, Indonesia, Laos, Malaysia, Myanmar (Burma), the Philippines, Singapore, Thailand, and Vietnam.   438

Asymmetrical warfare   A strategy by which a national military or other armed force, including a terrorist organization, that is relatively small and lightly equipped attacks a militarily stronger opponent by using unconventional means, such as terrorism, or with limited unconventional weapons, such as nuclear explosives and material, biological agents, or chemical agents.   56

Authoritarian government   A political system that allows little or no participation in decision making by individuals and groups outside the upper reaches of the government.

Authoritarianism   A type of restrictive governmental system where people are under the rule of an individual, such as a dictator or king, or a group, such as a party or military junta.   175

Balance of payments for current accounts   A measure of the entire flow of money into and out of a country's economy except funds for investments.   254

Balance of power   A concept that describes the degree of equilibrium (balance) or disequilibrium (imbalance) of power in the global or regional system.   44, 93

Beijing + 5 Conference   A meeting held at the UN in New York City in 2000 to review the progress made since the fourth World Conference on Women held in 1995.   162

Bilateral diplomacy Negotiations between two countries. 263

Bilateral (foreign) aid Foreign aid given by one country directly to another. 417

Bilateral trade agreement A free trade agreement between two countries or between a regional trade agreement and any other non-member country. 434

Biological Weapons Convention A multilateral treaty concluded in 1972. The parties to the treaty agree not to develop, produce, stockpile, or acquire biological agents or toxins of types and in quantities that have no justification for prophylactic, protective, and other peaceful purposes and to destroy any such material that they might have. 348

Biopolitics This theory examines the relationship between the physical nature and political behavior of humans. 68

Biosphere Earth's ecological system (ecosystem) that supports life—its land, water, air, and upper atmosphere—and the living organisms, including humans, that inhabit it. 491

Bipolar system A type of international system with two roughly equal actors or coalitions of actors that divide the international system into two poles. 45

Bureaucracy The bulk of the state's administrative structure that continues even when leaders change. 84

Capitalism An economic system based on the private ownership of the means of production and distribution of goods, competition, and profit incentives. 378

Carrying capacity The number of people that an environment, such as Earth, can feed, provide water for, and otherwise sustain. 492

Cartel An international agreement among producers of a commodity that attempts to control the production and pricing of that commodity. 403

Chemical Weapons Convention (CWC) A treaty that was signed and became effective in 1995 under which signatories pledge to eliminate all chemical weapons by the year 2005; to submit to rigorous inspection; to never develop, produce, stockpile, or use chemical weapons; and to never transfer chemical weapons to another country or assist another country to acquire such weapons. 350

Civil society The voluntary and private (not controlled by the government) economic, cultural, and other interactions and associations of individuals. 131

Clash of civilizations Samuel P. Huntington's thesis (1996, 1993) that the source of future conflict will be cultural. 151

Classic liberalism A subdivision of liberal thought that is optimistic about human nature and believes that people can achieve more collectively than individually, that people understand this, and therefore given the opportunity, people will seek to work together in their common, long-term interests. 24

Classic realism A subdivision of realist thought, which believes that the root cause of conflict is the aggressive nature of humans. 21

Codify To write down a law in formal language. 281

Coercive diplomacy The use of threats or force as a diplomatic tactic. 269

Cognitive decision making Making choices within the limits of what you consciously know. 66

Cold war The confrontation that emerged following World War II between the bipolar superpowers, the Soviet Union and the United States. Although no direct conflict took place between these countries, it was an era of great tensions and global division. 46

Collective security The original theory behind UN peacekeeping. It holds that aggression against one state is aggression against every member and should be defeated by the collective action of all. 362

Communism An ideology that originated in the works of Friedrich Engels and Karl Marx; it is essentially an economic theory. As such, it is the idea that an oppressed proletariat class of workers would eventually organize and revolt against those who owned the means of production, the bourgeoisie; a political system of government applied in China, and elsewhere, wherein the state owns the means of production as a system to expedite Engels and Marx's economic theory. 176

Communitarianism The concept that the welfare of the collective must be valued over any individual rights or liberties. 457

Comprehensive Test Ban Treaty (CTBT) A treaty that bans all testing of nuclear weapons. The treaty was signed in 1996 but will not go into force until ratified by the major nuclear weapons powers. The U.S. Senate rejected ratification in 2001. 350

Conditionality A term that refers to the policy of the International Monetary Fund, the World Bank, and some other international financial agencies to attach conditions to their loans and grants. These conditions may require recipient countries to devalue their currencies, to lift controls on prices, to cut their budgets, and to reduce barriers to trade and capital flows. Such conditions are often politically unpopular, may cause at least short-term economic pain, and are construed by critics as interference in recipient countries' sovereignty. 427

Confederation A group of states that willingly enter into an alliance to form a political unit for a common purpose, such as economic security or defense; it is highly interdependent, but has a weak directorate organization, thus allowing the individual states to maintain a fairly high degree of sovereignty. 203

Constructivism The view that the course of international relations is an interactive process in which the ideas of and communications among "agents" (or actors: individuals, groups, and social structures, including states) serve to create "structures" (treaties, laws, international organizations, and other aspects of the international system), which, in turn influence the ideas and communications of the agents.   30

Containment doctrine   U.S. policy that sought to contain communism during the cold war.   46

Convention on the Elimination of All Forms of Discrimination Against Women (CEDAW)   Adopted by the UN General Assembly in 1979 and subsequently adhered to by over 90% of all countries, the treaty defines what constitutes discrimination against women and sets forth an agenda for national action to end it.   466

Convention on the Rights of the Child   Adopted unanimously by the UN General Assembly in 1989, with sufficient ratifications to go into effect in 1990, the convention outlines a wide range of collective and individual rights for all persons under the age of 18.   469

Conventional Forces in Europe Treaty (CFE)   A treaty negotiated between the countries in NATO and the (now-defunct) Soviet-led Warsaw Pact that placed numerical limits on a range of conventional "heavy" weapons, including tanks and other armored combat vehicles, artillery, and fixed-wing and rotary combat aircraft permitted in the so-called Atlantic-to-the-Urals Zone (ATTU) region.   354

Conventional warfare   The application of force by uniformed military units usually against other uniformed military units or other clearly military targets using weapons other than biological, chemical, or nuclear weapons.   326

Council of the European Union   The most important decision-making body on the EU. The Council represents the member-states through each member's representatives, which can range from the head of state to specialized ministers (such as agriculture). Formerly known as the Council of Ministers.   226

Court of Auditors   An oversight institution within the EU. It is staffed by one individual from each member-country and monitors the implementation of EU budgets and policies.   228

Court of Justice   The most important court in the European Union.   228

Crisis situation   A circumstance or event that is a surprise to decision makers, that evokes a sense of threat (particularly physical peril), and that must be responded to within a limited amount of time.   79

Cultural imperialism   The attempt to impose your own value system on others, including judging others by how closely they conform to your norms.   456

Current dollars   The value of the dollar in the year for which it is being reported. Sometimes called inflated dollars. Any currency can be expressed in current value. *See also* Real dollars.   375

Debt service   The total amount of money due on principal and interest payments for loan repayment.   414

Decision-making process   The manner by which humans choose which policy to pursue and which actions to take in support of policy goals. The study of decision making seeks to identify patterns in the way that humans make decisions. This includes gathering information, analyzing information, and making choices. Decision making is a complex process that relates to personality and other human traits, to the sociopolitical setting in which decision makers function, and to the organizational structures involved.   65

Democracy   A system of government that at minimum extends to citizens a range of political rights and a range of civil liberties that are important to free government.   177

Democratic government   The governmental system a country has in terms of free and fair elections and levels of participation.   78

Democratic peace theory   The assertion that as more countries become democratic, the likelihood that they will enter into conflict with one another decreases.   183

Democratized diplomacy   The current trend in diplomacy where diplomats are drawn from a wider segment of society, making them more representative of their nations.   265

Demographic graying   The aging of a population, with the median age and the percentage of people who reach retirement age increasing.   244

Dependency theory   The belief that the industrialized North has created a neocolonial relationship with the South in which the less developed countries are dependent on and disadvantaged by their economic relations with the capitalist industrial countries.   379

Détente   A cold war policy involving the United States, the Soviet Union, and China, which sought to open relations among the countries and ease tensions.   48

Deterrence   Persuading an opponent not to attack by having enough forces to disable the attack and/or launch a punishing counterattack.   333

Development Assistance Committee (DAC)   The 22 member-countries of the Organization for Economic Cooperation and Development that give official development aid.   417

Development capital   Monies and resources needed by less developed countries to increase their economic growth and diversify their economies.   413

Direct democracy   Policy making through a variety of processes, including referendums, by which citizens directly cast ballots on policy issues.   17

Doha Round   The ninth and latest round of GATT negotiations to reduce barriers to international free economic interchange. The round is named after the 2001 WTO ministerial meeting in Doha, Qatar, where agreement to try to negotiate a new round of reductions in barriers by 2005 was reached.   423

Domestic terrorism   Attacks by local nationals within their country against a purely domestic target for domestic reasons.   316

Dual-use technology   Technology that has peaceful uses but also has military applications.   354

East-West axis   A term used to describe the ideological division between hemispheres following World War II. The East was associated with communism, while the West was associated with democracy.   46

Economic Community of West African States (ECOWAS)   A regional group of 15 countries founded in 1975. Its mission is to promote economic integration, and it has also taken on some peacekeeping activities through its nonpermanent function called Economic Community's African States Monitoring Group (ECOMOG).   361

Economic interdependence   See *Interdependence*.   57

Economic internationalism   The belief that international economic relations should and can be conducted cooperatively because the international economy is a non-zero-sum game in which prosperity is available to all. 29, 377

Economic nationalism   The belief that the state should use its economic strength to further national interests, and that a state should use its power to build its economic strength.   29, 376

Economic sanctions   Economic measures imposed by a country or international governmental organization on one or more countries to change their behavior. These sanctions include such tools as refusing to purchase another country's product, refusing to sell it something that it needs, freezing its accounts in your country, or imposing punitive tariffs and quotas on its products.   260

Economic structuralism   The belief that economic structure determines politics, as the conduct of world politics is based on the way that the world is organized economically. A radical restructuring of the economic system is required to end the uneven distribution of wealth and power.   29, 378

Economically developed country (EDC)   An industrialized country mainly found in the Northern Hemisphere. 58, 376

Environmental optimists   Those analysts who predict that the world population will meet its needs while continuing to grow economically through conservation, population restraints, and technological innovation.   492

Environmental pessimists   Those analysts who predict environmental and ecological problems, based on current trends in ecology and population pressure.   491

Escalation   Increasing the level of fighting.   327

Ethnonational group   An ethnic group in which a significant percentage of its members favor national self-determination and the establishment of a nation-state dominated by the group.   55, 104

Ethology   The comparison of animal and human behavior. 68

European Commission   A 20-member commission that serves as the bureaucratic organ of the European Union.   226

European Communities   (EC) Established in 1967, the EC was a single unit whose plural name (Communities) reflects the fact that it united the European Coal and Steel Community, the European Economic Community, and the European Atomic Energy Community under one organizational structure. The EC evolved into the European Union beginning in 1993.   223

European Economic Community (EEC)   The regional trade and economic organization established in Western Europe by the Treaty of Rome in 1958; also known as the Common Market.   223

European Ombudsman   An official of the European Union appointed by the European Parliament to investigate EU citizens' complaints about maladministration in the activities of EU bodies, excluding the Court of Justice and the Court of First Instance.   228

European Parliament (EP)   The 626-member legislative branch of the European Union. Representation is determined by population of member-countries and is based on five-year terms.   228

European Union (EU)   The Western European regional organization established in 1983 when the Maastricht Treaty went into effect. The EU encompasses the still legally existing European Community (EC). When the EC was formed in 1967, it in turn encompassed three still legally existing regional organizations formed in the 1950s: the European Coal and Steel Community (ECSC), the European Economic Community (EEC), and the European Atomic Energy Community (EURATOM).   223

Eurowhites   A term to distinguish the whites of Europe and of Australia, Canada, New Zealand, the United States, and other countries whose cultures were founded on or converted to European culture from other races and ethnic groups, including Caucasian peoples in Latin America, the Middle East, South Asia, and elsewhere.   42

Exceptionalism   The belief of some that their nation or group is better than others.   119

Exchange rate   The values of two currencies relative to each other—for example, how many yen equal a dollar or how many yuans equal a euro.   383

Extreme poverty   A World Bank term for the condition of those living on less than $1 per day.   389

Failed states   Countries in which all or most of the citizens give their primary political loyalty to an ethnic group, a religious group, or some other source of political identity. Such states are so fragmented that no one political group can govern effectively and, thus, these states are more legal entities than functioning governments.   114

Fascism   An ideology that advocates extreme nationalism, with a heightened sense of national belonging or ethnic identity.   176

Federation   Also called a federal government, this power-sharing governance structure is one in which the central authority and the member units each have substantial authority.   203

Feminism   The view that women have been suppressed and ignored in both politics and political scholarship and have had to strive to achieve greater equality.   28

Feudal system   Medieval political system of smaller units, such as principalities, dukedoms, and baronies, ruled by minor royalty.   38

First-use option   The possibility of a nuclear country using its nuclear weapons first in a war with another nuclear country or using its nuclear weapons against a non-nuclear country.   333

Fiscal year (FY)   A budget year, which may or may not be the same as the calendar year. The U.S. fiscal year runs from October 1 through September 30 and is referred to by its ending date. Thus, FY2007 ran from October 1, 2006, through September 30, 2007.   10

Foreign direct investment (FDI)   Buying stock, real estate, and other assets in another country with the aim of gaining a controlling interest in foreign economic enterprises. Different from portfolio investment, which involves investment solely to gain capital appreciation through market fluctuations.   138, 382

Foreign policy   The international goals of a country and how it uses its national capabilities to achieve those goals.   235

Foreign policy–making actors   The political actors within a state—including political executives, bureaucracies, legislatures, political opponents, interest groups, and the people—who influence the foreign policy process.   81

Foreign policy process   A concept that includes the influences and activities within a country that cause its government to decide to adopt one or another foreign policy.   65

Foreign portfolio investment (FPI)   Investment in the stocks and the public and private debt instruments (such as bonds) of another country below the level where the stock or bondholder can exercise control over the policies of the stock-issuing company or the bond-issuing debtor.   138, 382

Formal powers   Authority to act or to exert influence that is granted by statutory law or by the constitution to a political executive or to another element of government.   82

Fourth World Conference on Women (WCW)   The largest and most widely noted in a series of UN conferences on the status of women. This international meeting took place in Beijing, China, in 1995.   467

Free Trade Area of the Americas (FTAA)   The tentative name given by the 34 countries that met in December 1994 at the Summit of the Americas to a proposed Western Hemisphere free trade zone.   436

Frustration-aggression theory   A psychologically based theory that frustrated societies sometimes become collectively aggressive.   68

Functional relations   Relations that include interaction in such usually nonpolitical areas as communication, travel, trade, and finances.   279

Functionalism   International cooperation in specific areas such as communications, trade, travel, health, or environmental protection activity. Often symbolized by the specialized agencies, such as the World Health Organization, associated with the United Nations.   197

Fundamentalism   Religious traditionalism and values incorporated into secular political activities.   153

Gender opinion gap   The difference between males and females along any one of a number of dimensions, including foreign policy preferences.   69

General Agreement on Tariffs and Trade (GATT)   The world's primary organization promoting the expansion of free trade. Established in 1947, it has grown to a membership of over 100.   421

General and complete disarmament (GCD)   The total absence of armaments.   369

Global warming   The increase over time in Earth's average annual temperature and other associated climate changes.   518

Globalism   The view of the world as a whole, a single unit with many commonalities and connections that cut across political borders, national identities, and cultural differences.   131

Globalization   A multifaceted concept that represents the increasing integration of economics, communications, and culture across national boundaries.   54, 131, 380

Green accounting   An approach to measuring the comprehensive wealth of countries by calculating "human capital" (such as education, health, and equality) and "natural capital" (the quality and quantity of air, land, water, and natural resources), as well as such traditional economic measures as gross national product.   491

Greenhouse effect   The process by which the accumulation of carbon dioxide and other gases in Earth's upper atmosphere arguably cause an increase in temperature by creating a thermal blanket effect; this prevents some of the cooling that occurs at night as Earth radiates heat.   518

Greenhouse gases (GHGs)   Carbon dioxide, methane, chlorofluorocarbons, and other gases that create a blanket effect by trapping heat and preventing the nightly cooling of Earth.   518

Gross domestic product (GDP)   A measure of income within a country that excludes foreign earnings.   375

Gross national product (GNP)   A measure of the sum of all goods and services produced by a country's nationals, whether they are in the country or abroad.   58, 375

Group of Eight (G-8)   The seven economically largest free market countries: Canada, France, Germany, Great Britain, Italy, Japan, and the United States, plus Russia (a member on political issues since 1998).   431 ·

Group of 77 (G-77)   The group of 77 countries of the South that cosponsored the Joint Declaration of Developing Countries in 1963 calling for greater equity in North-South trade. This group has now come to include about 133 members and represents the interests of the less developed countries of the South.   421

Groupthink How an individual's membership in an organization/decision-making group influences his or her thinking and actions. In particular there are tendencies within a group to think alike, to avoid discordance, and to ignore ideas or information that threaten to disrupt the consensus. 72

Hard currency Currencies, such as dollars, euros, pounds, and yen, that are acceptable in private channels of international economics. 413

Hard power Assets that can be used negatively as a threat or a sanction, or positively as an inducement by one country to shape the behavior of another country. 236

Head of government The ranking official in the executive branch who is politically and constitutionally invested with the preponderance of authority to administer the government and execute its laws and policies. 82

Hegemonic power A single country or alliance that is so dominant in the international system that it plays the key role in determining the rules and norms by which the system operates. As the dominant power in the system, it has a central position in both making and enforcing the norms and modes of behavior. Hegemon is a synonym for a hegemonic power. 49, 93

Heuristic devices A range of psychological strategies that allow individuals to simplify complex decisions. Such devices include evaluating people and events in terms of how well they coincide with your own belief system ("I am anticommunist; therefore all communists are dangerous"), stereotypes ("all Muslims are fanatics"), or analogies ("appeasing Hitler was wrong; therefore all compromise with aggressors is wrong"). 66

Holy Roman Empire The domination and unification of a political territory in Western and Central Europe that lasted from its inception with Charlemagne in 800 to the renunciation of the imperial title by Francis II in 1806. 37

Horizontal authority structure A system in which authority is fragmented. The international system has a mostly horizontal authority structure. 91

Ideological/theological school of law A set of related ideas in secular or religious thought, usually founded on identifiable thinkers and their works, that offers a more or less comprehensive picture of reality. 280

Ideology Interconnected theological or secular ideas that establish values about what is good and what is not, and that indicate a course of action, create perceptual links among adherents, and perceptually distinguish those who adhere to a given ideology from those who do not. 104

Idiosyncratic analysis An individual-level analysis approach to decision making that assumes that individuals make foreign policy decisions and that different individuals are likely to make different decisions. 73

Imperial overstretch thesis The idea that attempting to maintain global order through leadership as a hegemon, especially through military power, is detrimental to the hegemon's existence. 252

Imperialism A term synonymous with colonization, meaning domination by Northern Eurowhites over Southern nonwhites as a means to tap resources to further their own development. 42

Individualism The concept that rights and liberties of the individual are paramount within a society. 457

Individual-level analysis An analytical approach that emphasizes the role of individuals as either distinct personalities or biological/psychological beings. 65

Industrial revolution The development of mechanical and industrial production of goods that began in Great Britain in the mid-1700s and then spread through Europe and North America. 42

Informal powers Authority to act or to exert influence that is derived from custom or from the prestige within a political system of either an individual leader or an institution. 82

Instrumental theory of government The notion that the purpose of political units and their governments is to benefit the people who established them and that the continued legitimate existence of these organizations rests on whether and how well they perform their tasks. 174

Instruments of foreign policy Tools countries use to implement their policies. 256

Interdependence The close interrelationship and mutual dependence of two or more domestic economies on each other. 137, 380

Interest group A private (nongovernmental) association of people who have similar policy views and who pressure the government to adopt those views as policy. 87

Intergovernmental organizations (IGOs) International/transnational actors that are composed of member-countries. 2, 195

Intermediate-Range Nuclear Forces Treaty (INF) A treaty between the United States and Soviet Union signed in 1987 that pledged the two countries to destroy all their ground-launched ballistic and cruise missiles with ranges of between 500 and 5,500 kilometers. 378

Intermestic The merger of *inter*national and *domestic* concerns and decisions. 8, 80

International Conference on Financing for Development (ICFD) A UN-sponsored conference on development programs for the South that met in Monterrey, Mexico, during March 2002. Fifty heads of state or government, as well as over 200 government cabinet ministers, leaders from NGOs, and leaders from the major IGOs attended the conference. 421

International Convention on the Elimination of All Forms of Racial Discrimination Adopted in 1965 and in effect in 1969, the treaty defines and condemns racial discrimination and commits the states that are party to it to "pursue by all appropriate means and without delay a policy of eliminating racial discrimination in all its forms and promoting understanding among all races."   472

International Court of Justice (ICJ)   The world court, which sits in The Hague, the Netherlands, with 15 judges and is associated with the United Nations.   285

International Criminal Court (ICC)   The permanent criminal court with jurisdiction over genocide and other crimes against humanity. The court, seated in The Hague, the Netherlands, began its operations in 2003.   467

International investment capital   The flow of money in and out of a country to buy companies, stocks, bonds, real estate, and other assets.   9

International Monetary Fund (IMF)   The world's primary organization devoted to maintaining monetary stability by helping countries to fund balance-of-payment deficits. Established in 1947, it now has 170 members.   424

International political economy (IPE)   An approach to the study of international relations that is concerned with the political determinants of international economic relations and also with the economic determinants of international political relations.   375

International system   An abstract concept that encompasses global actors, the interactions (especially patterns of interaction) among those actors, and the factors that cause those interactions. The international system is the largest of a vast number of overlapping political systems that extend downward in size to micropolitical systems at the local level. *See also* System-level analysis.   36

International terrorism   Terrorists involved in attacking a foreign target, either within their own country or abroad.   316

Iron triangle   An alliance between interest groups, bureaucracies, and legislators that forms a military-industrial-congressional complex.   360

Irredentism   A minority population's demand to join its motherland (often an adjoining state), or when the motherland claims the area in which the minority lives.   111

Issue areas   Substantive categories of policy that must be considered when evaluating national interest.   79

Jus ad bellum   The Western concept meaning "just cause of war," which provides a moral and legal basis governing causes for war.   292

Jus in bello   The Western concept meaning "just conduct of war," which provides a moral and legal basis governing conduct of war.   292

Kyoto Protocol   A supplement to the Global Warming Convention (1992) that requires the economically developed countries to reduce greenhouse gas emissions by about 7% below their 1990 levels by 2012 and encourages, but does not require less developed countries to reduce emissions.   524

Leader-citizen opinion gap   Differences of opinion between leaders and public, which may have an impact on foreign policy in a democratic country.   90

Leadership capabilities   A range of personal job skills including administrative skills, legislative skills, public persuasion abilities, and intellectual capacity that affect the authority of political leaders.   82, 248

League   A governmental arrangement in which the centralized government is mostly symbolic and has little or no functional authority.   198

League of Nations   The first, true general international organization. It existed between the end of World War I and the beginning of World War II and was the immediate predecessor of the United Nations.   198

Least developed countries (LLDCs)   Those countries in the poorest of economic circumstances. In this book, this includes those countries with a per capita GNP of less than $400 in 1985 dollars.   386

Less developed countries (LDCs)   Countries, located mainly in Africa, Asia, and Latin America, with economies that rely heavily on the production of agriculture and raw materials and whose per capita GDP and standard of living are substantially below Western standards.   58, 376

Levels of analysis   Different perspectives (system, state, individual) from which international politics can be analyzed.   65

Liberals   Analysts who reject power politics and argue that people are capable of finding mutual interests and cooperating to achieve them.   23

Liberalism   The view that people and the countries that represent them are capable of finding mutual interests and cooperating to achieve them, by forming ties between countries and also by working together for the common good through international organizations and according to international law. See *Classic liberalism* and *Neoliberalism*.   23

Limited membership council   A representative organization body of the UN that grants special status to members who have a greater stake, responsibility, or capacity in a particular area of concern. The UN Security Council is an example.   206

Limited unipolar system   A configuration of the international system in which there is one power center that plays something less than a fully dominant role because of a range of external and/or internal restraints on its power.   50

Maastricht Treaty   The most significant agreement in the recent history of the European Union (EU). The Maastricht Treaty was signed by leaders of the EU's 12 member-countries in December 1991 and outlined steps toward further political-economic integration.   225

MAD (mutual assured destruction) A situation in which each nuclear superpower has the capability of launching a devastating nuclear second strike even after an enemy has attacked it. The belief that a MAD capacity prevents nuclear war is the basis of deterrence by punishment theory. 333

Majority voting A system used to determine how votes should count. The theory of majoritarianism springs from the concept of sovereign equality and the democratic notion that the will of the majority should prevail. This system has two main components: (1) each member casts one equal vote, and (2) the issue is carried by either a simple majority (50% plus one vote) or, in some cases, an extraordinary majority (commonly two-thirds). 208

Manufactured goods Items that required substantial processing or assembly to become usable. Distinct from primary products, such as agricultural and forestry products, that need little or no processing. 379

Marxist theory The philosophy of Karl Marx that the economic (material) order determines political and social relationships. Thus, history, the current situation, and the future are determined by the economic struggle, termed dialectical materialism. 378

McWorld This concept describes the merging of states into an integrated world. Benjamin Barber coined this term to describe how states are becoming more globalized, especially with the growth of economic interdependence. 54

Merchandise trade The import and export of tangible manufactured goods and raw materials. 137, 380

Microstate A country with a small population that cannot survive economically without outside aid or that is inherently so militarily weak that it is an inviting target for foreign intervention. 123

Mirror-image perception The tendency of two countries or individuals to see each other in similar ways, whether positive or negative. 71

Missile Technology Control Regime (MTCR) A series of understandings that commits most of the countries capable of producing extended-range missiles to a ban on the export of ballistic missiles and related technology and that also pledges MTCR adherents to bring economic and diplomatic pressure to bear on countries that export missile-applicable technology. 348

Monarchism A political system that is organized, governed, and defined by the idea of the divine right of kings, or the notion that because a person is born into royalty, he or she is meant to rule. 176

Monetary relations The entire scope of international money issues, such as exchange rates, interest rates, loan policies, balance of payments, and regulating institutions (for example, the International Monetary Fund). 383

Moral absolutism A philosophy based on the notion that the ends never justify the means, or that morality should be the absolute guide of human actions, particularly in regard to international law. 300

Moral pragmatism The idea that there is a middle ground between amorality and moral absolutism that acts as a guide to human actions, particularly in regard to international law. 302

Moral relativism A philosophy that human actions must be placed in context as a means to inform international law. 300

Multilateral diplomacy Negotiations among three or more countries. 263

Multilateral (foreign) aid Foreign aid distributed by international organizations such as the United Nations. 417

Multilateralism Taking important international actions, especially those using military force, within the framework of a multilateral organization such as the United Nations. 263

Multinational corporations (MNCs) Private enterprises that have production subsidiaries or branches in more than one country. 138, 382

Multinational states Countries in which there are two or more significant nationalities. 109

Multipolar system A world political system in which power is primarily held by four or more international actors. 42

Multistate nation A nation that has substantial numbers of its people living in more than one state. 110

Munich analogy A belief among post–World War II leaders, particularly Americans, that aggression must always be met firmly and that appeasement will only encourage an aggressor. Named for the concessions made to Hitler by Great Britain and France at Munich during the 1938 Czechoslovakian crisis. 67

Munich Conference A meeting between France, Germany, Great Britain, and Italy in 1938, during which France and Great Britain, unwilling to confront Hitler, acquiesced with Germany's decision to annex the Sudetenland (part of Czechoslovakia). This appeasement of Germany became synonymous with a lack of political will. 45

Nation A group of culturally and historically similar people who feel a communal bond and who feel they should govern themselves to at least some degree. 103

National interest A term that is often loosely applied to mean the interests of a country or its government as defined subjectively by those in power in the country, but which more accurately means the interests of the country's nation, its people. 188

National technical means (NTM) An arms control verification technique that involves using satellites, seismic measuring devices, and other equipment to identify, locate, and monitor the manufacturing, testing, or deployment of weapons or delivery vehicles, or other aspects of treaty compliance. 357

Nationalism The belief that the nation is the ultimate basis of political loyalty and that nations should have self-governing states. *See also* Nation-state. 44, 104

Nation-state A politically organized territory that recognizes no higher law, and whose population politically identifies with that entity. *See also* State. 105

Naturalist school of law Those who believe that law springs from the rights and obligations that humans have by nature. 280

Neocolonialism The notion that EDCs continue to control and exploit LDCs through indirect means, such as economic dominance and co-opting the local elite. 376

Neofunctionalism The top-down approach to solving world problems. 197

Neoliberalism The view that conflict and other ills that result from the anarchical international system can be eased by building global and regional organizations and processes that will allow people, groups, countries, and other international actors to cooperate for their mutual benefit. 24

Neoliberals Analysts who believe that conflict and other ills resulting from the anarchical international system can be eased by building global and regional organizations and processes that will allow people, groups, countries, and other international actors to cooperate for their mutual benefit. 24

Neorealism The view that the self-interested struggle for power among countries is caused by the anarchical nature of the international system, which leaves each state solely responsible for its safety and welfare and forces each state to pursue its interests in competition with other states. 21

Neorealists Analysts who believe that the distribution across and shifting of power among states in the anarchical international system is a causal factor that determines the actions of states and, thus, the dynamics of world politics. 21

Net trade The difference between exports and imports, either overall or for specific commodities. For example, if a state exports $10 billion in agricultural products and imports $8 billion dollars in agricultural products, that country has a net agricultural trade surplus of $2 billion. 254

New International Economic Order (NIEO) A term that refers to the goals and demands of the South for basic reforms in the international economic system. 395

Newly industrializing countries (NICs) Less developed countries whose economies and whose trade now include significant amounts of manufactured products. As a result, these countries have a per capita GDP significantly higher than the average per capita GDP for less developed countries. 58, 386

Nongovernmental organizations (NGOs) International (transnational) organizations with private memberships. 2, 147

Non-Proliferation Treaty (NPT) A multilateral treaty concluded in 1968, then renewed and made permanent in 1995. The parties to the treaty agree not to transfer nuclear weapons or in any way to "assist, encourage, or induce any nonnuclear state to manufacture or otherwise acquire nuclear weapons." Nonnuclear signatories of the NPT also agree not to build or accept nuclear weapons. 347

Nontariff barrier (NTB) A nonmonetary restriction on trade, such as quotas, technical specifications, or unnecessarily lengthy quarantine and inspection procedures. 401

Non-zero-sum game A contest in which gains by one or more players can be achieved without offsetting losses for any other player or players. See *Zero-sum game*. 23, 237

North The economically developed countries (EDCs) including those of Western Europe, the United States and Canada in North America, Japan in Asia, and Australia and New Zealand in Oceania. 58, 386

North American Free Trade Agreement (NAFTA) An economic agreement among Canada, Mexico, and the United States that went into effect on January 1, 1994. It will eliminate most trade barriers by 2009 and will also eliminate or reduce restrictions on foreign investments and other financial transactions among the NAFTA countries. 434

North Atlantic Treaty Organization (NATO) An alliance of 26 member-countries, established in 1949 by Canada, the United States, and most of the countries of Western Europe to defend its members from outside, presumably Soviet-led, attack. In the era after the cold war, NATO has begun to admit members from Eastern Europe and has also expanded its mission to include peacekeeping. 46, 360

NUT (Nuclear Utilization Theory) The belief that because nuclear war might occur, countries must be ready to fight, survive, and win a nuclear war. NUT advocates believe this posture will limit the damage if nuclear war occurs and also make nuclear war less likely by creating retaliatory options that are more credible than massive retaliation. 333

Objective power Assets a country objectively possesses and has the will and capacity to use. 239

On-site inspection (OSI) An arms control verification technique that involves stationing your or a neutral country's personnel in another country to monitor weapons or delivery vehicle manufacturing, testing, deployment, or other aspects of treaty compliance. 357

Open diplomacy The public conduct of negotiations and the publication of agreements. 266

Operational code A perceptual phenomenon that describes how an individual acts and responds when faced with specific types of situations. 76

Operational reality The process by which what is perceived, whether that perception is accurate or not, assumes a level of reality in the mind of the beholder and becomes the basis for making an operational decision (a decision about what to do). 76

Organization for Economic Cooperation and Development (OECD) An organization that has existed since 1948 (and since 1960 under its present name) to facilitate the exchange of information and otherwise to promote cooperation among the economically developed countries. In recent years, the OECD has started accepting a few newly industrializing and former communist countries in transition as members. 431

Organization for Security and Cooperation in Europe (OSCE) Series of conferences among 34 NATO, former Soviet bloc, and neutral European countries that led to permanent organization. Established by the 1976 Helsinki Accords. 360

Pacificism A bottom-up approach to avoidance of war based on the belief that it is wrong to kill. 370

Pacta sunt servanda Translates as "treaties are to be served/carried out" and means that agreements between states are binding. 281

Parliamentary diplomacy Debate and voting in international organizations to settle diplomatic issues. 265

Peace enforcement The restoration of peace or the prevention of a breach of the peace by, if necessary, the assertive use of military force to compel one or more of the sides involved in a conflict to cease their violent actions. 365

Peacekeeping The use of military means by an international organization such as the United Nations to prevent fighting, usually by acting as a buffer between combatants. The international force is neutral between the combatants and must have been invited to be present by at least one of the combatants. *See also* Collective security. 363

Perceptions The factors that create a decision maker's images of reality. 70

Plenary representative body An assembly, such as the UN's General Assembly, that consists of all members of the main organization. 206

Poliheuristic theory A view of decision making that holds it occurs in two stages. During the first stage, nonrational considerations such as how an issue and the response to it will affect a decision maker's political or professional future are applied to narrow the range of choices. Then in the second stage decision makers use strategic considerations and other rational criteria to make a final policy choice. 78

Political culture A concept that refers to a society's general, long-held, and fundamental practices and attitudes. These are based on a country's historical experience and on the values (norms) of its citizens. These attitudes are often an important part of the internal setting in which national leaders make foreign policy. 81

Political executives Those officials, usually but not always in the executive branch of a government, who are at the center of foreign policy–making and whose tenures are variable and dependent on the political contest for power. 82

Political identity The perceived connection between an individual and a political community (a group that has political interest and goals) and among individuals of a political community. Nationalism is the dominant political identity of most people, but others, such as religion, do exist as a primary political identity and are becoming more common. 102, 146

Political theory An idea or connected set of ideas about why things happen and how events related to one another. 18

Popular sovereignty A political doctrine that holds that sovereign political authority resides with the citizens of a state. According to this doctrine, the citizenry grant a certain amount of authority to the state, its government, and, especially, its specific political leaders (such as monarchs, presidents, and prime ministers), but do not surrender ultimate sovereignty. 41, 106

Positivist school of law Those who believe that law reflects society and the way that people want the society to operate. 280

Postmodernism This theory holds that reality does not exist as such. Rather, reality is created by how we think and our discourse (writing, talking). As applied to world politics, postmodernism is the belief that we have become trapped by stale ways of conceiving of how we organize and conduct ourselves. Postmodernists wish, therefore, to "deconstruct" discourse. 27

Power The totality of a country's international capabilities. Power is based on multiple resources, which alone or in concert allow one country to have its interests prevail in the international system. Power is especially important in enabling one state to achieve its goals when it clashes with the goals and wills of other international actors. 235

Power capacity The sum of a country's power assets that determine its potential for exercising international power. 238

Power elite A relatively small group of people with similar backgrounds, values, and policy preferences who occupy most of the leadership positions in government, business, media, social, and other societal institutions and move back and forth among leadership positions in those institutions. 188

Power pole An actor in the international system that has enough military, economic, and/or diplomatic strength to often have an important role in determining the rules and operation of the system. Power poles, or simply poles, have generally been either (1) a single country or empire or (2) a group of countries that constitute an alliance or bloc. 44, 93

Power to defeat The ability to overcome in a traditional military sense—that is, to overcome enemy armies and capture and hold territory. 313

Power to hurt The ability to inflict pain outside the immediate battle area; sometimes called coercive violence. It is often used against civilians and is a particular hallmark of terrorism and nuclear warfare. 313

Prescriptive rights Obligations on a society and its government to try to provide a certain qualitative standard of life that, at a minimum, meets basic needs and perhaps does not differ radically from the quality of life enjoyed by others in the society. These rights are usually expressed in such terms as "the government shall . . ."   453

President of the Commission   Comparable to being president of the European Union (EU), this person is the director of the 25-member European Commission, the policy-making bureaucratic organ of the EU.   226

Primary products   Agricultural products and raw materials, such as minerals.   379

Procedural democracy   A form of democracy that is defined by whether or not particular procedures are followed, such as free and fair elections or following a set of laws or a constitution.   178

Proscriptive rights   Prohibitions to having something done to an individual or a group. These rights are usually expressed in such terms as "the government may not . . ."   453

Protectionism   Using tariffs or nontariff barriers such as quotas or subsidies to protect a domestic economic sector from competition from imported goods or services.   400

Protestant Reformation   The religious movement initiated by Martin Luther in Germany in 1517 that rejected the Catholic Church as the necessary intermediary between people and God.   40

Public diplomacy   A process of creating an overall international image that enhances your ability to achieve diplomatic success.   273

Purchasing Power Parity (PPP)   A measure of the relative purchasing power of different currencies. It is measured by the price of the same goods in different countries, translated by the exchange rate of that country's currency against a "base currency," usually the U.S. dollar.   59, 375

Rally effect   The tendency during a crisis of political and other leaders, legislators, and the public to give strong support to a chief executive and the policy that leader has adopted in response to the crisis.   79

Real dollars   The value of dollars expressed in terms of a base year. This is determined by taking current value and subtracting the amount of inflation between the base year and the year being reported. Sometimes called uninflated dollars. Any currency can be valued in real terms. *See also* Current dollars.   375

Realism   The view that world politics is driven by competitive self-interest, and, therefore, that the central dynamic of international system is a struggle for power among countries as each tries to preserve or, preferably, improve its military security and economic welfare in competition with other states. See classic realism and neorealism.   20

Realists   Analysts who believe that countries operate in their own self-interests and that politics is a struggle for power.   20

Realpolitik   Operating according to the belief that politics is based on the pursuit, possession, and application of power.   45

Regime   A complex of norms, treaties, international organizations, and transnational activity that orders an area of activity such as the environment or oceans.   201

Regional government   A possible middle level of governance between the prevalent national governments of today and the world government that some people favor. The regional structure that comes closest to (but still well short of) a regional government is the European Union.   203

Regional trade agreement   A broad term used by the World Trade Organization to define bilateral and cross-regional agreements as well as multilateral regional ones.   434

Relative power   Power measured in comparison with the power of other international actors.   237

Relativists   A group of people who subscribe to the belief that human rights are the product of cultures.   455

Renaissance   A period of cultural and intellectual rebirth and reform following the Dark Ages from approximately 1350 to 1650.   40

Role   How an individual's position influences his or her thinking and actions.   72

Secretariat   The administrative organ of the United Nations, headed by the secretary-general. In general, the administrative element of any IGO, headed by a secretary-general.   209

Self-determination   The concept that a people should have the opportunity to map their own destiny.   106

Services trade   Trade based on the purchase (import) from or sale (export) to another country of intangibles such as architectural fees; insurance premiums; royalties on movies, books, patents, and other intellectual properties; shipping services; advertising fees; and educational programs.   137, 380

Situational power   The power that can be applied, and is reasonable, in a given situation. Not all elements of power can be applied to every situation.   240

Social contract   The implicit understanding agreed to by those who merged into a society and created a government. The social contract details the proper functions of and prohibitions on government.   173

Social overstretch thesis   The idea that spending money on altruistic social welfare programs to support the least productive people in society financially drains that economy.   253

Soft power   Traits of a country that attract other countries to emulate it or otherwise follow its lead through the power of example.   236

South   The economically less developed countries (LDCs), primarily located in Africa, Asia, and Latin America.   58, 386

Southern Common Market (Mercosur)   A regional organization that emphasizes trade relations, established in 1995 among Argentina, Brazil, Paraguay, and Uruguay, with Bolivia, Chile, Peru, and Venezuela as associate members.   437

Sovereignty   The most essential characteristic of an international state. The term strongly implies political independence from any higher authority and also suggests at least theoretical equality. 2, 36

Special drawing rights (SDRs) Reserves held by the International Monetary Fund that the central banks of member-countries can draw on to help manage the values of their currencies. SDR value is based on a "market-basket" of currencies, and SDRs are acceptable in transactions between central banks. 425

Special operations The overt or covert use of relatively small units of troops or paramilitary forces, which conduct commando/guerrilla operations, gather intelligence, and perform other specialized roles. Special operations forces in the U.S. military include such units as the U.S. Green Berets, Seals, and Delta Force; Great Britain's Special Air Services (SAS); and Russia's Special Purpose Force (SPETSNAZ). 325

State A political actor that has sovereignty and a number of characteristics, including territory, population, organization, and recognition. 40

State building The process of creating both a government and other legal structures of a country and the political identification of the inhabitants of the country with the state and their sense of loyalty to it. 107

State of nature A theoretical time in human history when people lived independently or in family groups and there were no societies of nonrelated individuals or governments. 173

State terrorism Terrorism carried out directly by, or encouraged and funded by, an established government of a state (country). 317

State-centric system A system describing the current world system wherein states are the principal actors. 91

State-level analysis An analytical approach that emphasizes the actions of states and the internal (domestic) causes of their policies. 78

Statecraft The use of military, economic, diplomatic, and informational policy instruments to achieve the foreign policy goals of countries. 235

Stateless nation A nation that does not exercise political control over any state. 111

Strategic Arms Limitation Talks Treaty (SALT I) The Strategic Arms Limitation Talks Treaty signed in 1972. 347

Strategic Arms Limitation Talks Treaty (SALT II) The Strategic Arms Limitation Talks Treaty signed in 1979 but withdrawn by President Carter from the U.S. Senate before ratification in response to the Soviet invasion of Afghanistan. 347

Strategic Arms Reduction Talks Treaty I (START I) A nuclear weapons treaty signed by the Soviet Union and the United States in 1991 and later re-signed with Belarus, Kazakhstan, Russia, and Ukraine that will limit Russia and the United States to 1,600 delivery vehicles and 6,000 strategic explosive nuclear devices each, with the other three countries destroying their nuclear weapons or transferring them to Russia. 348

Strategic Arms Reduction Talks Treaty II (START II) A nuclear weapons treaty signed by the Soviet Union and the United States in 1993, which established nuclear warhead and bomb ceilings of 3,500 for the United States and 2,997 for Russia by the year 2003 and that also eliminated some types of weapons systems. As of February 1997 the treaty had not been ratified by the Russian parliament and, therefore, the treaty is not legally in effect. 348

Strategic Offensive Reductions Treaty (SORT) A treaty signed in 2002 by President George W. Bush and President Vladimir Putin. Under the treaty's provisions, the United States and Russia agree to reduce their nuclear arsenals of nuclear warheads and bombs to no more than 2,200 by 2012. When presidents Bill Clinton and Boris Yeltsin had earlier committed to the general levels established in the treaty, they had referred to the potential accord as the third Strategic Arms Reduction Treaty (START III), but that name was abandoned by Bush and Putin. 349

Strategic-range delivery vehicle A missile or bomber capable of delivering weapons at a distance of more than 5,500 kilometers (3,416.8 miles). 330

Subjective power A country's power based on other countries' perception of its current or potential power. 239

Substantive democracy A form of democracy that is defined by whether qualities of democracy, such as equality, justice, or self-rule, are evident. 178

Supermajority voting A voting formula that requires a two-thirds vote or some other fraction or combination of fractions for passage of a measure. 208

Superpower A term used to describe the leader of a system pole in a bipolar system. During the cold war, the Soviet Union and the United States were each leaders of a bipolar system pole. 46

Supranational organization An organization that is founded and operates, at least in part, on the idea that international organizations can or should have authority higher than individual states and that those states should be subordinate to the supranational organization. 203

Sustainable development The ability to continue to improve the quality of life of those in the industrialized countries and, particularly, those in the less developed countries while simultaneously protecting Earth's biosphere. 61, 493

System-level analysis An analytical approach that emphasizes the importance of the impact of world conditions (economics, technology, power relationships, and so forth) on the actions of states and other international actors. 91

Tariff A tax, usually based on percentage of value, that importers must pay on items purchased abroad; also known as an import tax or import duty. 400

Terrorism A form of political violence conducted by individuals, groups, or clandestine government agents that attempts to manipulate politics by attacking noncombatants and nonmilitary targets in order to create a climate of fear.   316

Theocracy   A political system that is organized, governed, and defined by spiritual leaders and their religious beliefs.   175

Third World   A term once commonly used to designate the countries of Asia, Africa, Latin America, and elsewhere that were economically less developed. The phrase is attributed to French analyst Alfred Sauvy, who in 1952 used *tiers monde* to describe neutral countries in the cold war. By inference, the U.S.-led Western bloc and the Soviet-led Eastern bloc were the other two worlds. But since most of the neutral countries were also relatively poor, the phrase had a double meaning. Sauvy used the older *tiers,* instead of the more modern *troisième,* to allude to the pre-Revolutionary (1789) third estate (*tiers état*), that is, the underprivileged class, the commoners. The nobility and the clergy were the first and second estates. Based on this second meaning, Third World came most commonly to designate the less developed countries of the world, whatever their political orientation. The phrase is less often used since the end of the cold war, although some analysts continue to employ it to designate the less developed countries.   46

Transnational advocacy networks (TANs)   IGOs, NGOs, and national organizations that are based on shared values or common interests and exchange information and services.   148

Transnational terrorism   Terrorism carried out either across national borders or by groups that operate in more than one country.   317

Transnational terrorist groups   Those that operate across borders or that have cells and members in more than one country.   317

Transnationalism   Extension beyond the borders of a single country; applies to a political movement, issue, organization, or other phenomena.   131

Treaty of Westphalia   The treaty that ended the Thirty Years' War (1618–1648). The treaty signals the birth of the modern state system and the end of the theoretical subordination of the monarchies of Europe, especially those that had adopted Protestantism, to the Roman Catholic Church and the Holy Roman Empire. While the date of 1648 marked an important change, the state as a sovereign entity had begun to emerge earlier and continues to evolve.   40

Tribalism   A term used by scholar Benjamin Barber to describe the internal pressure on countries that can lead to their fragmentation and even to their collapse.   55

Two-level game theory   The concept that in order to arrive at satisfactory international agreements, a country's diplomats actually have to deal with (at one level) the other country's negotiators and (at the second level) legislators, interest groups, and other domestic forces at home.   84, 265

UN Conference on Environment and Development (UNCED)   Often called Earth Summit I or the Rio Conference, this gathering in 1992 was the first to bring together most of the world's countries, a majority of which were represented by their head of state or government, to address the range of issues associated with sustainable development.   497

UN Conference on Population and Development (UNCPD)   A UN-sponsored conference that met in Cairo, Egypt, in September 1994 and was attended by delegates from more than 170 countries. The conference called for a program of action to include spending $17 billion annually by the year 2000 on international, national, and local programs to foster family planning and to improve the access of women in such areas as education.   500

UN Conference on Trade and Development (UNCTAD)   A UN organization established in 1964 and currently consisting of all UN members plus the Holy See, Switzerland, and Tonga, which holds quadrennial meetings aimed at promoting international trade and economic development.   421

UN Development Programme (UNDP)   An agency of the UN established in 1965 to provide technical assistance to stimulate economic and social development in the economically less developed countries. The UNDP has 48 members selected on a rotating basis from the world's regions.   421

UN General Assembly (UNGA)   The main representative body of the United Nations, composed of all 192 member-states.   206

UN Security Council   The main peacekeeping organ of the United Nations. The Security Council has 15 members, including 5 permanent members.   207

Unanimity voting   A system used to determine how votes should count. In this system, in order for a vote to be valid, all members must agree to the proposed measure. Abstention from a vote may or may not block an agreement.   208

Unconventional force   The application of force using the techniques of guerrilla warfare, covert operations, and terrorism conducted by military special forces or by paramilitary groups. Such groups frequently rely on external sources for funds and weapons. Unconventional warfare is sometimes waged against nonmilitary targets and may use conventional weapons or weapons of mass destruction.   323

Unilateralism   Occurs when a single country perhaps leading a small coalition of other countries, takes an important international action, such as using force, without the approval of an IGO.   263

Unipolar system   A type of international system that describes a single country with complete global hegemony.   93

Unitary government   One in which the central government has all or most of the power and the subordinate units have little or no functional authority.   203

United Nations (UN) An international body created with the intention to maintain peace through the cooperation of its member-states. As part of its mission, it addresses human welfare issues such as the environment, human rights, population, and health. Its headquarters are located in New York City, and it was established following World War II to supersede the League of Nations. 198

Universal Declaration of Human Rights Adopted by the UN General Assembly, it is the most fundamental internationally proclaimed statement of human rights in existence. 461

Universalists A group of people who subscribe to the belief that human rights are derived from sources external to society, such as from a theological, ideological, or natural rights basis. 455

Uruguay Round The eighth round of GATT negotiations to reduce tariffs and nontariff barriers to trade. The eighth round was convened in Punta del Este, Uruguay, in 1986 and its resulting agreements were signed in Marrakesh, Morocco, in April 1994. 423

Vertical authority structure A system in which subordinate units answer to higher levels of authority. 91

Veto A negative vote cast in the UN Security Council by one of the five permanent members; has the effect of defeating the issue being voted on. 209

Weapons of mass destruction (WMDs) Generally deemed to be nuclear weapons with a tremendous capability to destroy a population and the planet, but also include some exceptionally devastating conventional arms, such as fuel-air explosives, as well as biological, and chemical weapons. Weapons of mass destruction warfare refers to the application of force between countries using biological, chemical, and nuclear weapons. 56, 328

Weighted voting A system used to determine how votes should count. In this system, particular votes count more or less depending on what criterion is deemed to be most significant. For instance, population or wealth might be the important defining criterion for a particular vote. In the case of population, a country would receive a particular number of votes based on its population, thus a country with a large population would have more votes than a less-populated country. 208

West Historically, Europe and those countries and regions whose cultures were founded on or converted to European culture. Such countries would include Australia, Canada, New Zealand, and the United States. The majority of the populations in these countries are also "white," in the European, not the larger Caucasian, sense. After World War II, the term West took on two somewhat different but related meanings. One referred to the countries allied with the United States and opposed to the Soviet Union and its allies, called the East. The West also came to mean the industrial democracies, including Japan. *See also* Eurowhites. 42

Westernization of the international system A number of factors, including scientific and technological advances, contributed to the domination of the West over the international system that was essentially created by the Treaty of Westphalia (1648). 42

Will to power The willingness of a country to use its power capacity to influence global events. 238

World Bank Group Four associated agencies that grant loans to LDCs for economic development and other financial needs. Two of the agencies, the International Bank for Reconstruction and Development (IBRD) and the International Development Association (IDA), are collectively referred to as the World Bank. The other two agencies are the International Finance Corporation (IFC) and the Multilateral Investment Guarantee Agency (MIGA). 429

World Conference(s) on Women (WCW) A series of UN-sponsored global conferences on the status of women. Of these, the most recent was the fourth WCW held in Beijing in 1995. 162, 467

World Food Summit Specifically, a 1996 meeting in Rome attended by almost all the world's countries and dedicated to addressing both the short-term and long-term food needs of less developed countries. More generically, world food summit refers to any of a number of global meetings held on the topic. 480

World government The concept of a supranational world authority to which current countries would surrender some or all of their sovereign authority. 203

World Health Organization (WHO) A UN-affiliated organization created in 1946 to address world health issues. 484

World Summit on Sustainable Development (WSSD) Often called Earth Summit II, this conference was held in Johannesburg in 2002. It was attended by almost all countries and by some 8,000 NGOs, and it established a series of calls for action and timetables for ameliorating various problems. 498

World systems theory The view that the world is something of an economic society brought about by the spread of capitalism and characterized by a hierarchy of countries and regions based on a gap in economic circumstance, by a division of labor between capital-intensive activities in wealthy countries and labor-intensive activities in poor country, and by the domination of lower tier countries and regions by upper tier ones. 379

World Trade Organization (WTO) The organization that replaced the General Agreement on Tariffs and Trade (GATT) organization as the body that implements GATT, the treaty. 421

Xenophobia Fear of others, "they-groups." 119

Zero-sum game A contest in which gains by one player can only be achieved by equal losses for other players. See *Non-zero-sum game.* 20, 237

Zionism The belief that Jews are a nation and that they should have an independent homeland. 112

Abbott, Kenneth W., and Duncan Snidal. 1998. "Why States Act Through Formal International Organizations." *Journal of Conflict Organization,* 42:3–32.

Abrahams, Max. 2006. "Why Terrorism Does Not Work." *International Security,* 31/2:42–78.

Ajin, Choi. 2004. "Democratic Synergy and Victory in War, 1816–1992." *International Studies Quarterly,* 48/3:663–681.

Altman, Amnon. 2005. "Tracing the Earliest Recorded Concepts of International Law: The Old Akkadian and Ur III Periods in Mesopotamia." *Journal of the History of International Law,* 7/2:115–136.

Amstutz, Mark R. 2005. *International Ethics: Concepts, Theories, and Cases in Global Politics.* Lanham, MD: Rowman & Littlefield.

Andrade, Lydia M. 2003. "Presidential Diversionary Attempts: A Peaceful Perspective." *Congress & the Presidency,* 30: 55–79.

Antrobus, Peggy. 2004. *The Global Women's Movement: Issues and Strategies for the New Century.* New York: Palgrave Macmillan.

Arat, Zehra, and F. Kabasakal. 2006. "Forging a Global Culture of Human Rights: Origins and Prospects of the International Bill of Rights." *Human Rights Quarterly,* 28/2: 416–437.

Archer, Clive. 1983. *International Organizations.* London: Allen & Unwin.

Arnold, Samantha. 2004. "'May He Guide Us Now:' Religious Discourse and America's War on Terror." Paper presented at the annual convention of the International Studies Association, Montreal, Canada.

Art, Robert J., and Kenneth W. Waltz. 2003. *The Use of Force: Military Power and International Politics,* 6th ed. Lanham, MD: Rowman & Littlefield.

Asmus, Ronald D. 2003. "Rebuilding the Atlantic Alliance." *Foreign Affairs,* 82/5:20–31.

Atkinson, Carol. 2006. "Constructivist Implications of Material Power: Military Engagement and the Socialization of States, 1972–2000." *International Studies Quarterly,* 50/3: 509–537.

Axtmann, Roland. 2004. "The State of the State: The Model of the Modern State and Its Contemporary Transformation." *International Political Science Review,* 25/3: 259–279.

Balaam, David N., and Michael Veseth. 1996. *Introduction to International Political Economy.* Upper Saddle River, NJ: Prentice Hall.

Baradat, Leon P. 2003. *Political Ideologies.* 8th ed. Englewood Cliffs, NJ: Prentice-Hall.

Barber, Benjamin R. 1995. *Jihad vs. McWorld.* New York: Times Books/Random House.

Barber, Benjamin R. 1996. *Jihad vs. McWorld: How Globalism and Tribalism Are Reshaping the World.* New York: Ballantine Books.

Barber, James D. 1985. *Presidential Character,* 3rd ed. Englewood Cliffs, NJ: Prentice Hall.

Barnett, Michael, and Martha Finnemore. 2004. *Rules for the World: International Organizations in Global Politics.* Ithaca: Cornell University Press.

Beer, Francis A. 1990. "The Reduction of War and the Creation of Peace." In *A Reader in Peace Studies,* ed. Paul Smoker, Ruth Davies, and Barbara Munske. New York: Pergamon.

Bender, Peter. 2003. "America: The New Roman Empire?" *Orbis,* 47:145–159.

Benn, David Wedgwood. 2004. "Neo-Conservatives and Their American Critics." *International Affairs,* 80/5:963–969.

Bennett, Scott and Allan C. Stam. 2004. *The Behavioral Origins of War.* Ann Arbor: University of Michigan Press.

Beres, Louis Rene. 2004. "Israel and the Bomb." *International Security,* 29/1:175–180.

Betsill, Michele M., and Harriet Bulkeley. 2004. "Transnational Networks and Global Environmental Governance: The Cities for Climate Protection Program." *International Studies Quarterly,* 48/2:471–487.

Bhagwati, Jagdish. 2004. *In Defense of Globalization.* Oxford, U.K.: Oxford University Press.

Biddle, Stephen and Stephen Long. 2004. "Democracy and Military Effectiveness: A Deeper Look." *Journal of Conflict Resolution,* 48/4:525–546.

Boesche, Roger. 2002. *The First Great Realist: Kautilya and His Arthashastra.* Lanham, MD: Lexington Books.

Bohas, Henri-Alexandre. 2003. "A New Middle Age: A Post-Westphalian Approach to the European Union." Paper presented at "Challenge and Prospects for the European Union in a Globalizing World," Research Conference of the European Union Center of California, Claremont, CA.

Bond, Doug. 1992. "Introduction." In "Transforming Struggle: Strategy and the Global Experience of Nonviolent Direct Action." Program on Nonviolent Sanction in Conflict and Defense, Center for International Affairs, Harvard University, Cambridge, MA.

Bradley, Timothy. 2006. "Why a Ballistic Missile Defense Program Is the Wrong Path to U.S. National Security." *Defense & Security Analysis,* 22/1:95–99.

Brandes, Lisa C. O. 1994. "The Liberal Feminist State and War." Presented at the annual meeting of the American Political Science Association, New York.

Braun, Chaim, and Christopher F. Chyba. 2004. "Proliferation Rings: New Challenges to the Nuclear Nonproliferation Regime." *International Security,* 29/2:5–49.

Brecher, Jeremy. 1993. "Global Village or Global Pillage." *The Nation,* December 6.

Brecher, Michael and Jonathan Wilkenfeld. 1997. *A Study of Crisis.* Ann Arbor: University of Michigan Press.

Breuning, Marijke. 2003. "The Role of Analogies and Abstract Reasoning in Decision-Making: Evidence from the Debate over Truman's Proposal for Development Assistance." *International Studies Quarterly,* 47:229–245.

Brewer, Paul R., Kimberly Gross, Sean Aday, and Lars Willnat. 2004. "International Trust and Public Opinion about World Affairs." *American Journal of Political Science,* 48/1: 93–116.

Brooks, Stephen G., and William C. Wohlforth. 2005. "International Relations Theory and the Case against Unilateralism." Perspectives on Politics, 3/3:500–524.

Broomhall, Bruce. 2004. *International Justice and the International Criminal Court: Between Sovereignty and the Rule of Law.* Oxford, U.K.: Oxford University Press.

Brouard, Sylvain, and Vincent Tiberj. 2006. "The French Referendum: The Not So Simple Act of Saying Nay." *PS: Political Science & Politics,* 39/2:261–268.

Brown, Michael E., ed. 2003. *Grave New World: Security Challenges in the 21st Century.* Washington, DC: Georgetown University Press.

Brulé, David J. 2005. "Explaining and Forecasting Leaders' Decisions: A Poliheuristic Analysis of the Iran Hostage Rescue Decision." *International Studies Perspectives,* 6/1: 99–113.

Brzezinski, Zbigniew. 2004. "Hegemonic Quicksand." *The National Interest,* 74 (Winter 2003–2004):5–16.

Bueno de Mesquita, Bruce, and George W. Downs. 2006. "Intervention and Democracy." *International Organization,* 60/3:627–650.

Bueno de Mesquita, Bruce. 2002. "Domestic Politics and International Relations." *International Studies Quarterly,* 46:1–10.

Bueno de Mesquita, Ethan. 2005. "The Quality of Terror." *American Journal of Political Science,* 49/3:515–531.

Bugajski, Janusz. 2004. *Cold Peace: Russia's New Imperialism.* Westport, CT: Praeger.

Bunch, Charlotte, and Roxana Carillo. 1998. "Global Violence against Women: The Challenge to Human Rights and Development." In *World Security: Challenges for a New Century,* 3rd ed., ed. Michael T. Klare and Yogesh Chandran. New York: St. Martin's.

Bureau of the Census. *See* (U.S.) Bureau of the Census.

Burstein, Paul. 2003. "The Impact of Public Opinion on Public Policy: A Review and an Agenda." *Political Research Quarterly,* 56:29–40.

Butler, Michael J. 2003. "U.S. Military Intervention in Crisis, 1945–1994." *Journal of Conflict Resolution,* 47:226–248.

Byman, Daniel L., and Kenneth M. Pollack. 2001. "Let Us Now Praise Great Men." *International Security,* 25/4:107–146.

Calleo, David P. 2003. *Rethinking Europe's Future.* Princeton, NJ: Princeton University Press.

Campbell, Tom, Jeffrey Goldsworthy, and Adrienne Stone, eds. 2003. *Protecting Human Rights: Instruments and Institutions.* Oxford, U.K.: Oxford University Press.

Caplow, Theodore, and Louis Hicks. 2002. *Systems of War and Peace.* Lanham, MD: University Press of America.

Caporaso, James A. 2005. "The Possibilities of a European Identity." *Brown Journal of World Affairs,* 12/1:65–75.

Caprioli, Mary, and Peter F. Trumbore. 2005. "Rhetoric versus Reality: Rogue States in Interstate Conflict." *Journal of Conflict Resolution,* 49/4:770–791.

Caprioli, Mary. 2000. "The Myth of Women's Pacifism." In *Taking Sides: Clashing Views on Controversial Issues in World Politics,* 9th ed., ed. John T. Rourke. Guilford, CT: McGraw-Hill/Dushkin.

Caprioli, Mary. 2004. "Feminist IR Theory and Quantitative Methodology: A Critical Analysis." *International Studies Review,* 6/2:253–269.

Cardenas, Sonia, 2004. "Norm Collision: Explaining the Effects of International Human Rights Pressure on State Behavior." *International Studies Review,* 6/2:213–242.

Carter, Ralph G. 2003. "Leadership at Risk: The Perils of Unilateralism." *PS: Political Science & Politics,* 36/1: 17–22.

Cashman, Greg. 1999. *What Causes War? An Introduction to Theories of International Conflict.* Lanham, MD: Lexington Books.

Cha, Victor D., and David C. Kang. 2004. "The Debate over North Korea." *Political Science Quarterly,* 119/2: 229–254.

Chan, Steve. 2004. "Influence of International Organizations on Great-Power War Involvement: A Preliminary Analysis." *International Politics,* 41:27–143.

Chernoff, Fred. 2004. "The Study of Democratic Peace and Progress in International Relations." *International Studies Review,* 6/1:49–65.

Chicago Council on Global Affairs. 2004. *Global Views 2004: American Public Opinion and Foreign Policy.* Chicago Council on Global Affairs.

Chicago Council on Global Affairs. 2006. "Global Views 2006: The United States and the Rise of China and India." Chicago Council on Global Affairs.

Chittick, William O., and Lee Ann Pingel. 2002. *American Foreign Policy: History, Substance and Process.* New York: Seven Bridges Press.

CIA. *See* U.S. (CIA).

Cimballa, Stephen J. 2002. *Military Persuasion in War and Policy: The Power of Soft.* Westport, CT: Praeger.

Cimballa, Stephen J. 2003. *Shield of Dreams: Missile Defenses and Nuclear Strategy.* Westport, CT: Praeger.

Cline, William. 2004. *Trade Policy and Global Poverty.* Washington, D.C.: Institute for International Economics.

Coate, Roger, and Jacques Fomerand. 2004. "The United Nations and International Norms: A Sunset Institution?" Paper presented at the annual meeting of the International Studies Association, Montreal, Canada.

Coates, Neal. 2005. "The United Nations Convention on the Law of the Sea, the United States, and International Relations" Paper presented at the annual meeting of the International Studies Association, Honolulu, HI.

Cockburn, Alexander, and Jeffrey St. Clair. 2004. *Imperial Crusades: Iraq, Afghanistan and Yugoslavia.* New York: Verso.

Cohen, Raymond. 1987. *Theater of Power: The Art of Diplomatic Signaling.* Essex, U.K.: Longman.

Coker, Christopher. 2002. *Waging War Without Warriors? The Changing Culture of Military Conflict.* Boulder, CO: Lynne Rienner.

Conversi, Daniel. 2002. *Ethnonationalism in the Contemporary World: Walker Connor and the Study of Nationalism.* London: Routledge.

Conversi, Daniele, ed. 2004. *Ethnonationalism in the Contemporary World.* Oxford, U.K.: Routledge.

Conway, David. 2004. *In Defense of the Realm: The Place of Nations in Classical Liberalism.* Aldershot, U.K.: Ashgate.

Cowles, Maria Green, and Desmond Dinan. 2004. *Development in the European Union.* Houndsmills, U.K.: Palgrave Macmillan.

Cox, Dan G. 2002. "Making Sense of Poll Results: Ambiguity in the Interpretation of Foreign Policy Questions Regarding the United Nations." *International Journal of Public Opinion Research,* 14:218–219.

Cozette, Murielle. 2004. "Realistic Realism? American Political Realism, Clausewitz and Raymond Aron on the Problem of Means and Ends in International Politics." *Journal of Strategic Studies,* 23/3:428–453.

Cramer, Jane Kellett. 2006. "Just Cause or Just Politics? U.S. Panama Invasion and Standardizing Qualitative Tests for Diversionary War." *Armed Forces & Society,* 32/2:178–201.

Croucher, Sheila, L. 2003. "Perpetual Imagining: Nationhood in a Global Era." *International Studies Review,* 5:1–24.

Croucher, Sheila, L. 2003a. *Globalization and Belonging: The Politics of Identity in a Changing World.* Lanham, MD: Rowman & Littlefield.

Daalder, Ivo H., and James M. Lindsay. 2003. "The Bush Revolution: The Remaking of America's Foreign Policy." Paper presented at the conference on The Bush Presidency: An Early Assessment, Woodrow Wilson School, Princeton University, Princeton, NJ.

Dacey, Raymond, and Lisa J. Carlson. 2004. "Traditional Decision Analysis and the Poliheuristic Theory of Foreign Policy Decision Making." *Journal of Conflict Resolution,* 48:38–55.

Dahbour, Omar. 2003. *The Illusion of the Peoples: A Critique of National Self-Determination.* Lanham, MD: Lexington Books.

Dallin, David J. 1945. "Politics and World-Economy in the Great Depression of 1929–1934." *Review of Politics,* 7/1:15–28.

Danspeckgruber, Wolfgang. 2002. *The Self-Determination of Peoples: Community, Nation, and State in an Interdependent World.* Boulder, CO: Lynne Rienner.

Davenport, Christian. 2004. "The Promise of Democratic Pacification: An Empirical Assessment." *International Studies Quarterly,* 48/3:539–561.

De Bary, William Theodore. 2004. *Nobility and Civility: Asian Ideals of Leadership and the Common Good.* Cambridge: Harvard University Press.

de Nevers, Renée. 2006. "The Geneva Conventions and New Wars." *Political Science Quarterly,* 121/3:369–396.

Delahunty, Robert J. and John Yoo. 2005. "Against Foreign Law." *Harvard Journal of Law & Public Policy,* 29/1:291–329.

DeRouen, Jr., Karl, and Christopher Sprecher. 2004. "Initial Crisis Reaction and Poliheuristic Theory." *Journal of Conflict Resolution,* 48:56–68.

Diamond, Larry. 2003. "Universal Democracy?" *Policy Review,* 119:3–26.

DiIulio, John J. 2003. "Inside the Bush Presidency: Reflections of an Academic Interloper." Paper presented at the conference on The Bush Presidency: An Early Assessment, Woodrow Wilson School, Princeton University, Princeton, NJ.

Dinan, Desmond. 2004. *Europe Recast: A History of European Union.* Boulder, CO: Lynne Rienner.

Dollar, David, and Aart Kraay. 2001. "Trade, Growth and Poverty." *Finance & Development,* 38/3. Web edition at: http://www.imf.org/external/pubind.htm.

Dollar, David, and Aart Kraay. 2002. "Spreading the Wealth." *Foreign Affairs,* 81/1:1–18.

Donnelly, Jack. 2003. *Universal Human Rights in Theory and Practice.* Ithaca, NY: Cornell University Press.

Dowley, Kathleen. M., and Brian D. Silver. 2000. "Subnational and National Loyalty: Cross-national Comparisons." *International Journal of Public Opinion Research,* 12:357–371.

Doyle, Michael, W. 2005. "Three Pillars of the Liberal Peace." *American Political Science Review,* 99/3:463–466.

Drainville, André C. 2004. *Contesting Globalization: Space and Place in the World Economy.* Oxford, U.K.: Routledge.

Druckman, Daniel. 1994. "Nationalism, Patriotism and Group Loyalty: A Social Psychological Perspective." *Mershon International Studies Review,* supplement to *International Studies Quarterly,* 38:43–68.

Drury, A. Cooper, and Yitan Li. 2006. "U.S. Economic Sanction Threats Against China: Failing to Leverage Better Human Rights." *Foreign Policy Analysis,* 2/4:307–326.

Dyson, Stephen Benedict. 2006. "Personality and Foreign Policy: Tony Blair's Iraq Decisions." *Foreign Policy Analysis,* 2/3:289–306.

Dyson, Stephen Benedict, and Thomas Preston. 2006. "Individual Characteristics of Political Leaders and the Use of Analogy in Foreign Policy Decision Making." *Political Psychology,* 27/2:265–288.

Eatwell, Roger. 2006. "Explaining Fascism and Ethnic Cleansing: The Three Dimensions of Charisma and the Four Dark Sides of Nationalism." *Political Studies Review,* 4/3:263–278.

Economy, Elizabeth C. 2004. *The River Runs Black: The Environmental Challenge to China's Future.* Ithaca, NY: Cornell University Press.

Edwards, Martin S. 2006. Public Opinion Regarding Economic and Cultural Globalization: Evidence from a Cross-National Survey." *Review of International Political Economy,* 13/4:587–608.

Eichenberg, Richard C., Richard J. Stoll, and Matthew Lebo. 2006, "War President: The Approval Ratings of George W. Bush." *Journal of Conflict Resolution,* 50/4: 783–808.

Eland, Ivan. 2002. "The Empire Strikes Out: The 'New Imperialism': And Its Fatal Flaws." *Policy Analysis,* #469. Washington, DC: Cato Institute.

Elleiner, Eric, and Andreas Pickel, eds. 2005. *Economic Nationalism in a Globalizing World.* Ithaca, NY: Cornell University Press.

Elliott, Kimberly Ann, and Barbara L. Oegg. 2002. "Economic Sanctions Reconsidered—Again." Paper presented at International Studies Association Convention, New Orleans, LA, March 23–26, 2002.

Enders, Walter, and Todd Sandler. 2005. "After 9/11: Is It All Different Now?" *Journal of Conflict Resolution,* 49/2: 259–277.

Enders, Walters, and Todd Sandler. 2006. "Distribution of Transnational Terrorism among Countries by Income Class and Geography After 9/11." *International Studies Quarterly,* 50/2:367–394.

Ensalaco, Mark, and Linda C. Majka, eds. 2005. *Children's Human Rights: Progress and Challenges to Children Worldwide.* Lanham, MD: Rowman & Littlefield.

Eriksson, Mikael, and Peter Wallensteen. 2004. "Armed Conflict, 1989–2003." *Journal of Peace Research,* 41:625–636.

Erskine, Toni, ed. 2003. *Can Institutions Have Responsibilities: Collective Moral Agency and International Relations.* New York: Palgrave Macmillan.

Esposito, John. 2002. *Unholy War: Terror in the Name of Islam.* New York: Oxford University Press.

Etheredge, Lloyd S. 2001. "Will the Bush Administration Unravel?" The Government Learning Project, online.

Etzioni, Amitai. 1993. "The Evils of Self-Determination." *Foreign Policy,* 89:21–35.

Etzioni, Amitai. 2004. A Self-Restrained Approach to Nation-Building by Foreign Powers." *International Affairs,* 80/1: 1–17.

Everts, Philip, and Pierangelo Isernia, eds. 2001. *Public Opinion and the Use of Force.* London: Routledge.

Falk, Richard. 1986. "Normative International Relations: A General Introduction." In *The End of World Order: Essays on Normative International Relations,* ed. Richard Falk. New York: Holmes & Meier.

Falk, Richard. 1999. "World Prisms: The Future of Sovereign States and International Order." *Harvard International Review,* 21/3:30–35.

Farer, Tom J. 2003. "The Ethics of Interventions in Self-Determination Struggles." *Human Rights Quarterly,* 25: 382–406.

Farrell, Robert.1998. *The Dying President: Franklin D. Roosevelt, 1944–1945.* Columbia: University of Missouri Press.

Fearon, James D., and David D. Laitin. 2004. "Neotrusteeship and the Problem of Weak States." *International Security,* 28/4:5–43.

Fearon, James D., and David D. Laitin. 2003. "Ethnicity, Insurgency, and Civil War." *American Political Science Review,* 97:75–90.

Ferguson, Niall. 2004. "A World without Power." *Foreign Policy* 143 (July/August):32–40.

Ferguson, Yale H. 2005. "Institutions with Authority, Autonomy, and Power." *International Studies Review,* 7/2: 331–333.

Filson, Darren, and Suzanne Werner. 2004. "Bargaining and Fighting: The Impact of Regime Type on War Onset, Duration, and Outcomes." *American Journal of Political Science,* 48/2:296–317.

Finnemore, Martha. 2004. *The Purpose of Intervention: Changing Beliefs about the Use of Force.* Ithaca, NY: Cornell University Press.

Fish, M. Steven. 2005. *Democracy Derailed in Russia: The Failure of Open Politics.* New York: Cambridge University Press.

Fisher, Dana R. 2004. *National Governance and the Global Climate Change Regime.* Lanham, MD: Rowman & Littlefield.

Fitzsimons, David M. 1995. "Thomas Paine's New World Order: Idealistic Internationalism in the Ideology of Early American Foreign Relations." *Diplomatic History,* 19: 569–582.

Florea, Natalie, Mark A. Boyer, Michael J. Butler, Magnolia Hernandez, Kimberly Weir, Scott W. Brown, Paula R. Johnson, Ling Meng, Haley J. Mayall, and Clarisse Lima.

2003. "Negotiating from Mars to Venus: Some Findings on Gender's Impact in Simulated International Negotiations." Paper presented at the International Studies Association, Northeast Convention, Providence, RI.

Foot, Rosemary, S. Neil MacFarlane, and Michael Mastanudo, eds. 2003. *U.S. Hegemony and International Organizations.* New York: Oxford University Press.

Fordham, Benjamin O. 2002. "Domestic Politics, International Pressure, and the Allocation of American Cold War Military Spending." *Journal of Politics,* 64:63–89.

Fordham, Benjamin O. 2004. "A Very Sharp Sword: The Influence of Military Capabilities on American Decisions to Use Force." *Journal of Conflict Resolution,* 48/5: 632–656.

Forsythe, David P. 2006. "United States Policy toward Enemy Detainees in the 'War on Terrorism'" *Human Rights Quarterly,* 28/2:465–491.

Fortna, Virginia Page. 2004. "Does Peacekeeping Keep Peace? International Intervention and the Duration of Peace after Civil War." *International Studies Quarterly,* 48/2: 269–297.

Foster, Dennis M., and Glenn Palmer. 2006. "Presidents, Public Opinion, and Diversionary Behavior: The Role of Partisan Support Reconsidered." *Foreign Policy Analysis,* 2/3:269–290.

Foster, Dennis. 2006. "An 'Invitation to Struggle'? The Use of Force Against 'Legislatively Vulnerable' American Presidents." *International Studies Quarterly,* 50/2:421–444.

Fox, Jonathan, and Shmeul Sandler. 2004. *Bringing Religion into International Relations.* New York: Palgrave Macmillan.

Fox, Jonathan. 2004. "The Rise of Religious Nationalism and Conflict: Ethnic Conflict and Revolutionary Wars, 1945–2001." *Journal of Peace Research,* 41:715–731.

Foyle, Douglas C. 2004. "Leading the Public to War? The Influence of American Public Opinion on the Bush Administration's Decision to Go to War in Iraq." *International Journal of Public Opinion Research* 16/3: 269–294.

Fraser, Arvonne S. 1999. "Becoming Human: The Origins and Development of Women's Human Rights." *Human Rights Quarterly* 21:853–906.

Freedom House. 2006. *Freedom in the World: The Annual Survey of Political Rights & Civil Liberties, 2004–2005.* New Brunswick, NJ: Transaction.

Fukuyama, Francis. 1989. "The End of History?" *National Interest,* 16:3–18.

Fukuyama, Francis. 1998. "Women and the Evolution of Politics." *Foreign Affairs,* 77/5:24–40.

Fukuyama, Francis. 2004. *State-Building: Governance and World Order in the 21st Century.* Ithaca, NY: Cornell University Press.

Galtung, Johan. 1994. *Human Rights in Another Key.* Cambridge, U.K.: Polity Press.

Gartzke, Erik, and Quan Li, 2003. "War, Peace, and the Invisible Hand: Positive Political Externalities of Economic Globalization." *International Studies Quarterly,* 47/4:561–586.

Geisler, Michael, ed. 2005. *National Symbols, Fractured Identities.* Hanover, NH: University Press of New England.

Geller, Daniel S., and John A. Vasquez. 2004. "The Construction and Cumulation of Knowledge in International Relations: Introduction." *International Studies Review,* 6/4:1–12.

Gelpi, Christopher, and Peter D. Feaver. 2002. "Speak Softly and Carry a Big Stick? Veterans in the Political Elite and the American Use of Force." *American Political Science Review,* 96:779–793.

Ghobara, Hazem, Adam, Paul Huth, and Bruce Russett. 2004. "Comparative Public Health: The Political Economy of Human Misery and Well-Being." *International Studies Quarterly,* 48/1:73–101.

Gibler, Douglas M., Toby J. Rider, and Marc L. Hutchison. 2005. "Taking Arms against a Sea of Troubles: Conventional Arms Races during Periods of Rivalry." *Journal of Peace Research,* 42:131–147.

Gijsberts, Mérove, Louk Hagendoorn, and Peer Scheepers. 2004. *Nationalism and Exclusion of Immigrants: Cross-National Comparisons.* Aldershot, U.K.: Ashcroft.

Gilbert, Mark F. 2003. *Surpassing Realism: The Politics of European Integration since 1945.* Lanham, MD: Rowman & Littlefield.

Gilbert, Mark F. 2004. "A Fiasco but Not a Disaster: Europe's Search for a Constitution." *World Policy Journal,* 2 (Spring): 50–59.

Gilpin, Robert. 1981. *War and Change in World Politics.* Cambridge, U.K.: Cambridge University Press.

Gitlin, Todd. "America's Age of Empire." *Mother Jones* (January/February 2003): online.

Glaser, Charles L., and Steve Fetter. 2006. "Counterforce Revisited: Assessing the Nuclear Posture Review's New Missions." *International Security,* 30/2:84–126.

Goddard, C. Roe, Patrick Cronin, and Kishore C. Dash, eds. 2003. *International Political Economy,* 2nd ed. Boulder, CO: Lynne Rienner.

Goddard, Stacie E. and Daniel H. Nexon. 2005. "Paradigm Lost? Reassessing Theory of International Politics." *European Journal of International Relations,* 11/1:9–61.

Goff, Patricia M. 2000. "Invisible Borders: Economic Liberalization and National Identity." *International Studies Quarterly,* 44:533–62.

Goldsmith, Jack L., and Eric A. Posner. 2005. *The Limits of International Law.* New York: Oxford University Press.

Goldsmith, Jack, and Stephen D. Krasner. 2003. "The Limits of Idealism." *Daedalus,* 132:47–63.

Graber, Doris A. 2006. *Mass Media and American Politics.* Washington, D.C.: CQ Press.

Gray, Colin S. 1994. "Force, Order, and Justice: The Ethics of Realism in Statecraft." *Global Affairs,* 14:1–17.

Gray, Mark M., Miki Caul Kittilson, and Wayne Sandholtz. 2006. "Women and Globalization: A Study of 180 Countries, 1975–2000." *International Organization*, 60/2:293–333.

Greenfeld, Liah. 1992. *Nationalism: Five Roads to Modernity*. Cambridge, MA: Harvard University Press.

Greenstein, Fred I. 2003. "The Leadership Style of George W. Bush." Paper presented at the conference on The Bush Presidency: An Early Assessment, Woodrow Wilson School, Princeton University, Princeton, NJ.

Grossman, Gene M., and Elhanan Helpma. 2002. *Interest Groups and Trade Policy*. Princeton, NJ: Princeton University Press.

Gruenberg, Leon. 1996. "The IPE of Multinational Corporations." In *Introduction to International Political Economy*, ed. David N. Balaam and Michael Veseth. Upper Saddle River, NJ: Prentice Hall.

Hafez, Mohammmed. 2004. *Why Muslims Rebel: Repression and Resistance in the Islamic World*. Boulder, CO: Lynne Rienner.

Haftel, Yoram Z., and Alexander Thompson. 2006. "The Independence of International Organizations: Concept and Applications." *Journal of Conflict Resolution*, 50/2:253–275.

Haftel, Yoram Z. 2004. "From the Outside Looking In: The Effect of Trading Blocs on Trade Disputes in the GATT/WTO." *International Studies Quarterly*, 48/1:121–149.

Hall, Rodney Bruce. 1999. *National Collective Identity: Social Constructs and International Systems*. New York: Columbia University Press.

Halperin, Morton H., Joseph T. Siegle, and Michael M. Weinstein. 2004. *The Democracy Advantage: How Democracies Promote Prosperity and Peace*. Oxford, U.K.: Routledge.

Hammond, Ross A., and Robert Axelrod. 2006. "The Evolution of Ethnocentrism," *Journal of Conflict Resolution*, 50/6:926–936.

Handelman, Don. 2004. *Nationalism and the Jewish State*. Cambridge: Houndsmills, U.K.: Palgrave Macmillan.

Haseler, Stephen. 2004. *Super-State: The New Europe and Its Challenge to America*. New York: Palgrave Macmillan.

Hawkins, Darren. 2004. "Explaining Costly International Institutions: Persuasion and Enforceable Human Rights Norms." *International Studies Quarterly*, 48/4:779–806.

Hayden, Deborah. 2003. *Pox: Genius, Madness, and the Mysteries of Syphilis*. New York: Perseus.

Heasley, James E., III. 2003. *Organization Global Governance: International Regimes and the Process of Collective Hegemony*. Lanham, MD: Lexington Books.

Heater, Derek. 2004. *Citizenship: The Civic Ideal in World History, Politics, and Education*. Houndsmills, U.K.: Palgrave Macmillan.

Hechter, Michael. 2000. *Containing Nationalism*. Oxford, U.K.: York: Oxford University Press.

Heith, Diane J. 2003. "One for All: Using Focus Groups and Opinion Polls in the George H. W. Bush White House." *Congress & the Presidency*, 30:81–94.

Helco, Hugh. 2003. "The Bush Political Ethos." Paper presented at the conference on The Bush Presidency: An Early Assessment, Woodrow Wilson School, Princeton University, Princeton, NJ.

Henderson, Earl Anthony. 1999. "The Democratic Peace through the Lens of Culture, 1820–1989." *International Studies Quarterly*, 42/3:461–484.

Henderson, Errol A. 2002. *Democracy and War: The End of an Illusion?* Boulder, CO: Lynne Rienner.

Henderson, Errol A. 2004. "Mistaken Identity: Testing the Clash of Civilizations Thesis in Light of Democratic Peace Claims." *British Journal of Political Science*, 34/3:539–554.

Hermann, Richard K., Thomas Risse, and Marilynn B. Brewer. 2004. *Transnational Identities: Becoming European in the EU*. Lanham, MD: Rowman & Littlefield.

Herrmann, Richard K., and Jonathan W. Keller. 2004. "Beliefs, Values, and Strategic Choice: U.S. Leaders' Decisions to Engage, Contain, and Use Force in an Era of Globalization." *Journal of Politics*, 66/2:557–575.

Herspring, Dale R. 2006. "Undermining Combat Readiness in the Russian Military, 1992–2005." *Armed Forces & Society*, 32/4:513–531.

Herspring, Dale R., ed. 2004. *Putin's Russia: Past Imperfect, Future Uncertain*. Lanham, MD: Rowman & Littlefield.

Hetherington, Marc J., and Michael Nelson. 2003. "Anatomy of a Rally Effect: George W. Bush and the War on Terrorism." *Political Science and Politics*, 36:37–42.

Heymann, Philip B. 2002. "Dealing with Terrorism: An Overview." *International Security*, 26/3:24–38.

Hobol, Sara Binzer. 2006. "Direct Democracy and European Integration." *Journal of European Public Policy*, 13/1:153–166.

Hobsbawm, Eric J. 1990. *Nations and Nationalism since 1780: Programme, Myth, Reality*. Cambridge, U.K.: Cambridge University Press.

Hobsbawm, Eric J. 2001. "Democracy Can Be Bad for You." *New Statesman* 14/626 (March 5, 2001): 25–28.

Hobson, John M. 2005. "The Enduring Place of Hierarchy in World Politics: Tracing the Social Logics of Hierarchy and Political Change." *European Journal of International Relations*, 11/1:63–98.

Hoffmann, Stanley. 2003. "World Governance: Beyond Utopia." *Daedalus*, 132:27–35.

Holsti, K. J. 2004. *Taming the Sovereigns: Institutional Change in International Politics*. New York: Cambridge University Press.

Hooghe, Liesbet, and Gary Marks. 2006. "Europe's Blues: Theoretical Soul-Searching after the Rejection of the European Constitution." *PS: Political Science & Politics*, 39/2:251–255.

Horne, John. 2002. "Civilian Populations and Wartime Violence: Toward an Historical Analysis." *International Social Science Journal*, 26:426–435.

Horowitz, Michael, Rose McDermott, and Allan C. Stam. 2005. "Leader Age, Regime Type, and Violent International Relations." *Journal of Conflict Resolution*, 49/4: 661–685.

Hossay, Patrick. 2002. *Contentions of Nationhood: Nationalist Movements, Political Conflict and Social Change in Flanders, Scotland, and French Canada*. Lanham, MD: Lexington Books.

Howard, Peter. 2004. "Why Not Invade North Korea? Threats, Language Games, and U.S. Foreign Policy." *International Studies Quarterly*, 48/4:805–827.

Howell, William G., and Jon C. Pevehouse. 2005. "Presidents, Congress, and the Use of Force." *International Organization*, 59/1:209–232.

Hudson, Valerie M. 2005. "Foreign Policy Analysis: Actor-Specific Theory and the Ground of International Relations." *Foreign Policy Analysis*, 1/1:1–11.

Hufbauer, Cary Clyde, and Barbara Oegg. 2003. "The Impact of Economic Sanctions on U.S. Trade: Andrew Rose's Gravity Model." *International Economics Policy Briefs*, Number PB03-4, April 2003. Washington DC: Institute for International Economics.

Huntington, Samuel P. 1996. *The Clash of Civilizations and the Remaking of World Order*. New York: Simon & Schuster.

Huntington, Samuel. 1993. "The Clash of Civilizations." *Foreign Affairs*, 72(3):56–73.

Ignazi, Piero, and Mark Kesselman. 2004. "Extreme Right Parties in Western Europe." *Political Science Quarterly*, 119/2:369–371.

Ikenberry, G. John, ed. 2002. *America Unrivaled: The Future of the Balance of Power*. Ithaca, NY: Cornell University Press.

Ikenberry, G. John. 2004. "Liberalism and Empire: Logics of Order in the American Unipolar Age." *Review of International Studies*, 30:609–630.

Inglehart, Ronald, and Pippa Norris. 2002. "Islam and the West: Testing the Clash of Civilizations Thesis." Faculty Working Research Series. John F. Kennedy School of Government, Harvard University.

Inglehart, Ronald, and Pippa Norris. 2003. "The True Clash of Civilizations." *Foreign Policy*, 136:63–70.

Inglehart, Ronald. 2003. "How Solid Is Mass Support for Democracy—And How Can We Measure It?" *PS, Political Science and Politics*, 36/1:51–57.

International Institute for Strategic Studies (ISSI). Annual edition. *The Military Balance*. London: Taylor & Francis.

International Monetary Policy-Making after Bretton Woods. Albany: State University of New York Press.

Isernia, Pierangelo, Zoltan Juhasz, and Hans Rattinger. 2002. "Foreign Policy and the Rational Public in Comparative Perspective." *Journal of Conflict Resolution*, 46:201–225.

Jackson, Robert, and Georg Sørensen. 2003. *Introduction to International Relations: Theories and Approaches*, 2nd ed. Oxford, U.K.: Oxford University Press.

Jacobsen, John Kurt. 2003. "Dueling Constructivisms: A Post-Mortem on the Ideas Debated in Mainstream IR/IPE." *Review of International Studies*, 29:39–60.

James, Patrick, and Enyu Zhang. 2005. "Chinese Choices: A Poliheuristic Analysis of Foreign Policy Crises, 1950–1996." *Foreign Policy Analysis*, 1/1:31–46.

James, Patrick. 2002. *International Relations and Scientific Progress: Structural Realism Reconsidered*. Columbus: Ohio State University Press.

Jan Klabbers, Jan. 2006. "The Right to Be Taken Seriously: Self-Determination in International Law." *Human Rights Quarterly*, 28/1:186–206.

Jana Von Stein, Jana. 2005. "Do Treaties Constrain or Screen? Selection Bias and Treaty Compliance." *American Political Science Review*, 99/4:611–622.

Jaquette, Jane S. 1997. "Women in Power: From Tokenism to Critical Mass." *Foreign Policy*, 108:23–97.

Jayawickrama, Nihal. 2003. *The Judicial Application of Human Rights Law: National, Regional and International Jurisprudence*. Cambridge, U.K.: Cambridge University Press.

Johansen, Robert C. 2006. "The Impact of U.S. Policy toward the International Criminal Court on the Prevention of Genocide, War Crimes, and Crimes Against Humanity." *Human Rights Quarterly*, 28/2:301–331.

Johnson, Dominic D. P. 2004. *Overconfidence and War: The Havoc and Glory of Positive Illusions*. Cambridge, MA: Harvard University Press.

Johnston, Douglas, ed. 2003. *Faith-Based Diplomacy: Trumping Realpolitik*. New York: Oxford University Press.

Johnstone, Rachael Lorna. 2006. "Feminist Influences on the United Nations Human Rights Treaty Bodies." *Human Rights Quarterly*, 28/1:148–185.

Joyner, Christopher C. 2000. "The Reality and Relevance of International Law in the Twenty-First Century." In *The Global Agenda: Issues and Perspectives*, ed. Charles W. Kegley, Jr., and Eugene R. Wittkopf. Boston: McGraw-Hill.

Joyner, Christopher C. 2005. *International Law in the 21st Century: Rules for Global Governance*. Lanham, MD: Rowman & Littlefield.

Jung, Hwa Yol. 2002. *Comparative Political Culture in the Age of Globalization*. Lanham, MD: Lexington Books.

Jusdanis, Gregory. 2004. *The Necessary Nation*. Princeton, NJ: Princeton University Press.

Jutta, Joachim. 2003. "Framing Issues and Seizing Opportunities: The UN, NGOs, and Women's Rights." *International Studies Quarterly*, 47:247–274.

Kaltenthaler, Karl C., Ronald D. Gelleny, and Stephen J. Ceccoli. 2004. "Explaining Citizen Support for Trade Liberalization." *International Studies Quarterly*, 48/4: 829–851.

Kaplan, Lawrence F. 2004. "Springtime for Realism." *New Republic* (June 1), online.

Kenneally. Ivan. 2006. "Mansfield, Harvey C. *Manliness*" (Book review). *Perspectives on Political Science,* 35/2:104–106.

Kennedy, Paul. 1988. *The Rise and Fall of the Great Powers.* New York: Random House.

Kent, George. 2002. "Food Trade and Food Rights." *United Nations Chronicle,* 39/1, online.

Keohane, Robert O. 1998. "International Institutions: Can Interdependence Work?" *Foreign Policy,* 110:82–96.

Keohane, Robert O., and Joseph S. Nye, Jr. 1999. "Globalization: What's New? What's Not? (And So What?)." *Foreign Policy,* 114:104–119.

Kerr, Joanna, Ellen Spenger, and Alison Symington, eds. 2004. *The Future of Women's Rights: Global Visions and Strategies.* New York: Palgrave Macmillan.

Kerr, Rachel. 2004. *The International Criminal Tribunal for the Former Yugoslavia.* Oxford, U.K.: Oxford University Press.

Keshk, Omar M. G., Brian M. Pollins, and Rafael Reuveny. 2004. "Trade Still Follows the Flag: The Primacy of Politics in a Simultaneous Model of Interdependence and Armed Conflict." *Journal of Politics,* 66/4:1155–1182.

Kille, Kent J., and Roger M. Scully. 2003. "Executive Heads and the Role of Intergovernmental Organizations: Expansionist Leadership in the United Nations and the European Union." *Political Psychology,* 24:175–190.

Kimura, Masato, and David A. Welch. 1998. "Specifying 'Interests': Japan's Claim to the Northern Territories and Its Implications for International Relations Theory." *International Studies Quarterly,* 42:213–244.

Kinne, Brandon J. 2005. "Decision Making in Autocratic Regimes: A Poliheuristic Perspective." *International Studies Perspectives,* 6/1:114–128.

Kinsella, David, and Bruce Russett. 2002. "Conflict Emergence and Escalation in Interactive International Dyads." *Journal of Politics,* 64:1045–1069.

Kinsella, David. 2005. "No Rest for the Democratic Peace." *American Political Science Review,* 99/3:453–457.

Kissinger, Henry A. 1979. *The White House Years.* Boston: Little, Brown.

Kissinger, Henry A. 1982. *Years of Upheaval.* Boston: Little, Brown.

Kissinger, Henry A. 1994. *Diplomacy.* New York: Simon & Schuster.

Klare, Michael T., and Lora Lumpe. 2000. "Fanning the Flames of War: Conventional Arms Transfers in the 1990s." In *World Security: Challenges for a New Century,* 3rd ed., eds. Michael T. Klare and Yogesh Chandrani. New York: St. Martin's.

Kline, Scott. 2004. "The Culture War Goes Global: 'Family Values' and the Shape of U.S. Foreign Policy." Paper presented at the annual convention of the International Studies Association, Montreal, Canada.

Klinkner, Philip A. 2006. "Mr. Bush's War: Foreign Policy in the 2004 Election." *Presidential Studies Quarterly,* 36/2: 281–296.

Knecht, Thomas, and M. Stephen Weatherford. 2006. "Public Opinion and Foreign Policy: The Stages of Presidential Decision Making." *International Studies Quarterly,* 50/4: 705–727.

Koch, Michael, and Scott Sigmund Gartner. 2005. "Casualties and Constituencies: Democratic Accountability, Electoral Institutions, and Costly Conflicts." *Journal of Conflict Resolution,* 49/4:874–894.

Kolstø, Pål. 2006. "National Symbols as Signs of Unity and Division." *Ethnic and Racial Studies,* 29/4:67–701.

Krasno, Jean, Bradd C. Hayes, and Donald C. F. Daniel, eds. 2003. *Leveraging for Success in United Nations Peacekeeping Operations.* Westport, CT: Praeger.

Krauthammer, Charles. 1991. "The Unipolar Moment." *Foreign Affairs, America and the World, 1990/91,* 23–33.

Krauthammer, Charles. 2004. "In Defense of Democratic Realism." *The National Interest* (Fall), online.

Kuziemko, Ilyana, and Eric Werker. 2006. "How Much Is a Seat on the Security Council Worth? Foreign Aid and Bribery at the United Nations." *Journal of Political Economy,* 114/5:905–930.

Kydd, Andrew H., and Barbara F. Walter. 2006. "The Strategies of Terrorism." *International Security,* 31/1:49–79.

Lacina, Bethany, Nils Petter Gleditsch, and Bruce Russett. 2006. "The Declining Risk of Death in Battle." *International Studies Quarterly,* 5/30:673–680.

Lackey, Douglas. 1989. *The Ethics of War and Peace.* Englewood Cliffs, NJ: Prentice Hall.

Lacy, Dean, and Emerson M. S. Niou. 2004. "A Theory of Economic Sanctions and Issue Linkage: The Roles of Preferences, Information, and Threats." *Journal of Politics,* 66, 1:25–54.

Lai, Brian, and Daniel S. Morey. 2006. "Impact of Regime Type on the Influence of U.S. Foreign Aid," *Foreign Policy Analysis,* 2/4:385–412.

Lake, Daniel. 2005. "Why Play Hardball? The Political Incentives for Employing Coercive Statecraft." Paper presented at the annual convention of the International Studies Association, Honolulu, HI.

Lal, Deepak. 2004. *In Praise of Empires: Globalization and Order.* New York: Palgrave Macmillan.

Lang, Anthony F., Jr., ed. 2003. *Just Intervention.* Washington, DC: Georgetown University Press.

Langlois, Catherine C., and Jean-Pierre P. Langlois. 2006. "When Fully Informed States Make Good the Threat of War: Rational Escalation and the Failure of Bargaining." *British Journal of Political Science,* 36/4:645–669.

Lantis, Jeffrey S. 2005. "Strategic Culture: From Clausewitz to Constructivism." *Strategic Insights,* 4/10, online.

Laqueur, Walter. 2004. *No End to War: Terrorism in the Twenty-First Century.* New York: Continuum International.

Larémont, Ricardo Réne. 2005. *Borders, Nationalism, and the African State.* Boulder, CO: Lynne Rienner.

Larmer, Brook. 2005. "The Center of the World." *Foreign Policy,* 150:66–74.

Layne, Christopher. 2006. "Impotent Power? Re-examining the Nature of America's Hegemonic Power." *The National Interest,* 85:41–47.

Layne, Christopher. 2006a. "The Coming of the United States' Unipolar Moment." *International Security,* 31/2:7–41.

Lebovic, James H. 2004. "Uniting for Peace? Democracies and United Nations Peace Operations after the Cold War." *Journal of Conflict Resolution,* 48/6:910–936.

Lebow, Richard Ned. (2004). "Constructive Realism." *International Studies Review,* 6/2:346–348.

Legro, Jeffrey W. 1996. "Culture and Preferences in the International Cooperation Two-Step." *American Political Science Review,* 90:118–137.

Leitner, Kara, and Simon Lester. 2006. "WTO Dispute Settlement from 1995 to 2005: A Statistical Analysis." *Journal of International Economic Law,* 9/1:219–231.

Lensu, Maria, and Jan-Sefan Fritz, eds. 1999. *Value Pluralism, Normative Theory, and International Relations.* New York: St. Martin's.

Lentner, Howard. 2004. *Power and Politics in Globalization: The Indispensable State.* Oxford, U.K.: Routledge.

Leogrande, William M. 2002. "Tug of War: How Real Is the Rivalry between Congress and the President over Foreign Policy?" *Congress & the Presidency,* 29:113–118.

Levey, David H., and Stuart S. Brown. 2005. "The Overstretch Myth." *Foreign Affairs,* 84/3 (March/April), online.

Li, Quan, and Drew Schaub. 2004. "Economic Globalization and Transnational Terrorism: A Pooled Time-Series Analysis." *Journal of Conflict Resolution,* 48/2: 230–258.

Li, Quan, and Rafael Reuveny. 2003. "Economic Globalization and Democracy: An Empirical Analysis." *British Journal of Political Science,* 33:29–54.

Lieber, Keir A., and Daryl G. Press. 2006. "The End of MAD? The Nuclear Dimension of U.S. Primacy." *International Security,* 30/4:7–44.

Lieven, Anatol. 2004. *America Right or Wrong: An Anatomy of American Nationalism.* New York: Oxford University Press.

Lind, Michael. 1994. "In Defense of Liberal Nationalism." *Foreign Affairs,* 73(3):87–99.

Lindsay, James M. 1994. "Congress, Foreign Policy, and the New Institutionalism." *International Studies Quarterly,* 38: 281–304.

Lobell, Steven E. 2004. "Historical Lessons to Extend America's Great Power Tenure." *World Affairs* (Spring), online.

Lomborg, Bjørn, 2001. *The Skeptical Environmentalist: Measuring the Real State of the World.* New York: Cambridge University Press.

Lomborg, Bjørn. 2003. "Debating the Skeptical Environmentalist." In *Taking Sides: Clashing View on Controversial Issues in World Politics,* 11th ed., ed. John T. Rourke. Guilford, CT: McGraw-Hill/Dushkin.

Longman, Phillip. 2004. *The Empty Cradle: How Falling Birthrates Threaten World Prosperity and What to Do about It.* New York: Basic Books.

Luttwak, Edward. 2000. "Kofi's Rule: Humanitarian Intervention and Neocolonialism." *The National Interest* 58 (Winter): 57–62.

Mahmud, Sakah S. 2004. "Contesting Hegemony? The Islamic Nation as a Dominant Actor in International Relations." Paper presented at the annual convention of the International Studies Association, Montreal, Canada.

Maley, Willy. 2003. *Nation, State, and Empire in English Renaissance Literature: Shakespeare to Milton.* New York: Palgrave Macmillan.

Malone, David M., and Yuen Foong Khong, eds. 2003. *Unilateralism and U.S. Foreign Policy: International Perspectives.* Boulder, CO: Lynne Rienner.

Mandaville, Peter G. 2000. "Territory and Translocality: Discrepant Idioms of Political Identity." Paper presented at the International Studies Association Convention, Los Angeles, CA.

Mann, Michael. 2004. *The Dark Side of Democracy: Explaining Ethnic Cleansing.* New York: Cambridge University Press.

Mansfield, Harvey C. 2006. *Manliness.* New York: Yale University Press.

Marinov, Nikolay. 2005. "Do Economic Sanctions Destabilize Country Leaders?" *American Journal of Political Science,* 49/3:564–591.

Marshall, Andrew. 2006. "Making a Killing." *Bulletin of the Atomic Scientists,* 62/2:36–42.

Marshall, Bryan W., and Brandon C. Prins. 2002. "The Pendulum of Congressional Power: Agenda Change, Partisanship, and the Demise of the Post–World War II Foreign Policy Consensus." *Congress & the Presidency,* 29:195–212.

Marshall, Monty G., and Ted Robert Gurr. 2002. *Peace and Conflict, 2003: A Global Survey of Armed Conflicts, Self-Determination Movements, and Democracy.* College Park, MD: Center for International Development and Conflict Management.

Martin, Andrew, and George Ross, eds. 2004. *Euros and Europeans: Monetary Integration and the European Model of Society.* Cambridge, UK: Cambridge University Press.

Marx, Anthony W. 2003. *Faith in Nation: Exclusionary Origins of Nationalism.* New York: Oxford University Press.

Maurer, Andreas. 2003. "The Legislative Powers and Impact of the European Parliament." *Journal of Common Market Studies,* 41:227–248.

Mastanduno, Michael. 1998. "Economics and Security in Statecraft and Scholarship." *International Organization,* 52/4:825–854.

Mayda, Anna Maria and Dani Rodrik. 2005. "Why Are Some People (and Countries) More Protectionist than Others?" *European Economic Review,* 49/6:1393–1430.

McDonald, Patrick J. 2004. "Peace through Trade or Free Trade?" *Journal of Conflict Resolution,* 48/4:547–572.

McDowall, David. 2004. *The Modern History of the Kurds,* 3rd ed. Houndsmills, U.K.: Palgrave Macmillan.

Mearsheimer, John J. 2001. *The Tragedy of Great Power Politics.* New York: W. W. Norton.

Mearsheimer, John J., and Stephen Walt. 2003. "An Unnecessary War." *Foreign Policy,* 134:50–59.

Meernik, James, and Michael Ault. 2005. "The Diverted President: The Domestic Agenda and Foreign Policy." Paper presented at the annual convention of the International Studies Association, Honolulu, HI.

Melander, Erik. 2005. "Political Gender Equality and State Human Rights Abuse." *Journal of Peace Research,* 42: 149–166.

Mercer Jonathan. 2005. "Rationality and Psychology in International Politics. *International Organization,* 59/1: 77–106.

Meunier, Sophie. 2000. "What Single Voice? European Institutions and EU-US Trade Negotiations." *International Organization,* 54/2:103–135.

Migdal, Joel S. 2004. "State-Building and the Non-Nation-State." *Journal of International Affairs,* 58/1:17–47.

Milner, Helen V., and Benjamin Judkins. 2004. "Partisanship, Trade Policy, and Globalization: Is There a Left-Right Divide on Trade Policy?" *International Studies Quarterly,* 48/1:95–114.

Milner, Henry. 2006. "'YES to the Europe I want; NO to this one.' Some Reflections on France's Rejection of the EU Constitution." *PS: Political Science & Politics,* 39/2:257–260.

Mindich, David T. Z. 2004. *Tuned Out: Why Americans Under 40 Don't Follow the News.* New York: Oxford University Press.

Mintz, Alex. 2004. "How Do Leaders Make Decisions? A Poliheuristic Perspective." *Journal of Conflict Resolution,* 48/1:3–13.

Mitchell, David. 2005. "Centralizing Advisory Systems: Presidential Influence and the U.S. Foreign Policy Decision-Making Process." *Foreign Policy Analysis,* 1/2:181–203.

Mitchell, Sara McLaughlin and Brandon C. Prins. 2004. "Rivalry and Diversionary Uses of Force." *Journal of Conflict Resolution,* 48/6:937–961.

Moaz, Zeev. 2004. "The Mixed Blessing of Israel's Nuclear Policy." *International Security,* 28/2:44–77.

Monshipouri, Mahmood, Neil Englehart, Andrew J. Nathan, and Kavita Philip, eds. 2003. *Constructing Human Rights in the Age of Globalization.* Armonk, NY: M. E. Sharpe.

Monshipouri, Mahmood. 2004. "The Road to Globalization Runs through Women's Struggle: Iran and the Impact of the Nobel Peace Prize." *World Affairs,* 167/1:3–14.

Moore, Rebecca R. 2001. "China's Fledgling Civil Society." *World Policy Journal,* 18/1:56–66.

Moore, Will H., and David J. Lanoue. 2003. "Domestic Politics and U.S. Foreign Policy: A Study of Cold War Conflict Behavior." *Journal of Politics,* 65:376–397.

Morefield, Jeanne. 2004. *Covenants without Swords: Idealist Liberalism and the Spirit of Empire.* Princeton, NJ: Princeton University Press.

Morgan, T. Clifton. 2005. "When Threats Succeed: A Formal Model of the Threat and Use of Economic Sanctions." Paper presented at the annual convention of the International Studies Association, Honolulu, HI.

Morgan, T. Clifton, and Glenn Palmer. 2003. "To Protect and Serve: Alliances and Foreign Policy Portfolios." *Journal of Conflict Resolution,* 47:180–203.

Morgenthau, Hans J. 1945. "The Evil of Politics and the Ethics of Evil." *Ethics,* 56/1:1–18.

Morgenthau, Hans J. 1948. *Politics among Nations.* New York: Alfred A. Knopf.

Morgenthau, Hans W. 1973, 1986. *Politics among Nations.* New York: Knopf. Morgenthau's text was first published in 1948 and periodically thereafter. Two sources are used herein. One is the fifth edition, published in 1973. The second is an edited abstract drawn from pp. 3–4, 10–12, 14, 27–29, and 31–35 of the third edition, published in 1960. The abstract appears in Vasquez 1986:37–41. Pages cited for Morgenthau 1986 refer to Vasquez's, not Morgenthau's, book.

Mueller, John. 2004. *The Remnants of War.* Ithaca, NY: Cornell University Press.

Muldoon, James P., Jr. 2003. *The Architecture of Global Governance.* Boulder, CO: Westview.

Murphy, John. 2004. *The United States and the Rule of Law in International Affairs.* New York: Cambridge University Press.

Nabulsi, Karma. 2004. "The Peace Process and the Palestinians: A Road Map to Mars." *International Affairs,* 80/2:221–231.

Nathan, James A. 2002. *Soldiers, Statecraft, and History: Coercive Diplomacy and the International Order.* Westport, CT: Praeger.

Navaretti, Giorgio Barba, and Anthony J. Venables. 2004. *Multinational Firms in the World Economy.* Princeton: Princeton University Press.

Neack, Laura. 1995. "UN Peace-Keeping: In the Interest of Community or Self?" *Journal of Peace Research,* 32: 181–196.

Nelsen, Brent F., and James L. Guth. 2003. "Roman Catholicism and the Founding of Europe: How Catholics Shaped the European Communities." Paper presented at the annual meeting of the American Political Science Association, Philadelphia, August 2003.

Neumayer, Eric. 2005. "Do International Human Rights Treaties Improve Respect for Human Rights?" *Journal of Conflict Resolution,* 49/5:925–953.

Neustadt, Richard E. 1990. *Presidential Power: The Politics of Leadership from FDR to Carter.* New York: Wiley.

Norris, Pippa, and Ronald Inglehart. 2004. *Sacred and Secular: Religion and Politics Worldwide.* New York: Cambridge University Press.

Nye, Joseph S., Jr., 2000. *Understanding International Conflicts,* 3rd ed. New York: Longman.

Nye, Joseph S., Jr. 2002. "Globalism Versus Globalization." *The Globalist,* online. April 15, 2002.

Nye, Joseph S., Jr. 2004. *Soft Power: The Means to Success in World Politics.* New York: Public Affairs.

Nye, Joseph S., Jr. 2004a. "The Decline of America's Soft Power." *Foreign Affairs,* 83/3 (May/June 2004):16–21.

Nye, Joseph S., Jr., and Robert O. Keohane. 1970. "Transnational Relations and World Politics." In *Transnational Relations and World Politics,* ed. Joseph S. Nye, Jr. and Robert O. Keohane. Cambridge, MA: Harvard University Press.

O'Leary, Brendan. 1997. "On the Nature of Nationalism: An Appraisal of Ernest Gellner's Writings on Nationalism." *British Journal of Political Science,* 27:191–222.

O'Neill, Kate. 2004. "Transnational Protest: States, Circuses, and Conflict at the Frontline of Global Politics." *International Studies Review,* 6/2:233–249.

Oneal, John R., and Bruce M. Russett. 1997. "The Classical Liberals Were Right: Democracy, Interdependence, and Conflict, 1950–1985." *International Studies Quarterly,* 41:267–294.

Onuf, Nicholas. 2002. "Worlds of Our Making." In *Visions of International Relations,* Donald J. Puchala, ed. Columbia: University of South Carolina Press.

Opello, Walter C., Jr., and Stephen J. Rosow. 2004. *The Nation-State and Global Order: A Historical Introduction to Contemporary Politics.* Boulder, CO: Lynne Rienner.

Orford, Anne. 2003. *Reading Humanitarian Intervention: Human Rights and the Use of Force in International Law.* Cambridge, U.K.: Cambridge University Press.

Owen, John M. 2004. "Democratic Peace Research: Whence and Whither?" *International Politics,* 41:605–617.

Paquette, Laura. 2003. *Analyzing National and International Policy: Theory, Method, and Case Studies.* Lanham, MD: Lexington Books.

Park, Susan. 2005. "How Transnational Environmental Advocacy Networks Socialize International Financial Institutions: A Case Study of the International Finance Corporation." *Global Environmental Politics,* 5/4:95–119.

Patrick, Stewart, and Shepard Forman, eds. 2002. *Multilateralism and U.S. Foreign Policy: Ambivalent Engagement.* Boulder, CO: Lynne Rienner.

Patterson, Thomas E. 2005. *Young Voters and the 2004 Election.* Cambridge, MA: Joan Shorenstein Center on the Press, Politics, and Public Policy, John F. Kennedy School of Government, Harvard University.

Paul, T. V., G. John Ikenberry, and John A. Hall. 2004. *The Nation-State in Question.* Princeton, NJ: Princeton University Press.

Peterson, Peter G. 2001. "A Graying World: The Dangers of Global Aging." *Harvard International Review,* 23/3:1–4 (online).

Peterson, Susan, Michael J. Tierney, and Daniel Malinia. 2005. "Inside the Ivory Tower." *Foreign Policy* 51: 58–64.

Pevehouse, Jon C. 2004. "Interdependence Theory and the Measurement of International Conflict." *Journal of Politics,* 66/1:247–272.

Pew Research Center for the People and the Press. 2002. *Pew Global Attitudes Project 44-Nation Major Survey.* Washington, D.C.: Pew Research Center for the People and the Press.

Pew Research Center for the People and the Press. 2003. *Views of a Changing World, 2003.* Washington, DC: Pew Research Center for the People and the Press.

Phelps, Edward, 2004. "Young Citizens and Changing Electoral Turnout, 1964–2001." *Political Quarterly,* 75: 238–248.

Pickering, Jeffrey, and Emizet F. Kisangani. 2005. "Democracy and Diversionary Military Intervention: Reassessing Regime Type and the Diversionary Hypothesis." *International Studies Quarterly,* 49/1:23–46.

Pickering, Jeffrey, and Mark Peceny. 2006. "Forging Democracy at Gunpoint." *International Studies Quarterly,* 50/3: 539–566.

Pilch, Frances. 2005. "Developing Human Rights Standards in United Nations Peacekeeping Operations." Paper presented at the annual meeting of the International Studies Association, Honolulu, HI.

Plumper, Thomas, and Eric Neumayer. 2006. "The Unequal Burden of War: The Effect of Armed Conflict on the Gender Gap in Life Expectancy." *International Organization,* 60/3:723–754.

Poole, Peter A., and Michael Baun. 2004. "Europe Unites: The EU's Eastern Enlargement." *Political Science Quarterly,* 119/2 368–369.

Post, Jerrold M. 2004. *Leaders and Their Followers in a Dangerous World: The Psychology of Political Behavior.* Ithaca, NY: Cornell University Press.

Powell, Robert. 2006. "War as a Commitment Problem." *International Organization,* 60/1:169–203.

Price, Richard M., and Mark W. Zacher, eds. 2004. *The United Nations and Global Security.* New York: Palgrave Macmillan.

Quackenbush, Stephen L. 2006. "Not Only Whether but Whom: Three-Party Extended Deterrence." *Journal of Conflict Resolution,* 50/4:562–583.

Qvortrup, Mads. 2002. *A Comparative Study of Referendums: Government by the People.* Manchester, U.K.: Manchester University Press.

Rabkin, Jeremy. 1994. "Threats to U.S. Sovereignty." *Commentary,* 97(3):41–47.

Ralph, Jason. 2005. "International Society, the International Criminal Court, and American Foreign Policy." *Review of International Studies*, 31/1:27–44.

Ratha, Dilip. 2007. "Leveraging Remittances for Development." Paper presented at the Second Plenary Meeting of the Leading Group on Solidarity Levies to Fund Development, Oslo, Norway, February 6–7, 2007. Washington, D.C.: World Bank, Development Prospects Group.

Ratner, Steven R. 1998. "International Law: The Trials of Global Norms." *Foreign Policy*, 110:65–81.

Reardon, Betty A. 1990. "Feminist Concepts of Peace and Security." In *A Reader in Peace Studies*, ed. Paul Smoker, Ruth Davies, and Barbara Munske. Oxford, U.K.: Pergamon Press.

Redd, Steven B. 2005. "The Influence of Advisers and Decision Strategies on Foreign Policy Choices: President Clinton's Decision to Use Force in Kosovo." *International Studies Perspectives* 6/1:129–144.

Reed, Thomas C. 2004. *At the Abyss: An Insider's History of the Cold War.* New York: Ballantine.

Reimann, Kim D. 2006. "A View from the Top: International Politics, Norms and the Worldwide Growth of NGOs." *International Studies Quarterly*, 50/1:45–68.

Reiter, Dan, and Allan C. Stam. 2002. *Democracies at War.* Princeton, NJ: Princeton University Press.

Reiter, Dan, and Erik R. Tillman. 2002. "Public, Legislative, and Executive Constraints on the Democratic Initiation of Conflict." *Journal of Politics*, 64:810–837.

Renan, Ernest. 1995. "Qu'est-ce Qu'une Nation?" In *Nationalism,* ed. John Hutchinson and Anthony D. Smith. New York: Oxford University Press.

Rengger, Nicholas. 2002. "On the Just War Tradition in the Twenty-First Century." *International Affairs*, 78: 353–363.

Renshon, Stanley A. 1995. "Character, Judgment, and Political Leadership: Promise, Problems, and Prospects of the Clinton Presidency." In *The Clinton Presidency: Campaigning, Governing, and the Psychology of Leadership,* ed. Stanley Renshon. Boulder, CO: Westview.

Renshon, Stanley A., and Deborah Welch Larson, eds. 2002. *Good Judgment in Foreign Policy: Theory and Application.* Lanham, MD: Rowman & Littlefield.

Rhodes, Edward. 2003. "The Imperial Logic of Bush's Liberal Agenda." *Survival*, 45:131–154.

Ringquist, Evan J., and Tatiana Kostadinova. 2005. "Assessing the Effectiveness of International Environmental Agreements: The Case of the 1985 Helsinki Protocol." *American Journal of Political Science*, 49/1: 86–114.

Rodin, David. 2005. *War and Self-Defense.* New York: Oxford University Press.

Rodrigues, Maria Guadalupe Moog. 2004. *Global Environmentalism and Local Politics: Transnational Advocacy Networks in Brazil, Ecuador, and India.* Albany: State University of New York Press.

Romano, Cesare P. R., André Nollkaemper, and Jann K. Kleffner. 2005. *Internationalized Criminal Courts: Sierra Leone, East Timor, Kosovo, and Cambodia.* Oxford, U.K.: Oxford University Press.

Rosato, Sebastian. 2005. "Explaining the Democratic Peace." *American Political Science Review*, 99/3:467–472.

Rosen, Stephen Peter. 2004. *War and Human Nature.* Princeton: Princeton University Press.

Rosenau, James N. 2004. "Understanding World Affairs: The Potential of Collaboration." *Globalizations*, 1/2: 326–39.

Ross, Michael. 2006. "Is Democracy Good for the Poor?" *American Journal of Political Science*, 50/4:860–891.

Rothgeb, John M., Jr. 1993. *Defining Power: Influence and Force in the Contemporary International System.* New York: St. Martin's.

Rourke, John T. 1983. *Congress and the Presidency in U.S. Foreign Policy Making: A Study of Interaction and Influence, 1945–1982.* Boulder, CO: Westview.

Rourke, John T. 1993. *Presidential Wars and American Democracy: Rally 'Round the Chief.* New York: Paragon.

Rourke, John T., Richard P. Hiskes, and Cyrus Ernesto Zirakzadeh. 1992. *Direct Democracy and International Politics.* Boulder, CO: Lynne Rienner.

Rubin, Michael. 2006. "A Curiously Clintonian Turn in U.S. Foreign Policy." *The Weekly Standard*, online, June 12.

Ruggie, John Gerard. 1998. "What Makes the World Hang Together? Neo-Utilitarianism and the Social Constructivist Challenge." *International Organization*, 52:855–885.

Rummel, R. J. 1995. "Democracy, Power, Genocide, and Mass Murder." *Journal of Conflict Resolution*, 39:3–26.

Rusk, Dean, as told to Richard Rusk. 1990. *As I Saw It.* New York: W. W. Norton.

Schafer, Mark, and Stephen G. Walker. 2006. "Democratic Leaders and the Democratic Peace: The Operational Codes of Tony Blair and Bill Clinton." *International Studies Quarterly*, 50/3:561–583.

Schafer, Mark, and Scott Crichlow. 2002. "The Process-Outcome Connection in Foreign Policy Decision Making: A Quantitative Study Building on Groupthink." *International Studies Quarterly*, 46:45–68.

Schell, Jonathan. 2003. *The Unconquerable World: Power, Nonviolence, and the Will of the People.* New York: Metropolitan Books.

Schmidt, Brian C. 2004. "Realism as Tragedy." *Review of International Studies*, 30:427–441.

Schmitter, Philippe C. 2005. "Ernst B. Haas and the Legacy of Neofunctionalism." *Journal of European Public Policy*, 12/2:255–272.

Schmitz, Hans Peter. 2004. "Domestic and Transnational Perspectives on Democratization." *International Studies Review*, 6/3:403–421.

Schneider, Gerald, Katherine Barbieri, and Nils Petter Gleditsch, eds. 2003. *Globalization and Armed Conflict*. Lanham, MD: Rowman & Littlefield.

Schultz, Kathryn R., and David Isenberg. 1997. "Arms Control and Disarmament." In *A Global Agenda: Issues before the 52nd General Assembly of the United Nations*, ed. John Tessitore and Susan Woolfson. Lanham, MD: Rowman & Littlefield.

Schultze, Charles L. 2004. *Offshoring, Import Competition, and the Jobless Recovery*. Policy Brief 136. Washington, D.C.: Brookings Institution.

Schulzinger, Robert D. 1989. *Henry Kissinger: Doctor of Diplomacy*. New York: Columbia University Press.

Schulzinger, Robert D. 2006. "Comment on 'The Endgame of Globalization'." *Political Geography*, 25/1:15–17.

Schuman, Howard, and Amy D. Corning. 2006. "Comparing Iraq to Vietnam: Recognition, Recall, and the Nature of Cohort Effects." *Public Opinion Quarterly*, 70/1:78–87.

Schweller, Randall L. 2004. "Unanswered Threats: A Neoclassical Realist Theory of Underbalancing." *International Security*, 29/2:159–201.

Scott, James M., and Ralph G. Carter. 2002. "Acting on the Hill: Congressional Assertiveness in U.S. Foreign Policy." *Congress & the Presidency*, 29:151–170.

Scully, Roger, and David M. Farrell. 2003. "MEPs as Representatives: Individual and Institutional Roles." *Journal of Common Market Studies*, 41:269–288.

Seigfried, Charlene Haddock. 2006. "The Dangers of Unilateralism," *NWSA Journal*, 18/3:20–33.

Seligson, Mitchell A., and John T. Passé-Smith, eds. 2003. *Development and Underdevelopment: The Political Economy of Global Inequality*. Boulder, CO: Lynne Rienner.

Sen, Amartya. 1999. *Development as Freedom*. New York: Alfred A. Knopf.

Senese, Paul D. 2005. "Territory, Contiguity, and International Conflict: Assessing a New Joint Explanation." *American Journal of Political Science*, 49/4:769–791.

Shah, Timothy Samuel, and Monica Duffy Toft. 2006. "Why God Is Winning." *Foreign Policy*, 155:38–43.

Shaheed, Farida. 1999. "Constructing Identities: Culture, Women's Agency and the Muslim World." *International Social Science Journal*, 51:61–75.

Shambaugh, George E. 2004. "The Power of Money: Global Capital and Policy Choices in Developing Countries." *American Journal of Political Science*, 48/2:281–311.

Sherman, Dennis, and Joyce Salisbury. 2004. *The West in the World*, 2nd ed. Boston: McGraw-Hill.

Shinko, Rosemary. 2006. "Postmodernism: A Genealogy of Humanitarian Intervention." In *Making Sense of IR Theory*, ed. Jennifer Sterling-Folker. Boulder, CO: Lynne Rienner.

Silverman, Adam L. 2002. "Just War, Jihad, and Terrorism: A Comparison of Western and Islamic Norms for the Use of Political Violence." *Journal of Church and State*, 44:73–92.

Simmons, Beth A., and Daniel J. Hopkins. 2005. "The Constraining Power of International Treaties: Theory and Methods." *American Political Science Review*, 99/4: 623–631.

Simon, Craig. 1998. "Internet Governance Goes Global." In *International Relations in a Constructed World*, eds. Vendulka Kubalkova, Nicholas Onuf, and Paul Kowert. Armonk, NY: M. E. Sharpe.

Simonton, Dean Keith. 2006. "Presidential IQ, Openness, Intellectual Brilliance, and Leadership: Estimates and Correlations for 42 U.S. Chief Executives." *Political Psychology*, 27/4:511–526.

Sinclair, Andrew. 2004. *An Anatomy of Terror: A History of Terrorism*. New York: Palgrave Macmillan.

Singh, Sonali, and Christopher R. Way. 2004. "The Correlates of Nuclear Proliferation: A Quantitative Test." *Journal of Conflict Resolution*, 48/6:859–885.

(SIPRI) Stockholm International Peace Research Institute. Annual Editions. *SIPRI Yearbook*. Oxford, U.K.: Oxford University Press.

Skidmore, David. 2005. "Understanding the Unilateralist Turn in U.S. Foreign Policy." *Foreign Policy Analysis*, 1/2: 207–219.

Slantchev, Branislav L. 2003. "The Power to Hurt: Costly Conflict with Completely Informed States." *American Political Science Review*, 97:123–133.

Slantchev, Branislav L. 2005. "Military Coercion in Interstate Crises." *American Political Science Review*, 99/4: 533–547.

Slaughter, Anne-Marie. 2003. "The Global Community of Courts." *Harvard International Law Journal*, 44: 217–219.

Smith, Anthony D. 2004. *Chosen Peoples: Sacred Sources of National Identity*. Oxford, U.K.: Oxford University Press.

Smith, Anthony D. 2005. *The Antiquity of Nations*. Cambridge, U.K.: Polity.

Smith, Hugh H. 2005. "What Costs Will Democracies Bear? A Review of Popular Theories of Casualty Aversion." *Armed Forces & Society*, 31/4:487–512.

Smith, Tom W., and Seokho Kim. 2006. "National Pride in Comparative Perspective, 1995/96 and 2003/04." *International Journal of Public Opinion Research*, 18/1:128–136.

Snyder, Jack. 2002. "Myths of Empire, Then and Now." Morton-Kenney Public Affairs Lecture Series. Department of Political Science, Southern Illinois University, Carbondale, IL.

Snyder, Robert S. 2005. "Bridging the Realist/Constructivist Divide: The Case of the Counterrevolution in Soviet Foreign Policy at the End of the Cold War." *Foreign Policy Analysis*, 1/1:55–71.

Sørensen, Georg. 2001. *Changes in Statehood: The Transformation of International Relations*. London: Palgrave.

Sørensen, Georg. 2004. *The Transformation of the State: Beyond the Myth of Retreat*. New York: Palgrave Macmillan.

Speer, James P., II. 1968. "Hans Morgenthau and the World State." *World Politics*, 20/1:207–227.

Spruyt, Hendrik. 1994. *The Sovereign State and Its Competitors: An Analysis of Systems Change*. Princeton, NJ: Princeton University Press.

Stansfield, Gareth. 2005. "The Kurds: Nation without a State." Paper presented at the annual meeting of the International Studies Association, Honolulu.

Starkey, Brigid, Mark A. Boyer, and Jonathan Wilkenfeld. 2005. *Negotiating a Complex World: An Introduction to International Negotiation*, 2nd ed. Lanham, MD: Rowman & Littlefield.

Stefanova, Boyka 2006. "The 'No' Vote in the French and Dutch Referenda on the EU Constitution: A Spillover of Consequences for the Wider Europe." *PS: Political Science & Politics*, 39/2:257–260.

Steger, Manfred B., ed. 2003. *Rethinking Globalism*. Lanham, MD: Rowman & Littlefield.

Steinbruner, John. 2003. "Confusing Ends and Means: The Doctrine of Coercive Preemption." *Arms Control Today*, 33/1 (January/February). On the Web at http://www.armscontrol.org/.

Steiner, Barry H. 2004. "Diplomacy and International Theory." *Review of International Studies*, 30:493–509.

Sterling-Folker, Jennifer. 1997. "Realist Environment, Liberal Process, and Domestic-Level Variables." *International Studies Quarterly*, 41:1–26.

Sterling-Folker, Jennifer. 2002. *Theories of International Cooperation and the Primacy of Anarchy: Explaining U.S.*

Sutterlin, James. 2003. *The United Nations and the Maintenance of International Security*, 2nd ed. Westport, CT: Praeger.

Sylvester, Caroline. 1994. "A Review of J. Ann Tickner's *Gender in International Relations*." *American Political Science Review*, 87:823–824.

Szechenyi, Nicholas. 2006. "A Turning Point for Japan's Self-Defense Forces." *The Washington Quarterly*, 29/4: 139–150.

Tabb, William K. 2004. *Economic Governance in the Age of Globalization*. New York: Columbia University Press.

Taber, Charles S. 1989. "Power Capability Indexes in the Third World." In *Power in World Politics*, ed. Richard J. Stoll and Michael D. Ward. Boulder, CO: Lynne Rienner.

Tamir, Yael. 1995. "The Enigma of Nationalism." *World Politics*, 47:418–440.

Tammen, Ronald L., et al. 2002. *Power Transitions: Strategies for the Twenty-First Century*. New York: Chatham House/ Seven Bridges Press.

Tannenwald, Nima. 2006. "Nuclear Weapons and the Vietnam War." *Journal of Strategic Studies*, 29/4:675–722.

Tarar, Ahmer. 2005. "Constituencies and Preferences in International Bargaining." *Journal of Conflict Resolution*, 49/3:383–407.

Tarzi, Shah M. 2005. "Coercive Diplomacy and an 'Irrational' Regime: Understanding the American Confrontation with the Taliban." *International Studies*, 42/1: 21–41.

Telhami, Shibley, and Michael Barnett, eds. 2002. *Identity and Foreign Policy in the Middle East*. Ithaca, NY: Cornell University Press.

Tessman, Brock F., and Steve Chan. 2004. "Power Cycles, Risk Propensity, and Great-Power Deterrence." *Journal of Conflict Resolution*, 48/2:131–153.

Thies, Wallace J. 1998. "Deliberate and Inadvertent War in the Post–Cold War World." In *Annual Editions, American Foreign Policy 98/99*, ed. Glenn P. Hastedt. Guilford, CT: Dushkin/McGraw-Hill.

Thompson, Alexander. 2006. "Coercion Through IOs: The Security Council and the Logic of Information Transmission." *International Organization*, 60/1:1–34.

Thompson, William R. 2006. "Systemic Leadership, Evolutionary Processes, and International Relations Theory: The Unipolarity Question." *International Studies Review*, 8/1:1–22.

Tickner, J. Ann. 2005. "What Is Your Research Program? Some Feminist Answers to International Relations Methodological Questions." *International Studies Quarterly*, 49/1: 1–14.

Tomuschat, Christian. 2004. *Human Rights: Between Idealism and Realism*. Oxford, U.K.: Oxford University Press.

Travis, Rick, and Nikolaos Zahariadis. 2002. "A Multiple Stream Model of U.S. Foreign Aid Policy." *Policy Studies Journal*, 30:495–514.

Trumbore, Peter F. 1998. "Public Opinion as a Domestic Constraint in International Negotiations: Two-Level Games in the Anglo-Irish Peace Process." *International Studies Quarterly*, 42:545–565.

Trumbore, Peter F. 2003. "Victims or Aggressors? Ethno-Political Rebellion and Use of Force in Militarized Interstate Disputes." *International Studies Quarterly*, 47: 183–201.

Tsang, Steve, ed. 2004. *Peace and Security across the Taiwan Strait*. New York: Palgrave Macmillan.

Tsygankov, Andrei P. 2003. "The Irony of Western Ideas in a Multicultural World: Russia's Intellectual Engagement with the 'End of History' and 'Clash of Civilizations.'" *International Studies Review*, 5:53–76.

Tucker, Nancy Bernkopf, ed. 2005. *Dangerous Strait: The U.S.-Taiwan-China Crisis*. New York: Columbia University Press.

Turner, Frederick C., and Alejandro L. Corbacho. 2000. "New Roles for the State." *International Social Science Journal*, 163:109–120.

Tusicisny, Andrej. 2004. "Civilizational Conflicts: More Frequent, Longer, and Bloodier?" *Journal of Peace Research*, 41/2:485–498.

UN, Department of Economic and Social Affairs, Population Division. 2004. At http://www.undp.org/.

United Nations. *See* (UN).

(UN, UNICEF) United Nations Children's Fund. Annual editions. *State of the World's Children.* New York: Oxford University Press.

(UNDP) United Nations Development Programme. Annual editions. *Human Development Report.* New York: Oxford University Press.

(U.S.) Bureau of the Census. Annual editions. *Statistical Abstract of the United States.* Washington, DC.

U.S. (CIA) Central Intelligence Agency. Annual editions. *World FactBook.* Washington, DC: GPO.

Vandenbroucke, Lucien. 1993. *Perilous Options: Special Operations in U.S. Foreign Policy.* New York: Oxford University Press.

Vasquez, John, and Marie T. Henehan. 2001. "Territorial Disputes and the Probability of War, 1816–1992." *Journal of Peace Research* 38/2:123–138.

Vasquez, Joseph Paul, III. 2005. "Shouldering the Soldiering: Democracy, Conscription, and Military Casualties." *Journal of Conflict Resolution,* 49/4:849–873.

Voeten, Erik, and Paul R. Brewer. 2006. "Public Opinion, the War in Iraq, and Presidential Accountability." *Journal of Conflict Resolution,* 50/4:809–830.

Voeten, Erik. 2004. "Resisting the Lonely Superpower: Responses of States in the UN to U.S. Dominance." *The Journal of Politics,* 66:729–754.

Walker, Stephen G., Mark Schafer, and Michael D. Young. 1998. "Systematic Procedures for Operational Code Analysis: Measuring and Modeling Jimmy Carter's Operational Code." *International Studies Quarterly,* 42:175–189.

Wallerstein, Immanuel. 1974. *The Modern World System: Capitalist Agriculture and the Origins of the European World Economy in the Sixteenth Century.* New York: Academic Press.

Walt, Stephen M. 1996. "Alliances: Balancing and Bandwagoning." In *International Politics,* 4th ed., ed. Robert J. Art and Robert Jervis. New York: HarperCollins.

Walzer, Michael. 2004. *Arguing about War.* New Haven, CT: Yale University Press.

Wang, Kevin H., and James Lee Ray. 1994. "Beginnings and Winners: The Fate of Initiators of Interstate Wars Involving Great Powers since 1495." *International Studies Quarterly,* 38:139–154.

Watkins, Kevin. 2002. "Making Globalization Work for the Poor." *Finance & Development,* 39/1. Web edition at http://www.imf.org/external/pubind.htm.

Watson, James L. 2000. "China's Big Mac Attack." *Foreign Affairs,* 79/3:120–142.

Wead, Douglas. 2003. *All the President's Children: Triumph and Tragedy in the Lives of America's First Families.* New York: Atria.

Welsh, Jennifer M., ed. 2004. *Humanitarian Intervention and International Relations.* Oxford, U.K.: Oxford University Press.

Wendt, Alexander. 1992. "Anarchy Is What States Make of It: The Social Construction of Power Politics." *International Organization,* 46:335–370.

Wendt, Alexander. 2004. "The State as Person in International Theory." *Review of International Studies,* 30:289–316.

Werner, Suzanne, and Amy Yuen. 2005. "Making and Keeping Peace." *International Organization,* 59/2:261–292.

Wiebe, Robert H. 2002. *Who We Are: A History of Popular Nationalism.* Princeton, NJ: Princeton University Press.

Wilcox, Clyde, Lara Hewitt, and Dee Allsop. 1996. "The Gender Gap in Attitudes Toward the Gulf War? A Cross-National Perspective." *Journal of Peace Research,* 33/1:67–82.

Wilkinson, David. 2004. "Analytical and Empirical Issues in the Study of Power-Polarity Configuration Sequences." Paper presented at a Conference of a Working Group on Analyzing Complex Macrosystems as Dynamic Networks, Santa Fe Institute, Santa Fe.

Williams, Meryl J. 2005. "Are High Seas and International Marine Fisheries the Ultimate Sustainable Management Challenge?" *Journal of International Affairs,* 59/1:221–235.

Williams, Michael C. 2004. "Why Ideas Matter in International Relations: Hans Morgenthau, Classical Realism, and the Moral Construction of Power Politics." *International Organization,* 58/4:633–665.

Williams, Michael C. 2005. *The Realist Tradition and the Limits of International Relations.* New York: Cambridge University Press.

Williams, Rob M., Jr. 2003. *The Wars Within: People and States in Conflict.* Ithaca, NY: Cornell University Press.

Willinsky. John. 2006. "Access to Power: Research in International Policymaking." *Harvard International Review,* 28/2:54–57.

Wimmer, Andreas. 2002. *Nationalist Exclusion and Ethnic Conflict.* Cambridge, U.K.: Cambridge University Press.

Witko, Christopher. 2003. "Cold War Belligerence and U.S. Public Opinion toward Defense Spending." *American Politics Research,* 31:379–392.

Wohlforth, William C. 1999. "The Stability of a Unipolar World." *International Security,* 24/1:5–41.

Woodwell, Douglas. 2004. "Unwelcome Neighbors: Shared Ethnicity and International Conflict during the Cold War." *International Studies Quarterly,* 48/1:197–216.

World Almanac and Book of Facts. Annual editions. New York: Funk & Wagnalls.

World Bank. 2004. *World Development Indicators 2004.* Washington, DC: World Bank.

World Bank. Annual editions. *World Development Report.* New York: Oxford University Press.

World Resources Institute. Annual editions. *World Resources.* New York: Oxford University Press.

Yanik, Lerna K. 2006. "Major Powers, Global Arms Transfers, and Human Rights Violations." *Human Rights Quarterly,* 28/2:357–388.

Zakaria, Fareed. 1993. "Is Realism Finished?" *National Interest,* 32:21–32.

Zehfuss, Maja. 2002. *Constructivism in International Relations: The Politics of Reality.* New York: Cambridge University Press.

Zunes, Stephen. 2004. "U.S. Christian Right's Grip on Middle East Policy." *Foreign Policy in Focus,* online.

Zunes, Stephen. 2005. "The Two Faces of American Policy as a Generator of Anti-American Attitudes in the Middle East and North Africa." Paper presented at the annual convention of the International Studies Association, Honolulu.

Index

Page numbers in *italics* indicate boxes, tables, photos, charts, etc. Page numbers in **bold** indicate definitions.

Photo Credits

NORTH
PACIFIC
OCEAN

NORTH
ATLANTIC
OCEAN

U.S.

CANADA

UNITED STATES

MEXICO

Tropic of Cancer

U.S.

Equator

GUYANA
SURINAME
FRENCH
GUIANA
(FR)

COLOMBIA

VENEZUELA

ECUADOR

P E R U

B R A Z I L

BOLIVIA

WESTERN
SAMOA

TONGA

Tropic of Capricorn

PARAGUAY

CHILE

A
R
G
E
N
T
I
N
A

URUGUAY

SOUTH
ATLANTIC
OCEAN

SOUTH
PACIFIC
OCEAN

Antarctic Circle

U.S.

THE
BAHAMAS

0   300 Miles

0   300 Kilometers

CUBA

MEXICO

DOMINICAN
REPUBLIC

PUERTO RICO

JAMAICA

HAITI

ST. KITTS AND NEVIS
ANTIGUA AND BARBUDA
DOMINICA

BELIZE

CARIBBEAN
SEA

MARTINIQUE

ST. LUCÍA

GUATEMALA
HONDURAS

ST. VINCENT AND THE GRENADINES

BARBADOS
GRENADA

EL
SALVADOR

NICARAGUA

COSTA RICA

PANAMA

TRINIDAD AND TOBAGO

COLOMBIA

VENEZUELA

Scale: 1 to 125,000,000

0   1000   2000 Miles

0   1000   2000   3000 Kilometers